P9-BYA-179

International Architecture
Yearbook

International Architecture
Yearbook

The Images Publishing Group Pty Ltd

McGraw-Hill
New York Washington D.C. San Francisco
Montreal Toronto

ISBN 0 07 031811 5

Projects to be considered should be submitted to:
International Architecture Yearbook
The Images Publishing Group Pty Ltd
6 Bastow Place
Mulgrave, Victoria 3170
Australia
Telephone: +(61 3) 9561 5544
Facsimile: +(61 3) 9561 4860

10 CRITIQUE
Modern Architecture is Alive and Well, and Living All Over the World
by Michael Crosbie

CORPORATE

16 Brisbane Convention and Exhibition Centre
Philip Cox Richardson Rayner and Partners Pty Ltd

20 Charlotte Convention Center
Thompson, Ventulett, Stainback and Associates Inc

26 Dragon Centre
Wong Tung & Partners Limited

30 Edinburgh International Conference and Exhibition Centre
Terry Farrell and Partners

36 Embassy of Sweden
RTKL Associates Inc. in association with Stintzing Arkitekter, AB

38 ESEO Federal Credit Union
Elliott + Associates Architects

40 Gateway I, Harbour City
Wong & Ouyang (HK) Ltd

42 The Heierding Building
Elliott + Associates Architects

44 Hirsch, Robinson, Sheiness, Glover, PC., One Houston Center
Morris Architects

46 Hypo Bank London
Bernhard Blauel Architects

48 The Icehouse
Swatt Architects

54 The Ice House Renovation
Barton Myers Associates, Inc.

58 Kurfürstendamm 70
Murphy/Jahn, Inc. Architects

60 Kurfürstendamm 119
Murphy/Jahn, Inc. Architects

62 Lancaster Group Worldwide
Quantrell Mullins & Associates Inc

64 Li Po Chun Chambers Redevelopment
Wong Tung & Partners Limited

66 Long Beach Convention Center
Thompson, Ventulett, Stainback and Associates Inc

70 Modern Woodmen of America
Flad & Associates

74 Moscow Bank of the Russian Federation Savings Bank
Ellerbe Becket, Inc.

76 Northern States Power Company World Class Control Center
Ellerbe Becket, Inc.

78 Office in Helsinki
Hans Murman Arkitektkontor AB

80 Osaka World Trade Center Building
Nikken Sekkei Ltd in association with Mancini Duffy Associates

84 Pennsylvania Convention Center
Thompson, Ventulett, Stainback and Associates Inc

90 Silicon Graphics Entry Site
STUDIOS Architecture

96 State Farm Mutual Automobile Insurance Company South Texas Regional Office
Ellerbe Becket, Inc.

98 Surdiman Tower
RTKL Associates Inc. in association with PT. Airmas Asri

100 Truworths Head Office
Douglas Roberts Peter Loebenberg Architects

104 United Parcel Service Corporate Office
Thompson, Ventulett, Stainback and Associates Inc

EDUCATIONAL

112 Arts/Law Building, Northern Territory University
Daryl Jackson Architects in association with Woodhead (Aust) NT Pty Ltd

114 The Biocentre
Juhani Katainen Architects

120 Biology Building No. 68, Massachusetts Institute of Technology
Goody, Clancy & Associates, Inc.

122 Catholic University, Library and Lecture Hall
Young-sub Kim

126 City University of New York, New Library
Perry, Dean, Rogers & Partners: Architects, Inc.

132 Congressman Jerry Lewis Elementary School
HMC Group

138 Energy Systems Research Center, Ajou University
SAC International, Ltd.

140 Engineering Research Center, University of Cincinnati
Michael Graves Architect

144 Kungsängsskolan Upper Secondary School
Birgitta Holm Architects Inc. in association with STADION Architects Inc.

146 Medical Research Building II
The Stubbins Associates, Inc. in association with Earl Swensson and Associates

152 North View Primary School
DP Architects Pte Ltd

154 Perkins Elementary School
Martinez, Cutri & McArdle

156 Princeton Theological Seminary Henry Luce III Library
The Hillier Group

160 San Diego State University, Imperial Valley Campus
Martinez Cutri & McArdle

162 Seoul National University Museum
SAC International, Ltd.

164 St. Andrew's Junior College
DP Architects Pte Ltd

166 Tulane University Law School
Hartman-Cox Architects in association with The Mathes Group

168 National Center for Polymer Research, University of Massachusetts, Amherst
Ellenzweig Associates, Inc. Design Architect
Whitney Atwood Norcross, Inc., Architect of Record

174 Westside Middle School
Leo A. Daly

INDUSTRIAL

176 Building on the Prairie
Studio J.J. International

178 Eastern Counties Newspapers New Press Centre
Feilden & Mawson

180 Genzyme Corporation Biopharmaceutical Plant
Architectural Resources Cambridge, Inc.

184 Memorial Drive Flex-Use Industrial Facility
Herbert Beckhard Frank Richlan & Associates in association with Brandt-Kuybida Architects

186 Manufacturing Facility, Toppan Printing Company America, Inc.
Herbert Beckhard Frank Richlan & Associates in association with Brandt-Kuybida Architects

INSTITUTIONAL

188 Augusta Medical Center
Ellerbe Becket, Inc.

190 Bonita Professional Center
Martinez Cutri & McArdle

192 Cabrini Hospital
Bates Smart

194 Children's National Medical Center, Children's Research Institute
Ellerbe Becket, Inc.

196 Construction Industry Training Institute
DP Architects Pte Ltd

198 Cox Medical Center South Outpatient Center
The Wischmeyer Architects, Inc.

202 Cullman Regional Medical Center
TRO/The Ritchie Organization

204 Genentech Process Science Center
Flad & Associates

206 Grady Memorial Hospital
Kaplan/McLaughlin/Diaz in association with URS Consultants, Carl Trimble Architects, Stanley Love-Stanley and The Burlington Group

210 Health Central
HKS Inc.

214 Institute of Micro-Electronics/Information Technology Institute
DP Architects Pte Ltd

216 Joslin Diabetes Center Research and Clinical Facility Expansion
Ellenzweig Associates, Inc.

220 The Lighthouse Headquarters
Mitchell/Giurgola Architects

224 Mary Washington Hospital
HKS Inc.

230 The National Children's Center
Cooper•Lecky Architects, PC

232 Ohio Aerospace Institute
Richard Fleischman Architects, Inc.

234 Ronald McDonald House
Andrews, Scott, Cotton Architects Ltd

236 The Visby General Hospital
ETV Arkitektkontor AB

238 WestHealth
Ellerbe Becket, Inc.

240 Yuma Regional Medical Center
HKS Inc.

PUBLIC

242 Permanent Stage for the Botanic Gardens Symphony Lake
DP Architects Pte Ltd

244 Brisbane Airport International Terminal
Bligh Voller Architects

248 Control Tower, Sydney Airport
Ancher Mortlock & Woolley Pty Ltd

250 Crane Park Izumi
Nikken Sekkei Ltd.

256 Denver Central Library - Phase 1 Addition
Michael Graves Architect

260 Denver International Airport
C.W. Fentress, J.H. Bradburn and Associates

264 Dunhuang Cave Cultural Asset Reservation and Exhibition Center
Nikken Sekkei Ltd.

268 Ehime Museum of Science
Kisho Kurokawa Architect and Associates

272 Fire Station, Gennevilliers
Architecture Studio

276 Jerusalem City Hall Square
A.J. Diamond, Donald Schmitt & Company

278 New Wing and Renovation of the Joslyn Art Museum
Sir Norman Foster and Partners in association with Henningson Durham and Richardson

282 Korean War Veterans Memorial
Cooper•Lecky Architects, PC

284 Pacific Northwest Museum of Natural History
BOORA Architects, P.C.

286 Richmond Hill Central Library
A.J. Diamond, Donald Schmitt & Company

288 Techniquest
Ahrends Burton and Koralek

RECREATIONAL

290 Årsta Haninge Strand Golf Clubhouse
Hans Murman Arkitektkontor AB

294 The Belvedere
Mitchell/Giurgola Architects

296 Gund Arena
Ellerbe Becket, Inc.

298 Kiel Center Arena
Ellerbe Becket, Inc.

300 Night Safari
Consultants Incorporated

302 Porto Europa Wakayama Marina City
Ellerbe Becket, Inc.

304 Thomas Phillips Johnson Health & Recreation Center
MacLachlan, Cornelius & Filoni, Inc.

RESIDENTIAL

308 Alta Residence
House + House, Architects

310 Emerald Apartments
Enviro•Tec

312 Hight Residence
Bart Prince, Architect

316 Imperial Palace
G&W Architects, Engineers, Project Development Consultants

318 J. Tezzanos Pinto House
A.H. Ravazzani

320 Jay and Marilee Flood Residence
David Jay Flood

322 Jindal House
Gujrals

326 Joseph Pennock Farmstead Restoration
Susan Maxman Architects

328 Ka Hale Kukuna Residence
House + House, Architects

332 Laivapoika Housing Company
Helin & Siitonen Architects

338 Mead/Penhall Residence
Bart Prince, Architect

340 Mexx Farm
Gujrals

342 Millot-Gomez House
A.H. Ravazzani

344 Mount Royal in Morningside
Adrian Maserow Architects

346 Mr Eaton's Residence
Architects 49 Limited

350 Ocean View House
Swatt Architects

352 Permata Hijau Apartment
Pacific Adhika Internusa, PT

354 Powell House
Kanner Architects

356 Residence in Harvey Cedars
Susan Maxman Architects

360 Riverside Apartments
Hayball Leonard Stent

364 Segal House
Hugh Newell Jacobsen

366 Singer Residence
Kanner Architects

368 Waldhauer Residence
House + House, Architects

372 Villa Nuottaniemi
Arkkitehtitoimisto Paatela-Paatela & Co

RETAIL

374 Ever Commonwealth Commercial Complex
G&W Architects, Engineers, Project Development Consultants

376 Future Park Plaza
Architects 49 Limited

378 Phototime Processing Laboratory & Studio
House + House, Architects

382 Sainsbury's Supermarket
Terry Farrell and Partners

388 Tanglin Place
TSP Architects + Planners

OTHER

390 Apartment Building and Jeanine Manuel Bilingual Active School
Architecture Studio

394 Bamboo House (Restaurant) and Bamboo Gallery
Young-sub Kim

402 Bugis Junction
DP Architects Pte Ltd

404 Evercrest Golf Club & Resort
G&W Architects, Engineers, Project Development Consultants

406 Pepperdine University Student Dormitory
David Jay Flood Architect

408 Youth Hostels Association of Queensland Brisbane City Hostel
Bligh Voller Architects

415 BIOGRAPHIES

427 INDEX

432 ACKNOWLEDGMENTS

Modern Architecture is Alive and Well, and Living All Over the World

By Michael J. Crosbie

In reviewing the projects in this latest volume of the International Architecture Yearbook, one is struck by a certain sense of *deja vu*. This book is filled with fresh, inventive architecture, distinguished by expressive structure, crisp detailing, and carefully crafted materials. What is the current of architectural inquiry that seems to bind these projects of all different sizes, locations, and designers together? I believe that they represent a rebirth of the architecture that has become synonymous with the 20th century, the architecture that many of these buildings pay homage to at the close of the century. This architecture has now become part of our 'tradition': it is the architecture of Modernism.

Architecture's Materiality

Let us start with just one branch of this river of Modernist revival. Over the past few years there has been a resurgence of interest in the materiality of architecture. Where, during the height of Postmodernism, the materials of a building seemed to be secondary to the architect's fascination with classical detail, ornament, and colour, today more architects are exploring the implications of architecture as a material object: how are the building's materials expressed, how do they contrast with other materials used in the project, how should they be finished to reveal the material's essence, how does one material join to another, do the combination and placement of materials seem structurally and tectonically logical?

We see such an emphasis on materiality most often in the work of architects who have rediscovered Modernism as a design idiom, but it's also quite strong in the projects of such architects as Terry Farrell, who became closely identified with the Postmodern movement. For example, in his design for the Edinburgh International Conference and Exhibition Centre in Scotland, Farrell uses classical proportions and composition in the design of this 12,356 square metre (133,000 square foot) building. But this piece for a competition-winning master plan is vigorously expressive with its materials. Its exterior is light-coloured sandstone and precast concrete, meant to blend with the traditional sandstone of Edinburgh's most important buildings. The building's central drum element appears to be made of great blocks of stone, expressing the curvature of the element and reinforcing the point that this is an important civic structure in a city of stone buildings (even though the structure of Farrell's building is concrete and steel).

Another example of design that explores the power of material is the Korean War Veteran's Memorial in Washington, D.C. by Cooper•Lecky Architects. The major portion of the memorial is more than a dozen stainless steel statues of foot soldiers advancing towards a flagpole and a pool of contemplation. The statues are flanked by a wall of black granite, highly polished to reflect the surroundings and the visitors. Into the granite, a mural (by Louis Nelson Associates) has been sandblasted, depicting the faces of some 2,500 veterans of different branches of service, ethnic background, and gender. In this design it is the nature of the reflective material that joins the image of the visitor to the photo-realistic etchings of the veterans, making both appear as ghosts. The effect is quite dramatic.

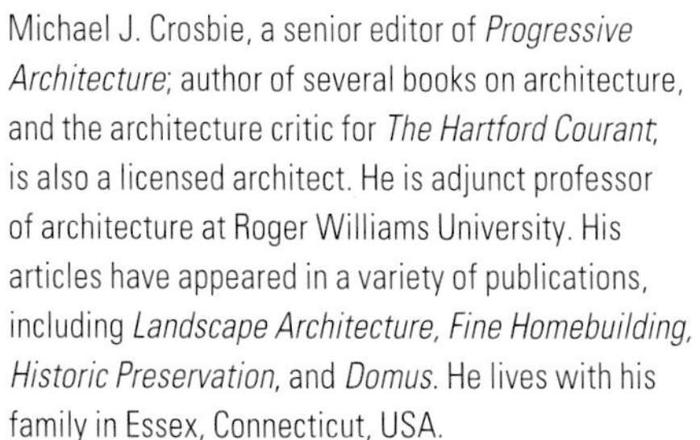

Michael J. Crosbie, a senior editor of *Progressive Architecture*; author of several books on architecture, and the architecture critic for *The Hartford Courant*, is also a licensed architect. He is adjunct professor of architecture at Roger Williams University. His articles have appeared in a variety of publications, including *Landscape Architecture, Fine Homebuilding, Historic Preservation*, and *Domus*. He lives with his family in Essex, Connecticut, USA.

A Late-Modernist Revival

The emphasis on architecture's materiality is just one element of our rediscovery of Modern architecture. Today's younger generation of architects is killing off their Postmodern fathers (and mothers) and embracing their late-Modern grandparents. It's important to stress here that this is not necessarily a return to the embryonic Modernism of Gropius, Le Corbusier, and Mies van der Rohe, but more a revival of such late-Modern architects as Eero Saarinen, John Johansen, and Paul Rudolph. The buildings of these late-Modern architects, who reached a 'high' period during the 1950s and early 1960s, might represent for today's architects a body of work that expresses the last vestiges of a spirit of optimism, progress, and certainty that Modern architecture had come to symbolise.

Crane Park Izumi in Kagoshima, Japan, by Nikken Sekkei is an example of such expressive Modernism. While this 2,315 square metre (24,920 square foot) building, intended for the study and appreciation of cranes, owes a certain debt to the legacy of the Japanese Metabolists, one sees in its strikingly pure geometry, pleated roof, and grand scale the late-Modern style of I.M. Pei. The underside of the pleated roof is expressive of its ribbed structure, while the generous use of natural lighting and simple detailing is also part of its late-Modern heritage.

In Australia, the Youth Hostels Association of Queensland Brisbane City Hostel employs raw and robust materials, as Bligh Voller Architects describe it. Here one finds the spare economy of materials with splashes of colour that suggest

a late-Modern landmark such as Johansen's Mummers Theater, which juxtaposed raw masonry with metal sheathing, just as the hostel does. In the latter case, the durability of the materials was a priority, given the building's use by boisterous backpackers. The hostel's 'kit-of-parts' quality and simple, powerful forms and planes employ Modernism to make it a memorable environment in the visitor's catalogue of mostly forgettable accommodations.

For a clientele that is anything but the backpacker set, the Phototime Processing Laboratory and Studio designed by House + House Architects in Palo Alto, California, USA, uses materials and forms with Modern rigour to distinguish an interior. The 185 square metre (2,000 square foot) project packs a lot into a small envelope, which is a *tour-de-force* of materials: highly polished stainless steel, lovingly finished maple, bright neon for signage, colourful plaster walls. One of the most lavish uses of material to best effect is the stainless steel railings with their burnished finish. Weaving through the railings are taut cables, secured with exposed hardware. Here are materials taken to lavish expression.

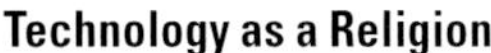

Technology as a Religion

One of the early tenets of Modernism was the romantic view of technology as saviour. Technology animated the spirit of Modernism, and in turn became the medium of Modernism's message. The Modern age was one of great technological breakthroughs, and architecture expressed the spirit of the time through sleek design and inventive construction. Much of that ethic lives on in the work of such architects as Norman Foster and Renzo Piano, and we find it cropping up in projects all over the world.

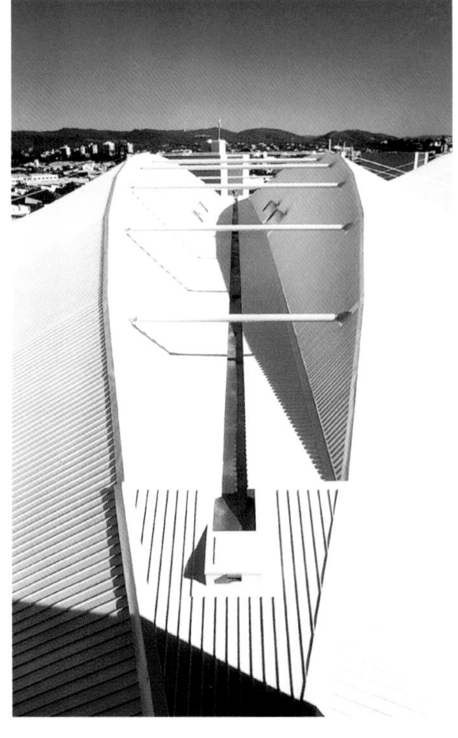

In Cardiff Bay, England, for example, Ahrends Burton and Koralek's Techniquest building seems to capture Modernism technological spirit. This 3,500 square metre (37,680 square foot) building houses science and technology exhibits for over 200,000 visitors a year. It incorporates the old wrought iron structure of an engineering workshop, making the building's skeleton essentially part of the exhibit. The vaulted roof is made up of lightweight trusses. Sun-shading structures of tubular steel hold canvas awnings that protect the building from solar heat gain, and also allude to the rigging and sails of boats in the bay. Technology is used here to give form to a building, the contents of which are the artefacts of our technical age.

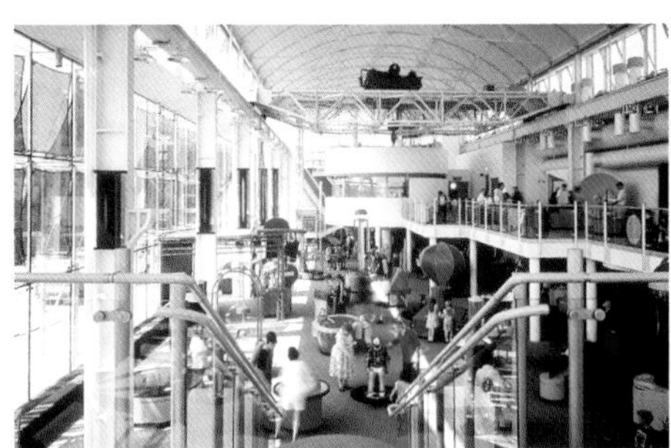

Two other projects in this volume share an expression of technological optimism.
In Australia, the Brisbane Convention and Exhibition Centre, designed by Philip Cox Richardson Rayner and Partners, uses structural gymnastics to give the building a civic presence. The 35,000 square metre (376,750 square foot) centre is sheltered under a prefinished steel roof that takes the form of hyperbolic paraboloids. The shell-like roofs are supported with large triangular trusses set diagonally to the building's streetfront, which helps to keep the scale of the building manageable. One can view the underside of the roof structure from the street entrance through the glassy walls, as well as from the exhibit spaces. Thus, one is constantly aware of this building's muscular technology. And a late-Modern architect appears to be the inspiration: the convention centre's shell-like roofs have a certain resemblance to Jørn Utzon's Sydney Opera House.

At the new Denver International Airport Passenger Terminal in Colorado, USA, C.W. Fentress, J.H. Bradburn and Associates have created an architectural oasis in the desert of the American Southwest. Although the project was plagued with delays and cost over-runs (one theory for the troubles was that the unappeased spirits of long-dead Native Americans were distressed by the site selection) the result is truly spirited. High above the desert, tall masts rise to give support to a white fabric roof. When illuminated at night, the roof appears to be a lounging cloud. The expression of the terminal's technology dovetails with the building's service to air travel, and seems an heir to the Modernism of Eero Saarinen, as expressed in his air terminals at JFK and Dulles.

A branch of late-Modernism that has received scant attention over the years is that of the Organic School, represented by such architects as Bruce Goff, Herb Greene, and John Lautner. In this volume, it is a tradition carried forward by Bart Prince, who worked with Goff for a number of years. In Prince's design for the Hight Residence in Mendocino County, California, USA, the building's wood-frame structure undulates like a wave. Inside, you read the framing as it warps above your head, rolling from one end of the house to the other. The interiors of Prince's houses are always spatial spectacles, and the Hight Residence is no exception.

Where Do We Go From Here?

Modernism's chief historian and cheerleader, Sigfried Giedion, wrote in his bible of the movement, *Space, Time, and Architecture*, that Modernism was truly suitable for any site, in any country, in any climate. Giedion believed that Modernism's strength was that it was international: it could provide an architectural answer to the particulars of any locality. Somehow this potential became obscured as Modernism developed. Its most abusive manifestation was in the work of Mies van der Rohe, who provided a one-size-fits-all version of Modernism: the same solution for every site. Mies's architecture became the epitome of the International Style, but it was anything but international. Anti-international was more like it.

The work in this yearbook might provide a new direction. It shows that architecture in the Modern idiom can be adapted around the globe. It also demonstrates that it can accommodate the local architectural heritage. Nikken Sekkei's design for the Dunhuang Cave Cultural Asset Reservation and Exhibition Centre in China reveals a Modern architecture that is responsive to the vernacular tradition. It's possible that Modern architecture still has enough life in it to provide a special answer to wherever we build. This sensitivity can only be realised through a fresh, inventive approach to every design problem, not with cookie-cutter solutions, or mindless historical pastiche.

Selected Projects

Brisbane Convention and Exhibition Centre

Philip Cox Richardson Rayner and Partners Pty Ltd

Completion: May 1995

Location: Brisbane, Queensland, Australia

Client: Queensland Government/Leighton Contractors

Area: 35,000 square metres; 376,750 square feet

Structure: Precast concrete; aluminium cladding; steel framing; prefinished steel roof

Materials: Steel; glass

Cost: A$138 million

Brisbane's new landmark Convention and Exhibition Centre is one of the most innovative in the world. Its structure uses hyperbolic paraboloids on an unprecedented scale, incorporates conventional building materials in an exciting and imaginative way. Despite the overall curved steel shapes, all members used in the structure are straight. The Centre is also the first in Australia to incorporate both convention and exhibition areas inside one volume.

The 'hypar' roof shapes are derived from a need to minimise the scale of a vast building, 450 metres (1,476 feet) long and 22 metres (72 feet) high, situated in an area of gardens and smaller buildings. As the hypar roofs geometrically span the halls diagonally, they present a less confrontational scale to the streets and edges than would a conventional orthogonal structure.

The spaces formed by the shell structure are considerably more voluminous than in other large scale exhibition centres, and create dramatic areas for conferences and performances. This feature is combined with a high level of flexibility in layout which is achieved by operable walls, and seats which can be raised to the ceiling for exhibition space, or lowered to the floor for conventions. Numerous configurations are possible in both the exhibition space and the meeting and breakout rooms, while at the same time discrete food and beverage service areas are provided.

A feature of the Centre is a large terrazzo artwork in the foyer, designed by artist John Olsen and based on his impressions of Lakefield National Park in North Queensland. This permanent artwork is accompanied by a vast range of contemporary Australian and Aboriginal artworks.

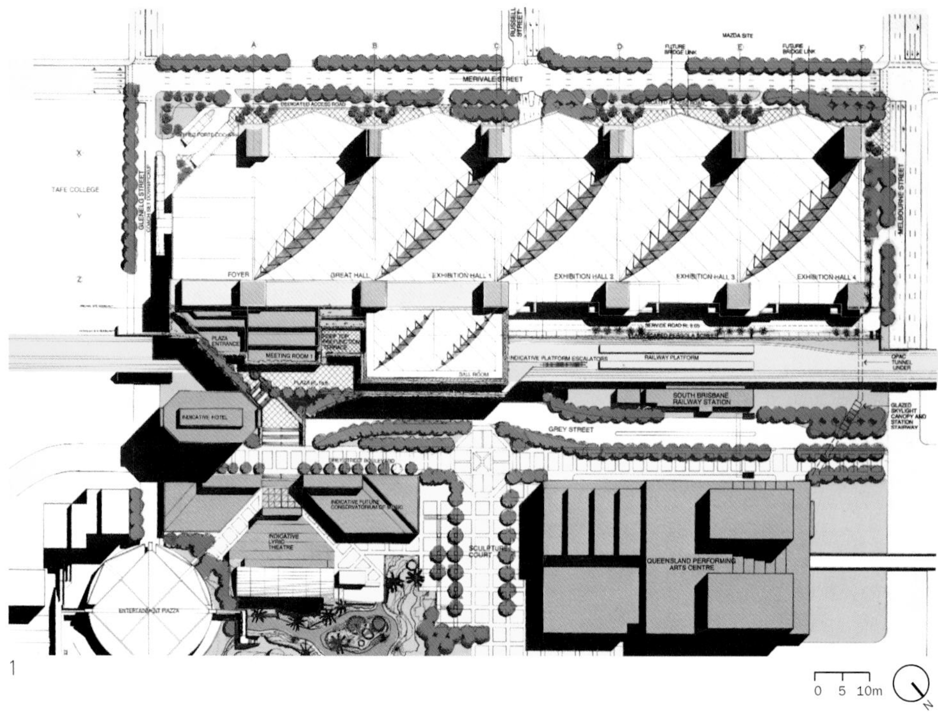

1

2

1 Site plan
2 Centre with city in background
3 Entrance foyer
4 Exhibition hall entry

3

4

5

6

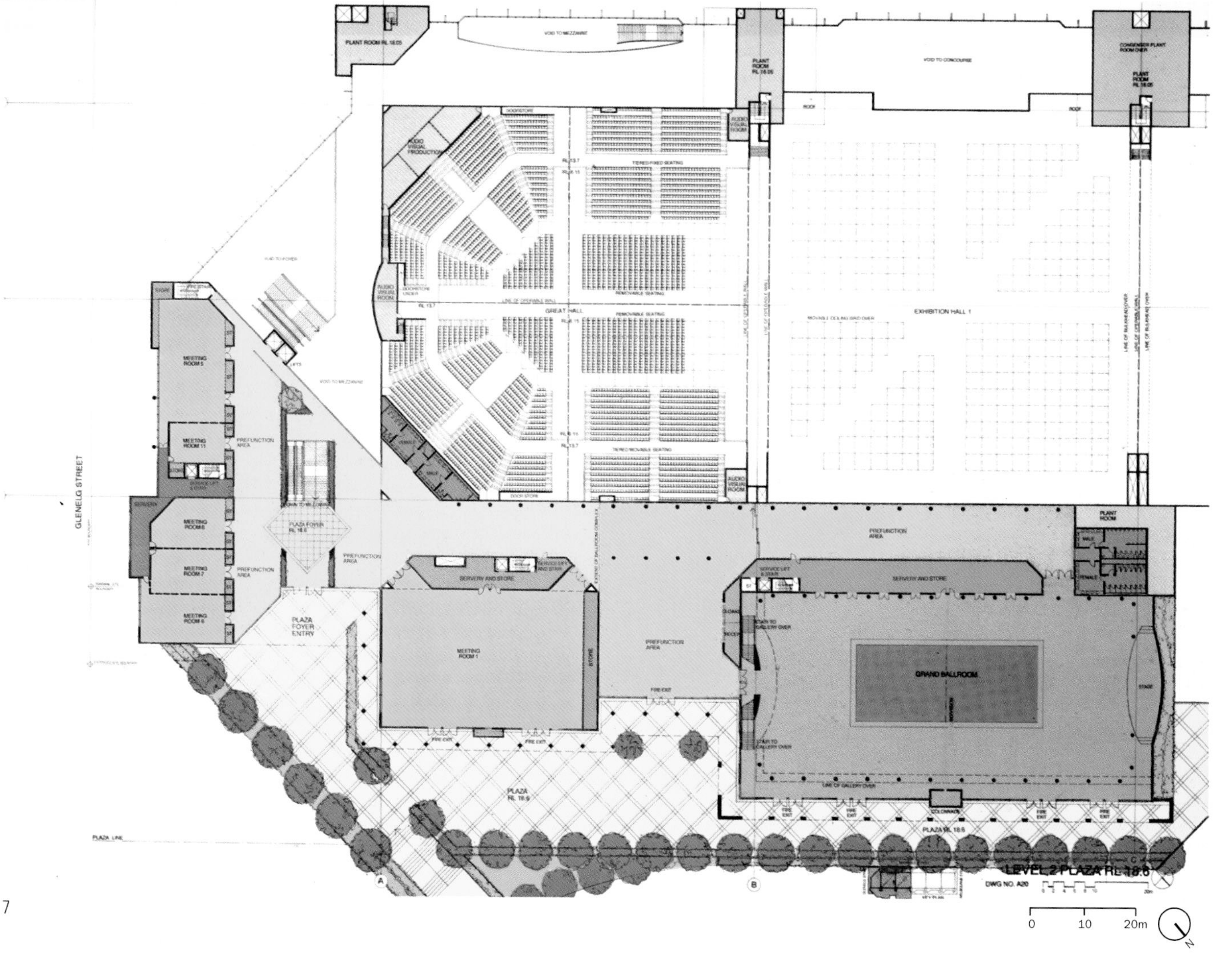

GREAT HALL

EXHIBITION HALL 1

GRAND BALLROOM

MEETING ROOM 1

PREFUNCTION AREA

PLAZA FOYER ENTRY

PLAZA RL 18.5

GLENELG STREET

LEVEL 2 PLAZA RL 18.6

DWG NO. A20

0 10 20m

N

7

5 Interior view primary roof truss
6 Exterior view of primary roof truss
7 Upper level plan
8 Great Hall
9 Ballroom
Photography: Patrick Bingham-Hall

8

9

Charlotte Convention Center

Thompson, Ventulett, Stainback and Associates Inc

Completion: January 1995

Location: Charlotte, North Carolina, USA

Client: The City of Charlotte

Area: 79,801 square metres; 859,000 square feet

Structure: Steel frame

Materials: Concrete masonry; precast concrete

Cost: US$86 million

Awards: Honour Award, AIA/Charlotte
1994 Community Enhancement Award, First Place

1995 Design Award, ASID/GA

1995 Winner, Public Spaces Interiors Magazine Annual Awards

In addition to providing a functionally state-of-the-art convention centre and a building that is an urbanistically responsible contribution to the city of Charlotte, TVS&A explored and sought to express other architectural values that will reveal themselves to be meaningful as the building is experienced over time.

The building is organised in three levels. Below grade is the exhibition space with truck loading areas; the street level L-shaped concourse consists almost entirely of public circulation space, and the upper level contains meeting rooms and a ballroom, as well as the administrative offices and a cafe.

The cross form of the building plan has a harmonic relationship to Charlotte's urban form and its cultural and geographical origins as a 'crossroads' town. The City grew from the intersection of Native American trade routes (now Trade and Tryon Streets) and the four wards of the City are defined by this intersection.

The basic form of the building is therefore defined by intersecting circulation axes laid over an L-shaped plan. The circulation spaces themselves are formally exploded (roof planes separated from walls, large amounts of glass with views to gardens) to visually open the interior to the exterior. The circulation spaces (concourses) are identified with a shallow vaulted roof, which provides a centralising effect without being overtly traditional, and which balances the asymmetrical gestures of the concourse piers.

A large central hall at the crossing of the building's axes serves as a meeting place. It is crowned by a large skylight structure above an oculus which appears as a lantern at night. The cross-form and the L-form of the plan become motifs that are employed at a variety of scales throughout the building.

The project also provided an opportunity to work out architectural ideas that are of ongoing concern: a primary use of materials, forms, and colour; a tension between centred and non-centred compositions; a juxtaposition of massiveness and lightness; and generally, a freedom from cultural assumptions and an amplification of the essential aspects of architecture.

1 Site location map
2 Perspective view of west entrance
3 Upper level floor plan
4 Entrance level floor plan
5 Exhibit hall/lower level floor plan
6 West entrance

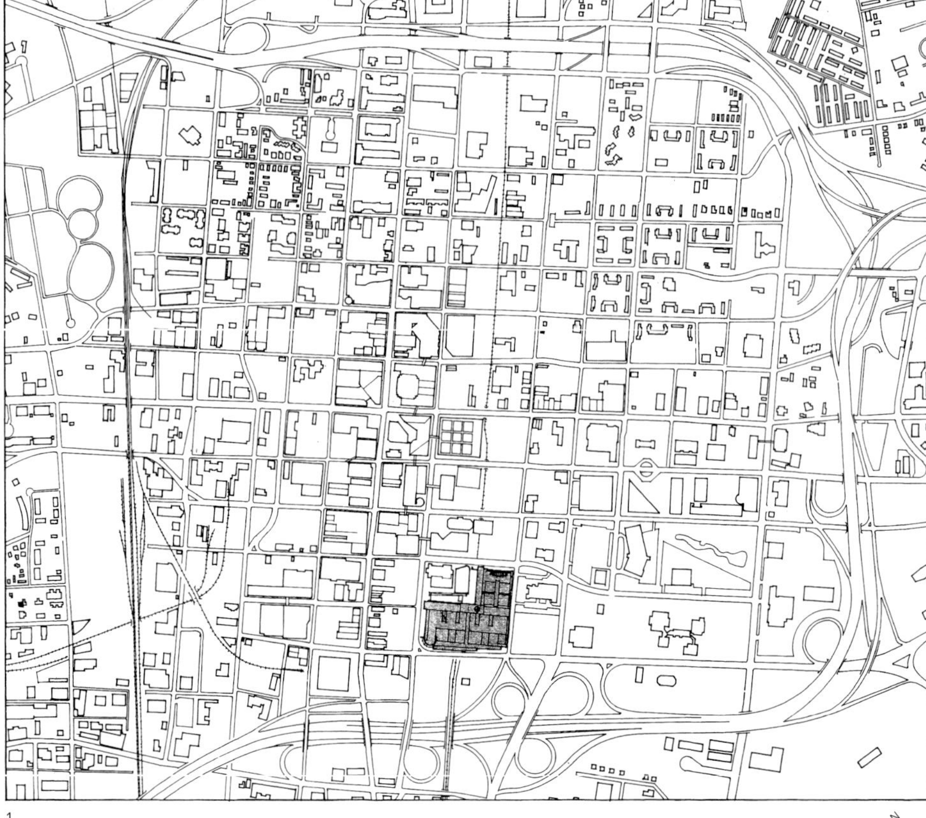

1

2

2
5
2
3
2
6
4
4
7
0
150
300ft
N

3

2
2
3
0
150
300ft
N

4

1
1
1
0
150
300ft
N

5

CONVENTION CENTER
CHARLOTTE
CONVENTION
CENTER

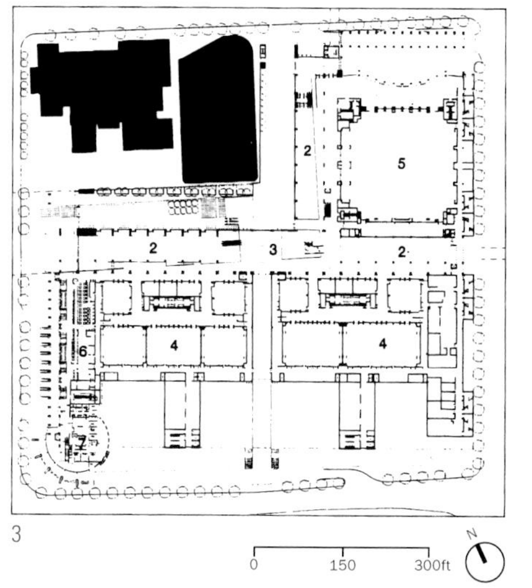

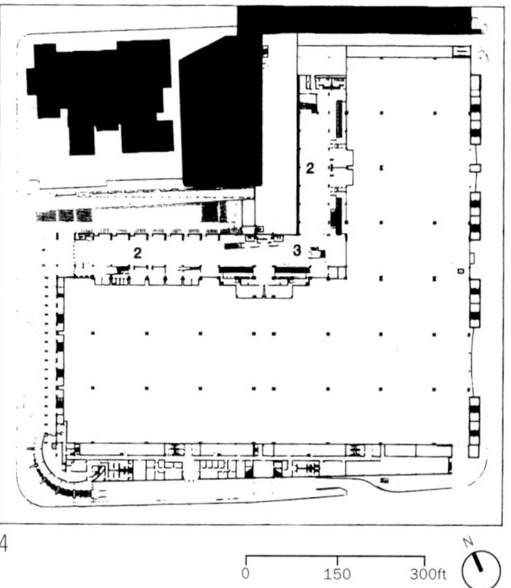

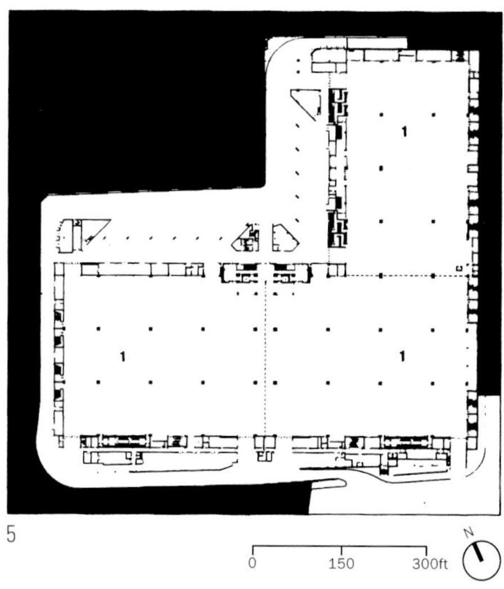

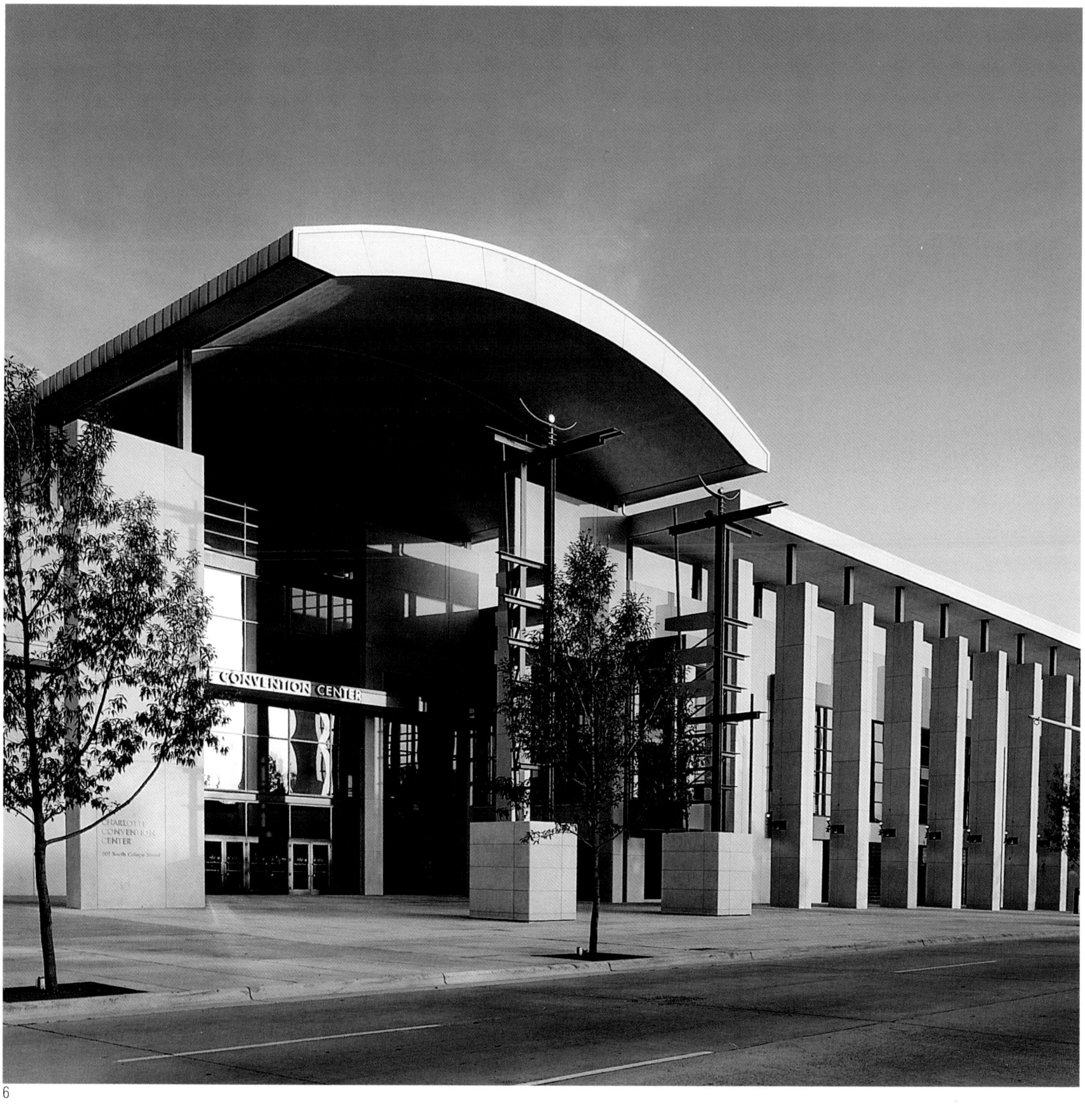

6

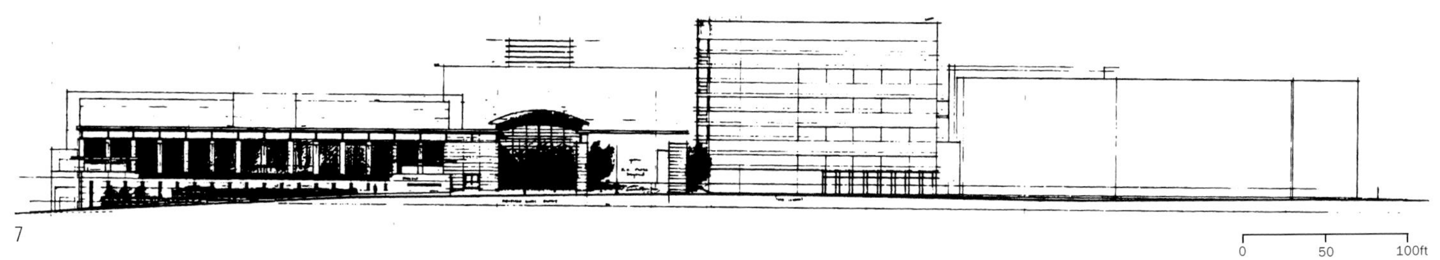

7

8

9

10

7 North elevation
8 East elevation
9 West elevation
10 South elevation
11 Typical meeting room entry
12 Exterior view at public circulation concourse

11

12

13

14

13 View into Grand Hall
14 Interior of public circulation concourse
15 Entrance at night
Photography: Brian Gassell/TVS&Associates

15

Dragon Centre

Wong Tung & Partners Limited

Completion: September 1994

Location: Hong Kong

Client: Fotosky Investment Limited

Area: 8,175 square metres; 88,000 square feet

Structure: Reinforced concrete; steel columns for basement

Materials: Glazed ceramic tiles; painted steel; glass; stainless steel; metal cladding; terrazzo slab flooring; metal and gypsum board ceilings

Cost: HK$800 million

Awards: 1994 Certificate of Merit from the Hong Kong Institute of Architects

The brief for this project called for an all commercial building for retail, restaurants and entertainment while accommodating the lease requirements of a large ground floor six-bay public transport terminus and spaces for the parking of 550 private cars and 210 lorries.

While the total building area is more than 12 times the area of the site, the building is subjected to severe height restriction of ten storeys due to its location directly under a flight path.

Five levels of basements were required to house all the car and lorry spaces and created the deepest basement in Hong Kong at the time. A top-down construction method which permitted the superstructure to go up simultaneously with the basement construction was used to achieve the shortest building program.

The 45,000 square metre (484,392 square foot) commercial portion is arranged around an elliptical skylit atrium which is expressed as a crystalline centrepiece on the elevation, with a 28 metre (92 foot) wide by 32 metre (105 foot) high curved suspended glass wall that flares out at the bottom to form the glass roof of the main entrance, an engineering feat in itself. This together with the feature staircase—columns, masts and fabric features at the roof—dissolve the large flat-top building mass to a collage of interesting forms that are compatible in scale with the environment.

Continued

1

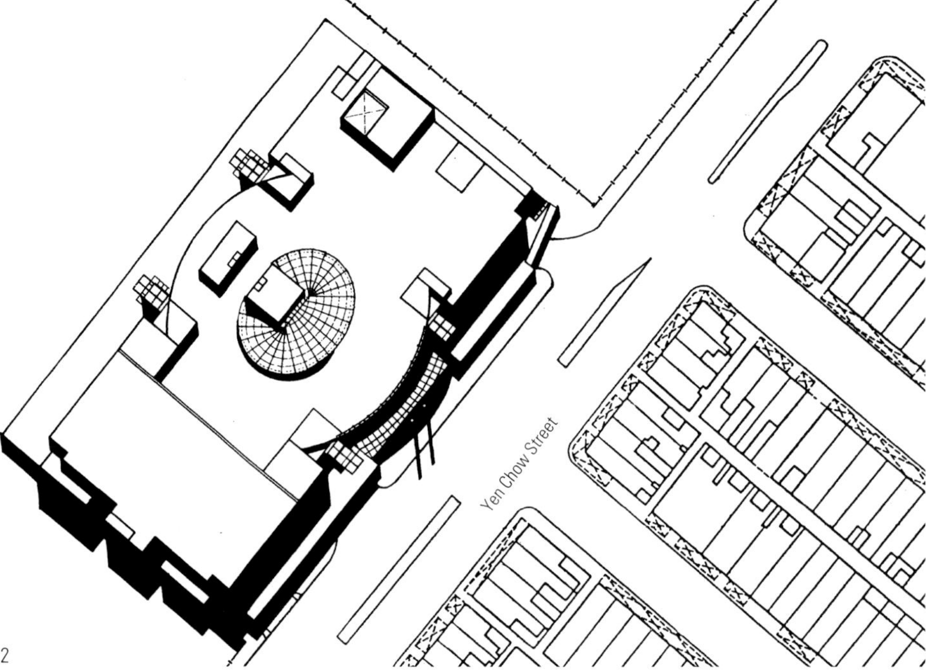

2

3

1 Rooftop fabric features
2 Site plan
3 Main street elevation
4 Main entry lobby
5 Express escalator lobby
6 Central feature glass wall

4

5

6

Two 'magnets'; the entertainment floor featuring an ice-skating rink and the first indoor roller coaster in Hong Kong, and the food hall are located at the top of the building. The vertical transportation system comprises escalators, observation lifts and an additional 'floor skipping' escalator system that provides shoppers with express service to reach the high floors of the complex.

Very basic and friendly materials, earth tone brick tiles and painted steel were chosen for the exterior to set the building comfortably in the rather industrial neighbourhood. Yet its bold forms, bright colours, transparency and its myriads of details of steel and glass render a totally contrasting image of robustness and festivity that suits a building of this nature. The crown of fabric canopies and features reinforces the image and reaches out to address the surrounding area.

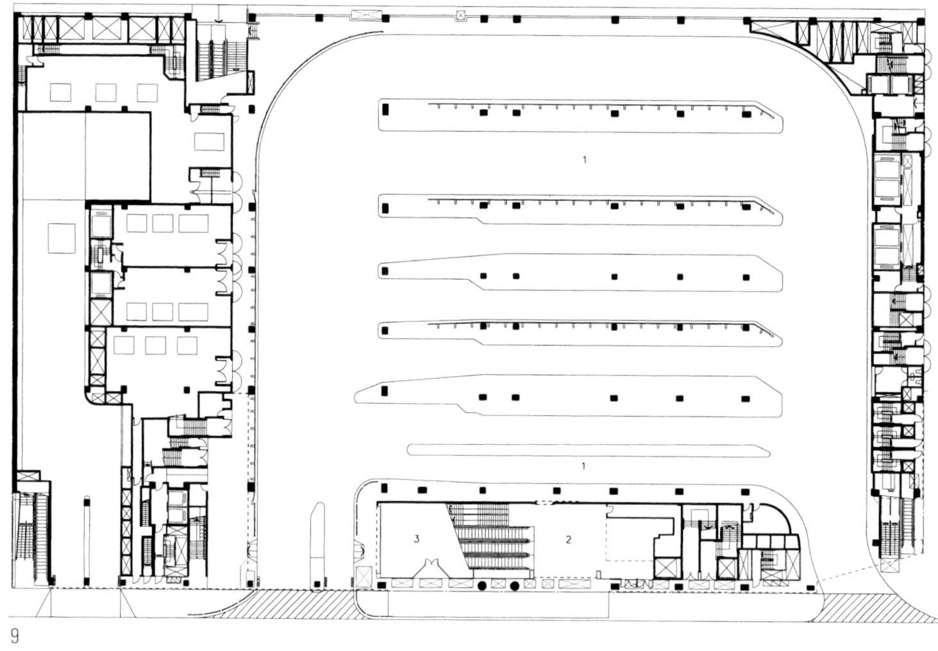

9

7

10

8

11

7 Typical arcade
8 Skylight and indoor roller coaster
9 Ground floor public transport terminus
10 Retail floor
11 Entertainment floor
12 Central atrium

0 5 10m

12

Edinburgh International Conference and Exhibition Centre

Terry Farrell and Partners

Completion: September 1995

Location: Edinburgh, Scotland

Client: Edinburgh District Council, Lothian & Edinburgh Enterprise Limited and Lothian Regional Council

Area: 12,356 square metres; 133,000 square feet

Structure: In situ concrete frame; steel frame

Materials: Sandstone; architectural precast concrete; metal rails; profiled metal panels and louvres; structural double glazing; glass blocks; membrane roof

Cost: GB£38 million

The development of the winning master plan proposals by Terry Farrell during 1989 and 1990 led to the location of the Conference Centre at the crossing of Morrison Street and the West Approach Road: a prominent position at the centre of the emerging West End/Port Hamilton/ Haymarket business district, on the western approach to the city.

The Conference and Exhibition Centre design has been influenced by the shape of the site, the difference in levels between Morrison Street and the West Approach Road, budget restrictions, and its role in the realisation of the master plan. It establishes the setback and curve of the Morrison Street frontage and pedestrian access from Morrison Street.

A simple, strong architecture is intended to give the building both civic presence appropriate to its Scottish setting, and an international image. In keeping with the master plan principles, the elevations will be light buff/ grey in colour, harmonising with the traditional sandstone of Edinburgh.

1

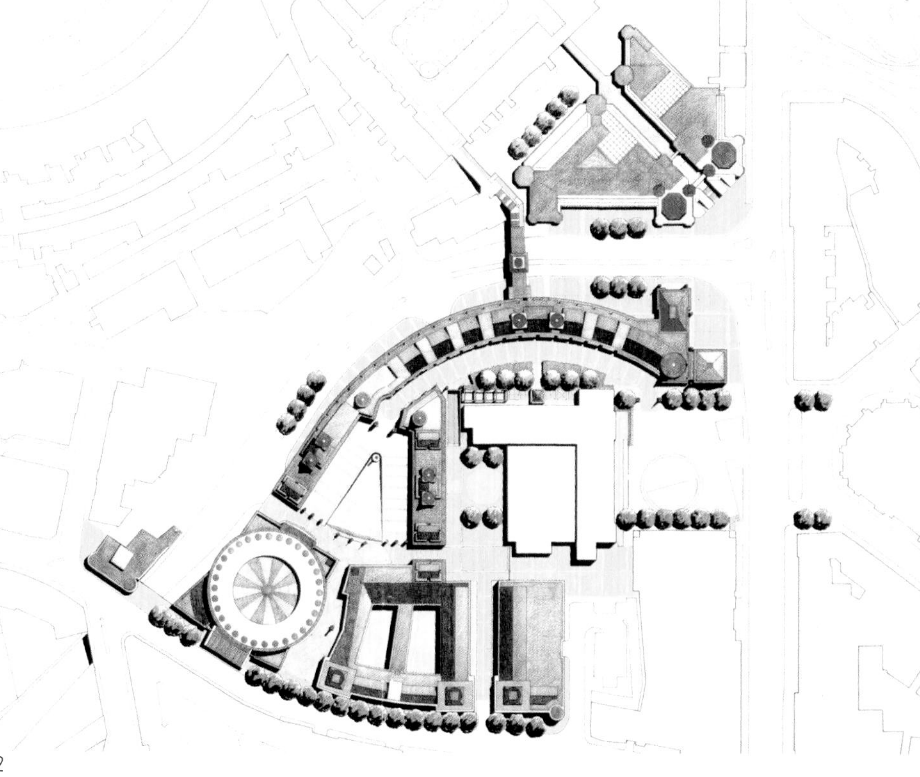

2

1 Model: detail of south elevation, main entrance
2 Master plan 1993
3 Level 5: ground floor, mezzanine 1
4 Level 7: auditorium
5 Level 11: roof plan
6 Model: south and east elevations
7 Model: aerial view
8 Model: main entrance elevation

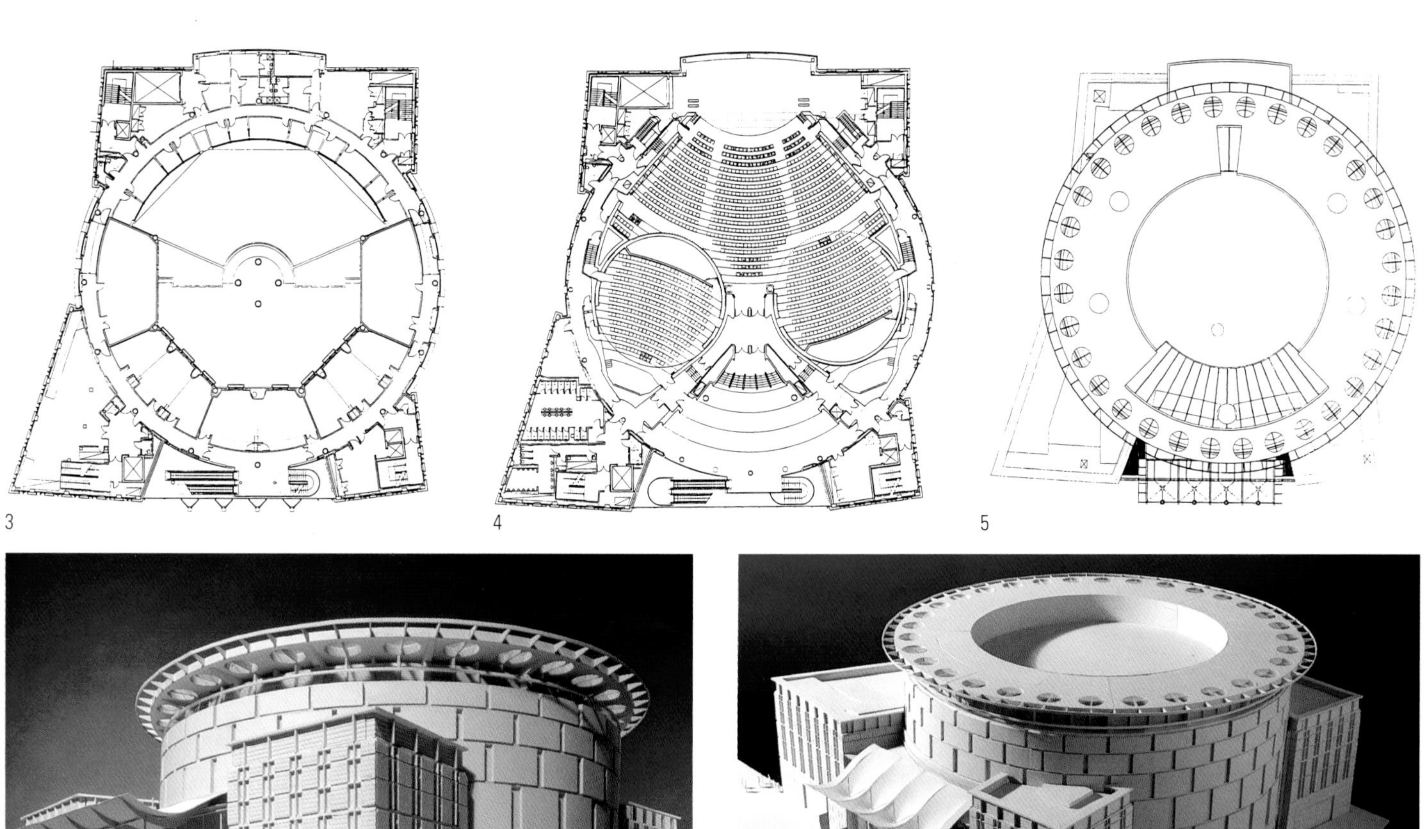

3 4 5

6 7

8

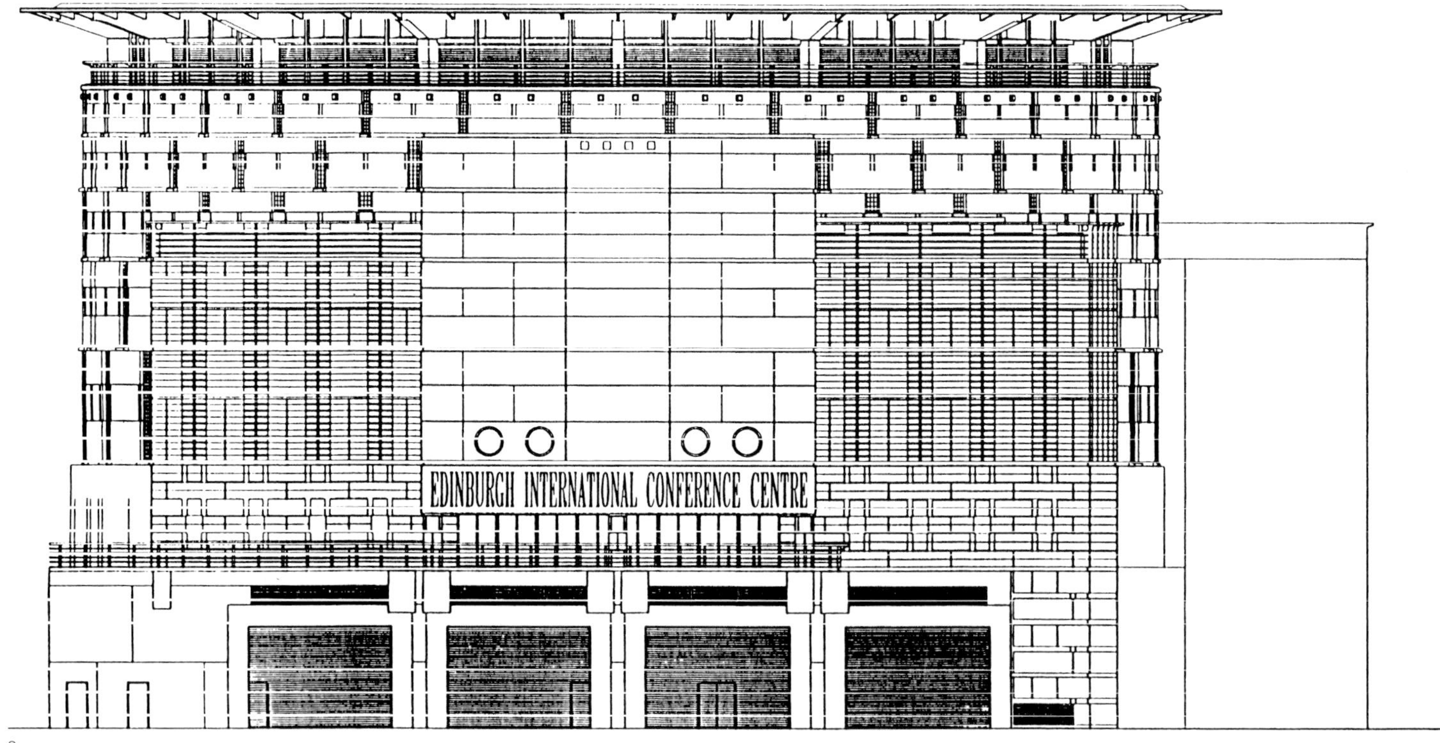

9

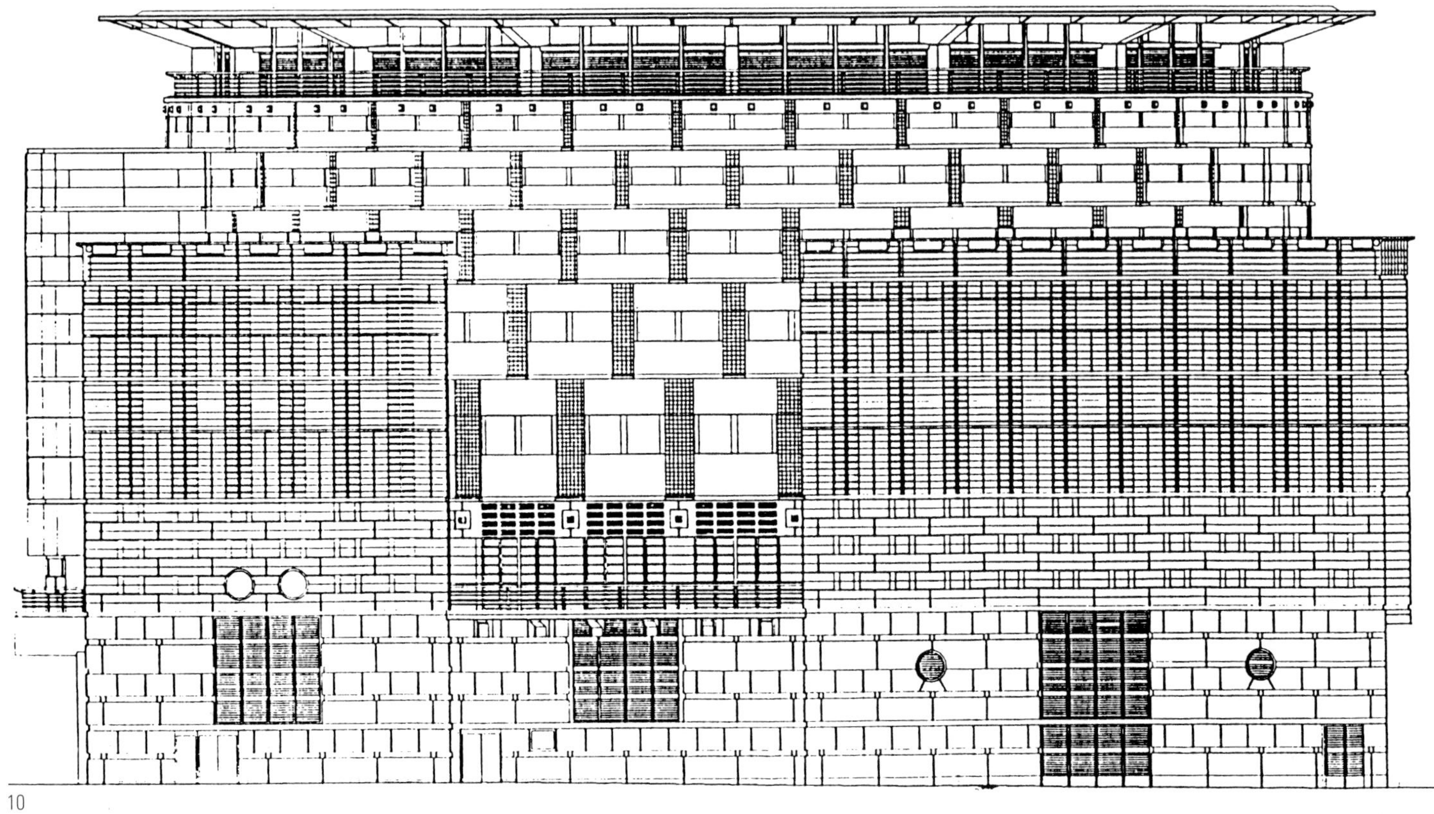
10

9 North elevation
10 West elevation
11 Aerial photograph of Conference Centre

11

12

13

12 Elevation detail
13 South elevation looking down Morrison Street
14 Entrance canopy
15-16 Entrance canopy detail
Photography: Nigel Young

14

15

16

Embassy of Sweden

RTKL Associates Inc.
in association with Stintzing Arkitekter, AB

Completion: June 1994

Location: Washington, D.C., USA

Client: The Government of Sweden

Area: 2,787 square metres; 30,000 square feet

Materials: Oak floors; wood panels; wool carpet

RTKL provided interior architecture services for the Embassy of Sweden's 2,787 square metre (30,000 square foot) Washington office.

Located on two floors, the new space houses embassy personnel and support staff and includes a multi-purpose room, library, secure storage rooms, luncheon room, and conference and reception areas.

Incorporating both Swedish and American materials, the embassy reflects Swedish aesthetic and cultural influences. It also responds to specific Swedish requirements, such as the provision of windows for every employee.

RTKL worked in conjunction with a Swedish design architect for planning and design. Also part of the team were local embassy personnel and National Property Board of Sweden representatives.

1

1 Ambassador's office
2 Lobby
3 Multi-purpose room
4 Lunch room
Photography: Hedrich Blessing

2

Carl Johan De Geer
TRIVSEL
Norrköpings Konstmuseum
WACHTMEISTER
SOTHEBY'S
19 OKT - 11 NOV 1994

3

4

ESEO Federal Credit Union

Elliott + Associates Architects

Completion: June 1994

Location: Oklahoma City, Oklahoma, USA

Client: ESEO Federal Credit Union

Area: 725 square metres; 7,800 square feet

Structure: Steel tube columns; wood truss roof

Materials: Destin field stone; insulated glass; green composition shingle roof

Cost: US$912,000

Awards: 1995 American Institute of Architects, Oklahoma Council Honour Award

IDEA95/Business Week Magazine, National Environments, Gold Award

1994 Interiors Magazine National Big 'I' Award

The site concept for this project was to develop a master plan that allowed for a second structure and an expanded drive-in, in addition to creating a Redbud (State tree) orchard with 53 trees to commemorate the age of the institution at the time of construction.

The architectural concept was to: create an architectural statement that was a 'portrait' of the Credit Union that combines the business philosophy with the personality of the membership; respond to climatic conditions of Oklahoma; define a patch of ground with a sheltering roof and steel columns supporting the canopy roof much as a tree trunk and branches support the leaf canopy of a tree; integrate the honesty and integrity of the membership personality with local native American folklore and indigenous materials; and, create a space that evokes the sensation of working out-of-doors under the shade of a giant tree.

Rusting steel 'branches', field stone, aggregate floors and exposed wood structure communicate a frugal, unpretentious, 'lodge' atmosphere; the symbolic stone 'campfire' recognises historical Native American presence on the site and the four sacred colours (red, yellow, black and white) appear on the conference room storage cabinet. The conference room roof stands as the 'bird' soaring through the space.

Mechanical systems include nine gas fired, roof top units with electric cooling for nine zones; large glass areas are accommodated with clear 2.5 cm (1 inch) insulated glass and low-e coating on the north and underfloor supply overall. Condensing units are hidden from view and located on the roof of the mechanical rooms. There are no visible roof penetrations.

Halogen ambient lighting systems are used throughout to reduce computer eye strain and to enhance the architectural volume of the spaces and structural detailing. H.I.D. uplighting provides inexpensive security lighting while making a dramatic statement at night.

1

2

3

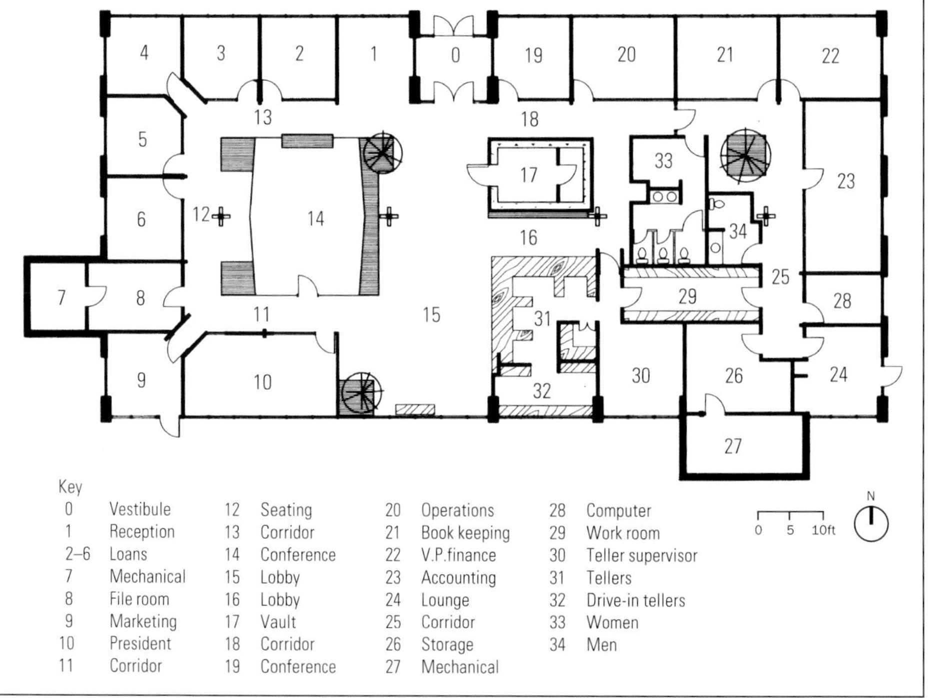

4

5

1 Northwest corner showing clerestory skylight and entry stone wall
2 View from office towards stone vault
3 Northeast corner illustrating 'floating roof'
4 Floor plan
5 Nighttime exterior illustrating 'floating roof'
6 Building section
7 Entry elevation with super beam support
8 Drive-in canopy 'bridge' connection
9 Interior view

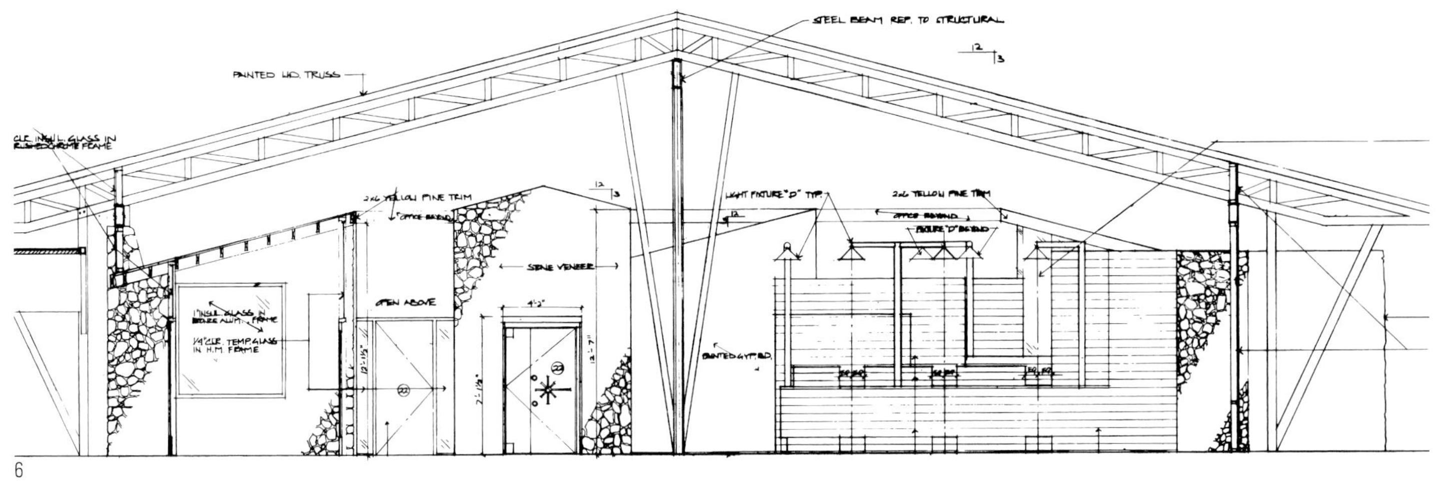
STEEL BEAM REF. TO STRUCTURAL
PAINTED WD. TRUSS
2x6 YELLOW PINE TRIM
OFFICE BEYOND
STONE VENEER
OPEN ABOVE
LIGHT FIXTURE "D" TYP.
FIXTURE "D" BEYOND
PAINTED GYP. BD.

6

7

8

9

Gateway I, Harbour City

Wong & Ouyang (HK) Ltd

Completion: October 1994

Location: Harbour City, Hong Kong

Client: Wharf Group

Area: 123,400 square metres; 1,328,310 square feet

Structure: Reinforced concrete flat slab

Materials: Granite; glass

Cost: HK$800 million

The Gateway development was born from the desire of the Wharf Group to revamp their mainstay headquarters at Harbour City. The whole of Harbour City is 400,000 square metres (4,305,705 square feet) in area, but due to the 60 metre (197 foot) Principle Datum Limit (PDL), the site development in the early 1960s had not been fully optimised. Relaxation of the PDL coupled with the new airport proposals resulted in the commissioning of Wong & Ouyang to redevelop the northern part of the site, known as Pentland and Trinity Courts.

The rectangular site, over 51,000 square metres (548,977 square feet) in area, is flanked by China Harbour City to the north, Harbour City to the south, Canton Road to the east and a praya to the west. The brief was to optimise the views of the harbour and at the same time maximise the full development plot ratio of the site. The development was also to be linked to the rest of the Harbour City arcades to the south.

The design incorporates twin 36-storey towers linked up to 27th floor level, where they are intentionally separated to accentuate the identity of each of the towers. The towers are rotated 45 degrees of the orthogonal which enables three elevations of each tower to have a frontage to Victoria Harbour. The corners of the towers are chamfered and rounded off to eliminate the oppressive angles, and the windows are taken down to floor level to maximise the vistas. The building is clad in alternating bands of coolite green glass and polished Azalea granite.

The towers sit on a 3-storey podium, below which is a 2-storey basement. The podium design had to accommodate four cinemas, retail shops and an arcade to be linked to the existing Harbour City arcades at second and third floor level. This had resulted in the location of the lift lobbies, incorporating 24 lifts at second floor, reached by two escalators from the main entrance at Canton Road.

The structural design incorporated the reuse of as much of the existing basement as possible to Pentland and Trinity Courts, thus saving on time and cost. After the foundation caisson work was completed, construction was top down with the erection of skeletal columns and the simultaneous construction of the super structure and basement excavation. The podium and towers were designed for maximum flexibility, with flat slab and drop panels using post tensioned tendons to eliminate any tie beams to the slab soffites.

The building services provision is modelled on the Times Square project at Causeway Bay. Grade A office and retail mechanical/engineering facilities with high tech optical fibre cabling are provided for any future needs. Radio and paging facilities are integrated with the existing Harbour City.

1

2

3

4

5

6

1 Main entrance from Canton Road, Kowloon
2 View of Gateway 1 from the harbour
3 Main office lobby
4 Retail atrium
5 Main entrance lobby showing escalator access to office main lobby
6 Main entrance lobby showing escalator access to retail atrium

The Heierding Building

Elliott + Associates Architects

Completion: May 1995

Location: Oklahoma City, Oklahoma, USA

Client: Rand and Jeanette Elliott

Area: 472 square metres; 5,080 square feet

Cost: US$545,362

This renovation of a 1914 building needed to address the following program points: the building was to be restored to its original condition, and is on the National Register of Historic Places, it had to meet the ADA requirements without compromising the integrity of the historic structure; it moved the office of Elliott + Associates back downtown to set an example in the community showing the importance of preservation; and the building was to be used as an opportunity to showcase both architectural preservation and modern thinking. The immediate site and sidewalks were to be restored to useable condition, and a 'patch of green' to be created on the adjacent property in direct contrast to the hardness of the downtown setting.

Functional considerations included creating a gallery/ conference space on the first level to accommodate project meetings, small social gatherings, the display of project photographs and the exhibition of one changing work.

Workstations were located on the north side of level two to benefit from the soft light while the lunch room/library was placed on the south in the south sunlight. A large central work counter/material library allows open access to all professionals.

The architectural concept is called 'Light Shrines'. The idea is to use the daylight coming into the space to create the atmosphere. There are six light shrines in the building that illustrate how light (daylight and electric) can behave as it interacts with the architecture. It was the goal to use light as a design element and 'paint with light'. Light is the art and the spirit of the space.

Common materials have been used in unusual and thought provoking ways, showing visitors new possibilities and creative thought.

1

2

3

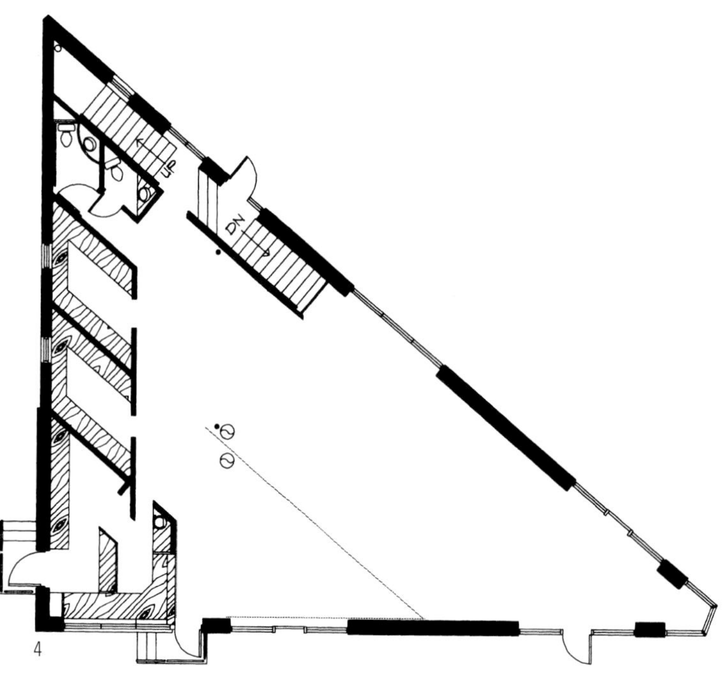

4

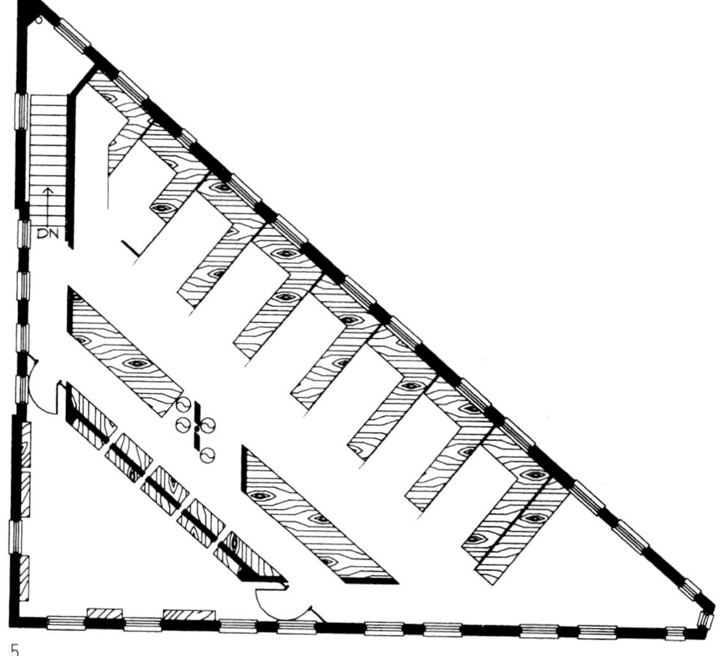

5

6

7

8

9

10

11

12

13

14

15

1 Exterior 'nose' elevation
2 South elevation
3 Entry detail
4 First floor
5 Second floor
6 Gallery/reception view with theatre scrim
7 Gallery/reception intersection showing clear fibreglass duct, scrim divider, light switch pull-chains and perforated ceiling
8 A view of the dividing 'scrim wall' between receptionist and reception
9 Gallery view looking east with glass 'nose' stained concrete floor with floor lights. Fibreglass HVAC duct and mesh window panels
10 Toilet ceiling glass detail
11 Stair detail—light detail and stamped brick wall
12 Studio 'light wall' and pole lighting
13 Studio central work and counter/materials library
14 'Nose' office looking east with rolling desk and solar window mesh panels
15 West elevation

Hirsch, Robinson, Sheiness, Glover, PC, One Houston Center

Morris Architects

Completion: September 1994
Location: Houston, Texas, USA
Client: Hirsch, Robinson, Sheiness, Glover, PC
Area: 5,110 square metres; 55,000 square feet
Materials: Steel; granite; glass; wood; silk

Located on two floors in the prestigious One Houston Center building, this law firm occupies 5,110 square metres (55,000 square feet). The two floors are connected by a steel and granite monumental staircase that is flanked by a 6.7 metre (22 foot) tall interior glass wall. The reception rooms, conference rooms and custom secretarial stations are panelled in Fiddleback Makore veneers. The flooring is granite and a custom designed carpet.

The secretarial stations are designed for efficiency, privacy and provide an ergonomically correct working environment featuring indirect and task lighting, and adjustability to various users. All shared facilities, i.e. copy centre, central files, library, supply centre, computer centre and the employee facility are centrally located. The office also features a mock court facility and special project workrooms for intense casework.

The granite, wood and carpet are rich in colour, contrasting with the soft neutrals of the silk wall panels, paint and plastic laminate work surfaces. Reddish brown and charcoal grey enhance the parchment colour of the wall materials. The patterned carpet was designed specifically to hide soiling while the lighter vertical surfaces visually enlarge the spaces. The use of opaque glass adds the image of transparency while providing privacy for the conference rooms. The lighting was designed to enhance the panelling and artwork in the public spaces while the indirect lighting in the work areas add a softness to the space, reducing eye fatigue to the computer operations. The overall effect of the interior architecture has reinforced the image of this aggressive and predominantly youthful law firm.

1

2

3

1 Level 37 reception room
2 Level 36 elevator lobby
3 Level 36 reception room
4 Typical secretarial area
5 Main conference room

4

5

Hypo Bank London

Bernhard Blauel Architects

Completion: April 1995

Location: London, United Kingdom

Client: Hypo Bank

Area: 2,500 square metres; 27,000 square feet

Structure: Reinforced concrete

Materials: Granite curtain wall; dry lining; limestone; glass

Cost: GB£2.9 million

The building is located in the heart of the City of London and accommodates 125 workstations including over 20 dealer positions for one of Germany's major banks. The relatively low slab to slab heights of the original structure required the mechanical and electrical installation heights to be minimised. A chilled ceiling, relatively new in the UK market, provided reduced fresh air duct sections due to the split cooling and heating installations and a reduced energy requirement due to the low temperature differentials.

A flexible floor layout is achieved with fully drylined and glazed demountable partitions on a raised floor. All installations are centrally controlled via a BMS, which can be adjusted individually to suit the individual needs of the occupants in each room.

Generous reception and circulation areas provide exhibition space for an exquisite collection of modern art.

1

2

3

1 Entrance foyer and lift lobby with marble plastered wall
2 Reception desk arrival point—displaying contemporary art collection
3 Office floor with flexible glass screens
4 Entrance from Moorgate
5 Staff cafe
6 Management floor reception area
7 Dealing room

Photography: Dennis Gilbert

4

5

6

7

The Icehouse

Swatt Architects

Completion: November 1994

Location: San Francisco, CA, USA

Client: Levi Strauss & Co.

Area: 18,580 square metres; 200,000 square feet

Structure: Timber frame; exposed steel seismic bracing; brick bearing walls

Materials: Exposed brick and wood; painted steel bracing; gypsum board; translucent industrex glass; maple wood panelling

The Icehouse is San Francisco's largest masonry complex, built in 1914 to manufacture ice for the city's fishing industry. The new owner, one of San Francisco's oldest businesses, has a 150 year history of apparel products that have been associated with everything from gold mining to rock and roll. Currently, they are also known and respected for cutting edge corporate policy regarding employee empowerment, teamwork and environmental responsibility.

Swatt Architects' task was to express the philosophy, history and image of the client with a new, modern, efficient headquarters facility in the historic building that was designed and built for other uses.

In keeping with the client's image and style, the design needed to be casual and comfortable with a sense of genuine quality. Expressing the owner's history and commitment to San Francisco, the design respects and reuses the best of the old buildings and celebrates the contrast of new and old. Irregular brick walls, stained timber columns and beams, steel bracing and industrial sash curtain walls have been uncovered and left exposed.

New elements include common amenity spaces located in a 5-storey steel and glass bridge that was restored to its original transparency. A new 6-storey mural tops the main conference room with an image from the company's archives.

The success of The Icehouse project is in the creation of a contemporary workplace with architecture that respects and honestly expresses the history of these great buildings. The recycling of The Icehouse is a lasting contribution to the City of San Francisco.

1

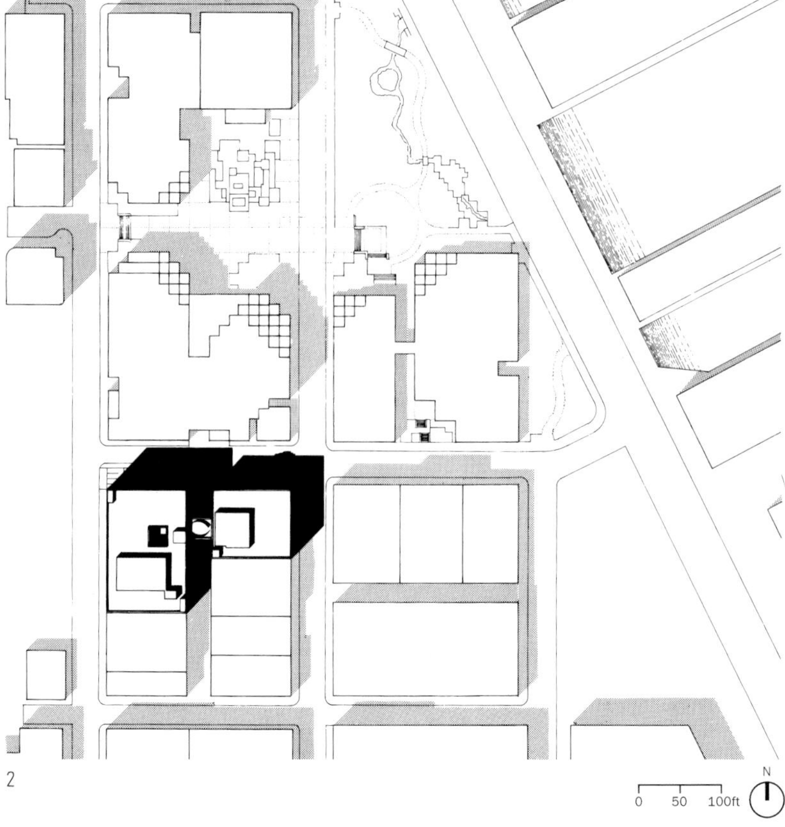

2

3

1 Building construction prior to renovation
2 Site plan
3 Exterior view of Icehouse Two
4 Longitudinal section through lightwell and bridge
5 Lounge at bridge

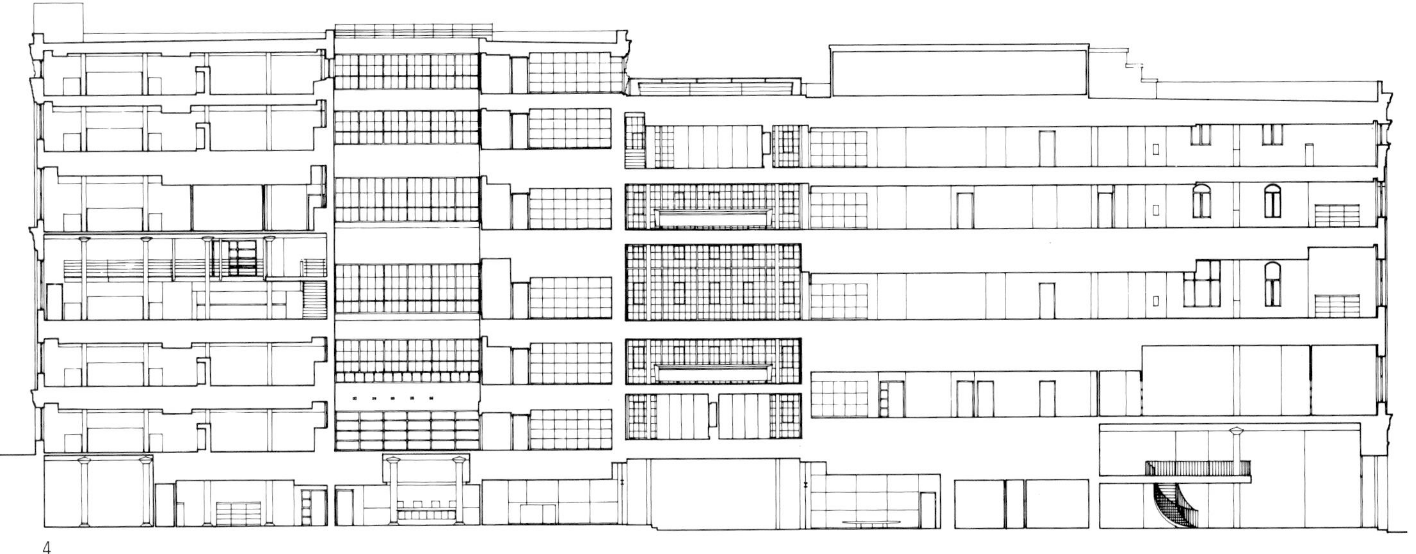

4

5

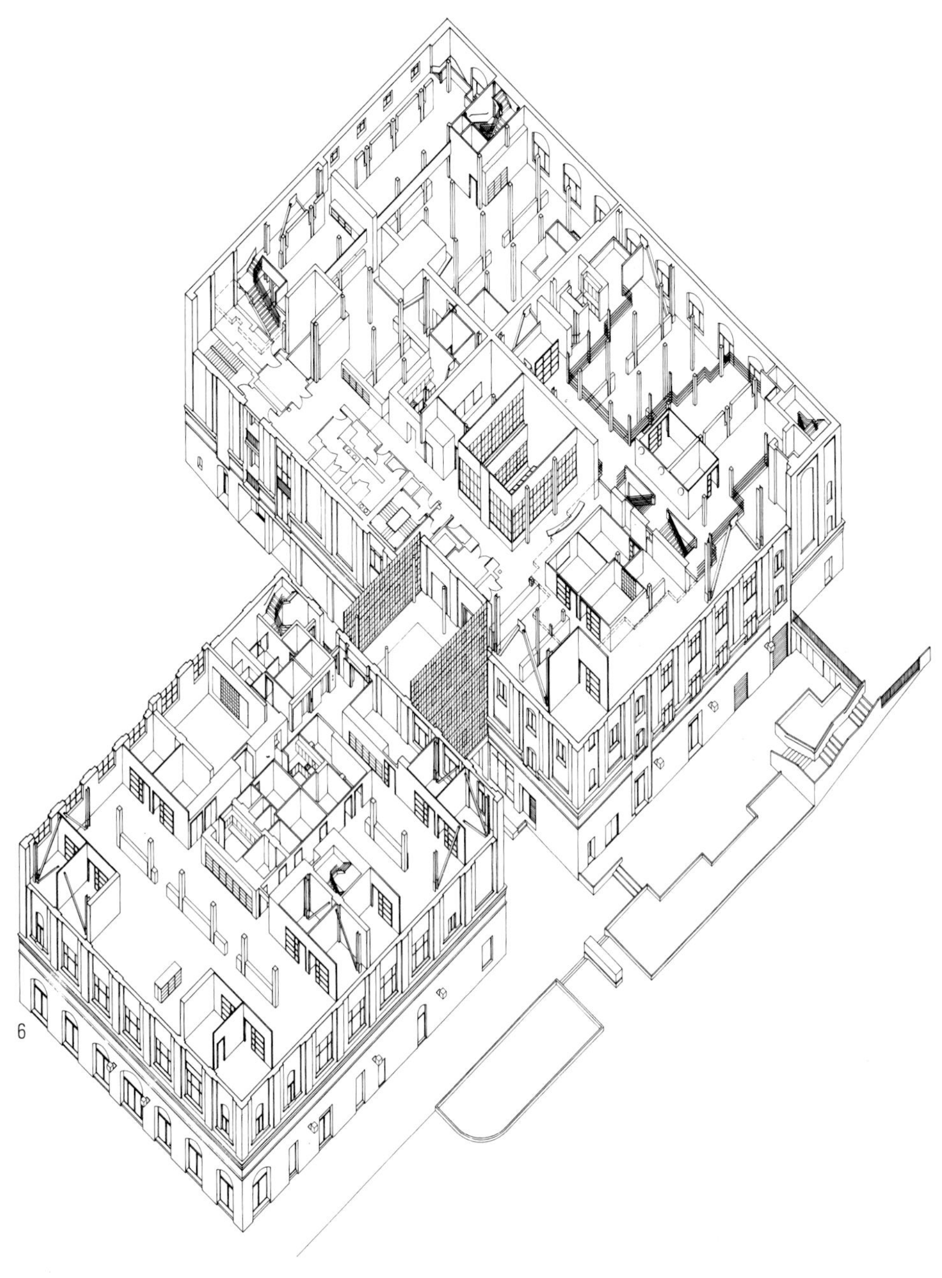

6

7

8

9

6 Axonometric
7 New stair at bridge
8 Double stair at mezzanine
9 Steel bracing at brick bearing wall
10 Exterior view of bridge

10

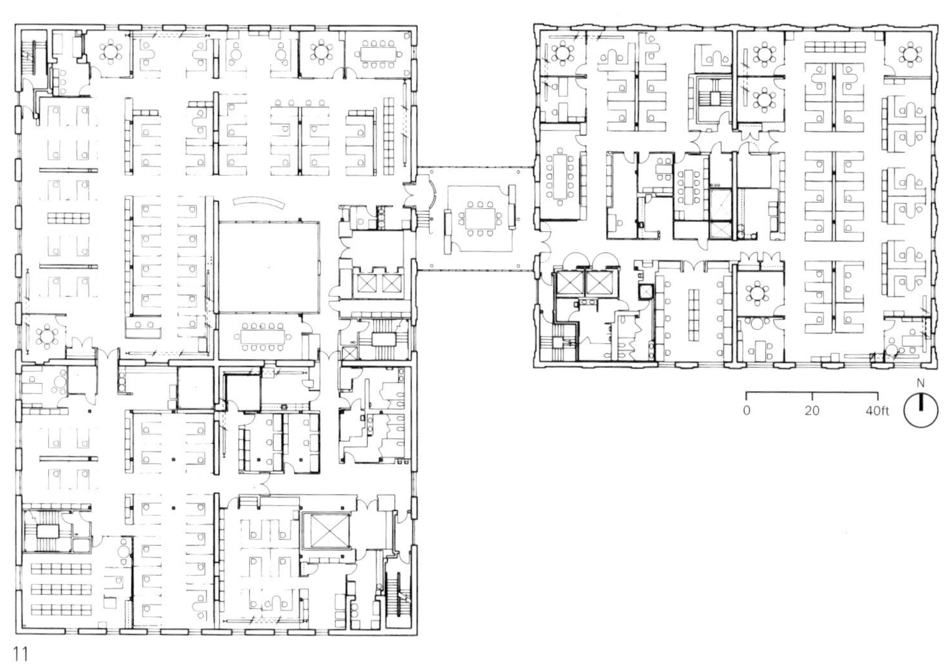

11

13

12

14

15

11 Fifth level floor plan
12 Sixth level floor plan
13 Detail at lunchroom
14 Mural at lightwell
15 Circulation and open office area
16 Conference room
Photography: Chas McGrath

16

The Ice House Renovation

Barton Myers Associates, Inc.

Completion: January 1994
Location: Beverly Hills, California, USA
Client: The McGregor Company
Area: 4,180 square metres; 45,000 square feet
Structure: Reinforced concrete; steel frame
Materials: Cement plaster; steel; glass; slate; wood

The building was constructed in 1925 as the ice storage house for Beverly Hills. When this use became outdated, the building was altered and reused for storage until 1961 when it was first converted to office uses and a fourth floor was added. Further renovations were initiated and abandoned in 1982 at which time the building fell into disrepair and remained only partially occupied.

Barton Myers Associates' design for the renovation transforms The Ice House into an elegant modern office building, while celebrating the industrial character of its history. The building plays a key role in the City of Beverly Hills' plan to revitalise the light industrial area around Civic Centre Drive and Third Street.

The project was undertaken as a speculative office development with no potential tenants as the renovation began. It was fully leased over the course of the renovations and in its first few months of operation. The renovated building seems to have had a special appeal to the entertainment industry with several film companies opening offices on the first and third floors; an entertainment lawyer occupying the second floor; and a director in a special studio space at the rear of the building. The top floor of the building is shared by Barton Myers Associates, architects of the building, and a property management group who remained in the building through the renovation.

The shell and core work includes: a full renovation of exterior elevations including new window openings and fenestration; a new glass and steel front facade; extensive seismic reinforcing; the gutting of the interior and the creation of 4,180 square metres (45,000 square feet) of office space on four floors; and, new gardens and landscaping around the building. Barton Myers Associates' offices are designed as an open studio space with generous work areas, meeting rooms, library, archives and terrace. Barton Myers Associates has also been responsible for the design of several offices within The Ice House building.

Continued

1

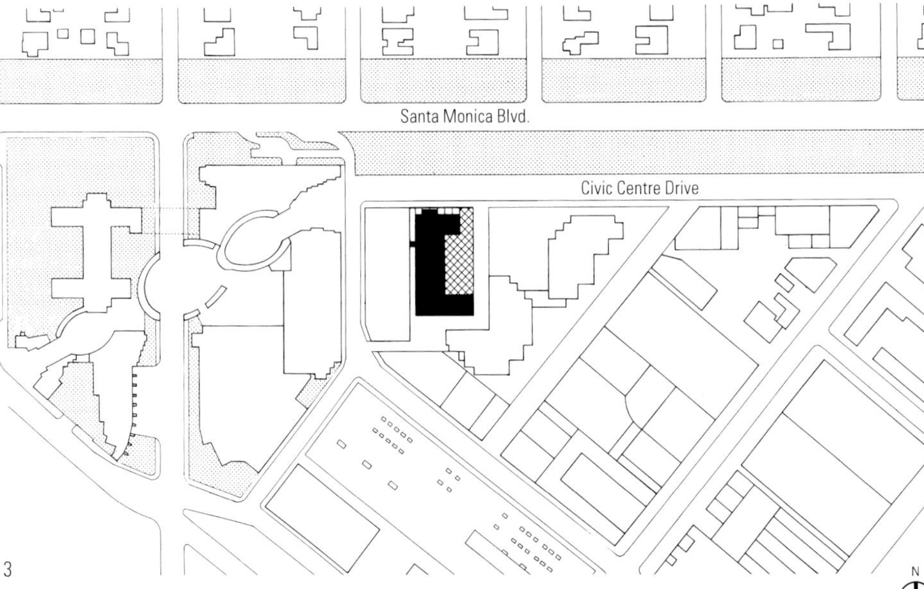

3

2

1 A corner of the steel beam and glass screen which define the facade
2 The glass screen across the facade
3 Site plan
4 View of the front of the building from the northeast
5 View of the front of the building at night
6 Overview of the building at dusk

4

5

6

In maintaining an industrial aesthetic, the massive concrete building is now punctuated by a rhythm of large steel and glass factory sash windows. New additions to the building, such as exterior stairs and canopies, are elegant steel structures which play against the solidity of the concrete building. A 46 metre (150 foot) long steel beam spans the front of the building, acting as both a new vehicular and pedestrian entrance gate, and supporting a glass skylight over the front office terrace. An integral component of the beam is a 14 metre (45 foot) steel and glass screen across the front facade which serves as a new symbol for the building. The beam and screen unify the composition of the facade, and announce the renovation with deference to the original building.

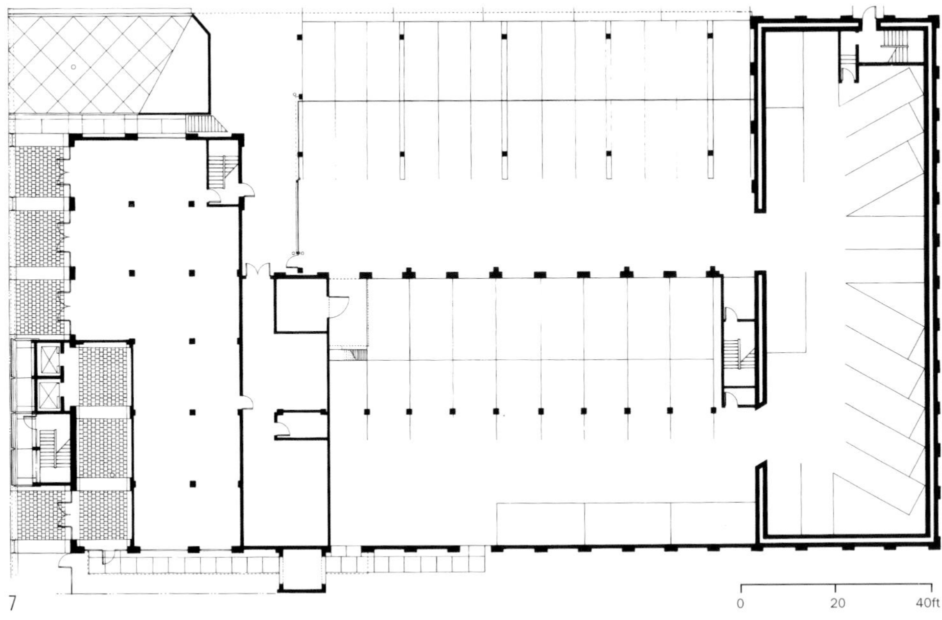

7

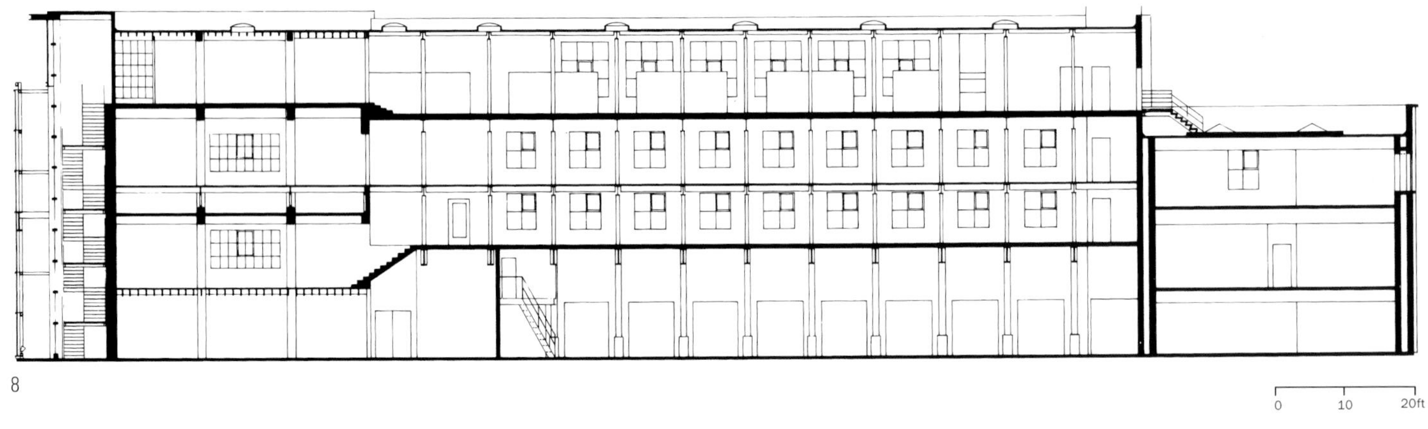

8

9

10

7 Ground floor plan
8 North–south section
9 Terrace of Barton Myers Associates (BMA) office
10 BMA Office, meeting room at dusk
11 BMA Office, library
12 BMA Office, design studio
Photography: Tim Griffith; Erhard Pfeiffer

11

12

Kurfürstendamm 70

Murphy/Jahn, Inc. Architects

Completion: June 1994

Location: Berlin, Germany

Client: EUWO Unternehmensgruppe

Area: 1,142 square metres; 12,000 square feet

Structure: Concrete core; steel floors; steel trusses

Materials: Fritted glass; aluminium mullions and panels

Awards: AIA Chicago Chapter Award; AIA National Award

This is the first building of a series on Ku-Damm. It is urban repair, covering the end of a building exposed through insensitive and destructive street planning in the 1950s. In its attitude the building is an urban intervention against the mediocrity of the 'new' city along the Ku-Damm and the nostalgia for the 'lost' Berlin tradition.

Due to an available site width of only three metres, the city allowed to cantilever the building over the sidewalk on Ku-Damm and Lewishamstraße and exceed the height of the adjacent building.

This makes the building a 'marker' on Ku-Damm and solitary sign, reinforced through its knife-like plan configuration and its steel mast with sign.

The tension between the changing volume, the varying treatments of the surface, with its projecting 'mendelsonian' blades and its mast gives the building a rich dynamic quality.

The steel floors are hung from the three metre wide service core in concrete. Cladding is of an all glass skin accentuated by the hangers and alternating floors. The glass is fritted to create different transparencies in response to the view conditions from the inside, resulting in an intended decorative pattern, within this strong construct.

At the ground floor, a vestibule leads to one elevator which, like a moveable lobby, makes all floors accessible. On a 60 metre square (197 foot) site area, 800 square metres (8,611 square feet) of office space is built. The building is totally sealed, air-conditioned and sprinklered.

1

2

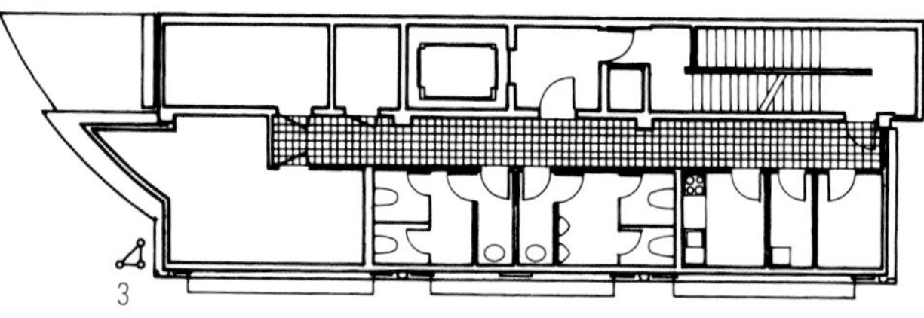

3

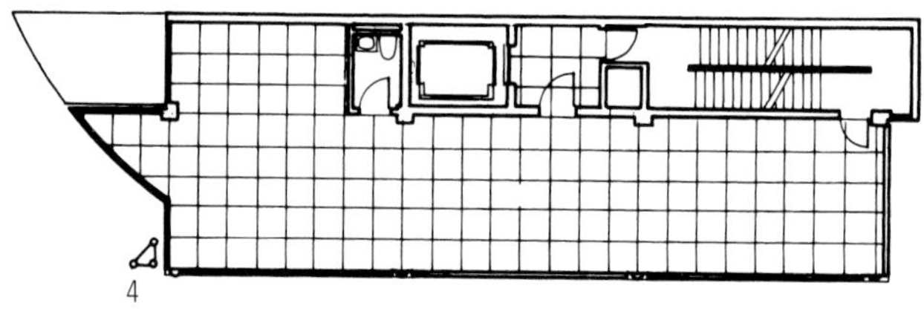

4

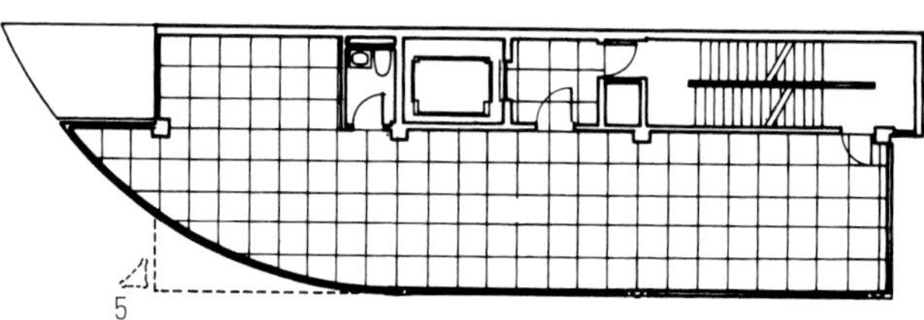

5

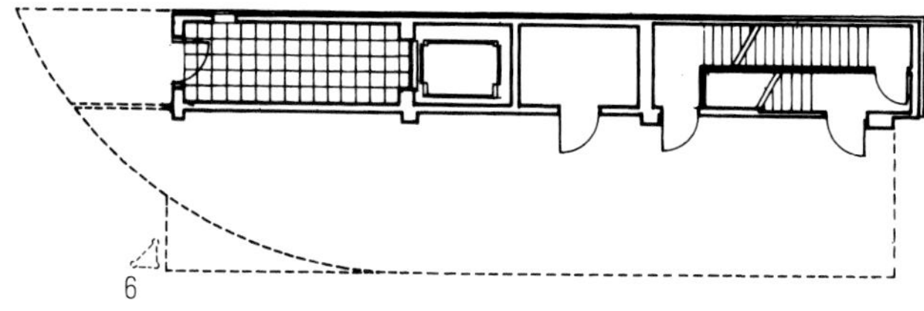

6

1 View from the southeast
2 View from the east
3 Top level plan
4 Upper levels plan
5 Lower levels plan
6 Ground floor plan
7 East elevation
8 View of the entrance
9 Elevator cab
10 Interior view at point

Photography: H.G. Esch

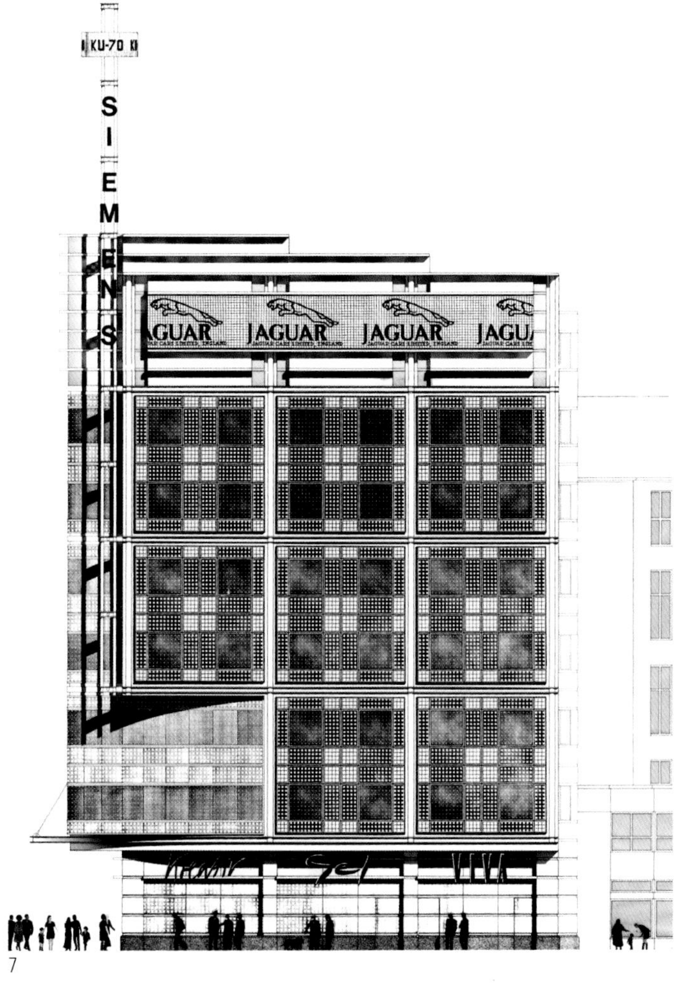

7

8

9

10

Kurfürstendamm 119

Murphy/Jahn, Inc. Architects

Completion: March 1995

Location: Berlin, Germany

Client: Athena Grundstuecks AG; Vebau GmbH Frankfurt/Berlin

Area: 15,000 square metres; 150,000 square feet

Structure: Poured-in-place reinforced concrete

Materials: Aluminium/glass curtain wall; aluminium panels; black granite; steel structures

Urbanistically the building is a completion of a partially existing block-configuration, though the adjacent low-cost, mediocre post-war residential buildings offer no clues for this relationship. It adjusts to the irregular site with rounded corners acting like hinges and steps down from eight floors at the Ku-Damm to five floors at the Kronfrinzen Damm, and at the corners of the building has special features, like 'faces' acting as urban signs towards the streets. Here projecting Glass-Bays, steel brows and steel masts, reflect features of the historic city in a new way.

The rounded ends and the landscaping make the courtyard an accessible urban space, offering additional urban linkages within this city quarter.

The linear nature of the building is reinforced through a banded aluminium and glass facade, which turns into all glass at the two upper floors to correspond to the lower cornice height of the adjacent buildings.

The building has a centre core configuration allowing for flexible lease configurations and multiple tenant use.

Except for limited commercial use on the ground floor near the Ku-Damm the 15,000 square metres (161,464 square feet) are for office use. Below grade are 180 parking spaces, service and technical areas.

1

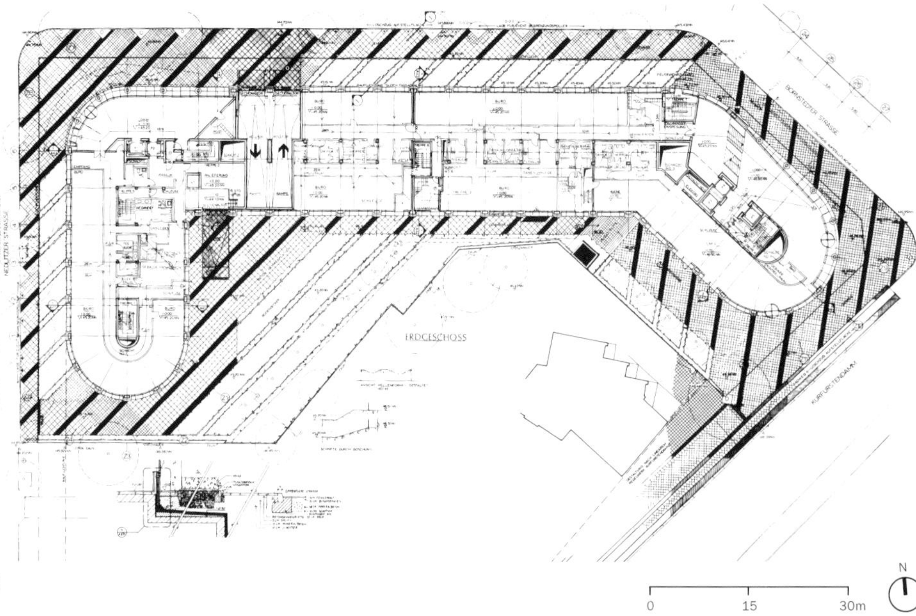

2

3

1 Elevation Ku-Damm
2 1st floor plan
3 Elevation from northeast
4 Elevation from southwest
5 Lobby Ku-Damm
6 Entrance Ku-Damm
7 Glass stair
8 Elevator cab
9 Elevator lobby
10 Night view

Photography: H.G. Esch

4

5

6

7

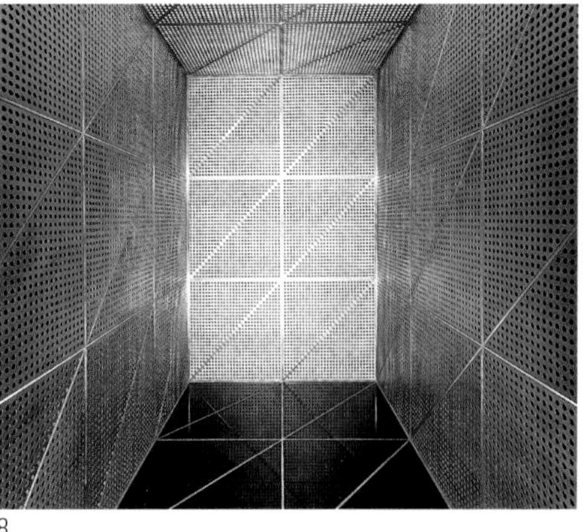
8

9

10

Lancaster Group Worldwide

Quantrell Mullins & Associates Inc

Completion: February 1994

Location: New York, New York, USA

Client: Lancaster Group Worldwide, Inc.

Area: 6,503 square metres; 70,000 square feet

Structure: Granite; glass

Materials: Gypsum board; glass; sycamore panelling; tile

The project consisted of three floors in a new Midtown Manhattan building. Separate offices were included in the design for an outside Advertising and Public Relations agency that will serve Lancaster. A strong emphasis was placed throughout on the incorporation of state-of-the-art technology, including video and teleconferencing facilities to enable Lancaster to communicate with its other operations worldwide. Quantrell Mullins & Associates also developed their corporate image and physical identity.

The client requested the space be open and airy with high ceilings and a generous use of daylight. The interior environment was to be open, functional, distinctive and elegant without appearing opulent.

Quantrell Mullins & Associates addressed this charge by using glass extensively as office 'fronts' as well as dividers and screen walls to create an open, airy feeling. Sand blasted patterns of stars and waves are derived from the corporate logo and are a recurring motif. Custom lacquer and sand blasted glass reception desks also serve as functional, sculptural elements as does the stainless steel and black marble staircase.

In addition to providing full service architectural design for the new headquarters offices, Quantrell Mullins & Associates utilised their extensive experience in strategic environmental planning to co-ordinate the involvement of all participants and maintained the project's time and budget guidelines.

1

2

3

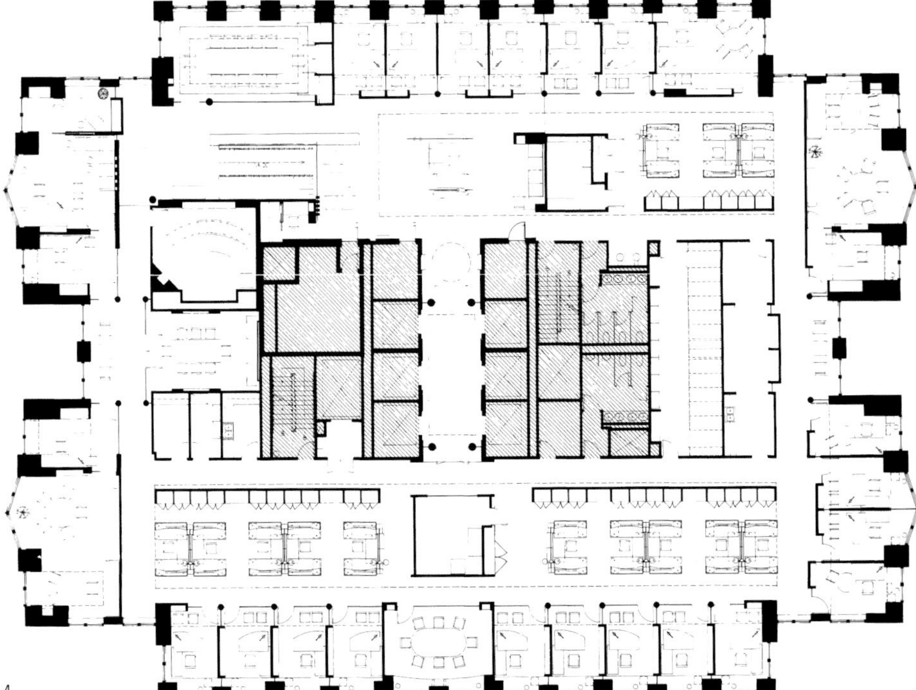

4

1 Open work space
2 Conference room
3 Floor plan 33rd floor
4 Floor plan 34th floor
5 Open work space
6 Elevator lobby
7 Stair
8 Reception area 34th floor
9 President's office
10 Reception area 34th floor

Photography: Paul Warchol

5

6

7

8

9

10

Li Po Chun Chambers Redevelopment

Wong Tung & Partners Limited

Completion: April 1995

Location: Hong Kong

Client: Aucilla & Arracourt Partnership

Area: 29,000 square metres; 312,165 square feet

Structure: Reinforced concrete

Materials: Coated aluminium; reflective glass; granite; gypsum board; marble

Cost: HK$354 million

The commercial redevelopment is a 28-storey office tower with retail on ground and first floors and parking, loading/unloading areas in the basement. It occupies a narrow urban lot with adjoining buildings on both sides in downtown Central. The office tower enjoys prime proximity to the waterfront with uninterrupted views of the harbour.

The ground floor of the building is set back to create wider pavements to cater for the large pedestrian flow due to the nearby mass transit railway entrances. Main entrance of the tower is off Des Voeux Road Central where three long escalators lead visitors to the third floor grand lobby, which is elevated above the waterfront flyover and features generous 11 metre (36 foot) ceiling height and all glass external walls.

The column-free typical office floor plan is symmetrical on plan with a side core that contains a central lift lobby which serves the low- and high-zone lifts and permits the low-zone bank to drop off to create extra prime useable floor space at upper floors. Both the north and south facades are set back at the corners, creating prestigious executive corner offices and allowing an articulated facade at the same time. The bow shaped centre further enhances the powerful column-like image of the tower which will be visually prominent from Victoria Harbour.

The topmost two floors are taken up by penthouse offices which have enhanced ceiling heights and can be interconnected by an internal stair. The sculptural form at the top of the building ensures a strong and dignified identity in the city skyline. Illumination of the top and other highlights of the building is carefully considered. All light fittings are integrated into the building fabric.

A blue-green reflective glass and an American granite are used for the exterior of the reinforced concrete building. These are complemented by trims, suspended canopies and other features in fluorocarbon coated aluminium. 'Ventrows' are incorporated in each and every panel of the unitised curtain wall system for emergency ventilation. They form continuous horizontal recesses on the elevation adding depth and a new dimension to the glass wall. The overall image is that of dignity and subtle elegance befitting the high quality of the building.

1

2

3

1 Layered roof features
2 Suspended canopy
3 Elevation with recessed ventrows
4 Foyer level
5 Ground floor plan
6 Third floor lobby
7 Lift lobby

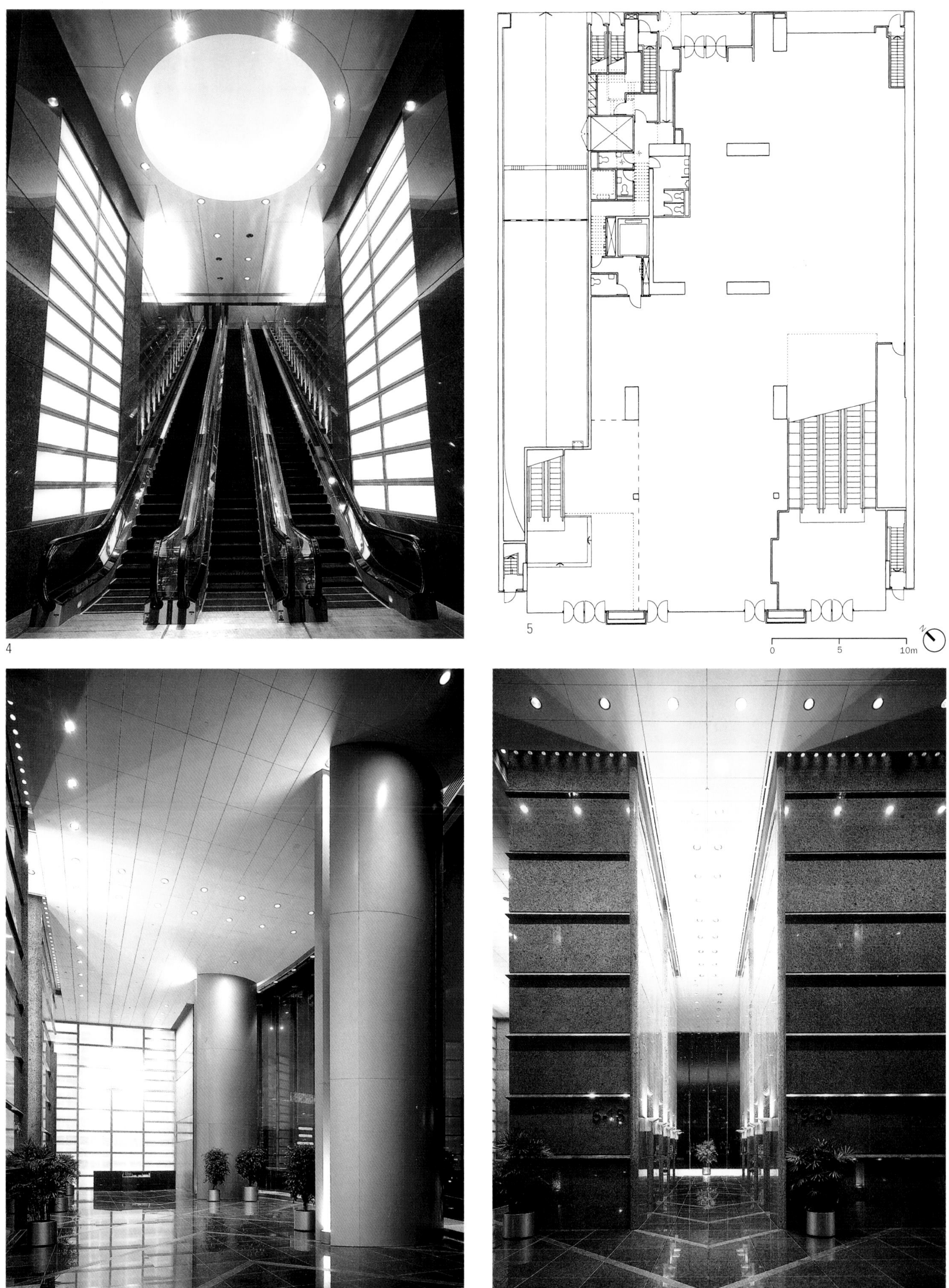

4
5
6
7

Long Beach Convention Center

Thompson, Ventulett, Stainback and Associates Inc

Completion: July 1994

Location: Long Beach, California, USA

Client: City of Long Beach

Area: 63,172 square metres; 680,000 square feet

Structure: Concrete/steel frame

Materials: Concrete; steel; glass

Cost: US$81,215,000

Awards: 1995 Design Award, AIA/Cabrillo
1994 Concrete Industry Award

The US$80 million expansion of the Long Beach Convention Center included an expansion of an existing exhibition hall (from 8,360 to 20,900 square metres/90,000 to 225,000 square feet), new lobby/prefunction space, meeting rooms (3,160 square metres/34,000 square feet), ballroom (1,860 square metres/20,000 square feet), as well as support service space and parking for 1,500 cars.

The design concept takes advantage of two special site opportunities: first, the extraordinary 180 degree, panoramic view to the California Palos Verdes Mountains and the Pacific Ocean; and second, to animate an existing windswept pedestrian promenade that linked the Long Beach business district to the more recent waterfront development (including retail, hotel, and marina). Both of these opportunities were realised by stretching a new, grandly scaled, glazed concourse along the existing promenade.

A pair of stylised elevator towers topped with dramatic light fixtures mark the main entrance and flank a grand ceremonial staircase. At the main entrance, the linear concourse gives way to a semicircular lobby space defined by a curved wall which rises 16.8 metres (55 feet) from the main floor through the mezzanine and features a distinctive skylit 'fish scale' texture.

The architectural imagery was influenced by the seaside location and especially the adjacent marina. The exterior steel framing suggests sailboat masts and rigging. The brightly coloured banners recall nautical flags, custom carpet patterns depict the ocean surf, and the handrail detail from the Queen Mary (permanently docked across the bay) is borrowed to serve as a chair rail.

The project was integrated into (and partially on top of) three existing buildings whose continuous operation was required.

1 Site plan
2 View from waterfront
3 Concourse level floor plan
4 Exhibit Hall level floor plan
5 Evening activity of nearby Pine Street cafes is extended to the Promenade

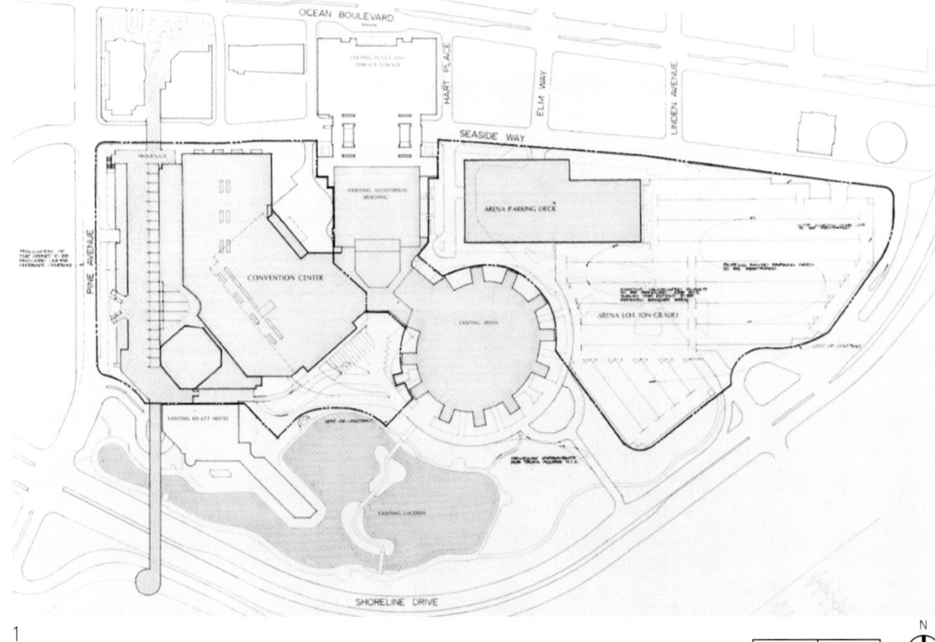

1

2

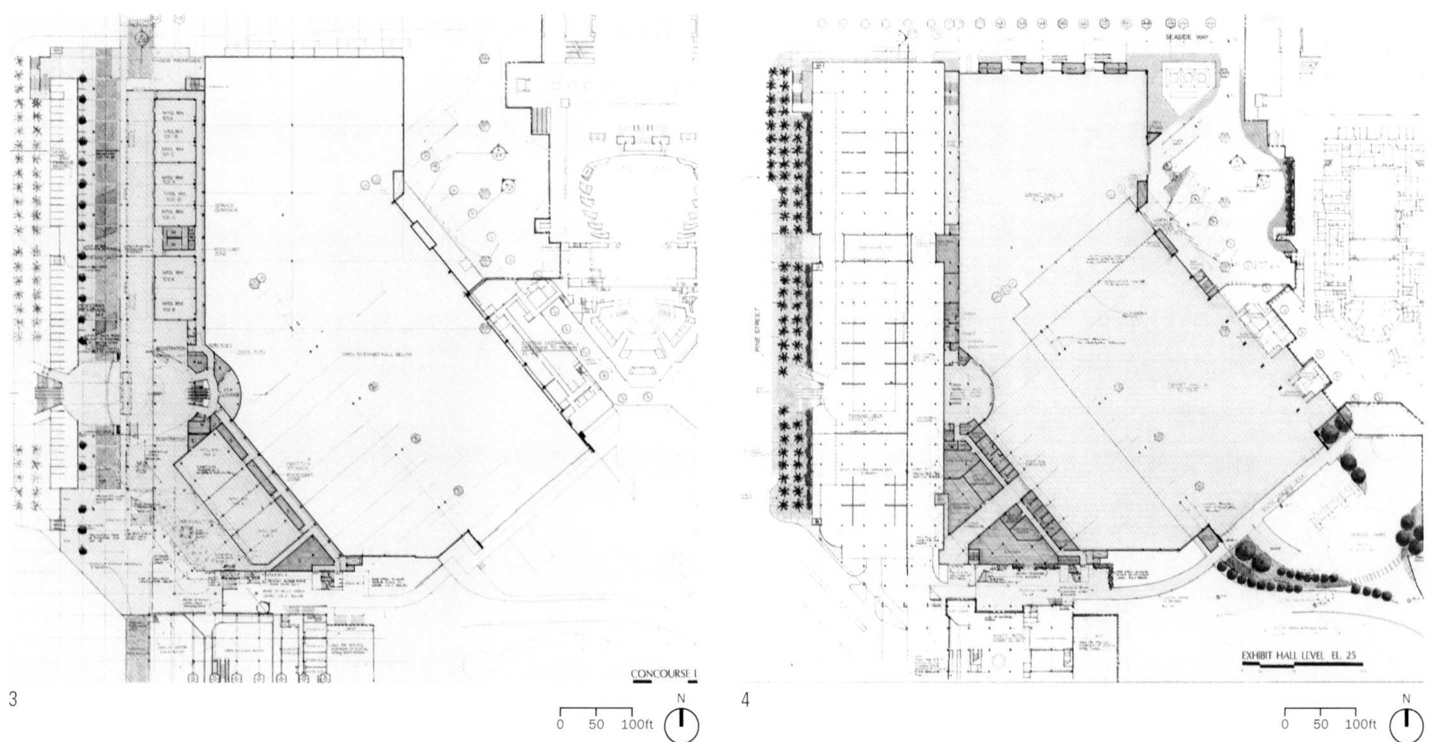

CONCOURSE I
0 50 100ft
N

3

SEASIDE WAY
PINE STREET
EXHIBIT HALL LEVEL EL. 25
0 50 100ft
N

4

Shoreline Dr

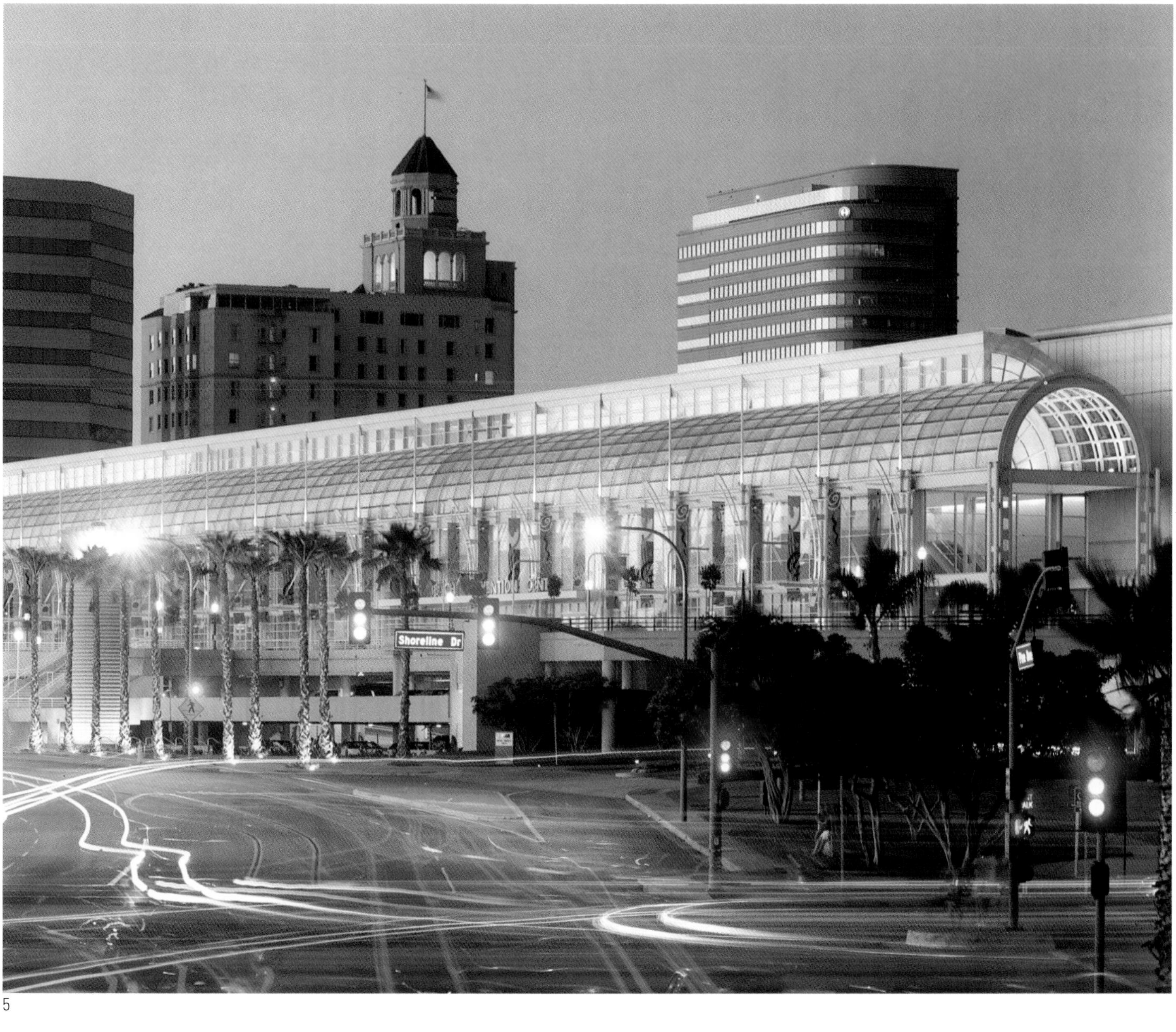

5

6 Stylised elevator towers/light fixtures marking the main entrance

7 Elevated pedestrian promenade and public circulation concourse

8 Colourful banners recall nautical flags

Photography: Brian Gassell/TVS&Associates

6

7

8

Modern Woodmen of America

Flad & Associates

Completion: June 1995

Location: Rock Island, Illinois, USA

Client: Modern Woodmen

Area: 8,361 square metres; 90,000 square feet

Structure: Cast-in-place, post-tensioned concrete

Materials: Granite and curtain wall cladding; ribbon mahogany; travertine and thincoat plaster walls; terrazzo

Cost: US$18 million

Modern Woodmen's freestanding addition to their existing headquarters in Rock Island, Illinois, offers a simple plan that maximises the quality of the workplace through the strategic arrangement of its components. This 3-storey facility over two levels of parking, accommodates office space, a corporate data centre, and a training centre.

Open office space dominates the north side of the plan, where the building's transparent, multi-layered exterior reveals pleasant views to the Mississippi River. A perimeter free of enclosed offices allows indirect northern light to fill the offices. The building's south side takes on a more solid approach as the horizontal floor plates lock into three granite-clad masses, which block the direct light and less pleasing views to the south. Vertically stacked behind this solid facade lies the facility's training centre, data centre, and mechanical support.

The approach to this west addition of the Modern Woodmen campus is through a glass enclosed skywalk leading into a lobby of travertine marble walls and terrazzo floors with insets of brass and zinc, creating a stately image of function and durability. To the north, a 3-storey atrium stairway connects all office floors and offers views of the river. A curved wall of ribbon mahogany blends drama with function as it draws visitors into the office area from the public lobby.

1

3

2

4

1 View from Centennial Bridge
2 Glass enclosed skywalk from above
3 Mississippi River facade
4 View across Mississippi
5 View of atrium stair

5

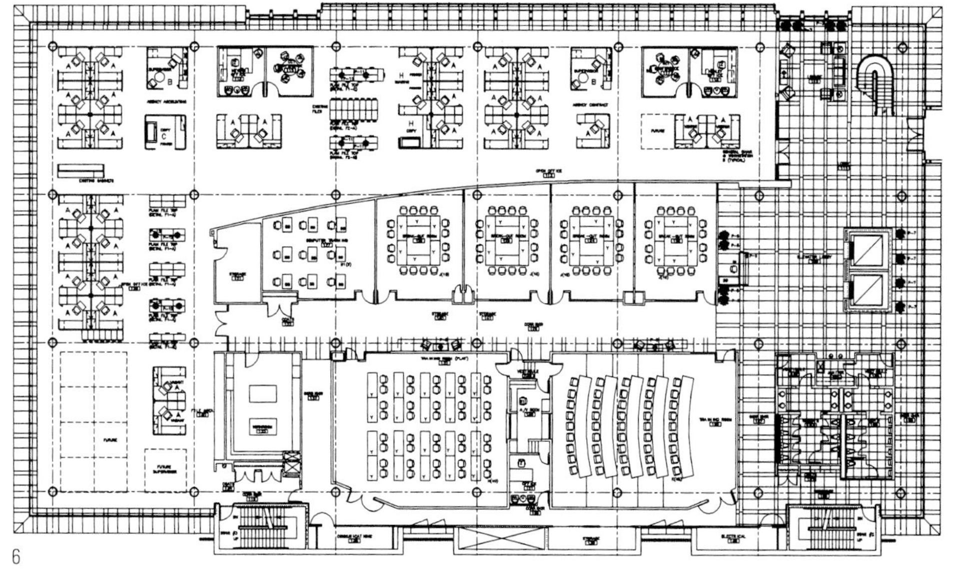
6

8

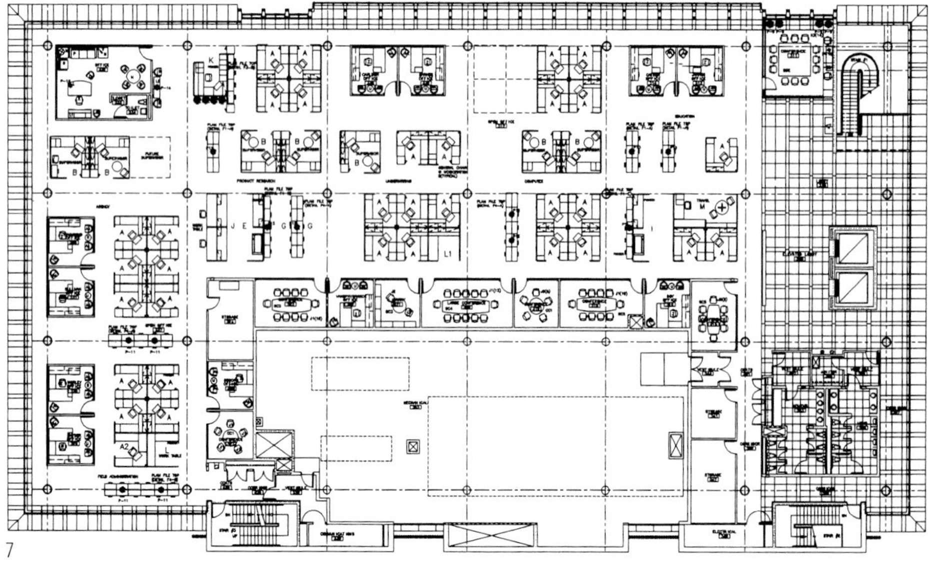
7

9

10

6 First floor plan
7 Third floor plan
8 Granite-clad interior columns
9 Curved ribbon mahogany wall
10 View along corridor
11 Training centre classroom
12 Offices at perimeter
13 View through glass enclosed skywalk
Photography: Steve Hall, Hedrich-Blessing

11

12

13

Moscow Bank of the Russian Federation Savings Bank

Ellerbe Becket, Inc.

Completion: July 1995

Location: Moscow, Russia

Client: Sberegatelniy Bank

Area: 27,870 square metres; 300,000 square feet

Structure: Precast concrete

Materials: Brick; Russian granite; dry-vit; stucco; curved, 2.5 cm (one inch) bullet proof glass

Cost: US$40 million

Ellerbe Becket Construction Services was selected to design and manage construction of the Moscow Bank of the Russian Federation Savings Bank. The 27,870 square metre (300,000 square foot) project expands the existing headquarters into a world class banking facility, and also houses the brokerage offices of the Moscow Commodity Exchange.

To accommodate both the public and private functions of the facility, the design is organised into two L-shaped sections, with separate lobbies and elevator cores, enclosing a central banking hall. This daylight atrium space provides natural light and views to the interior offices.

The Commodity Exchange occupies approximately a third of the office space in the facility. The 2-storey drum of the trading circle is the functional and symbolic centre of the Commodity Exchange.

The proportion and detailing of the design and the use of brick and Russian granite relate the state-of-the-art facility to its immediate physical context and to the rich heritage of Russian architecture.

1

2

1 North elevation—main bank entrance—auditorium at far right
2 Main atrium—office, conference room and cafeteria overlooking main floor banking and teller functions
3 Executive Boardroom—translation booths concealed behind sliding sound panels
4 Special translation stations
5 Executive vice president office
6 400-seat auditorium with eight translation booths at upper level mezzanine
7 Main atrium
8 Main bank entrance lobby

Photography: Steven Levy PhotoGraphics Studio

3

4

5

6

7

8

Northern States Power Company World Class Control Center

Ellerbe Becket, Inc.

Completion: May 1995

Location: Minneapolis, Minnesota, USA

Client: Northern States Power Company

Area: 2,583 square metres; 27,800 square feet

Materials: Bullet resistant glass; fabric; custom millwork

Cost: US$6 million

Awards: First Place, American Society of Interior Designers, Midwest Design Awards

Ellerbe Becket's Interiors Group was commissioned by Northern States Power Company (NSP) to create a theatre and support facility for the command and control of electrical generation, transmission and distribution. This new Control Theater is the merger of five former operational groups into one unified centre. NSP is the largest company in the country which incorporates all of these electricity utility processes into one centralised facility.

Renovation of the 1,300 square metre (14,000 square foot) office interior included complete demolition and new construction which resulted in the 24-hour, high security, black-box theatre on access flooring.

The Control Center includes the Control Theater, a 20-person Observation Room with gallery, a complete Training Simulation Facility, hotelling space for trainees, and breakroom, exercise, restroom and shower facilities.

NSP's desire for a clean, open and warm atmosphere led the design concept towards the simple, direct approach of the 'International' style. An overall timeless character is achieved through the use of simple building materials and a neutral colour and materials palette. Prime consideration was placed on the integration of ergonomic design with sophisticated technology.

1

2

3

1 Detail of entry graphics
2 Display vitrines
3 System map board detail
4 Observation room
5 Systems control theatre overview
6 Training simulator
7 Training area
8 Observation room
9 View of observation room

Photography: Koyama Photographic

4

5

6

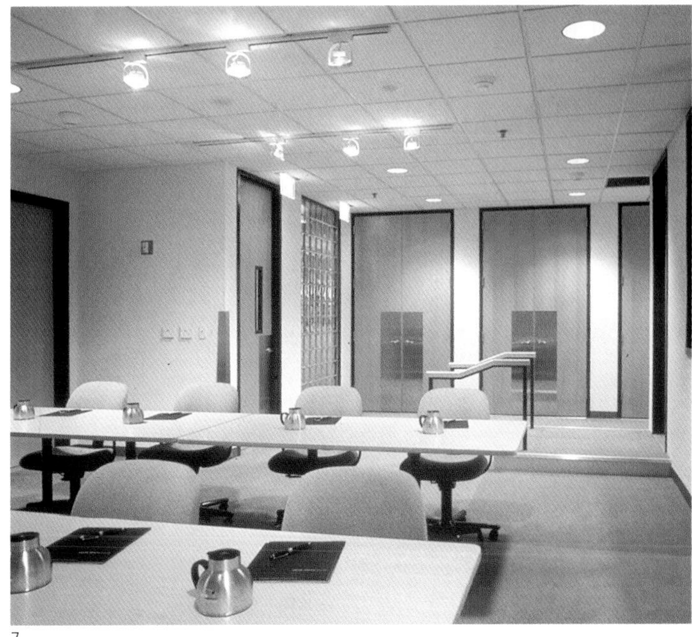
7

8

9

Office in Helsinki

Hans Murman Arkitektkontor AB

Completion: March 1995

Location: Helsinki, Finland

Client: Stockman OY

Area: 575 square metres; 6,190 square feet

Materials: Glass; Oregon pine

Cost: 2,500,000 SEK

Alvar Aalto designed the building in which this office is situated, in 1966. In the refurbishment of this office, attention was paid to the original design of the building.

An airy interior was created, by making daylight a feature through the use of enormous windows. Floors were made from birch, with white walls, and original fluorescent light fittings designed by Aalto were used along the rear of the office. Tables and chairs are designed by Aalto complete with classic and new Scandinavian design.

To let daylight into the middle of the office, glass walls were designed in Oregon pine (used in the original design of the building, as window frames and doors).

1

2

1 Glass sliding doors of Oregon Pine
2 Exterior view of the building where the office is on the third floor and the Academic Bookshop on the ground floor
3 Plan
4 Glass partitions giving daylight to the inner part of the office
5 Conference room with a curved wall of birchwood for Audio-visual projections
6 Reception area
7 The walls between the rooms consist of white screens with glass against the facade and above the screen

Photography: Åke E-son Lindman

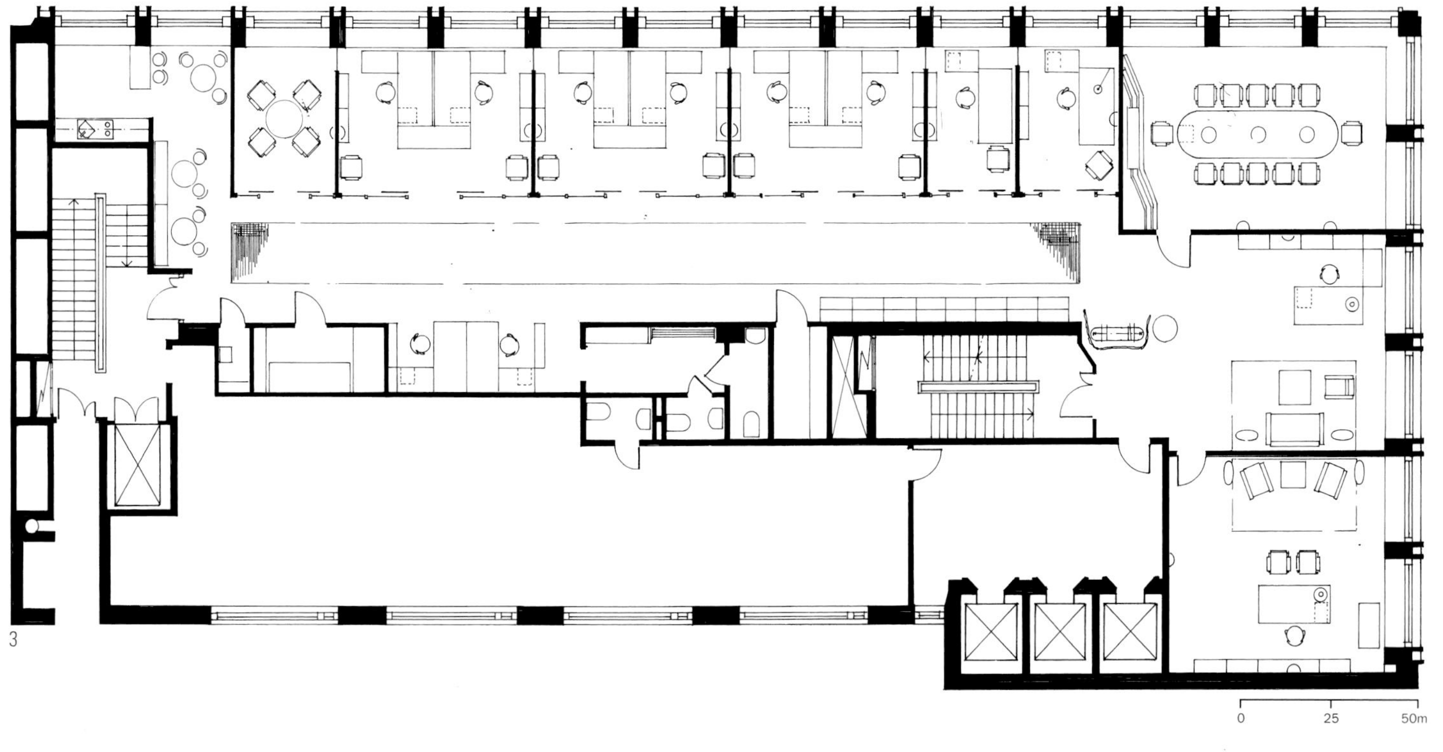

3

4

5

6

7

Osaka World Trade Center Building

Nikken Sekkei Ltd
in association with Mancini Duffy Associates

Completion: February 1995
Location: Osaka, Japan
Client: Osaka World Trade Center Building
Area: 11,000 square metres; 118,406 square feet
Structure: Steel frame; reinforced concrete
Materials: Glass

The Osaka World Trade Center Building, a core facility of 'Cosmo Square'; a new urban centre in the Osaka bay area; is a home of the World Trade Center—an organisation affiliated with the Global World Trade Center network interconnecting similar centres in about 200 cities all over the world. As such, this building is expected to perform a central role in the city's internationalisation and thus become Osaka's new symbolic landmark.

The building, which is the tallest in western Japan with a total height of 256 metres (840 feet), is clad in reflective glass curtain walls which emphasise the white structural elements within, accentuating the slim verticality of the high-rise tower. Furthermore, the inverted pyramid atop the building overhanging the glass walls below and accommodating the observation deck, delineates a unique geometry in the Cosmo Square skyline.

Except where the beams are located, the curtain walls are composed of transparent pair glass throughout, from floors to ceilings. This design brings natural sunlight into the office zones during daytime, while it takes the appearance of an attractively lit tower during the night.

In addition, the entrance lobby with its 20 metre (66 foot) high hall has elevators coming down towards the glass-clad shafts on the lower level, and the atrium with a space of about 3,000 square metres (32,293 square feet) that can be used for a variety of events; add the impressive features to this unique building.

1

2

3

1 South elevation with Asia & Pacific Trade Center (front)
2 Southeast elevation
3 Attractively lit tower at night
4 First floor plan
5 Spacious atrium 'Fespa' for various events
6 Entrance lobby (2F)

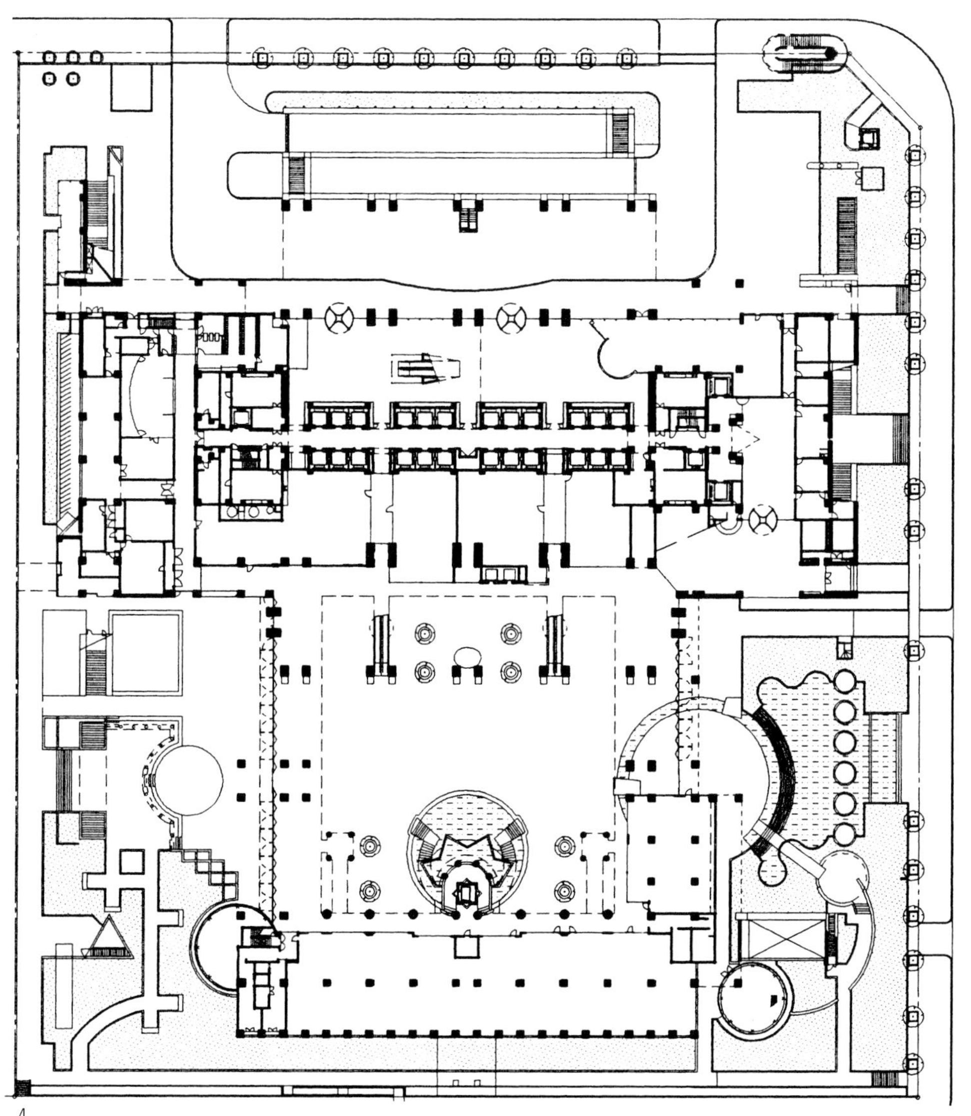

4

6

5

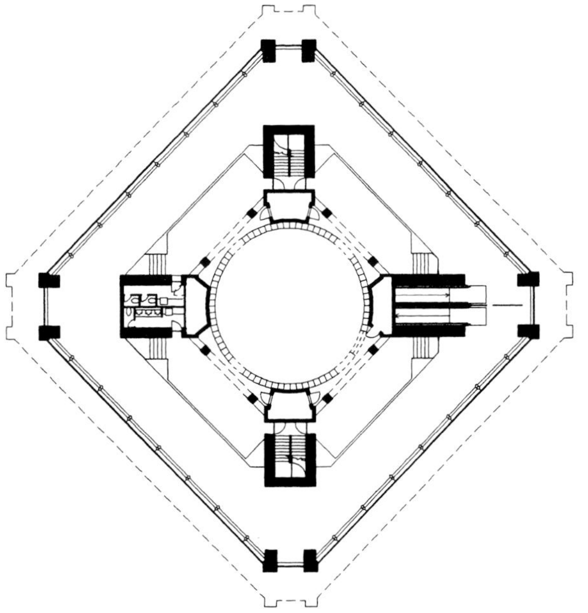

7

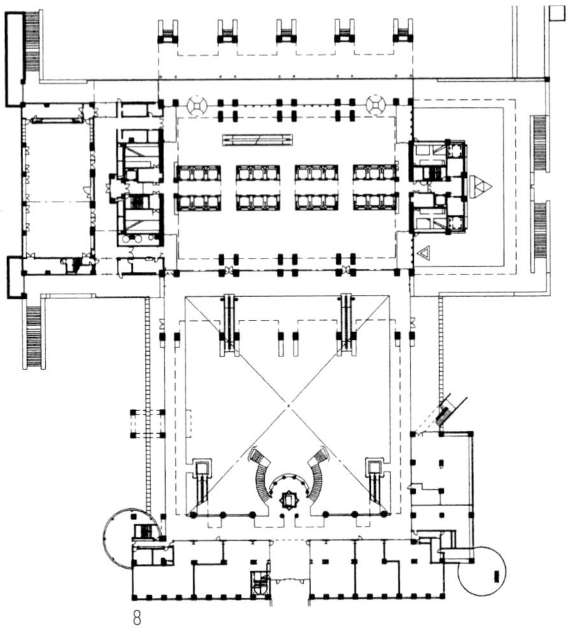

8

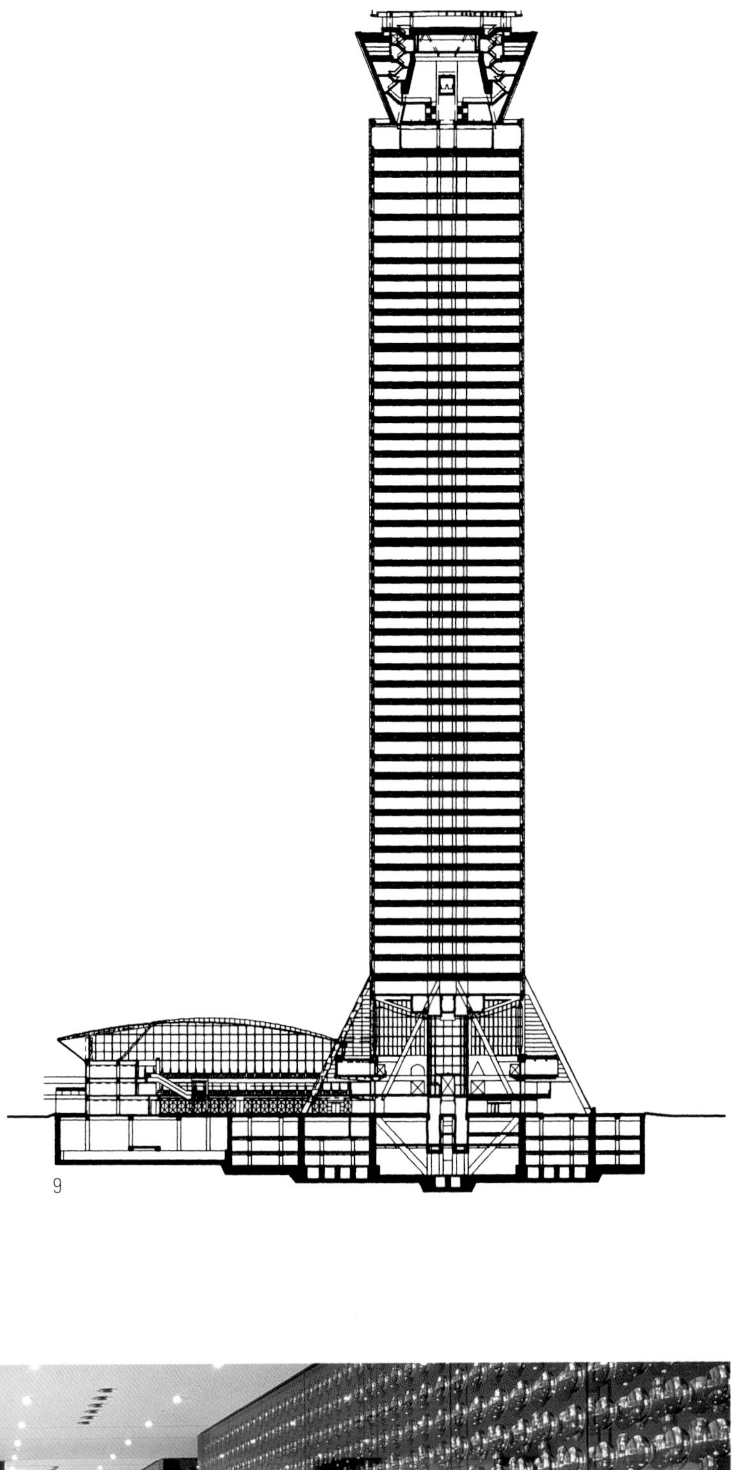

9

10

7 Observatory floor plan
8 Second floor plan
9 Section
10 Entrance lobby (2F)
11 Large conference hall (2F)
12 Elevator hall (2F)
Photography: Y. Takase

11

12

Pennsylvania Convention Center

Thompson, Ventulett, Stainback and Associates Inc

Completion: April 1994

Location: Philadelphia, Pennsylvania, USA

Client: The Pennsylvania Convention Center Authority

Area: 120,770 square metres; 1,300,000 square feet

Structure: Steel frame; concrete frame

Materials: Brick; limestone; granite; precast concrete

Cost: US$212 million

Awards: 1995 Historical Preservation Award, Historical and Museum Commission, Philadelphia, PA

1995 Design Award, AIA/GA

1995 Honorable Mention for Sustainable Design, AIA/GA

1995 Project of the Year, National Commercial Builders Council

The Pennsylvania Convention Center Authority wanted to minimise the problematic aspects of placing a convention centre in the centre of downtown Philadelphia, yet there was also a desire to maximise the potential that it would have to revitalise an area of downtown that is almost within the shadow of William Penn, the statue high atop City Hall. TVS&A designed a facility encompassing over 120,000 square metres (1.3 million square feet), including the once dilapidated historic Reading Terminal Train Shed.

Linking the facility to Philadelphia's famous and historic Market Street, the 100-year old train shed is a major entry point for the facility. Also, while displaying its original 76 metre (250 foot) span steel truss arches, it houses a 2,787 square metre (30,000 square feet) ballroom and 2,787 square metres (30,000 square feet) of meeting rooms.

The main floor level of the Convention Center was designed to align with the existing floor level of the Train Shed, approximately 8 metres (26 feet) above street level, allowing major streets in the area to remain open and separated from the truck traffic which is ramped to that main floor level via the abandoned train viaduct. The 29,264 square metre (315,000 square feet) Main Exhibition Hall spans a major street, creating a block long drop-off corridor for buses and taxis beneath the building. An additional 5,574 square metres (60,000 square feet) of meeting rooms and a 11,612 square metre (125,000 square feet) ground floor exhibition hall fill the area beneath the elevated main level.

Continued

1

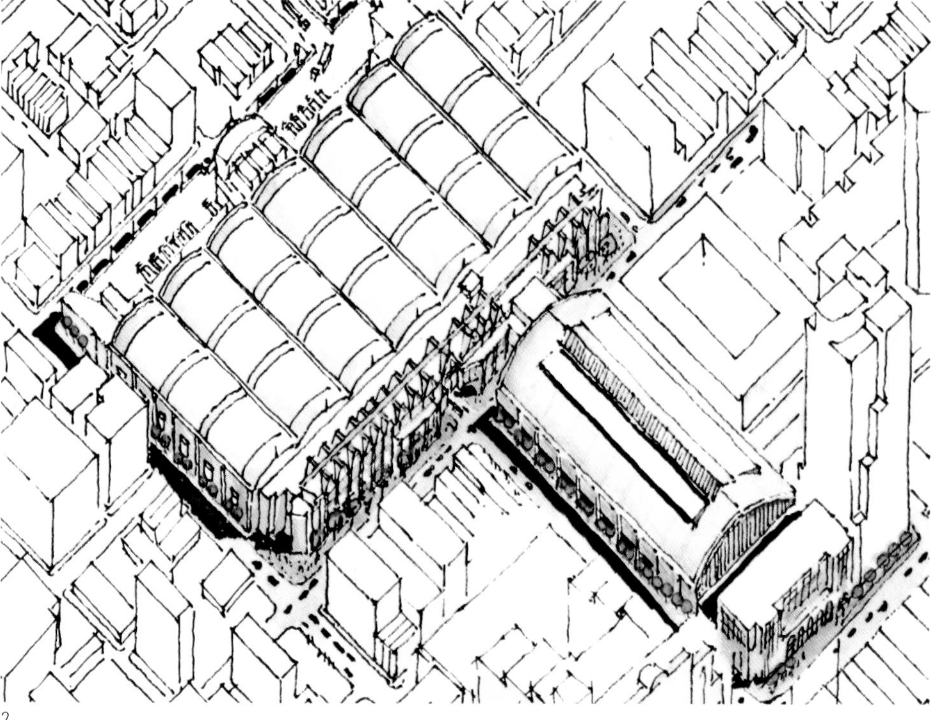

2

3

1 Pylon marking convention centre complex
2 Aerial perspective showing Philadelphia context
3 Public circulation concourse along Arch Street
4 Ground level floor plan
5 Exhibit Hall/Train Shed level floor plan

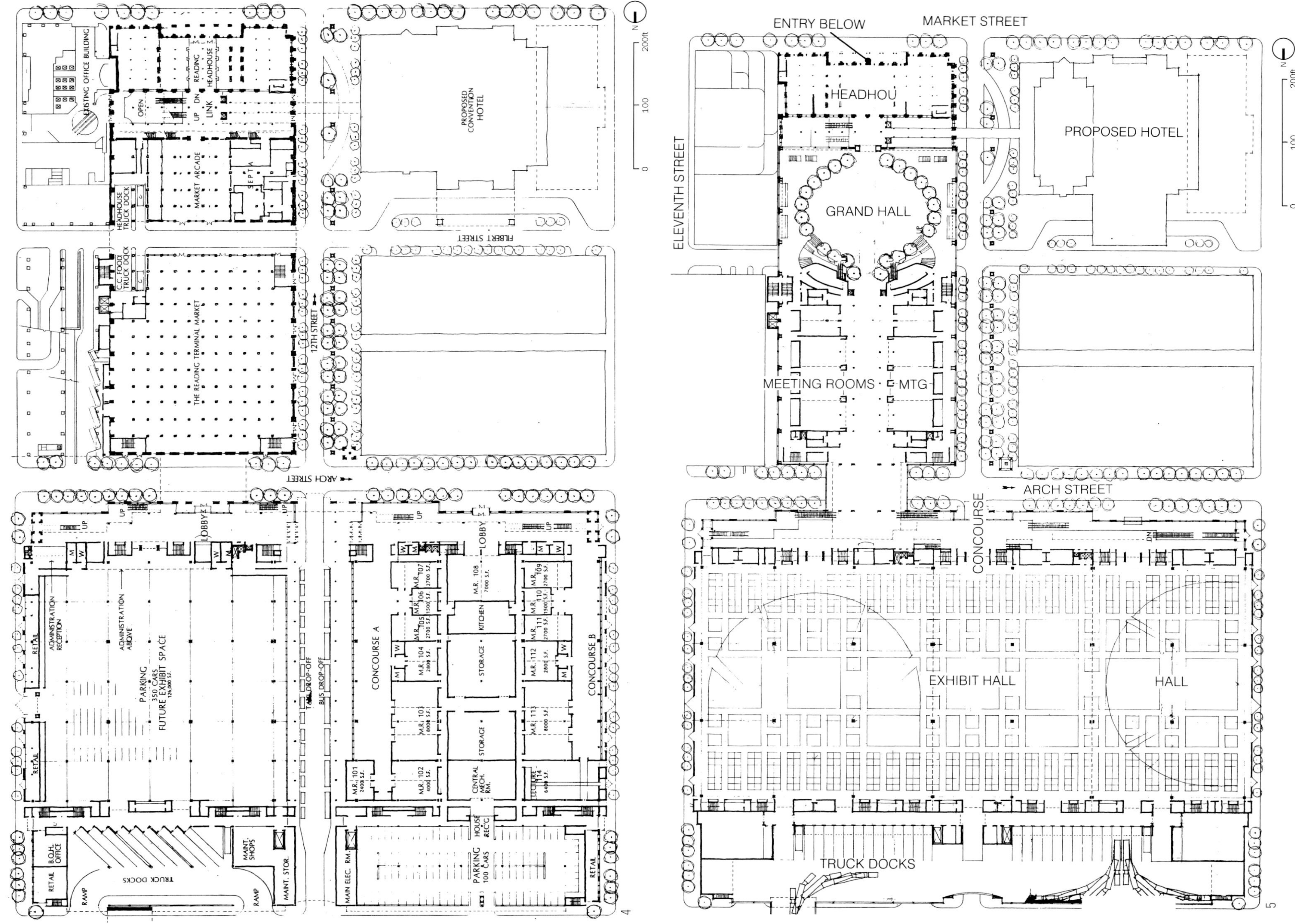
RETAIL
B.O.H. OFFICE
RAMP
TRUCK DOCKS
MAINT. SHOPS
MAINT. STOR.
ADMINISTRATION RECEPTION
ADMINISTRATION ABOVE
PARKING
350 CARS
FUTURE EXHIBIT SPACE
126,000 S.F.
LOBBY
UP
TAXI DROP-OFF
BUS DROP-OFF
ARCH STREET
C.C. FOOD TRUCK DOCK
HEADHOUSE TRUCK DOCK
EXISTING OFFICE BUILDING
OPEN
THE READING TERMINAL MARKET
MARKET ARCADE
LINK
READING HEADHOUSE
SEPTA
12TH STREET
MAIN ELEC. RM.
CONCOURSE A
M.R. 101
M.R. 102
M.R. 103
M.R. 104
M.R. 105
M.R. 106
M.R. 107
PARKING
100 CARS
HOUSE REC'G
CENTRAL MECH. RM.
STORAGE
KITCHEN
M.R. 108
LECTURE 114
M.R. 113
M.R. 112
M.R. 111
M.R. 110
M.R. 109
CONCOURSE B
FILBERT STREET
PROPOSED CONVENTION HOTEL
4
0
100
200ft
N
ELEVENTH STREET
TRUCK DOCKS
EXHIBIT HALL
HALL
CONCOURSE
ARCH STREET
MEETING ROOMS
MTG
GRAND HALL
HEADHOU
ENTRY BELOW
MARKET STREET
PROPOSED HOTEL
5
0
100
200ft
N

The multi-level public circulation concourse which runs the full length of the building provides access to the exhibit halls and meeting rooms, features food service facilities and provides views into the city. At street level this concourse wraps around three sides of the facility with meeting room space and retail components to help animate and encourage interaction at the sidewalk plaza areas.

6 Facade detail at concourse
7 Exhibit Hall bay windows
8 Terminus of public circulation concourse
9 Streetscape along Arch Street with bridge to Train Shed

6

7

8

9

10 Interior of public circulation concourse at Exhibit Hall level

11 Evening view along Arch Street

12 Interior of renovated Train Shed from Ballroom prefunction area

Photography: Brian Gassell/TVS&Associates

10

11

12

Silicon Graphics Entry Site

STUDIOS Architecture

Completion: December 1994
Location: Mountain View, California, USA
Client: Silicon Graphics
Area: 10,368 square metres; 111,600 square feet
Structure: Steel braced frame; supporting metal deck
Materials: Metal panels; glass with masonry outcrops; metal exposed roofs

The direct influence of the client has been very significant in the design of this project. Silicon Graphics, a highly optimistic, innovative and prosperous company requested that Studios Architecture provide them, not with an anonymous high-tech 'facility', but a building with an architectural presence. They have chosen a site that is amongst the most highly visible remaining in Silicon Valley so that their building will be seen by thousands of travellers every day.

Silicon Graphics (SGI) desires a building which articulates the idea of 'openness', in order that their company be accessible, both visually and psychologically, to the community at large. The building accomplishes this on several levels. The passerby in an automobile is given a high-speed glimpse of the inner workings of the building via the large screened element along the west facade, a 'bay window' built in clear glass with operable shading within. At the north end of the building, the main entry is a clear glass vitrine to allow the activity within to project outside on a macro scale. Communication and orientation within the building are essential to Silicon Graphics.

Continued

1 Site plan
2 View from visitor entry
3 *Brise-soleils* on southwest side of building

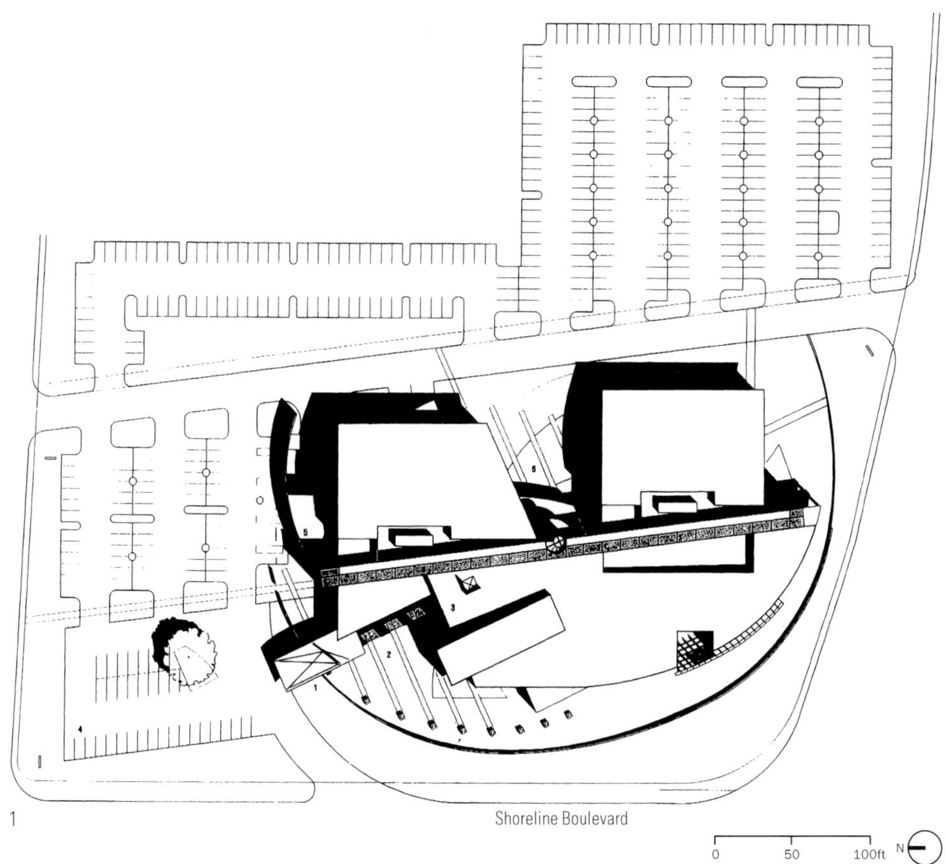

1

2

3

The plan can be understood as a simple rectangle, where two courtyards, one peripheral and one central, have been carved out. Overlaid upon this is a circulation spine, essentially central to the plan, and connecting stairs, bathrooms, and other building services. The rotated structural grid at the entry, which is in alignment with the grid of SGI's existing campus further north, opens the building lobby to the street, and further peels away at the rectangle. The central hub serves as a culmination of the entry sequence, a binder for the divergent grids, and a central focus to the plan.

The client's intention was not to have suspended ceilings in the office areas of this building; as a result, the spatial play of the exterior will be fully tangible within, but scaled by exposed structure and human activity.

4

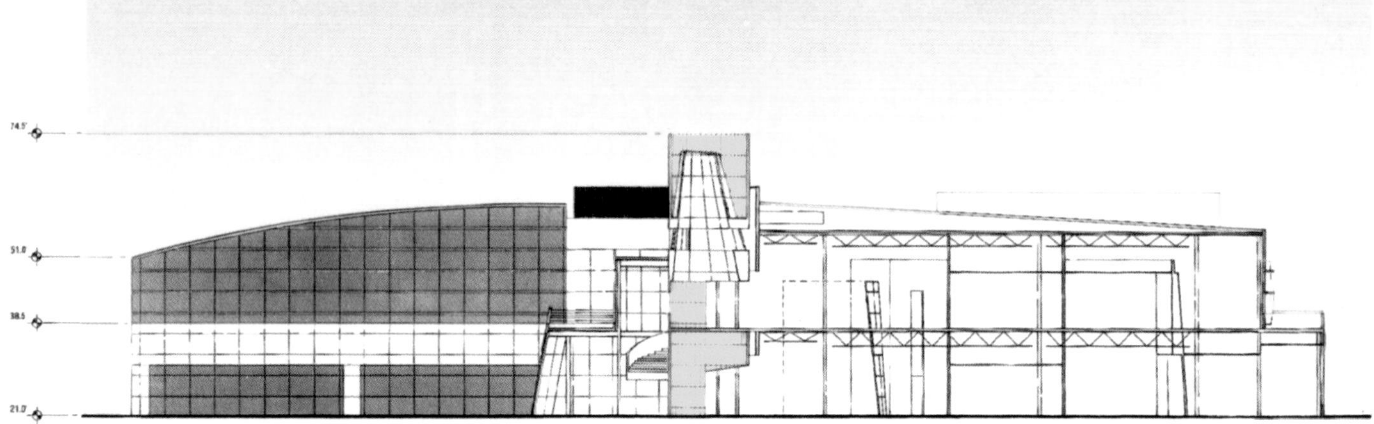

5

6

4 Courtyard
5 Building section
6 North elevation
7 Reflection detail

7

8

9

8 Canopy at visitor entry
9 Night view of lobby
10 South side of building
11-12 Central 'spine' corridor
Photography: Paul Warchol; Michael O'Callahan

10

11

12

State Farm Mutual Automobile Insurance Company South Texas Regional Office

Ellerbe Becket, Inc.

Completion: June 1994

Location: Austin, Texas, USA

Client: State Farm Mutual Automobile Insurance Company South Texas Regional Office

Area: 43,663 square metres; 470,000 square feet

Structure: Steel frame; composite deck

Materials: Brick

Cost: US$31.8 million

This 3-storey Regional Office for State Farm Insurance Companies is located on 80 acres in the verdant Texas hill country surrounding Austin. Strong concern for the environment and strenuous zoning regulations led to a design that minimised man-made intrusions onto the site. The cruciform plan takes advantage of topography and natural clearings in the woods to break down the large scale of the project into discrete vignettes of the building. Access roads and parking for over 1,200 cars are woven through the natural landscape. Ellerbe Becket carefully master planned the site to accommodate building expansion to 55,740 square metres (600,000 square feet) with parking growing proportionally.

The facility functions as an operation centre for maintenance and processing of policies in Southern Texas.

At the heart of the operation is a 2,230 square metre (24,000 square foot) raised access floor computer centre. The majority of the project is highly flexible open office planned on a 9.1 metre (30 foot) module assuring communication and environmental controls for all of the building. A state-of-the-art classroom complex provides education and training for local employees and field agents.

At the hub of the building is an atrium linking and orienting all three floors. Pinwheeling off this centralised community space are employee break rooms, a credit union, a dining room and an outdoor terrace.

1

2

3

4

5

1 North employee entry
2 North employee entry detail
3 Lobby entry detail
4 Employee entry/drop-off detail
5 North employee entry/drop-off detail at night
6 Lobby entry detail
7 South employee entry detail
8 Main lobby
9 Employee dining room
10 Atrium
11 Main Lobby

Photography: R. Greg Hursley, Inc.

6

7

8

9

10

11

Surdirman Tower

RTKL Associates Inc.
in association with PT. Airmas Asri

Completion: January 1994

Location: Jakarta, Indonesia

Client: Lippoland Development

Area: 18,580 square metres; 200,000 square feet

Materials: Brazilian rose grey granite; metal panel (Alucabond with silver fluorocarbon coating); Red Breccia stones

RTKL provided architectural design services for Lippo Bank's 20-storey headquarters office tower located in the southern tip of Jakarta's 'Golden Triangle' commercial zone.

Clad in polished granite and glass, the tower will be a memorable image against the urban skyline. A 3-storey combined office lobby/banking chamber will serve as a monumental entry leading visitors and workers to 18,580 square metres (200,000 square feet) of leasable space. Restaurants on the 19th and 20th floors will feature 360 degree views of the city and provide a glow to the tower penthouse at night.

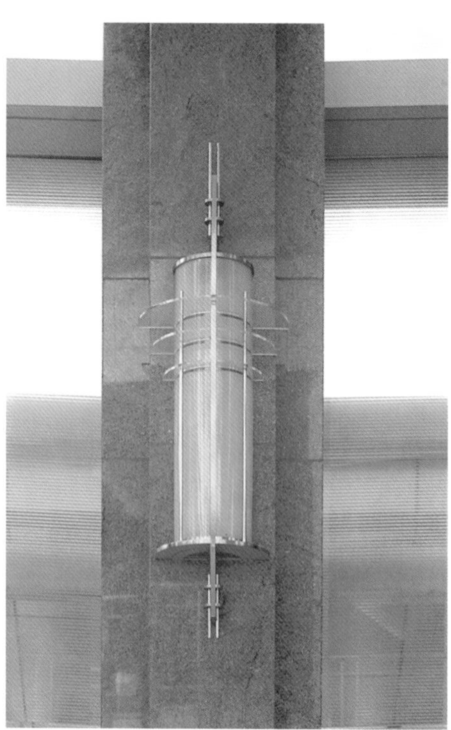

1

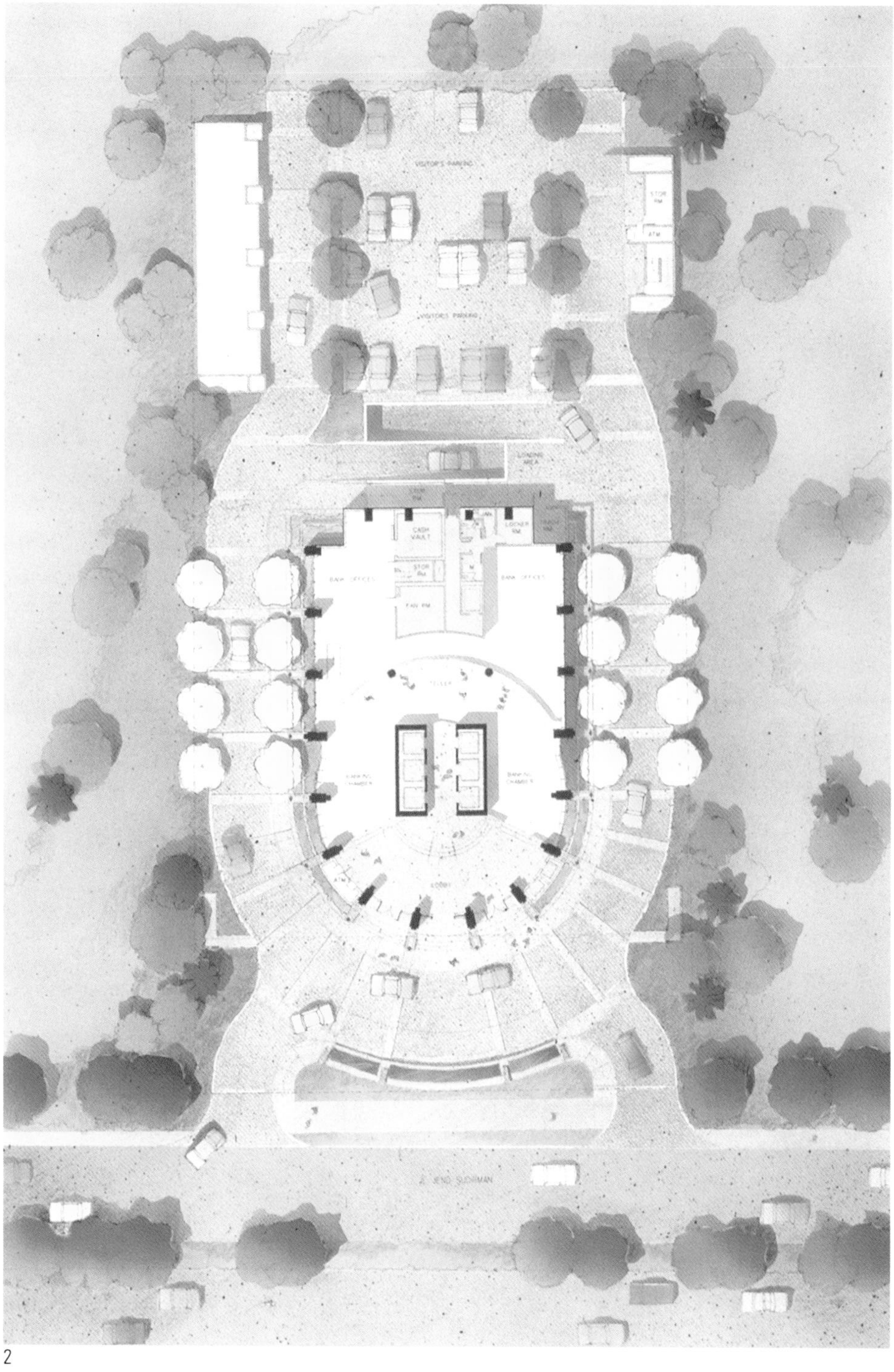

2

3

1 Detail of lighting source
2 Site plan
3 Exterior
4 Lobby
Photography: Tim Griffith

4

Truworths Head Office

Douglas Roberts Peter Loebenberg Architects

Completion: April 1995
Location: Cape Town, South Africa
Client: Wooltru Properties
Area: 40,000 square metres; 430,570 square feet
Structure: Framed concrete; precast concrete
Materials: Glass; marble cladding
Cost: R85 million

Wooltru is a leading Southern African Retail and Wholesale Group operating 671 stores and employing close to 1,700 people. The Group comprises three major trading companies, one of which is the Select Retail Group. Ten years previously, the Roberts & Loebenberg team designed a Corporate Head Office for the Group, including 35,000 square metres (376,750 square feet) of office accommodation. Due to a natural growth and acquisition the Truworths Head Office component had to move into a new building nearby.

The building is designed to house Truworths initially on four floors, and over a period, the full eight floors of office accommodation. Parking is available for 400 motor vehicles on lower levels and the ground floor has off-street shops.

1

2

3

1 Glass-clad canopies and automatic revolving glass door
2 Dining atrium lit by clear glass skylights
3 The building reflects three distinct functions including a parking podium, rentable office space for future expansion and Truworths Head Office
4 Concrete landings supporting the steel staircase
5 The entrance foyer is clad in polished and sand-blasted reconstructed marble and local granite
6 Curved forms of the building perimeter are reflected in the Truworths atrium
7 Atrium successfully linking four open planned office levels

4

5

6

7

8

9

8 Reception counter clad in teak veneer and solid stained ash

9 The Truworths auditorium is designed to hold both fashion shows and garment and audio visual presentations

10 Coffee area alongside the dining area, hard finished in various Italian reconstructed marbles and natural African granites

10

United Parcel Service Corporate Office

Thompson, Ventulett, Stainback & Associates Inc

Completion: August 1994

Location: Atlanta, Georgia, USA

Client: United Parcel Service

Area: 57,598 square metres; 620,000 square feet

Structure: Cast-in-place concrete; precast concrete

Materials: Precast concrete; glass

Awards: 1995 Award for Design Excellence, Architectural Precast Association

1994 American Concrete Institute, Georgia Chapter

1995 Design Award, ASID/GA

1995 Design Award, AIA/GA

1995 Environmental Planning Award, International Development Research Council

1995 National Design Award, Precast/Prestressed Concrete Institute

United Parcel Service's new corporate offices are located on a heavily wooded 35 acre site in the northern suburbs of Atlanta. Special care was taken to preserve as much of the site's natural setting as possible. Thompson, Ventulett, Stainback & Associates' design responsibilities includes land use master planning, interior programming, complete architectural/engineering design, interior design, and furnishings selection.

The structure includes almost 57,600 square metres (620,000 square feet), and averages seven storeys in height, the approximate height of the tree canopy. Offices and support areas accommodate approximately 2,000 employees and include a 600-seat cafeteria, central conference/training facilities and more than 400 pieces of artwork. Parking is provided in two structured parking decks accommodating over 1,800 cars.

Positioned on a steeply sloped site, the building is designed to have minimal impact on the surrounding environment. The construction contract required trees to be saved as close as 4.5 metres (15 feet) from the face of the building. The design called for the building to capture—rather than destroy—an existing stream that runs through the middle of the site. The two main office structures parallel the topography on either side of the site dividing ravine and the multi-storey bridge connects those elements with conference, cafeteria, and other public oriented spaces.

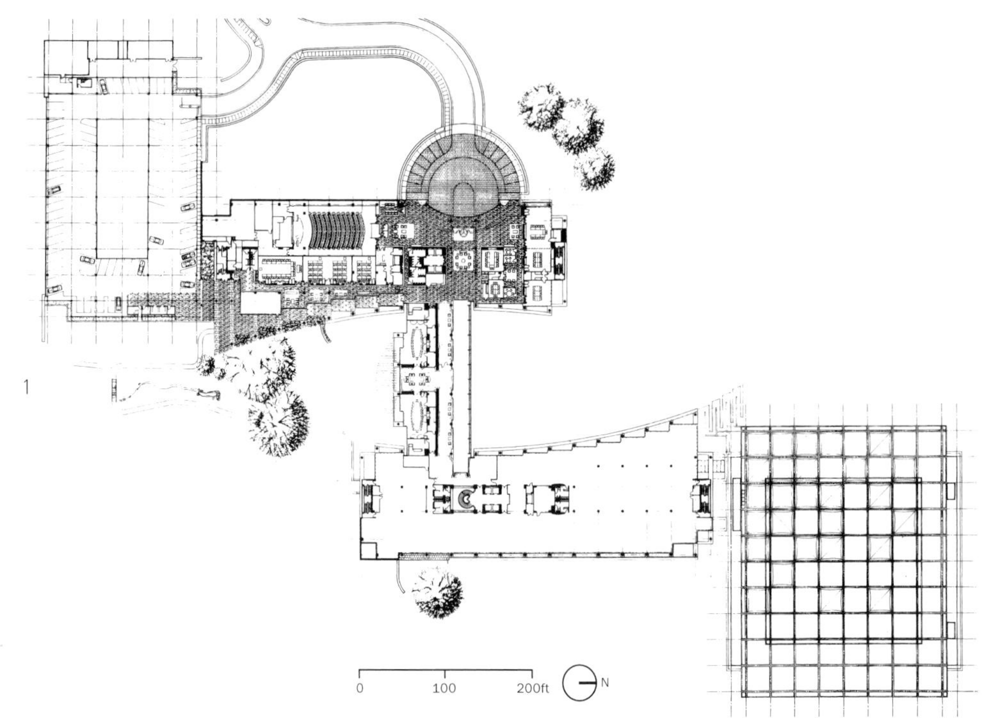

1 Main lobby level
2 Aerial view
3 View from south between building wings

2

3

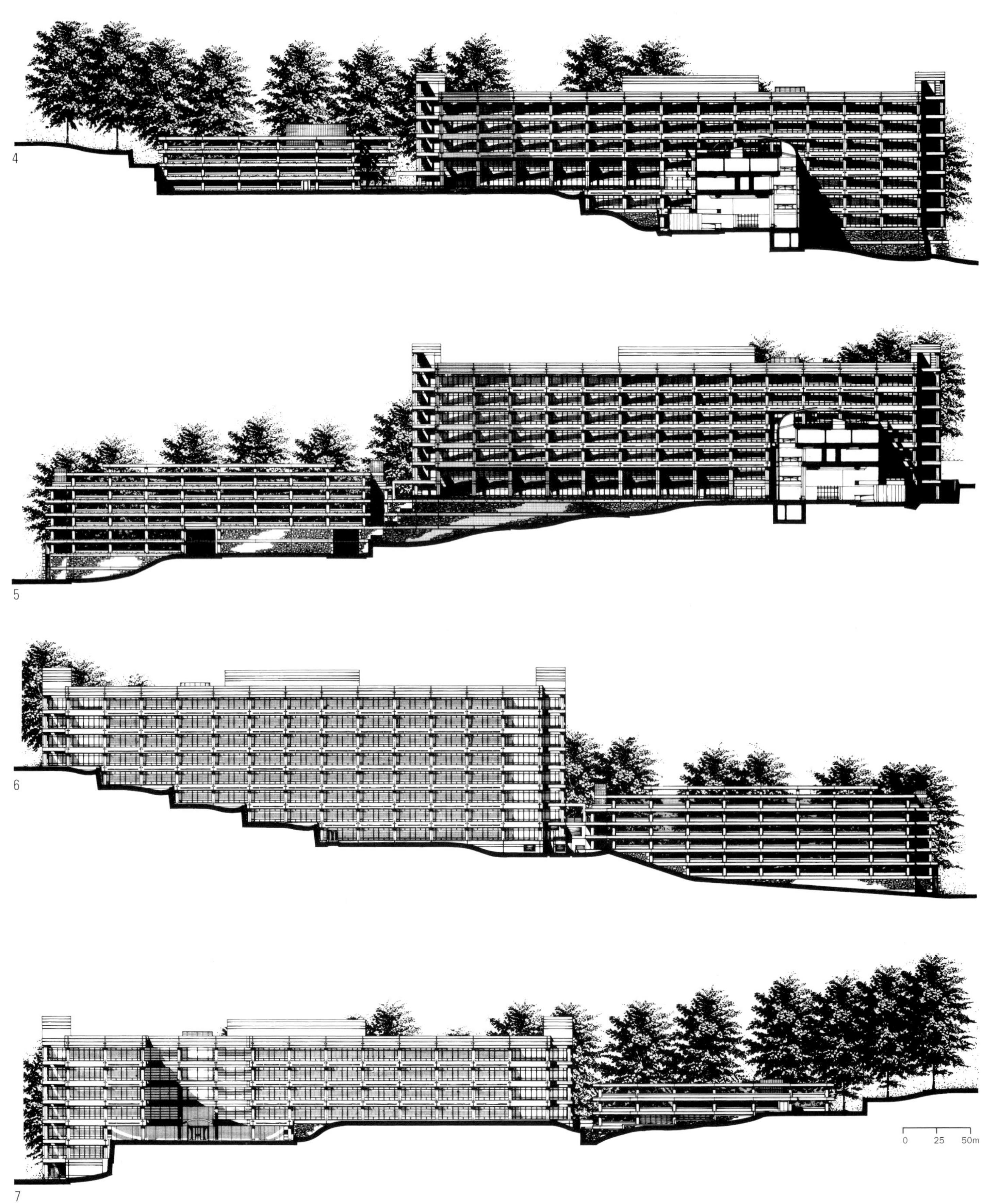
4
5
6
7
0 25 50m

8

9

10

11

4 East elevation of west wing
5 West elevation of east wing
6 East elevation of east wing
7 West elevation of west wing
8 Corner detail
9 West facade of east wing
10 Main entrance
11 View of cafeteria and exterior dining terrace

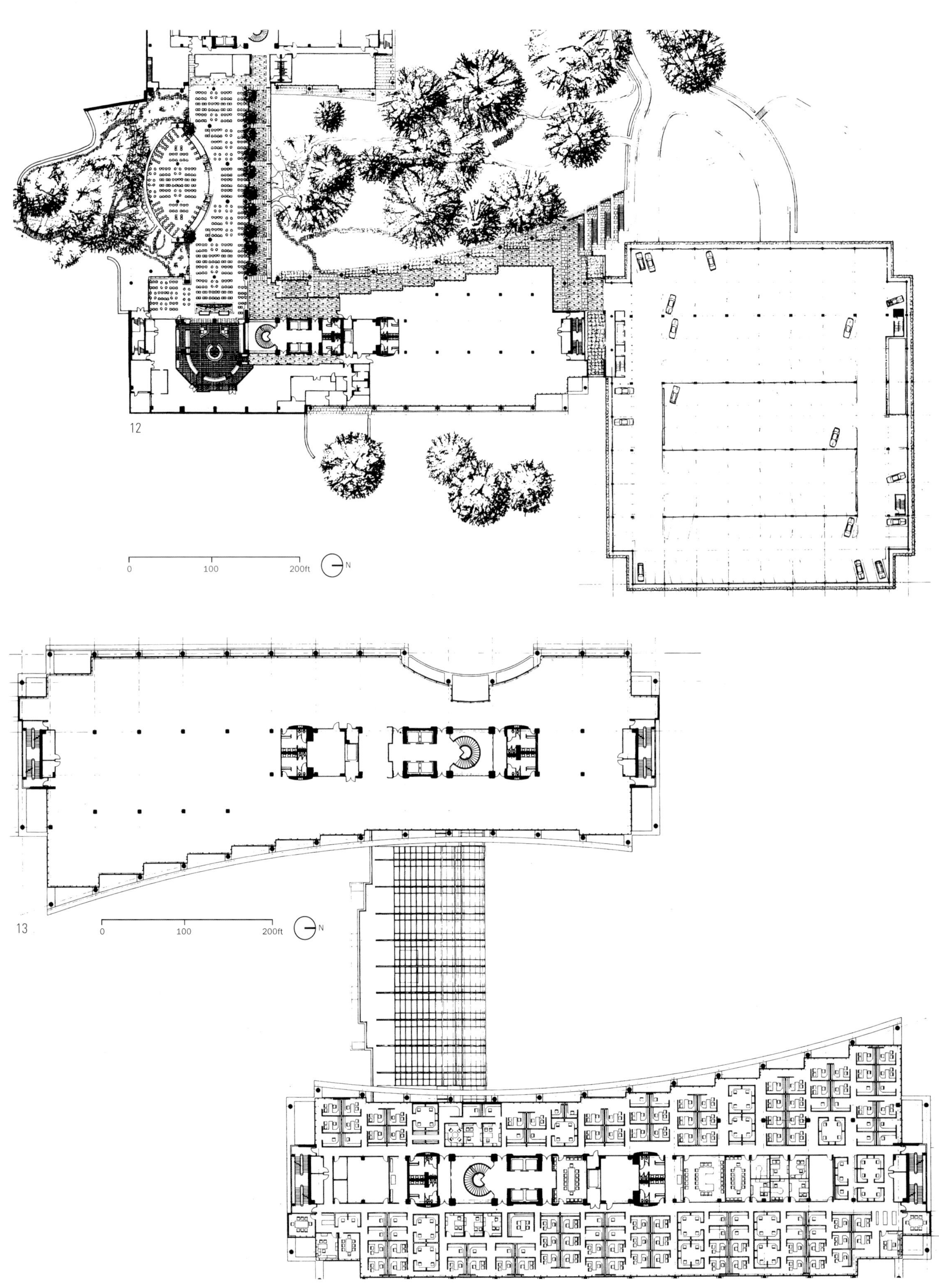
12
0
100
200ft
N
13
0
100
200ft
N

12 Cafeteria level
13 Typical floor
14 Atrium view from main lobby

14

15 Executive offices
16 Main lobby
17 Detail at monumental spiral stairs
Photography: Brian Gassel/TVS&Associates

15

16

17

Arts/Law Building, Northern Territory University

Daryl Jackson Architects
in association with Woodhead (Aust) NT Pty Ltd

Completion: December 1994

Location: Brinkin, Northern Territory, Australia

Client: Northern Territory University

Area: 5,500 square metres; 59,203 square feet

Structure: Reinforced concrete; in situ band beams; concrete slabs

Materials: Rendered blockwork; corrugated metal; steel; metal

Darwin is tropical, the climate typically wet and hot, or dry and hot. Sun protection, air movement and roof cover are of paramount importance. A long thin academic building with an 'open' central loggia or veranda, forms a common entry to the separate faculties of Arts and Law. Long rows of private offices for staff contrast with cubist blocks, wrenched out of the basic block, which offer identity to the library, moot courts and other special uses.

Strong primary colours; shaded, deeply recessed lightweight walls; and skeletal steel stairs complete the assemblage.

1 Window detail
2 Building in its landscape
3 Staircase detail

1

2

3

The Biocentre

Juhani Katainen Architects

Completion: April 1995

Location: Helsinki, Finland

Client: University of Helsinki

Area: 15,417 square metres; 165,953 square feet

Structure: Reinforced concrete

Materials: Reinforced concrete; steel coffers; wood; aluminium siding

Cost: 90 million FIM

The Biocentre of the University of Helsinki was completed in April 1995. The building is located in the Viikki district of Helsinki and forms part of the University Science Park currently under construction. The Biocentre contains research and teaching facilities for the biosciences (pharmacy, genetics and biochemistry). The gross floor area of the building is 15,417 square metres (165,953 square feet), and its volume 60,000 square metres (645,856 square feet).

In the master scheme for the area, the institution buildings were placed along Viikinkaari. The massing principle featured high tower blocks linked by a low lamellar building following the curve of the road. Functionally, the research laboratories were placed in the tower blocks, while the office space was concentrated in the linking lamellar building. The jointly used lecture theatres are between the towers on the ground level, and the teaching laboratories are also on the ground floor. The research facilities are organised around a core of service facilities in each tower.

The building has a foundation of reinforced concrete piles. The construction comprises reinforced concrete bearing walls and pillars. The floors are hollow slab in reinforced concrete. The elevations are finished in clinker-faced reinforced concrete elements and partly in painted steel coffers. The triple-glazed windows are made of wood, with stove-enamelled aluminium siding on the outside. The windows in the stairwells have steel frames. The floors are mainly linoleum.

1

2

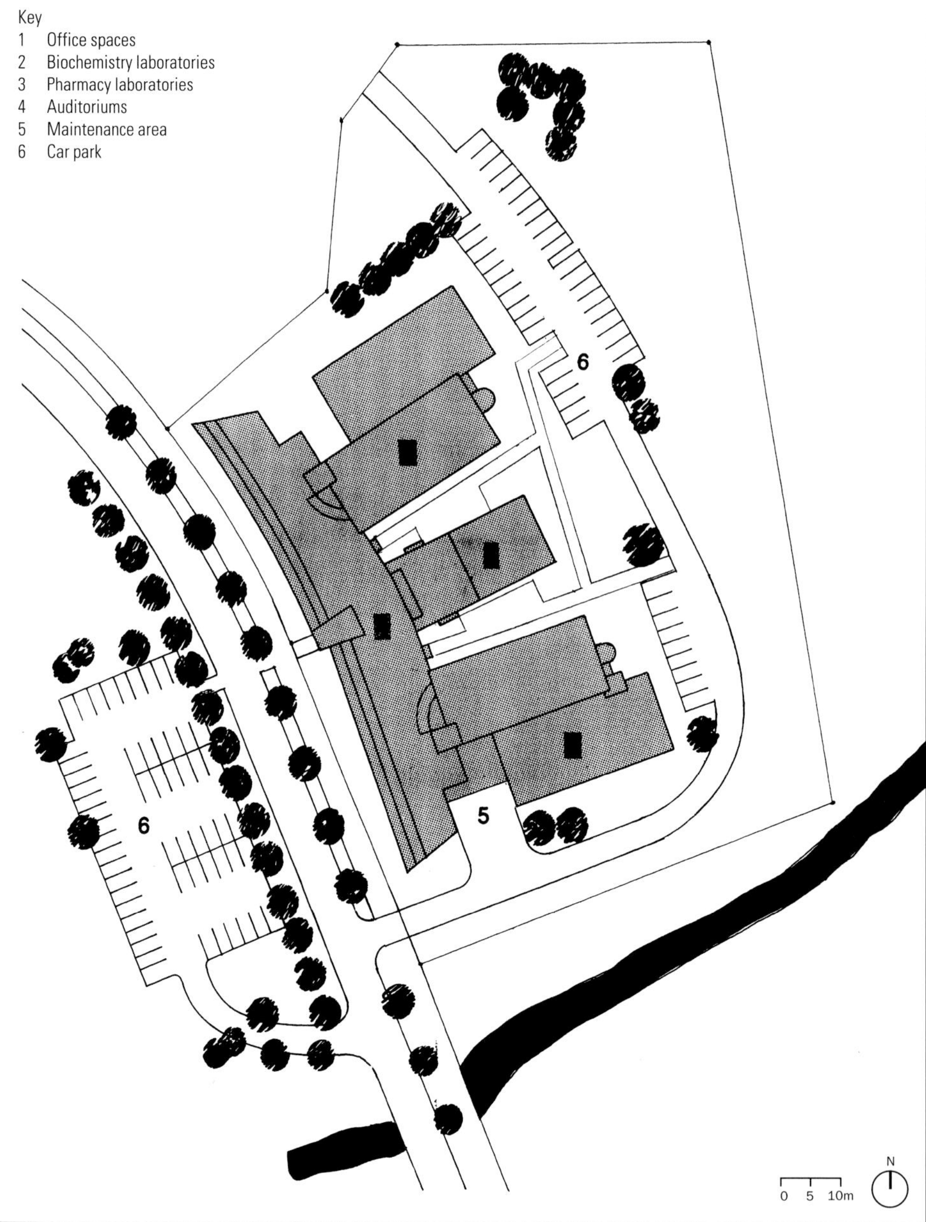

3

1-2 The main entrance

3 Site plan

4 Exterior view

5 The building seen across the surrounding fields

4

5

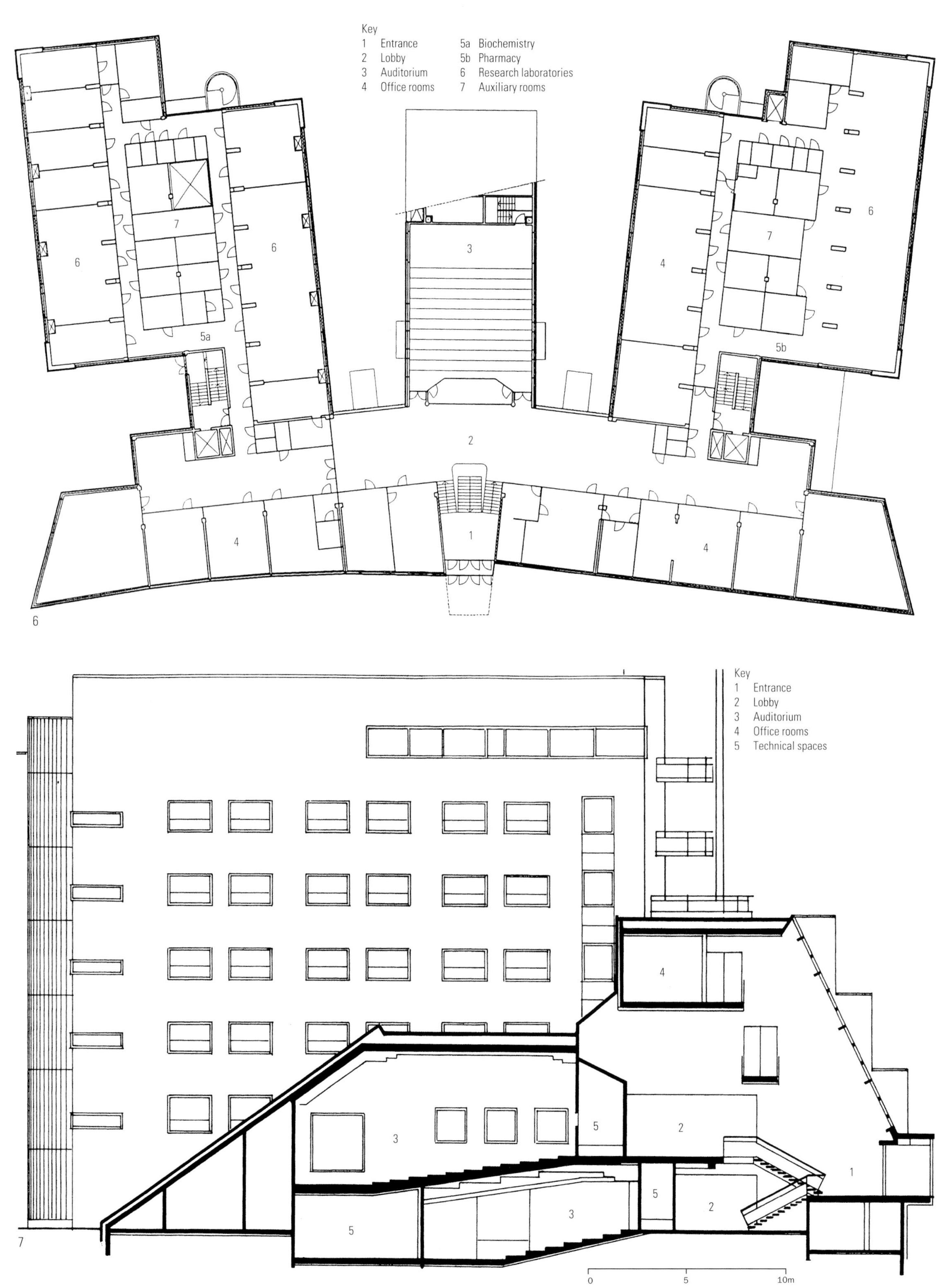
Key
1 Entrance
2 Lobby
3 Auditorium
4 Office rooms
5a Biochemistry
5b Pharmacy
6 Research laboratories
7 Auxiliary rooms
Key
1 Entrance
2 Lobby
3 Auditorium
4 Office rooms
5 Technical spaces
0
5
10m

6

7

8

6 First floor

7 Section

8 Spaces for pharmacy

9 The spaces for pharmacy in the foreground, auditorium and biochemistry in the background

9

10

11

12

10 Auditorium
11 Laboratory spaces
12 The entrance hall
Photography: Hannu Koivisto

Biology Building No. 68, Massachusetts Institute of Technology

Goody, Clancy & Associates, Inc.

Completion: June 1994
Location: Cambridge, Massachusetts, USA
Client: Massachusetts Institute of Technology
Area: 23,410 square metres; 252,000 square feet
Structure: Cast-in-place reinforced concrete; steel
Materials: Indiana limestone cladding; prefinished aluminium panels; glass; tiles; wood; plaster
Cost: US$53.2 million

As the first building of MIT's Northeast Sector, the Biology Building had to not only meet the intended program but also establish a strong precedent for future development. The design approach expresses the distinctions between the laboratory modules and the social spaces which occur at the major vertical circulation 'nodes' of the building. Exterior materials selected are consistent with the palette of the Main Campus.

Five floors of laboratories, support spaces and faculty offices form the heart of the building. The floor layouts are designed to foster communications among research groups, both in the shared equipment areas and in social spaces. The plan is based on a flexible lab module which can be modified to suit a variety of research activities, and which is on the perimeter of the building for daylight and views. A highly efficient single corridor scheme is utilised, with instrument rooms in the central shared equipment zone doubling as cross-corridors.

In the spirit of the original campus, the design of the Biology Building allows for a great deal of change over time, for continued use as a biological research facility or for other uses. Each of the nearly 150 hoods has its own riser, located on the exterior (within a prefinished metal enclosure) which connects to an exhaust manifold plenum in the Penthouse. This approach permits the use of heat recovery and provides redundancy and improved occupant safety. Furthermore, only six major exhaust fans are utilised instead of the traditional one-hood-one-fan approach, thus simplifying maintenance and operations. Air supply and exhaust systems were designed to facilitate the addition or deletion of a fume hood in any laboratory without the need to shut down or rebalance the entire system. Special energy conservation measures, including occupancy sensors to control lights, and variable frequency fan drives, are integrated into the electrical and lighting systems.

1

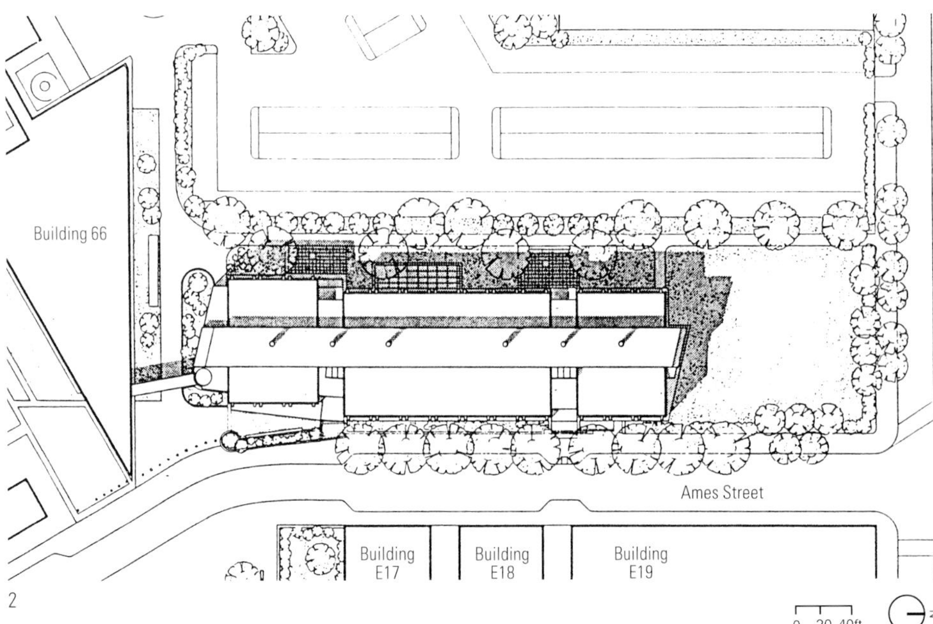

2

3

1 Detail of east elevation
2 Site plan
3 West elevation
4 Typical laboratory floor plan
5 First floor plan
6 East elevation
7 View from Building 66 at bridge
8 Open stairways connect all floors in each of two atria
9 Typical four-person laboratory module
10 Lounge, showing lower floor of 2-storey space
Photography: Steve Rosenthal

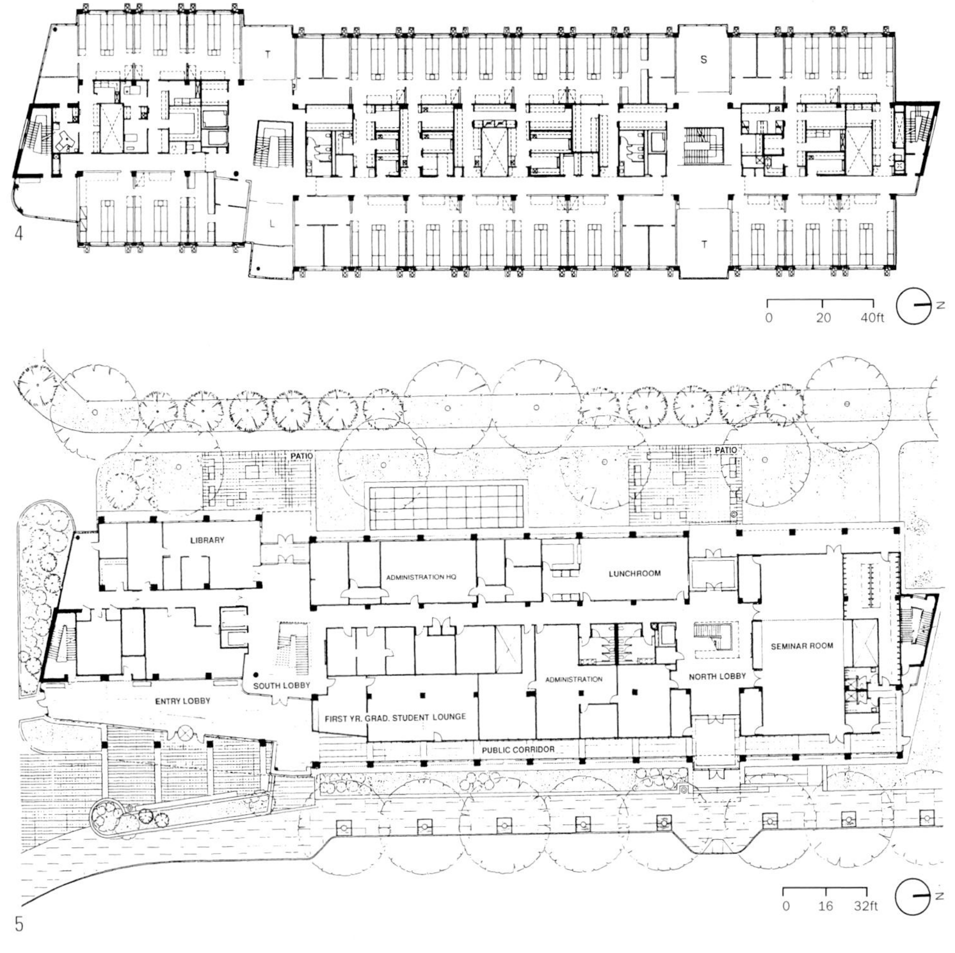
T
S
L
T
0 20 40ft
PATIO
PATIO
LIBRARY
ADMINISTRATION HQ
LUNCHROOM
SEMINAR ROOM
SOUTH LOBBY
ENTRY LOBBY
ADMINISTRATION
NORTH LOBBY
FIRST YR. GRAD. STUDENT LOUNGE
PUBLIC CORRIDOR
0 16 32ft

4

5

6

7

8

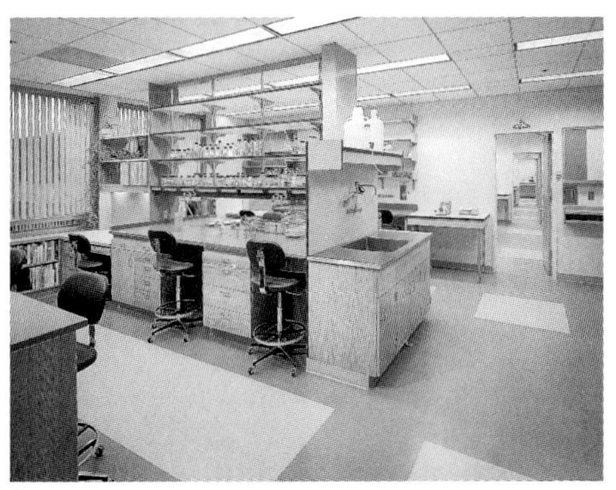

9

10

Catholic University, Library and Lecture Hall

Young-sub Kim

Completion: January 1995

Location: Seoul, Korea

Client: Foundation Catholic School Parish

Area: 1,650 square metres; 17,760 square feet

Structure: Reinforced concrete

Materials: Red brick; copper plate roof

Awards: First prize 6th Annual Korean Environmental Design and Architectural Culture Award

The site where the Catholic University is located is near the active and vibrant neighbourhood of Dong Sung-dong. Yet just over the hill where the university is actually located, it is surprisngly peaceful, surrounded by trees. In late 1992, Choi, the principal of the Catholic University, requested four specific program requirements: first, the red brick with pitched roof—the architecture of the old Catholic school built in 1920 and completely destroyed in the early 1970s could be echoed in the new structure; second, the building was to be redesigned around a tree, the oldest standing on the campus; third, the administration building was to be considered when placing the library and the lecture hall within the campus so that the students' circulation was controlled.

In the beginning of the design, the library and the lecture hall were housed in the same building. However, due to the different loading calculations of each structure, it was decided to locate them separately, connecting the two structures by corridor. The sunken garden blocks the circulation by students to the professors' quarter, but at the same time provides students space for 24 hour access to the library and a place for outdoor activity.

The most important concept in the design of this project was to invite nature into the building. In other words, trees, greenery and lights were brought into the library to change the image of the university as a conservative institute. The connecting hall was enveloped with glass windows on three sides, and faces the historical two Zelkova trees and light shining between the tree branches. The lecture called 'Haksa-dong' also was designed to facilitate an open atmosphere, as well as providing heterogenous experiences moving through the building. The circulation elements such as stairs, corridors and bridges are exposed.

1

2

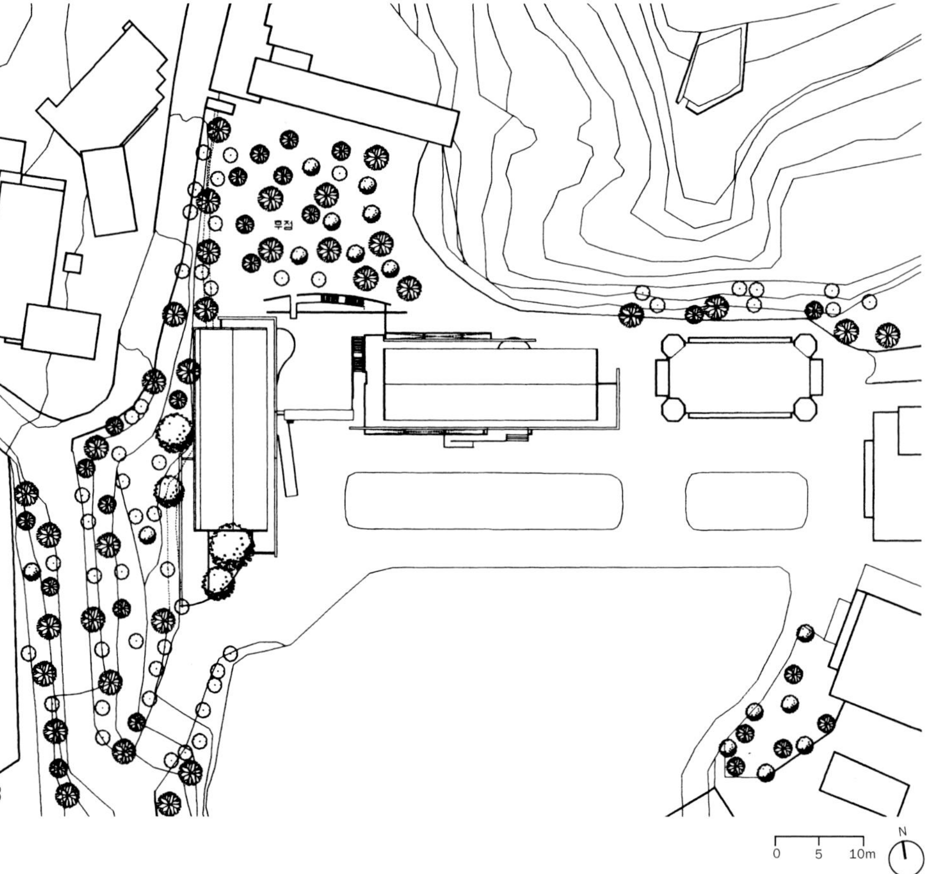

3

4

1 View from approach road
2 View from play yard
3 Site plan
4 View from east road in Soung Shin campus
5 Basement floor plan
6 Connection roof between library and lecture hall

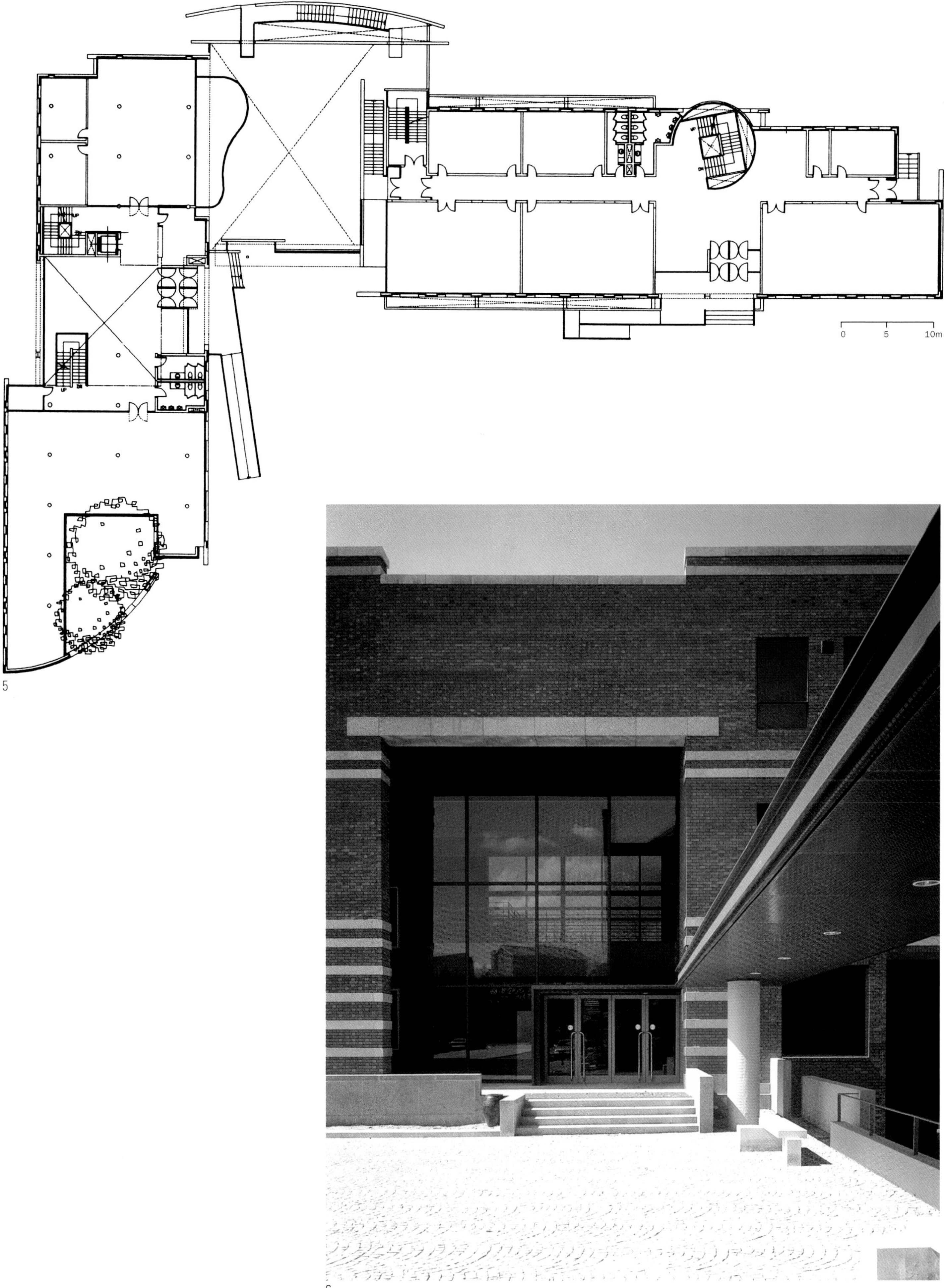

5

6

7

8

9

10

11

7 View of sunken garden
8 Details of stair in library
9 Entrance gate of library (view from landing place)
10 Reading room below ground floor
11 Skylight in book stack
12 Staircase in lecture hall
13 Large window in entrance hall
Photography: Kim, Young-sub

12

13

City University of New York, New Library

Perry, Dean, Rogers & Partners: Architects, Inc.

Completion: April 1994

Location: Staten Island, New York, USA

Client: Dormitory Authority, State of New York

Area: 10,498 square metres; 113,000 square feet

Structure: Steel/concrete frame; exposed steel curtain wall

Materials: Brick; stucco; glass block

Cost: US$23 million

The Library and Student Center for the College of Staten Island at Willowbrook are a joint design effort of two architectural firms, each of which developed one building after collaboration on the conceptual design. The buildings are organised along the primary campus axis, and define the centres of the north and south academic quadrangles which are linked by a broad alley. They are conceptually related in parti, massing and choice of materials, while the diverse nature of the respective programs is expressed in the different formal approaches to the plan; the Library maintains a more classical stance against the more dynamic, fluid aspects of the Student Center, which serves to heighten the tension between the structures.

The Library is a 3-storey, square structure made of brick, stucco and steel curtain wall, with a central rotunda into which is inserted a large, octagonal screen. Entry is from the north through a smaller rotunda made of glass block and flanked with glazed curtain wall. At the south side of the building is a large double height reading room, which recalls, in its space and use of natural light, traditional reading rooms such as those found in the Boston Public Library and the Bibliotheque Ste. Genevieve in Paris.

The rotunda is naturally lit through clerestory windows behind the octagonal screen, and a glass block lantern. Night lighting will be from a variety of indirect sources; one will illuminate the glass block lantern, which speaks to an identical structure at the peak of the student centre. These will serve as beacons defining the centre of the campus. The roof structure in this central space is entirely exposed, and the play of light and shadow among the network trusses, rafters, cables and fluted deck will contribute to the quality of this room.

Functionally, the building is divided into six discrete facilities, each with separate internal entrances. Beside the library, the program includes a Snack Bar, Tutorial Learning Center, Academic Computing Center, Media Center, and the Professional Staff Congress. The primary library user functions are immediately adjacent to the central rotunda on the first and second floors, with the bulk

Continued

1

2

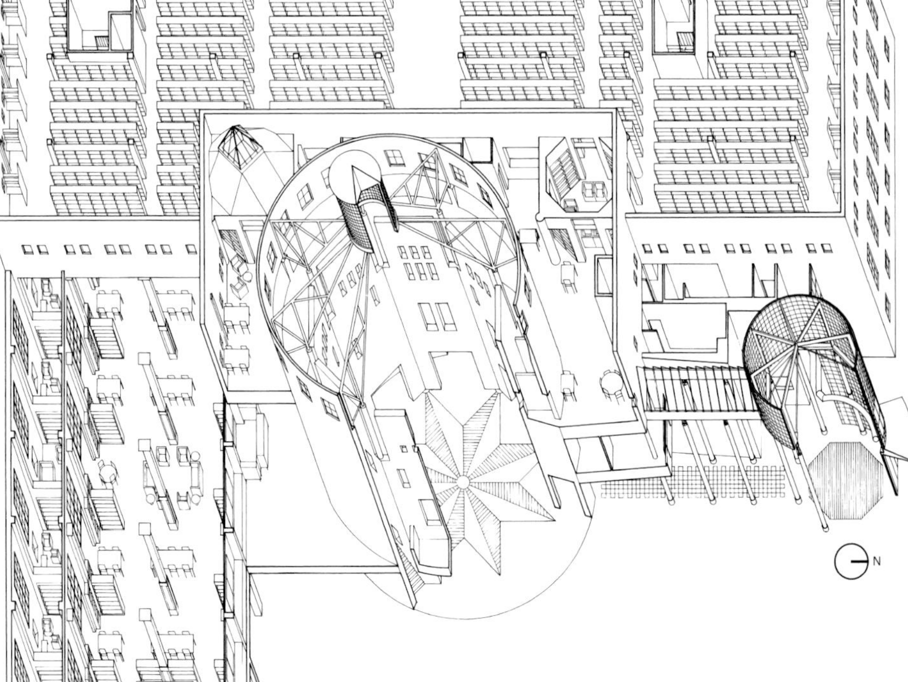

3

4

1 Entrance detail
2 Entrance facade at night
3 Axonometric showing spatial sequence
4 View from alley
5 Main floor plan
6 Third floor plan
7 Rotunda looking north
8 Natural light in the rotunda

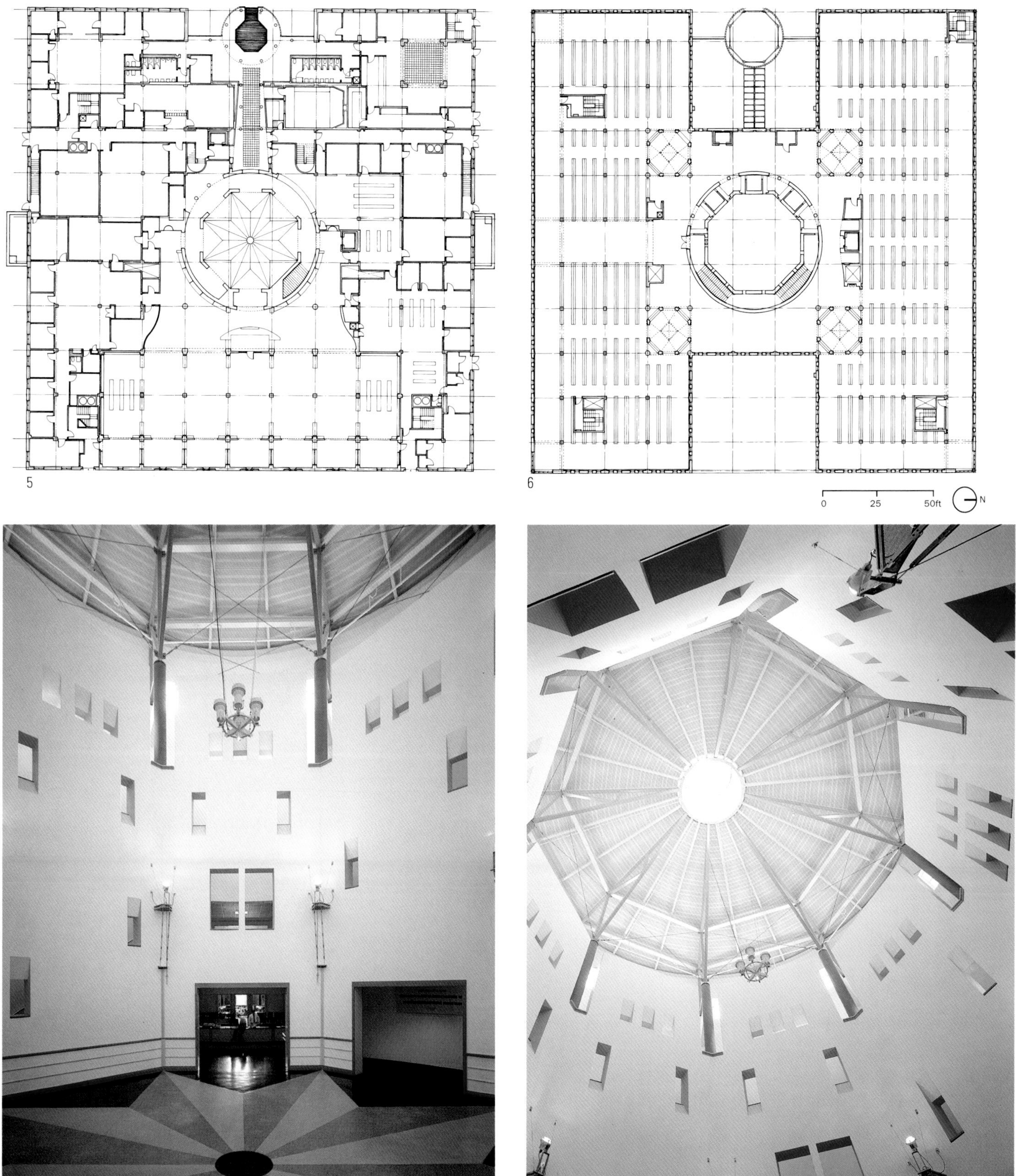

5

6

7

8

of the collection being housed on the top floor of the building. Overlooking the double height reference room on the second floor is a large balcony containing the periodicals collections and its attendant services. Small skylit studies define a raised central area around the rotunda on the third floor which, with the glazed, open corners on this level, provide oases for readers among the expanse of stacks.

The Academic Computing and Media Center incorporate state-of-the-art information technologies to handle a wide variety of computer and audio-visual applications. These facilities are designed to eventually be networked to remote locations on campus. The library will utilise three online catalogue systems, which will enable users to more easily access the resources of the CUNY libraries and the OCLC system.

9 Study carrel
10 Reading room
11 Reference room
12 The rotunda

9

10

11

12

13

13 Study alcoves in the reference room
14 The foyer looking east

14

Congressman Jerry Lewis Elementary School

HMC Group

Completion: December 1994

Location: Fort Irwin, California, USA

Client: Silver Valley Unified School District, San Bernadino County, California

Area: 4,645 square metres; 55,000 square feet

Structure: Steel frame; steel stud wall

Materials: Concrete blocks; plaster; gypsum board; tackable vinyl

Cost: US$9 million

Awards: 1995 Honor Award, American Institute of Architects, Inland Chapter

1995 Honor Award, Coalition for Adequate School Housing

1994 Citation of Merit Design, National School Boards Association

1993 Merit Award, Coalition for Adequate School Housing

The design of the school was derived from a series of metaphors that describe the desert context. The forms, massing, and colour scheme were selected to create a sympathetic link between the school and the natural landscape. Located in the midst of multi-family military housing, the project responds to site orientation, pedestrian and vehicular access, scale, and other planning issues by directly addressing the surrounding neighbourhood.

Situated atop a small knoll, visitors are drawn towards the school's long low buildings. Jutting towers punctuate the primary building massing in a reference to the way the distant mountains punctuate the horizon. Landscaped berms slope gently away from the building, imitating sparsely vegetated alluvial plains. An extended covered walkway welcomes students and visitors to the school, offering an escape from the unrelenting sun. The horizontal scoring of the supporting piers alludes to fractured strata exposed over millennia. During torrential summer thunderstorms, run-off from the awning gathers to a scupper where it splashes into a stone-filled cistern and disappears in the timeless manner of the desert.

Dark lava soils, purple and violet mountains, ochre mesquite and chaparral, and deep blue skies are the basis of the school's colour scheme. Aggregated and intensified, these colours create a vibrant statement about the school's philosophy. Trees are laid out in a rigid grid to enhance their effectiveness as windbreaks and to reinforce the incongruence of finding alien plant life in the high desert.

The focus of school activities is directed inward due to the harsh climate. A sheltered courtyard and covered play area are provided to shield students from seasonal high winds and extreme heat. A tower and sundial provide the focus of attention in the courtyard, marking the passage of the sun, and connecting students to their physical environment. The school's circulation elements describe axial relationships that are long sweeping gestures that, like the desert, stretch to the horizon. The interior of the school is characterised by cool dark passages punctuated by brightly lit colour wells placed at important circulation nodes, creating an inviting interior oasis that assists students in wayfinding and minimises the effect of long narrow corridors.

Continued

1

2

3

4

5

6

1 Main entrance to school
2 Architectural exterior detail
3 Courtyard sundial
4 Site plan
5 Kindergarten
6 Road to Fort. Irwin, California desert
7 Rock garden outside Multipurpose Room

7

The design incorporates energy conservation and management systems, extra insulation, daylighting, and xeroscape landscaping. The structural system utilises a steel brace frame with metal stud framing. The building is clad in exterior plaster with gypsum board interior finishes. Concrete block is used as an accent material both inside and outside the building.

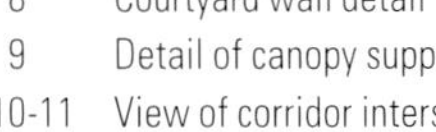

8 Courtyard wall detail
9 Detail of canopy support
10-11 View of corridor intersection
12 Drinking fountain alcove
13 View of entry from under canopy
14 View of reception desk in Administration

8

9

10

11

12

13

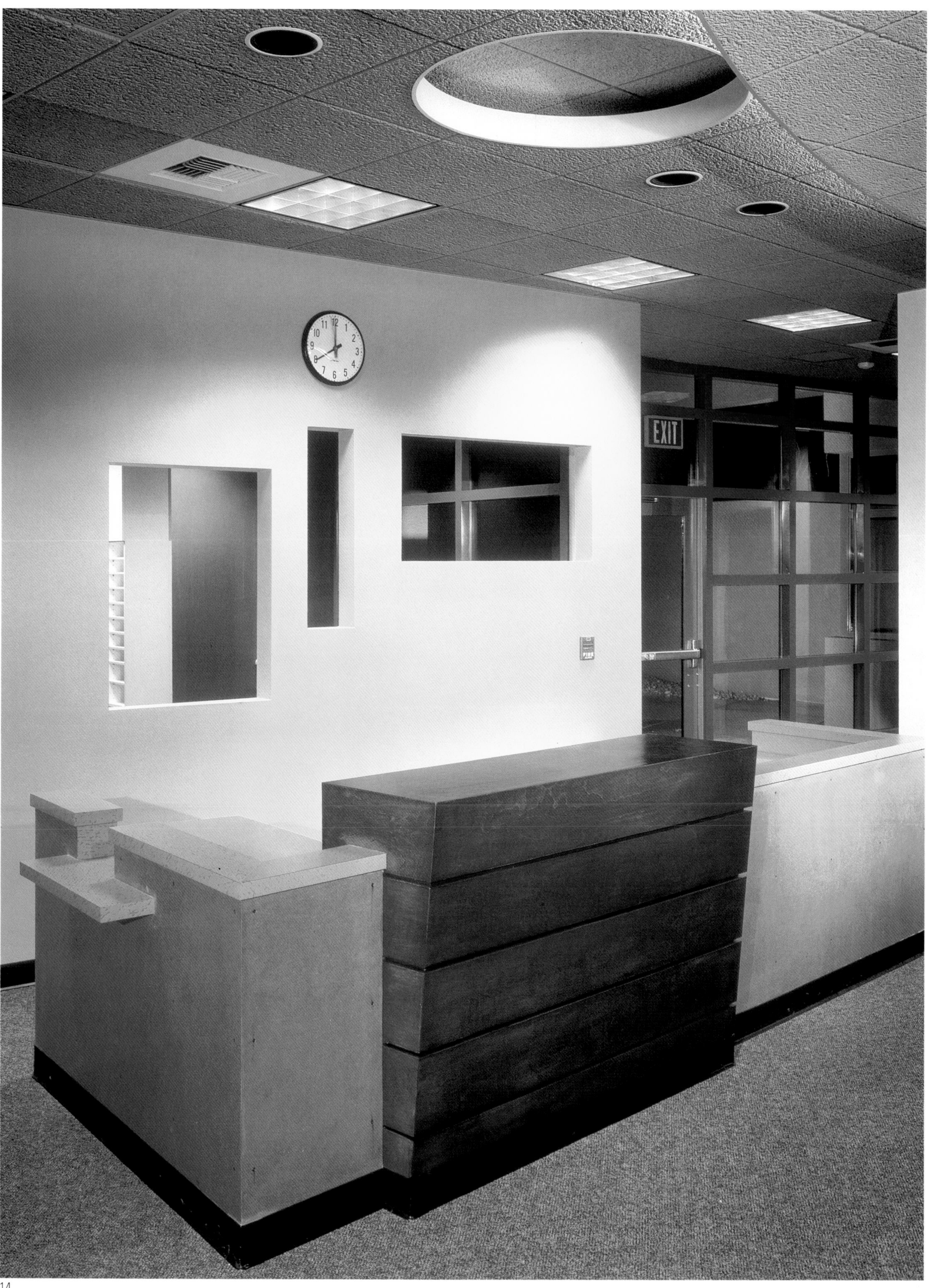

14

15 Corridor intersection
16 View of entry of library skylight well
17 Principal's office
18 View towards principal's office
19 Typical classroom
20 Multipurpose room

Photography: Barton Anderson; Wolfgang Simon; Fred Licht; Klyde Wilson

15

16

17

18

19

20

Energy Systems Research Centre, Ajou University

SAC International, Ltd.

Completion: August 1994

Location: Ajou University, Suwon, Korea

Client: Ajou University

Area: 5,115 square metres; 55,060 square feet

Structure: Steel; steel reinforced concrete

Materials: Epoxy painting; aluminium panel; double glazing; aluminium grill sun breaker

Cost: US$7.8 million

The building houses the University computer centre as well as the Energy Systems Research Centre consisting of classrooms, faculty offices, the computer room, dry laboratories, double height process laboratories and a lecture theatre. It is organised as a simple, double-loaded rectangular volume, and is located at the western edge of the Ajou University campus. As there is heavy pedestrian traffic from other science and engineering buildings to the north of the Centre, a generous exterior stair is attached to the rectangular volume on the north side.

While the majority of buildings on the Ajou University campus are built of red face brick with exposed concrete, the Energy Systems Research Centre stands out as the only exposed steel structure. This was designed intentionally to be a visual expression of the science and technology component of the University. Because the building is oriented east and west on the long elevations, metal sunbreakers are attached to the volume, making the texture of the enclosure richer and constantly changing. The sunbreakers remind onlookers of energy, the main theme of the activity inside.

1

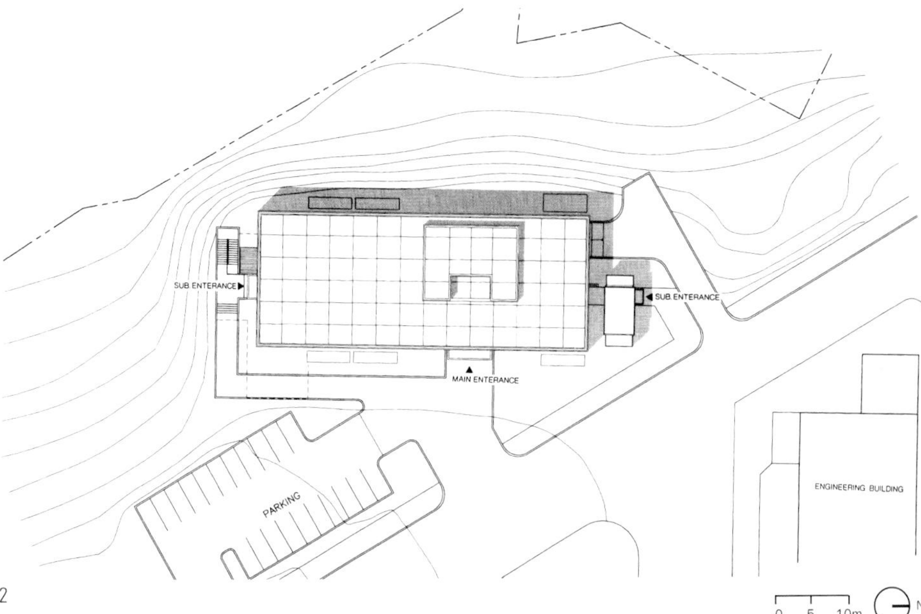

2

3

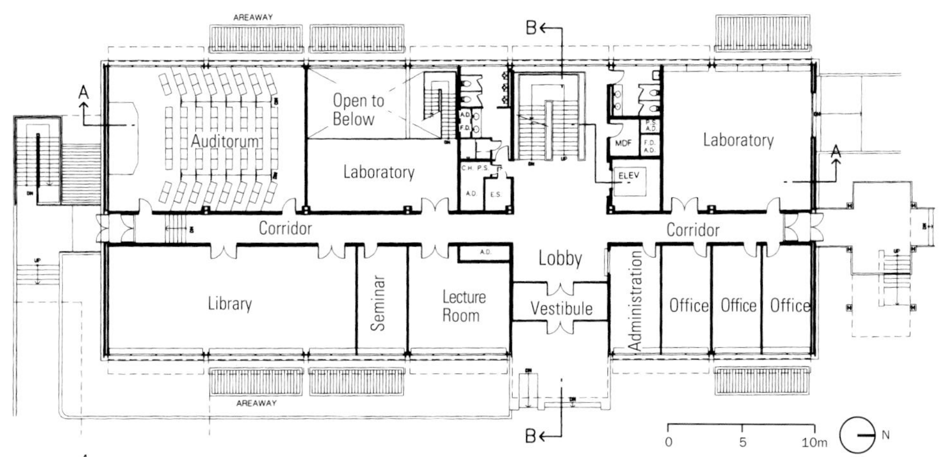

4

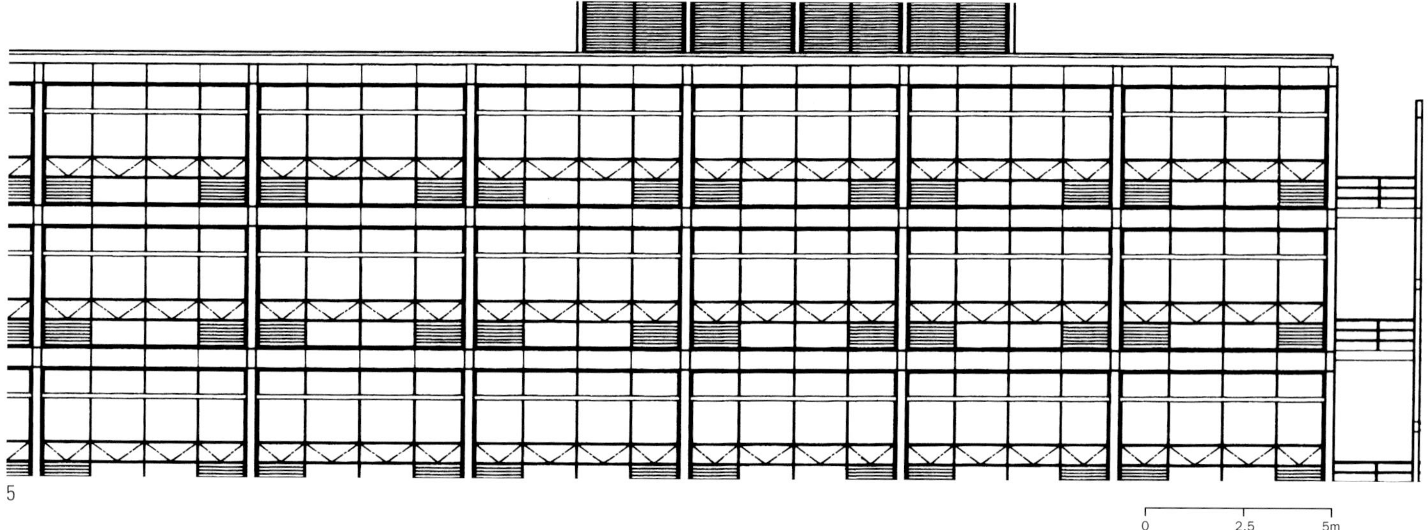

5

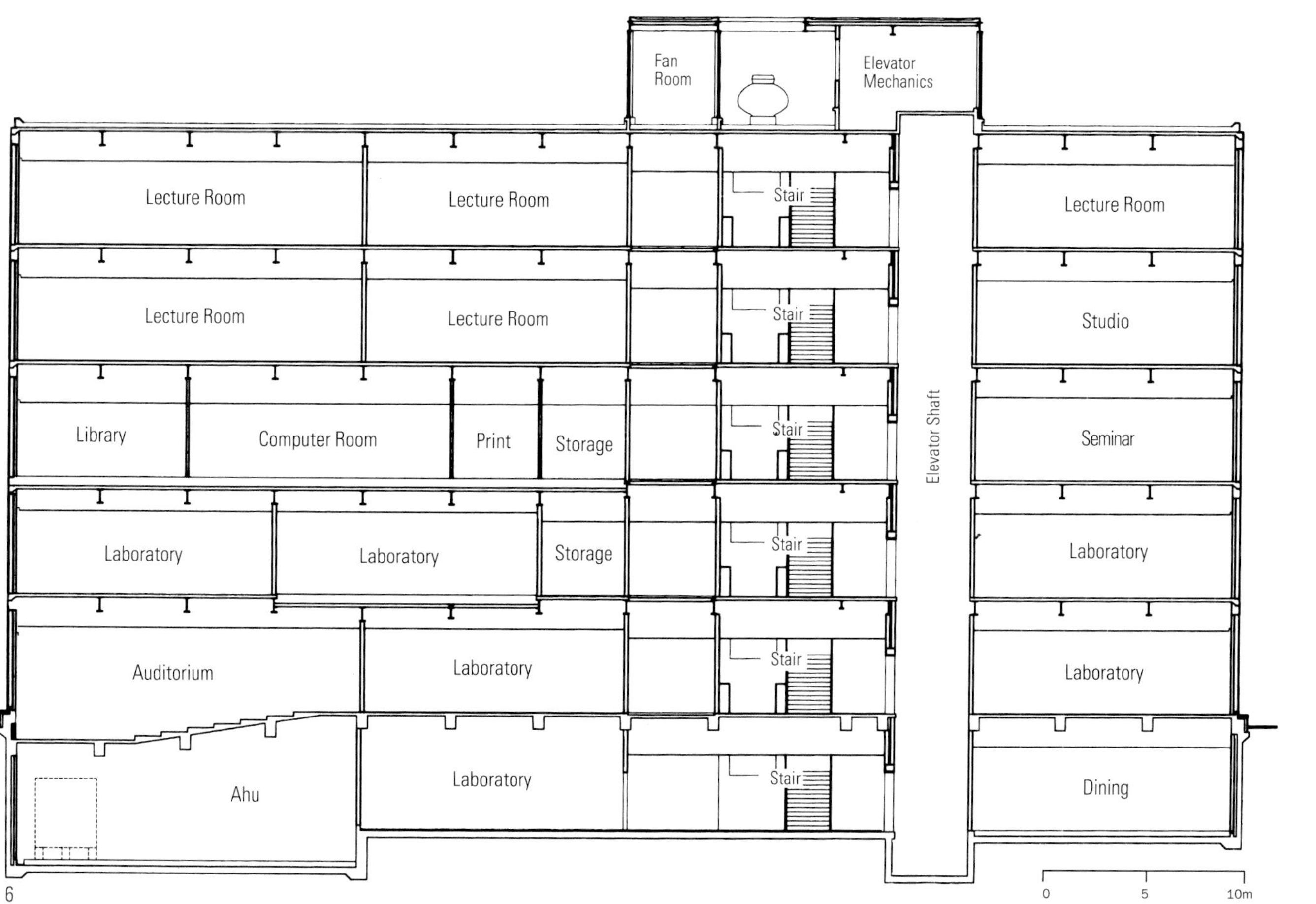

6

1 Details for the sun-breaker
2 Site plan
3 View from southeast
4 Ground floor plan
5 East elevation
6 Longitudinal section
Photography: SAC International, Ltd.

Engineering Research Center, University of Cincinnati

Michael Graves Architect

Completion: May 1995

Location: Cincinnati, Ohio, USA

Client: University of Cincinnati

Area: 15,533 square metres; 167,200 square feet

Structure: Steel frame

Materials: Terracotta brick; cast stone; copper sheathing

Cost: US$27.5 million

Award: 1991 New Jersey Society of Architects Design Award

The building program for this science and engineering research building provides approximately 8,826 square metres (95,000 square feet) and 15,533 gross square metres (167,200 square feet) within six storeys above ground and one below. The building is sited to accommodate existing roadways, paths, steps and grades and to connect to Rhodes Hall which is part of the School of Engineering.

A focal point is provided on the existing axis of University Place, the main approach to the campus from the east, through the placement of the building entrance at the centre of a 6-storey pavilion pulled forward from the body of the building. The pavilion contains faculty offices, clerical space and conference rooms above an open loggia at the plaza level. The elevator lobby and the main stair tower link the entrance pavilion to the laboratories, graduate study areas, additional faculty offices and conference rooms in the body of the building.

The building itself is organised as a series of equal bays or pavilions; two to the south and one to the north of the entrance pavilion. Exterior and interior public stairs accommodate the 5.2 metre (17 foot) change in grade from the building entrance to the plaza levels, where entrances to the library and other buildings are located. The exterior stairs and terraces are planted and provided with seating to encourage use as a gathering place and means of access. Within the building, a generous public stair and hall link University Place with the plaza levels. This interior space is anticipated to be a major circulation route for the general student population as well as for those working in the building.

The exterior skin of the building is terracotta and ochre brick with cast stone detailing, consistent with the older sections of the campus. The vaulted roof, dormers and stacks, suggestive of industrial forms appropriate to the building program, are sheathed in copper.

1

2

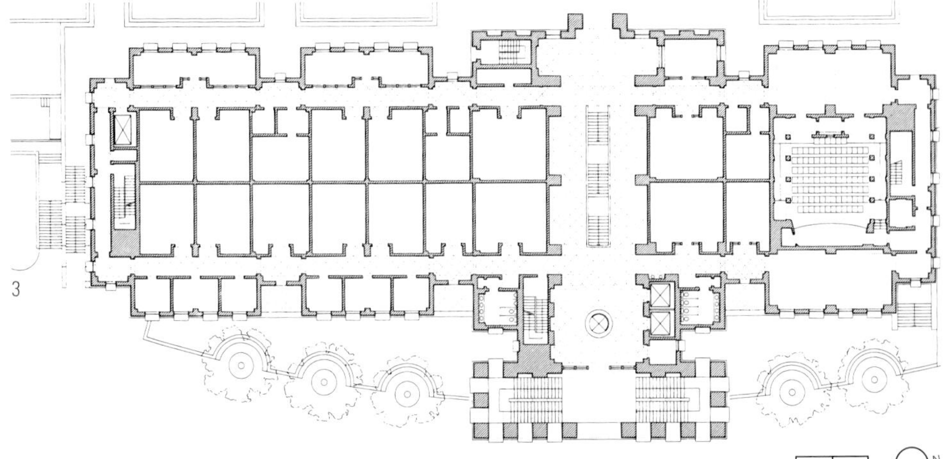

3

4

1 View of northeast
2 Three-quarter view of front facade
3 First floor plan
4 Entrance facade
5 Copper roof detail

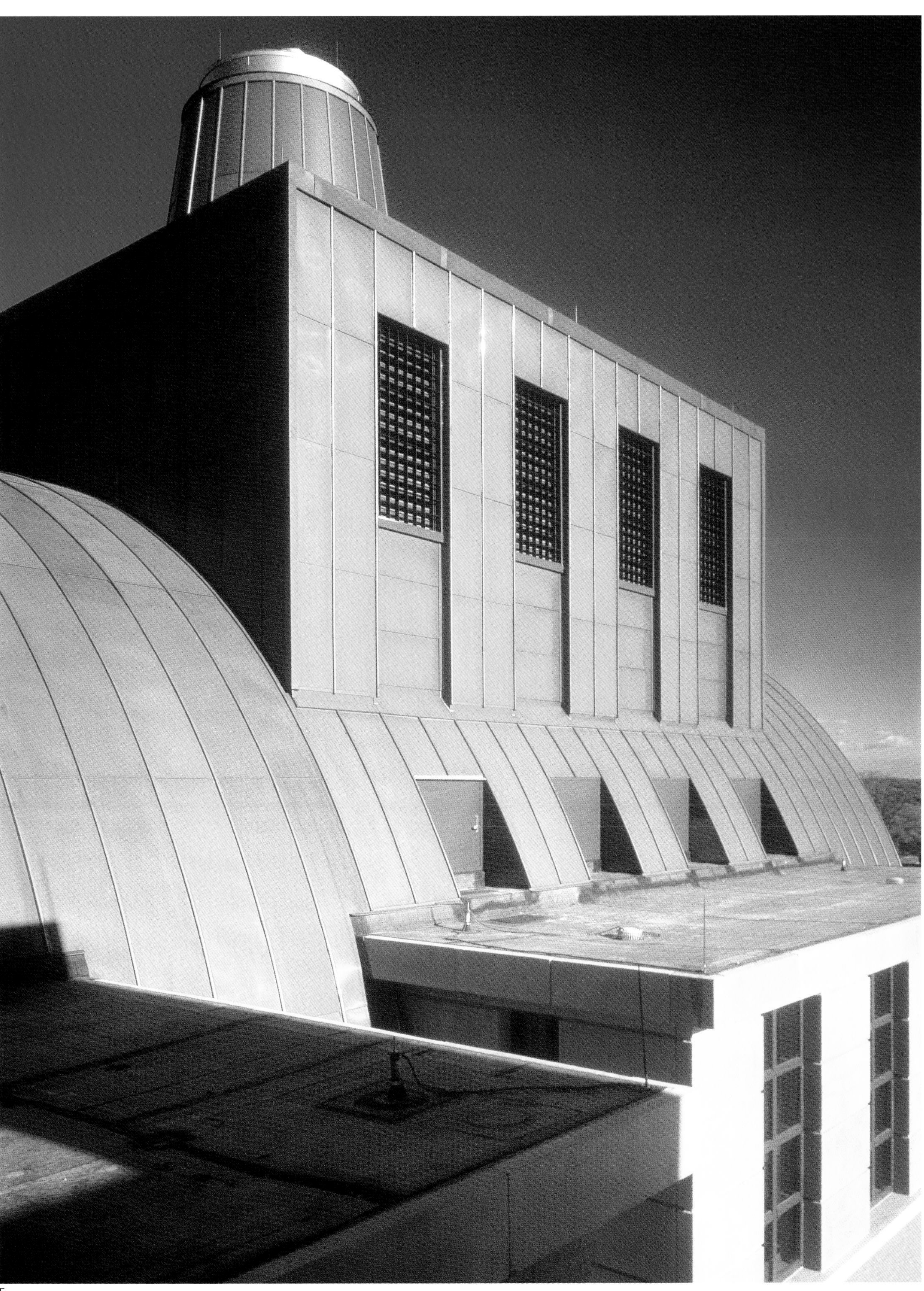

5

6 Stairway
7 East–west section
8 Second level of entrance stair
Photography: Steven Brooke

6

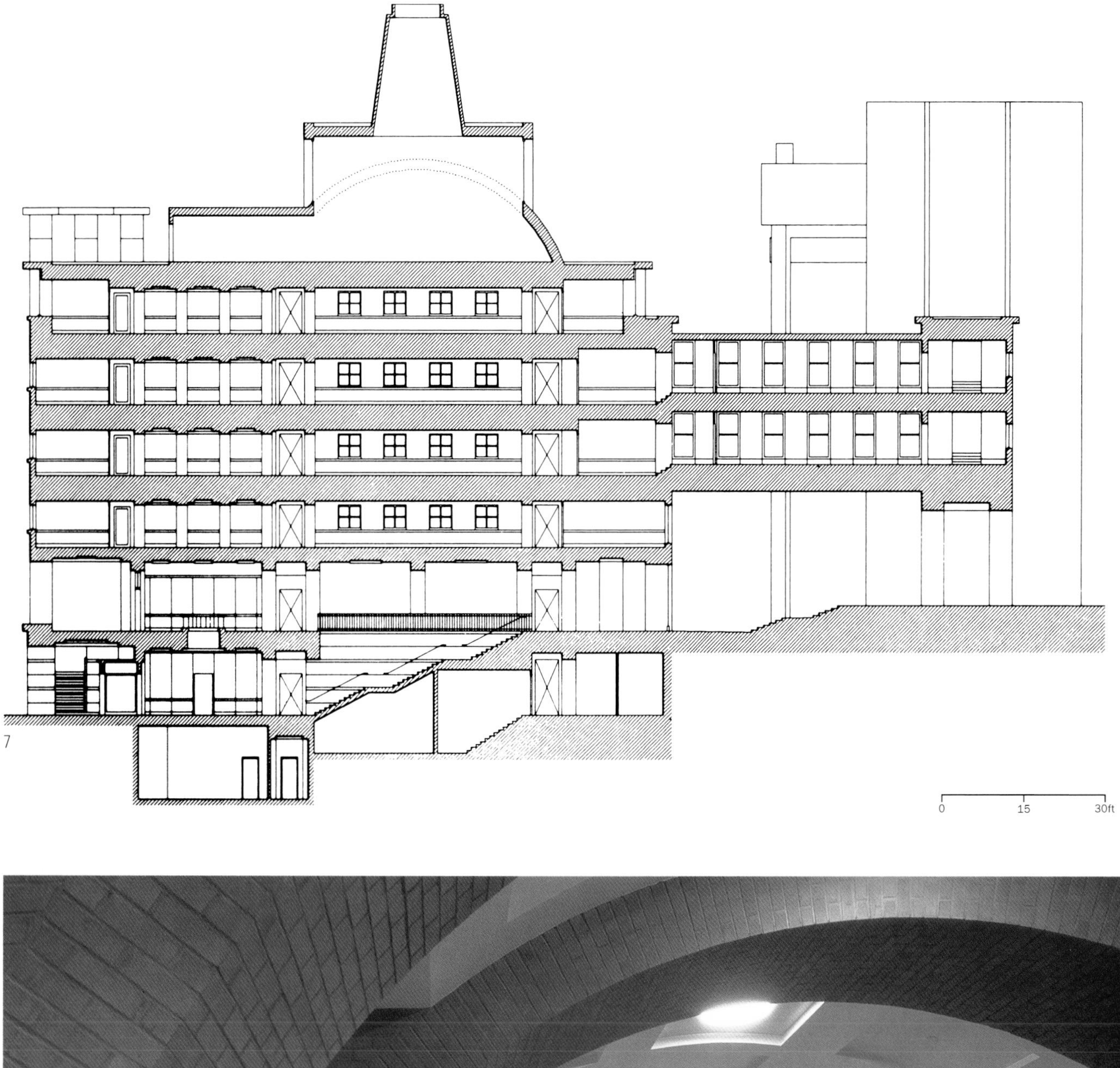

7

0 15 30ft

8

Kungsängsskolan Upper Secondary School

Birgitta Holm Architects Inc.
in association with STADION Architects Inc.

Completion: August 1995
Location: Sala, Midsweden, Sweden
Client: Sala Community
Area: 4,600 square metres; 49,515 square feet
Structure: Massive brick; steel; wood
Materials: Wood; steel; gypsum
Cost: 18.5 million Skr

This project is a renovation and extension of an upper secondary school built between 1959 and 1975. The extension is shown here. The old school consists of three blocks, A, B and C, with no indoor communication. The new building (house D) was located between house A and B. On the ground floor in house D are classrooms. A partly glass covered entrance hall connects the new building with house B where the practical education is given. The library is located in the upper floor. An aerial passage connects this floor with house A holding the theoretical education.

The client wanted the new building to be ecological both in materials and technical systems. A big wall of massive brick separates the library/classroom building from the entrance hall and stabilises the indoor climate. The air treatment is partly based on natural ventilation. Outdoor air is distributed down to an air conditioning chamber, 'calorifer', in the basement, to be chilled or heated by passive accumulation. From the calorifer the supply air is distributed in underground ducts to floor-supported supply air diffusers in the classrooms on the first floor and the library on the upper floor. In the library it is possible to open windows in the lantern light to let the warm air out.

1

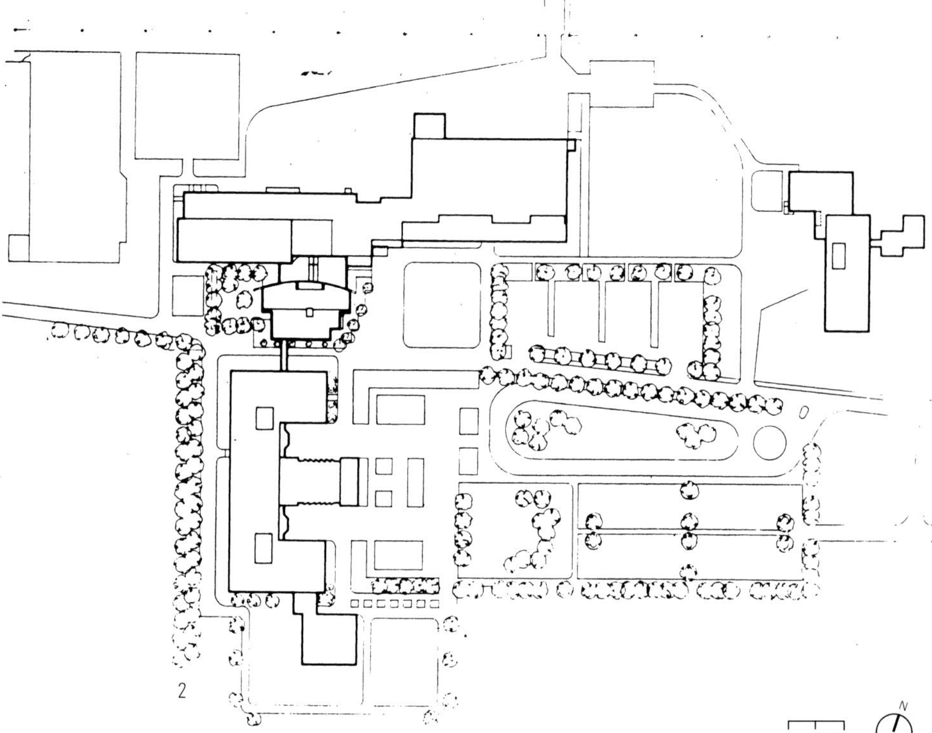

2

3

1 Detail of the new building from the west
2 Site plan
3 New building from the east
4 Section
5 Ground floor and upper floor plans
6 Outside detail from the north
7 Library
8 Classroom for music

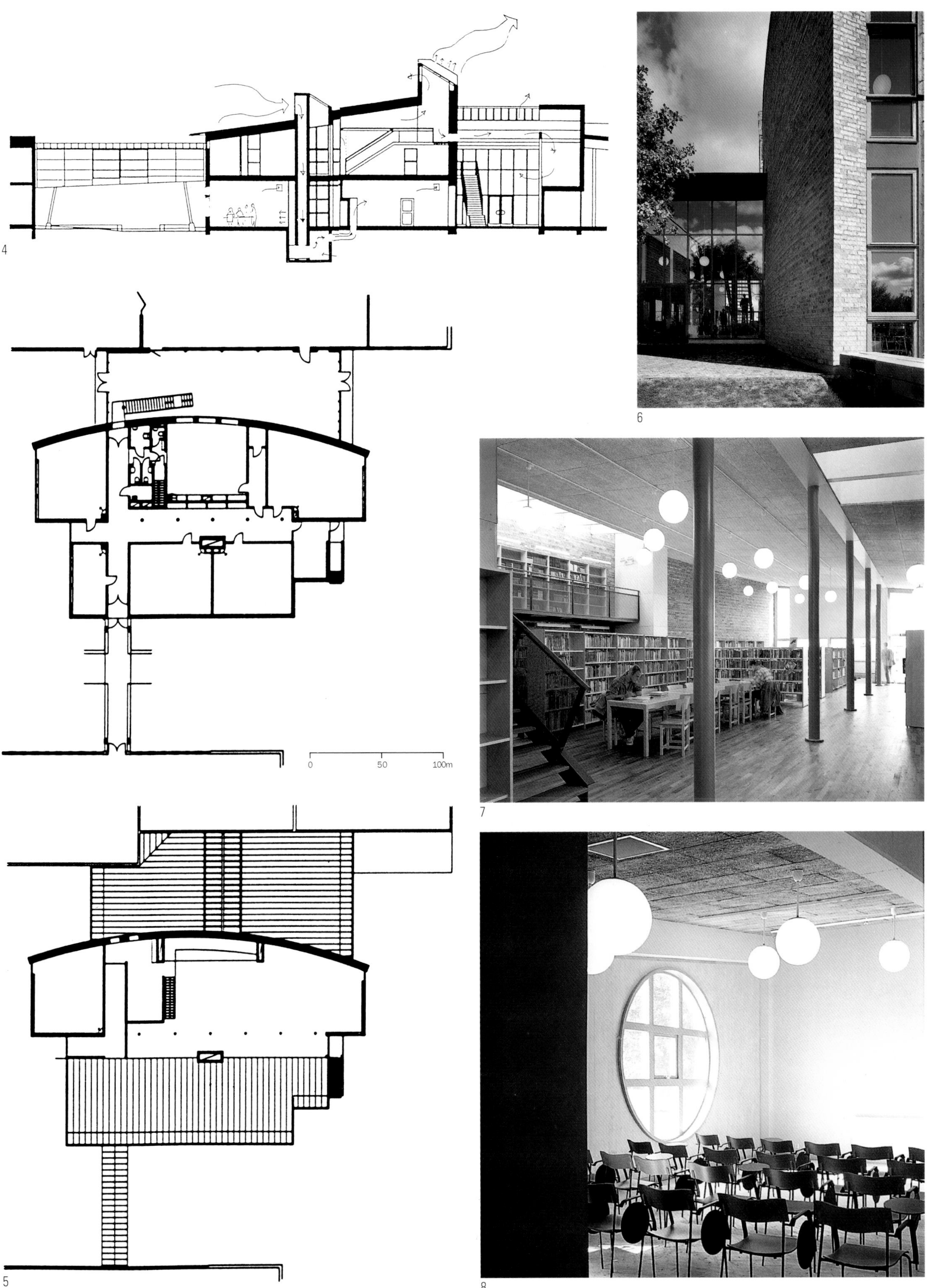

4
5
6
7
8

Medical Research Building II

The Stubbins Associates, Inc.
in association with Earl Swensson and Associates

Completion: April 1995

Location: Nashville, Tennessee, USA

Client: Vanderbilt University

Area: 21,589 square metres; 231,000 square feet

Structure: Post-tensioned concrete

Materials: Brick facade; limestone; precast concrete accents

Cost: US$34 million

Due to the success of previous work for Vanderbilt University, The Stubbins Associates were recommended to the University's Medical Center. They were the first architectural firm to be awarded a commission from both the Medical Center and the University.

Vanderbilt University's Medical Center has expanded its biomedical research facilities with the addition of over 21,589 square metres (231,000 square feet) of laboratories built over an existing single-storey, outpatient clinic, the building contains five floors of research, one floor of vivarium space and one floor for mechanical services.

Laboratories of 46.5 and 70 net square metres (500 and 750 net square feet) are paired for flexibility. Each is adjoined by an office and multi-purpose space. The core area on each floor includes four laboratories, two instrument rooms, four cold rooms, glass wash and autoclave, and administrative space.

The building creates a new entry to the Medical Center from the south for staff and faculty who will park in the new garage. Two new landscaped courtyards have been created on the second level adjacent to the building.

The exterior character of the facility is designed to harmonise with existing buildings on the campus. The primary materials are brick with limestone accents.

1

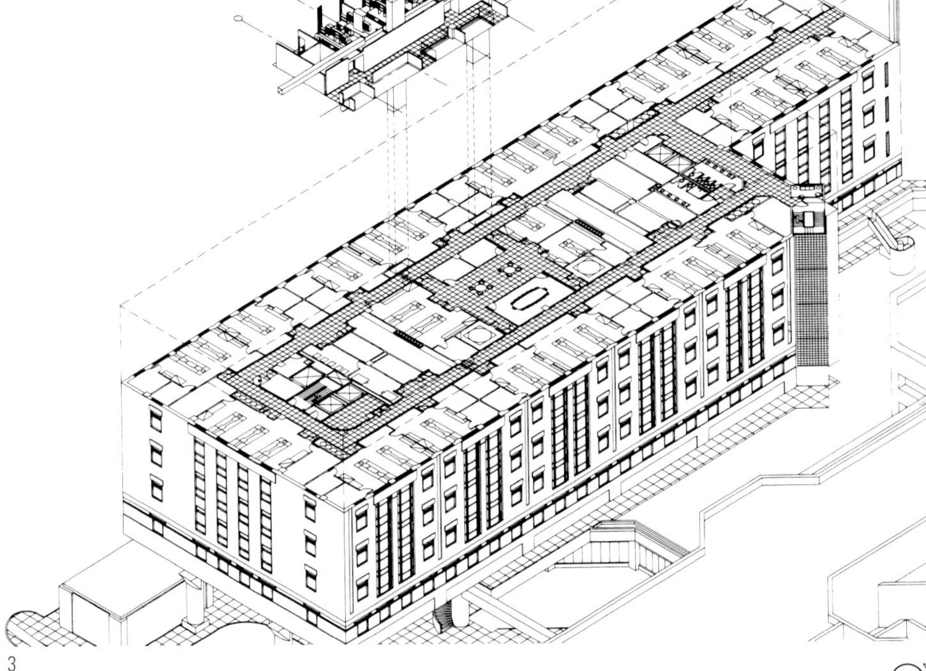
3

2

4

1 North entrance
2 Landscaped courtyard
3 Axonometric plan
4 Main entrance
5 Night view featuring stacked meeting rooms

5

6

7

8

9

6 Main entrance detail
7 Main entrance canopy
8 Elevator lobby
9 Corridor with view into meeting room
10 Wet lab
11 Wet lab

10

11

12 Lab module
13 Rendering
14 Facade detail
Photography: Jonathan Hillyer

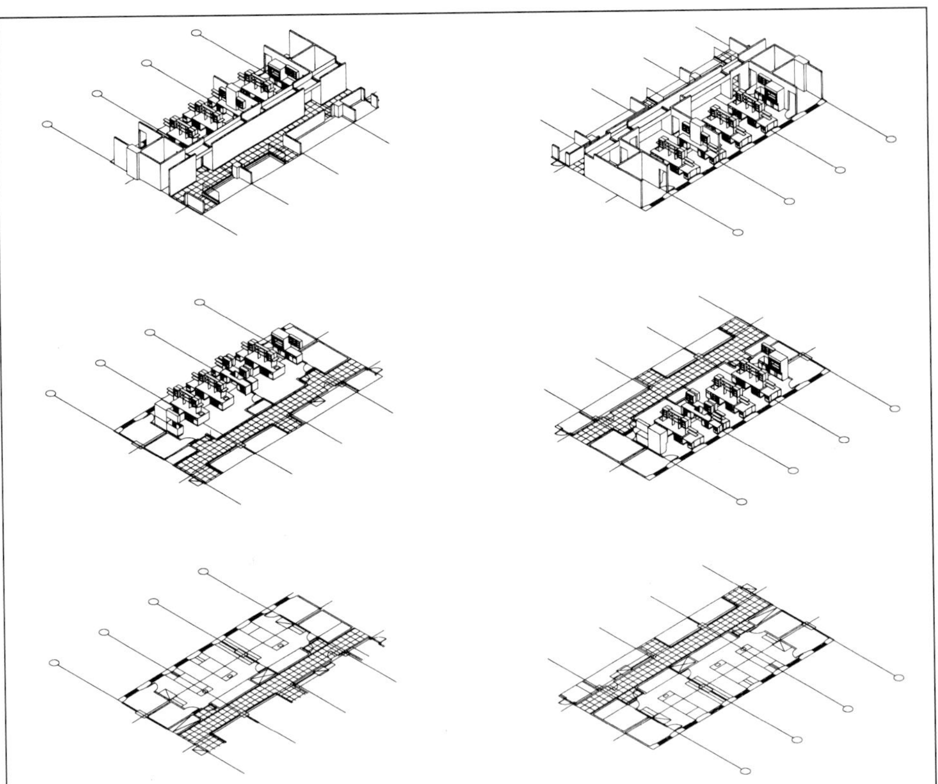
12

13

14

North View Primary School

DP Architects Pte Ltd

Completion: August 1994

Location: Singapore

Client: Public Works Department, Ministry of Education

Area: 10,000 square metres; 107,643 square feet

Structure: Post and beam reinforced concrete; steel truss

Materials: Plaster and painted walls; aluminium windows

Cost: S$8.2 million

This new school is situated in a high density residential area of north central Singapore. Designed for a student population of 1,440 the concept is based on an idea of a 'mini-city', comprising staggered blocks of classrooms winding around each other forming courtyards between.

Essentially arranged as two embracing 'arms', bridges link the two classroom blocks at all levels providing a visual identity to each courtyard. Symbolically, the Library acts as a pivotal point at the centre of the entire school, around which all elements are organised.

Architecturally the theme involves the framing and layering of views. The design aims to create an introspective labyrinth of buildings and garden courts which together create a sense of a huge complex in what is essentially a tiny plot. Part theatrical, part civic, part residential, the experience of being in the school is never static but ever changing instead.

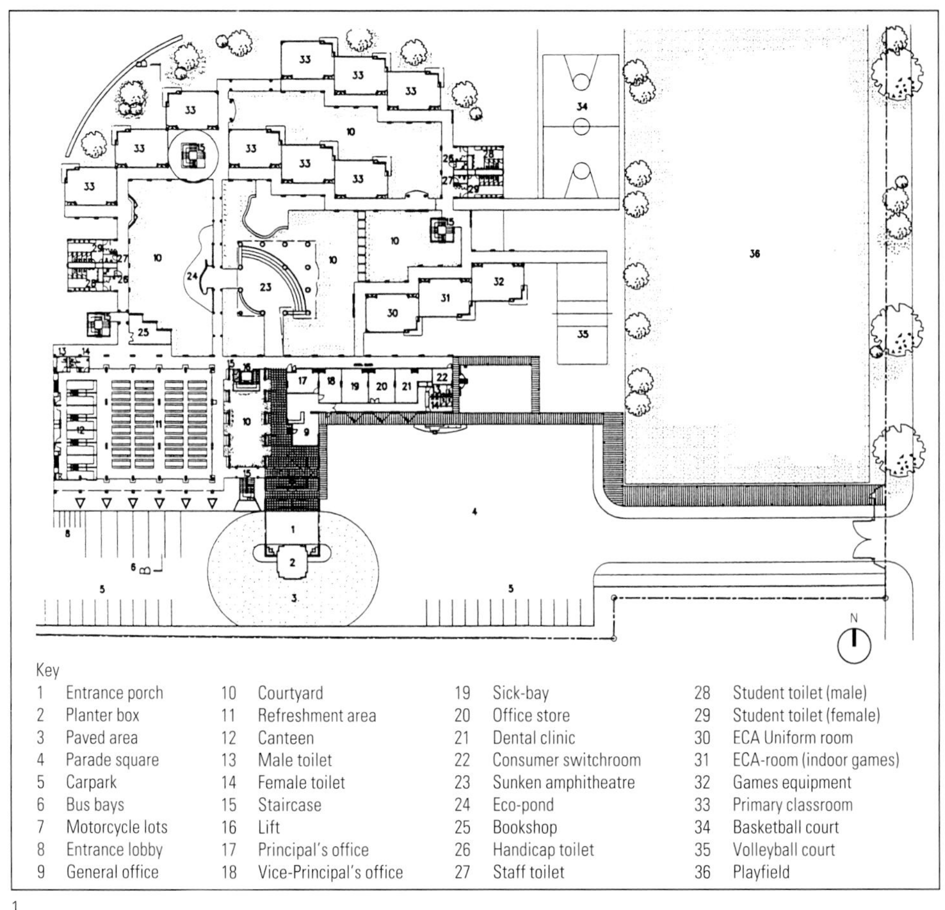

1

2

1 Site plan
2 View from parade square
3 South elevation
4 North–south section
5 Partial south elevation
Photography: Chan Sui Him; Tai Chooi Mee

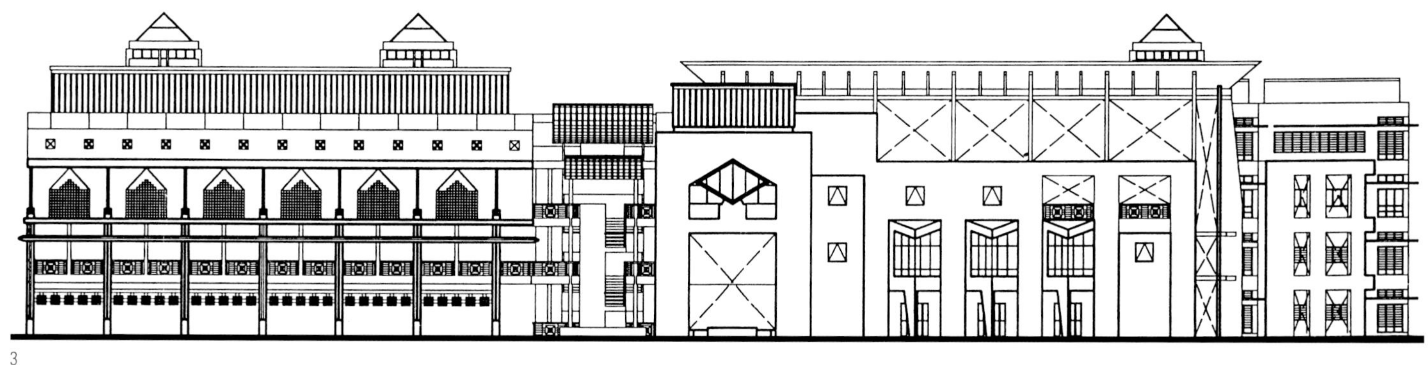

3

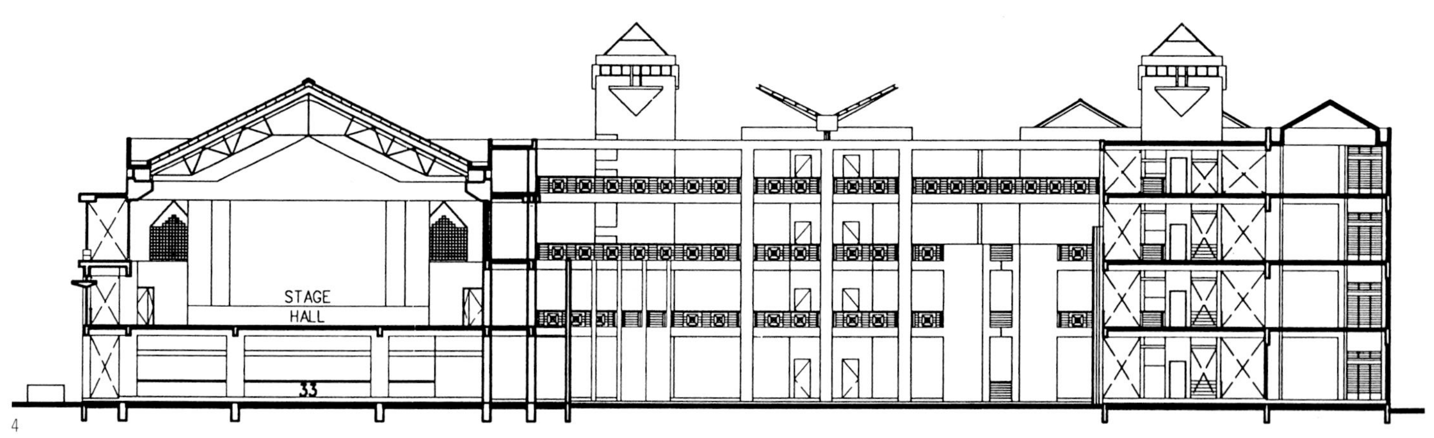

4

5

Perkins Elementary School

Martinez, Cutri & McArdle

Completion: June 1994
Location: San Diego, California, USA
Client: San Diego Unified School District
Area: 4,110 square metres; 44,250 square feet
Structure: Concrete slabs; wood/steel frame
Materials: Exterior stucco; accent ceramic tiles
Cost: US$3.6 million

Located in the Hispanic community of San Diego, this elementary school contains 25 classrooms, a media-library centre, a 400-seat multi-purpose 'cafetorium' and an administration area.

The aesthetics of the school are drawn from the Hispanic heritage of the area, employing strong planar forms and vibrant colours.

The site layout as well as the massing of the architecture relies on the extensive use of natural daylighting, sun control, natural ventilation, and other energy saving design solutions. The scale of the principle street elevation is consistent with the non-residential/industrial structures of the neighbourhood. On the interior side of the site, the scale is tailored to the children.

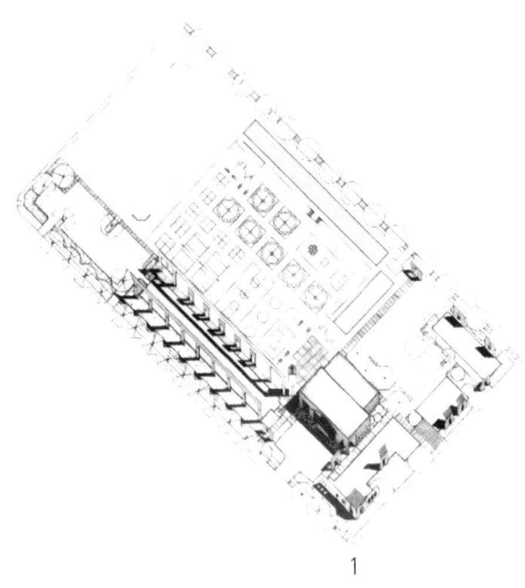

1

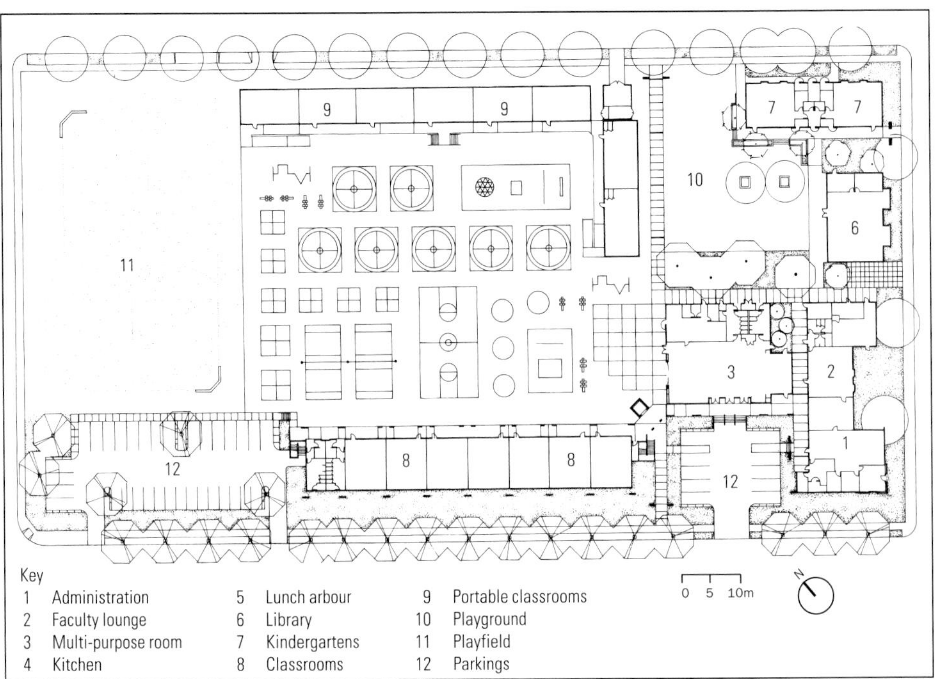

2

3

1 Icon-axonometric
2 Site plan
3 Aerial rendering
4 Administration building
5 Multi-purpose building (left), administration
6 Classroom building and playground
Photography: Jim Brady

4

5

6

Princeton Theological Seminary Henry Luce III Library

The Hillier Group

Completion: October 1994
Location: Princeton, New Jersey, USA
Client: Princeton Theological Seminary
Area: 3,716 square metres; 40,000 square feet
Structure: Steel frame; concrete deck
Materials: Limestone; brownstone
Cost: US$7.6 million

The Hillier Group provided site design, program review, and architectural services for The Henry Luce III Library, a 3,716 square metre (40,000 square foot), 2-storey research library addition housing rare books, special collections, and study areas for graduate students. The new building is organised around an atrium and a garden courtyard located between the addition and the original building. A 3-storey glass enclosed bridge unifies the two buildings into one complex. The collections are housed in an environmentally separated enclosure.

Designed to be compatible with the original building and sympathetic to its historic neighbours, the typical wall is constructed of coursed ashlar limestone and brownstone trim. The tower, entry, and typical window distinguish the addition from its neighbour and give it a civic presence. The library has a 350,000 volume capacity, seating for 260 and a 40-seat Meeting Center.

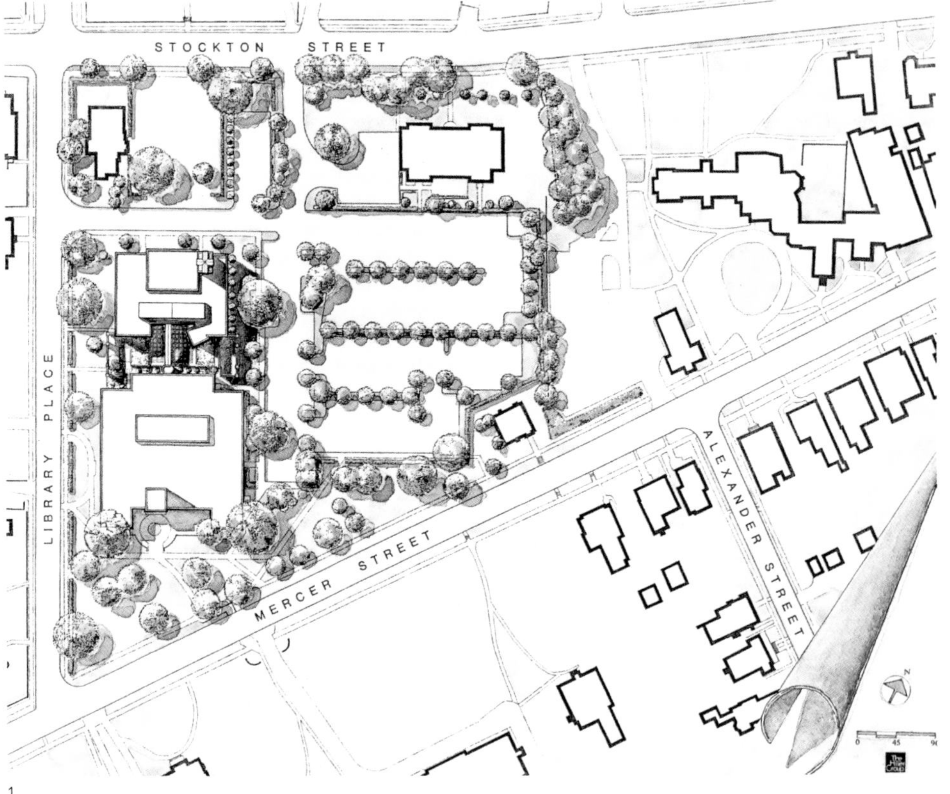

1

2

1 Site plan indicating the original library, the addition and environs
2 North/entry facade facing new campus lawn and public street
3 Garden courtyard showing south facade of addition and bridge

3

4

5

6

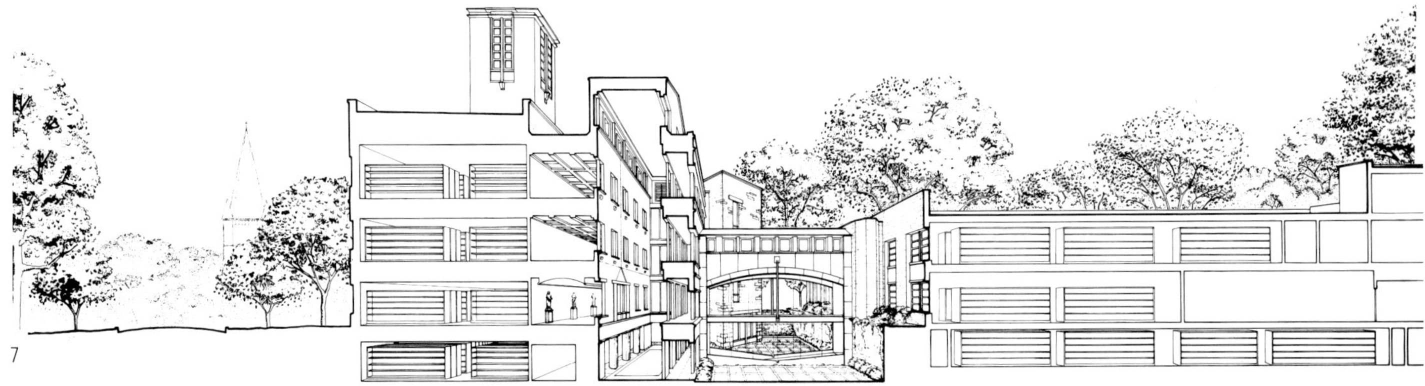

7

4 West facade/library place illustrating original library, new garden wall and new addition
5 North facade/entry
6 South facade/garden courtyard
7 Sectional perspective illustrating the original library, the addition, garden courtyard and connecting bridge
8 Basement level floor plan
9 First floor plan
10 Second floor plan
11 Atrium reading room
12 PhD candidate study suite

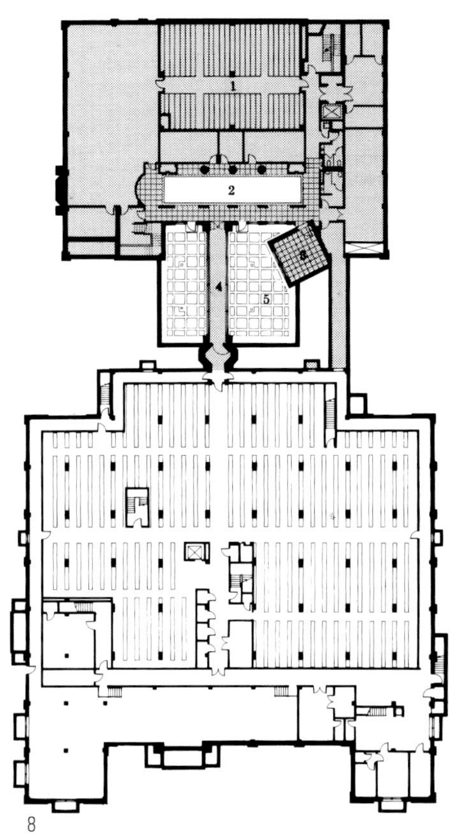
8

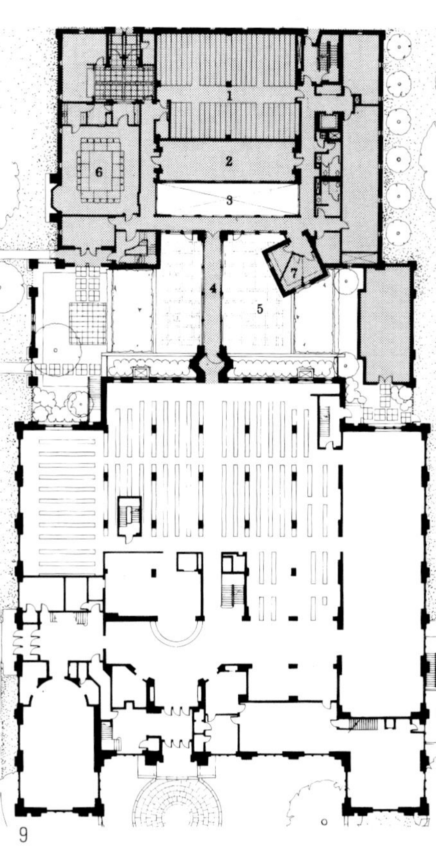
9

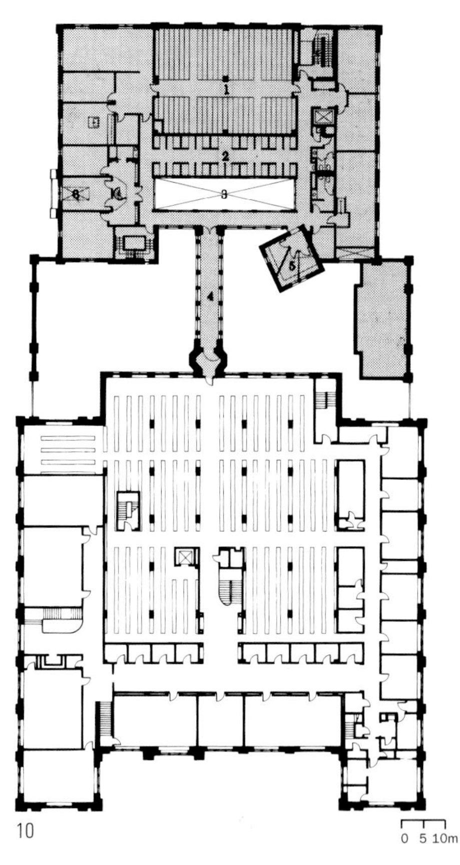

10

11

12

San Diego State University, Imperial Valley Campus

Martinez Cutri & McArdle

Completion: August 1995

Location: Calexico, California, USA

Client: Trustees, California State University

Area: 5,119 square metres; 55,100 square feet

Structure: Concrete slabs; wood/steel frame

Materials: Exterior stucco; ceramic tile accents; mission tile roofs

Cost: US$6.6 million

The campus master plan for this complex is centered around two important goals: first, the establishment of a framework plan which will unify old and new structures into a clear hierarchy of buildings and spaces; and, second, the identification and articulation of important campus landmarks which contribute to the greater community/region.

The architectural design of the seven new structures; Administration, Art Gallery, Faculty Offices, Research Institute, Library expansion, Student Lounge/Bookstore, and Physical Plant; takes its inspiration from the existing 1927 Spanish Colonial architecture, and the emerging binational/bicultural spirit of the Pacific Rim.

The 'jewels' of the campus are the Neo-Atzlan aesthetic of the Art Gallery, the creation of an 'outdoor room' (academic yard) and the regional landmark character of the telecommunications tower.

1

2

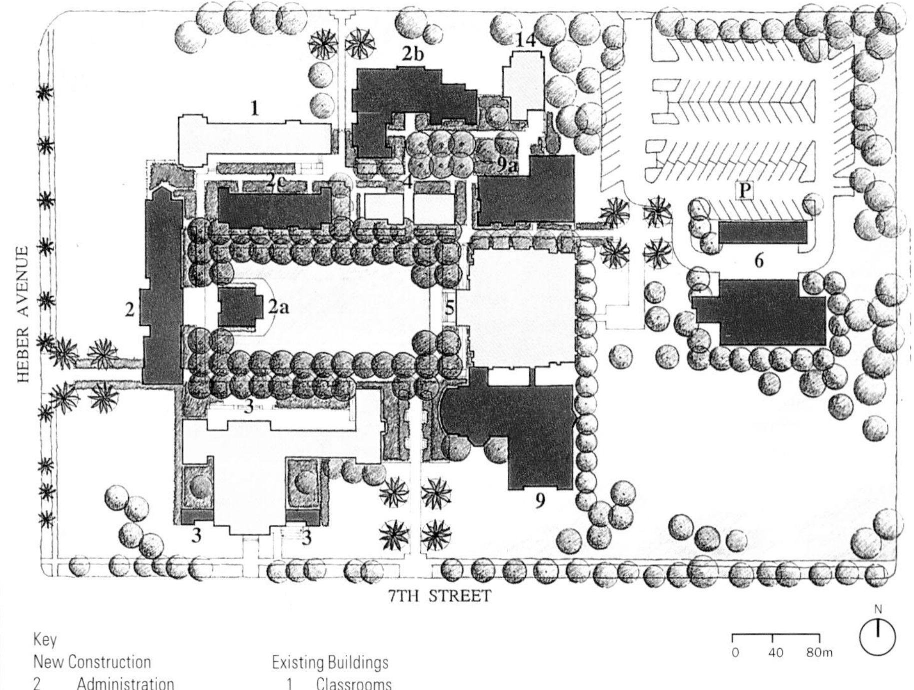

Key

New Construction
2 Administration
2a Gallery
2b Faculty offices
2c Faculty offices
3 Auditorium restrooms
6 Physical plant
9 Library addition
9a Library addition

Existing Buildings
1 Classrooms
3 Auditoriums/classrooms
4 Classrooms
5 Library
14 Student union
P Existing parking lot

3

4

1 Art Gallery
2 Entry portico
3 Site plan
4 Academic courtyard
5 Library
6 Administration building
7 Reading room, library

Photography: Jim Brady

5

6

7

Seoul National University Museum

SAC International, Ltd.

Completion: August 1994
Location: Shinlim-dong, Gwanak-gu, Seoul, Korea
Client: Seoul National University
Area: 6,165 square metres; 66,362 square feet
Structure: Reinforced concrete
Materials: Pink-grey granite; copper sheathing
Cost: US$9.3 million

The campus of the Seoul National University is situated on the slopes of Kwanak mountain at the southwestern edge of greater Seoul. The University Museum occupies a prominent spot above a ball field to the east of the main gate, forming an entry point to the Fine Arts/Music ensemble.

Compositionally, the Museum is made up a single-storey gallery volume to the north and a 2-storey gallery plus curatorial volume to the south between which a transparent lobby, a courtyard and an auditorium are inserted creating a circulation spine. The gallery volumes are characterised by two rows of quarter cylinder shape skylights clad in copper.

As the Museum serves diverse disciplines of archaeology, anthropology, natural history and fine arts, there are galleries dedicated to those fields as well as a temporary exhibition. The promenade on either side of the courtyard and the auditorium offer additional exhibition spaces.

The major finishes are flame-finished pink-grey granite panels and polished granite fascias on the exterior, ultra-violet ray filtering, laminated clear glass for skylights sheathed in copper, oak panelling around the auditorium, and, a neutral fabric wall covering on the gallery walls.

1 Site plan
2 View of the main entrance
3 Axonometric drawing
4 Ground floor plan
5 Longitudinal section
6 Main exhibition hall
7 Courtyard view from lobby
Photography: SAC International, Ltd.

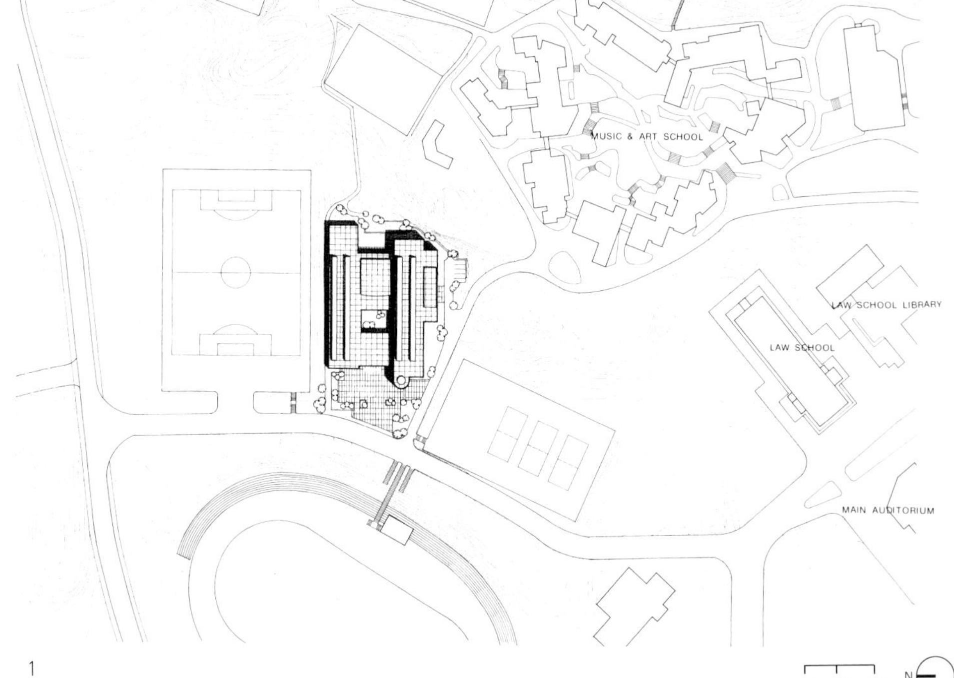

1

2

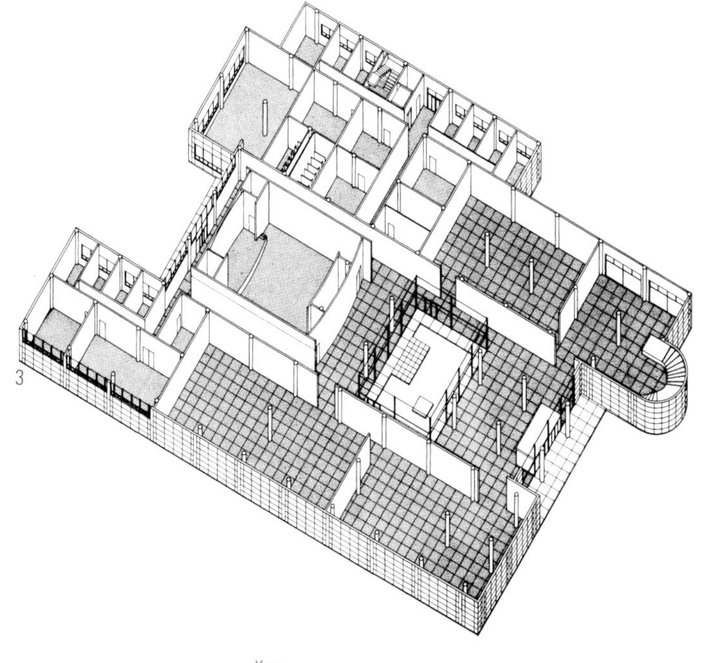

3

Key
1 Workshop (Modern Art)
2 Director of Modern Art
3 Research room
4 Storage (Modern Art)
5 Photo Lab
6 Storage
7 Library
8 Faculty reading room
9 Laboratory
10 Seminar
11 Disinfection room
12 Packing room
13 Guard
14 Control
15 Broadcasting
16 Workshop (Natural History)
17 Director of Natural History
18 Projection room
19 Modern gallery
20 Changing exhibition
21 Courtyard
22 Outdoor exhibition area
23 Gallery (Natural History)
24 Lobby
25 Lounge
26 Museum store

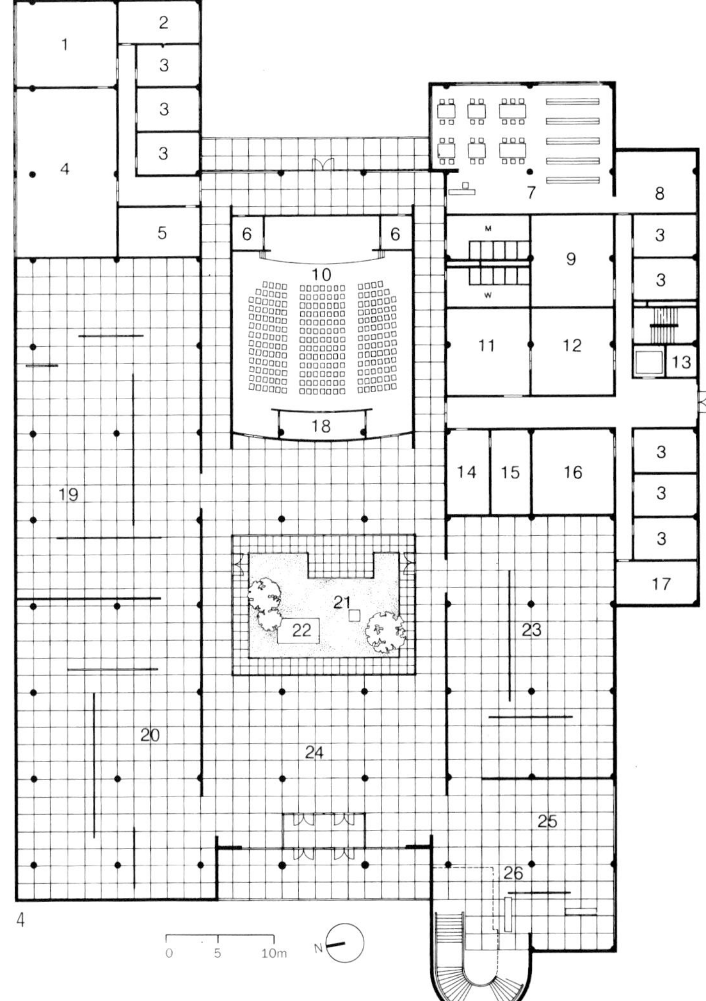

4

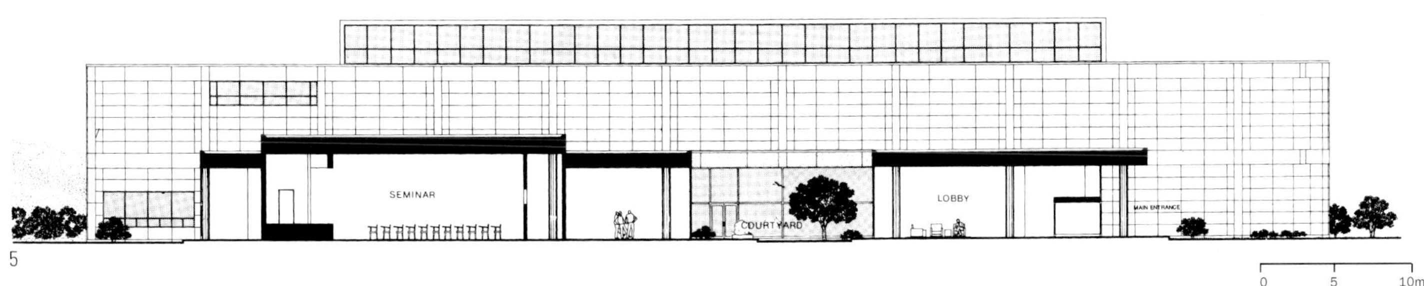

5

6

7

St Andrew's Junior College

DP Architects Pte Ltd

Completion: July 1994

Location: Singapore

Client: The Synod of the Diocese of Singapore

Area: 20,258 square metres; 218,062 square feet

Structure: Post and beam reinforced concrete

Materials: Plaster wall; homogenous tile; texture coating; clay roof tile; aluminium windows

Cost: S$16 million

Awards: 1983 SIA Honours Awards (Institute/Religious Category)

Sited on a verdant slope, St. Andrews Junior College was one of the early pioneers in experimental design for educational facilities. Completed in 1978, the seminal design by DP Architects was based on encouraging student/teacher interaction through the creation of flexible, informal spaces. It won an honourable mention in the 1983 SIA Awards.

With a growing student population, from an initial 1,200 to 1,800 in 1990, the need for expansion and upgrading became inevitable. The new extension was designed to both harmonise as well as to reinforce the original concept.

The initial formal move was to extend the existing circulation spine and create a continuous loop in the process. New faculties are then subtly inserted into this critical spine. The location of the various new blocks respect the contours and views, exploiting them to create a multiplicity of intimate spaces, layered views and interesting vistas.

A new open-air amphitheatre was designed at the top of a hillock. Defined by a pavilion, this gathering space marks the beginning of the extension. New walkways extending from this space are defined by columns that frame a variety of vistas.

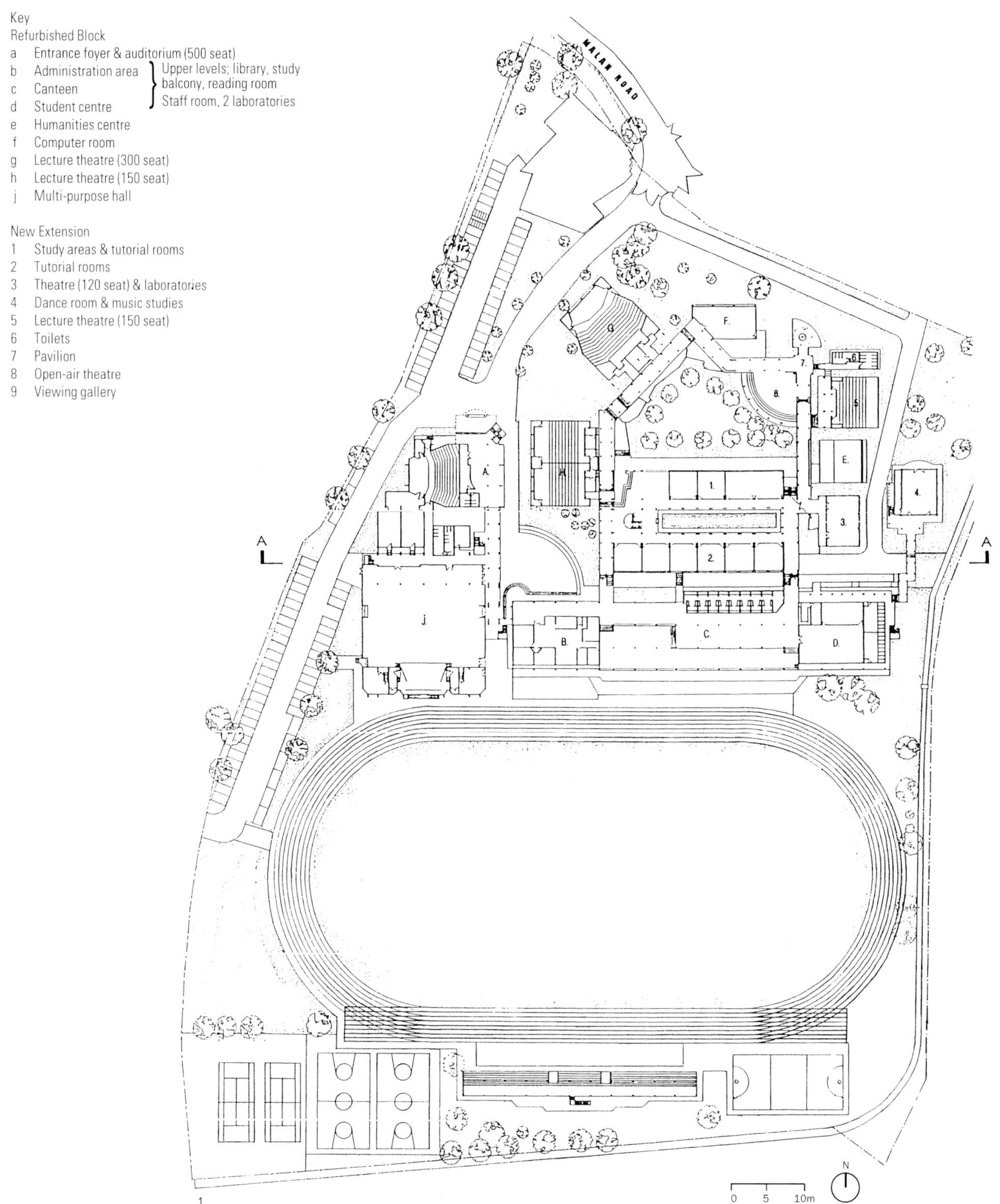

1

2

3

4

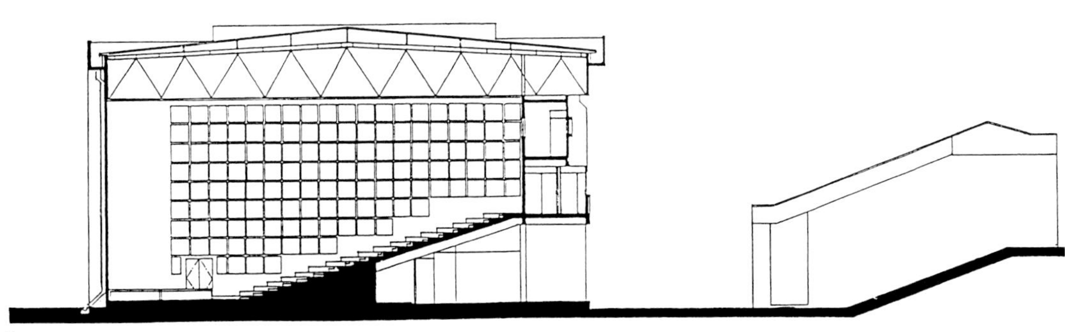
5

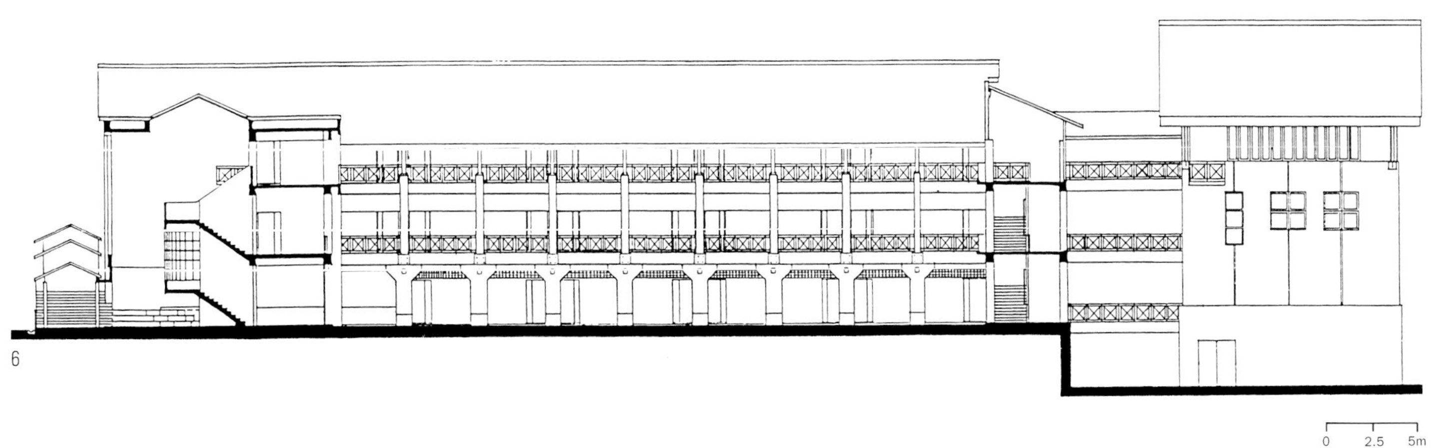

6

1 First storey plan
2 Tutorial blocks courtyard
3 Stairwell atrium
4 Layered views along the circulation loop
5 Section AA through the auditorium
6 Section AA through the tutorial courtyard
Photography: Maria Hartati

Tulane University Law School

Hartman-Cox Architects
in association with The Mathes Group

Completion: January 1995

Location: New Orleans, Louisiana, USA

Client: Tulane University

Area: 13,935 square metres; 150,000 square feet

Structure: Concrete frame; concrete beams and pan system; pile foundations

Materials: Brick on CMU; custom aluminium curtain wall; built-up roof; tile floor; custom wood trim

This new law school building containing library, classrooms, clinic, offices and computer lab is located on a mid-campus site that forms the fourth side of a quadrangle. The other buildings are two high-rise, 1960s gridded apartment slabs and the new, high-rise post-modern business school. These buildings do not relate well to each other, and none offered a style to emulate.

The new law school buildings, while drawing certain design references—such as the ground floor arches and centre bay—from the other, more handsome buildings elsewhere on the campus, attempts to emulate the character of a traditional law school building. This prototype is essentially neo-Romanesque, or collegiate Gothic in character. The design places the library in a central, higher block with courtyards (a New Orleans tradition as well as a collegiate tradition) on either side. This allows the rest of the building to be three storeys high, preserving the scale along Freret Street to the south and echoing the campus proper.

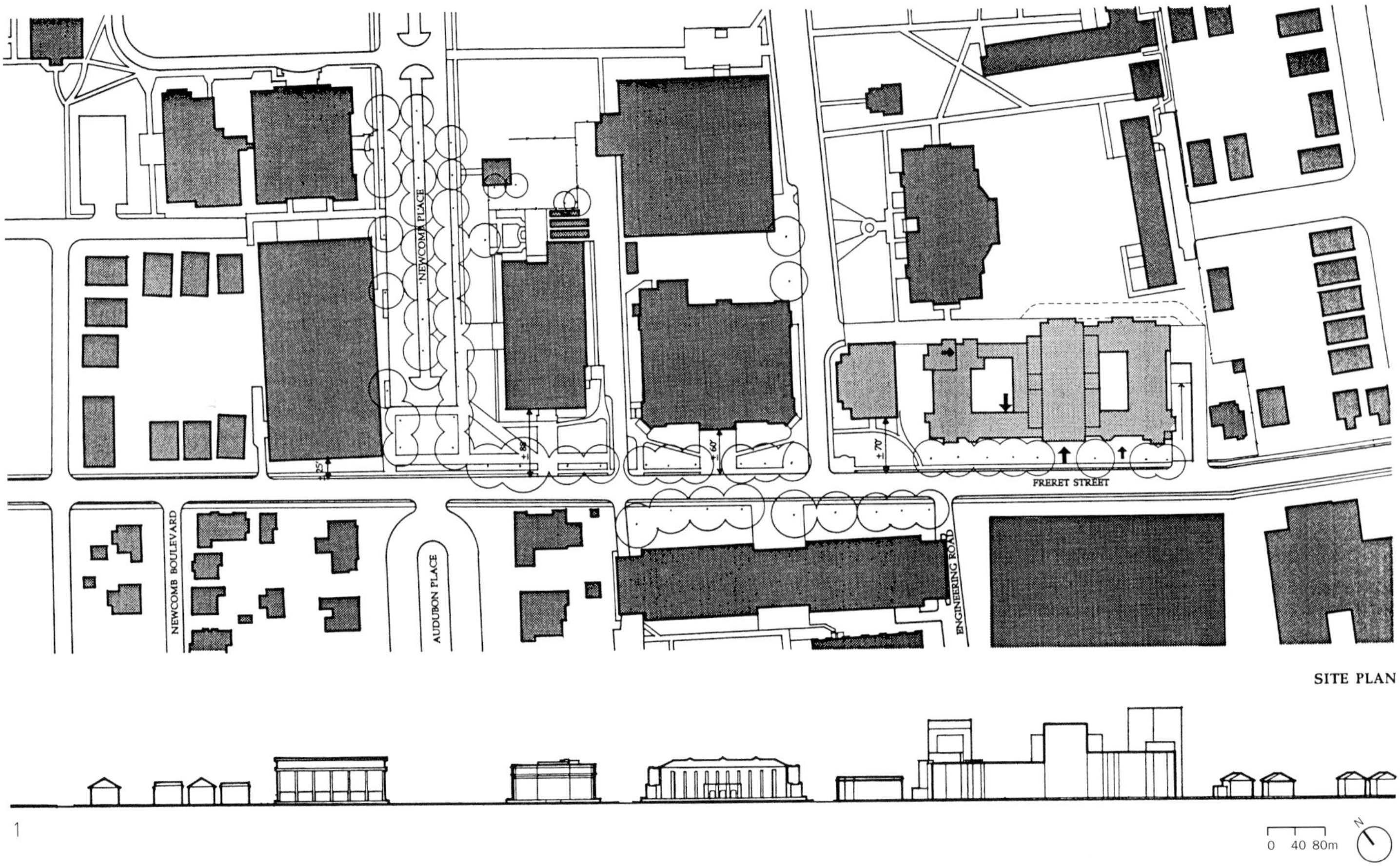

NEWCOMB PLACE

FRERET STREET

NEWCOMB BOULEVARD

AUDUBON PLACE

ENGINEERING ROAD

SITE PLAN

1

0 40 80m

N

2

3

1 Site plan and site elevation
2 Freret Street or entrance tower
3 North elevation
4 Ground floor plan
5 West Courtyard
6 Reading room
Photography: ©Peter Aaron/Esto

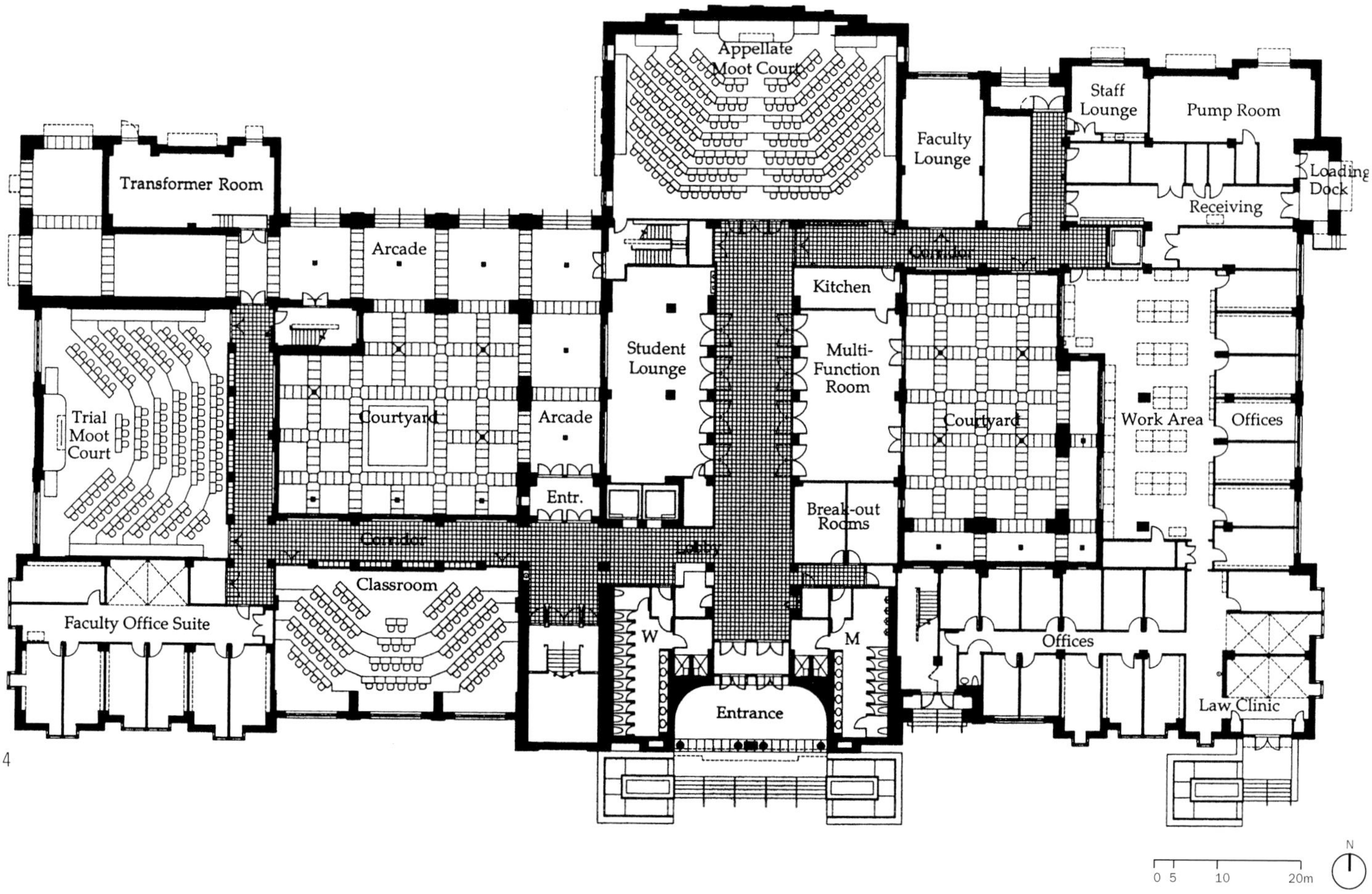

4

5

6

National Center for Polymer Research, University of Massachusetts, Amherst

Ellenzweig Associates, Inc., Design Architect

Whitney Atwood Norcross, Inc., Architect of Record

Completion: May 1995
Location: Amherst, Massachusetts, USA
Client: University of Massachusetts
Area: 16,285 square metres; 175,300 square feet
Structure: Cast-in-place concrete; steel frame
Materials: Metal panels; limestone; glass; granite
Cost: US$32.8 million

The new National Center for Polymer Research is designed as two 6-storey buildings, a limestone-clad laboratory block and a curved, metal-clad office wing, which are linked by an elevator tower and step down in height from an existing 16 storey research tower. The laboratory building was designed to meet the particular needs of the various polymer sub-disciplines, and structured with a cast-in-place concrete frame to reduce vibration which would jeopardise experimentation. The office block, by contrast, is located in a separate building, both to address safety issues and to foster interaction among researchers. The steel-frame structure of the office building yielded overall project cost savings.

Materials and details accentuate the bipartite massing. Silver metal panels sheath the curvilinear form which contains offices, lounges and conference facilities, while contrasting buff-coloured limestone clads the rectilinear laboratory block. The stepped-height composition is achieved by a vaulted, lead-coated copper, mechanical penthouse which graces the top of the laboratory block. The covered drive-through features glass block composed with elegant metal detailing. A continuous granite base unifies the design.

Connecting the 6-storey office and laboratory buildings is an elevator lobby which appears to vanish beneath shimmering metal and glass curtainwall. The windows themselves are aluminium framed and feature a three coat fluoropolymer surface, demonstrating the contribution of polymer research to high performance metal finishes.

In the laboratories, vinyl composition tile provides a resilient flooring; ceilings are made of acoustical tile; and casework is composed of oak wood with unistrut framing and epoxy counters.

The new National Center for Polymer Research consolidates the University of Massachusetts' facilities for this cutting-edge science and engineering discipline while making a significant contribution to the University's main campus. The new centre accommodates diverse interdisciplinary facilities, including laboratories for electron-microscopy, nuclear magnetic resonance, and mass spectrometry. The lower floors house the engineering division, which requires heavy, vibration-sensitive equipment, while the upper floors accommodate the fume-hood intensive synthetic division.

The two-building arrangement reduces the apparent mass of this large program and reconciles the height of the connecting 16-storey graduate chemistry research tower with the predominantly low-rise surroundings.

1

2

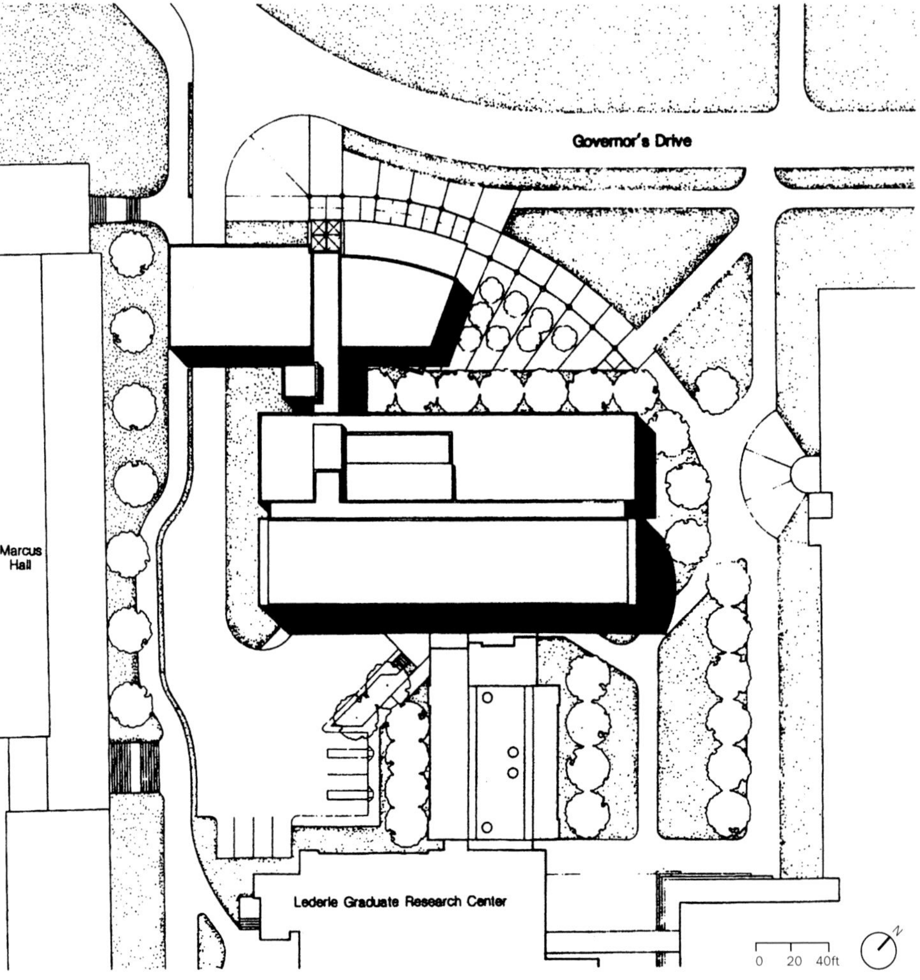

3

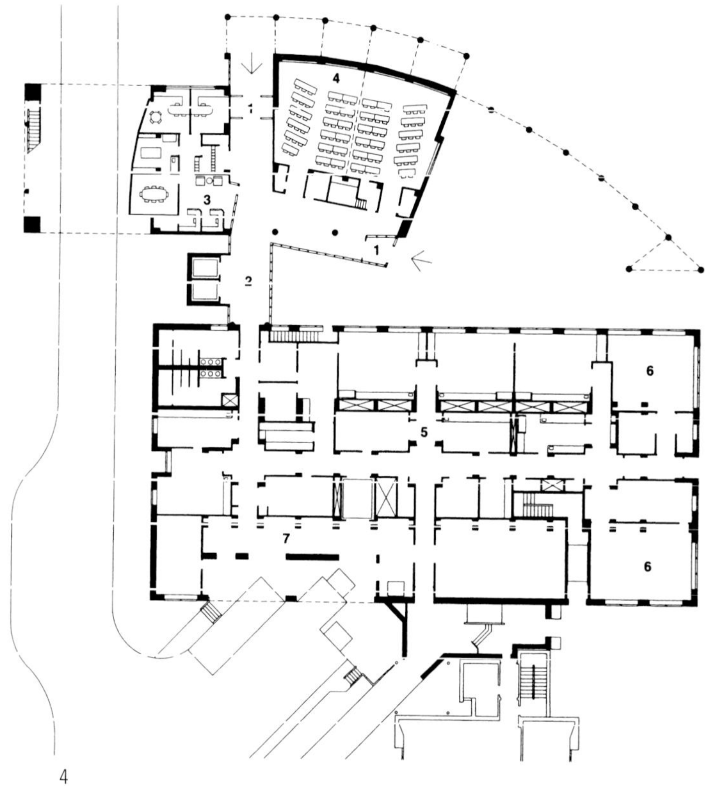

4

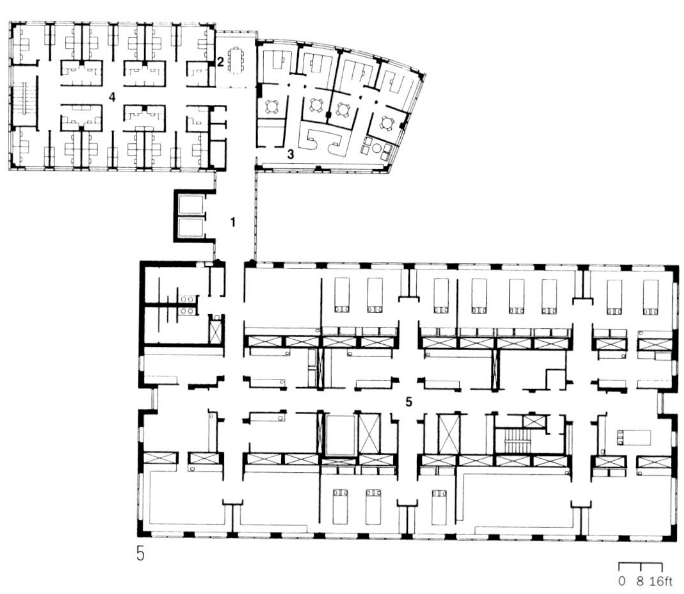

5

6

7

1 View from the northeast
2 View from the west
3 Site plan
4 Ground floor plan
5 Typical floor plan
6 Laboratory entries and circulation
7 Research laboratory

8 Detail of limestone cladding
9 South elevation
10 Detail of stair

8

9

0 8 16ft

10

11 Section of mechanical penthouse
12 View from south
13 Detail of metal panel cladding
Photography: Steve Rosenthal

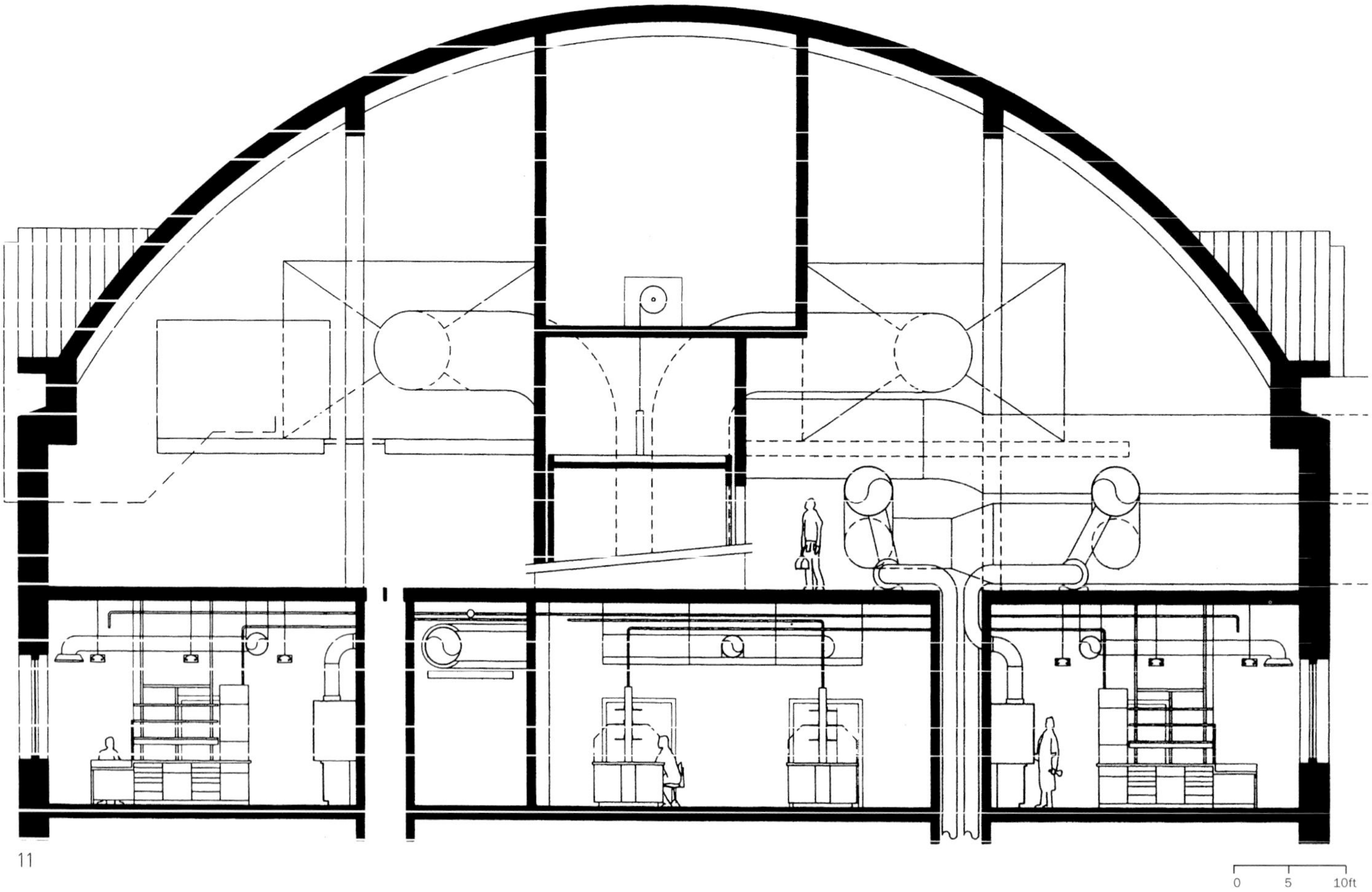

11

0 5 10ft

12

13

Westside Middle School

Leo A. Daly

Completion: August 1995
Location: Omaha, Nebraska, USA
Client: District 66 - Westside Community Schools
Area: 12,080 square metres; 130,000 square feet
Structure: Precast concrete
Materials:
Cost: US$3.4 million

Westside Community School District (NE District 66) asked Daly to assist them in creating an environment to encourage students and faculty to participate in a technologically revised educational atmosphere. Full services were provided for the reprogramming, renovation, and expansion to an existing Daly-designed 12,080 square metre (130,000 square foot) building to change its personality.

Westside Middle School was reprogrammed and renovated to accommodate four academic 'Houses'. Each 'House' integrates Math, Science, English and History classes around a technology resource hub, called a 'Discovery Center'. 'Discovery Centers' are linked to a 790 square metre (8,500 square foot) central, hi-tech Media Center. They act as local extensions of the Center. A new skylit 930 square metre (10,000 square foot) administrative/entry/commons area was added to the existing building. Phasing plans for temporary and permanent classroom relocation to allow continuation of classes during construction, were also part of the work.

Phase I achieved the major goals; upgrading the existing building to allow installation of 'Discovery Centers', completing the new Media Center, and, adding the new commons/entry area. In Phase II, total window replacement to reduce energy loads and improve lighting for computer screens will be completed. Phase III provides the addition of an 745 square metre (8,000 square foot), 400-seat auditorium.

1 Entry to commons
2 Discovery Center
3 Media Center
Photography: Douglas Kahn

1

2

3

Building on the Prairie

Studio J.J. International

Completion: March 1995
Location: Middleton, Wisconsin, USA
Client: Saco Foods Inc.
Area: 1,605 square metres; 17,280 square feet
Structure: Steel frame
Materials: Steel truss; glass; concrete blocks
Cost: US$1.4 million

The varied bay-system is the result of building in a system that will accommodate Building 2, the office complex made of six bays each 11 x 7.3 metres (36 x 24 feet) in area. A certain flexibility is maintained with only four interior columns in each building. Steel frame and bays with steel truss joists are connected on the exterior with steel truss elements filled with glass acting as lateral stiffening elements. Face panels are made of 30.5 cm (12 inch) thick concrete block elements that are face ground on the outside to show the character and colour of the beautiful moraine gravel found in this area.

It is a belief that only architecture which is of its time can be significant. Therefore the firm builds only within those general confines of the principles of architecture which it understands. It seems that there is no architectural form specific to the form of a prairie, desert or a mountain which can be understood in a historical context without being formalistic in concept. 'Prairie Architecture' is not unique. It is like all other architecture, perhaps just more quietly set. It is a geometricising or crystallisation of space within the space formed by the natural elements of the landscape—unobtrusive, natural, reflective to its surroundings, clear in structure and barely noticeable. Projects, if poorly conceived within a rich and delicate area, such as the mid-west prairie, produce a constant irritant upon not only the landscape and those immediately involved, but also on everyone who is concerned with the fragile ecological balance within these particular areas.

1

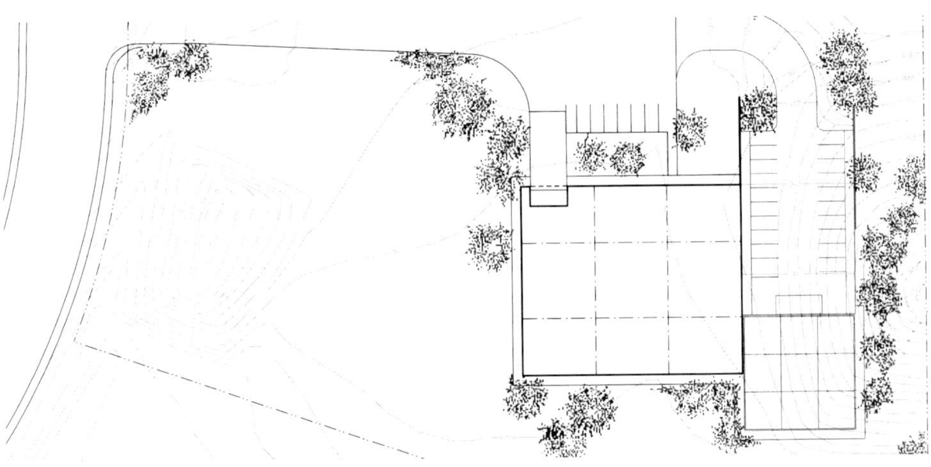

2

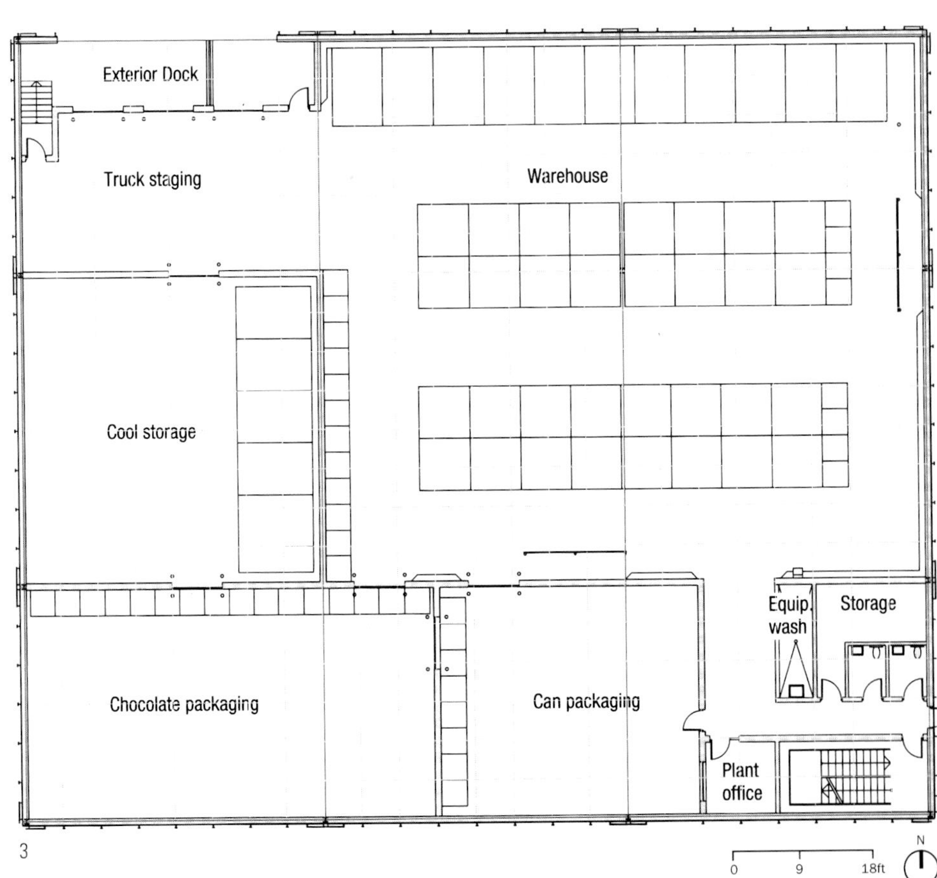

3

1 Loading dock
2 Site plan
3 Floor plan of packaging plant
4 South elevation
5 North elevation
6 Chocolate packaging
7-8 Docking area
9 South elevation

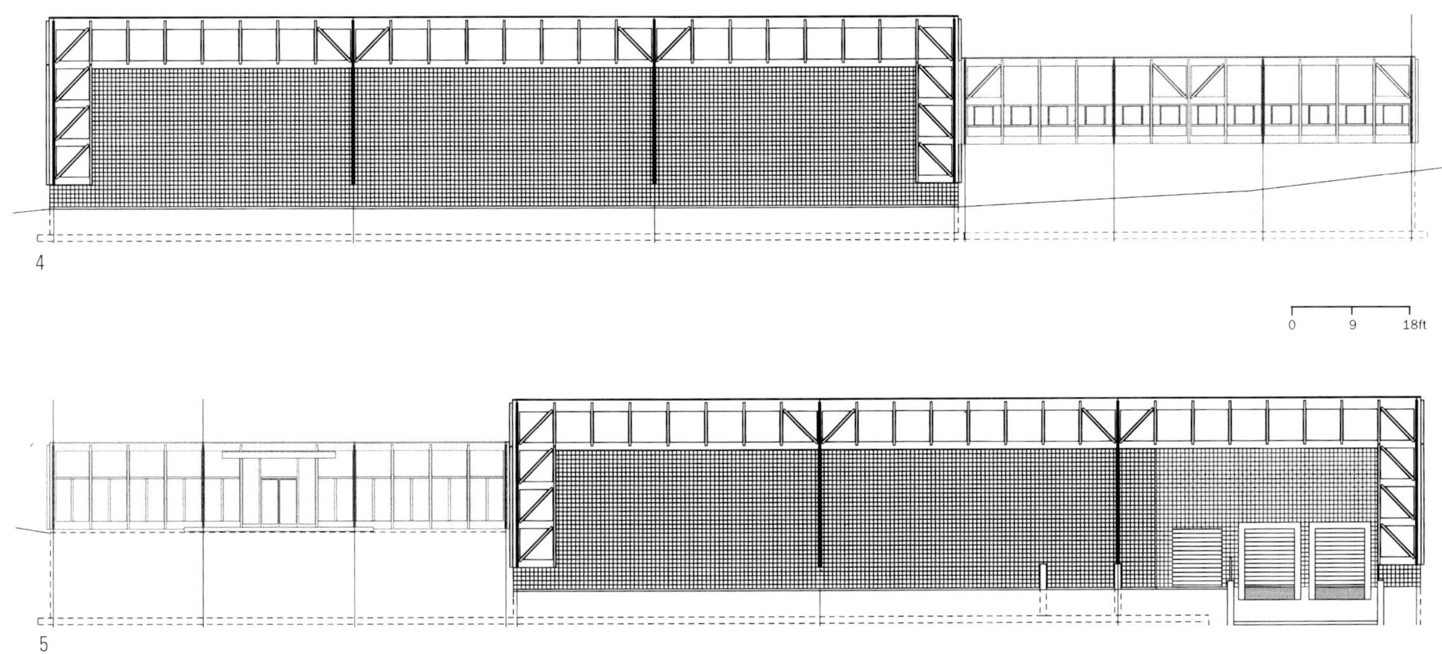

4

5

6

7

8

9

Eastern Counties Newspapers New Press Centre

Feilden & Mawson

Completion: March 1995

Location: Norwich, UK

Client: Eastern Counties Newspapers Ltd.

Area: 8,240 square metres; 88,168 square feet

Structure: Steel frame; reinforced concrete

Materials: Composite steel insulated panels; aluminium curtain wall

Cost: GB£6.5 million

1

1 Corner detail
2 View from northeast
3 Northeast elevation
4 Southeast elevation
5 Southwest elevation
6 Southwest sectional elevation
Photography: John Critchley

The client's brief included a two phase removal of their entire newspaper operation on a prominent city centre site in Norwich. The transfer had two practical reasons: the advantages of a site adjacent to the southern bypass to maintain and improve delivery journey times; and the inadequate room on their previous site to build and commission a new press alongside their existing machinery, which would have to continue in operation until this was complete. Construction was envisaged in two phases; the first being the press and delivery operation, the editorial facility moving at a later stage.

The client had admired the Surun Turamat newspaper building in Istanbul where, on an urban site, the press and editorial operations were very closely integrated physically and visually. On their spacious greenfield site, however, and with an independent timescale for these two components, a more organic concept was preferred.

The press centre constituting the first phase therefore has four boldly expressed and contiguous elements, the relationship between them constituting the principal architectural statement. They are: (a) Reel store, to which the basic raw material is continually delivered and where it is stored and prepared for use. It was found convenient to locate the press centre offices and hospitality suite on a first floor above within the same envelope. (b) Press hall, accommodating a Goss HT 70 Highliner 4 high tower press with foundations and enclosure for 40 percent expansion in the future. With reel stands below and a gantry crane above, the dimensions of the Press hall were settled at an early stage as 61.4 metres (202 feet) long, 17.3 metres (57 feet) wide and 20.5 metres (67 feet) high. Some ancillary processes such as platemaking, together with mechanical plant, had also to be included. (c) Dispatch hall parallel to the press to accommodate insertion machines, packaging and consignment by conveyor to six vehicle delivery points. Space was also required in this area for a number of smaller in-house short-run press facilities moved from existing premises in Norwich. (d) Main entrance hall to be shared with the second phase.

In locating the main elements on site, a major consideration was the scale of the 62 metre (203 foot) by 43 metre (141 foot) rectangle produced by placing the press and dispatch halls side by side. The relationships of the other elements to this rectangle were more flexible, but two further considerations had to be borne in mind: space to turn large delivery vehicles in association with the reel store, and the desirability of the press itself being visible from the editorial floorspace.

In achieving these objectives, the Phase 1 building was set on the axis of an adjacent 19th century building which is in close visual contact, rather than conforming to a new axis determined for the rest of the new business park from which there is a measure of visual separation by existing trees. A curving footprint for the future editorial wing attached to the main entrance hall would feature views both of the press through glazing and the attractive prospect southwards over the river, whilst permitting its further end to confront the business park on the new axis.

The geography of the site ruled out a public view of the press at close quarters. Instead the bold curves of the cross section adopted for the press hall generate a more distant but prominent object of landmark status, visible to the passing traffic on the bypass 1.2 kilometres (0.75 miles) away, without contravening the client's initial desire for an attractive but simple shed without prestigious accoutrements. At the same time it conforms to the visual standards required of its location in a business park.

2

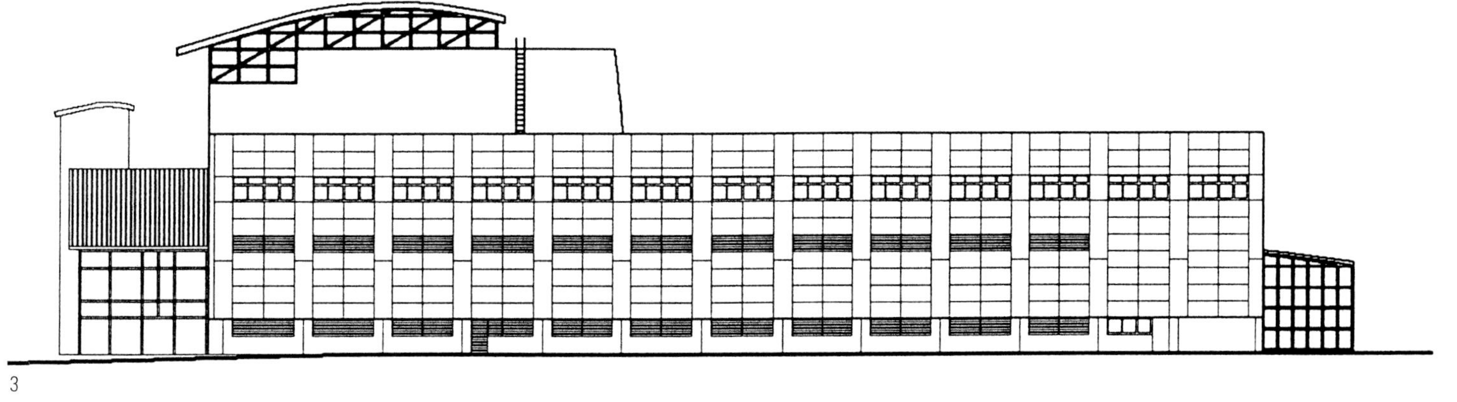

3

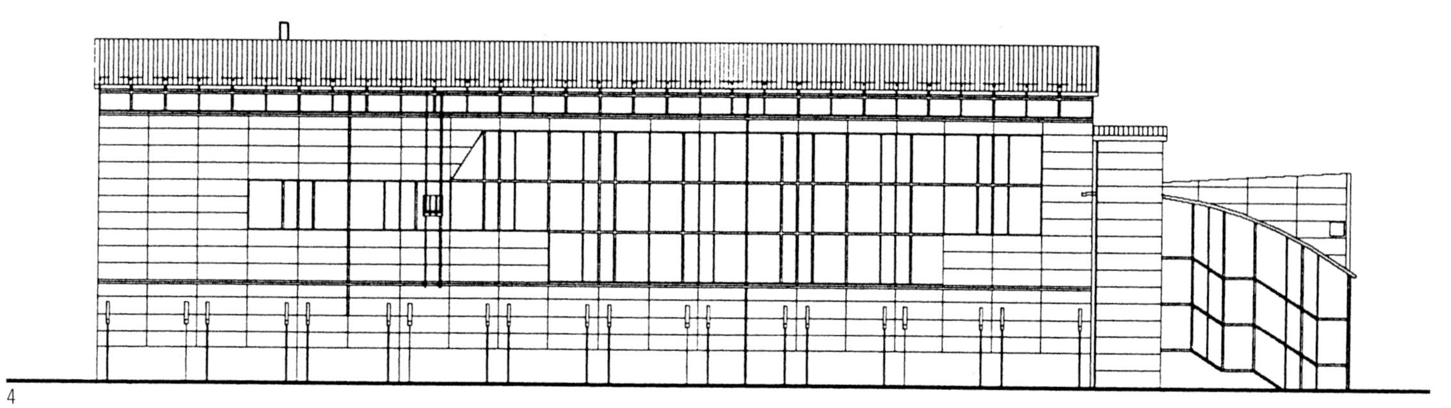

4

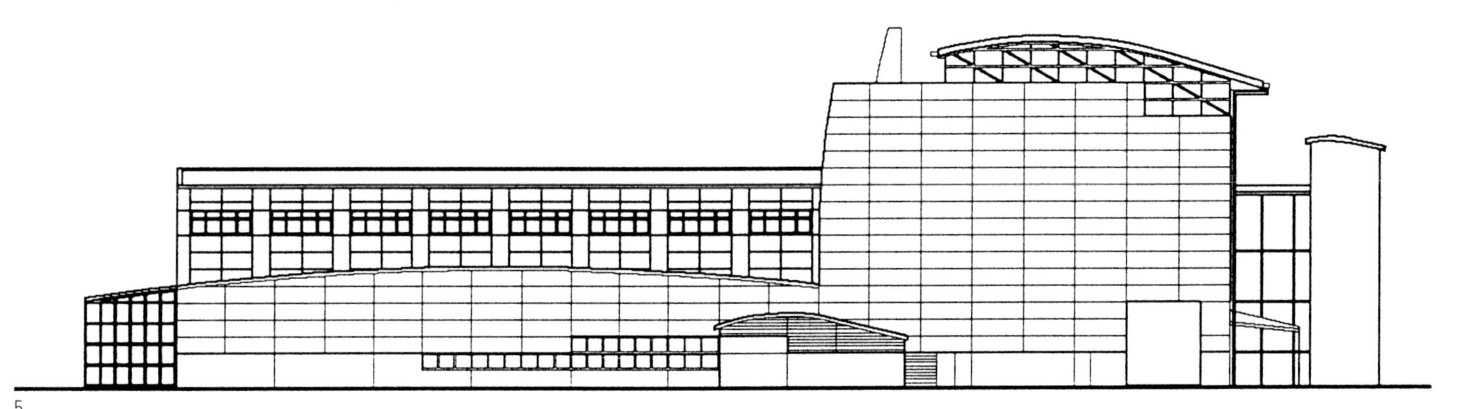

5

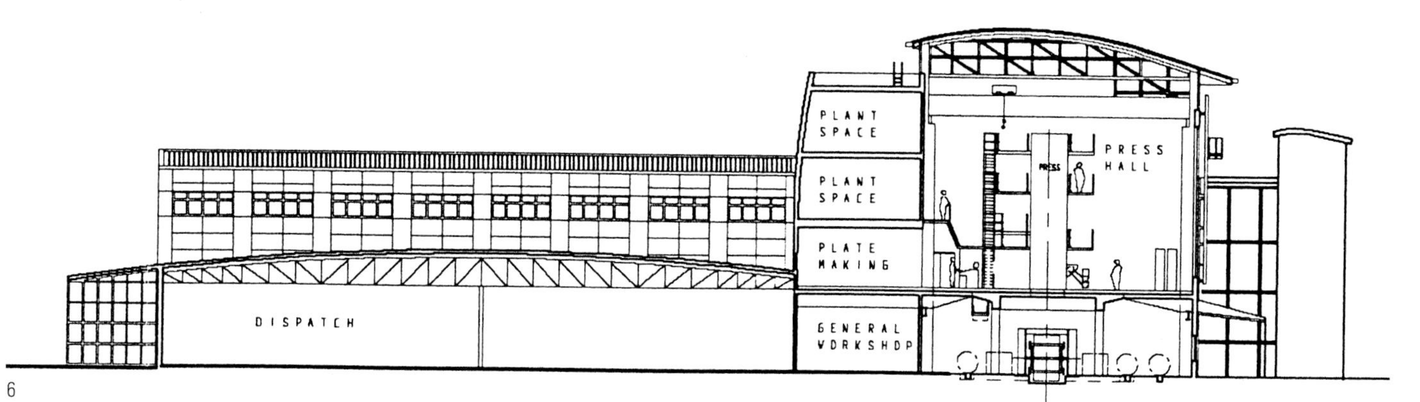
PLANT SPACE
PLANT SPACE
PLATE MAKING
GENERAL WORKSHOP
PRESS HALL
PRESS
DISPATCH

6

Genzyme Corporation Biopharmaceutical Plant

Architectural Resources Cambridge, Inc.

Completion: January 1994
Location: Boston, Massachusetts, USA
Client: Genzyme Corporation
Area: 17,187 square metres; 185,000 square feet
Structure: Brick
Materials: Brick
Cost: US$100 million

Genzyme's new biopharmaceutical manufacturing plant is prominently located on the Charles River in Boston, Massachusetts. The client's primary requirement for the exterior expression was to fit harmoniously into an architectural context comprised of historic Harvard University buildings and industrial plants along the river. Detail elements from neighbouring structures were combined and reinterpreted in the design to establish a strong link to the surrounding academic community. The bridges spanning the river, for example, reappear in the arches along the facade and the rounded windows reflect those of the neighbouring industrial buildings.

The manufacturing building houses large-scale bioreactors for mammalian cell culture, protein purification sites and sterile filling operations for the production of a recombinant drug therapy. The facility, which currently employs more than 130 people in Massachusetts, was designed to produce Cerezyme recombinant enzyme, a drug developed to succeed Ceredase enzyme, a tissue-derived drug, utilising state-of-the-art mammalian cell culture technology . Before Cerezyme was developed, Ceredase was the only effective therapy for Gaucher disease (characterised by an enlarged liver or spleen, anaemia, significant bone and joint pain, fatigue and orthopaedic complications) and represented a scientific breakthrough. People with Gaucher disease lack the normal form of glucocerebrosidase (GCR) and are unable to break it down.

Building materials such as metal panels and precast concrete were considered during design, but the tight schedule did not permit a lengthy shop drawing and manufacturing process. A dull masonry wall bearing on its own foundation was the ultimate solution to accommodate both the schedule and the client's aesthetic goals. To expedite the fast-track process, the exterior skin bears on the grade beams and is not carried on the structural frame, allowing the schedule for construction of the building shell to be independent of the structural shell.

Continued

1

1 Return corridor
2 Site plan
3 Rowers in the 'Head of the Charles Regatta' pass by the Genzyme plant on the way to the finish line
4 Level 1
5 Level 2
6 Level 3

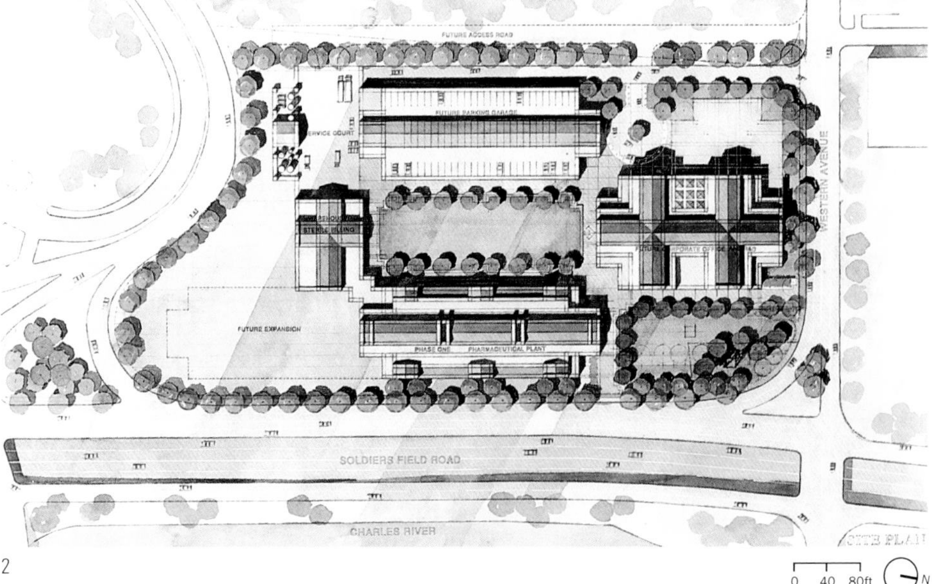

2

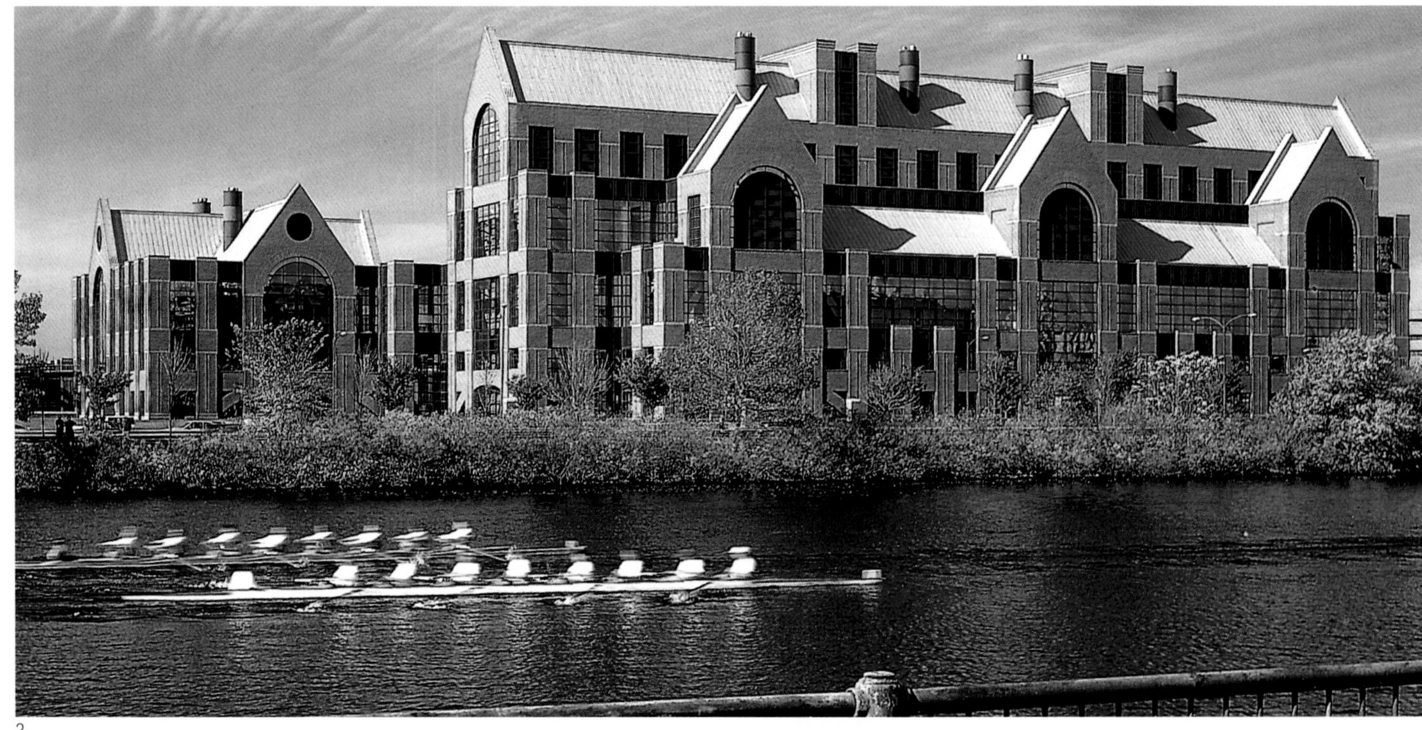

3

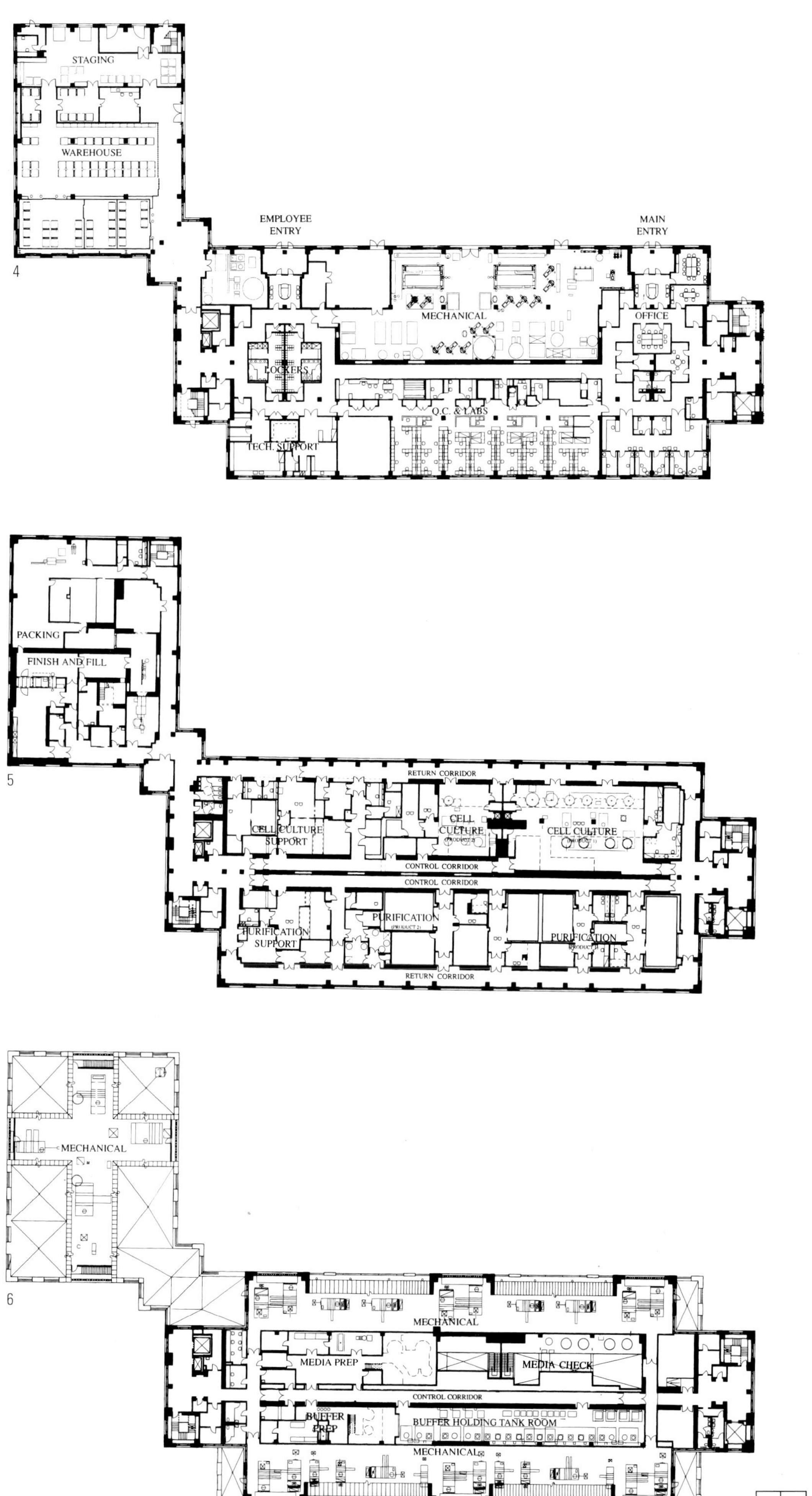
STAGING
WAREHOUSE
EMPLOYEE ENTRY
MAIN ENTRY
4
MECHANICAL
OFFICE
LOCKERS
Q.C. & LABS
TECH. SUPPORT
PACKING
FINISH AND FILL
5
RETURN CORRIDOR
CELL CULTURE SUPPORT
CELL CULTURE
CELL CULTURE
CONTROL CORRIDOR
CONTROL CORRIDOR
PURIFICATION SUPPORT
PURIFICATION
PURIFICATION
RETURN CORRIDOR
MECHANICAL
6
MECHANICAL
MEDIA PREP
MEDIA CHECK
CONTROL CORRIDOR
BUFFER PREP
BUFFER HOLDING TANK ROOM
MECHANICAL
0 16 32ft

With its extraordinary depth and range of texture and colour, a Kane Gonic waterstruck brick was selected to recall the traditional waterstruck brick of the nearby university buildings. Brick details are expressed through intricate corbelling, coursing and colour striping. The wide arches at the base of the facade and the high arches in the gables are framed with soldier courses and have hand-cast tapered bricks at the radius joints, specially sized at each course. The windows sit on deep brick sills, designed and cast with an integral wash at the top face. The projecting sills create a shadow line and the windows are framed at the top and bottom with stretcher and soldier courses of brick.

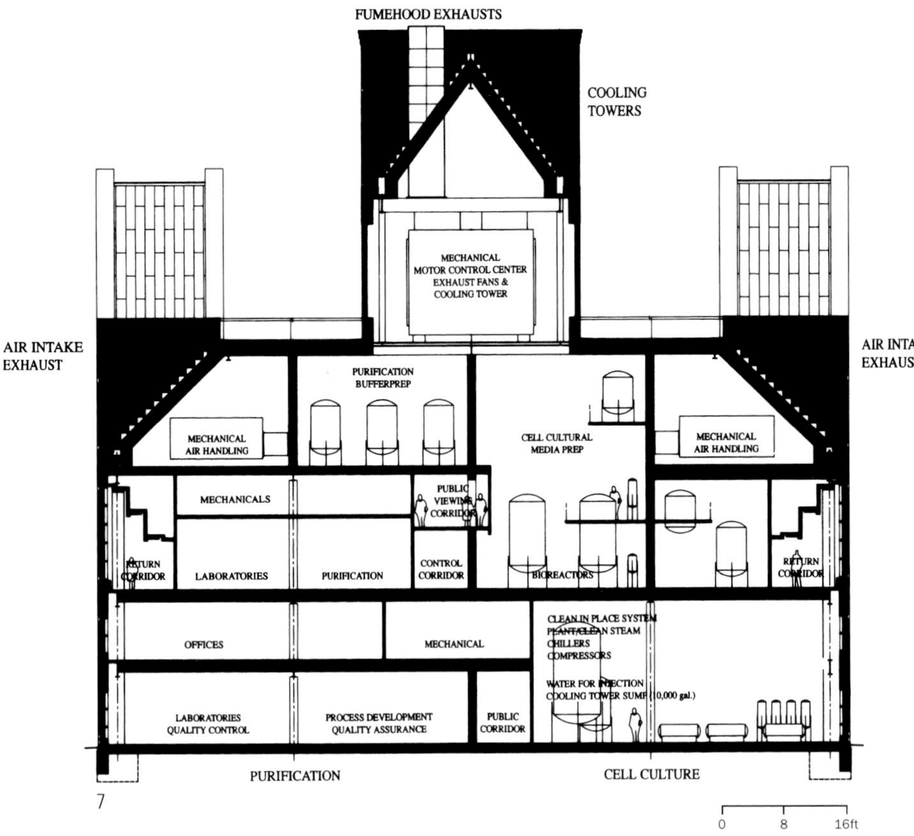

7

7 Section showing interior organisation
8 Quality assurance/quality control laboratory
9 Cell culture hall
Photography: John Horner; Nick Wheeler; Peter Vanderwarker

8

STERILE PROCESS
PROCESS DRAIN
CLEAN STEAM
CIP SUPPLY
CIP RETURN
STERILE PROCESS
PROCESS DRAIN
CIP SUPPLY
CIP RETURN
X-2105B
PRODUCTION BIOREACTOR

9

Memorial Drive Flex-Use Industrial Facility

Herbert Beckhard Frank Richlan & Associates
in association with Brandt-Kuybida Architects

Completion: September 1994

Location: Franklin Township, New Jersey, USA

Client: Cali Associates

Area: 13,935 square metres; 150,000 square feet

Structure: Steel frame; load-bearing masonry envelope

Materials: Scored concrete block with glazed block bands; metal; glass

Cost: US$5.8 million

Awards: American Concrete Masonry Institute Honorable Mention Award (New Jersey Chapter)

The design goal of this project was to take a prosaic, utilitarian building and generate a better level of architecture, within stringent economic constraints.

Typical of new 'flex-use' buildings, increments of 2,323 square metres (25,000 square feet) are leased for warehousing and light manufacturing.

Even within the framework of extremely economical construction materials, detailing and planning can create appealing and inviting buildings. The facade is articulated by using masonry piers—expressing the necessary expansion joints—and recessed, metal-clad entrances, which contrast with the spirit of the concrete block facade. The economical block construction is further enhanced with red-glazed block horizontal bands.

1

2

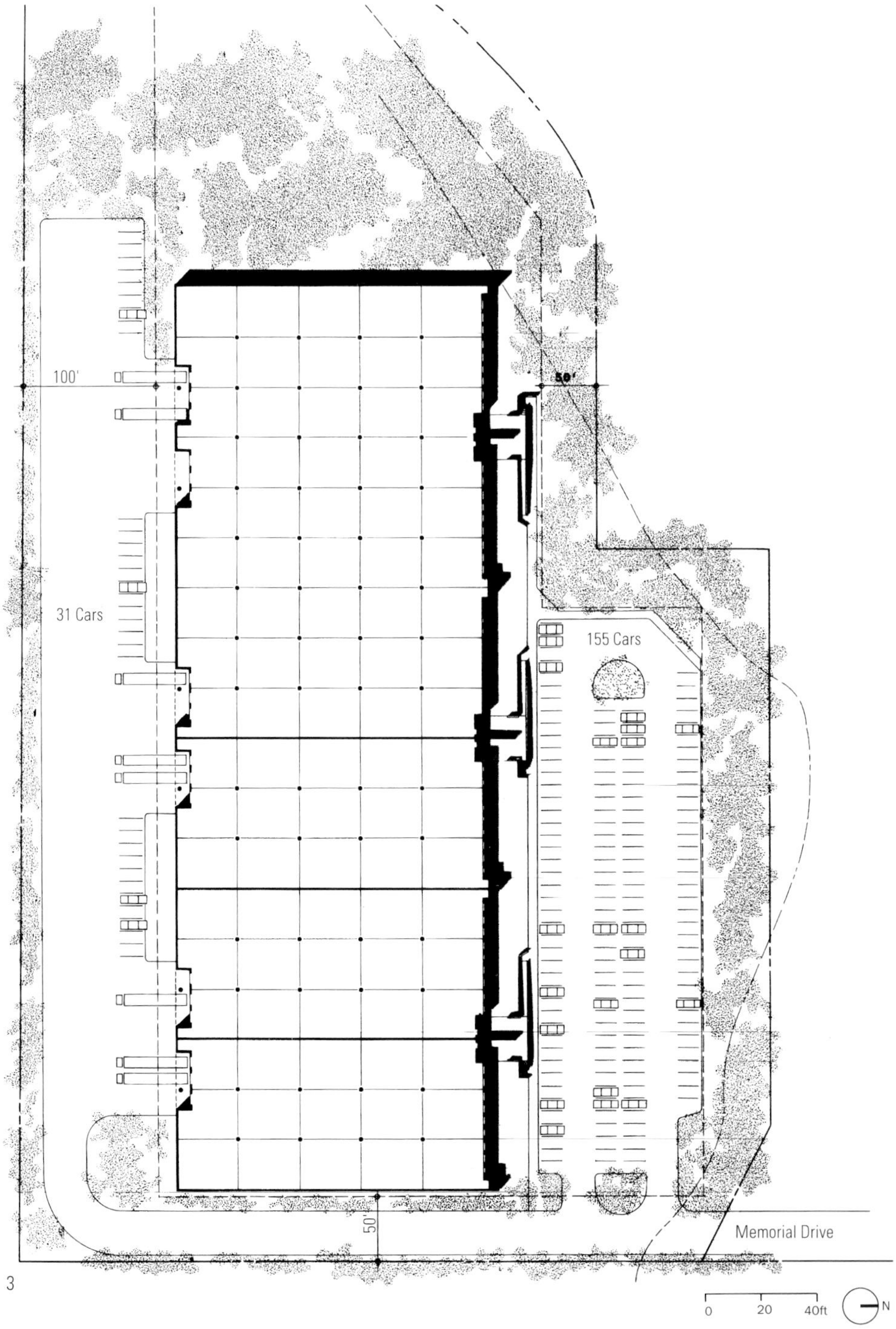

100'

50'

31 Cars

155 Cars

Memorial Drive

0 20 40ft

N

3

1 Lateral view of typical office zone
2 Detail view of masonry piers articulating expansion joints and rentable modules
3 Site plan
4 Detail plan at paired rentable modules
5 Typical paired entrance recess serving two rentable modules

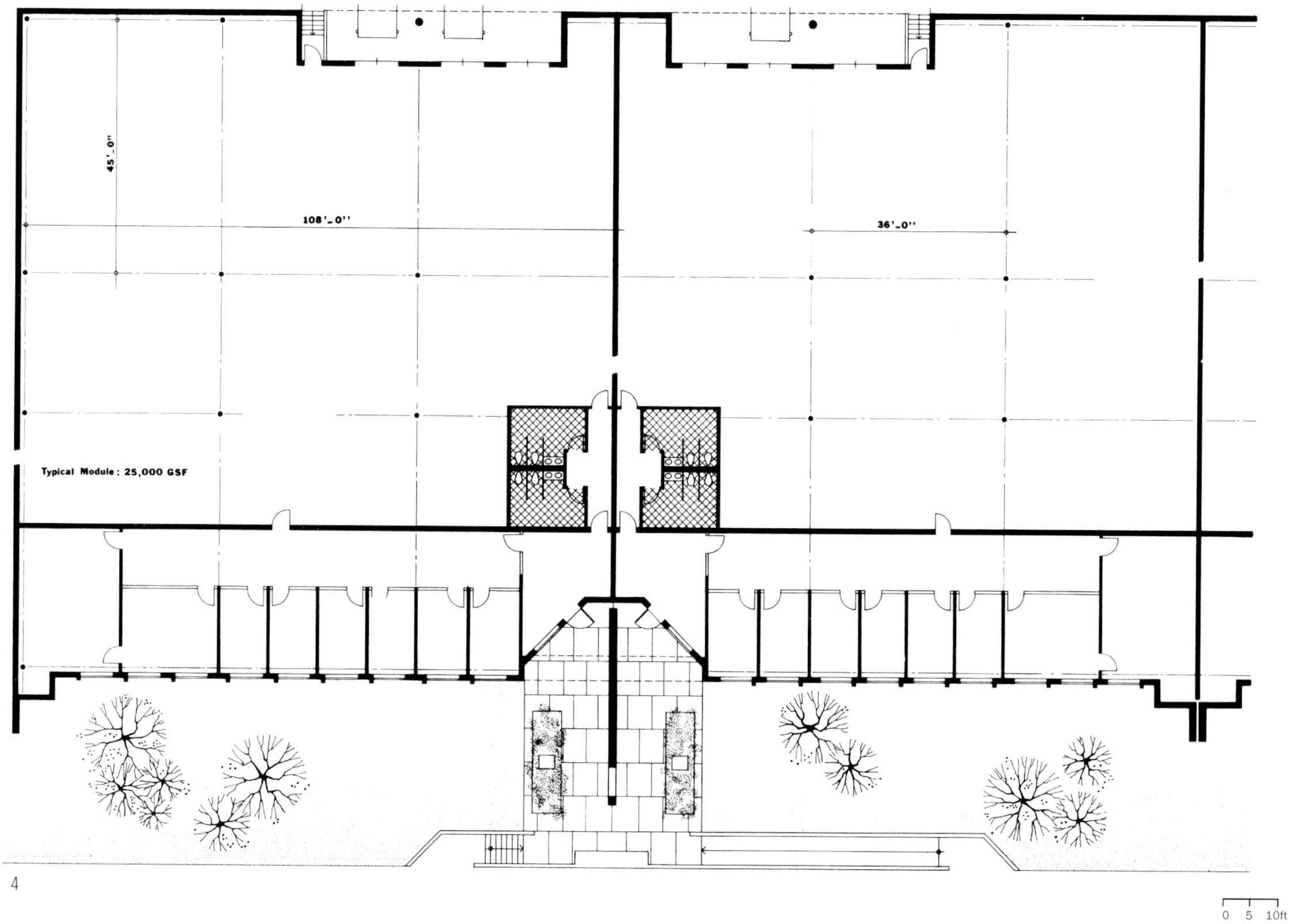

45'-0''

108'-0''

36'-0''

Typical Module: 25,000 GSF

4

0 5 10ft

5

Manufacturing Facility, Toppan Printing Company America, Inc.

Herbert Beckhard Frank Richlan & Associates
in association with Brandt-Kuybida Architects

Completion: June 1994

Location: Somerset, New Jersey, USA

Client: CLD Associates

Area: 18,580 square metres; 200,000 square feet

Structure: Steel frame

Materials: Precast concrete exterior panels

Cost: US$12.7 million

Awards: 1994 Design Award for excellence in architectural and engineering design by the Precast/Prestressed Concrete Institute for the 'Best Industrial Building'

Manufacturing buildings, once prosaic and ordinary, have changed. Today, higher standards are demanded, for both positive corporate identity and worker morale. Economics are always a prominent factor and constraint.

For this project, the architects managed to take simple rectangular shapes and transformed them, with modest intrusions at the principal facade, into non-routine, visually arresting forms: a recessed entrance, deeply set articulated window elements, and grooved precast concrete.

The site has two main vehicular access points, the first for truck use and employee parking at the rear of the building, and the second for visitor parking. By placing the bulk of the cars and trucks in the back, the building front, pleasantly landscaped, allows a car-free approach.

The advantages of precast concrete included speed of erection during winter months and factory reliability.

1

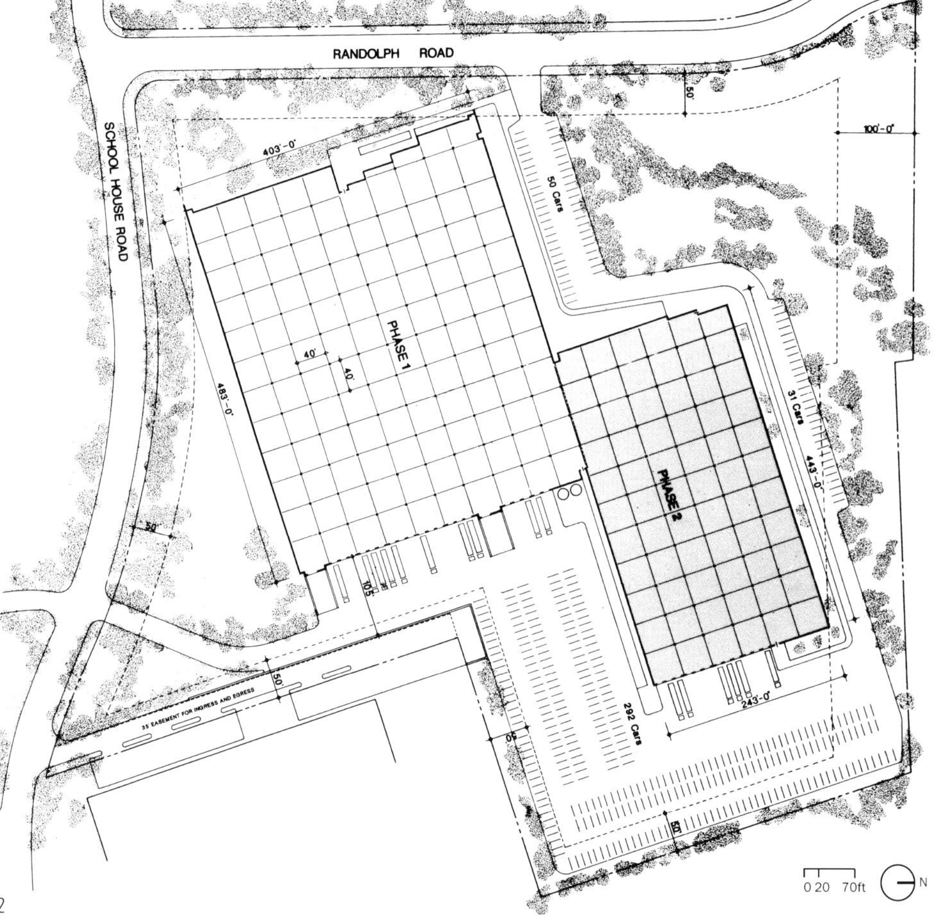

2

3

1 Detail view of stepped facade at corner offices
2 Site plan
3 View looking toward entrance and administrative offices
4 First floor plan administrative area
5 Second floor plan administrative area
6 Detail view of main entrance
7 Typical segment of manufacturing area facade

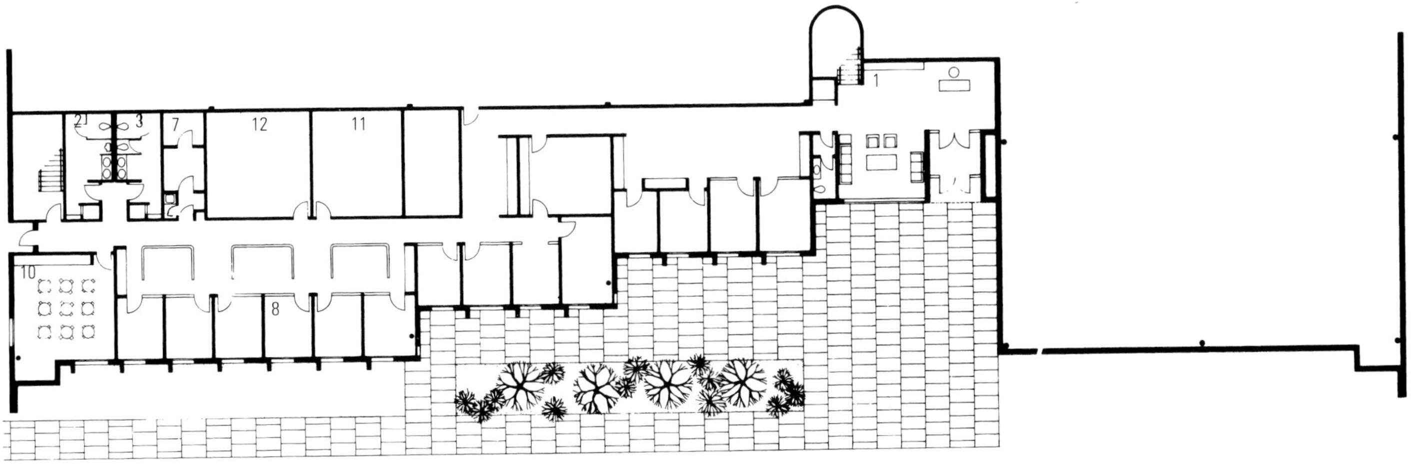

4

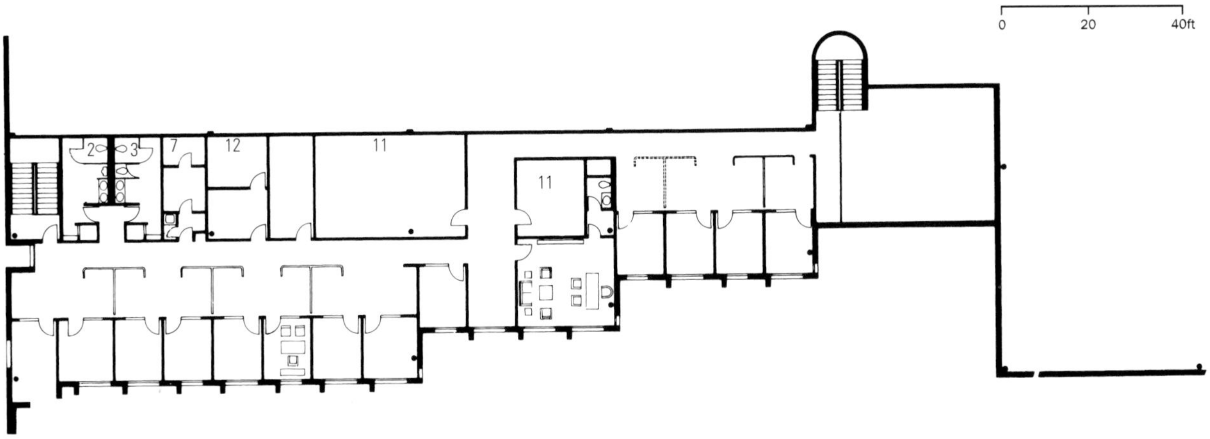

0 20 40ft

5

Key
1 Lobby
2 Men's toilet
3 Women's toilet
4 Janitor's closet
5 Coat
6 Xerox room
7 T/E room
8 Typical office
9 Manager's office
10 Lunch room
11 Conference room
12 Core room

6

7

Augusta Medical Center

Ellerbe Becket, Inc.

Completion: August 1994
Location: Fishersville, Virginia, USA
Client: Augusta Hospital Corporation
Area: 36,198 square metres; 389,640 square feet
Structure: Concrete pan and joist
Materials: Brick; concrete; metal
Cost: US$48 million

The Augusta Medical Center is a 256-bed replacement hospital serving two nearby communities. The 127 acre rural site has been master planned as a comprehensive collection of health-related components. The Phase I hospital includes inpatient, outpatient, high-tech ancillary, logistical and administrative services. The building has been planned for growth and change, responding to federal healthcare legislation and workload demands. The total project budget is US$70 million.

Ellerbe Becket responded with a design that respects the natural terrain of the site, incorporates architectural and interior design elements familiar to both communities, organises hospital functions to achieve optimal operating efficiencies, and utilises natural light and the outdoors to orient patients, visitors and staff throughout the facility.

The hospital design is focused on efficiencies in construction, patient care staffing, and building and grounds operating costs. All beds are private and half of the rooms can be converted to two bedrooms for maximum flexibility. Back-to-back nursing stations improve staffing efficiency. A simple circulation system segregates patient, staff and materials traffic, while easing visitor access. The site design integrates patient, staff, visitor, emergency and service traffic along with 850 parking spaces and a helicopter pad.

1

2

3

4

1 Main entry drop-off showing canopy, rotunda and medical main street
2 Exterior view of patient wing
3 View showing secondary patient entry, chapel, stair tower, flag and administration wing
4 Front entrance, evening
5 Close-up of stair tower with flag
6 Exterior view showing cardiopulmonary exercise area
7 Maintenance area and smokestack
8 Typical private patient room
9 View from ICU showing chairing network
10 Interior view of rotunda and atrium
11 View of cafeteria, dining area, overlooks main entry

Photography: Maxwell Mackenzie

5

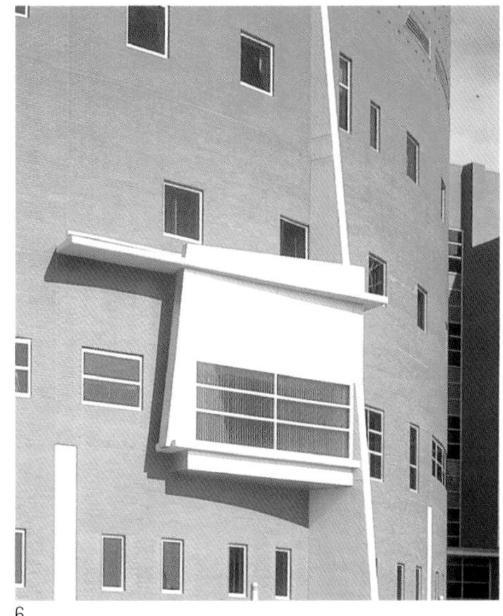
6

7

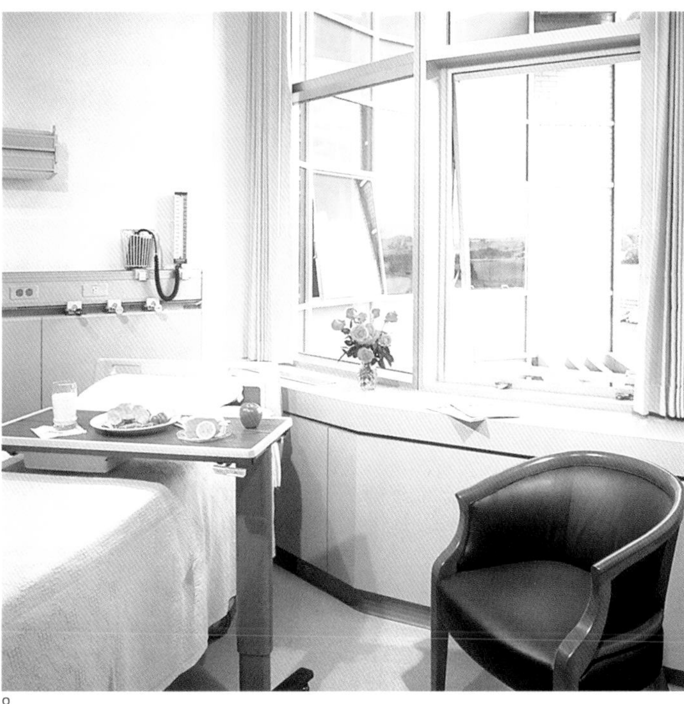
8

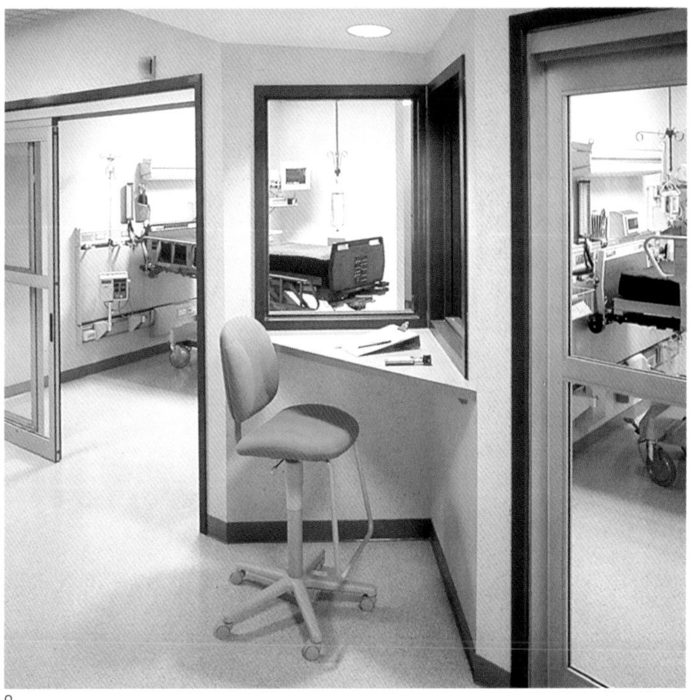
9

10

11

Bonita Professional Center

Martinez Cutri & McArdle

Completion: March 1994

Location: Bonita, California, USA

Client: The Pieri Company and Phair Company

Area: 4,664 square metres; 50,200 square feet

Structure: Concrete slabs; wood/steel frame

Materials: Exterior stucco; stone accents; Mission Tile roofs

Cost: US$5.5 million

This 3-storey medical facility is located at one of the most prominent intersections/thoroughfares of this small rural community. Inherent to the region is a strong Mission Style aesthetic. The design parti takes architectonic elements of the residential neighbourhood—entry arches, window mouldings, pergolas, colouration, etc.—and amplifies their scale and proportion to create a facility which is immediately reminiscent of its origins, typological in line with its program, and in concert with its rural environs.

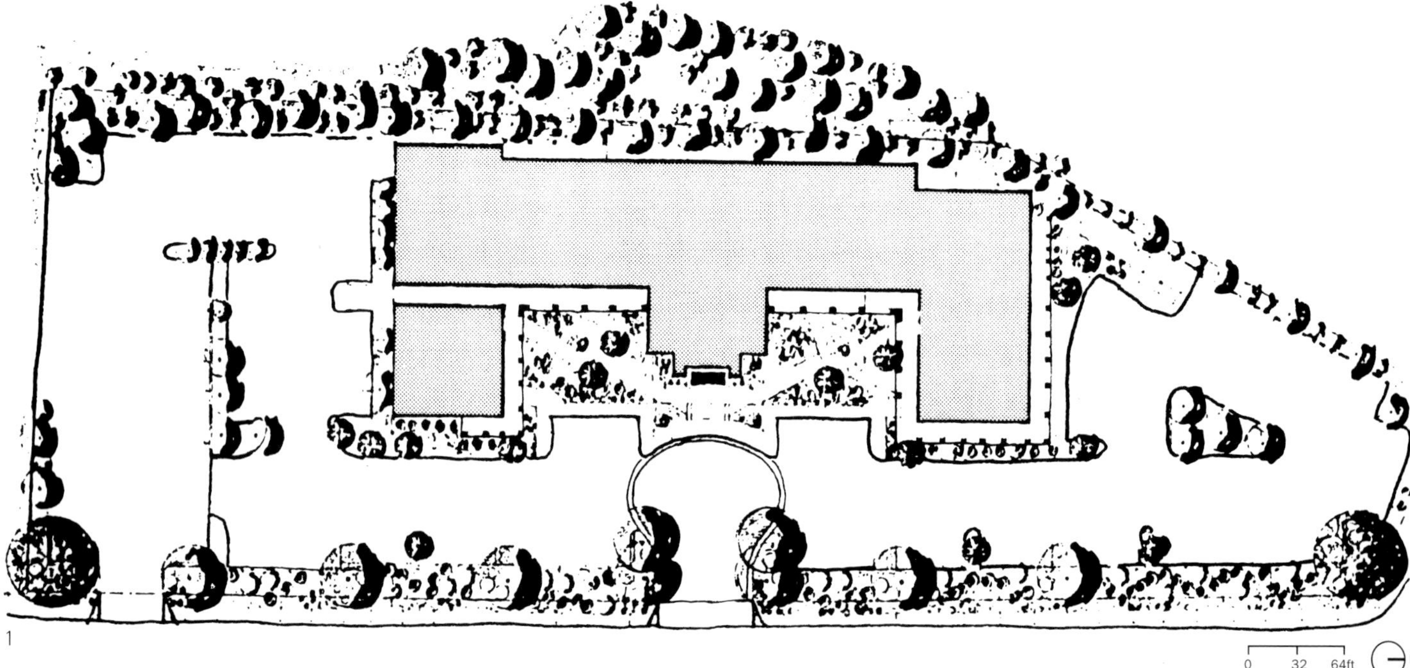

1

2

1 Site plan
2 Entry facade and courtyards
3 Ground floor plan
4 Second floor plan
5 Third floor plan
6 Entry pavilion
Photography: Jim Brady

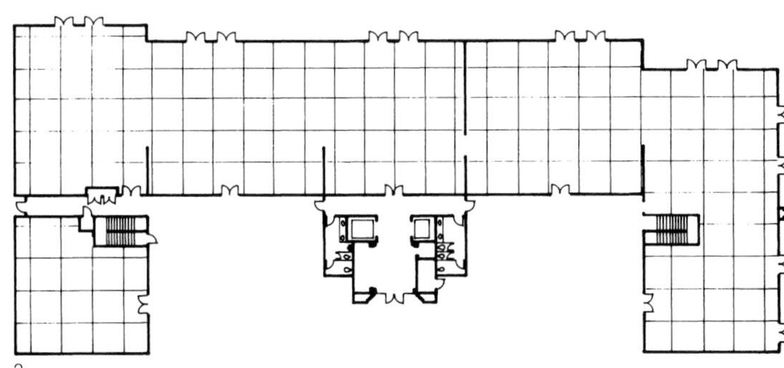

3

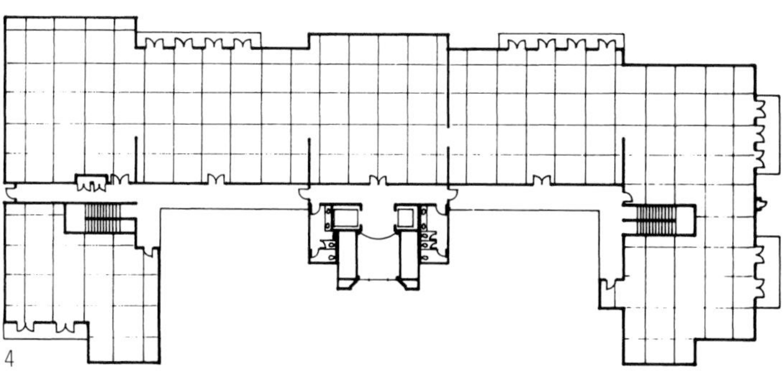

4

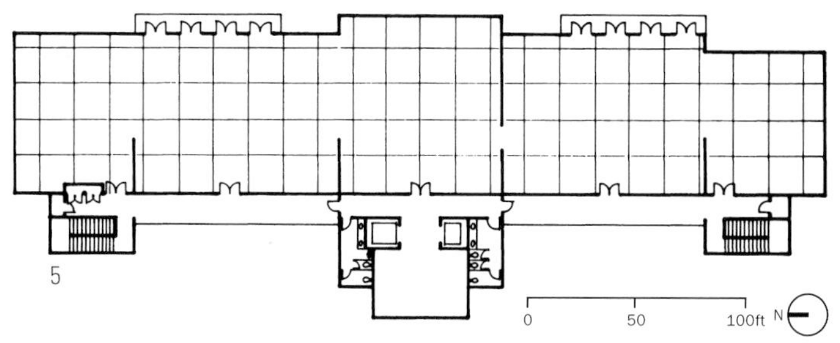

5

6

Cabrini Hospital

Bates Smart

Completion: August 1994

Location: Malvern, Victoria, Australia

Client: St Frances Xavier Cabrini Hospital

Area: 5,750 square metres; 61,895 square feet

Structure: Face brickwork; precast and in situ concrete

Materials: Fibrous cement sheet; kliplok roofing

Cost: A$20.3 million

Awards: 1995 Royal Australian Institute of Architects Commendation

Bates Smart were briefed to 'de-institutionalise' the new facility which includes a new ward block, Chapel, and consulting suites to the rear of the existing hospital.

Externally these are presented as three buildings but the linkages and treatment of interiors provide a sense of wholeness. The hospital's main frontage is Wattletree Road, whilst the site for the new building is on the eastern side of the property addressing a residential street with low-scale housing on the other side. Clever traffic management has closed this street but allows access to the carpark under the new complex. Consulting rooms which face this street present a 'frayed' low scale edge which mimics the Edwardian housing opposite. The visitor to this hospital would have little difficulty in negotiating this large and complex institution.

1

2

3

4

5

6

7

1 Cabrini Chapel
2 Chapel from Coonil Crescent
3 North block from Coonil Crescent
4 Terrace cafe, garden terrace
5 Terrace cafe, interior dining area
6 Terrace cafe, servery
7 Chapel Altar (stained glass window by David Wright)
Photography: John Gollings

Children's National Medical Center, Children's Research Institute

Ellerbe Becket, Inc.

Completion: January 1995
Location: Washington, D.C., USA
Client: Children's National Medical Center
Area: 4,645 square metres; 50,000 square feet
Structure: Steel frame; composite concrete decks
Materials: Glazed aluminium glass curtain wall
Cost: US$8 millioin

Ellerbe Becket is responsible for the planning and design of a 2-storey, phased expansion to the research and support needs of the Children's Research Institute. The first phase is a 4,645 square metre (50,000 square foot) single floor rooftop addition. Approximately 50% of the initial lab program area is built out with the rest as shelled space to be incrementally fitted out. Laboratory planning flexibility was a primary concern to support six research centres including: Virology, Immunology & Infectious Diseases; Tumour Cell/Transplantation Biology; Molecular and Cellular Biology; Applied Physiology; Neurobiology; and, Clinical Research.

To maximise laboratory flexibility for both Phase I and Phase II, an interstitial service deck with modular access strips is used above the Phase I laboratory. Utility and service distribution occurs in horizontal zones within the service level to avoid conflicts. Penetrations through the service deck necessary for laboratory build-out below can occur as required through the accessible deck sections. This arrangement allows future Phase II work to progress without impacting existing laboratories below, and provides for complete freedom of layout and placement of mechanical equipment within the laboratories.

Appropriate placement of the addition maximises expansive views of Washington, D.C.'s monuments and skyline. The clear, peaked skylight in the central atrium space creates an appealing environment for ceremonial functions, seminars and conferences. Workstations for the senior research staff are located adjacent to the standardised laboratory benches which are custom fitted with cabinetry suitable for specific research needs.

1

2

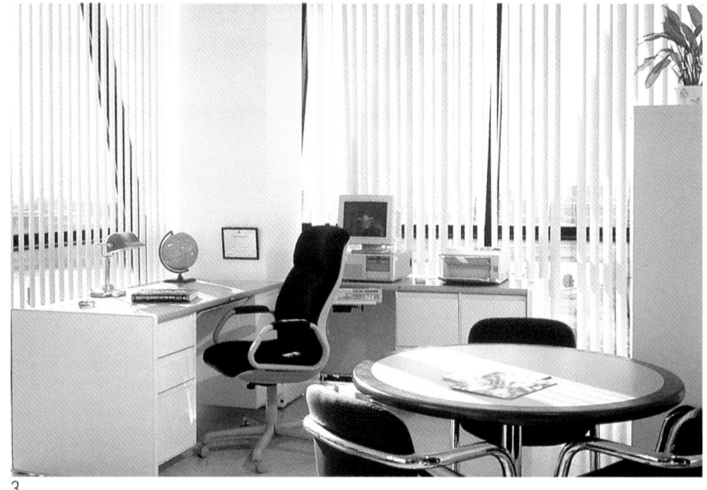

3

4

5

1 Conference room with access to rooftop deck

2 The skylit central atrium, with a view of Washington's skyline, creates an appealing space for ceremonial functions, seminars and conferences

3 Office of the executive director of the CRI

4 Workstation for research staff

5 Research laboratory with custom fitted cabinetry suitable for specific research needs

Photography: Maxwell Mackenzie

Construction Industry Training Institute

DP Architects Pte Ltd

Completion: July 1994
Location: Singapore
Client: Construction Industry Development Board
Area: 25,653 square metres; 276,136 square feet
Structure: Precast and pre-stressed concrete
Materials: Concrete; steel; glass
Cost: S$25 million
Awards: 1994 CIDB Best Buildable Design Award

The Construction Industry Training Institute at Bishan is a training school for construction workers and others involved in the building industry. The accommodation consists of seminar rooms, workshops, a lecture theatre, library, administration building and other support facilities.

The main access to the complex is through the entrance foyer in the administrative block; a naturally ventilated, double height space. The two rows of double height workshops run parallel to the Central Expressway, their single span lightweight roof form affording column free interior spaces. The courtyards created between are used for outdoor projects and recreation. Circulation between the workshops is by raised, covered walkways which span the courtyards.

In line with the brief, the concept of buildable design is given practical demonstration. The proposals were simplified according to a modular system using prefabricated elements. Combined with innovative materials both cost and construction time were reduced.

1

2

3

1 Main entrance elevation
2 Side elevation
3 View across a courtyard
4 Entrance foyer
Photography: Hans Schlupp

4

Cox Medical Center South Outpatient Center

The Wishcmeyer Architects, Inc.

Completion: April 1995
Location: Springfield, Missouri, USA
Client: Cox Medical Center South
Area: 15,773 square metres; 169,779 square feet
Structure: Steel frame; glue-laminated beams
Materials: Precast concrete; aluminium panels; insulated glass brick; standing seam metal roof
Cost: US$19.86 million

A shift in emphasis to 60-70% outpatient procedures led this 500-bed hospital to commission a new Outpatient Center.

Two of Wischmeyer's previous projects on this 60 acre campus reinforce the design vocabulary throughout the base of the building. The emergency department addition and pedestrian bridge utilise glass, red aluminium panels and window mullions, and precast concrete to create a brighter, more inviting context and counterpoint to the weighty appearance of the existing brick tower.

The Outpatient Center continues this concept with a precast concrete portico which creates an 'inside/outside' space that shades the interior from direct midday sun. Floor to ceiling glazing enhances the concept of 'building as pavilion'. At night, the illuminated interior acts as a beacon, marking the entrance.

The healing process begins as people enter the building. The focal point of the facility is the lobby/entrance. It combines an information centre, patient registration, pre-examination, waiting, cafe, and pharmacy. Jointly, these functions draw a critical mass of people together in a larger, open space which is inviting and comfortable to use. Daylighting and the use of natural materials are the key to the airy, warm feeling of the space. Clerestory light boxes direct and filter the daylight across warm-toned oak panels. Glue-laminated beams order the space, creating an unexpected, fresh image for this healing environment. The column bases contain integrated halogen up-lighting which further accents the beam construction. In the evening the warm glow of these fixtures creates a shadow play and secondary rhythms on the ceiling that reflect and enhance the welcoming atmosphere.

Five patient modules of Same Day Surgery (two shelled for future growth), a renovated Endoscopy suite, and a new Special Delivery Maternal Care Center (including LDR's and Perinatal ICU) complete the ground floor. The tunnel floor accommodates the expansion of biomedical engineering, print shop, and communications departments.

1

2

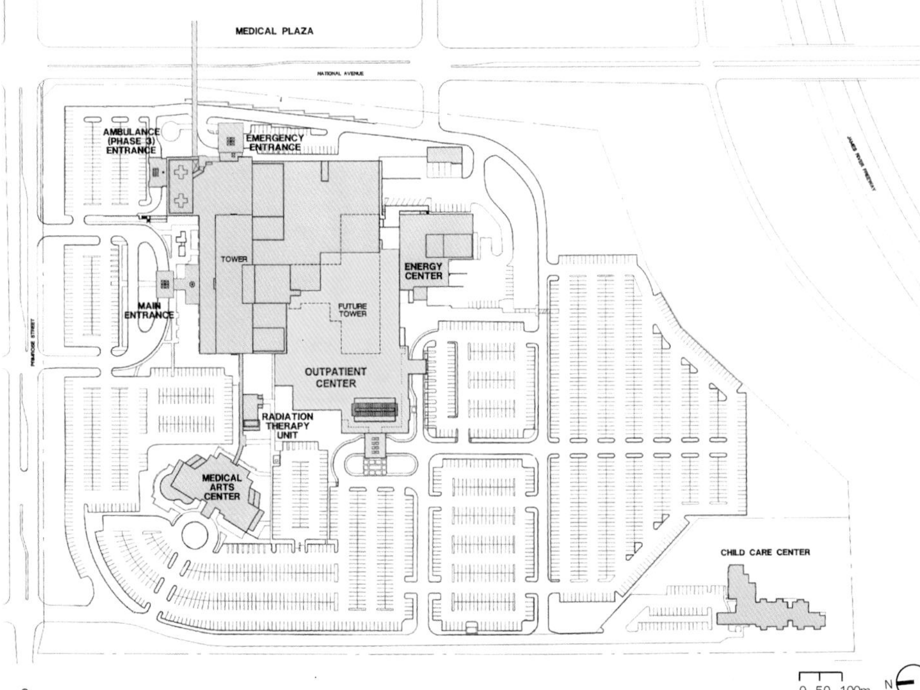

3

4

1 South entry elevation
2 Portico with cafe seating
3 Site plan
4 Main outpatient center entrance
5 East–west cross section
6 Longitudinal section through lobby
7 Ground floor plan

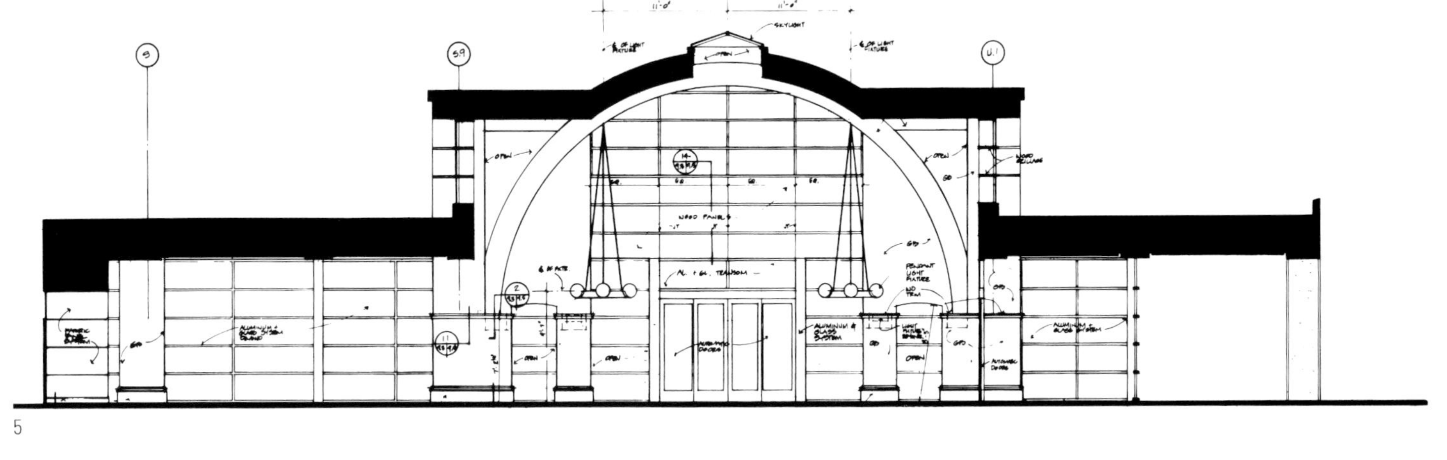

5

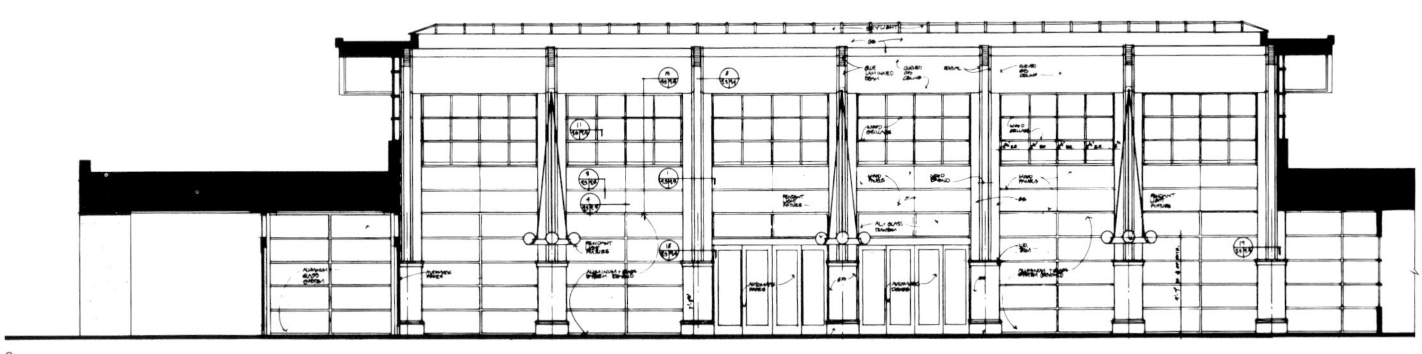

6

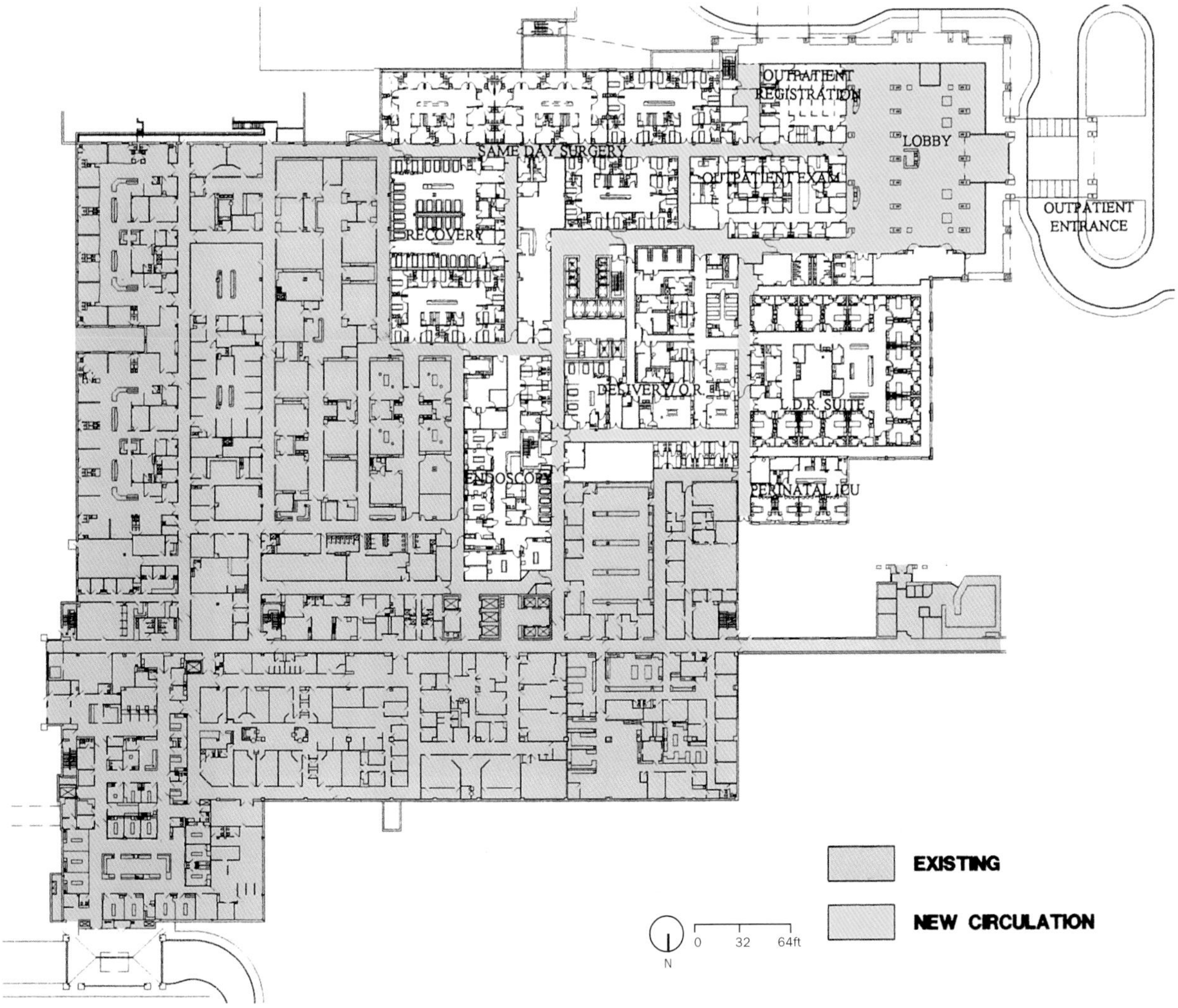

OUTPATIENT REGISTRATION

LOBBY

SAME DAY SURGERY

OUTPATIENT EXAM

RECOVERY

OUTPATIENT ENTRANCE

DELIVERY/O.R.

D.R. SUITE

ENDOSCOPY

PERINATAL ICU

EXISTING

NEW CIRCULATION

N

0 32 64ft

7

8

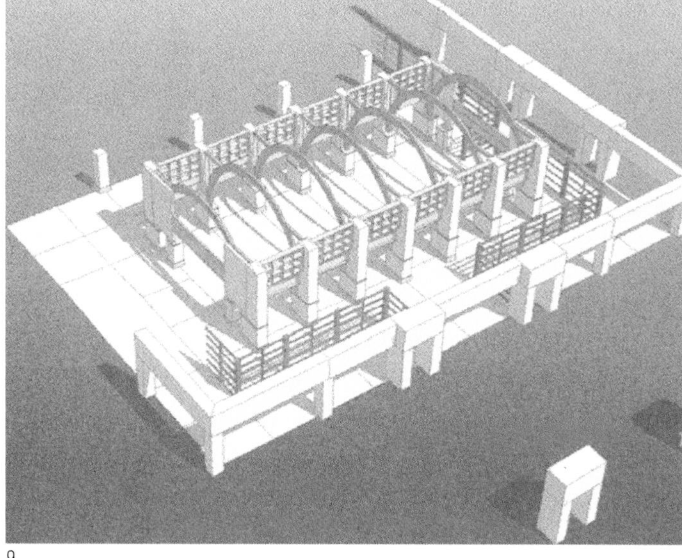
9

10

11

8 Computerized lobby view
9 Computer model—organizational concept
10 Detail—glue-laminated structure
11 Same-day surgery family waiting
12 Lobby at dusk
Photography: Alise O'Brien (Interior); Robert Pettus (Exterior)

12

Cullman Regional Medical Center

TRO/The Ritchie Organization

Completion: January 1995
Location: Cullman, Alabama, USA
Client: Cullman Regional Medical Center
Area: 20,243 square metres; 217,900 square feet
Structure: Concrete
Materials: Brick; glass
Cost: US$26,050,000

This 115-bed hospital replaces an existing facility which had become obsolete in its ability to serve an ever-increasing demand for outpatient and emergency services. Among the owner's primary concerns were building efficiency, user convenience and flexibility. The visual connection between the building's interior and the exterior environment was a guiding principle in the development of the design.

The hospital is situated along a ridge running east to west on the site. As an organising element, this ridge establishes the axis of a major public corridor. Roads, walkways and a line of trees extending from the site entry to the hospital, create an intersecting axis which guides patients and visitors to the patient drop-off. This visual axis extends into the hospital directing visitors to the public lobby and elevators beyond. Views of the exterior along corridors and at nodes help maintain a sense of orientation.

Hospital functions are grouped together for optimum efficiency. The Emergency Center doubles the capacity of the previous facility with separate entries for walk-in emergencies and trauma patients. Outpatient Services, including a Day Hospital, Women's Center and a Cancer Center are accessed by a separate Outpatient Entry on the west side of the Hospital.

Abundant use of glass gives the building a transparent quality and allows pleasant views from many perspectives. A corridor with views to an interior courtyard and the front of the hospital, conveniently links the main lobby to Outpatient Services. A 2-storey atrium provides views to a landscaped courtyard from the dining room below and from the main lobby above.

1

2

3

4

5

6

7

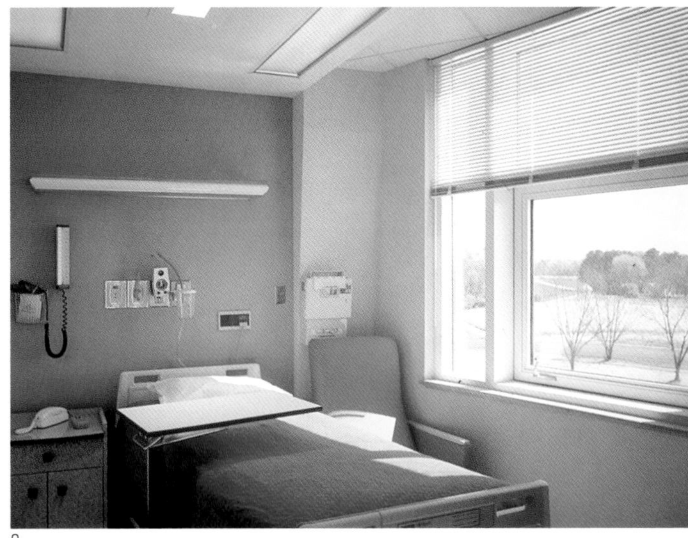
8

9

1 A curved landscaped walkway directs patients and visitors to the hospital's main entry
2 Exterior columns are detailed to lend aesthetic appeal to the hospital
3 An enclosed courtyard provides a pleasant amenity for patients/visitors
4 Building design provides visual clues for orientation and wayfinding
5 Principle diagnostic/treatment departments are configured with flexibility for future growth
6 The building design incorporates the natural healing qualities of the landscape; sunlight, views, vegetation
7 The public elevator lobby provides pleasant views and aids in orientation
8 Views to the outside from all patient rooms was a guiding principle for design
9 A dining area provides a pleasant amenity for patients, visitors and staff

Genentech Process Science Center

Flad & Associates

Completion: July 1995

Location: South San Francisco, California, USA

Client: Genentech

Area: 15,328 square metres; 165,000 square feet

Structure: Precast concrete

Materials: Aluminium and glass curtain wall; painted metal

Cost: US$48 million

Genentech's new Process Science Center was developed to shorten the time from product discovery to market delivery. The building brings process science researchers and production together on the lower part of their campus, overlooking San Francisco Bay. Views of water, mountains, and the coastal landscape are a part of every major interior space.

The layout of this complex centres around a 2-storey scale-up pilot plant and a 2-storey lunchroom/cappuccino bar. These spaces share a common window and a grand view of the bay, and together function as a large 'commons' for the users of the building.

A 3-storey lab wing to the east connects along a primary corridor. Research labs along the perimeter connect across the corridor to shared wet labs in the middle, and a 3-storey skylit stair in the centre of each floor connects labs on all levels.

Office spaces occupy the perimeter for maximum daylight and views. Glass sliding entry doors bring light into the office corridor and allow maximum floor space use in the offices. Third floor offices enjoy the use of terraces with 'nautical' white railings overlooking the water.

Rooftop mechanical systems are contained and centralised in a gently curving metal panel penthouse which derives its form from the silhouette of Mt. San Bruno to the west.

The exterior spaces formed with adjacent buildings mix the urban scale hardscape of the manufacturing campus with the natural dune forms of the indigenous coastal landscape. A double-helix exterior pathway recalls the geometry of DNA strands, which are the focus of Genentech's research.

1

3

4

5

2

6

7

1 Building entry and bridge connection
2 View from San Francisco Bay
3 View from public street
4 Office terrace, third level
5 Laboratory casework
6 View from the bridge
7 Central stair
8 Lunchroom/cappuccino bar

Photography: Peter Malinowski, Insite Photography

8

Grady Memorial Hospital

Kaplan/McLaughlin/Diaz
in association with URS Consultants, Carl Trimble Architects, Stanley Love-Stanley and The Burlington Group

Completion: May 1995

Location: Atlanta, Georgia, USA

Client: Fulton-Dekalb Hospital Authority, Grady Memorial Hospital

Area: 206,572 square metres; 2,223,600 square feet

Structure: Steel; concrete

Materials: Terrazzo; sheet vinyl; vinyl tile; stone; wood; plaster; precast concrete; metal panels; insulating glass

Cost: US$180 million

Awards: 1996 National Commercial Builders Council of the National Association of Home Builders Award of Excellence

Kaplan/McLaughlin/Diaz is the programming, planning and design consultant for renovation and expansion of this large urban hospital. The hospital is jointly funded by two counties and functions as a teaching hospital for Emory University and Morehouse College medical schools.

The renovation and expansion project includes a new 10-storey 34,560 square metres (372,000 square foot) clinic/diagnostic and treatment building which will provide new facilities for surgery, labour and delivery, a 120-bassinette neonatal intensive care unit, 88 intensive care beds, and outpatient clinics which will accommodate between 2,000 and 3,000 people per day.

A new 14-storey bed tower was created by 'laminating' 24,340 square metres (262,000 square feet) of new construction to 24,619 square metres (265,000 square feet) of renovation to provide 86% of the hospital's 944 adult beds in efficiently organised 41-bed nursing units. A new 1,580 square metre (17,000 square foot) service building relocates the loading dock and includes a direct tunnel connection for the hospital's basement building service level. Renovation of the existing building focuses on a series of infrastructure upgrades of engineering systems, replacement of windows for energy conservation, and two new stair/mechanical towers to resolve code compliance issues.

An entire floor is dedicated to mental health services including emergency, crisis, a 24-bed inpatient nursing unit and administrative and support services.

A formerly independent hospital will be renovated to house a 9,847 square metre (106,000 square foot) paediatric pavilion. The pavilion and a new 1,180 square metre (12,700 square foot) outpatient imaging facility will be connected to the main hospital via a below grade pedestrian link.

Continued

1

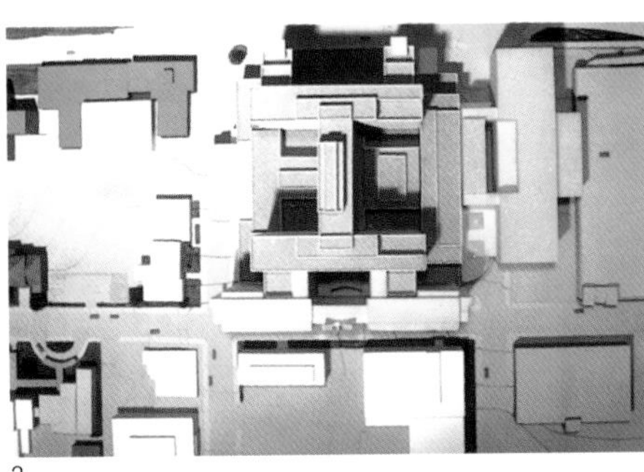
2

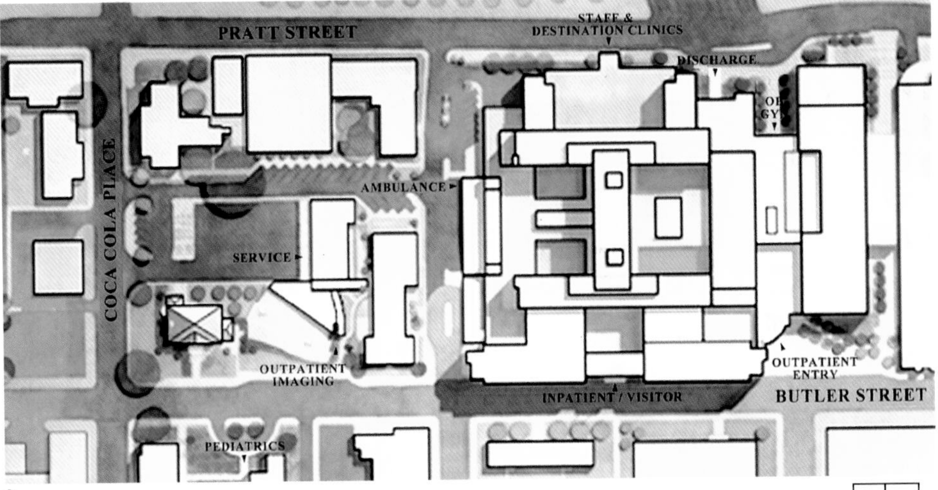

3

4

5

1 Exterior detail at new clinic and D&T building
2 Plan view of study model; new construction shown in blue
3 Site plan
4 New outpatient entry and new building for ICU, surgery, labour/delivery, NICU and clinics
5 Canopy detail
6 Ambulance canopy at Emergency and Trauma Centre addition
7 Arcade at Butler Street entry zone
8 Southwest corner of new clinics and D&T building

6

7

8

Relocation of the emergency entrance and a new two block long entry zone along Butler Street will reduce pedestrian/vehicle conflicts and provide separate access points for clinics, inpatients and visitors, staff and the perinatal centre. Concentrating on the Butler Street side of the building is a key element in the organisation concept, which zones the hospital laterally by function (diagnostic and treatment, clinics, administrative, etc.) and vertically by service (surgery, obstetrics, etc.) and will enable the hospital to grow either to the north or south. The combination of the service building, emergency relocation and 'laminated' bed tower permitted Grady to maintain full trauma centre operations (up to 1,000 patients per day) and a full bed complement during the four and a half year construction process.

9

9 Public corridors and atrium in new clinic and D&T building

10 Typical patient room

11 Cafeteria interior

Photography: Gabriel Benzur; Rion Rizzo/Creative Sources

10

11

Health Central

HKS Inc.

Completion: February 1994

Location: Ocoee, Florida, USA

Client: West Orange Hospital

Area: 24,154 square metres; 260,000 square feet

Structure: Glass; brick; metal cladding

Cost: US$34.8 million

Awards: Citation of Excellence AIA Architecture for Health Facilities Review

Central Florida has long been known as an area of innovation—from Walt Disney World Resort to Cape Canaveral. Now it is also the site of innovation in health care. A former orange grove on the west side of Metropolitan Orlando is home to a new model for a healthier future.

Traditionally, patients have gone to one place to see their doctor, another to the hospital and still somewhere else for health services such as eye care or pharmacy. Health Central seeks to change all that. Designed to serve as a 'one-stop shopping centre' for heath care services, it combines a 141-bed acute care hospital with physician suites, health services and related retail shops. Patients will use the medical centre as a source for health promotion and wellness, as well as rehabilitation from injury and disease. The hospital and physicians work in partnership to provide convenient, efficient health care using emerging technologies and computer link-ups. The centre contains more than 4,645 square metres (50,000 square feet) of physician office space.

The 836 square metre (9,000 square foot) atrium is surrounded by glass: palm trees and greenery create a feeling of bringing the 'outdoors' indoors. The atrium hosts a variety of community events, from art shows and children's choir concerts, to health fairs and screenings. Registration for hospital services resembles a hotel check-in desk and most outpatient testing procedures may be found just a few steps from the registration area.

With the building being seen as a forced perspective using a play on scale, Health Central makes people question and ask why. These questions draw people into the building. Outwardly, the building appears much larger than it really is. Dividing the project into specific components turns the building into one; the red component being the heart, the ancillary area the major organs, the nursing tower as the arms and legs, with the colour acting as freckles. The soul becomes all the people who utilise the building, giving body to the life that exists. Ultimately, the owner wanted the building to evoke emotion—be it positive or negative—just as long as it produced an emotion, because health care is emotional.

Continued

1

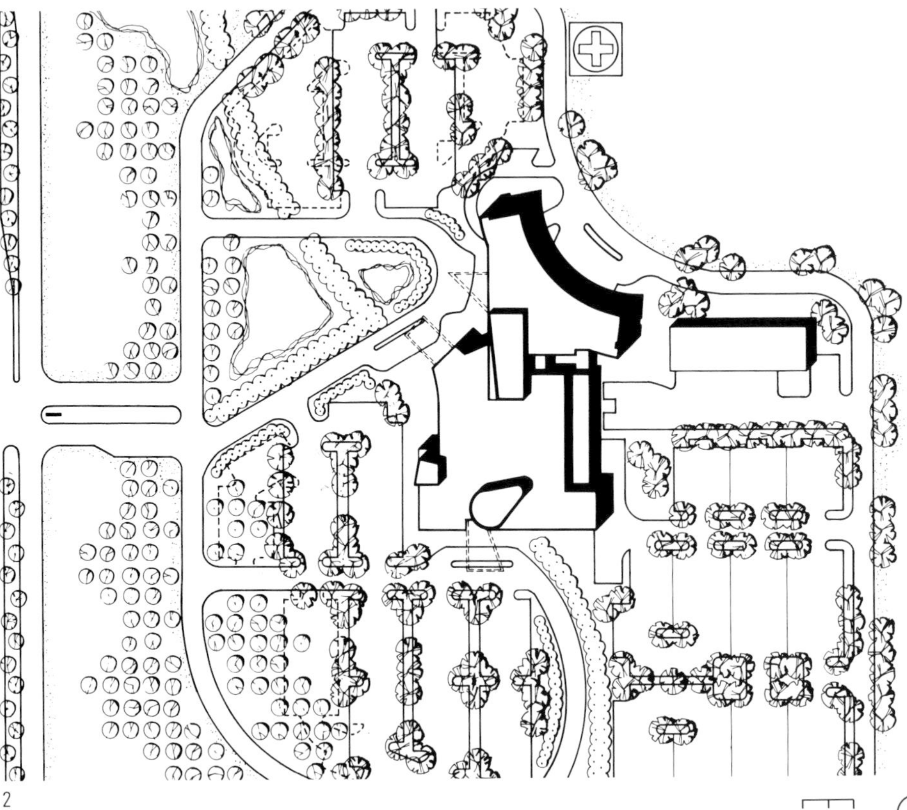

2

1 Facade detail
2 Site plan
3 Overall exterior
4 Exterior entry

3

4

One unique design element is called a 'mobile technology port'. As new medical advances emerge, before the hospital makes a permanent investment in the equipment, a truck carrying the technology will back-up to the mobile technology port, and by using an airport-like couple, the truck will actually become part of the hospital as patients are wheeled directly onto and off the vehicle. In this way, patients receive the benefit of new technology as soon as it is available.

Health Central has been designed with flexibility in mind. It can expand easily as new programs and services are needed. As the needs of the community change and grow, so will the new medical campus.

5 Axonometric
6 Level 1
7 Lobby atrium
Photography: Michael Lowry

7

Institute of Micro-Electronics / Information Technology Institute

DP Architects Pte Ltd

Completion: March 1995

Location: Singapore

Client: National University of Singapore

Area: 12,600 square metres; 135,630 square feet

Structure: Reinforced concrete

Materials: Aluminium cladding; sandstone; aluminium curtain wall; homogenous tiles; plaster; aluminium windows

Cost: S$27.5 million

Occupying a site area of 17,369 square metres (186,965 square feet), the design of this arrangement conforms to the simulated L-shaped building form in the Singapore Science Park Phase 2 master plan. The courtyards not only provide a refreshing sense of general openness to the complex, but also afford natural lighting into the building. This also provides splendid views of the surrounding lush greenery bringing nature closer to the workplace.

The formal as well as the informal arrangement of various building components basically fulfil two requirements in both architectural planning and functional requirement. Besides creating interesting spaces and opportunities to promote greater integration amongst staff members, the design also clearly differentiates the locations of the two institutes. The laboratories sit directly on the ground and are structurally separate from the administration building; this ensures the provision of good acoustic and a vibration-free environment for high-precision work.

1

2

3

4

5

6

7

8

1 Detail of ceiling in the ITI lounge
2 Escape stair between laborratory blocks four and five
3 Rear elevation of the laboratory blocks
4 Front elevation
5 View from second level into the reception space
6 Detail of reception feature wall
7 Rear of reception drum
8 Reception feature wall

Joslin Diabetes Center Research and Clinical Facility Expansion

Ellenzweig Associates, Inc.

Completion: April 1994

Location: Boston, Massachusetts, USA

Client: Joslin Diabetes Center

Area: 10,219 square metres; 110,000 square feet

Structure: Steel frame

Materials: Metal panels; glass; aluminium; rubber membrane; stainless steel; cherry wood panelling; oak; granite

Cost: US$18.2 million

Awards: American Institute of Architects Honour Award for Design Excellence

American Institute of Architects New England Design Awards

American Institute of Architects, Boston Society of Architects, Architecture Honour Award

Boston Society of Architects and the New England Healthcare Assembly, Honour Award for Design Excellence

Metal Construction Association, Scholarship Award

R&D Magazine, Lab of the Year Award, Special Mention

Designed to express the leadership of this world-renowned medical institution in the field of diabetes research and treatment, the expansion of the Joslin Diabetes Center doubles the facility's capacity, providing additional space for research, support (including animal facilities), clinical and administrative functions, as well as a new research library, cafeteria, entrance lobby, skylit atrium and landscaped courtyard. The expanded facilities provide state-of-the art research laboratories for up to 64 biomedical researchers and enhance Joslin's leading research, clinical, and teaching programs.

This major 3-storey addition and renovation was required to accommodate a complex, high technology program on a restricted urban site. The project demonstrates innovation both in the way it solves challenging mechanical and structural issues and how it maintains operations of the underlying 1976 building. The design reconciles the austere style of the older exposed concrete structure with a contemporary addition, producing a unified statement which reflects both Joslin's history and its vision for the future.

1

2

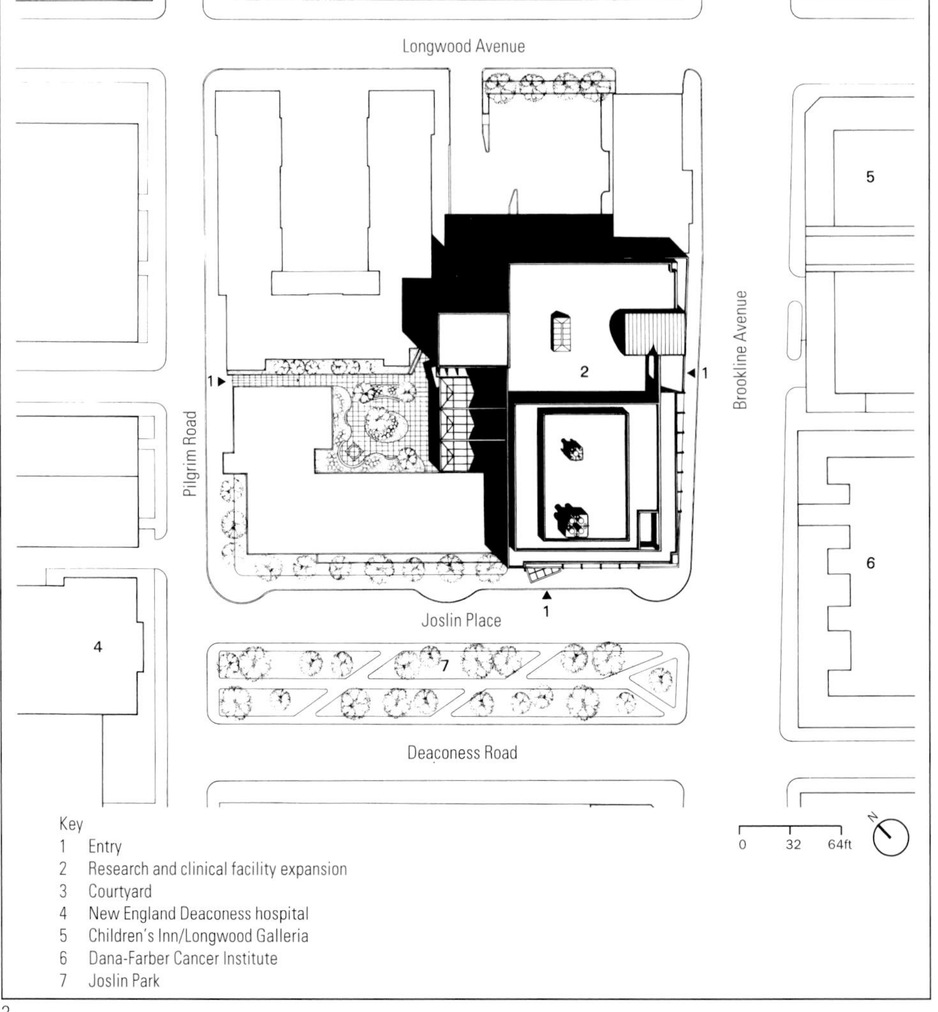

3

1-2 Before expansion
3 Site plan
4 View from south
5 View from west

4

5

6

7

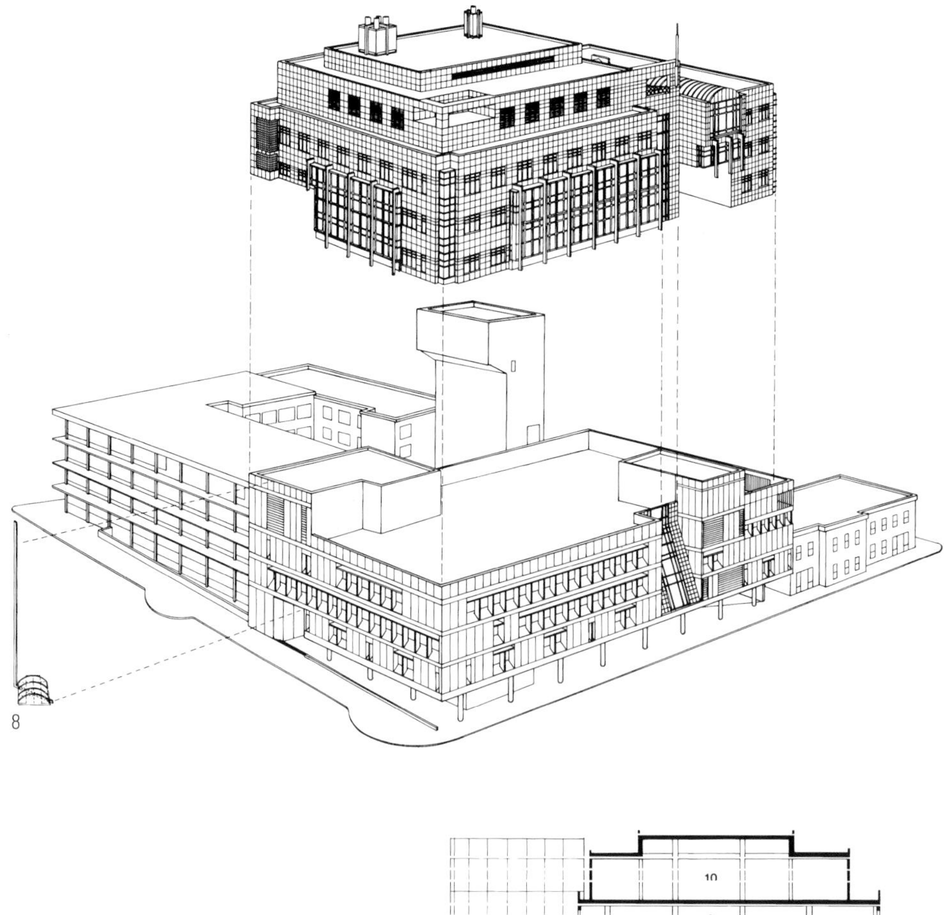
8

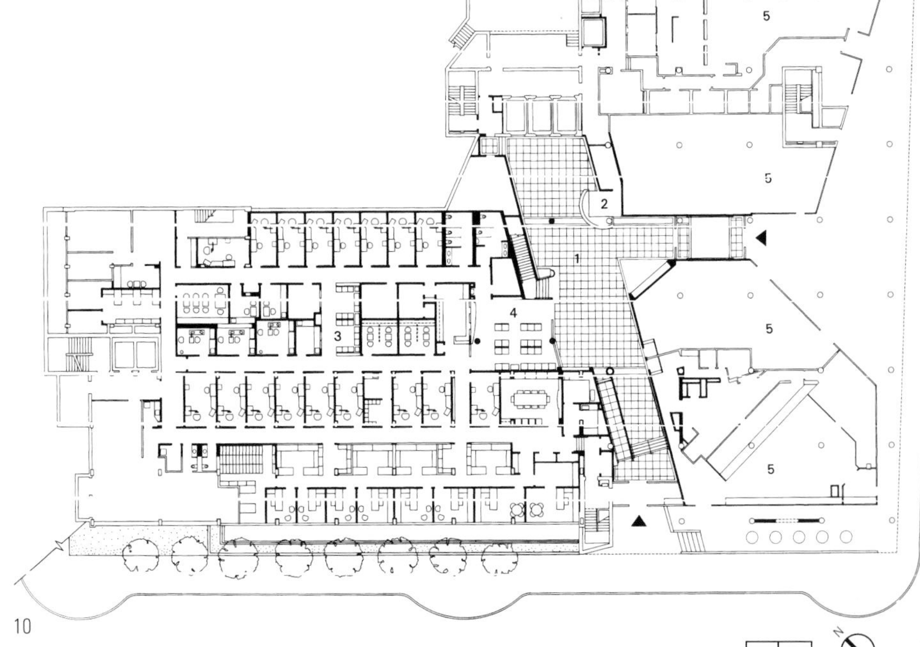

9
10

6 View from southwest
7 Detail
8 Exploded axonometric
9 Section
10 Ground floor plan
11 Main lobby
12 Atrium
13 Cafeteria
14 Laboratory entry and circulation
15 Research laboratory
Photography: Steve Rosenthal

11

12

13

14

15

The Lighthouse Headquarters

Mitchell/Giurgola Architects

Completion: June 1994

Location: New York, New York, USA

Client: The Lighthouse Inc.

Area: 15,793 square metres; 170,000 square feet

Structure: Steel frame

Materials: Buff coloured brick; cast stone spandrels

Awards: 1996 American Institute of Architects Honor Award for Interior Design

1995 Access New York Award

1994 Insight Award, Society of Environmental Graphic Designers

Situated on the same site since 1906, this building had undergone several expansion and modernisation programs, reflecting the institution's evolution. Moving from self-segregated activities for the blind to inclusion in all activities in society, the client's goals were to reflect the changing philosophy in the disabilities community and provide a new headquarters where people who are visually impaired can come to learn to adapt and develop the necessary skills for functioning in the mainstream. The existing 1960s building was gutted to steel framing on 59th Street and the site expanded to include the through-block area to 60th Street.

The design resolution expresses the client's concept of mainstreaming, from the establishment of new street edges, to the creation of an open and light-filled 2-storey public entry which gives the institution a new, vitalised street presence. The introduction of natural light has been maximised through new window openings in the party walls, as well as a continuous ribbon of windows along the front and rear facades. The prominent southeast corner was given a strong expression with floor-to-ceiling windows and double-height spandrels, culminating in a symbolic room on the 15th floor containing a lighted colour spectrum (the visible light which enables us to see) on the ceiling. Seen from the street, this spectrum, as well as glowing buff coloured brick and cream cast stone spandrels, reinforces the concept of the facility as a community beacon in midtown. Public spaces are organised along the busy streetfront on 59th Street. To encourage wider public use and after hours functions, the 3-storey conference centre is located at the base of the building and interconnected by a prominent, central staircase. Offices and administrative areas on the middle floors feature a clear plan organisation with consistency from floor to floor to facilitate movement through the building. The top floors contain executive offices and the boardroom.

Continued

1

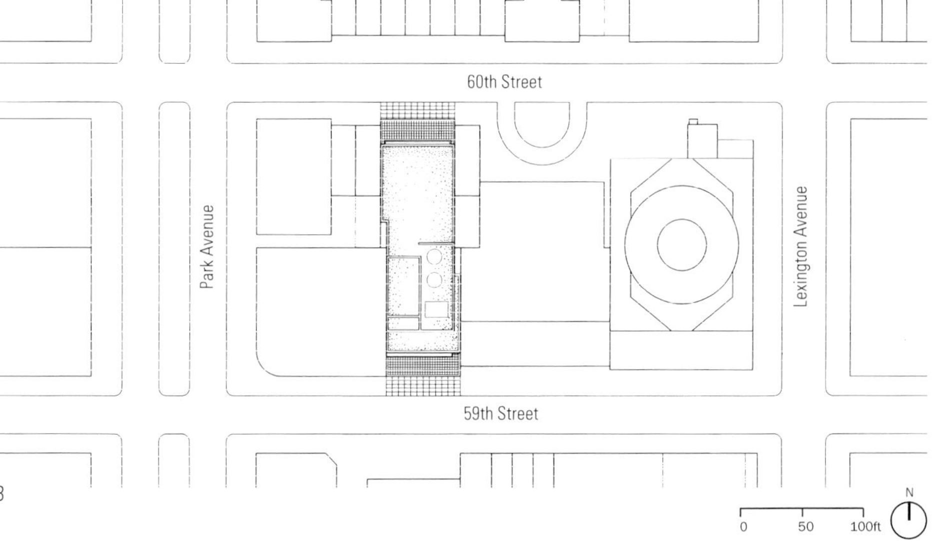

3

2

4

1 Entry detail with ground level retail store and 2-storey cafeteria at the second level with an enclosed children's play terrace on the third level
2 2-storey glass enclosed balcony accents highly visible southeast corner. Spandrel extensions at corner cover frame of reused 1964 tower structure
3 Site plan
4 New 2-storey base fills a former plaza on 59th Street
5 Ground level plan
6 11th floor plan, typical office floor
7 Axonometric of completed facility
8 Curved seating in lobby is wide enough for seeing-eye dogs to tuck under

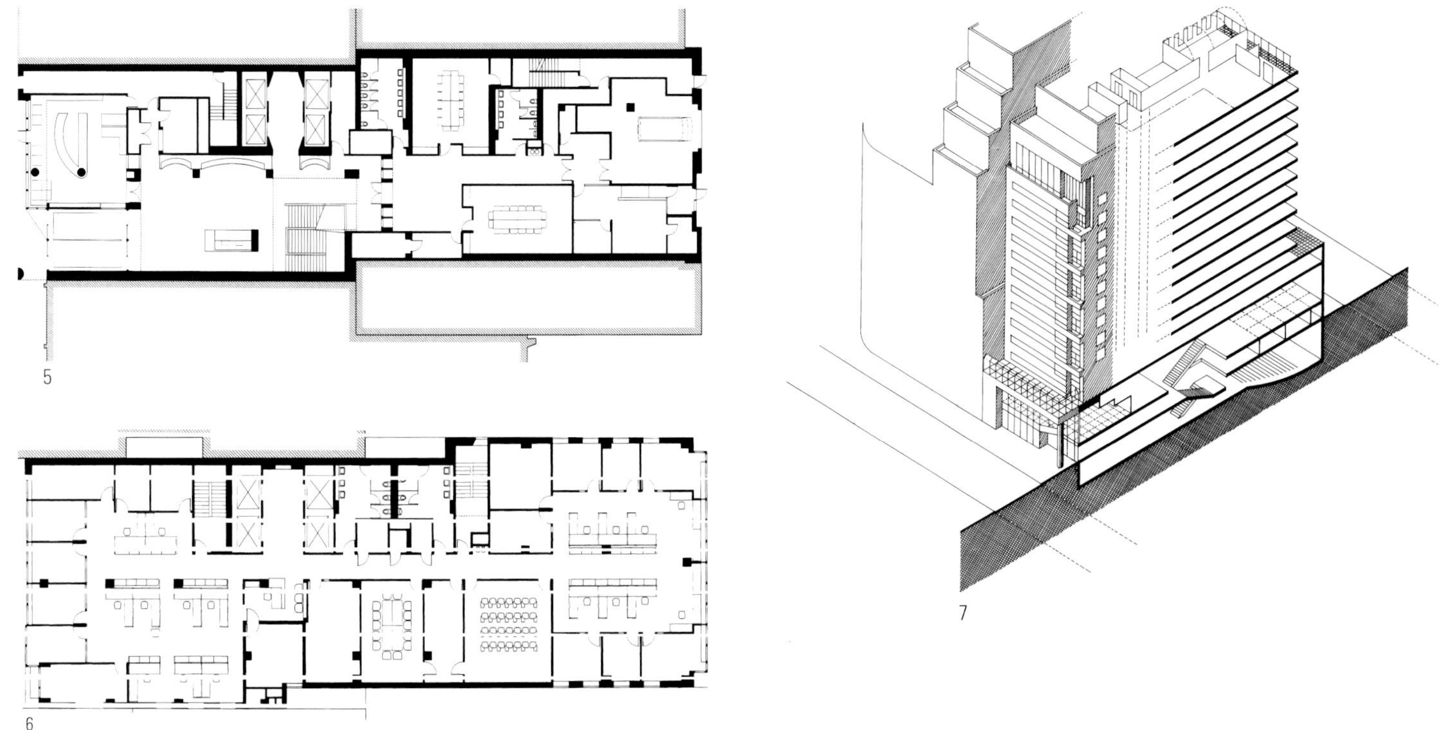

5

6

7

8

Nearly every aspect of the building, from circulation to colour selection, was tested through workshops and focus groups. The design process included the needs of people with vision, hearing and mobility impairments in a systematic manner, using the best knowledge currently available. As a result, this is one of the world's first facilities in which the architecture, engineering, lighting and information components, developed by a co-ordinated design team, create a unique level of accessibility. Reflecting the warmth and vitality of the institution, the design resolution gives equal sensitivity to both aesthetic sensibility and special needs.

9

10

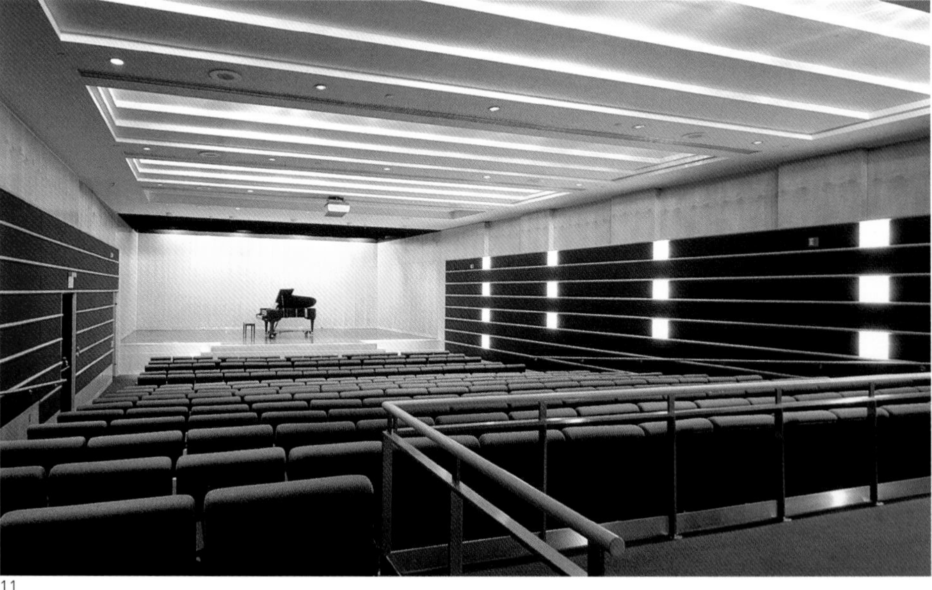

11

9 Window over delivery entrance is detailed with masonry recesses at window frames

10 The artwork throughout the facility has been chosen for its tactile as well as visual qualities. Contrast at the stair treads and risers in all public areas assist in navigation

11 Auditorium has strongly contrasted lighting

12 Light-filled cafeteria is an attractive gathering place for the Lighthouse Community

13 Boardroom features vaulted ceiling

Photography: Jeff Goldberg/Esto

12

13

Mary Washington Hospital

HKS Inc.

Completion: July 1994

Location: Fredericksburg, Virginia, USA

Client: Mary Washington Hospital

Area: 39,947 square metres; 430,000 square feet

Structure: Steel frame; brick

Cost: US$62.25 million

Awards: Citation of Excellence: AIA Architecture for Health Facilities Review

Mary Washington Hospital is a 310-bed replacement regional hospital consisting of 256 medical/surgical beds, 22 LDRP's, 32 special care beds and a full range of ambulatory care diagnostic and treatment and ancillary support services.

The building site is a plateau which overlooks a small canal, wetlands and the city of Fredericksburg, Virginia. All inpatient rooms provide the patients with a panoramic view to the north and east, featuring a dramatic glimpse of the city. And when viewed from a distance, the main hospital presents a sleek, engaging non-institutional profile.

Other components of the hospital were broken down and expressed individually, creating a more 'human' scale. In recognition of the historical area, brick was used to complement and soften the impact of the glass.

Acute care units were separated from the critical care units and have been tightly clustered around nurse work stations, with support services shared between units. These units were clustered around public and service elevators in a shared central core, while separate outpatient elevators transport patients to same day surgery, endoscopy and labour and delivery.

Radiology and emergency, same day surgery, and surgery, and medical records and medical staff services are clustered and share support spaces wherever possible.

Environmental awareness was extremely important in the design and construction of the hospital. The building rests on a hill and covers approximately 70 acres of sloping ground. To preserve the original landscape, minimal earth work was performed during the building's construction. Site development was eased between two bed towers and flows into a landscaped plaza.

Northeast of the site lies protected wetlands. Under the Snowden Wetlands Project this area was preserved and expanded. The facility opens towards this landmark, providing a stunning view to all visiting patients. The hospital's orientation acknowledges the importance of enhancing and respecting the nation's natural resources.

Continued

1

1 Courtyard
2 Site plan
3 Overall exterior
4 Exterior view from courtyard

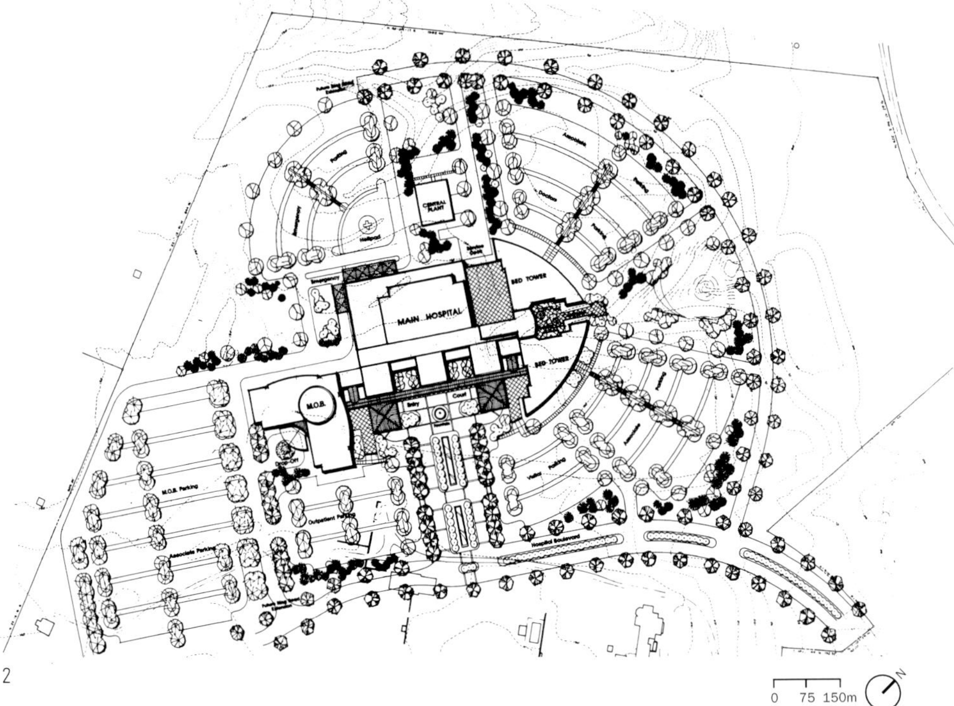

2

3

4

The hospital's internal, horizontal and vertical flexibility will allow the facility to grow, with few problems in any transitional state. The ancillary block is based on a nine metre (30 foot) structural module and is both horizontally and vertically expandable. Those departments most likely to expand are located on the exterior to facilitate immediate, smooth growth.

The hospital is organised along a public concourse. Departments are attached for easy expansion or relocation. The concourse terminates at the patient tower which is also vertically expandable.

As inpatients become more critical the patient rooms are designed to easily convert to a higher intensity of care. Full capability rooms with built-in features for conversion to critical care were provided.

This project recognises that careful selection of interior architectural features can reduce stress and thus enhance healing. Measures to provide a familiar and less stressful environment include custom woodworking and window treatments; artwork and shelves relocated in the patient's line of vision, for cards and flowers foster nurturing. Patient activity rooms and a television and video recorder in each room enhance education and entertainment.

A strong ambulatory care emphasis was incorporated into the overall project. An integrated physician office building was designed for high efficiency and direct access.

5

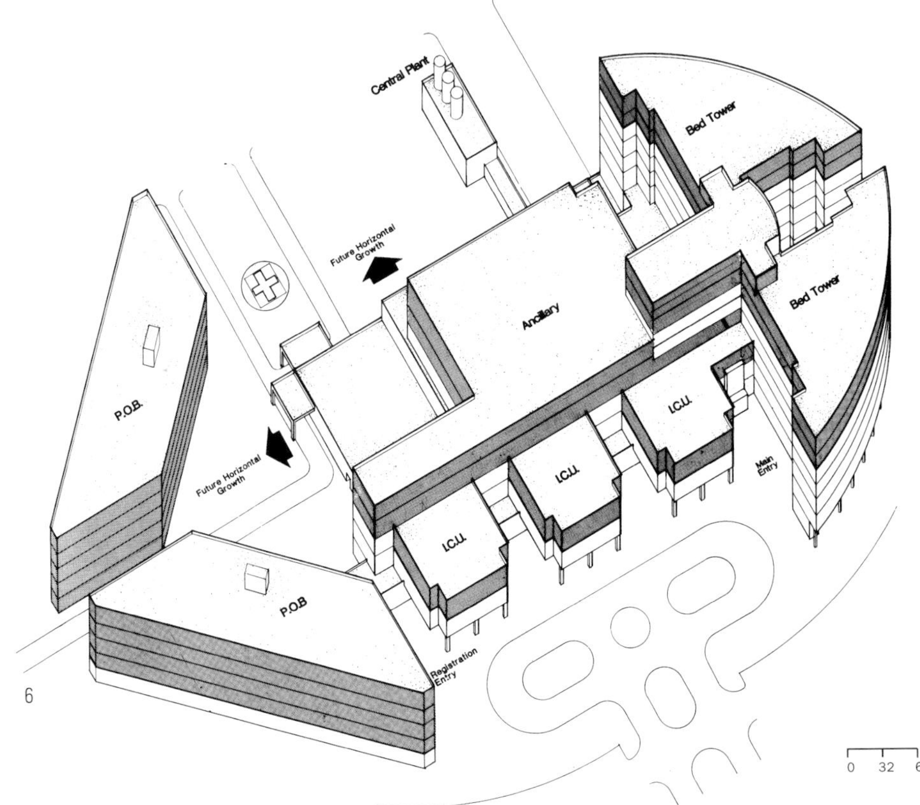

6

5 Facade detail
6 Axonometric
7 Lower level floor plan
8 Typical patient unit
9 First floor plan

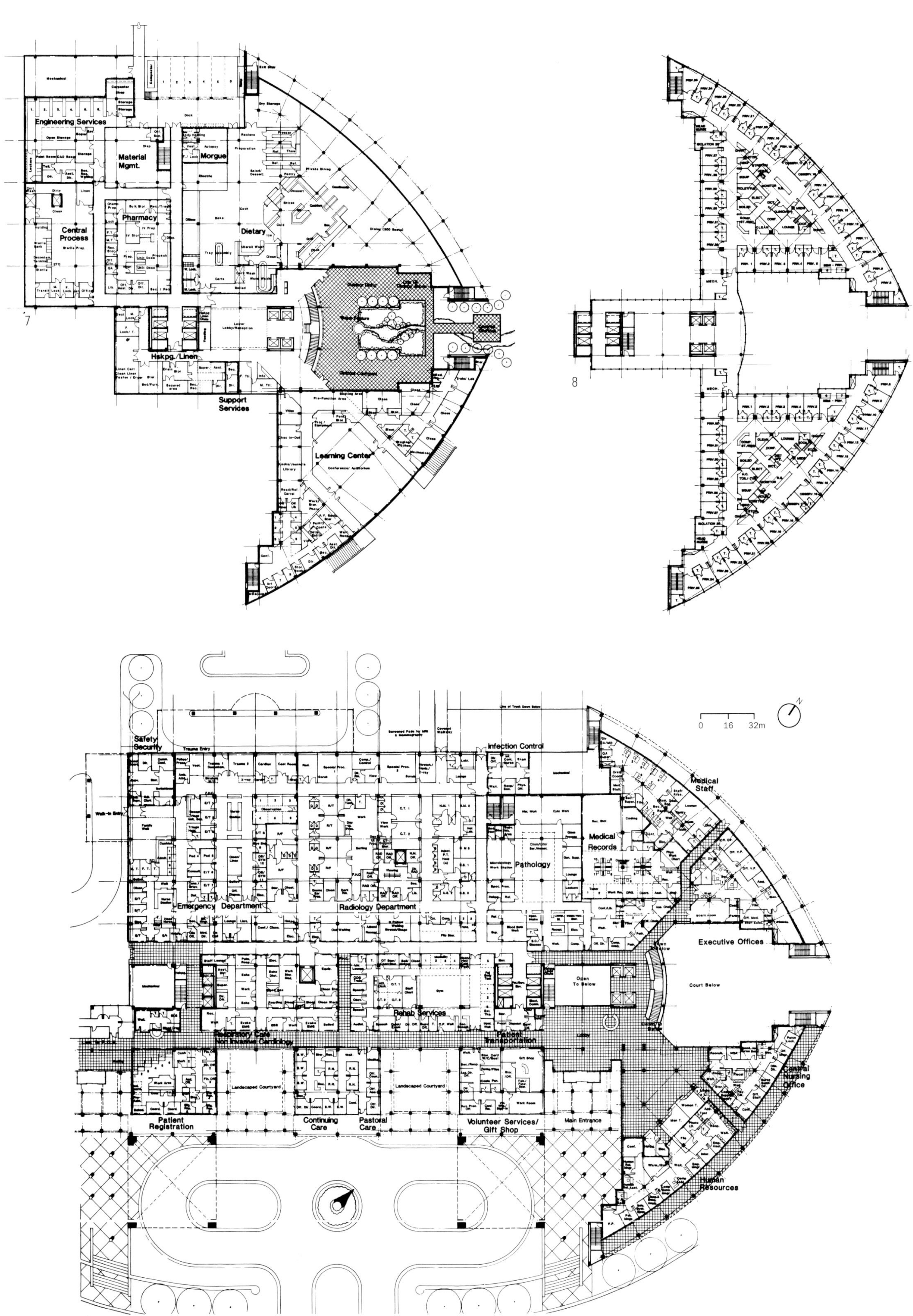
7
Engineering Services
Material Mgmt.
Morgue
Central Process
Pharmacy
Dietary
Hskpg./Linen
Support Services
Learning Center
8
Safety Security
Infection Control
Medical Staff
Medical Records
Pathology
Emergency Department
Radiology Department
Executive Offices
Court Below
Rehab Services
Respiratory Care Non Invasive Cardiology
Patient Transportation
Landscaped Courtyard
Landscaped Courtyard
Central Nursing Office
Patient Registration
Continuing Care
Pastoral Care
Volunteer Services/ Gift Shop
Main Entrance
Human Resources
0
16
32m
9

10 Lobby atrium
11 Grand stair
12 Reception/information desk
Photography: Rick Granbaum

10

11

12

The National Children's Center

Cooper•Lecky Architects, PC

Completion: July 1995

Location: Anacostia, Washington, D.C., USA

Client: The National Children's Center

Area: 5,200 square metres; 56,000 square feet

Structure: Precast concrete; masonry; steel columns; glulam beams

Materials: Brick; concrete blocks; pre-fabricated ribbed metal

Cost: US$7 million

The National Children's Center is a privately owned, non-profit facility offering programs to the severely disabled, mentally retarded, and emotionally disturbed. The 5,200 square metre (56,000 square foot) building offers three different programs—early intervention for the very young up to age two; pre-school for children from three to six; and, an adult program for those over 18.

Building on Cooper•Lecky's 25-year history of designing environments for children, the design objectives were simple: de-institutionalise the look and feel of the building; keep the scale down—for many of these children, this will be their first exposure to the world away from home; provide a colourful, varied and exciting environment that will encourage curiosity and mental exploration; try to promote as much residential recall as possible; simplify personal orientation—make it obvious and clear how one is supposed to find his or her way around the building; and, provide an environment that is barrier free and sensitive to potential accidents from falling, seizures, or play, yet still offering a sense of challenge and exploration.

The development of the architectural form for the Center was largely driven by the site. The client had acquired a narrow, finger shaped peninsula of land surrounded by major arterial roadways. The topography from one side of the finger to the other sloped as much as 4.5 metres (15 feet) in some locations. Because of accessibility requirements, all the major functions were kept on one floor. This seemed to suggest a very linear floor plan with a lengthy corridor connection between the various functions. Rather than distort or disguise the inevitable, it was elected to embrace it—even celebrate it. The solution became a sunlit interior street extending some 158.5 metres (520 feet) from one end of the site to the other. The 'street' serves as the main corridor circulation path that opens along the way to 'interior plazas'. These, in turn, are surrounded by village clusters of residentially scaled blocks that form the classrooms.

1 The building adopts the residential character of the houses across the street and uses this imagery to create a non-institutional look and feel
2 A welcoming main entrance canopy serves as a covered bus drop off
3 The long, wide corridor shown in the plan serves as a strong organiser of interior spaces
4 A welcoming reception area introduces the visitor to the light filled, airy and commodious interior spaces of the Center
5 The building is designed like a toy construction kit resulting in instructive and playful spaces
6 Architectural play sculptures designed by the architect become transitional scale elements in the interior courtyards to relate to the children
7 Personal orientation is made simple and clear by spaces viewing into each other

Photography: Ron Blunt
Drawings: James P. Clark, AIA

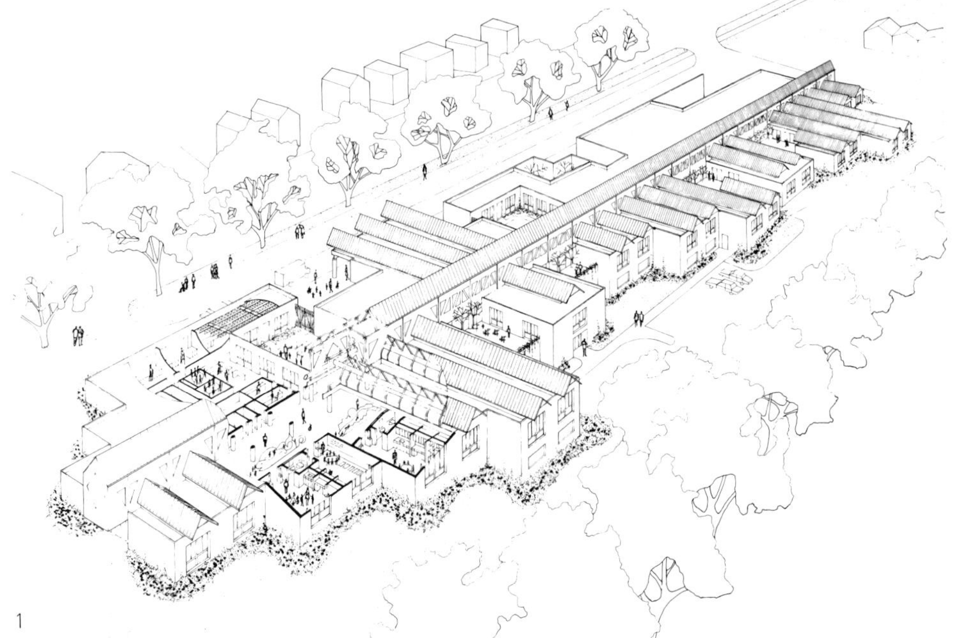

1

2

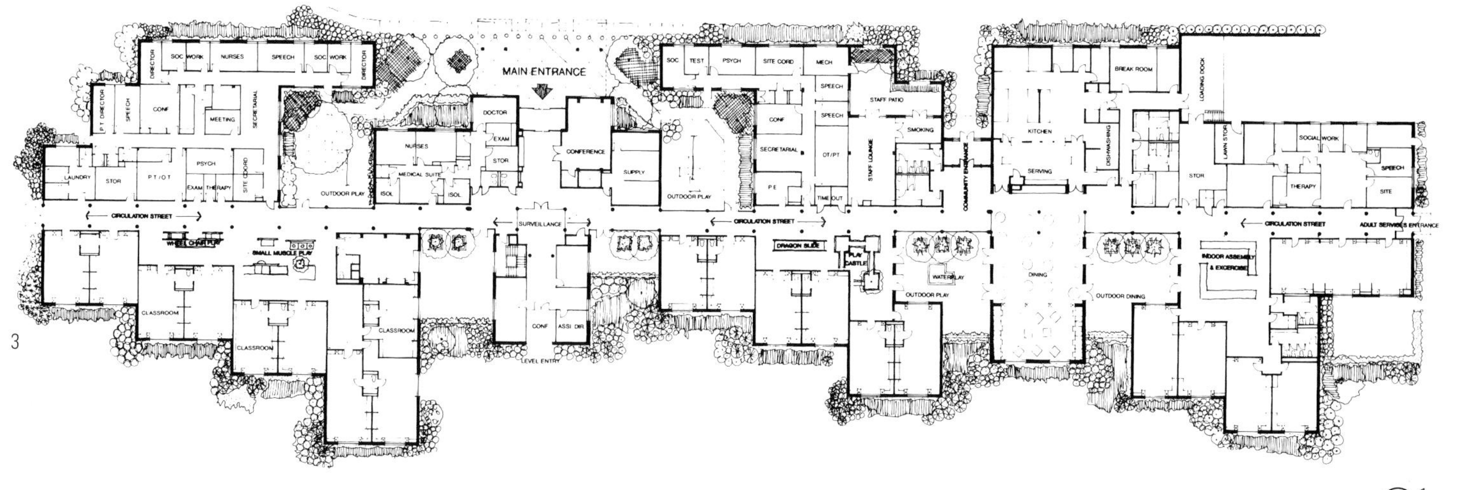
MAIN ENTRANCE
CIRCULATION STREET
CIRCULATION STREET
CIRCULATION STREET
CIRCULATION STREET
ADULT SERVICES ENTRANCE
COMMUNITY ENTRANCE
LOADING DOCK
LEVEL ENTRY
SOC WORK
NURSES
SPEECH
DIRECTOR
CONF
MEETING
SECRETARIAL
LAUNDRY
STOR
PT/OT
PSYCH
EXAM
THERAPY
OUTDOOR PLAY
NURSES
MEDICAL SUITE
ISOL
DOCTOR
EXAM
CONFERENCE
SUPPLY
SURVEILLANCE
SOC
TEST
PSYCH
SITE COORD
MECH
STAFF PATIO
SECRETARIAL
OT/PT
SMOKING
STAFF LOUNGE
TIME OUT
KITCHEN
SERVING
DISHWASHING
BREAK ROOM
SOCIAL WORK
THERAPY
SITE
SMALL MUSCLE PLAY
CLASSROOM
CLASSROOM
CLASSROOM
CONF
DRAGON SLIDE
PLAY CASTLE
WATER PLAY
DINING
OUTDOOR DINING
INDOOR ASSEMBLY & EXERCISE
0 20 40ft
3

4

5

6

7

Ohio Aerospace Institute

Richard Fleischman Architects, Inc.

Completion: January 1994

Location: Brook Park, Ohio, USA

Client: State of Ohio

Area: 6,560 square metres; 71,000 square feet

Materials: Glass

Cost: US$7,225,746

Awards: 1994 Citation Award; American Association of School Administrators, American Institute of Architects and The Council of Educational Facility Planners, Int.

1994 Global Recognition - MDO Monte Carlo, Monaco; Outstanding Educational Facility

1994 Honorable Mention Award; Public/ Institutional; IBD-CID

1994 Citation Award; American School & Universities

1994 Honor Award; American Institute of Architects, Cleveland Chapter

1994 Merit Award; American Institute of Architects

The Ohio Aerospace Institute is made up of nine universities, private corporations and two federal laboratories who together built an Aerospace Research and Education Center. This consortium identified a parcel of land that was part of the NASA Lewis Research Center. The State of Ohio provided US$10 million for the total development of the complex.

The Institute created an atmosphere which is stimulating to resident and visiting scholars and makes unplanned contact easy, and, indeed, unavoidable. To this end, single or double offices are interspersed with open office workstations. Common areas are located at key points of circulation so that chance encounters can be turned into productive conversations around tables or in lounge furniture.

This dual nature of the Institute is reflected in its design. The public side is entered through a 3-storey atrium, serving as the entry point for the two building functions. A lecture hall, equipped for many forms of electronic communications, opens off the atrium. The second floor houses classrooms, seminar rooms and a multi-purpose room. The administrative staff are on the third floor.

Both in its interior spaces and as an object in the landscape, the building's design is intended to reflect the excitement of the aerospace enterprise. Because of its proximity to the Cleveland Hopkins Airport, its appearance from the air is considered important. While a literal reference to spacecraft is not appropriate, the forms convey an image consistent with the building's use.

Modern technology is utilised to maximise energy efficiency and acoustical quality in the building. The specially coated window assemblies are filled with argon gas and lined with tailor-made gaskets for optimum insulation.

Three different types of glass make up the curtain wall; reflective glass for areas that house closed offices, classrooms, administrative offices, the auditorium and the skylight; tinted glass for the front of the building where the entrance and 3-storey atrium are located; and, tinted glass with a low-emissivity coating for scholar work areas.

Although the scholar portion of the facility is not open to the public, it is visually accessible. This has been accomplished by offsetting each of the three floor levels. The two upper floors, mezzanine and balcony, step back in plan, so that they overlook the floor. The entire space, including the atrium, is enclosed by a softly curved roof.

This multi-level educational and research facility is essentially one larger volume. It allows for scholars to interact as they pursue collaborative projects. Since all the student population continues to be enrolled at their specific universities, time constraints are critical.

1

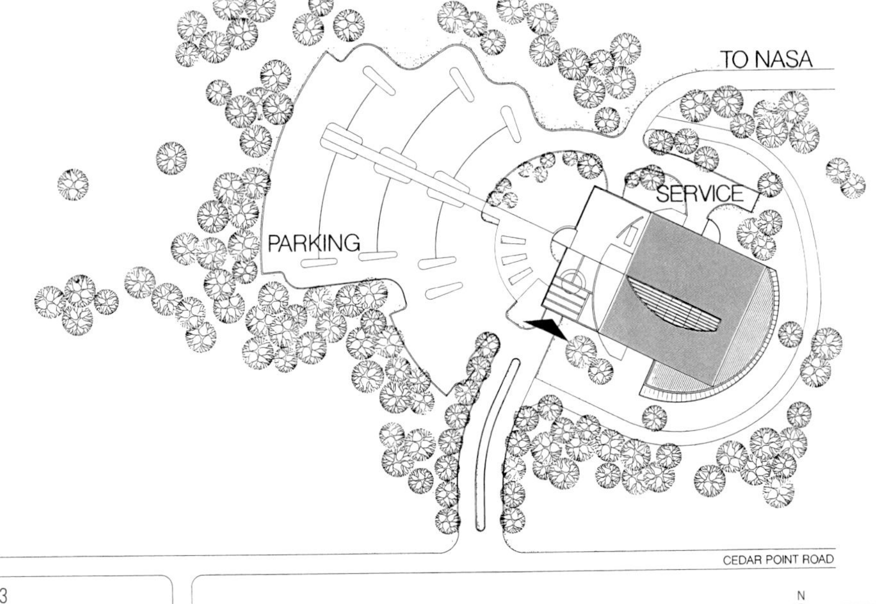

3

2

4

1 Library
2 View of front at night
3 Site plan
4 Front of Ohio Aerospace Institute
5 Section
6 Entrance atrium
7 First floor
8 Conference space
9 Third floor

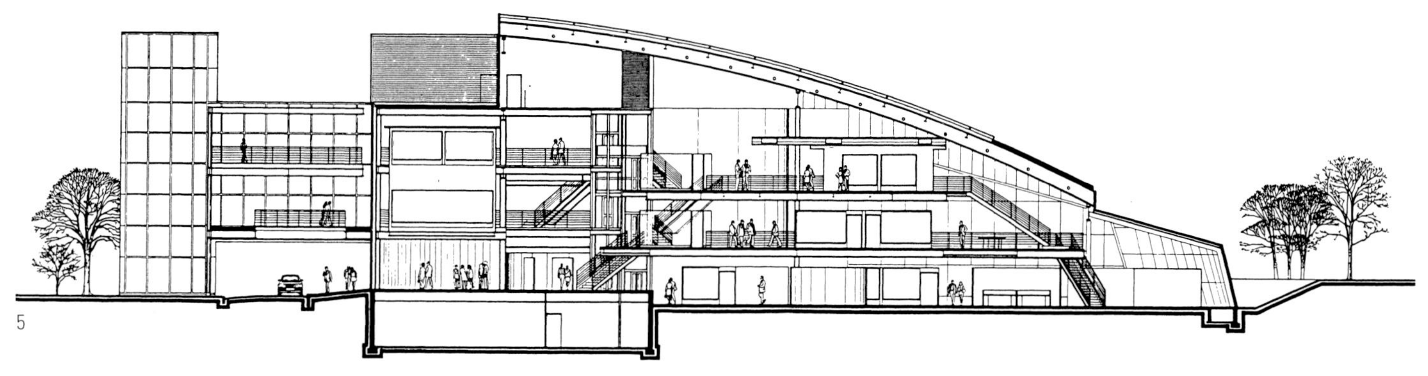
5

6

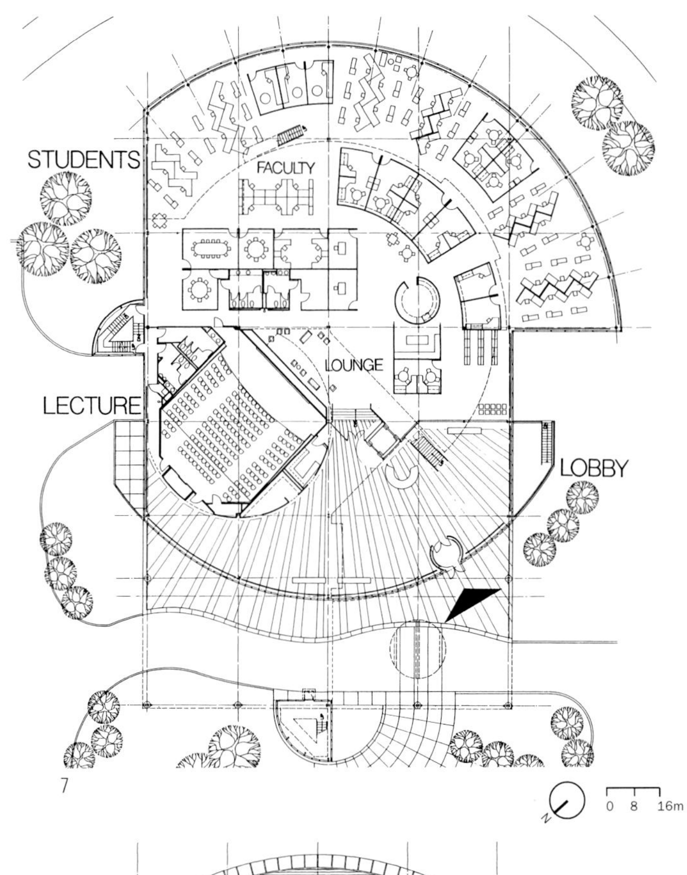
STUDENTS
FACULTY
LOUNGE
LECTURE
LOBBY
0 8 16m
7

8

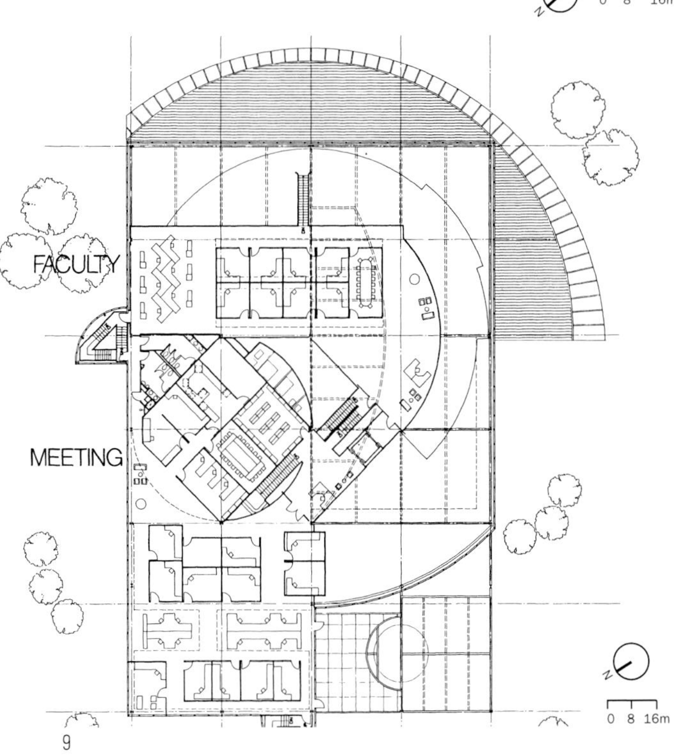
FACULTY
MEETING
0 8 16m
9

Ronald McDonald House

Andrews, Scott, Cotton Architects Ltd

Completion: November 1994

Location: Auckland, New Zealand

Client: Ronald McDonald House Trust

Area: 1,355 square metres; 14,585 square feet

Structure: Precast concrete; steel frame; timber infill

Materials: Solid plaster walls; membrane and metal roofs; glass infill panels

Cost: NZ$2.1 million

Awards: 1995 New Zealand Institute of Architects Regional Award

A 'home away from home' for families of children with life threatening conditions receiving treatment at Auckland Hospital. An accommodation 'house' that was to appear non-institutional, and positively assist in the support of families in crisis.

1

2

3

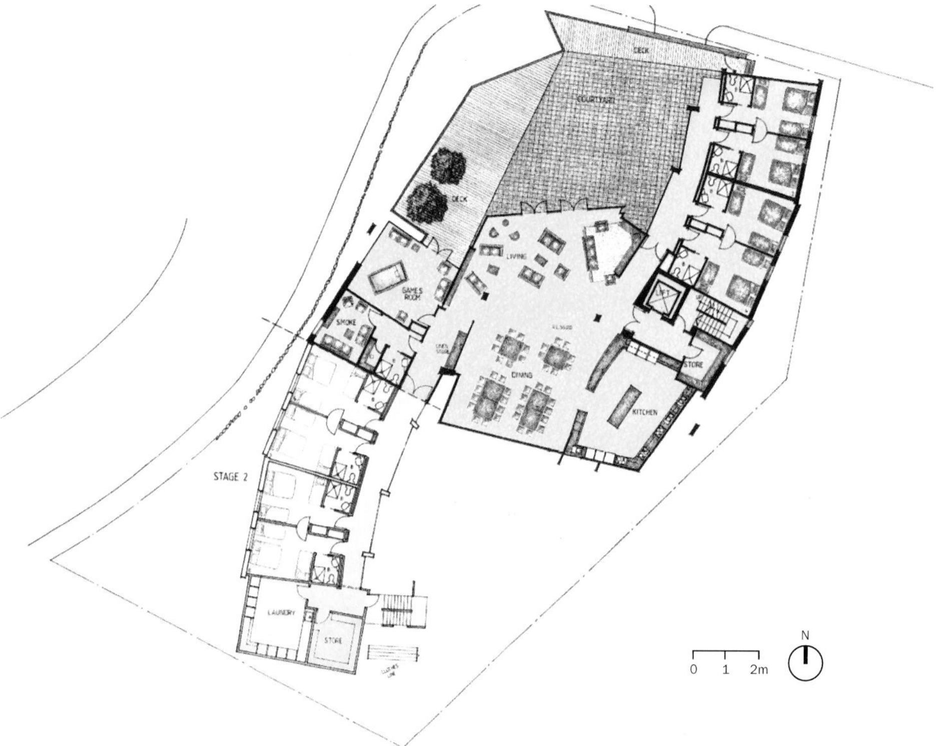

0 1 2m N

4

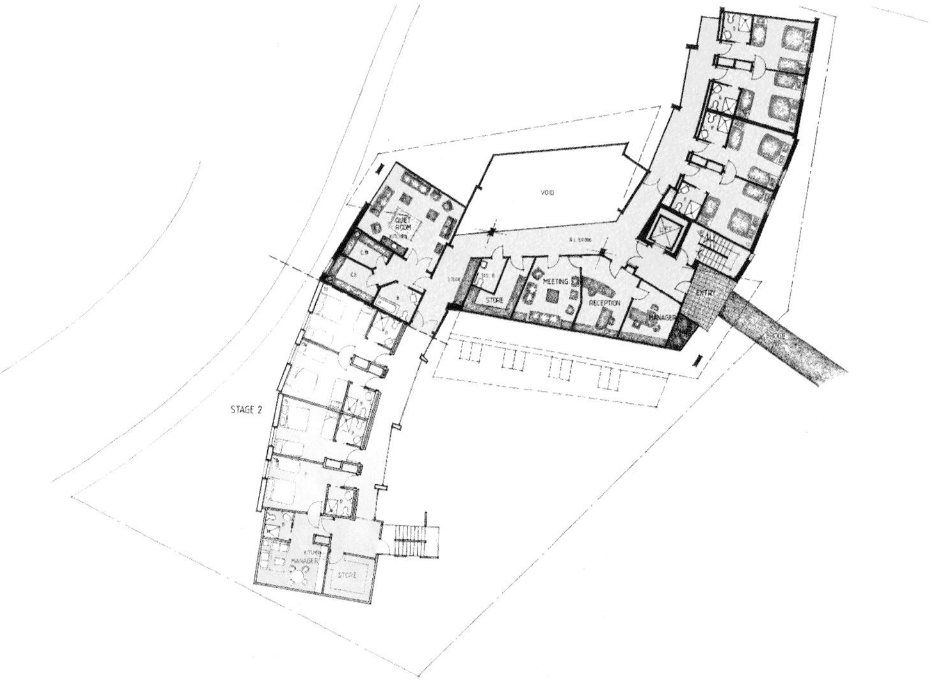

5

6

7

1 View of west elevation
2 Courtyard
3 Dining room
4 Lower ground floor plan
5 Upper ground floor plan
6 North elevation
7 West elevation
8 Bridge entry
Photography: John Pettitt

8

The Visby General Hospital

ETV Arkitektkontor AB

Completion: April 1995

Location: Visby, Gotland, Sweden

Client: The Gotland Local Authority

Area: 29,000 square metres; 312,164 square feet

Structure: In situ concrete

Materials: Brick; steel cladding; sheet metal roofing

Cost: 475 million SEK

Responsible in the office: Gösta Eliasson, Paul Gilbert and Ahmed Radwan, interior design: Walter Weis

The hospital is located just outside the medieval city wall of Visby and facing the Baltic Sea on the island of Gotland on a site sloping west towards the sea. The hospital offers full medical services for the entire island of Gotland. The client's brief called for a complete modernisation of the hospital which was no longer up to date. The existing hospital, originally built in 1903, has been continuously expanded over the years. This latest renewal has given the hospital a new and clear layout, removing many of the confusing mass of buildings from earlier additions but incorporating the original building. A new main corridor forming a north–south axis on all levels overlooking the sea and park connects the different buildings. Walking along the corridor on the entrance level, visitors meet various activities, such as a restaurant and cafe, pharmacy, auditorium and library.

The hospital's supply and service areas have been placed furthest south. New wards and treatment wings have been built north of the existing hospital. The north end of the site has been left free for future expansion.

A new round nursing unit facing the sea, where all patients have their own rooms, has proven to be very space saving since there is very little corridor space. The number of beds has been reduced since single patient rooms give total flexibility. It is even possible for visitors to stay overnight in the patient rooms. The new radiology department is fully digital.

The existing hospital functioned normally during the construction, additions and renovations.

1

2

3

4

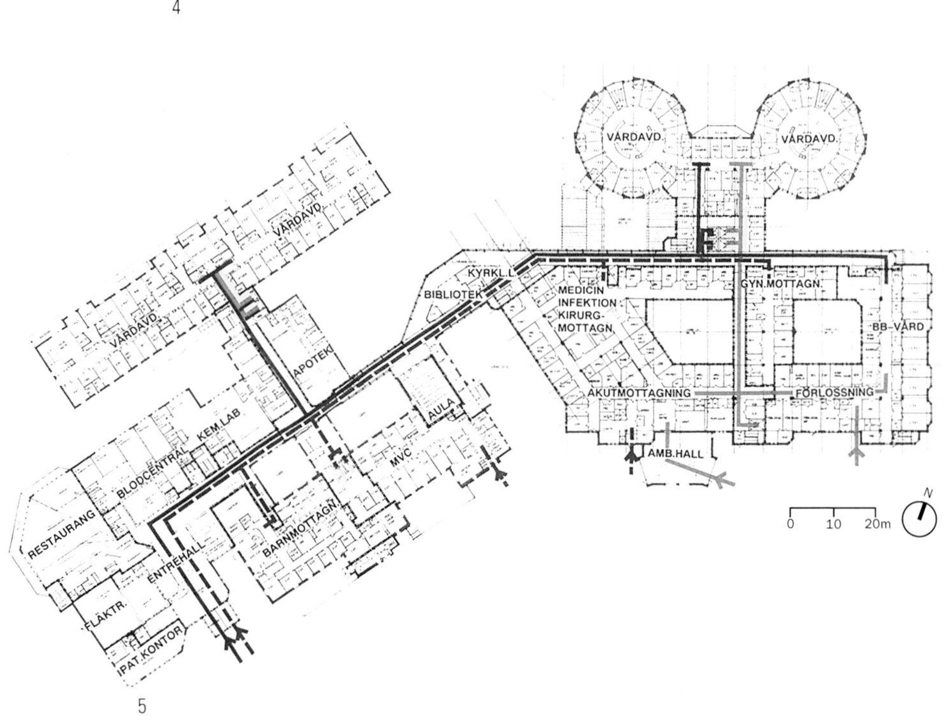

5

1 View of the ward buildings
2 Exterior view of the restaurant
3 View of the main entrance
4 Axonometric perspective of the hospital
5 Ground floor plan, main entrance level
6 Interior of the entrance hall
7 Waiting room
8 Entry doors, detail
9 The round ward with centrally located nurses' station
10 Main corridor and library looking south
11 Main corridor looking south

6

7

8

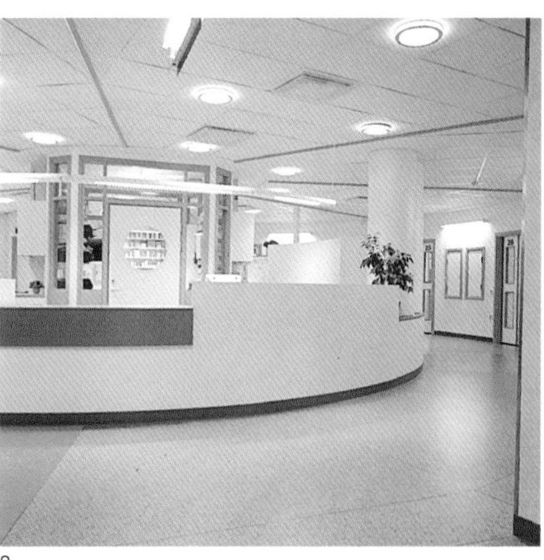
9

10

11

WestHealth

Ellerbe Becket, Inc.

Completion: September 1994
Location: Minneapolis, Minnesota, USA
Client: WestHealth
Area: 10,219 square metres; 110,000 square feet
Cost: US$12.5 million

Ellerbe Becket provided interior design and medical planning services for WestHealth, a community-based health care partnership of Abbott Northwestern Hospital and North Memorial Medical Center. The new facility represents the first phase of the partnership's lifetime of wellness campus; providing ambulatory care services that include wellness screening, preventive care, urgent care, medical offices, same-day surgery and community health education.

Ellerbe Becket's innovative design for this non-institutional, friendly environment reinforces efficient communication and circulation by organising diagnostic and treatment spaces along a central spine. This strong circulation concept for the 6-storey building creates an easily recognisable main thoroughfare from which all clinical departments are accessed, lessening the amount of signage needed for visitor orientation. Each entry way is a distinctive landmark, distinguished by changes in materials, lighting, plants and windows. A centrally located town square acts as a focal point for orientation, with shared services and information.

Throughout public areas the design features details such as stone paving, wood panelling, trees, etched glass, potted plants, and benches, all reinforcing the community environment. The focus on wellness, healing and a sense of community has been picked up by local artists whose work has been incorporated into the overall design.

1

2

3

4

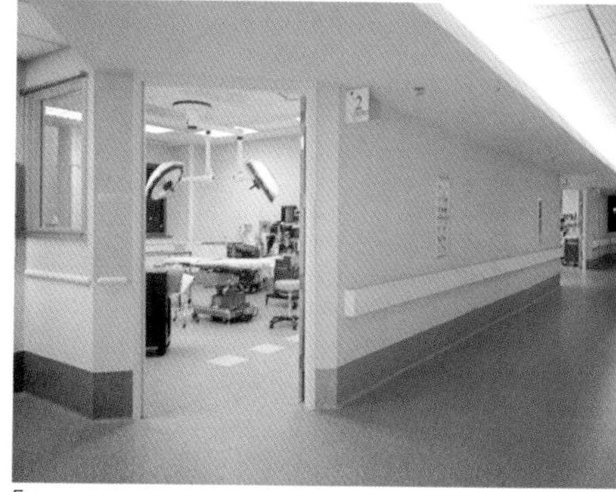
5

6

7

8

9

10

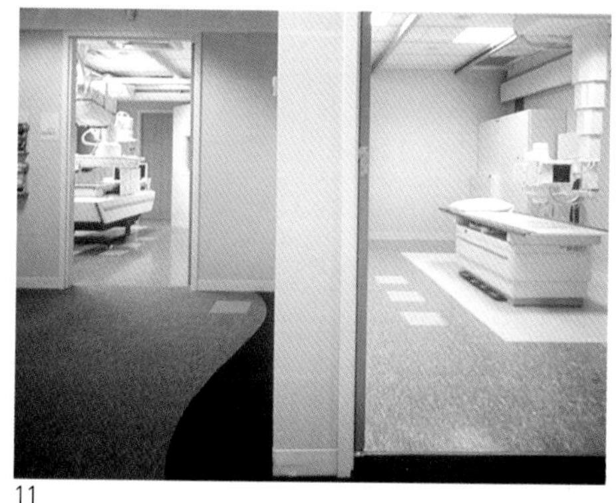
11

12

13

14

15

1 Department entry detail
2 Exam corridor
3 View of lobby/atrium from surgery waiting
4 Main lobby/atrium
5 Same day surgery
6 Main lobby/atrium
7 Patient registration wing
8 Education centre
9 Patient registration waiting
10 Public elevator lobby
11 Radiology exam rooms
12 Patient registration desk
13 Same day surgery patient care suites (pre- and post-operation)
14 Same day surgery waiting
15 Concierge desk

Photography: Koyama Photographic

Yuma Regional Medical Center

HKS Inc.

Completion: May 1994
Location: Yuma, Arizona, USA
Client: Yuma Regional Medical Center
Area: 7,432 square metres; 63,500 square feet
Cost: US$11.1 million
Awards: Modern Healthcare Design Competition

1

The 5,900 square metre (63,500 square foot) addition and 1,533 square metre (16,500 square foot) renovation provides expanded maternal and child care needs for the Yuma Regional Medical Center.

The project centralised obstetrical services with inpatient and outpatient (off-site) gynaecological services including a surgical suite designated for OB/GYN needs. These facilities consisted of: an LDRP-based obstetrical service of 24 rooms; an antepartum service of seven private rooms; an outpatient labour evaluation and antenatal testing area; a five bassinette normal newborn nursery (integrated with neonatal intensive care bassinettes) and a surgical/ C-Section suite capable of accommodating four rooms plus outpatient prep/recovery areas. All of these OB/GYN services were centralised on the first floor with reception and admitting services dedicated to this building. OB/GYN clinics were located in remodelled space vacated by the former postpartum and nursery areas to be accessible from the new lobby/reception area.

A state-of-the-art paediatric inpatient service was created on the second floor consisting of 20 initial private rooms with capability to expand to 24 total. Isolation capability and provision for intermediate care of multiple patient with high acuity in one room was included in the design. To accommodate surges in inpatient paediatric service during the winter months, some rooms were designed with capability to become semi-private rooms as needed. Overnight rooming-in of parents was provided in the paediatric unit, and a private room for similar use was provided in the neonatal ICU of ten bassinettes. Expansion of a special outpatient clinic for chid rehabilitation was faced within the outpatient zone of the project in remodelled old labour/delivery space.

A key challenge in the design was the development of a configuration which provided close proximity of all 24 LDRP rooms to the surgical suite and the nurseries. The form of the footprint was driven by this design criterion. Other challenges included: programming and design of the project; careful phasing of site development and internal operations was necessary to maintain existing OB/ GYN services throughout construction which occurred adjacent to the existing labour/delivery, postpartum and nursery areas; material and administrative management integration between the existing medical centre departments and the newly created was a particular challenge which affected programming, site location, internal patient and material flow and facility design; and, site topography and existing utilities required finessing the impact of the best functional footprint of the building with numerous external constraints.

Of particular interest on this project was the fact that the transition from a traditional labour/delivery/postpartum service to an LDRP service was facilitated by the design in a special way. Rather than implement the LDRP service overnight when the staff moved into the new building, the clustering of six LDRP's and the seven antepartum private rooms around a nurse station adjacent the surgical suite allowed a continuation of the traditional labour/delivery/ postpartum concept for the first six months of occupancy. This unique capability minimised the 'shock' to staff and physicians moving into a new building and allowed a more gradual transition period into the LDRP concept over time.

2

3

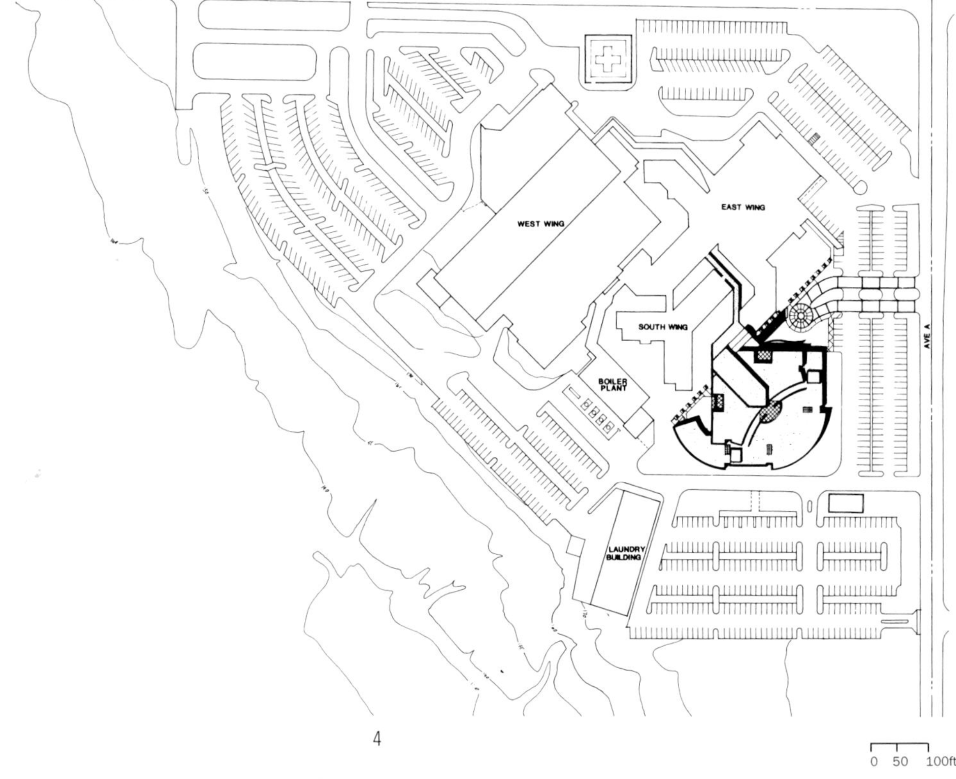

4

1 Facade detail
2 Lobby/information desk
3 Facade detail
4 Site plan
5 Level 1
6 Level 2
7 Overall exterior
Photography: Wes Thompson

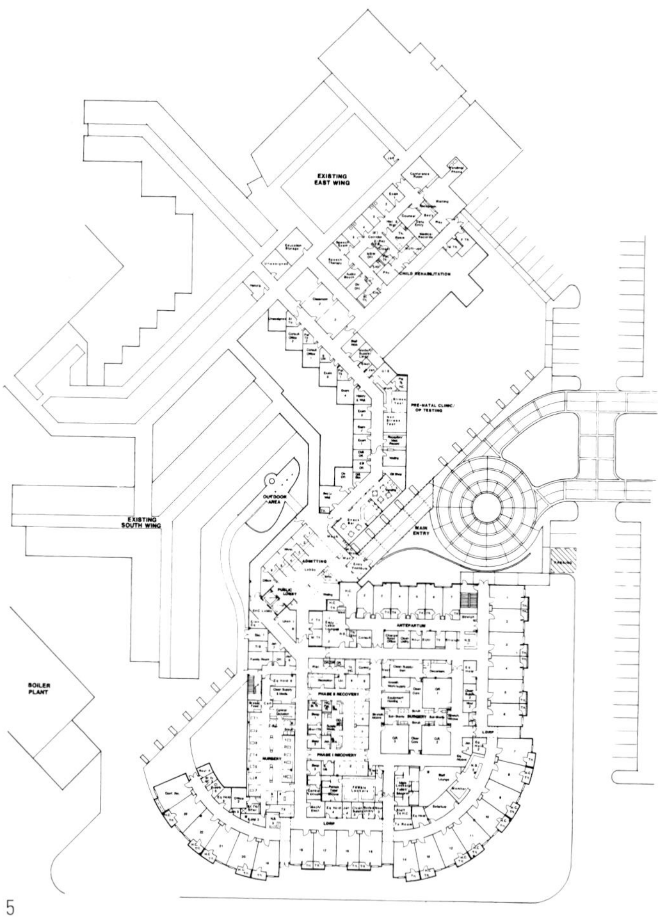
EXISTING EAST WING
EXISTING SOUTH WING
BOILER PLANT
OUTDOOR AREA
MAIN ENTRY
CHILD REHABILITATION
PRE-NATAL CLINIC/ OP TESTING

5

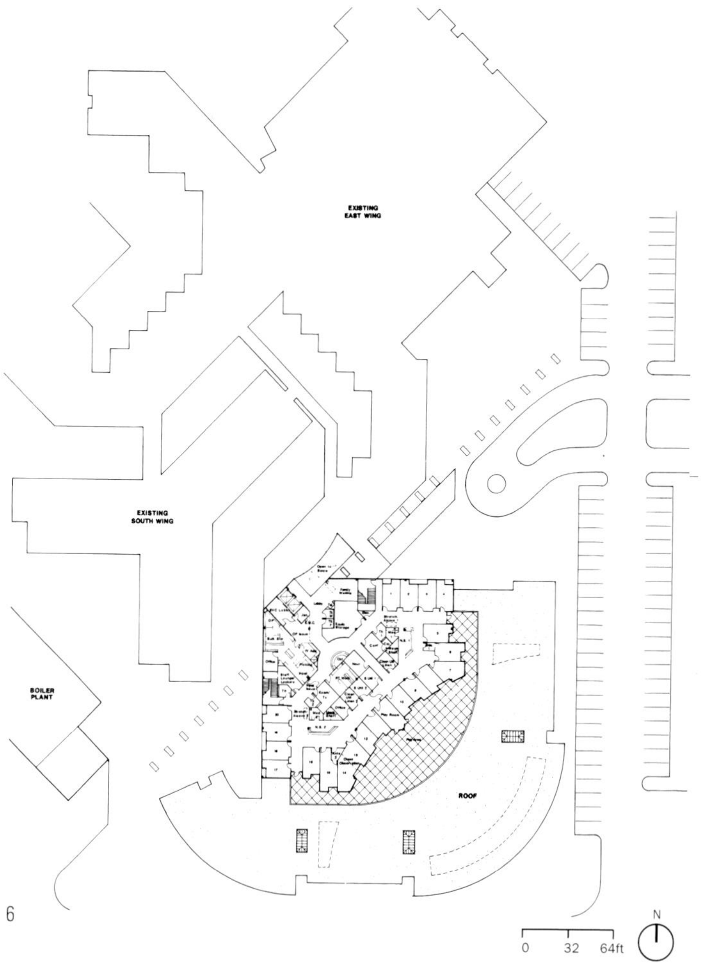
EXISTING EAST WING
EXISTING SOUTH WING
BOILER PLANT
ROOF
0 32 64ft
N

6

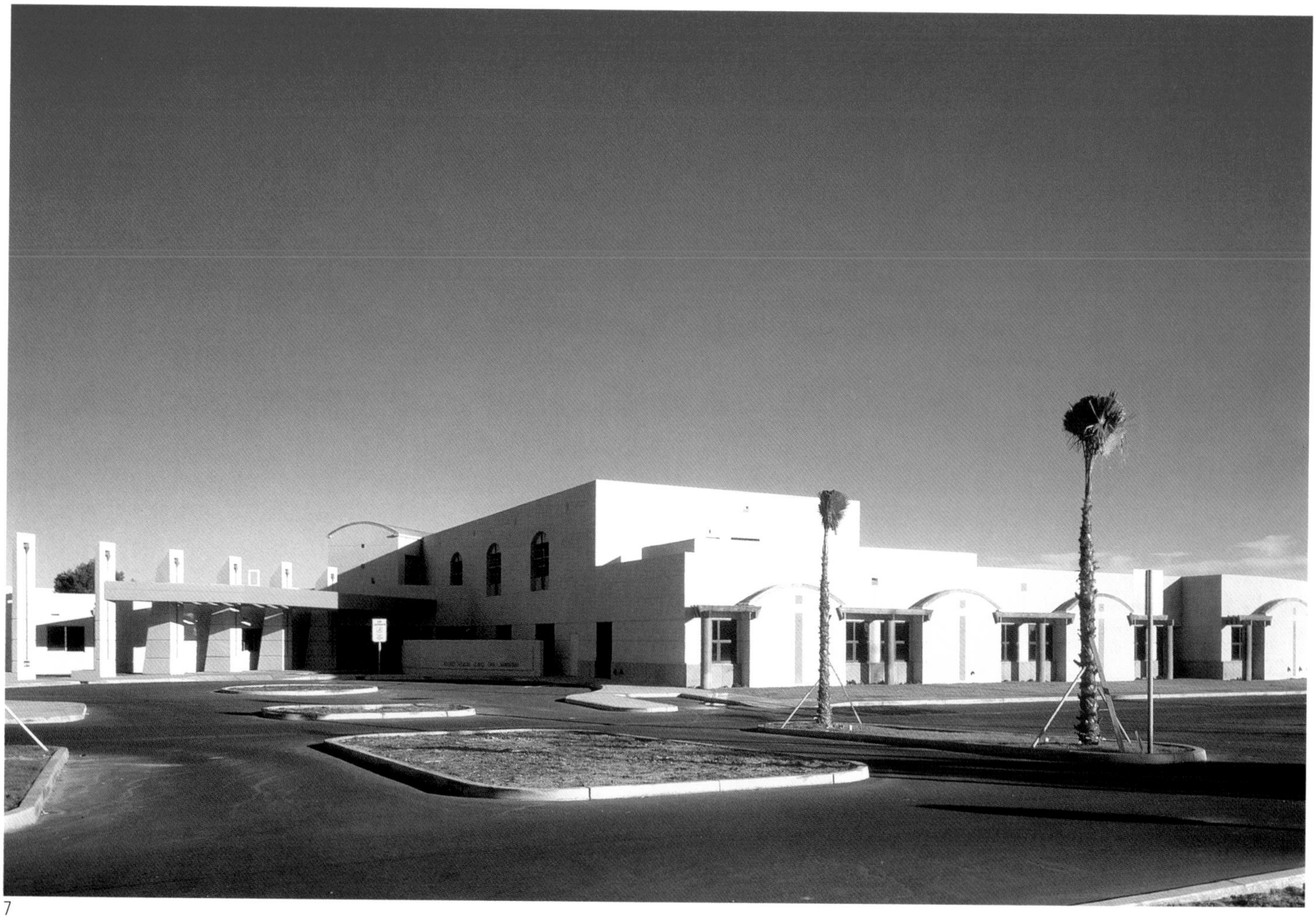

7

Permanent Stage for the Botanic Gardens Symphony Lake

DP Architects Pte Ltd

Completion: July 1995
Location: Botanic Gardens, Singapore
Client: Singapore Symphony Co Ltd
Area: 200 square metres; 2,153 square feet
Structure: Steel cable suspended metal structure
Materials: Steel; wood-acoustic panels
Cost: S$1.5 million

The brief called for a sheltered structure to be built permanently for both symphony and other stage performances in the Botanic Gardens. Located at the lake next to the Orchid Terrace and Palm Valley it is part of the master plan to enhance the facilities for the Botanic Gardens redevelopment.

The design is acoustically adjusted for outdoor stage performances. The metal roof is suspended on steel cables to simulate a natural leaf form, floating on the landscaped lake.

1

2

3

4

5

6

1 Detail of stair to the second level
2 The stage in relation to Palm Valley
3 Front elevation
4 Side elevation
5 The inaugural concert in progress
6 Detail of roof structure
Photography: Chan Hui Min

Brisbane Airport International Terminal

Bligh Voller Architects

Completion: September 1995
Location: Brisbane, Queensland, Australia
Client: Federal Airport Corporation
Area: 65,000 square metres; 699,677 square feet
Structure: Steel frame; concrete floor slab
Materials: Glass; aluminium; vitrified tiles
Cost: A$250 million

Bligh Voller were requested as part of a design and construct venture with Civil and Civic, to develop the architectural and interior design brief for the new International Airport Terminal.

The brief entailed sizing of the terminal to suit projected passenger numbers, developing plans to suit clear passenger flows, a strong emphasis on retail design—both landside and airside—and a suitable gateway building for southeast Queensland.

Brisbane's new international terminal is currently designed to serve 1,200 passengers per hour with eight gates and three stand-off positions.

However, this can be readily expanded to increase gate capacity. The terminal has been designed to suit incremental growth to approximately 24 aircraft parking positions and a tripling in size of the initial terminal. The terminal building is also being designed to suit various passenger streaming arrangements including domestic, pre-cleared and uncleared international passenger categories.

The building is designed to be flexible to cater for changes in passenger processing and technical changes due to changes in types of aircraft and future changes in the baggage handling system. There is considerable emphasis in the design of the terminal complex on the retail aspects, to encourage passengers and their friends to remain longer in the terminal and, as a consequence, increase revenues for the client.

The terminal includes landside retail facilities with observation over the departure lounge and through to aircraft on the apron, to heighten the awareness of aircraft activity to the landside occupants of the building. This is an Australia-first concept for international aircraft planning.

The new terminal is a spacious and comfortable building where passengers and friends feel welcome and relaxed in the airport environment.

The ambience and colour of southeast Queensland are reflected through the use of local landscaping and an emphasis on daylight into the major public spaces. Finishes are robust yet suitable, to add to the environmental qualities making the terminal a special 'gateway' building.

Key
1 Stage 1
2 Future extension
3 Bus park
4 Customer parking
5 Taxi parking
6 Shell service station
7 Kingsford Smith Memorial
8 Staff parking
9 Apron

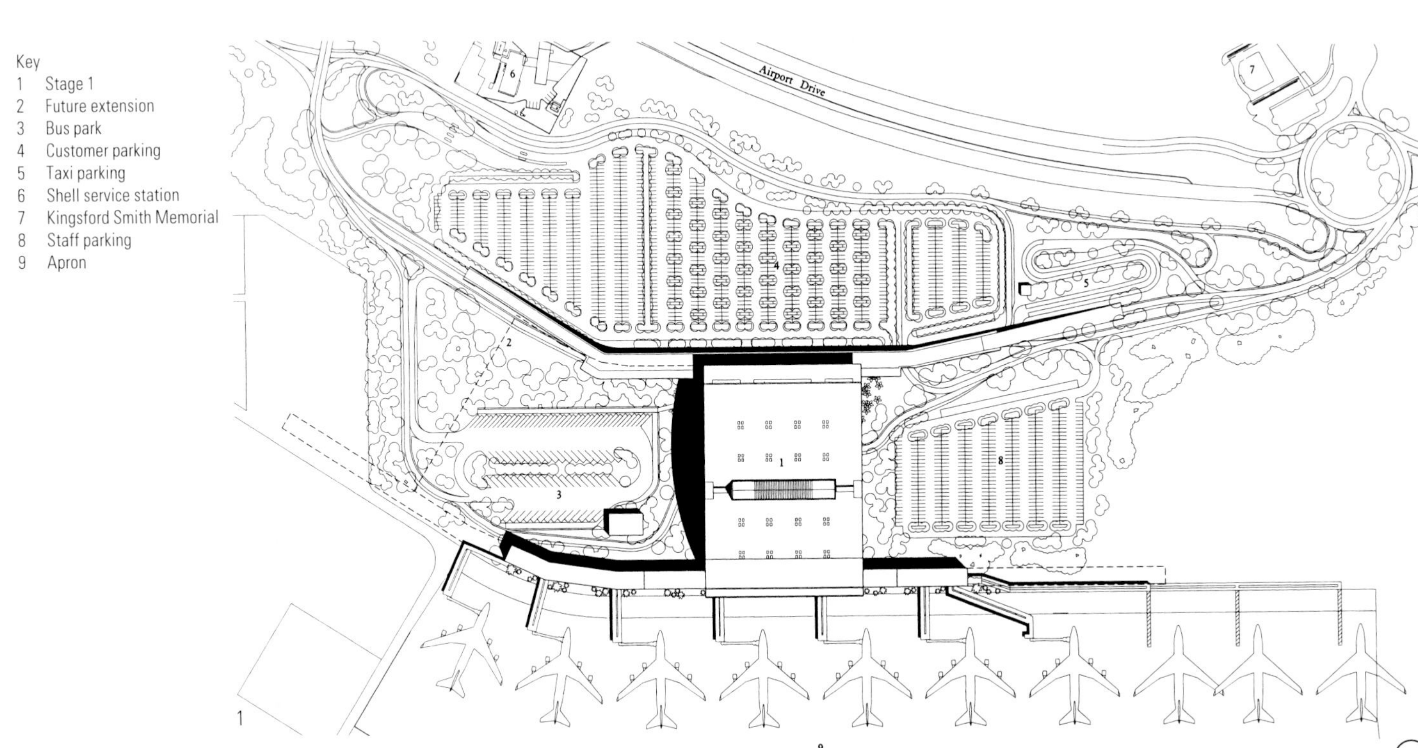

1

2

1 Site plan
2 Aerial perspective
3 Cross section
4 Departures road
5 From carpark
6 Night view
7 From airside
8 Departures level
9 Carpark entry

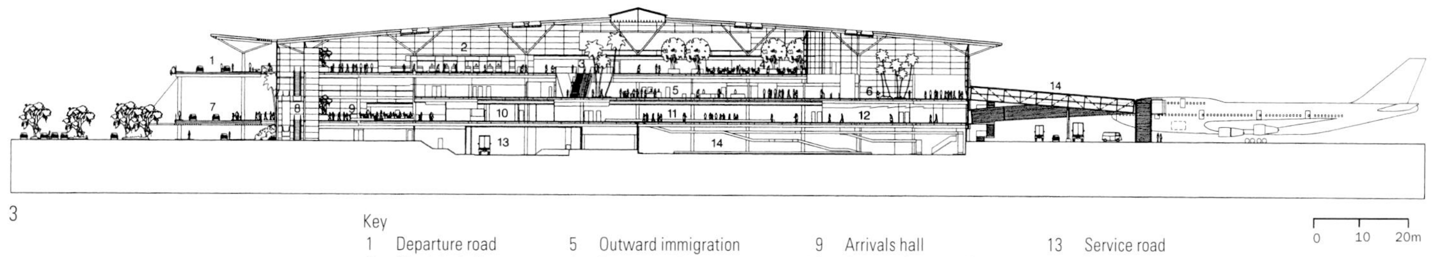

3

Key
1 Departure road
2 Check-in hall
3 Central void
4 Retail terrace
5 Outward immigration
6 Departures lounge
7 Arrivals road
8 Vertical circulation
9 Arrivals hall
10 Customs bag search
11 Baggage claim
12 Inward immigration
13 Service road
14 Fixed link

4

5

6

7

8

9

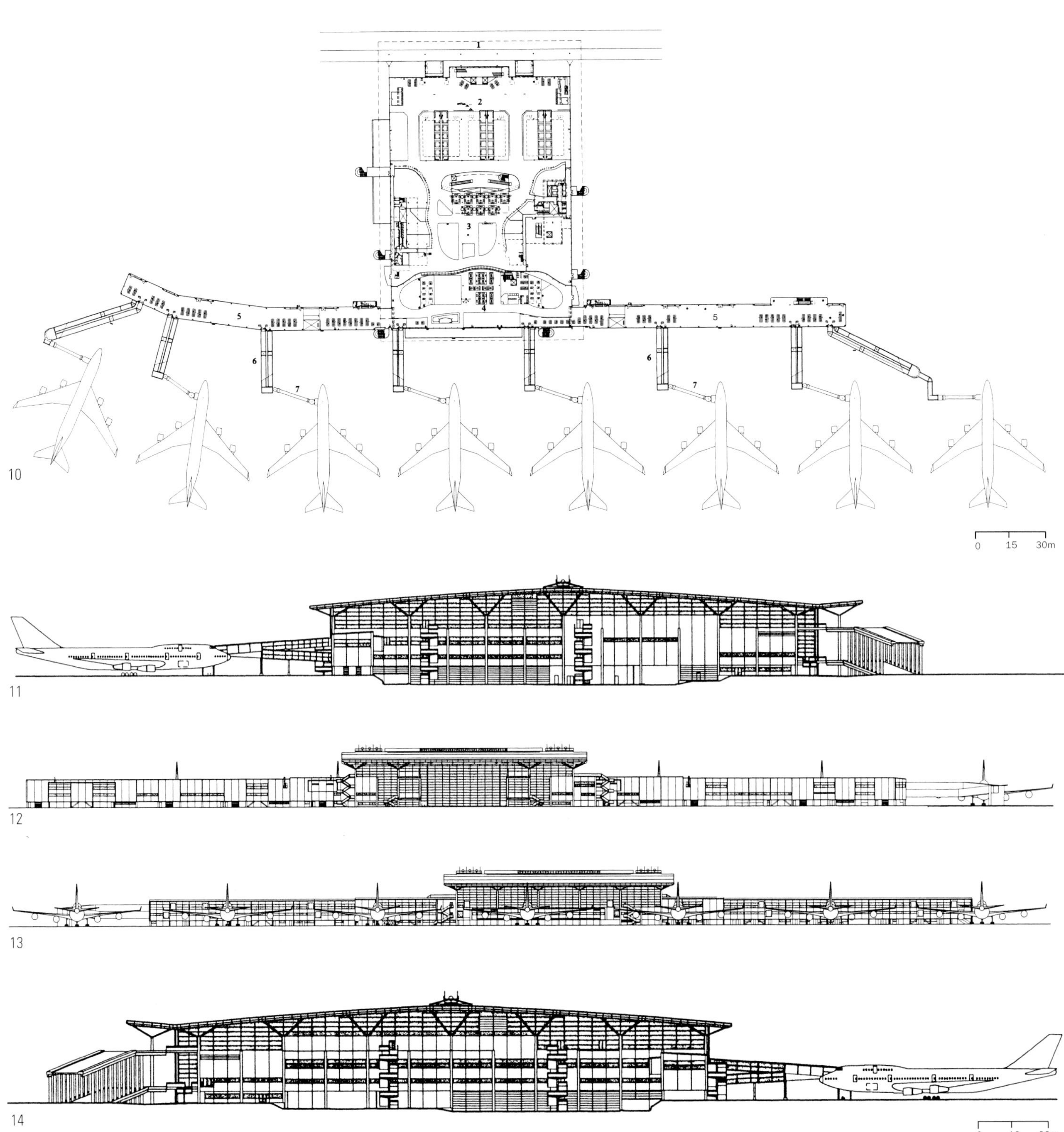
1
2
3
4
5
5
6
6
7
7
10
0 15 30m
11
12
13
14
0 10 20m

15

10 Site location plan
11 North elevation
12 West elevation
13 East elevation
14 South elevation
15 Departure portal
16 Departure levels
17 Departure lounge
18 Departure atrium
19 Vertical circulation
Photography: David Sandison

16

17

18

19

Control Tower, Sydney Airport

Ancher Mortlock & Woolley Pty Ltd

Completion: September 1994

Location: Sydney, New South Wales, Australia

Client: Civil Aviation Authority

Structure: Precast, prefabricated concrete; post-tensioned steel

Materials: Stainless steel; aluminium sheeting; glass

Cost: A$6,418,390

Awards: 1995 AISC NSW Architectural Steel Design Award for Buildings, High Commendation

1995 Finalist BHP Australian Steel Awards

1994-95 BHP Metal Building Award of Merit

Airport control towers are the lighthouses of the 20th century. At Sydney the new control tower has been completed for the Civil Aviation Authority as part of the parallel runway project. Being located next to General Holmes Drive, a major public viewpoint, the impact is dramatic and in civic design terms is a symbol of the airport and of Sydney.

As air transport has become more elaborate, squat brick control towers have evolved to taller steel frames and in the most familiar form, tall cantilevered concrete shafts with a large bubble on top, using the technology of water towers. In designing for Sydney, Ancher Mortlock & Woolley, as architects, challenged this convention. A cantilever out of the usually swampy ground of airports and another cantilever at the top encourages movement, while the massive loads of water towers do not apply. As there must be a lift, services and emergency stairs, the shaft is grossly oversized for the loads involved.

This unique control tower consists of a top 'cabin' with all round visibility achieved by angled frameless glass and minimal support. This design has only one central column from which the roof cantilevers, stabilised by stainless steel rods at the glass joints. Located at the perimeter, the air traffic control consoles enable controllers to survey the parallel runway systems, the first time this has been done in Australia. Above the cabin is the surface movement radar sensor and a corona of aerials and lightning conductors. Immediately below the main platform is a smaller one on which the spiral stair lands and which provides a balcony for attachment of microwave dishes and other aerials as they are required.

Below the cabin is the main deck, designed as six pods, like a cloverleaf, which accommodate electronic equipment and plant rooms, staff rest area, toilets and management office. The overall height of the structure is 45 metres (148 feet) and at the base is a circular building with plantroom, standby generator, uninterrupted power supply, equipment rooms, staff amenities and management offices. The geometry of the design is based on a equilateral triangle or tri-star plan with a slim precast central column in which services run, supporting a steel strutted and cantilevered platform and braced by post-tensioned steel rods to three points on the base building. This ensures the most rigid, sway-free structure with the advantage of prefabrication for rapid construction.

Maintaining the visual clarity of this stayed-mast structure, the lift runs on the outside of the central column and the escape stair is arranged in a large spiral well away from it. The effect is a striking one, demonstrating the advanced technology appropriate to its purpose and its associations with aircraft technology. All of the construction is lightweight, prefabricated and weather-protected, essential for the extreme terrain of its location. This solution arose from a reassessment of the logic of the conventional towers.

1

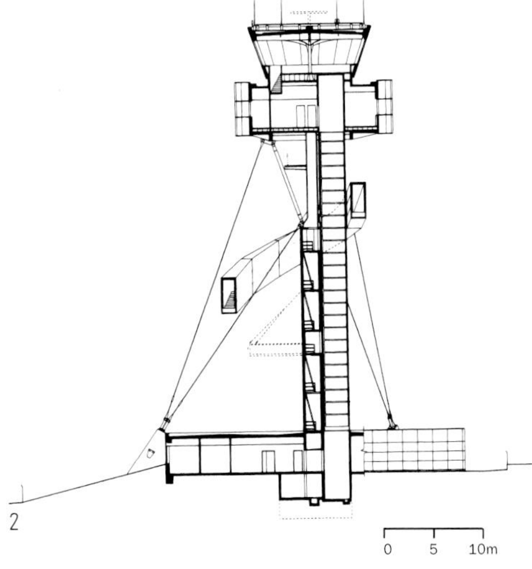

2

3

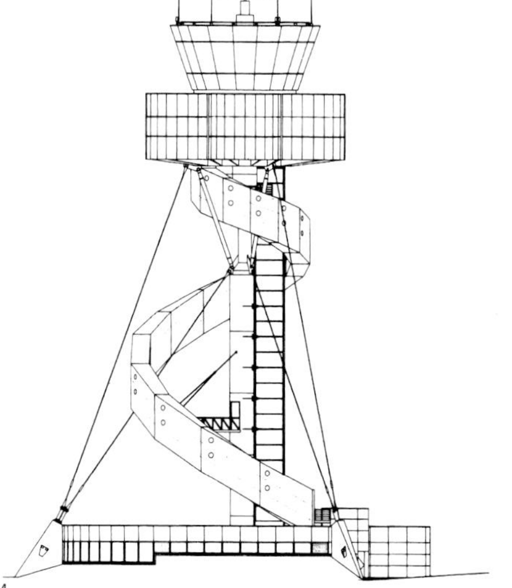

4

1 From Botany Bay
2 Section
3 Concept development
4 East and north elevations
5 Rest area and office
6 Control cabin
7 From southeast
8 Entrance court, looking up
9 Plans

Photography: Eric Sierens

5

6

7

8

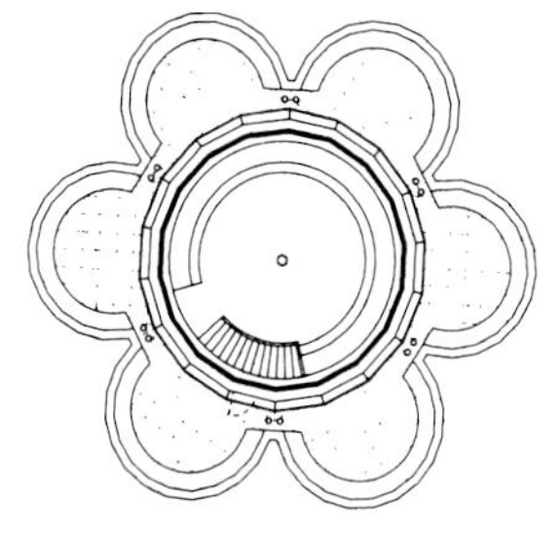

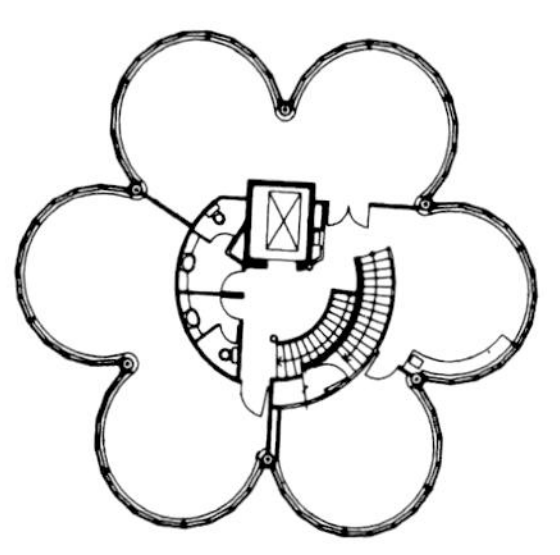

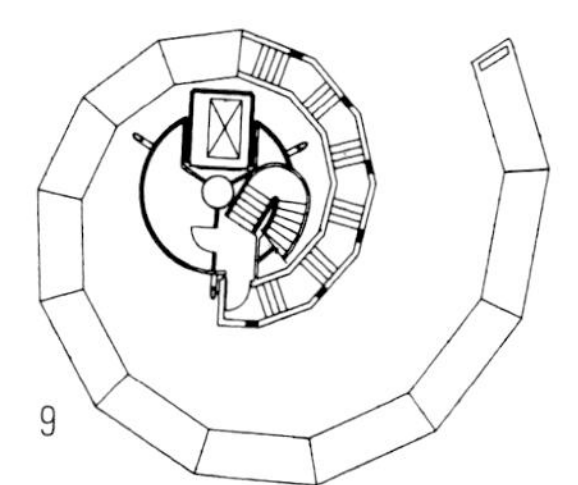
9

Crane Park Izumi

Nikken Sekkei Ltd.

Completion: March 1995

Location: Kagoshima, Japan

Client: Izumi City

Area: 2,315 square metres; 24,920 square feet

Structure: Reinforced concrete; steel frame; wood

Materials: Wood; stone; resin paints

The city of Izumi in the southern district of Kyushu Island is renowned for a yearly migratory visit of about 10,000 cranes. This building is intended to serve as a comprehensive crane museum provided with facilities for collection, storage and display of scientific materials concerning cranes and also as a place for study and information exchange, both at a citizens' hobby level and at a high academic level addressing experts specialised in this field of study worldwide. Furthermore, the building is intended to attract tourists year-round.

The building is ideally located in a large riverbed of the attractive Yonemozu River. In planning, positive attempts were made to utilise these natural environmental elements to advantage in creating a park that can serve as a paradise for cranes which seek a place of calm repose in this restless world. The planning was primarily aimed at the creation of a place for interchange between cranes and people. While the buildings were located according to a dispersed layout concept to match the geographical feature, an attempt was made to integrate the buildings and the park into a unified whole using expansive timber roofs and pergolas which were designed to blend the buildings with the natural setting. This setting was designed to create an image of a crane family having communication and to be a landmark of this park that has rather a special character.

Continued

1

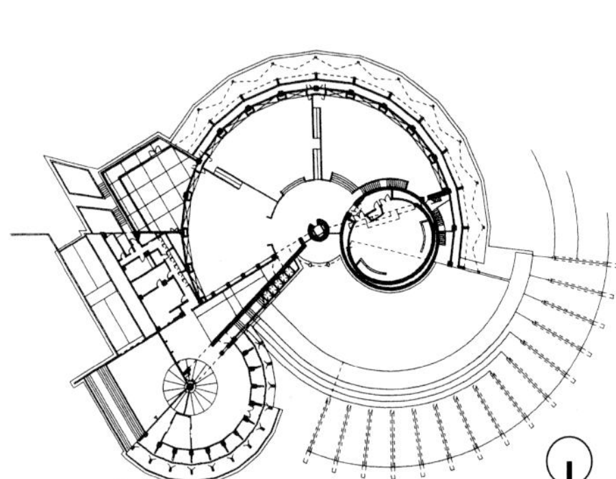

2

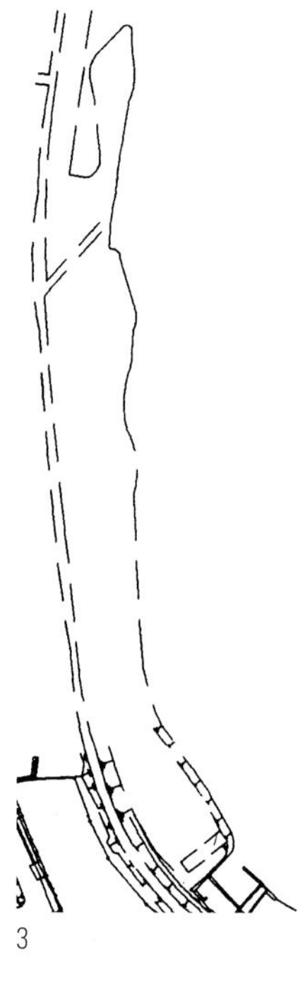

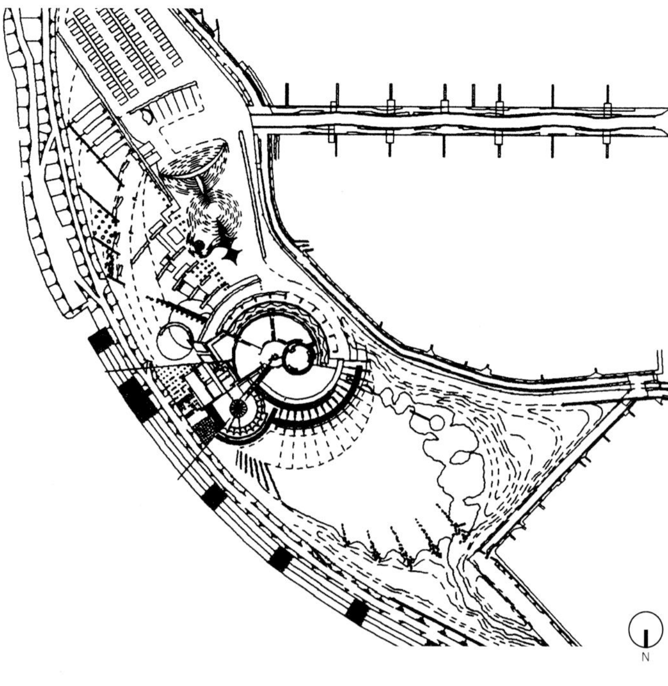

3

4

1 North elevation
2 First floor plan
3 Site plan
4 Aerial view
5 Kid's field
6 West elevation in twilight

5

6

Natural materials such as stone, woods and also natural sunlight were used for the interior of the exhibition room. This room also enables visitors to visualise large timber frames and creates a heart-warming space which is suggestive of the crane wings embracing the visitors.

To solve problems caused by typhoons and sea air, the buildings were provided with semi-spherical roofs which were made to hang low at the eaves to prevent the buildings from being directly hit by the winds. Also, the roofs and windows were coated with fluorine-contained-resin paints.

7

8

7 Facade from approach
8 Pond seen from passage
9 Section
10 Passage to Exhibition Hall
11 Library

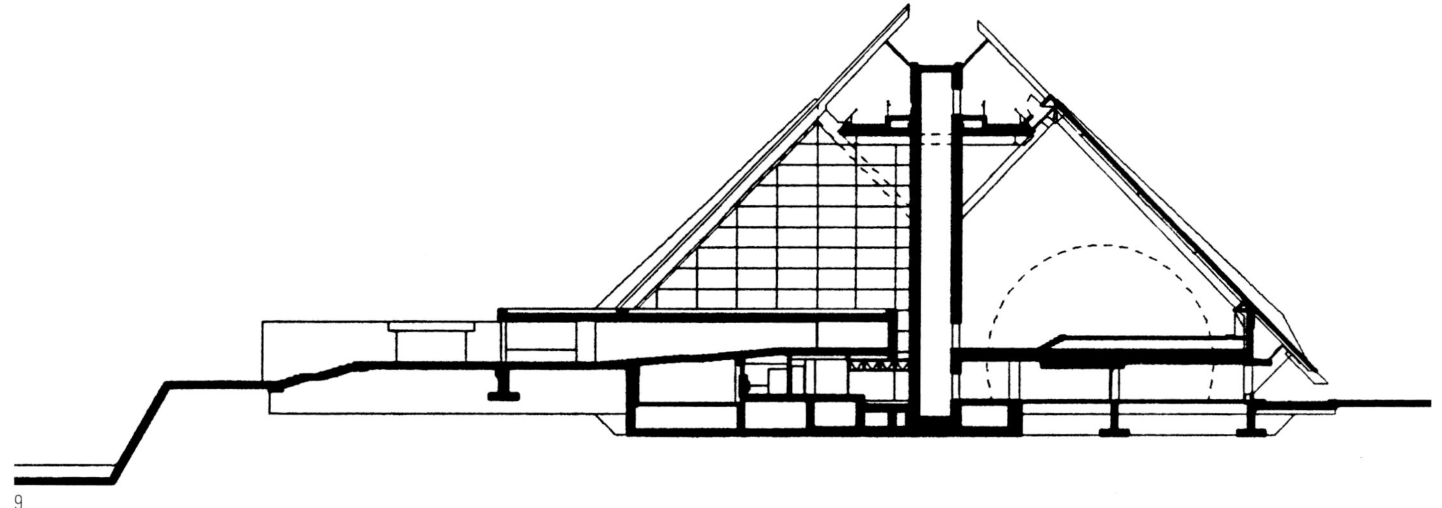

9

10

11

12

12 Lobby
13 Detail of ceiling of Exhibition Hall
14 Exhibition Hall
Photography: Nishinihon Shaboh

13

14

Denver Central Library - Phase I Addition

Michael Graves Architect

Completion: March 1995

Location: Denver, Colorado, USA

Client: City and County of Denver

Area: 36,231 square metres; 390,000 square feet

Structure: Cast-in-place concrete

Materials: Cast stone and natural stone; maple wood

Cost: US$46.5 million

Awards: 1992; 1995 New Jersey Society of Architects Design Awards

This project involves complete renovation and significant expansion of the original library building designed by Burnham Hoyt in 1956. This building is part of the Civic Center Historic District, and is listed on the National Register of Historic Places.

The Graves' design envisions the expanded Denver Central Library as an important civic structure reflecting the activities and architecture of its community. The original building maintains the institution's presence on Civic Center Park. The 36,231 square metre (390,000 square foot) addition stands to the south, forming a backdrop for Hoyt's composition. A strong new public image is established along Thirteenth Avenue, facing future development and parking to the south.

The scale and colouration of the addition allows the original library building to maintain its own identity as one element of a larger composition. Two major public entrances establish an east–west axis through the expanded building, developed as a Great Hall. This 3-storey vaulted space is the central public room of the building, allowing visitors to become oriented to the facilities provided on all levels. Special rooms at the edge of the building offer visitors views of the city and mountains beyond.

1

2

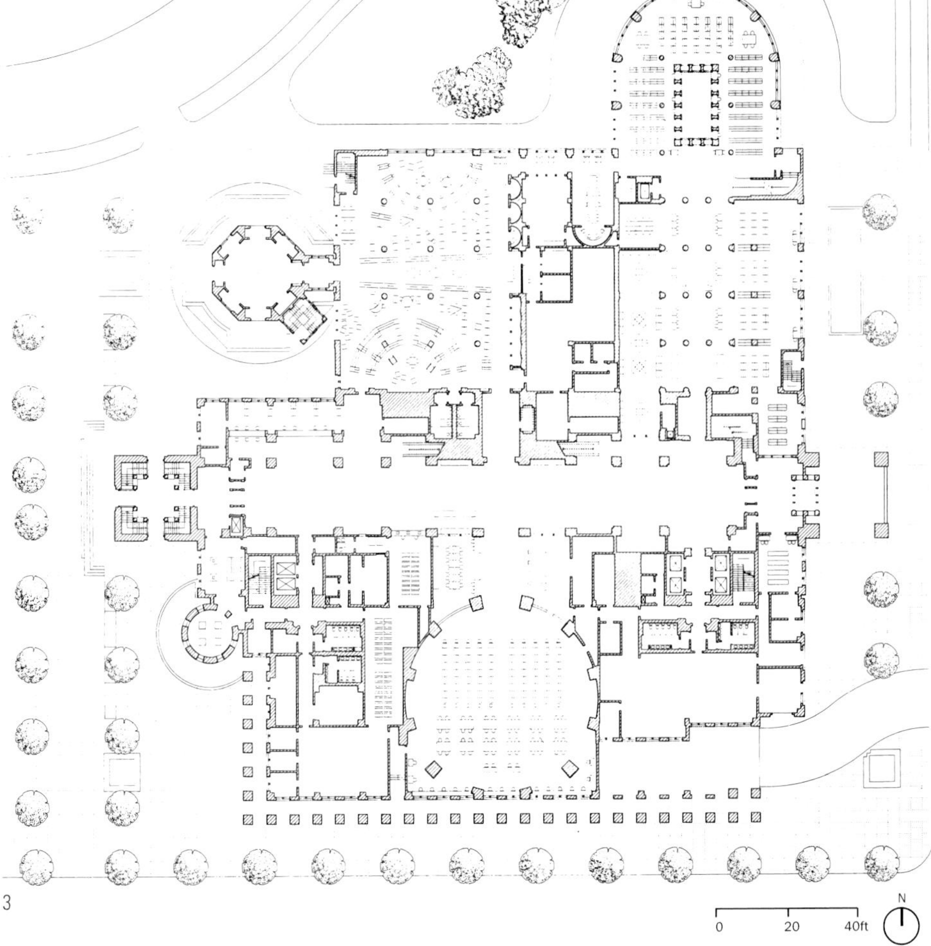

3

4

1 View from south
2 Detail of south facade and rotunda
3 Site and ground floor plan
4 View from southwest
5 Southwest view from Acoma Plaza
6 Fifth floor plan
7 North–south section through existing building, the Great Hall and rotunda

5

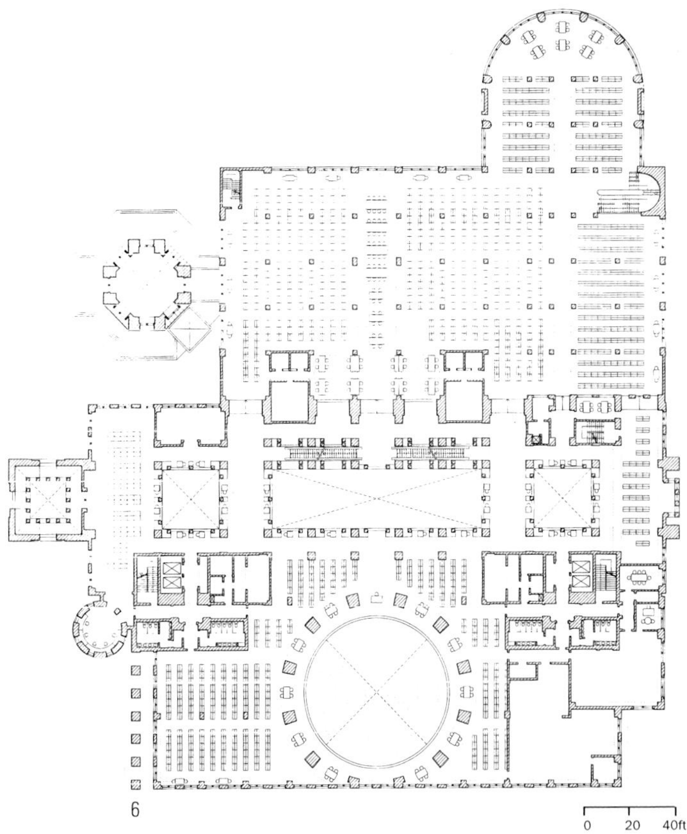

6

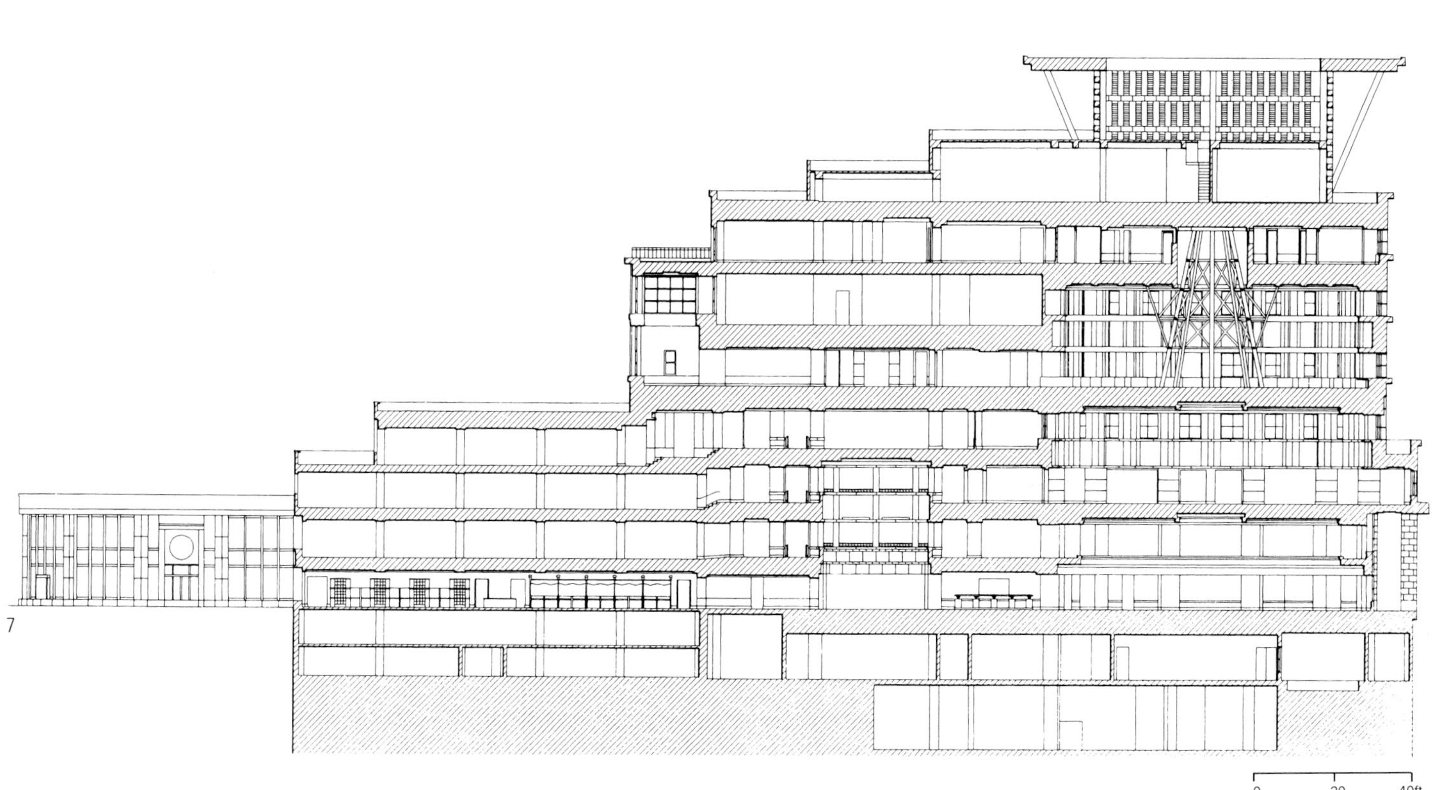

7

8

9

10

11

8 The Great Hall
9 Circulation desk
10 Western history reading room
11 Third floor periodicals reading room
Photography: Timothy Hursley/The Arkansas Office

12

Denver International Airport

C.W. Fentress, J.H. Bradburn and Associates

Completion: February 1995
Location: Denver, Colorado, USA
Client: City and County of Denver
Area: 185,800 square metres; 2,000,000 square feet
Cost: US$455 million

Inspired by the majestic Rocky Mountains, the terrain and Colorado's own sense of destiny, Denver's new International Airport is designed to be a memorable expression of civic pride and sense of place. The 21st century traveller to the west will be greeted by a vision of the future. Set against a breathtaking view of the Rocky Mountains, this terminal design looks into the future for its references and creates a new space age image, symbolising Denver's confidence in the future of the new west.

The local passenger will approach the terminal on a six-lane highway and from parking have a mere 90 metre (300 foot) walk to the terminal. In the centre is a train station which transports the passenger to the airside concourses and departure gates. From a design standpoint, the terminal rises from a solid stone-like base landform into a spectacular pavilion, enclosed by the largest tensile member structures in the world.

The moment one approaches the building, the visual sensation is unique. At night the building will emit a soft glow. The roof transmits about 12percent of the interior light. Entering the main terminal, the traveller is struck by the enormous scale of the environment, with the roof peaks rising 40 to 46 metres (130 to 150 feet). This soft glow and the magnificent scale will create a calming effect on the busy traveller. In a terminal which may serve 50,000 to 100,000 people a day, the primary goal of the design is to simplify everything. This elegant and unusual solution will influence terminal design for years to come.

1

1 Aerial view
2 Site plan
3 Night view of terminal and parking structure
4 South elevation
5 West elevation
6 Curbside approach road

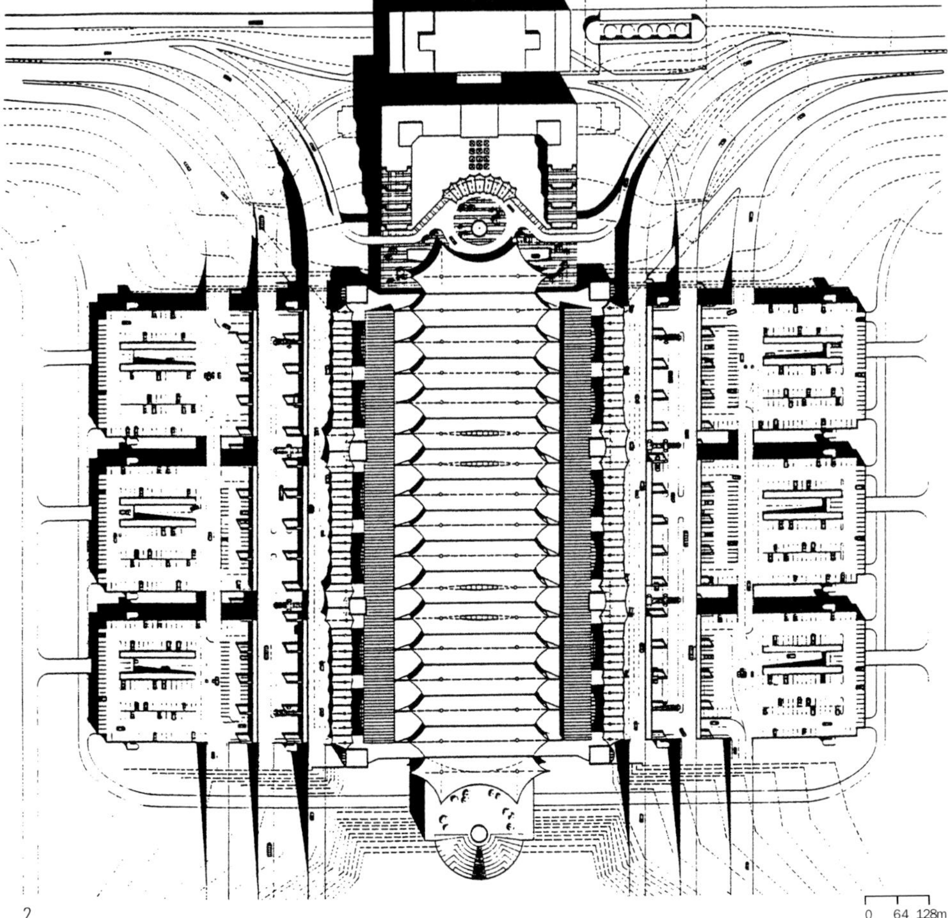

2

3

0 32 64m

4

0 32 64m

5

United/United Express
United/United Express
d Express

6

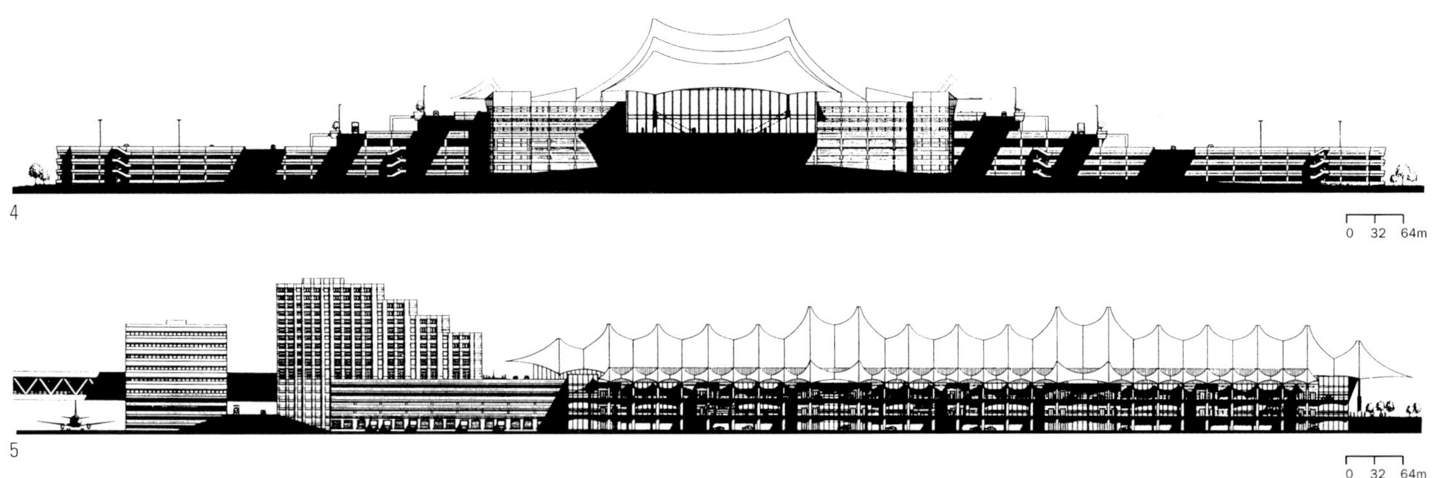

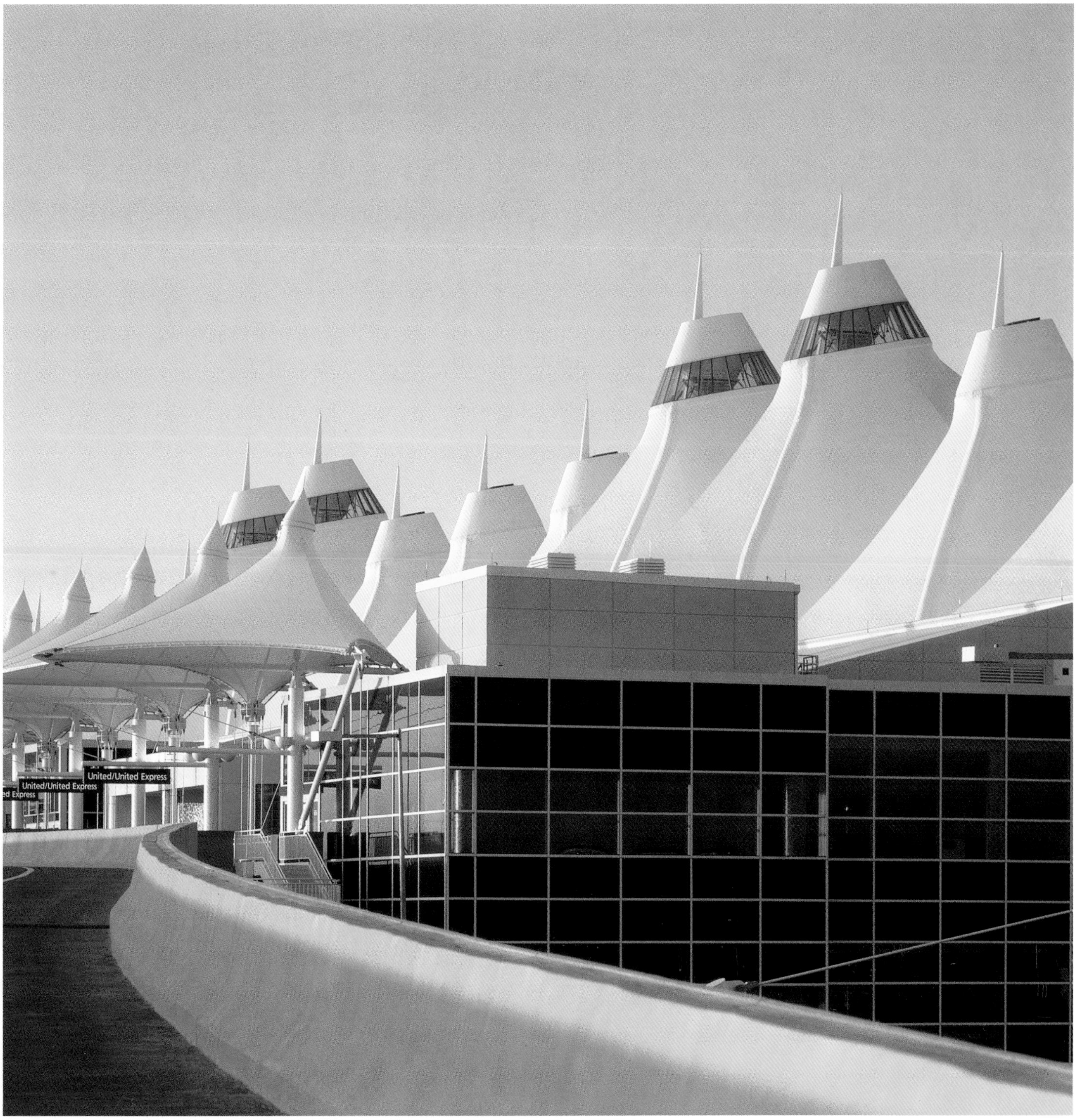

7

8

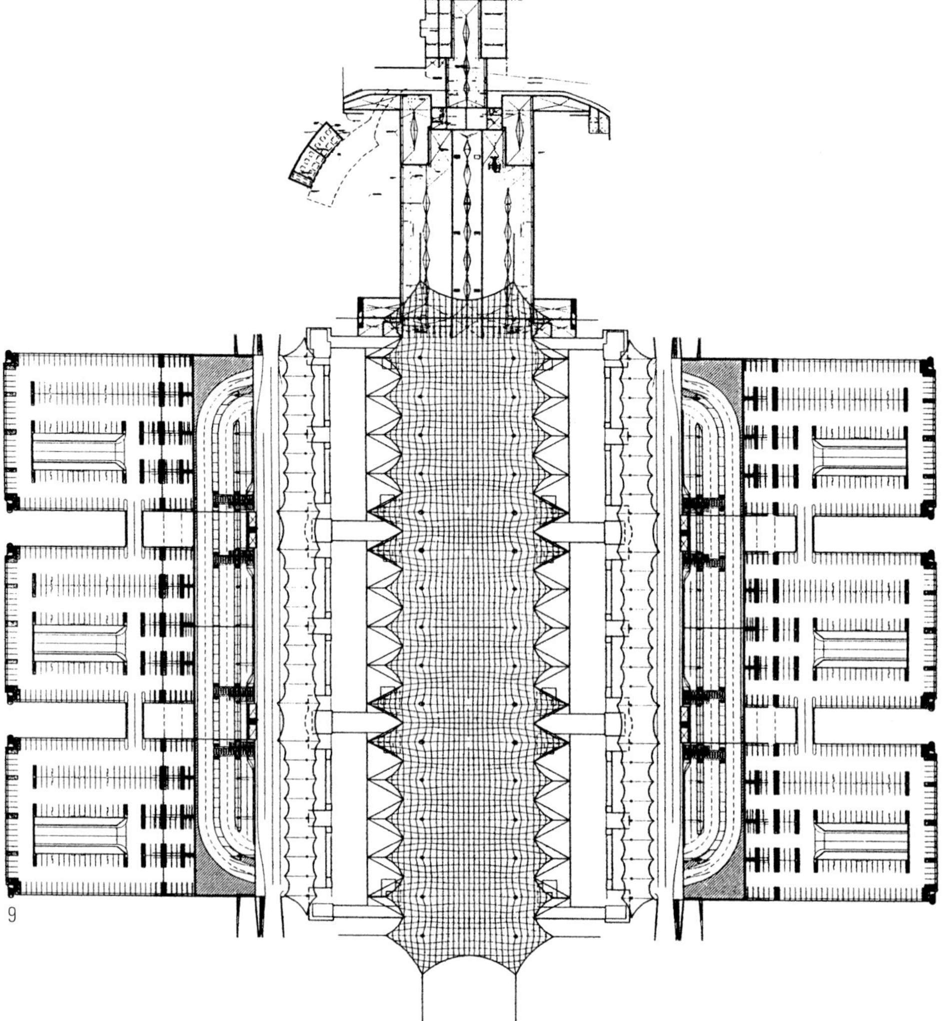
9

10

7 Aerial view
8 Roof detail
9 Roof plan
10 Curbside passenger pick-up

11

12

Dunhuang Cave Cultural Asset Reservation and Exhibition Center

Nikken Sekkei Ltd

Completion: August 1994

Location: Dunhuang, China

Client: Dunhuangology Academy (ODA Project of Japanese Government)

Area: 5,050 square metres; 54,360 square feet

Structure: Reinforced concrete

Materials: Large-size brick

Cost: ¥942,615,000

This exhibition centre consists of two facilities and is given three main purposes, i.e. conservation, study and the exhibition of 'Magao Grottoes'. A world cultural legacy located in Dunhuang, the People's Republic of China; this centre was built to deal with the critical conditions that this cultural asset is facing—a crisis of the collapse due to approaching cracks and breaks in the precipice, and a natural collapse from fading, abrasion and chipping to the wall paintings and clay statues.

At the conservation/study facility, in addition to scientific studies on conservation of the asset; keeping images, records, distribution and registration for the data of the cultural assets such as stone caves, wall paintings and others are undertaken. At the exhibition facility, mockups of eight stone caves, copied wall paintings and excavated cultural findings are shown representing each era. These exhibitions facilitate visitors to understand the Dunhuang arts and in addition, aid researchers in avoiding damages to the precious stone caves by visitors.

The Magao Grottoes, located 1,800 km (1,120 miles) west of Beijing and 25 km (15.5 miles) southeast of Dunhuang are an oasis located at the eastern edge of Takla Makan Desert. The Dunhuang Caves are a great Buddhist vestige constructed between the 4th and 14th century AD, taking about 1,000 years to complete; with the site extending over 1.6 km (1 mile) along the precipice of Mingsha Shan, having about 492 caves, wall paintings of total area 45,000 square metres (484,392 square feet), and clay statues of about 2,000 bodies. Special considerations were necessary on the surrounding environments prior to designing this exhibition centre at the Dunhuang Cave, a great world precious legacy.

Continued

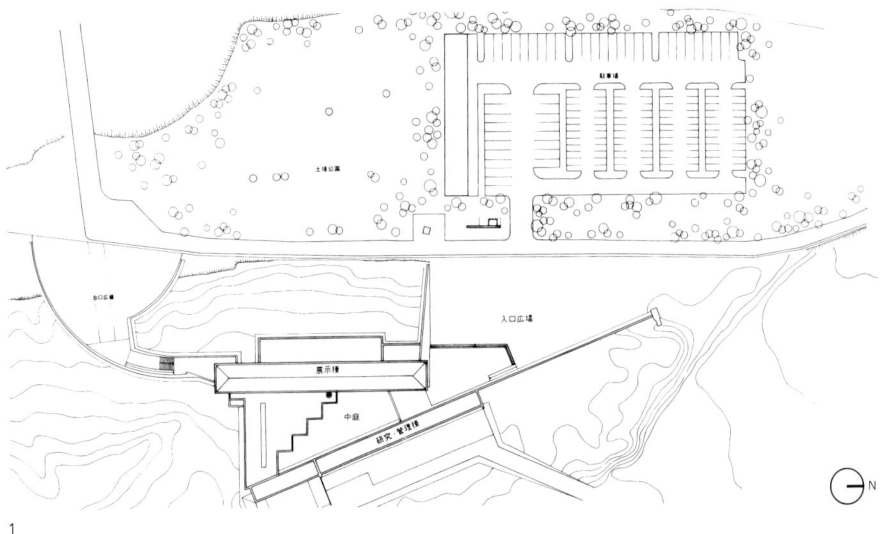

1

2

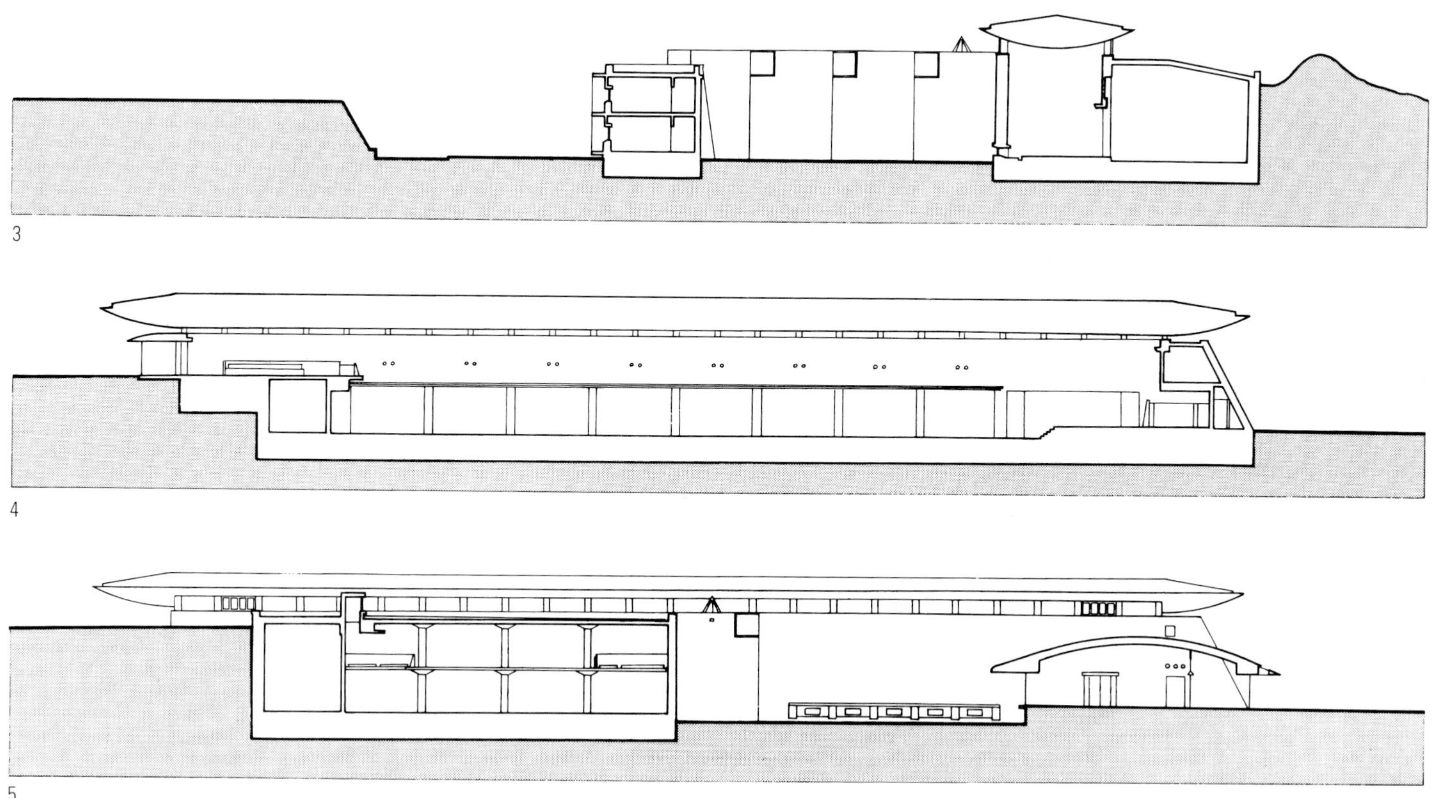

3

4

5

6

1 Site plan
2 View from Buddha Temple and cave 96
3 East–west section
4 North–south section
5 North–south section of courtyard
6 Entrance

In addition to the geological site conditions mostly holding a wide extended desert of yellowish colour (with the exception of a very limited green zone existing between the Magao Grottoes and Daquan Cave) and its peculiar geography with Gilian Shan mountains running at a distance, the site is located in a location which has a continental climate with high dryness, little rainfall, strong seasonal winds and severe temperature differences between day and night.

Thorough consideration was given to these geographical and weather conditions and, to a special circumstance, constructing beside the remains. This is a concept of 'Oneness in Architecture and Geographical Features' which was applied to make it possible to build a structure in accordance with its environment without damaging the surrounding historical environment.

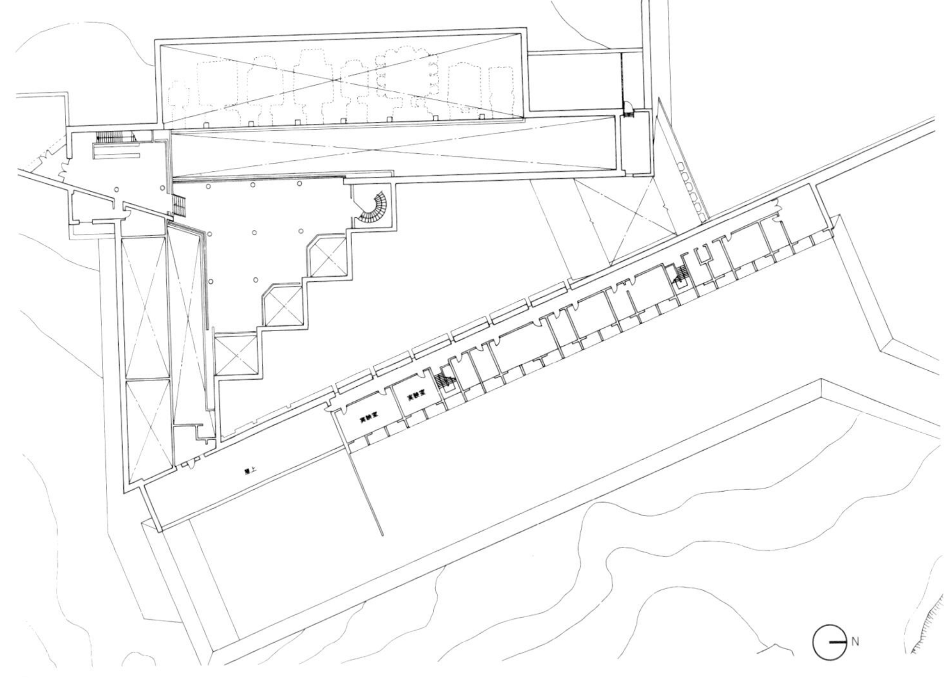

7

8

7 Second floor plan
8 Exhibition hall
9 Exhibition hall (cave model)
10 Exit lobby
Photography: Yoshio Takase (GA Photographers)

9

10

Ehime Museum of Science

Kisho Kurokawa Architect and Associates

Completion: September 1995
Location: Ehime, Japan
Client: Ehime Museum
Area: 24,290 square metres; 261,464 square feet
Structure: Partly reinforced concrete; steel
Materials: Aluminium; glass

The site is located in the suburb of Niihama, on the island of Shikoku, Japan, where a future highway interchange is planned adjacent to the site, at the foot of the mountains.

In order to create relations with the surrounding area, buildings would be individually articulated into four fragments. Each fragment functions as an administrative facility and a planetarium.

Simple geometric forms are adopted; a crescent, a cube, a square, a cone, and a triangle. The layout of each fragment is designed to reflect the free arrangement of stepping stones in a Japanese garden. This is another way of expressing the asymmetry of Japanese traditions.

As one takes a careful look at the exterior of the square Exhibition hall, it can be seen as slightly shifted and tilted to emphasise the composition of four different square exterior surfaces. Various finishes were applied for the facade; aluminium, glass and exposed concrete.

The spherical planetarium located on the artificial pond, is connected with the Entrance hall by an underground passage below the pond. This is to express the abstract invisible relationship.

1

2

3

4

1 View of Planetarium (left), Exhibition Hall (right), and Entrance Hall (middle) over the pond
2 Site plan
3 Multi-storey parking lot seen from the restaurant
4 Overall view
5-6 Sections
7 View of Education Hall (right), Exhibition Hall (left) and outdoor exhibition space (front)

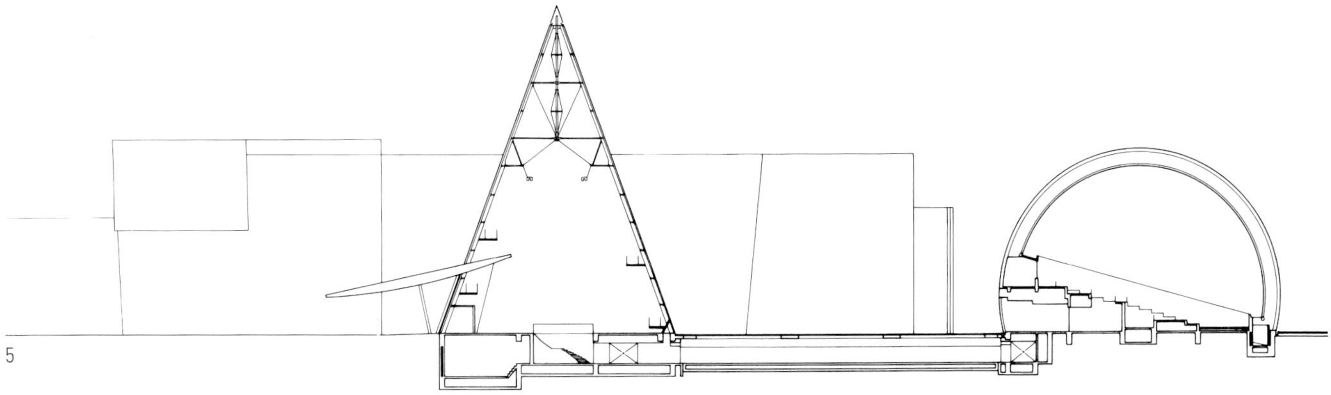

5

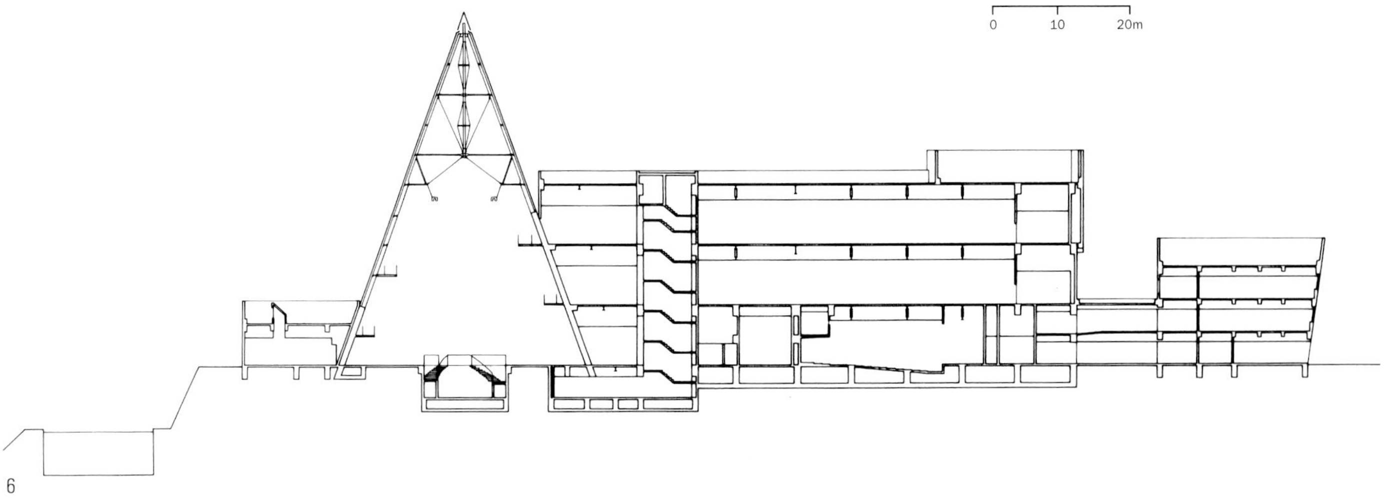

0 10 20m

6

7

8

9

10

11

8 Exhibition Hall, titanium plate striked concrete exterior wall and cleaning robot

9 Exhibition Hall (left) and Planetarium (right) seen over the pond from the restaurant

10 Exhibition Hall, corridor to the outdoor exhibition space

11 Exhibition Hall

12 Fourth floor at the multi-purpose hall

Photography: Tomio Ohashi

12

Fire Station, Gennevilliers

Architecture Studio

Completion: June 1995

Location: Gennevilliers, France

Client: Prefecture de police, Ville de Paris

Area: 13,500 square metres; 145,320 square feet

Structure: Concrete; staple stone; steel; metal girder; aluminium; glass

Cost: 63 million French francs

The fire station inscribes its complex program in the scattered suburban environment: the firemen's accommodation, the telephone exchange, the exercise tower, some offices. On this site which lacks togetherness, the fire station introduces drama, a meaningful opposition.

At the bow, the articulation of two buildings is designed to match each other. One of them leans forward, the other straightens up; one submits, the other swaggers about; one slides, the other flies off. It is a necessary choreographic figure: the mastery of alignments.

On the flank, a third figure is introduced which upsets this harmony. The battering ram makes a hole and extracts an unpredictable element from it. Detached, dissymmetrical, almost unbalanced, the instruction tower advances into the limelight and reveals gable walls.

The colours contribute to the contrapuntal writing of the architectural project. Therefore, they constitute neither an analysis nor a companion. Like the architectural shape, the colours assert the buildings, not as singular entities, but as figures of a set.

1

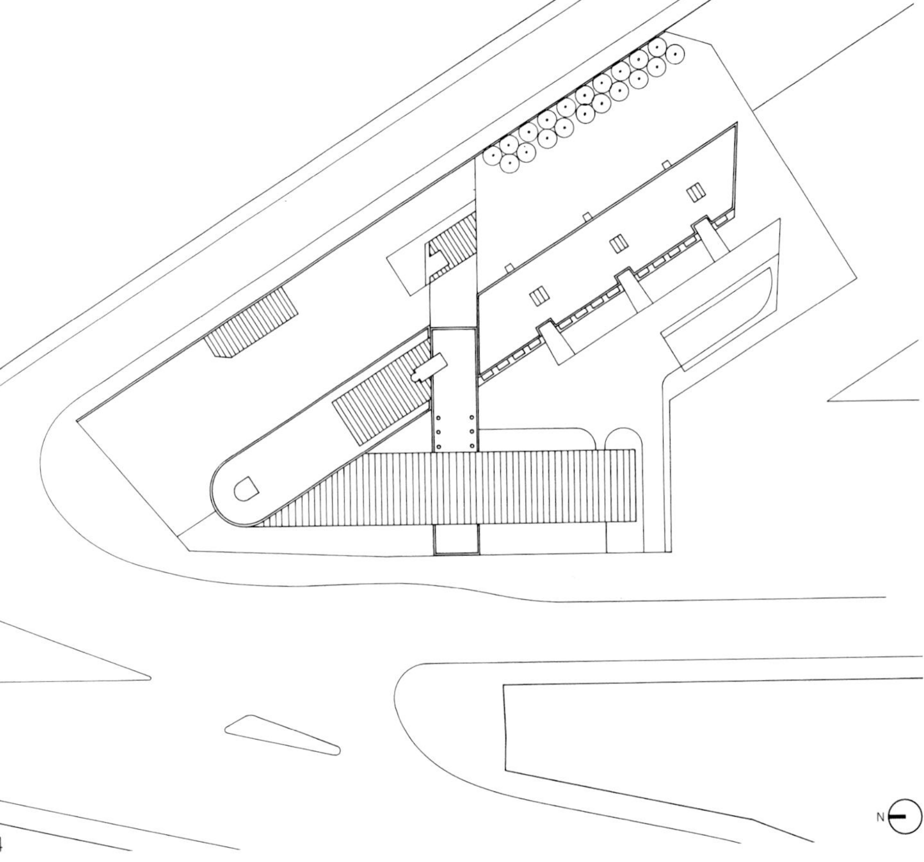

4

2

3

5

1 Terrace
2 Exercise Tower
3 Circulation into the housing of the firemen
4 Block Plan
5 Housing of the firemen and exercise tower
6 Ground floor plan
7 Exercise Tower
8 Eastern frontage

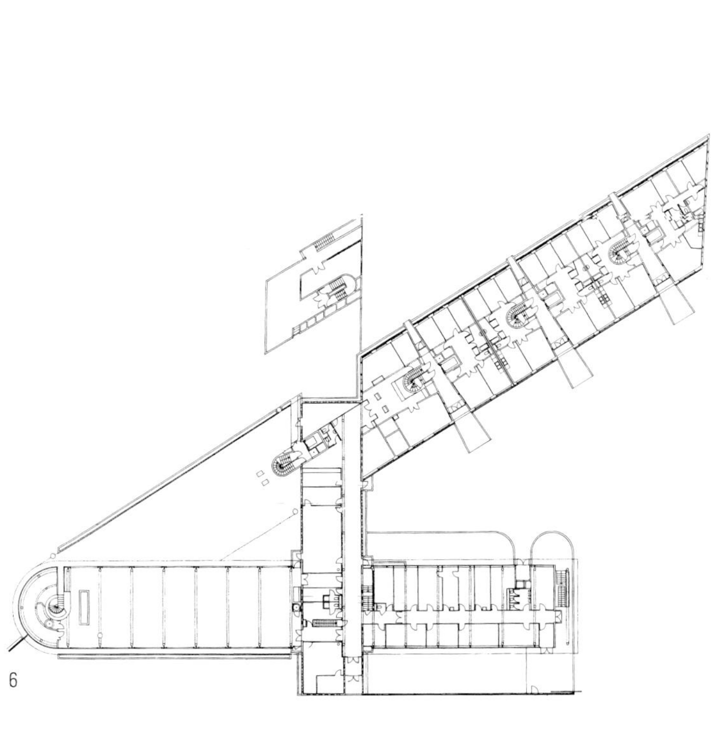

6

7

8

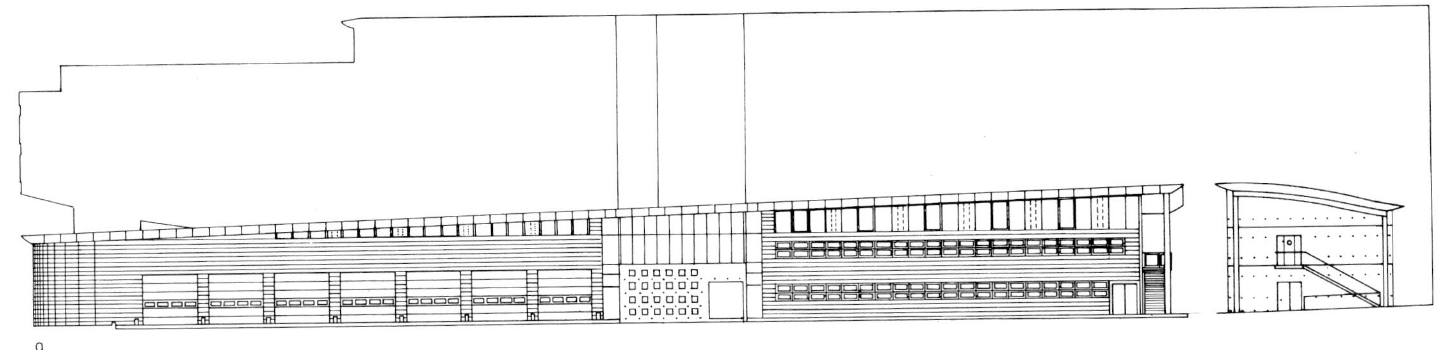
9

10

11

12

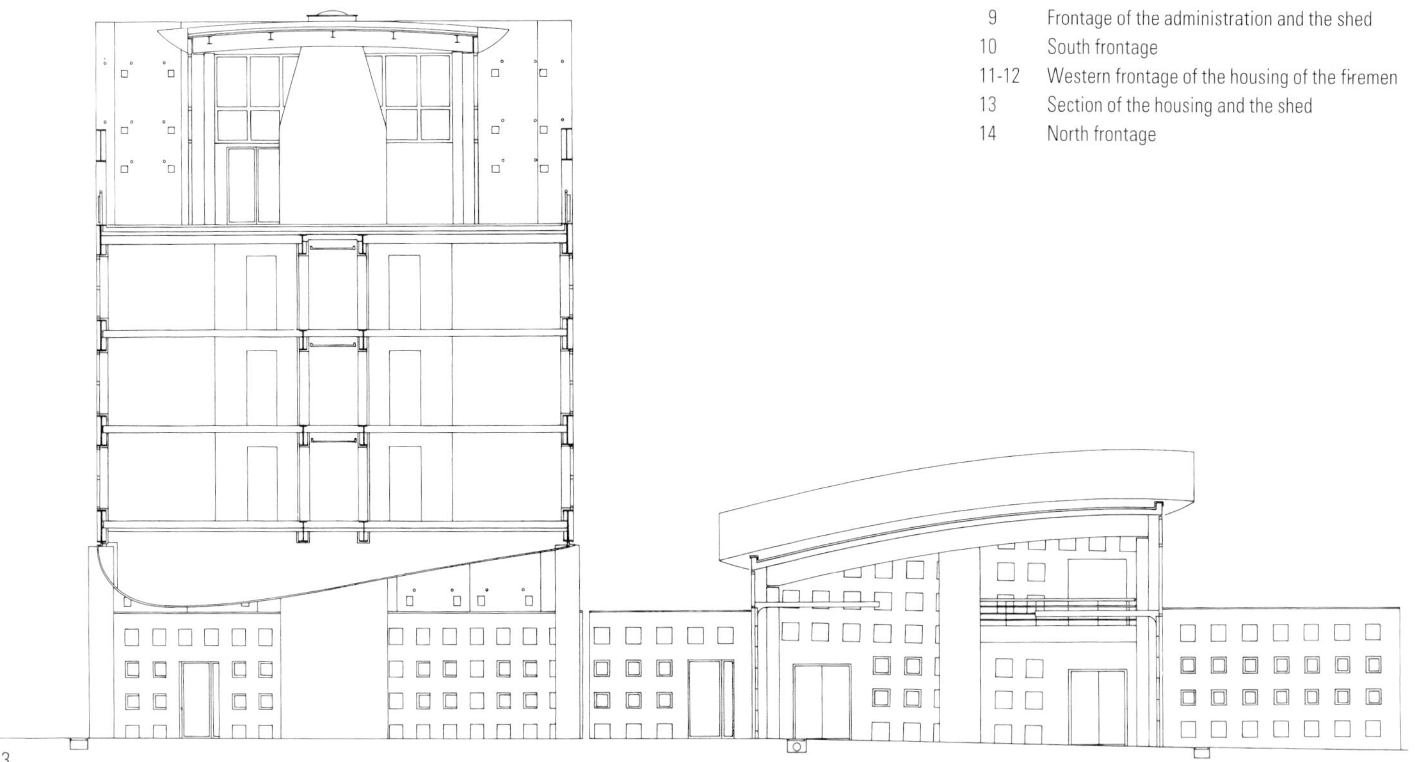

13

9	Frontage of the administration and the shed
10	South frontage
11-12	Western frontage of the housing of the firemen
13	Section of the housing and the shed
14	North frontage

14

Jerusalem City Hall Square

A.J. Diamond, Donald Schmitt & Company

Completion: November 1994

Location: Jerusalem, Israel

Client: City of Jerusalem

Area: 52,367 square metres; 563,692 square feet

Structure: Poured-in-place concrete

Materials: Jerusalem stone; bronze; stainless steel; pre-painted steel; pre-finished aluminium; glass; red oak; carpet

Cost: CA$100 million

Awards: 1990 Canadian Architect Award of Excellence

1

A civic campus, rather than a city hall, more accurately describes the collection of ten existing and three new buildings, together with the main plaza, minor plaza, courts and gardens that make up this municipal complex. The main plaza, bordered by colonnades, new and renovated structures and gardens, will serve as a focus for all citizens and is positioned to be equally accessible from both East and West Jerusalem. Dramatic contrast has been achieved between the formal plaza, on which programmed activities will be staged, and the gardens in which cafes have been placed to serve informal functions.

Access to the main new municipal building is varied: via the palm court from Jaffa Road to the west; up the landscaped ramps and from the Damascus Gate to the east; through a series of passages, courts and gardens to the south; and, directly from the Russian compound to the north.

All the buildings are faced with Jerusalem stone. A masonry scale, commensurate with the size and importance of the building, has been achieved in the Mamluke manner by alternating double courses of the light ochre and the deep rose of the Jerusalem limestone. Fine iron work railings and sun screens, in the Turkish manner, act as foils to the weight of the trabeated structure.

The primary driving force behind the urban design and landscape was to provide the first secular public gathering space in the City of Jerusalem, with equal access from all sectors. The second driving force of the design was to create a subtle connective tissue that would unite and strengthen the whole and make the complex more than the sum of its parts.

Although the common building material, Jerusalem stone, provides architectural unity, the primary cohesive links are the spaces between the buildings which form a rich sequence of experiences in the passage from the surrounding areas to the main plaza located on the highest portion of the site. Some of these routes are axial, as in the formal route leading directly from Zahal Square to the entrance of the main municipal building on the plaza. Others are much less formal where the relationship of the building to the exterior space is incidental, containing the space rather than dominating it. The character of each open space is different and these differences are contrasted sharply to give richness and drama: the formal simplicity of the hard urban square and the lush green informality of Daniel Auster Gardens; the small sunlit court and the dappled shade of the trellised triangular garden; the angular ramped approach to the plaza from the east and the ordered palm grove on Jaffa Road to the west.

2

3

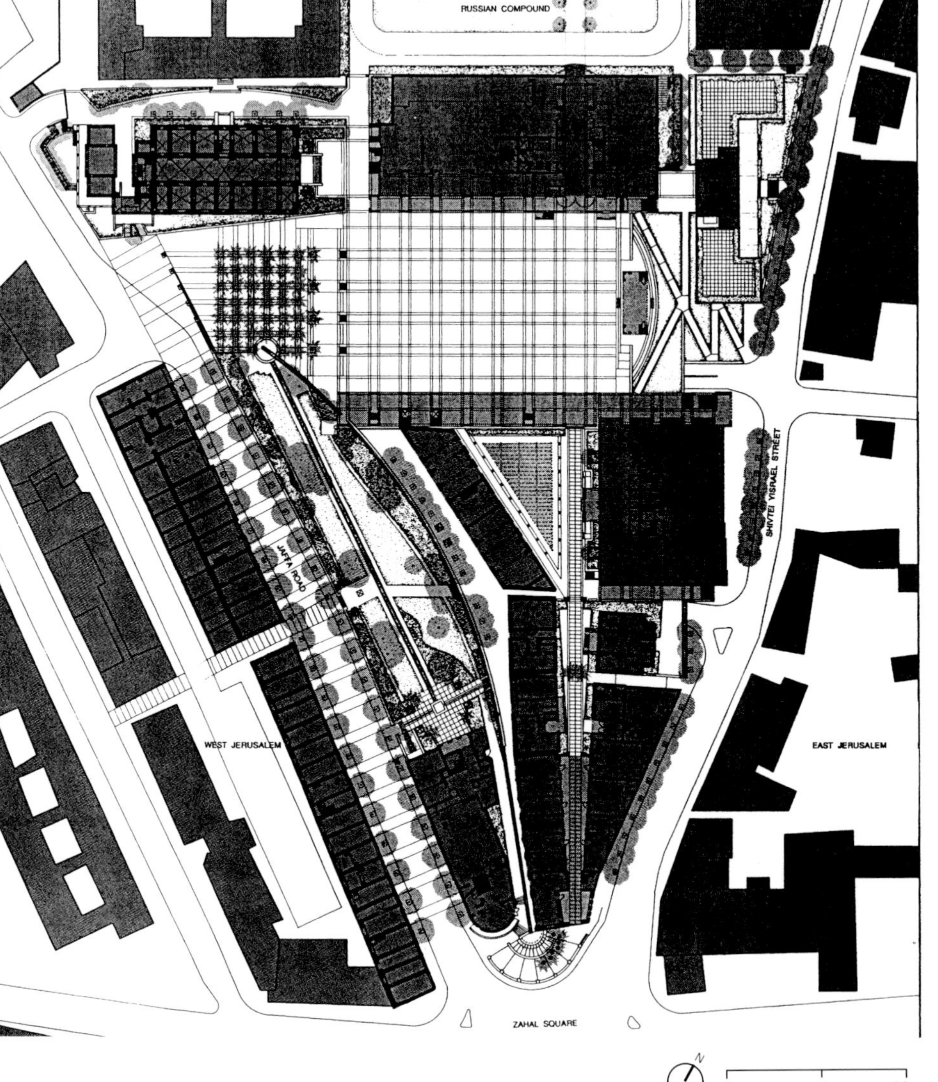

4

1 Aerial view from west
2 Main municipal building, Palm Court, Archimedes Screw, and plaza from west
3 Arcade of main municipal building
4 Ground floor plan of municipal complex
5 North–south site section
6 East elevations
7 Looking north to main building from colonnade
8 View of main municipal building through aqueduct
9 Main municipal building, Russian Orthodox church and Russian hospital
10 View through colonnade to entrance of main municipal building
11 Main municipal building and Palm Court
12 Main plaza, colonnade, east municipal building and restored Zoology building

Photography: Steven Evans

5

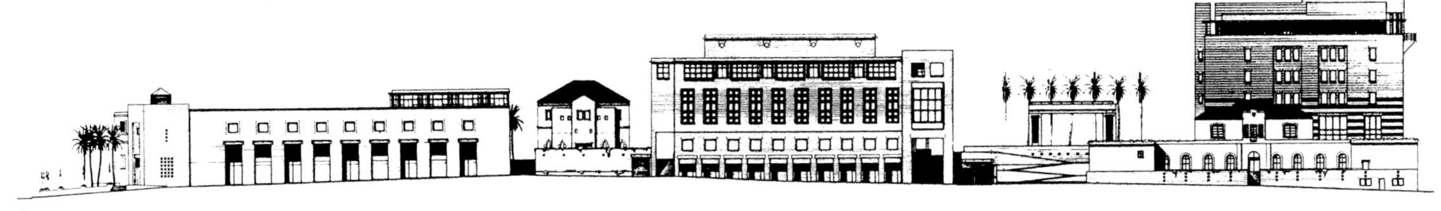
6

7

8

9

10

11

12

New Wing and Renovation of the Joslyn Art Museum

Sir Norman Foster and Partners
in association with Henningson Durham and Richardson

Completion: November 1994

Location: Omaha, Nebraska

Client: Joslyn Art Museum

Area: 5,388 square metres; 58,000 square feet

Structure: Precast concrete; steel

Materials: Marble 'Etowah Fleuri' clad pre-cast concrete panels; 'Veudi lavas' granite floor in atrium; steel and glass atrium skylight; Douglas Fir end grain wood block flooring in galleries; plywood backed plasterboard walls and ceiling in galleries

Cost: US$15,950,000

In June 1992, Sir Norman Foster and Partners were selected to design the addition to the Joslyn Art Museum, Omaha, Nebraska, following interviews attended by a group of international architects.

The Joslyn Art Museum, built in 1931 as a cultural centre to embrace both art and music, is one of the finest examples of Art Deco architecture in America. The handsome structure is clad in an unusual pink Etowah Fleuri marble from Georgia.

A grand stone staircase leads to an imposing classical entrance portico and beyond to a symmetrical series of exquisite spaces; a huge entrance lobby, a top lit foundation court, and a 1,200-seat concert hall. These central spaces are flanked by two wings of gallery spaces.

After 60 years of use, many of the building's facilities had become antiquated and there was a desperate need for additional space.

The client's brief included a new building of approximately 4,650 square metres (50,000 square feet) to house new gallery spaces and collection management facilities, as well as limited renovation and refurbishment work in the original building.

A new master plan was developed following analysis of the existing facilities. Over the years, the use of the main entrance had been greatly reduced, with the majority of visitors entering the building via a small door adjacent to the car park.

The public emphasis has been restored to the grand east entrance by reinstating the access road and car parking towards the front of the Joslyn. The site's replanning includes a new landscaped amphitheatre for summertime concerts.

Continued

1 Site plan
2 Main entrance
3 East elevation
4 North–south section
5 Interior of glazed atrium

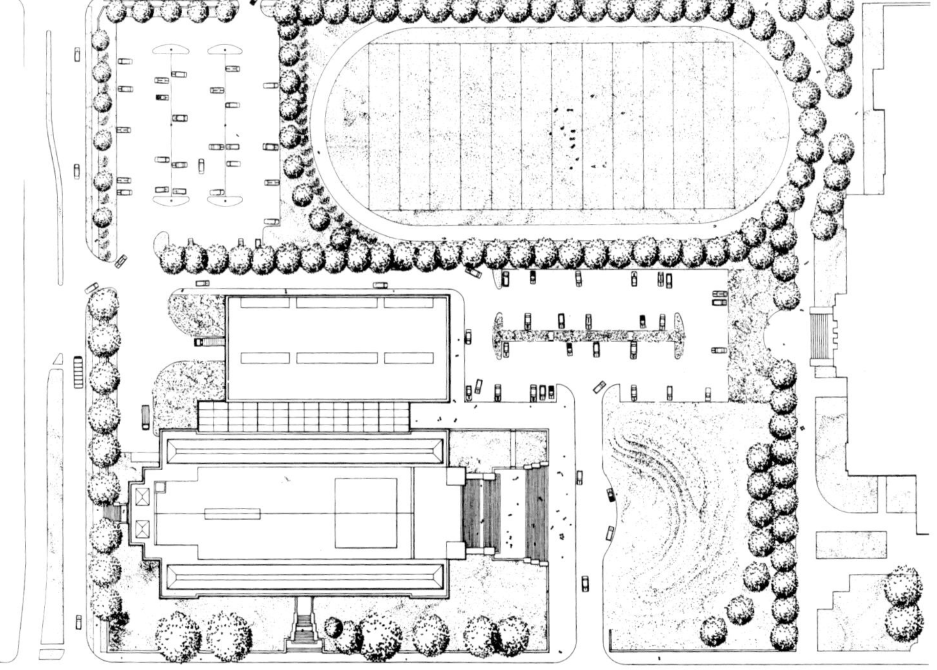

1

2

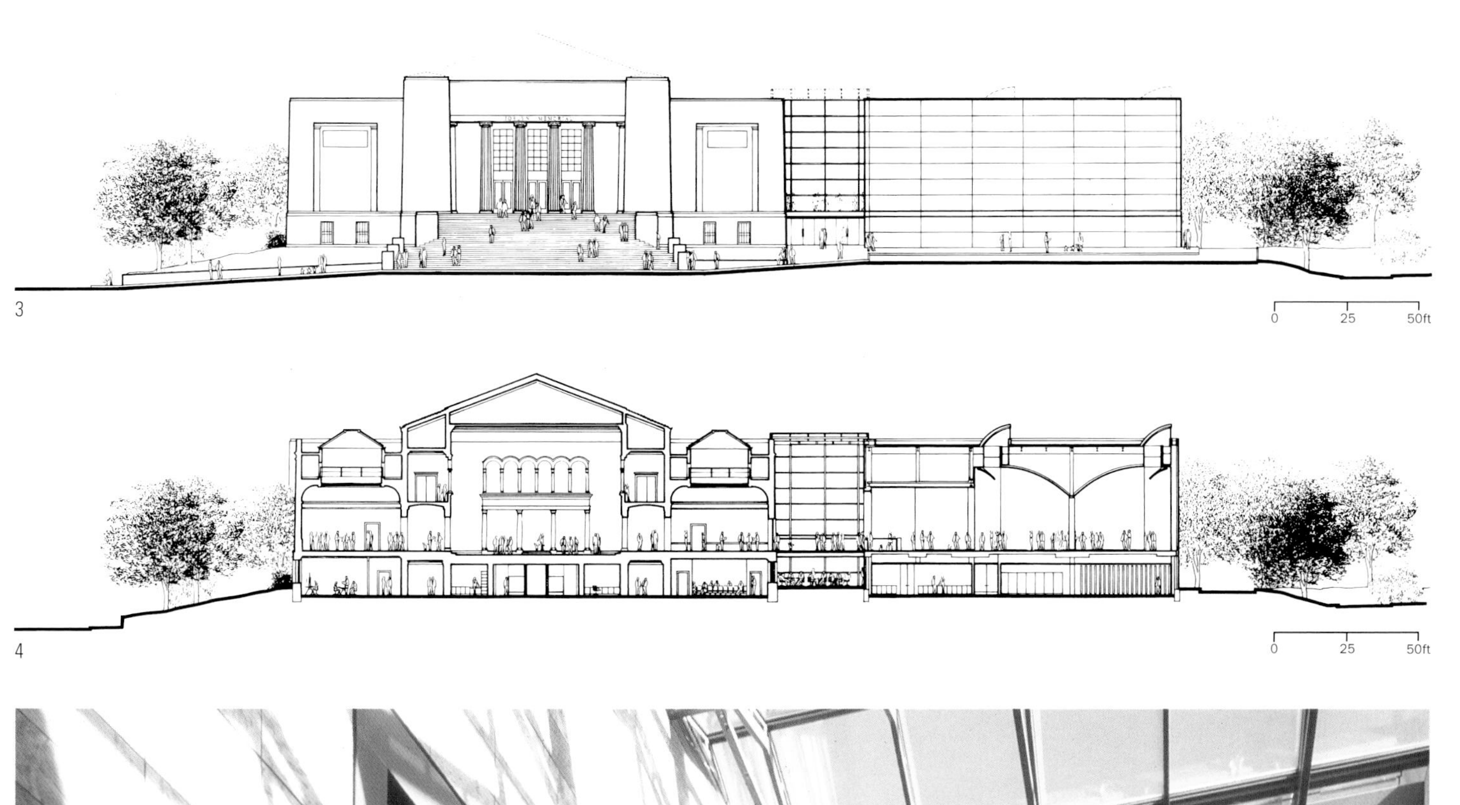

3

4

5

New accommodation is contained within a new wing which defers to the monumental simplicity of the original design. Its solid rectangular form is minimally articulated, but similarly proportioned to the original building. It is clad in identical pink 'Etowah Fleuri' marble from the quarry in Georgia used for the original building back in the 1930s.

A glass atrium, firmly but sensitively, unites these two buildings, without causing undue alteration to the essential profile of the original building. This provides new restaurant space and a secondary public entrance and reception area.

The main level of the new wing contains temporary exhibition gallery space with indirect controllable daylight. Beneath this gallery level are state of the art collection management facilities and art storage vaults. There are also support spaces including cloakrooms, restrooms and a new kitchen and servery for the atrium restaurant.

The work undertaken in the original building has included significant improvements to the concert halls' lighting and acoustics, restoration of the existing galleries, renovated restroom facilities and administration departments, and a remodelled museum shop.

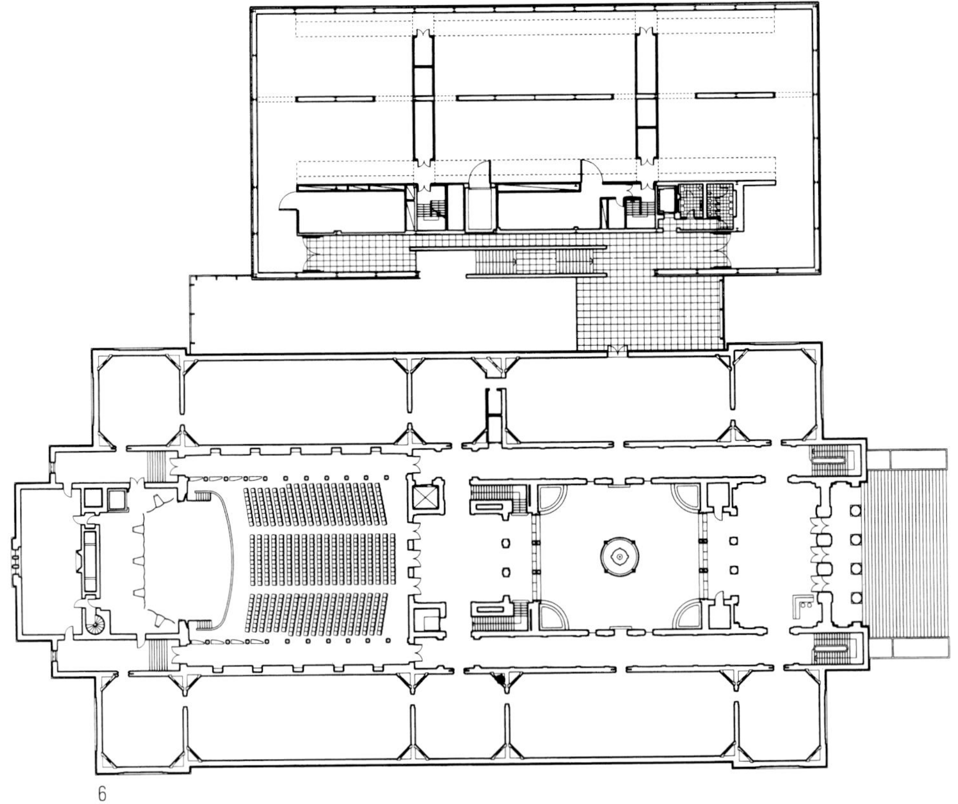

6

6 Gallery level floor plan
7 North elevation
8 East–west section through galleries
9 Gallery
10 Gallery
Photography: Patrick Drickey

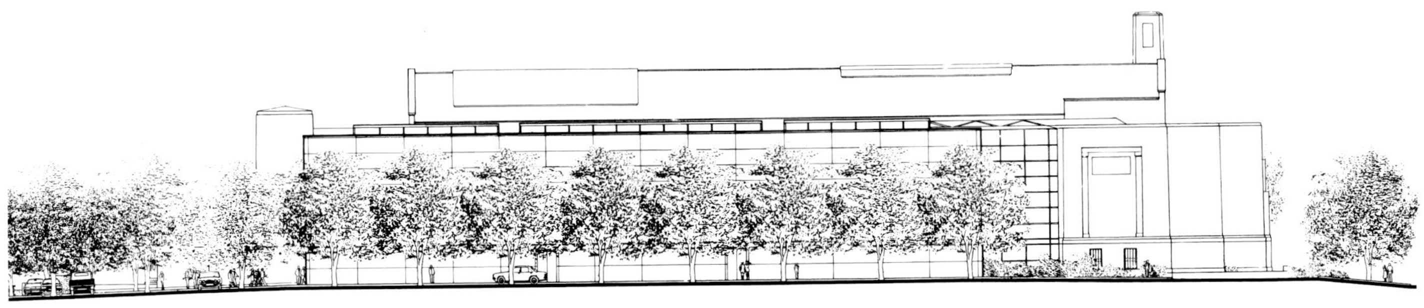

7

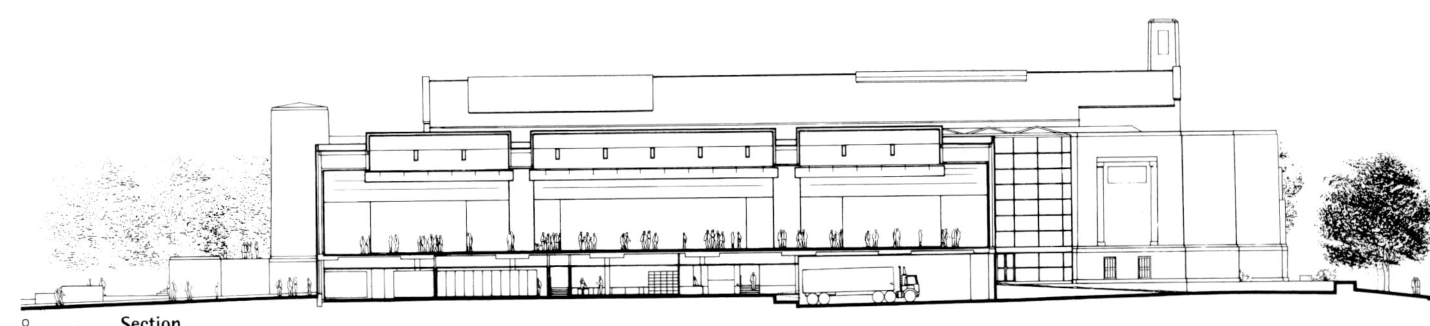

8 **Section**

9

10

Korean War Veterans Memorial

Cooper•Lecky Architects, PC

Completion: July 1995

Location: Washington, D.C., USA

Client: American Battle Monuments Commission

Area: 6 acres

Structure: Reinforced concrete on steel piles

Materials: Granite; stainless steel

Cost: US$8 million

Charles Moore, an early chairman of the Commission of the Fine Arts, observed that in the monuments of the Capital one can read the country's history. The National Mall, at the heart of the Monumental Core, is where much of that 'reading' takes place. To be worthy of a place on the Mall, a memorial must embody a message of such significance that it often surpasses the event or the person commemorated. This is so with the Korean War Veterans Memorial as it expresses both the enduring gratitude of the nation to those who served and fell in Korea, and also proclaims a broader message about the willingness to serve in a citizens' armed forces which lies at the heart of American democracy. It is a message for all time and for all people.

The Korean War Veterans Memorial completes the triad of memorials on the west end of the National Mall's reflecting pool in Washington, D.C.. Standing on the steps of the Lincoln Memorial; the Korean War Veterans Memorial is located to the right and the Vietnam Veterans Memorial to the left.

The Memorial is formed in two major geometric components, a triangular 'Field of Service', and a circular 'Pool of Remembrance'. They are overlapped and joined together by the Memorial's focal element, an American Flag.

The triangular field contains the elements which symbolise service to country: 19 ground troopers, clad in foul weather ponchos, fully equipped for battle, emerge from the shadows and protection of a forest. All are tense, alert, and driven forward by his resolve in the cause of freedom. The cast stainless steel figures form two seemingly endless columns moving forward uphill, over a cultivated terrain. They recall the Korean War as the last true foot soldier's war. Looking out on these columns are thousands of faces etched on a polished granite wall; they are photographs of support forces taken from military archives. These faces are now imprinted forever in the wall which slices through the landscape reflecting the adjacent columns of troopers. Completing this field of service at the north edge, a raised granite curb lists the 22 nations that contributed to this first United Nations effort.

A dark, circular reflecting pool lies at the apex of the triangular field. The pool is surrounded by a circular bosque of clipped Linden trees. A triangular peninsula, formed by the convergence of the main walkways which bound the field, extends into the quiet water. A low wall forms the edge to this peninsula on the south, upon which a reminder of the sacrifices has been carved:

"FREEDOM IS NOT FREE"

1

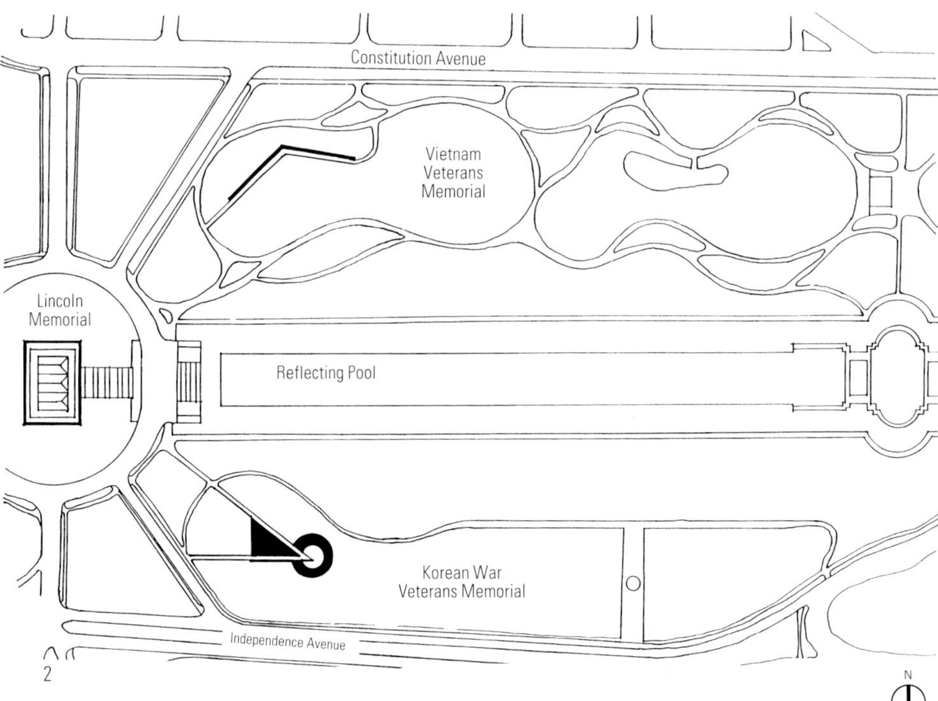

2

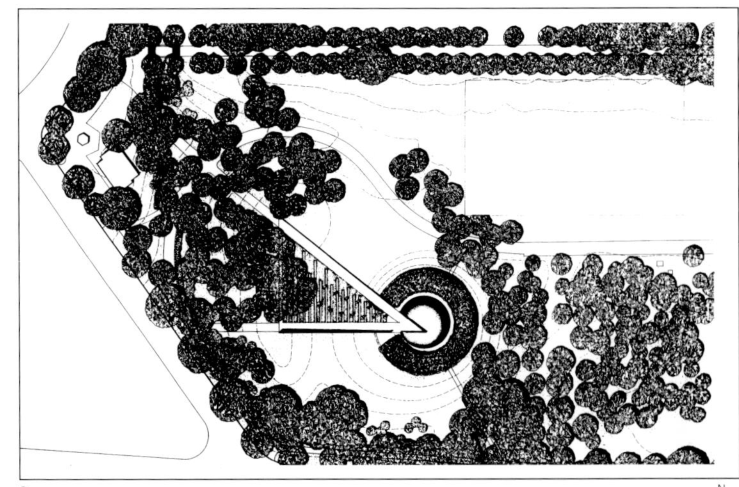

3

1 The circulation design leads visitors around a simple 'V' configuration allowing the Memorial to be experienced from two different directions without loss of content or message

2 Two major axis, the Mall's east–west alignment and the Lincoln-Jefferson vista, are employed as the site orienting principles of the design

3 The architectural design concept is based on a formal geometric composition of 'overlapping' the interpretive elements, sculpture, mural wall and pool

4 The cast stainless steel figures form two seemingly endless columns moving forward uphill recalling the Korean War as the last true foot soldier's war

5 Under a shady bower of trees, visitors are received with a place to pause and reflect, to remember or to learn of the enormous sacrifice of the Korean War

Photography: Carol Highsmith

4

5

Pacific Northwest Museum of Natural History

BOORA Architects, P.C.

Completion: July 1994

Location: Ashland, Oregon, USA

Client: Pacific Northwest Museum of Natural History

Area: 2,493 square metres; 26,840 square feet

Structure: Cast-in-place concrete; steel roof supports

Materials: Sandblasted concrete; regional stones; metal roofing

Cost: US$3.4 million

Awards: American Institute of Architects, Portland, Oregon Chapter, Citation Award

The US$3.4 million Pacific Northwest Museum of Natural History in Ashland, Oregon, serves as a scientific, research, and cultural centre for the public, nearby Southern Oregon State College and research organisations. The 14 acre site offers panoramic views of the Cascade Range and the Siskiyou Mountains. The building is designed on one level to hug the gently sloping site and provide maximum sunlight. The design recalls the distant mountain organic landscape forms that can clearly be seen by interstate travellers.

The museum is less ambitious than when BOORA was hired in 1986 and when supporters launched their fundraising campaign. What was to be a US$21 million facility was scaled down to a US$9 million project, and again to its current US$3.4 million size. The necessary funds were raised through federal, state and private sources. But what the facility lost in size it gained in educational value. The museum offers public education to provide a basis for informed dialogue and problem solving on critical natural resource issues.

The museum's captivating indoor and outdoor exhibits and engaging educational programs provide a comprehensive view of nature past, present and future, that includes an examination of plants and animals, minerals, fossils, land formation, ecosystems of the Northwest and human history and prehistory. Other program areas include offices, lecture and conference space, science classroom, 100-seat theatre and gift shop.

The concrete entry plaza and lobby floor are articulated with a variety of regional stone types which increase in area as one passes through the transparent vestibule and approaches the exhibit entry. A water feature and rock formation at the edge of the plaza appear to pass through the vestibule wall, becoming a pool, waterfall and finally a lava tube cave which is the entry to the exhibits.

The primarily orthogonal walls that enclose the offices, classroom and exhibits are made of exposed cast-in-place concrete while, in contrast, the curvilinear shaped section of the central axis and the cross-axial entry are made of steel and metal panels.

Sustainable building strategies incorporate low maintenance, enduring materials, natural lighting of public spaces admitted through high performance glazing, on-site water retention, drought resistant landscaping, and minimal disruption of existing site contours.

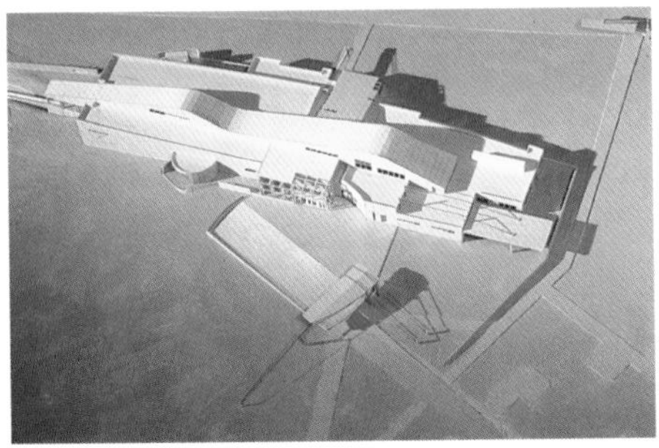

1

2

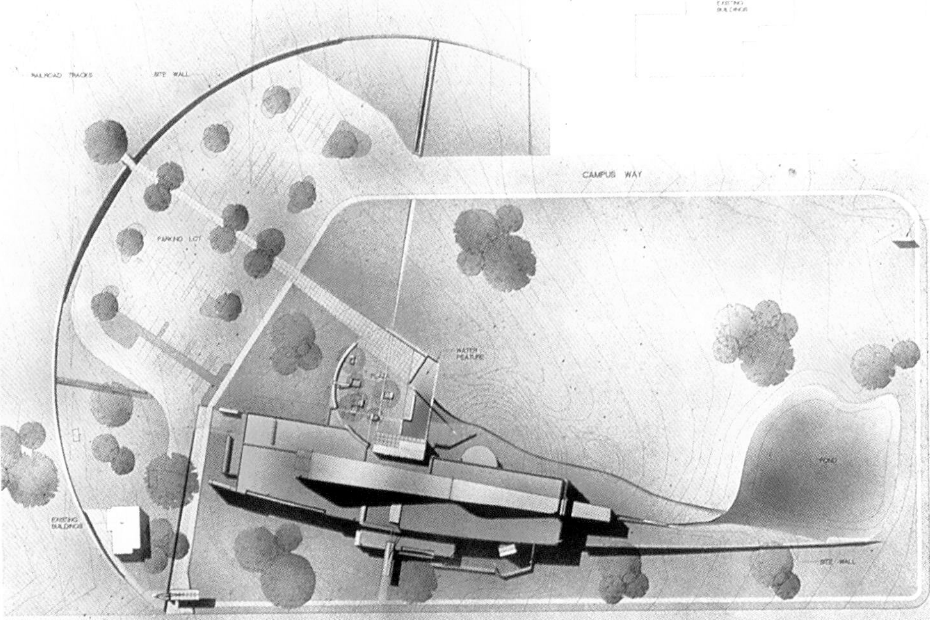

3

4

1 Overall site organisation
2 North view
3 Site plan
4 Northwest view of building and area for future exterior exhibits
5 Entry plaza
6 Waterfall feature in lobby
7 Contemplative area
8 Gift shop
9 Systems detail
10 Outdoor gathering space

Photography: C. John Hughel, Jr.

5

6

7

8

9

10

Richmond Hill Central Library

A.J. Diamond, Donald Schmitt & Company

Completion: October 1994

Location: Richmond Hill, Ontario, Canada

Client: Town of Richmond Hill

Area: 7,000 square metres; 75,350 square feet

Structure: Poured-in-place concrete

Materials: Precast concrete cladding; glass; steel; carpet; wood; slate; polished plaster

Cost: CA$17 million

Awards: 1994 Concrete Building Award of Excellence

1994 Governor Generals Award of Merit

The Richmond Hill Central Library is not only the major component of the library system for the Town, but also a key component of the Richmond Hill Civic Centre.

The library houses 170,000 volumes, and occupies 7,000 square metres (75,350 square feet) of space. The most advanced technologies for libraries have been incorporated into the design—for example, computerised cataloguing and retrieval systems, including on-line access to all branches and the centralised Ontario-wide catalogue.

A hallmark of the design is the high level of integration between structural, mechanical and electrical systems, and the manner in which the structure has been used as an element of the architecture. The structure has been utilised to define and give the appropriate proportion to the various rooms within the library.

While natural light is harmful to print material, it is also an essential ingredient in the achievement of satisfying, humane buildings. Thus light has been given much consideration, and is admitted, filtered, screened or blocked as appropriate to each of the library activities and spaces.

Provision for growth has been made in two ways. First the structure is designed to accept another floor of construction which will allow the administration, now housed above the stacks, to relocate to the penthouse floor, in turn allowing collection and stack extension. Second, the plan has been configured to allow strategic horizontal expansion for the growth of administrative facilities.

1

2

3

4

0 5 10m

5

0 5 10m

1 View of main facade from east
2 Main entrance, south elevation
3 View from southeast
4 North–south section
5 East–west section
6 North elevation
7 Entrance colonnade looking east
8 Main stair from ground floor
9 South reading room
10 Main reading room from 3rd floor balcony
11 South reading room
12 Entrance corridor, handicap ramp and display cases

Photography: Steven Evans

6

7

8

9

10

11

12

Techniquest

Ahrends Burton and Koralek

Completion: May 1995
Location: Cardiff Bay, UK
Client: Cardiff Bay Development Corporation
Area: 3,500 square metres; 37,675 square feet
Structure: Existing iron frame; steel; concrete
Materials: Glass; brick; aluminium cladding
Cost: GB£7.4 million

1

2

The new building for Techniquest, which retains and gives new life to the structure of the Bailey's Heavy Engineering workshop, will be one of the principle visitor attractions in the Inner Harbour area of Cardiff Bay.

Techniquest is an educational charity with one of the leading 'hands on' science and technology exhibitions in the country. The new building presented the challenge of accommodating a three-fold increase in their previous facilities, whilst maintaining the intimate and very personal character of the exhibition. It is anticipated that the project will attract over 200,000 visitors per year.

The exhibition space is designed onto and around the mid-19th century cast and wrought iron structure, completely transforming this, whilst preserving its integrity. This structure consists of heavy cast iron columns and beams supporting a 25 ton transporter crane as well as a relatively light wrought iron roof structure consisting of arched trusses. The crane has been retained as an exhibit.

The exhibition space, which incorporates mezzanine floors, occupies the full 11 metre (36 foot) high volume of the old engineering works. Adjacent to this is a workshop area for the construction and maintenance of exhibits. The upper floors are reached by two generous open tread stairs and an open hydraulic scissor lift in a glazed enclosure. The first floor includes an exhibition area of a more enclosed character to allow for light sensitive exhibits and a small library and reference area. At second floor level there is a circular mushroom shaped viewing platform overlooking the main exhibition areas. The scheme also includes a science laboratory and a mini planetarium known as 'Starlab' as well as a small semicircular lecture theatre, the design of which is based on the theatre at the Royal Society in London. Administrative offices and staff accommodation are also located on the first floor mezzanine.

There are entrances on both sides of the building from Stuart Street to the north and from the visitors car park adjacent to the Graving Docks to the south. A large glazed wall, shaded by an external sunscreen, overlooks the old graving docks to the south whilst a series of curved and stepped brick walls, in Staffordshire Blue engineering bricks, shelter the building to the north, establishing a generous entrance forecourt on Stuart Street. 'Starlab' is contained within a small concrete sphere clad in aluminium triangular panels and marks the location of the north entrance. The other elevations are largely of glass, consisting of double planar glazing supported on lightweight tubular steel space frame structures. On the south facing elevation this steel structure is external and also supports the external sun shading in a transparent black fabric. The two gable walls are set back from the ends of the roof structure and are supported on internal tubular steel structures. The existing arched roof trusses are exposed internally and externally, supporting a thin curved roof clad with standing seam aluminium in single sheets across the entire span. Internal finishes, as well as the building fabric itself, are in muted neutral colours, silver, and various shades of grey and white, which complement and provide an effective background to the bright primary colours of the Techniquest exhibits.

3

4

5

6

7

8

9

1 Sketch from east
2 Sketch from south
3 Original mid-19th century iron structure
4 View across Inner Harbour
5 View from the 'Graving Docks' looking north
6 Entrance canopy
7 Detail of sunscreen from outside
8 Detail of sunscreen from inside
9 View of exhibition space
Photography: Peter Cook

Årsta Haninge Strand Golf Clubhouse

Hans Murman Arkitektkontor AB

Completion: August 1995

Location: Sweden

Client: Skanska

Area: 530 square metres; 5,705 square feet

Structure: Concrete; wood frame

Materials: Pinewood panels

Cost: 3.5 million SEK

The site is on a small elevation with a wide view of the golf course. The national land use planning had put out the countryside here and in the neighbourhood of highest interest of the Swedish agricultrual landscape. As such, Hans Murman had to be careful with both location and design of the clubhouse.

In the lobby, stone was used on the floor to make it possible for golfers to walk on with nails under their shoes.

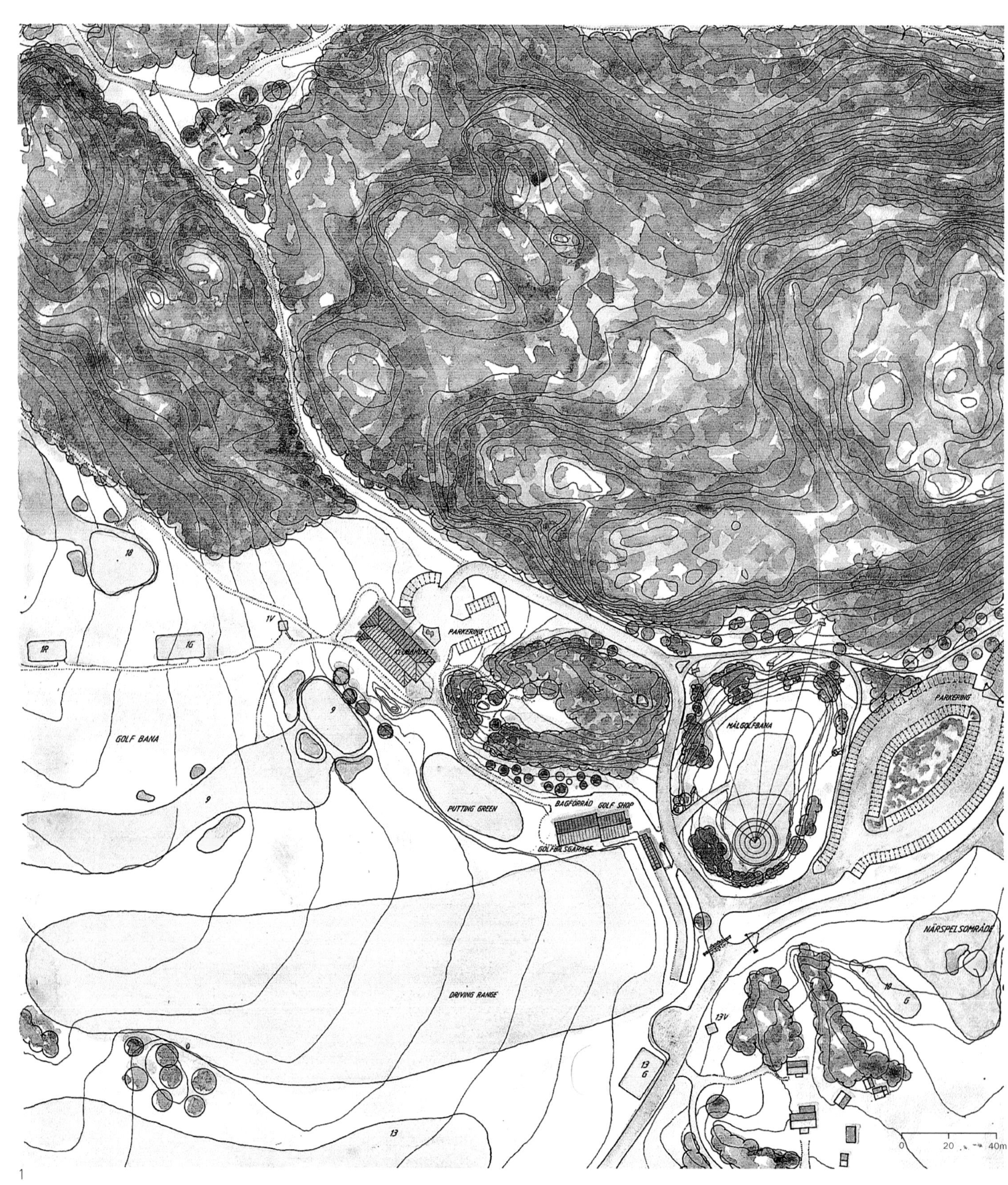

1

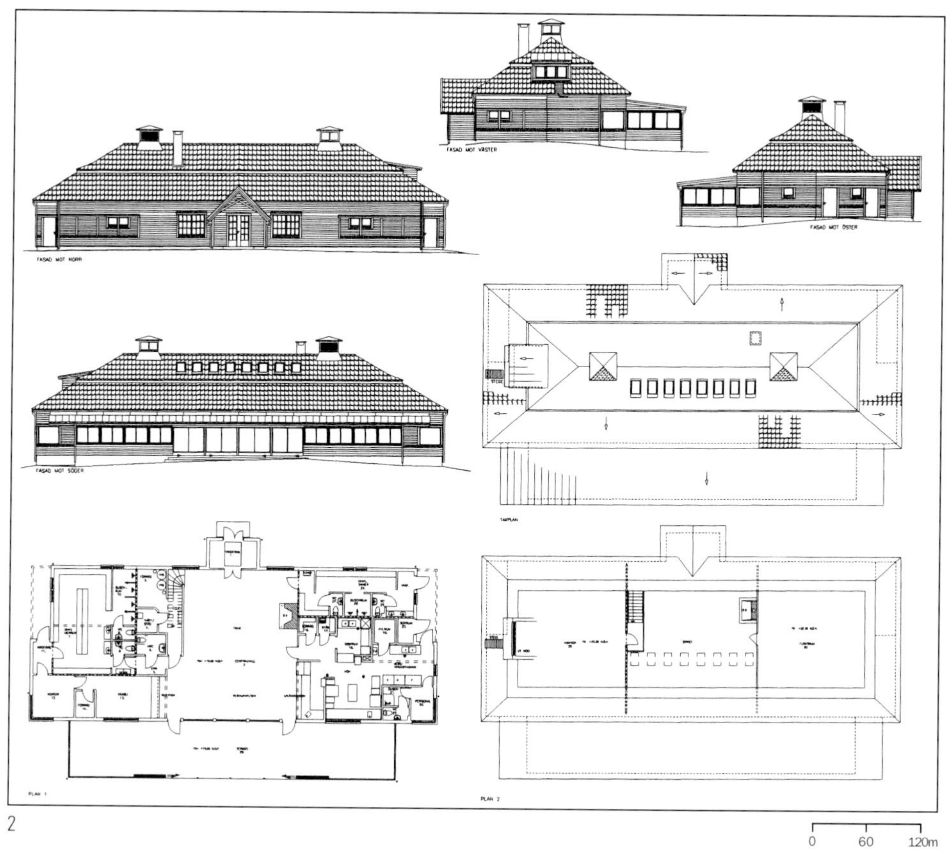

2

0 60 120m

3

1 Site plan
2 Elevation and plans
3 Early cross section through the lobby

4 The stone paved terrace with overview over the golfcourse
5 The roof over the terrace also gives shelter from rain
6 The clubhouse seen from the 9th fairway

4

5

6

The Belvedere

Mitchell/Giurgola Architects

Completion: August 1995

Location: Battery Park City, New York, USA

Client: Battery Park City Authority

Area: 1.6 acres

Materials: Dakota granite stone wall; stainless steel pylons; teak and stainless steel railings; English Oak trees; Honey Locust trees

Cost: US$6 million

Awards: 1996 National Honor Award for Urban Design, The American Institute of Architects

1995 International Excellence on the Waterfront Award

1. Stainless steel pylons by Martin Puryear
2. View of south wall showing pedestrian linkage to the World Financial Center
3. Site plan
4. Aerial view of the site
5. View of the esplanade along south wall looking west
6. Arrival at the water's edge
7. View south on the esplanade towards the pylons and Statue of Liberty
8. View from the Belvedere to the Statue of Liberty and the New Jersey shoreline

Photography: Jeff Goldberg/Esto Photographics

The Belvedere is among the most prominent and pivotal sites in lower Manhattan, a 1.6 acre parcel located at the north corner of North Cove, a marina at the foot of the World Financial Center. Surrounded by water on two sides, with views of the Hudson River, Ellis Island, Liberty Island and the New Jersey shoreline, the site is part of the continuous sequence of public open spaces along the river's edge. The client called for the park to accommodate both residential and commercial aspects of the site, including thousands of commuters from the Trans-Hudson ferry terminal. The new park connects the World Financial Center Plaza to North Park, and provides an informal relaxation place for residents of the adjacent neighbourhood and employees of the commercial district. The design is the result of a collaboration between the architect, landscape architect and artist, co-ordinated by a public arts consultant representing the client.

The site was previously interrupted by a turnaround cul-de-sac roadway. By shortening the street and relocating it to the north, visual and physical connections to the water were, for the first time, reestablished for over 40,000 employees of the World Financial Center. In addition, for ferry commuters, the Belvedere becomes a new waterfront gateway into lower Manhattan. Primary elements of the park are: an elevated platform area with a bosque of trees and a belvedere for viewing the New York Harbour; the Esplanade; and, a battered stone wall. A formal densely planted bosque of English Oak trees provides a high canopy to shade the site in contrast to informal groves of Honey Locust at the Belvedere and Esplanade. Paths through the trees lead to the Belvedere, the Esplanade and a lower level viewing area at the water's edge. Benches are located throughout the bosque. At the lower level, the Esplanade runs along the edge of the Hudson River and continues as a consistent strip of waterfront walk. Mediating the two levels is a Dakota granite battered stone wall which changes configuration as it curves around the Belvedere and becomes serpentine to reflect the curvilinear walls along the river's edge in Hudson River Park. The battered wall recalls the stone fortifications at the base of the Statue of Liberty. The wall and teak railing also provide a continuous seating surface, offering views of the harbour and activity along the water's edge. Broad steps and ramps are cut into the wall to connect the upper level with the lower Esplanade, At the bosque, 24 metre (80 foot) wide steps provide areas for sitting and sunning, leading to the river's edge. Two striking multi-storey stainless steel light pylons, designed by a noted sculptor, serve as distinctive markers of the park as well as provide a symbolic welcome to those entering the site by ferry.

The park is formal and informal, resolving a critical connection between two landscapes; a modern and corporate open plaza to the east and a romantic park to the north. Linear and informal tree arrangements, framed views and traditional materials provide the framework within which a very flexible and free use of the space is possible, a rare amenity in New York City.

1

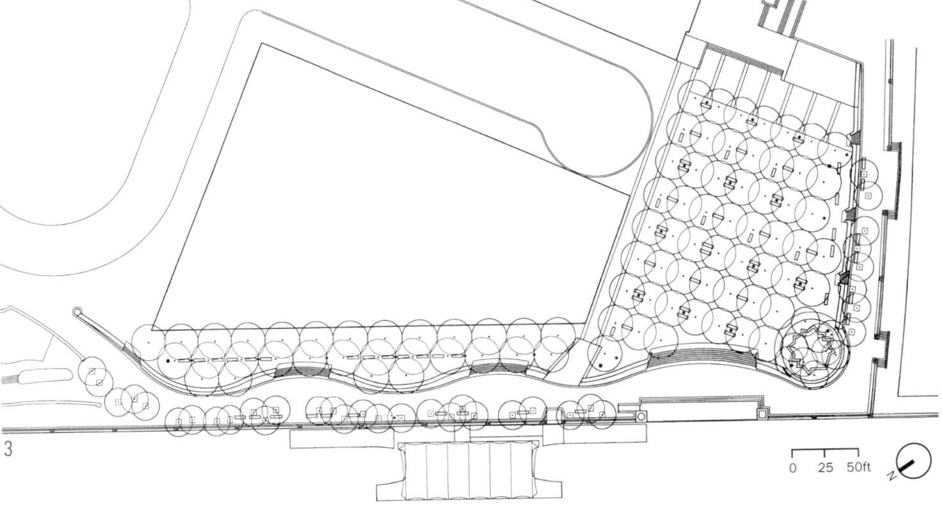

3

2

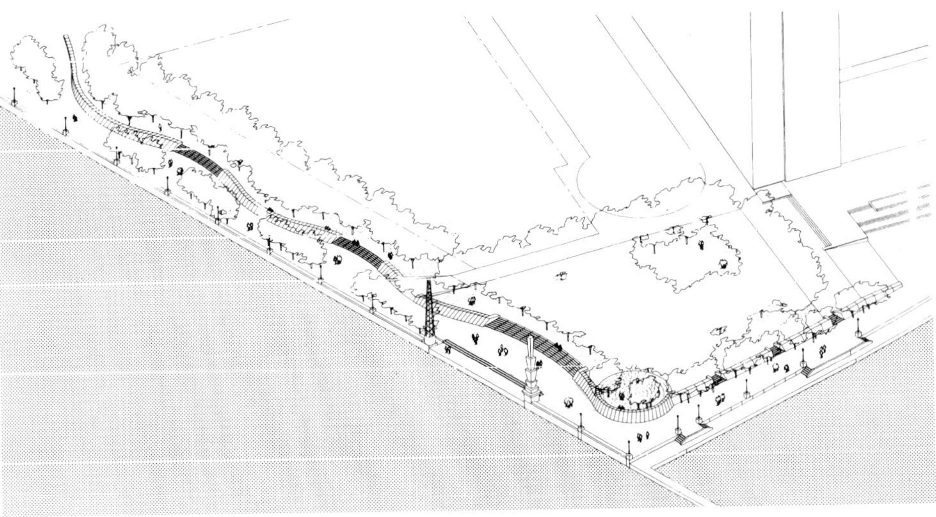

4

5

6

7

8

Gund Arena

Ellerbe Becket, Inc.

Completion: August 1994

Location: Cleveland, Ohio, USA

Client: Gateway Development Corporation

Area: 68,746 square metres; 740,000 square feet

Structure: Steel superstructure; long span steel truss roof

Materials: Exterior precast concrete panels; glass curtain wall

Cost: US$136 million

Ellerbe Becket was commissioned to design Cleveland's Gund Arena for the NBA Cavaliers. The prominent downtown site of the arena is part of an overall Gateway Complex which also includes a new baseball stadium, shared public space, structured parking and retail/office facilities. The Complex is envisioned as an important landmark and civic development. The design accommodates 20,000 seats for basketball and includes 96 luxury 'loge' boxes, restaurants, a practice court, internal ticket arcade, a variety of food courts, parking for 3,000 cars and an underground service area that can accommodate up to 19 semi-tractor trailer trucks simultaneously.

The arena is based on a split loge design concept featuring 28 loges in the lower deck and 68 loges just below the upper deck. The seating split is such that 60% of spectators will be located in the lower deck, with the remainder in the upper. The seating is as close to the event floor as possible and viewing is unobstructed by the structure. In planning the arena, the sightline focal point is set at the top of the hockey dasher. This point establishes the slope of the seating sections and provides excellent sightlines for professional basketball and hockey.

The arena is sited in the northern portion of the 18 acre Gateway site which serves as a transition zone between the interstate and industrial zone to the south, and the central business district, including historic Terminal Tower, to the north. The Cuyahoga River and the historic 'Flats' area are just to the west.

The arena design responds to the rich architectural heritage of Cleveland and its historical context, but also looks forward to the new century and to the spirit of Cleveland and its people.

1

2

3

4

1 Arcade entrance
2 Cav's Town—team store
3 Exterior at day
4 Exterior at night
5 Sammy's restaurant
6 Sports bar
7 Front entry detail

Photography: Timothy Hursley

5

6

7

Kiel Center Arena

Ellerbe Becket, Inc.

Completion: September 1994

Location: St Louis, Missouri, USA

Client: Kiel Partners, L.P.

Area: 60,664 square metres; 653,000 square feet

Structure: Poured-in-place concrete; long span steel truss roof

Materials: Precast concrete

Cost: US$84 million

The Kiel Center Arena, designed by Ellerbe Becket, will be home to the NHL St. Louis Blues and to St. Louis University's basketball team, the Billikins. In addition to being able to accommodate a possible NBA team in the future, the facility is capable of hosting a full spectrum of sports, civic and entertainment events.

The multi-functional arena incorporates a maximum total spectator capacity of 20,500 seats, and contains a hockey rink and multipurpose floor. The main arena accommodates 18,500 hockey fans, including up to 1,500 premium seats, 85 private suites and four party suites. A restaurant and lounge space will overlook the event floor.

The auditorium portion of the existing 1930s Kiel Opera House, and an adjacent parking structure will be demolished to provide the site in downtown St. Louis. The new arena will be attached to the remaining Opera House, which provides an appropriate frontice piece for the project on the Market Street Mall. The Opera House and its exhibit hall, also owned and operated by the arena's owner, will be restored and will share the use of the arena's service facilities, creating a multi-faceted entertainment complex.

The new facility is seen as a catalyst in the development of an entertainment district. A new metro link station is being constructed across the street to the south. A new 1,250 car attached parking structure will be built to the west by the City of St. Louis and has been designed as an integral part of the composition of the buildings.

1

2

3

1 Existing Opera House entrance
2 Exterior at day
3 Exterior at dawn
4 New arena and existing Opera House
5 Front entry detail
6 Main concourse
7 Sports bar
Photography: Heidrich Blessing

4

5

6

7

Night Safari

Consultants Incorporated

Completion: June 1994
Location: Singapore
Client: Singapore Zoological Gardens
Area: 100 acres
Structure: Exposed timber trusses
Materials: Slate tiles
Cost: S$60 million

Open only at dusk, the warm glow of the Entrance Area welcomes visitors who can choose to begin their twilight adventure with a ride on the tram or walk the trails through carefully planned representations of eight major habitat zones.

Throughout the design phase of the exhibits, the architect had to resolve a myriad of issues. Three major factors had to be balanced at all times—the needs of the visitor, the needs of the animals and the operational needs of the ground staff. With every animal having different requirements, each exhibit posed its own challenges. Within each of the design solutions can also be found a unique marriage of architectural expertise with civil and structural expertise, zoological expertise as well as landscape expertise.

The single common denominator throughout all the exhibit designs is the desire to always create a close relationship between man and nature. This can be seen in the respect for the site, its natural existing physical formations and its fauna—where possible, much of the existing site is retained. The front barriers are also deliberately designed to be unobtrusively seamless and are either hidden from view or disguised and merged as part of the landscape. The constant interplay of light, sound and vista also have an important role in creating the right scenario. At many points along the way, spectacular views of the surrounding waters can be enjoyed as well as lingering journeys through tracts of flora and fauna. At every turn, there is a surprise to delight the visitor.

The design of the building embraces much of the same principles. Mainly low, single-storey structures, the buildings are deliberately kept without walls unless absolutely necessary. This allows the free flow of the inside spaces to the outside spaces and vice versa.

A case in point is the Toilet design where a private garden is made an integral component of the toilet, i.e. without any wall separating the toilet from the garden. The garden lends effect to the overall ambience in which visitors can wash their hands amidst lush and tropical planting.

Visitors are also always given an option to lounge or dine in attractive outdoor spaces. Such terraces and plazas with spectacular views and open to the sky are found both at the Entrance Area and the East Lodge.

1

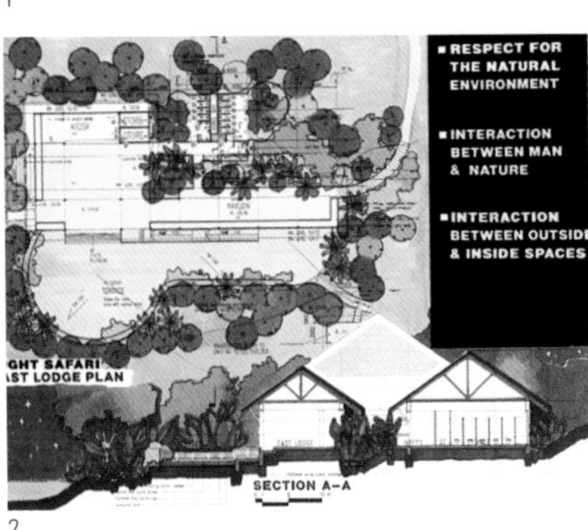

2

3

4

1 Sections through exhibits
2 East lodge plan and section
3 Site plan
4 Entrance area plan
5 Ghavial & Owl exhibit at dusk
6 Entrance area restaurant
Photography: Stefen Byfield

5

6

Porto Europa Wakayama Marina City

Ellerbe Becket, Inc.

Completion: July 1994

Location: Wakayama, Japan

Client: MCA Recreation Services, North Hollywood

Area: 20,558 square metres; 221,295 square feet

Structure: Structural steel

Materials: Exterior precast concrete panels; glass curtain wall

Cost: US$120 million

Ellerbe Becket provided architectural design services to support the owner's art directors and concept designers in the development of a concentrated and highly themed Mediterranean Seaport Village, an entertainment complex located in Wakayama Marina city in Japan. The complex, which opened in July 1994, includes an enclosed stunt show theatre, water flume ride and simulator attraction, as well as food and retail facilities. The project consists of three buildings plus area development work.

Building 1 is a 7,539 square metre (81,150 square foot) castle-like structure containing a live action stunt show arena and support areas for employee lockers and break rooms. The main mechanical and electrical rooms for the entire entertainment district are also contained in Building 1. Included as part of this building is a Chute thrill ride which is physically separated from the building but does pass through it and is integral with portions of it. A terrace, fast food facility and a queue area structure for the chute ride are also included in Building 1.

Building 2 is a 4,660 square metre (50,170 square foot) multi-use building containing a disco, jazz club, retail areas, fast food facility, casino/arcade area and virtual game facility. The building has four distinct massing elements separated above grade by narrow exterior alleys and a courtyard. This design approach gives the building a village-like image.

Building 3 is located adjacent to the main plaza on the site. It is an 8,359 square metre (89,975 square foot) building designed as a 'Town Hall' type of structure. It contains two motion base theatres, uni-simulator ride theatres and a 277-seat cinema theatre. In addition, there is a cafe, retail space and administrative offices for this portion of the entertainment district.

Two streets are included as part of the project area development. They are designed primarily for pedestrian use and, other than for service or emergency vehicles, there will be no vehicular traffic on the site. Themed paving, lighting, landscaping and other site systems and amenities are also included.

1

2

3

4

5

6

7

8

1 One of the three entry points
2 'Seafari' adventure motion base theatre and simulator, Games/Cinema building
3 Fountain in Main Plaza
4 View from Castle Terrace
5 View from Castle Terrace with flume ride in foreground
6 View toward Spanish Castle and flume ride 'chute'
7 View from Main Plaza toward arcade (left) and simulator building (right)
8 Internal 'streetscape'
Photography: MCA Recreational Service

Thomas Phillips Johnson Health & Recreation Center

MacLachlan, Cornelius & Filoni, Inc.

Completion: October 1994
Location: Bethany, West Virginia, USA
Client: Bethany College
Area: 4,830 square metres; 52,000 square feet
Structure: Steel frame
Materials: Shingle roofs; masonry
Cost: US$5.1 million

The Thomas Phillips Johnson Health & Recreation Center is a complex of renovated and newly constructed health, recreation and varsity sports facilities. Projects completed include the renovation of the Hummel Field House, construction of Bethany Stadium, a 400-metre running track with a 1,000-seat grandstand, Hoag Soccer Field, and the Ewing Tennis Center.

The complex is designed to be compatible with both the collegiate Gothic architecture of Bethany College and the rural setting of historic Bethany Village in West Virginia. Sloped roofs recall the lines of the bucolic buildings that dot the countryside and meet the high headroom clearances required for athletic activities; the dormers that punctuate these roofs are reminiscent of those found throughout the campus. In plan, the complex adjoins the Hummel Field House and each successive segment of the building is subtly canted to embrace the end of the track and field, and provide a sense of closure to the stadium. A tower is topped by the Bethany Thistle logo and six flags acknowledging the College's allegiance to country, state and athletic conferences.

Building costs were limited through the efficient use of building materials: pre-engineered building systems customised with dormers, shingle roofs, masonry, exposed structure, and sandwich-panel walls.

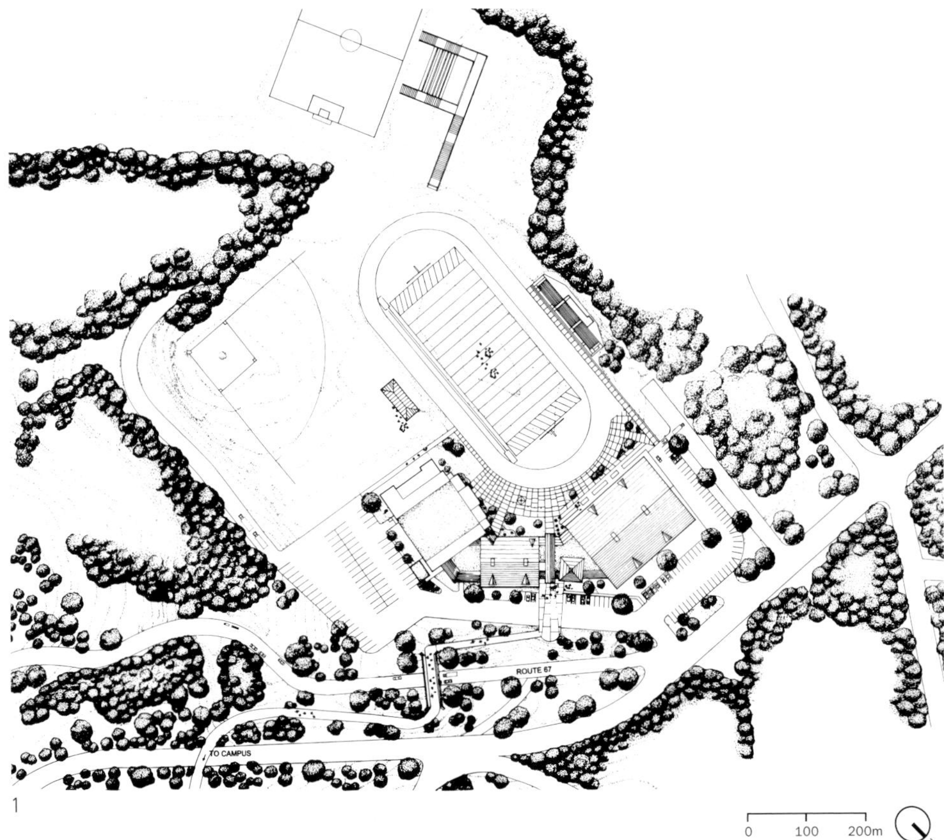

1

2

1 Site plan
2 Aerial view of Bethany College
3 Main entrance
4 Sports plaza

3

4

5

6

7

5 Pool wing
6 Sandwen Gymnasium
7 Bethany stadium and running track
8 Axonometric
9 Entrance
10 Gallery
Photography: Dennis Marsico

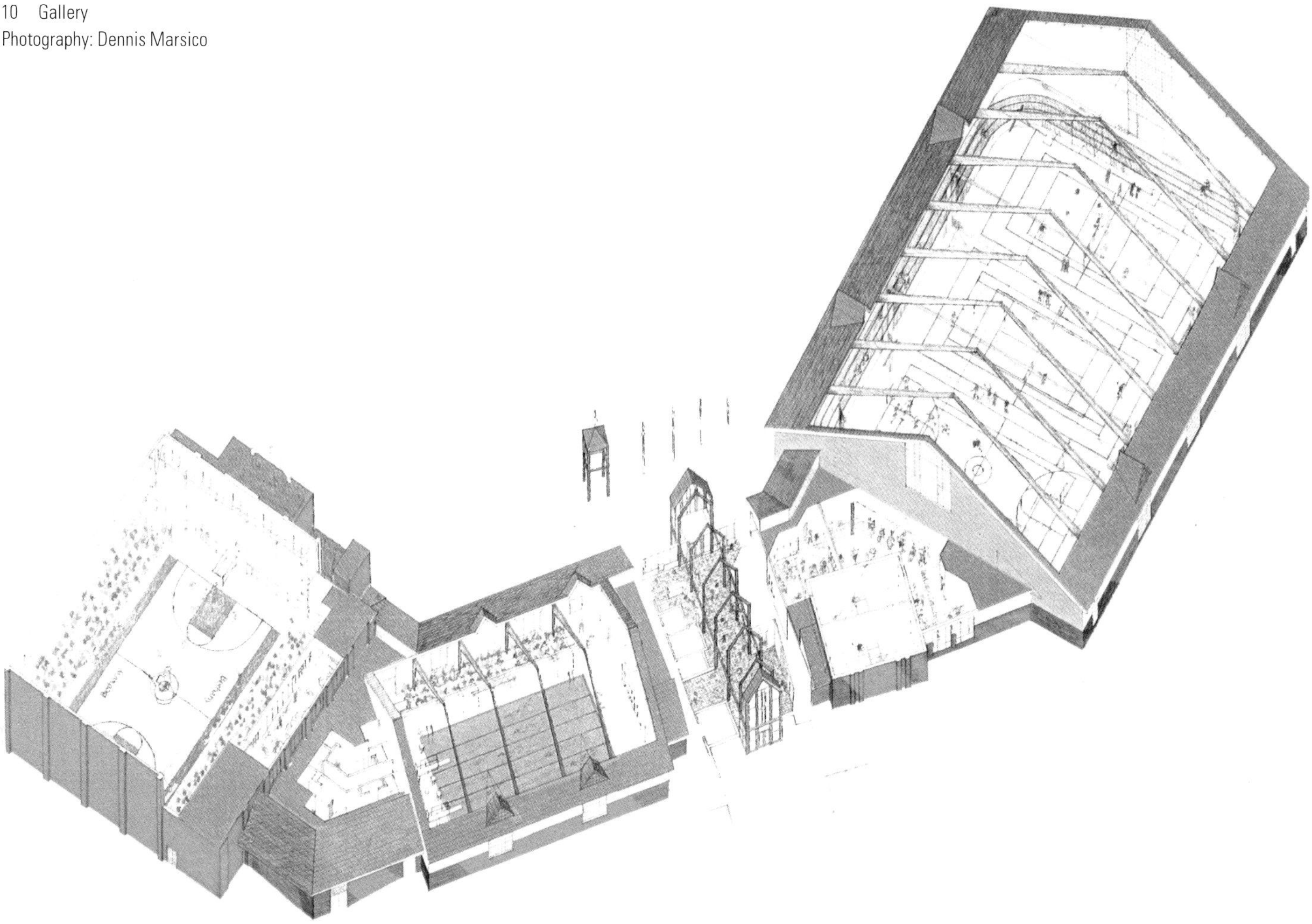

8

9

10

Alta Residence

House + House Architects

Completion: November 1994

Location: Oakland, California, USA

Client: Peterson-Mullin Construction

Area: 204 square metres; 2,200 square feet

Structure: Wood frame

Materials: Cedar siding; stucco; stainless steel cable railings; oak flooring; granite counters; fireplace surrounds; ceramic tile

On a dramatic sloping site in the Oakland Hills, this 204 square metre (2,200 square foot) home was designed to capture views to the San Francisco Bay, Angel Island and the Marin Headlands. After the Oakland Hills firestorm, this property was purchased for development as a speculative venture. Expansive views compensated for the severity of the slope, which proved to be the site's greatest challenge.

The two car garage necessitated a huge cut into the base of the slope, requiring complex shoring for the installation of 5.5 metre (18 foot) high retaining walls. A galvanised gate with curling ribbons of steel invites passage up stairs past the raspberry coloured stucco tower to the tiled entry terrace above the garage. The living room, with high ceilings and bold 2-storey windows, spans the full width of this terrace, taking full advantage of the views. Kitchen, dining and powder rooms step up and back and open onto a very private rear garden surrounded with terraced walls and dense planting. A 3-storey window follows the stairs up to the third floor family room, laundry and two bedrooms which share a bath, and on to the fourth floor master suite with study and private terrace.

Bold cutouts on each floor link the levels in a very sculptural manner and allow, through the careful placement of windows, each part of the house to share in the drama of the views. The sun's path throughout the day helped determine interior volumes and sectional relationships. Stainless steel cable railings with shaped wood detailing and dramatic lighting add interest to the interior and focus to the vertical cutouts. Soft greys and mauves in the walls, carpet and granite provide a touch of colour and complement the turquoise stained cedar sidings and the raspberry stucco.

1

2

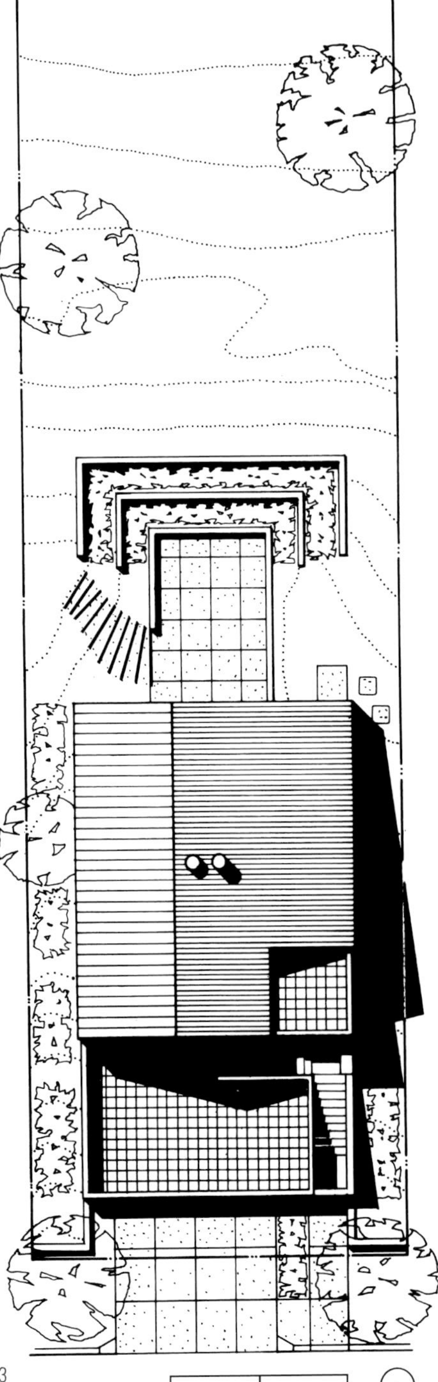

3

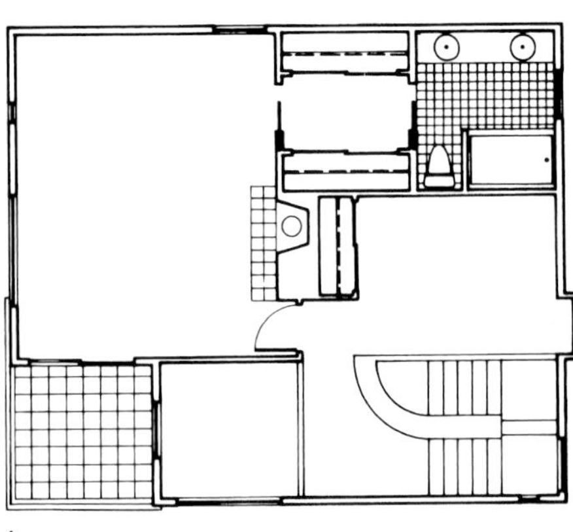

4

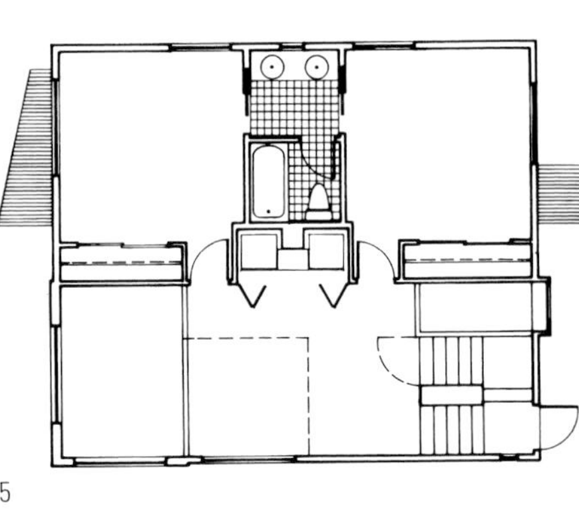

5

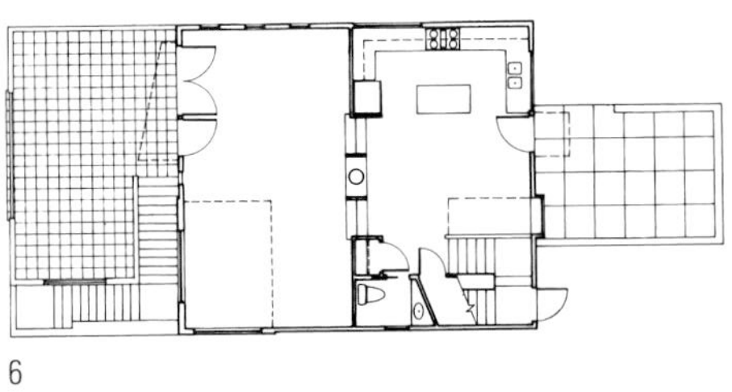

6

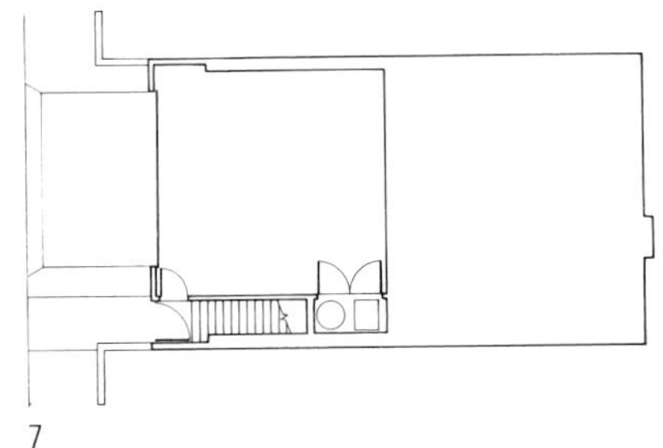

7

1 Evening view of west facade
2 South facade
3 Site plan
4 Third floor plan
5 Second floor plan
6 First floor plan
7 Garage floor plan
8 West facade
9 Living room
10 View of stairway from family room
11 Detail of cable railing
12 Dining room

Photography: Mark Johnson

8

10

11

9

12

Emerald Apartments

Enviro • Tec

Completion: June 1995

Location: Jakarta, Indonesia

Client: PT Niaz Emerald

Structure: Reinforced concrete column; beam frames; precast reinforced concrete piles

Materials: Reinforced concrete; marble; ceramic tiles; anodised aluminium; float glass; wood

Cost: US$15 million

The site consists of two land parcels with a combined net area of 7,500 square metres (80,732 square feet). At the initial stage of conceptual design, the clients called for a single block of service apartments on half of the total land area targeted for leasing purposes with the remaining vacant lot earmarked for future expansion. During the process of conceptualising the architectural design, the local property market for apartments took a brighter turn and it was then decided that two 16-storey apartment blocks of identical layout with a two level basement carpark be constructed as a single phase development.

Prior to finalisation of the apartment layouts, the architectural design of the project had undergone two major revamps; the first restructuring the layouts from smaller service apartments to larger strata units for sale, and then, increasing the overall building height from the original eight storeys to the current height of 16 storeys. The result was a pair of mirror imaged apartment towers with five apartment units per floor, topped with two Penthouse units per tower. The development is supported by a two level basement car park.

Communal facilities include a swimming pool with changing rooms, a tennis court, putting green, lounge bar, gym, restaurant and private residences lounges.

1

2

3

4

1 View of curvilinear glass block wall
2 Exterior view of Tower I
3 View of Tower II
4 Facade treatment
5 View of Twin Towers from Main Road
6 Entrance to Tower I
7 View of reception and security counter
8 View of lobby
9 Atrium planter and skylight
10 Atrium, typical link to apartments

5

6

7

8

9

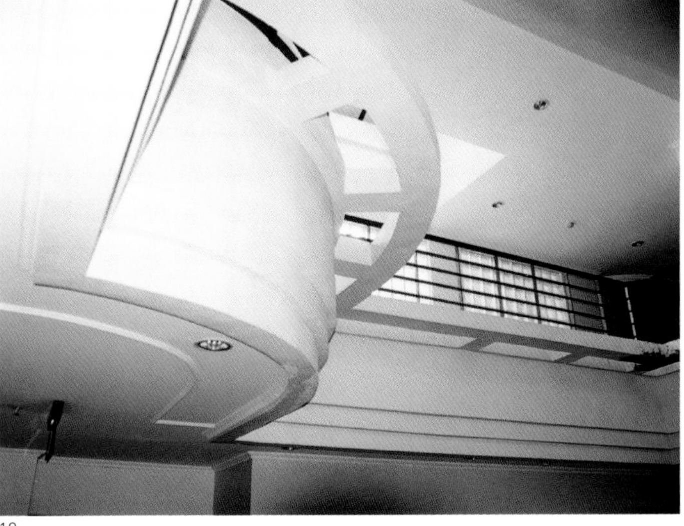
10

Hight Residence

Bart Prince, Architect

Completion: September 1995

Location: Mendocino County, California, USA

Client: Boyd and Mary Kay Hight

Area: 372 square metres; 4,000 square feet

Structure: Concrete; exposed masonry; glue-laminated wood

Materials: Exposed masonry; structural wood beams; cedar; copper; stucco

Cost: US$490,000

This house is designed for a beautiful two acre windswept site above the cliffs overlooking the Pacific Ocean north of the seaside village of Mendocino. The other houses in the area are built on similarly large tracts but are traditional wood/frame structures spaced among the existing cypress trees. This house is designed to initially function as a vacation or weekend home but one which will become the owners' main residence in a few years. It is sited to take advantage of the views to the south and southwest while shielding the occupants from the near constant winds from the north.

On the ground floor the house is divided at the entry by a breezeway which separates the garage with a guestroom above from the main living areas and other bedrooms, The cedar-shingled covered glue-laminated undulating roof parts at this entry point to allow the visitor to take cover from the wind and rain and yet see entirely through the structure to the sea and rock islands beyond. To the right centre of this breezeway is the entrance doorway which leads the occupants past the kitchen and behind the large fireplace mass around to the steps leading up to the main living level. Above and to the west of this living room is the master bedroom suite and to the east is the dining area and kitchen.

The roof structure is visible from inside as a series of glue-laminated beams which create an undulating surface of wood, copper, and glass forming a large space visible from one end to the other over the partitions of the bedrooms at each end. The roof extends nearly to the ground on the north side allowing the wind an easy path over the structure and opening high on the south to the views. Decks and terraces on the south side of the house are protected from the wind and rain water is carried off in channels from the roof to the north.

1

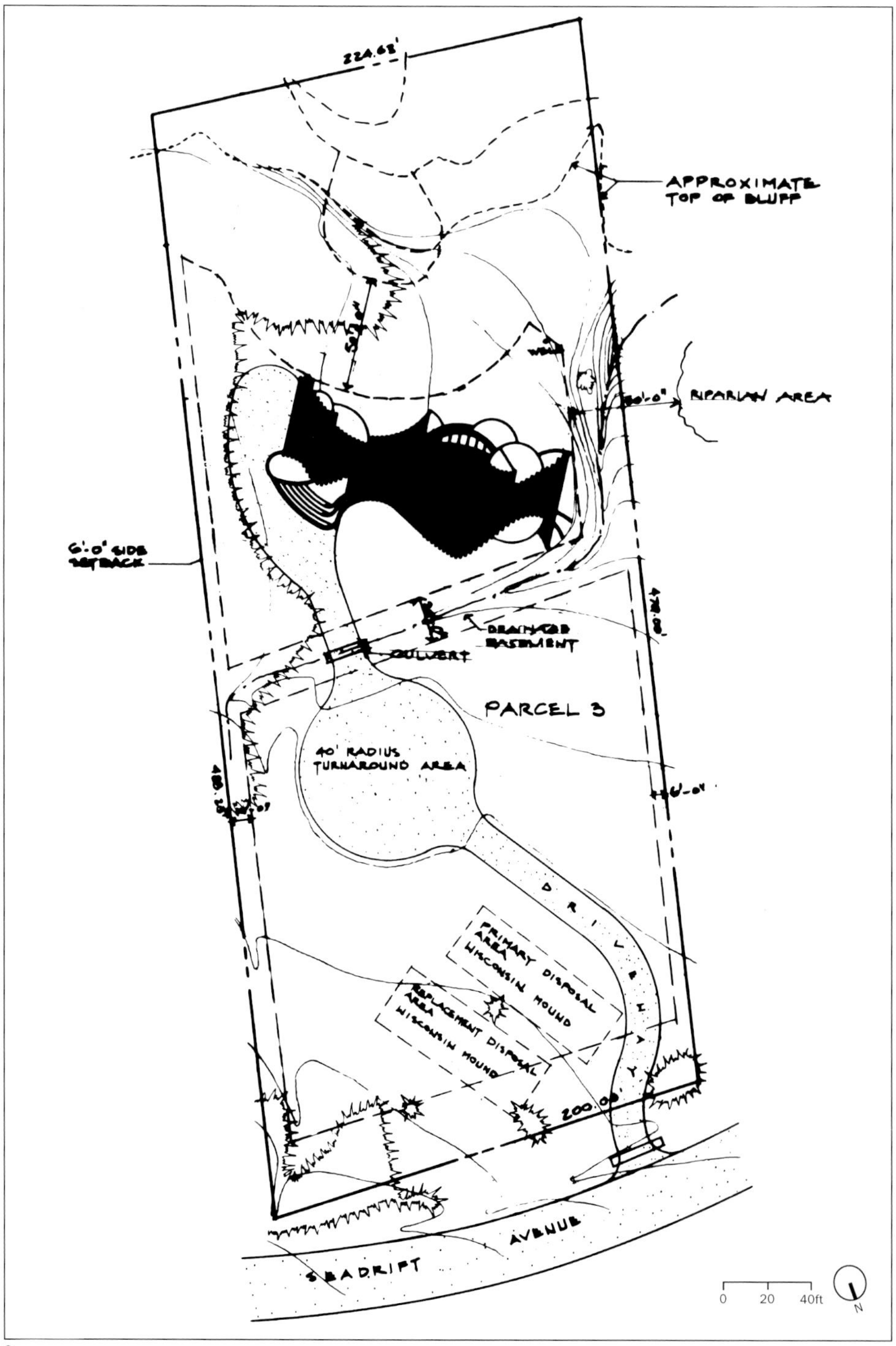

2

1 Interior view of entry
2 Site plan drawing
3 Ground level floor plan
4 View from ocean side looking north

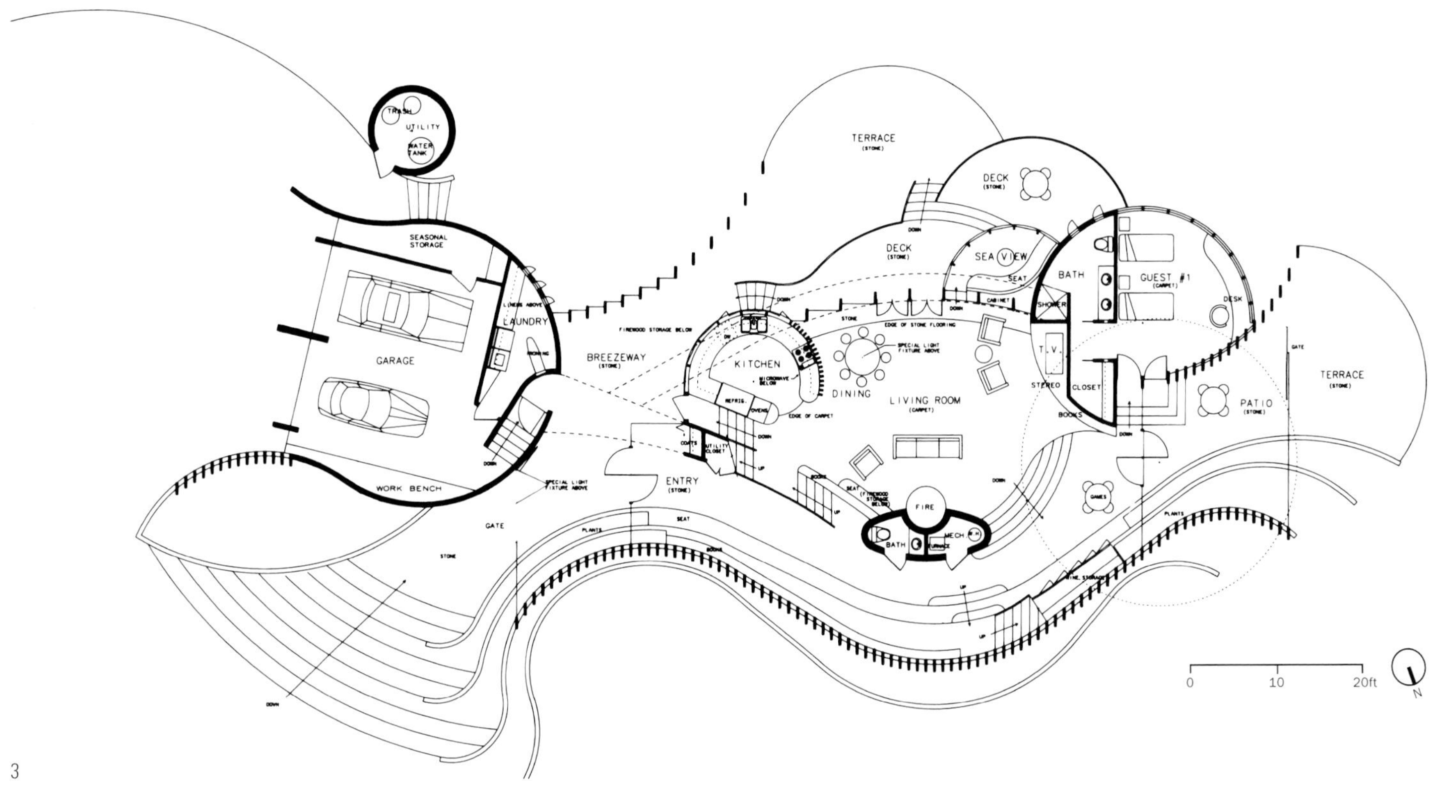
TRASH
UTILITY
WATER TANK
SEASONAL STORAGE
GARAGE
LAUNDRY
WORK BENCH
BREEZEWAY
(STONE)
KITCHEN
DINING
LIVING ROOM
(CARPET)
ENTRY
(STONE)
TERRACE
(STONE)
DECK
(STONE)
DECK
(STONE)
SEA VIEW
BATH
GUEST #1
DESK
T.V.
STEREO
CLOSET
BOOKS
PATIO
(STONE)
TERRACE
(STONE)
FIRE
BATH
MECH
GATE
0
10
20ft
N

3

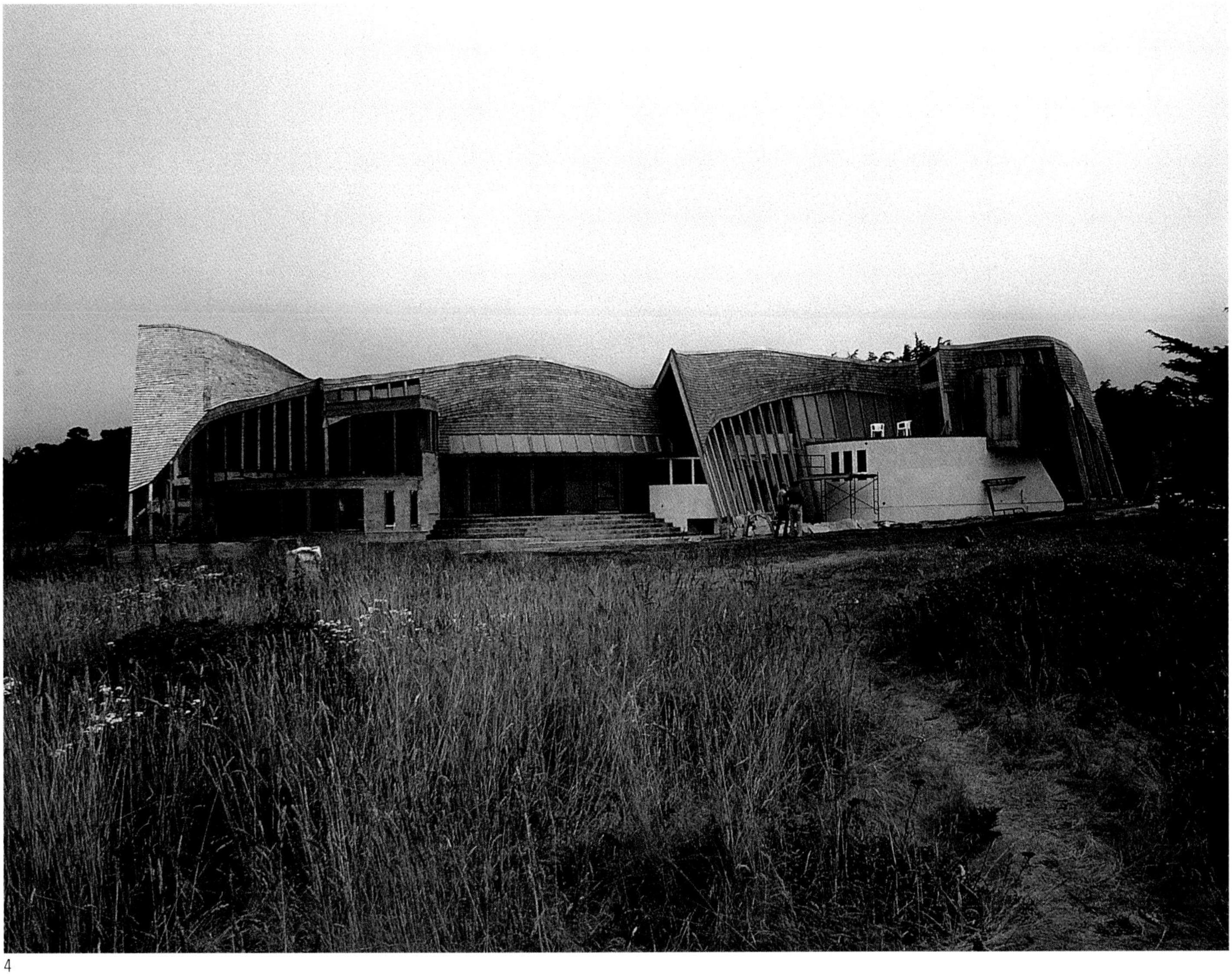

4

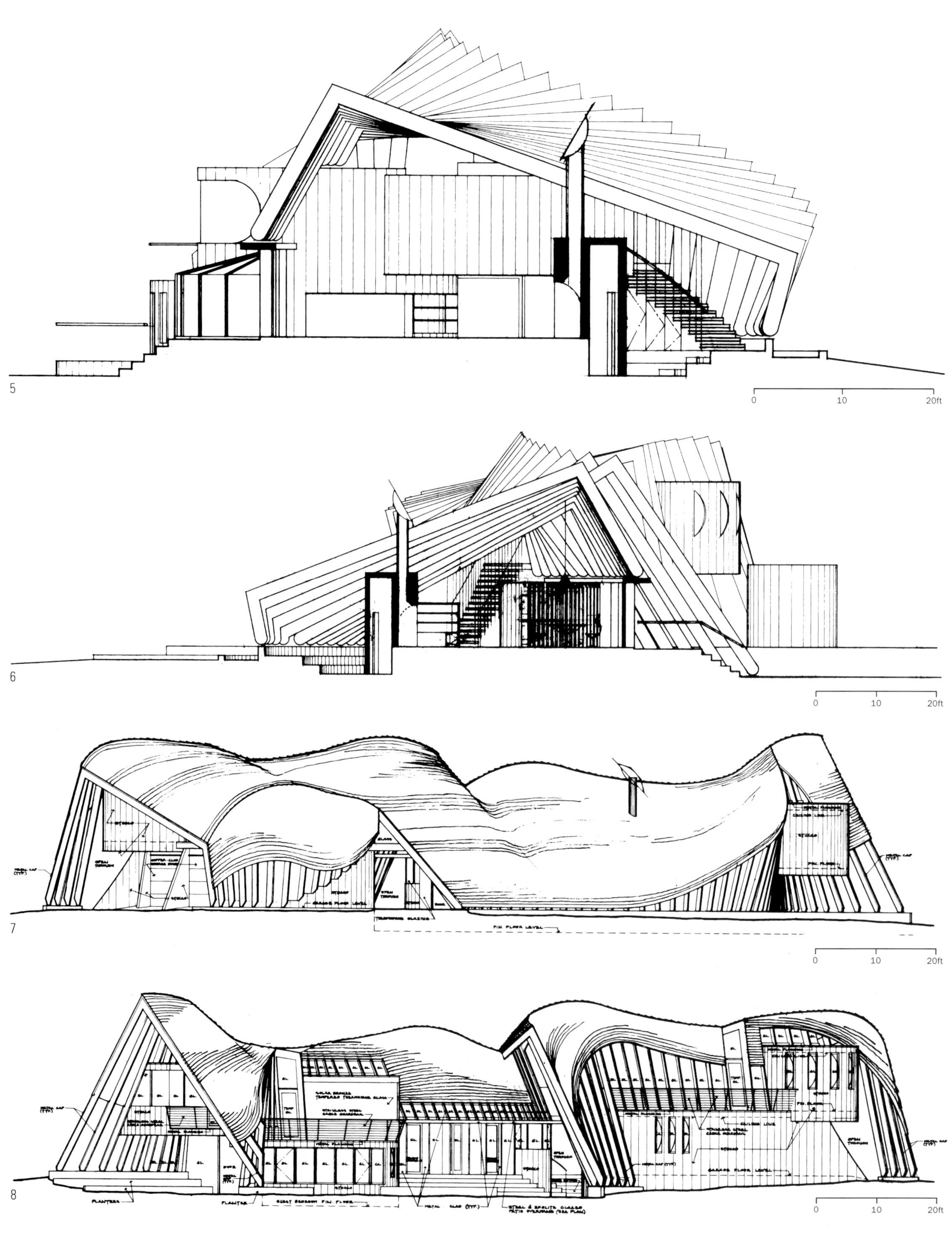
5
0
10
20ft
6
0
10
20ft
7
0
10
20ft
8
0
10
20ft

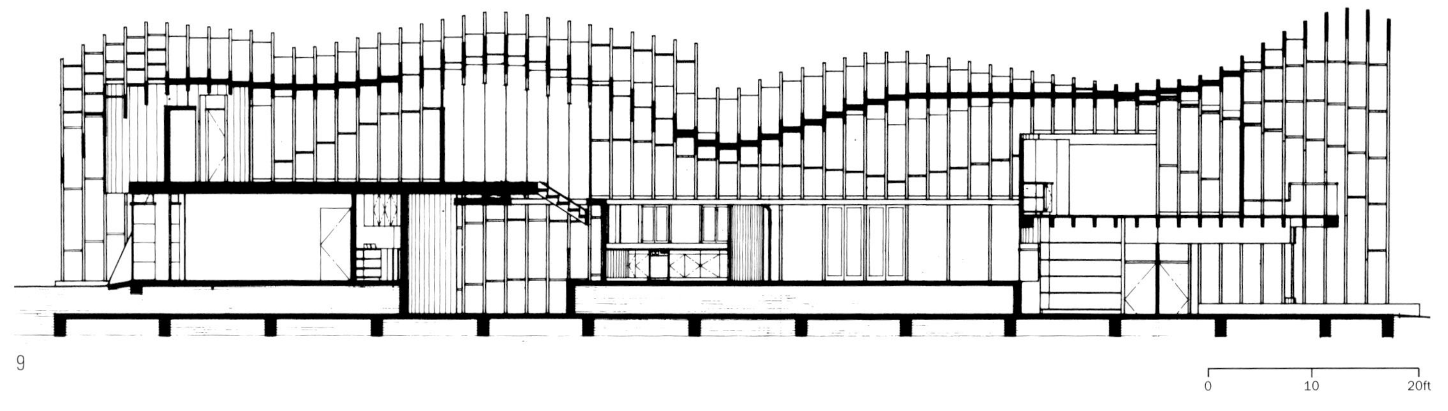

9

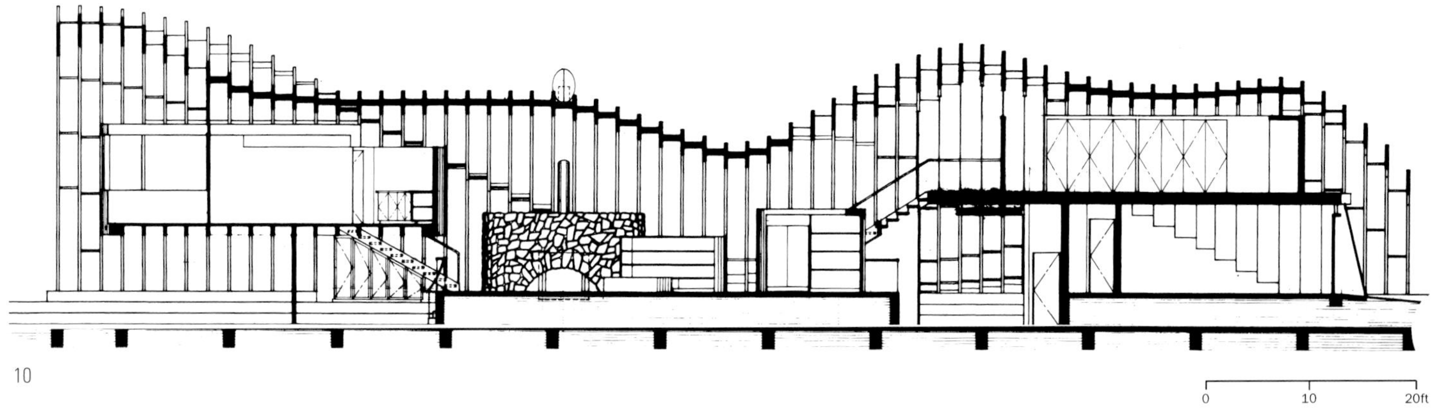

10

11

12

13

5 Building section looking west
6 Building section looking east
7 Street side (north) elevation
8 Ocean side (south) elevation
9 Longitudinal section looking south
10 Longitudinal section looking north
11 View of exterior looking southeast
12 View of exterior looking south
13 Detail of south side at breezeway

Imperial Palace

G&W Architects, Engineers, Project Development Consultants

Completion: October 1995
Location: Quezon City, Philippines
Client: N & M Land Development, INC.
Area: 14,000 square metres; 150,700 square feet
Structure: Reinforced concrete

Imperial Palace is a 12-storey service apartment complex, featuring basement valet parking and amenities including a gymnasium, swimming pool with adjacent coffee shop, and spaces for commercial lease.

1

1-2 Apartment facade

2

J. Tezzanos Pinto House

A.H. Ravazzani

Completion: January 1995

Location: Punta del Este, Uruguay

Client: Mr J. Tezzanos Pinto

Area: 372 square metres; 4,000 square feet

Structure: Reinforced concrete; pattern boards; tile

Materials: Natural brick; ceramic tiles; local stones; granite cobbled stone; wood

Cost: US$100,000

The house is located on the road of the highest real estate value in the area, fifty metres from the ocean, with an eastern exposure. Located on a corner property, covering an area of 1,858 square metres (20,000 square feet) with a constructed area of 372 square metres (4,000 square feet).

The basic features of this property are its transparency, interrelationship to surroundings, circulation via double stairs, architectural and interior composition, easy and immediate reading, and material value.

The property was constructed of reinforced concrete walls, with pattern boards 1.8 metres (6 feet) wide. The roof is similar, with floors constructed of tile stone. In the low area of the exterior, natural local stone was used. In the other levels, granite cobbled stones, taken from Montevideo's older streets, and reinforced double wall concrete has been utilised.

No finish was used in the bathroom or kitchen, with only a transparent resin coating protecting against water.

A technical and non-absorbent isolating plaque was installed inside the concrete wall and the exterior stone wall. Doors and windows are made from natural wood, as is the deck.

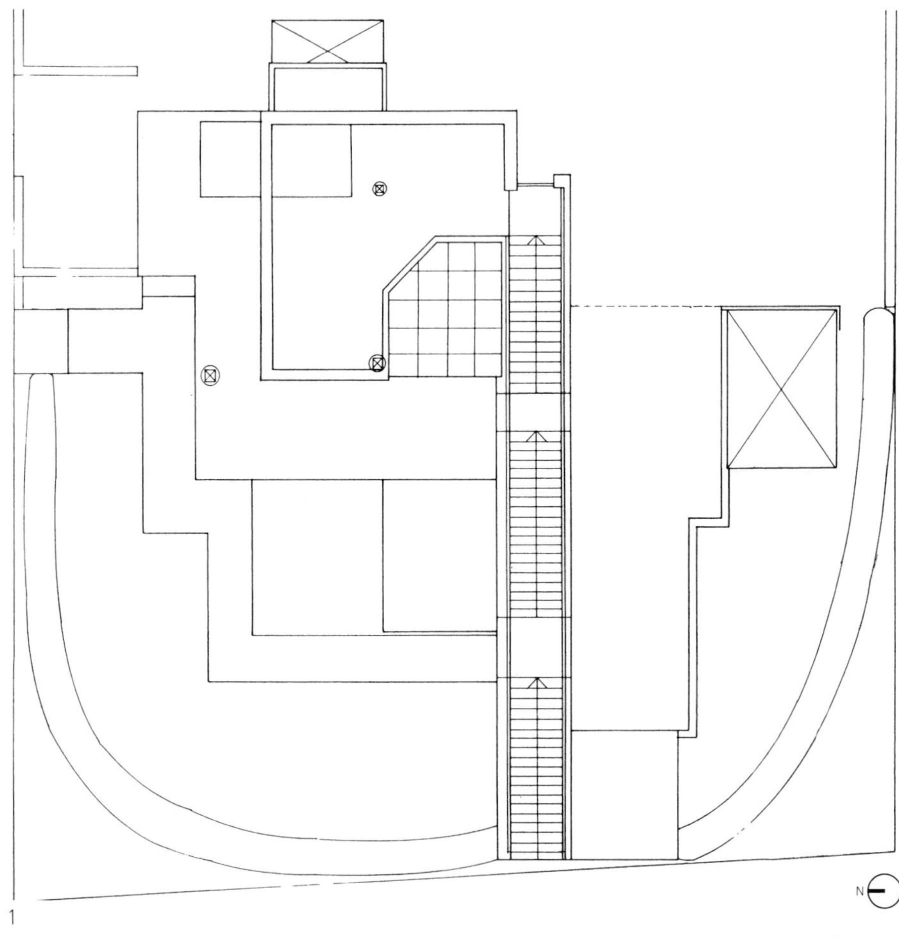

1

2

3

1 Site plan
2 View looking west
3 View looking southwest
4 North facade
5 South facade
6 Level 1
7 Patio
8 Detail exterior stairs

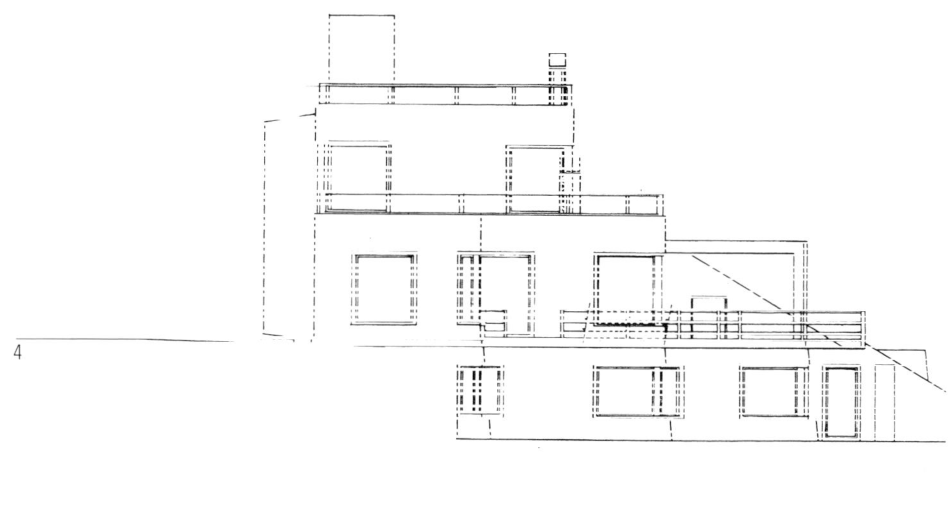
4

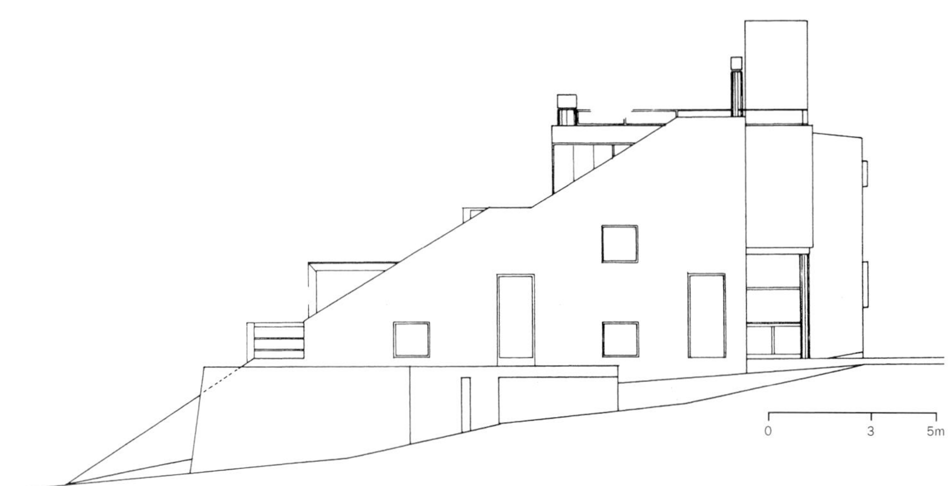

5

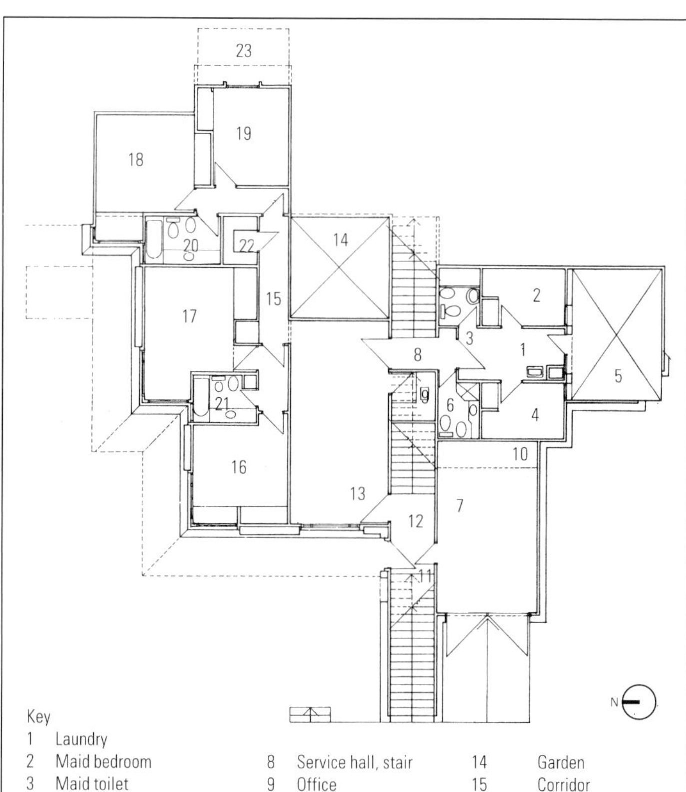

6

7

8

Jay and Marilee Flood Residence

David Jay Flood

Completion: January 1994

Location: Maui, Hawaii, USA

Client: Jay & Marilee Flood

Area: 353 square metres; 3,800 square feet

Structure: Wood frame

Materials: Exterior cement plaster over wood frame construction; asphalt shingles; aluminium frames

Cost: US$500,000

This 353 square metre (3,800 square foot) house, situated on the west side of the Island of Maui, Hawaii, is designed to respond to an informal lifestyle and to reflect a design philosophy that relies on a regional concern for architectural appropriateness of use, function, and location.

The house is designed to capture and respond to the sun from morning's first rays, caught by the floor-to-ceiling corner glass walls of the breakfast room to the end of the day with views from the living room of the sun, framed by trees, setting over the ocean.

Two existing Monkey trees located on the front and rear sides of a 2-storey high, glazed central entry are a key design element. An exterior stair/bridge, wrapping the trunk of one of the trees, announces the arrival. The house is entered through a fern patterned, etched glass front door with views to the ocean beyond. The entry and a second floor bridge connect the house's public and private wings.

To maximise the view potential, the living room, dining room, kitchen, and master bedroom are located on the second floor. Guest bedrooms, the garage and recreation/ office spaces are on the first floor.

The structure is dominated by a strong hipped roof shape with deep overhangs. The wood truss structural system, exposed throughout the living, dining, and kitchen spaces, is uninterrupted by dividing walls, allowing for a visual continuity between areas and continuous air movement through all spaces.

The shape of the plan allows for continuous visual connections from inside the house to other portions of the colourful exterior and landscaping.

The exterior colour palette was inspired by the colours of a Maui sunset as viewed through trees—mauve, peach, and vermilion wall colours with moss green window corner and teal roof overhangs.

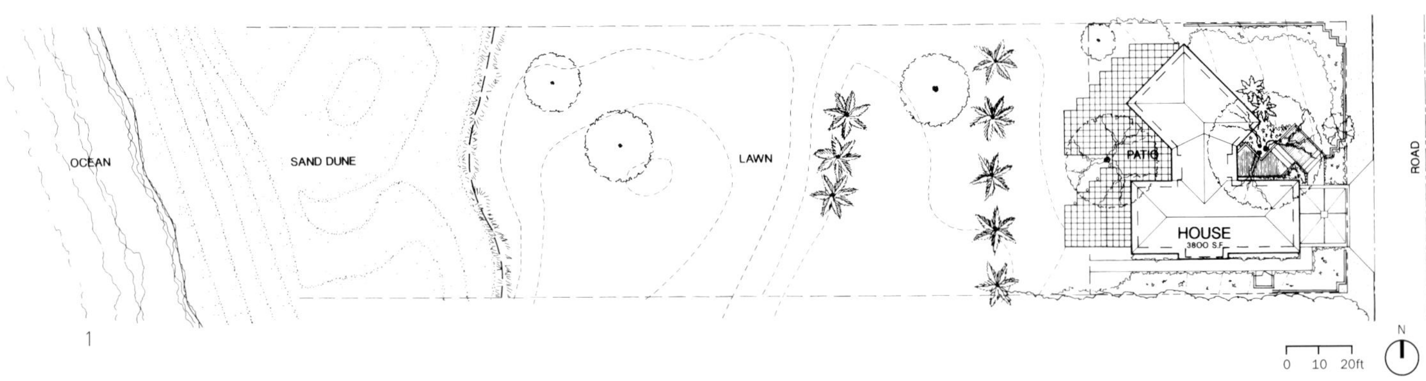

1

2

3

4

1 Site plan
2 Rear view
3 Interior view of living room
4 Front view
5 Upper level floor plan
6 Ground level floor plan

Photography: David Watersun

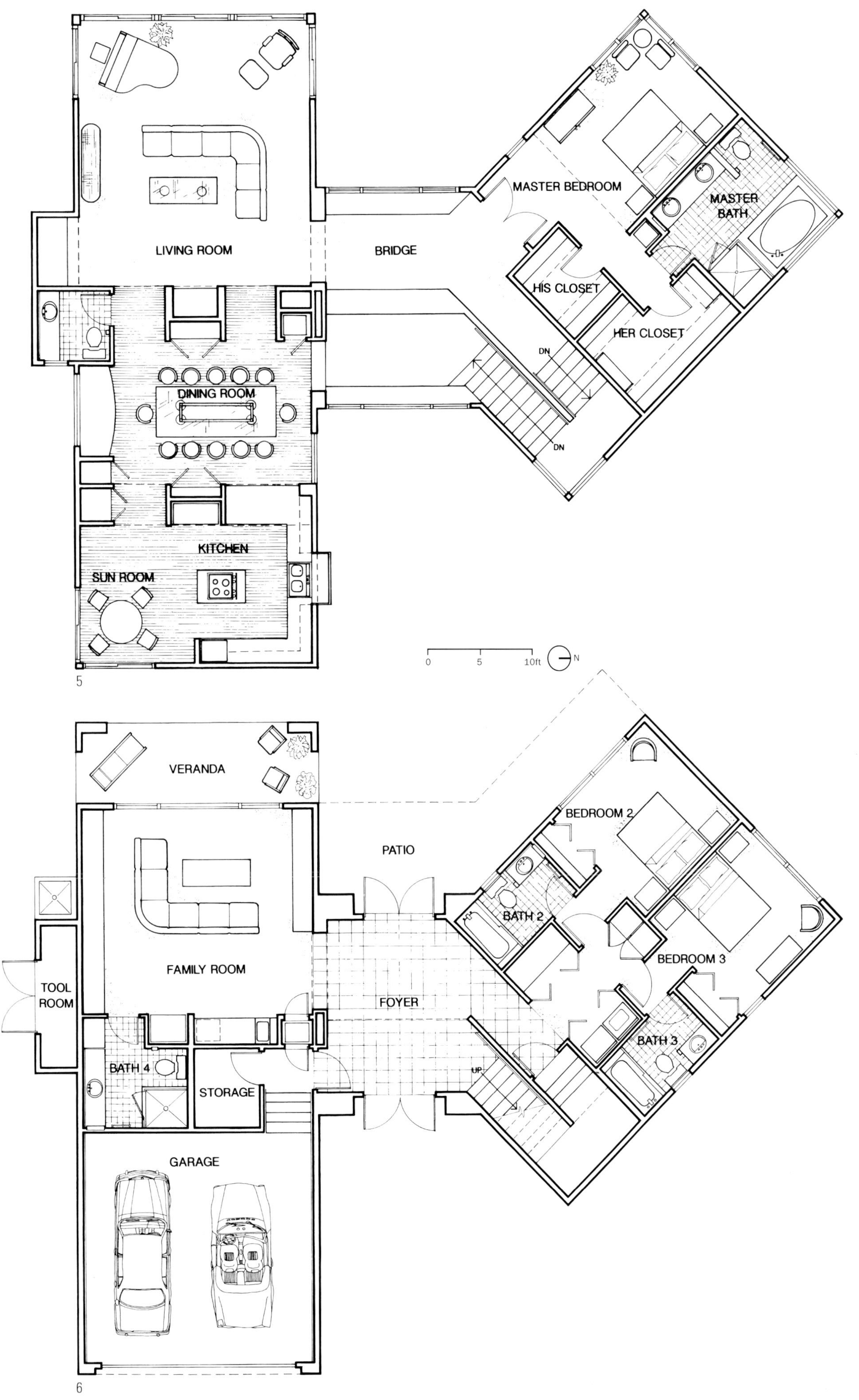
LIVING ROOM
BRIDGE
MASTER BEDROOM
MASTER BATH
HIS CLOSET
HER CLOSET
DN
DN
DINING ROOM
KITCHEN
SUN ROOM
0 5 10ft
N
5
VERANDA
PATIO
BEDROOM 2
BATH 2
FAMILY ROOM
BEDROOM 3
TOOL ROOM
FOYER
BATH 3
UP
BATH 4
STORAGE
GARAGE
6

Jindal House

Gujrals

Completion: January 1994

Location: New Delhi, India

Client: Mr Jindal

Area: 500 square metres; 5,382 square feet

Structure: Brick

Materials: Plaster; slate

The project was commenced in 1991 and completed in 1994. It is a country house for Mr Jindal, who has a small family. The building, covering 500 square metres (5,382 square feet), is built on a two and a half acre piece of land and part of a large complex of similar country houses about 15 kilometres from the centre of New Delhi.

The materials used included rough plaster on brick walls (all load bearing). Boundary walls, planters and structures around the house were clad in black slate. The plastered portion of the house is a biscuit shade.

1 Side of the front
2 Rear view seen from the pool
3 Interior with front door in centre as seen from the inside

1

2

3

4

5

6

7

4 Rear side view
5 Interior lounge seen from entrance
6 Swimming pool as seen from rear

7 Interior seen from entrance, with swimming pool in the distance
8 Interior view with stairs leading from lounge to the entrance level

8

Joseph Pennock Farmstead Restoration

Susan Maxman Architects

Completion: May 1994
Location: London Grove, Pennsylvania, USA
Area: 372 square metres; 4,000 square feet
Structure: Masonry; wood frame
Materials: Brick; stone; wood
Awards: 1995 Grand Prize; Great American Home Awards, National Trust for Historic Preservation

Abandoned for thirty years before Susan Maxman Architects began restoration, the Joseph Pennock House is a significant example of Chester country architecture. The building was composed over time, from a three room house of 1760 and stone kitchen of 1760-80, to a four-bay Georgian plan in 1800-1812. Architectural services included an existing conditions assessment, preparation of existing drawings and restoration of the interior and exterior of the building.

To update the house for modern living, new heating, plumbing and concealed wiring were added. A later existing porch was removed and reinstalled, and a new porch was added in the rear. A new garage was constructed on the ruins of a wagon shed. There are plans to restore the corn crib and barn in the future.

Because all efforts were made to preserve the original fabric of the building, these interventions have limited impact on the visual integrity of Pennock House and its surrounding buildings. An application has been made for inclusion in the National Register of Historic Places.

1

2

3

1 Summer kitchen fireplace
2 View from the east
3 View from the west
4 Floor plans
5 View into parlour
6 Kitchen fireplace
Photography: Catherine Bogert

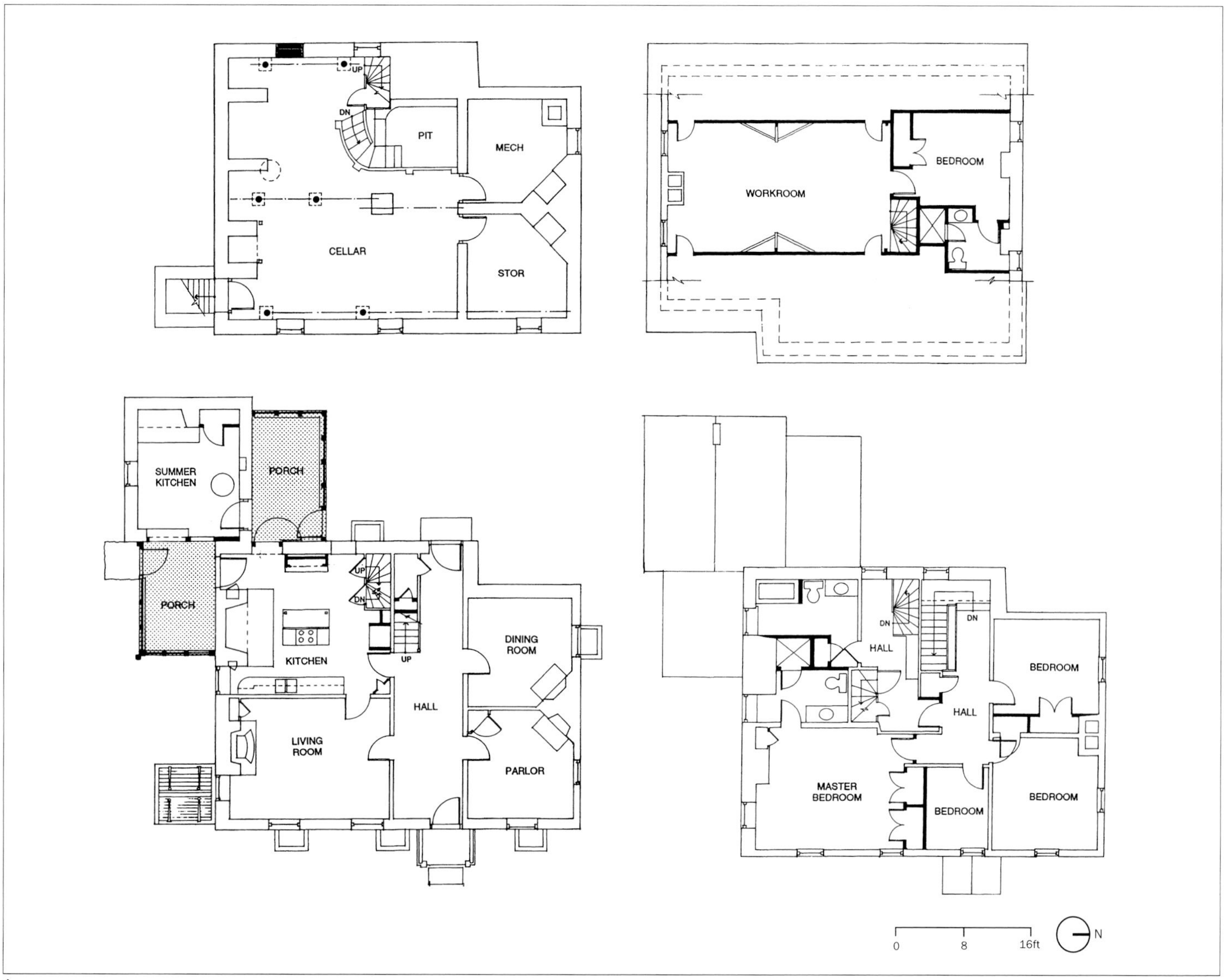

UP
DN
PIT
MECH
CELLAR
STOR

WORKROOM
BEDROOM

SUMMER KITCHEN
PORCH
PORCH
UP
DN
KITCHEN
UP
HALL
DINING ROOM
LIVING ROOM
PARLOR

DN
DN
HALL
BEDROOM
HALL
MASTER BEDROOM
BEDROOM
BEDROOM

0 8 16ft
N

4

5

6

Ka Hale Kukuna Residence

House + House, Architects

Completion: September 1994

Location: Maui, Hawaii, USA

Client: Dennis & Michelle Kleid

Area: 279 square metres; 3,000 square feet

Structure: Wood frame

Materials: Stucco; redwood; glass block; lava stone; concrete roofing tiles; cabinetry; tile

A massive curving wall anchored in lava encircles and protects a lush, tropical retreat on the Hawaiian island of Maui. This bold new residence, responds to the island's temperate climate and casual lifestyle. By turning its back on the intense south and west sun the house shields a very private world.

Activities are separated into two wings that are divided by a fountain and linked with stepping stones and a skylit bridge. The sweeping wall is thick, heavy stucco with tall, deep set windows as it encloses the living, dining and kitchen wing—and lacy, woven wood lattice casting glittering patterns of light and shadow into the garden as it embraces the bedroom wing. A natural lava crevice high on the cliffs spills a stream of water through the garden and the home into the entry fountain with its mosaic tile story of the mythic creation of the island. Indoor spaces become a part of the garden with walls which disappear, opening each room onto lanais. Tropical vegetation cascades down the lava cliffs and spills inside, intimately tying the feeling in this home to the lush, garden nature of the site. The tower studio with stairs to a lookout perch above offers distant views to the volcano of Haleakala and the Pacific Ocean beyond.

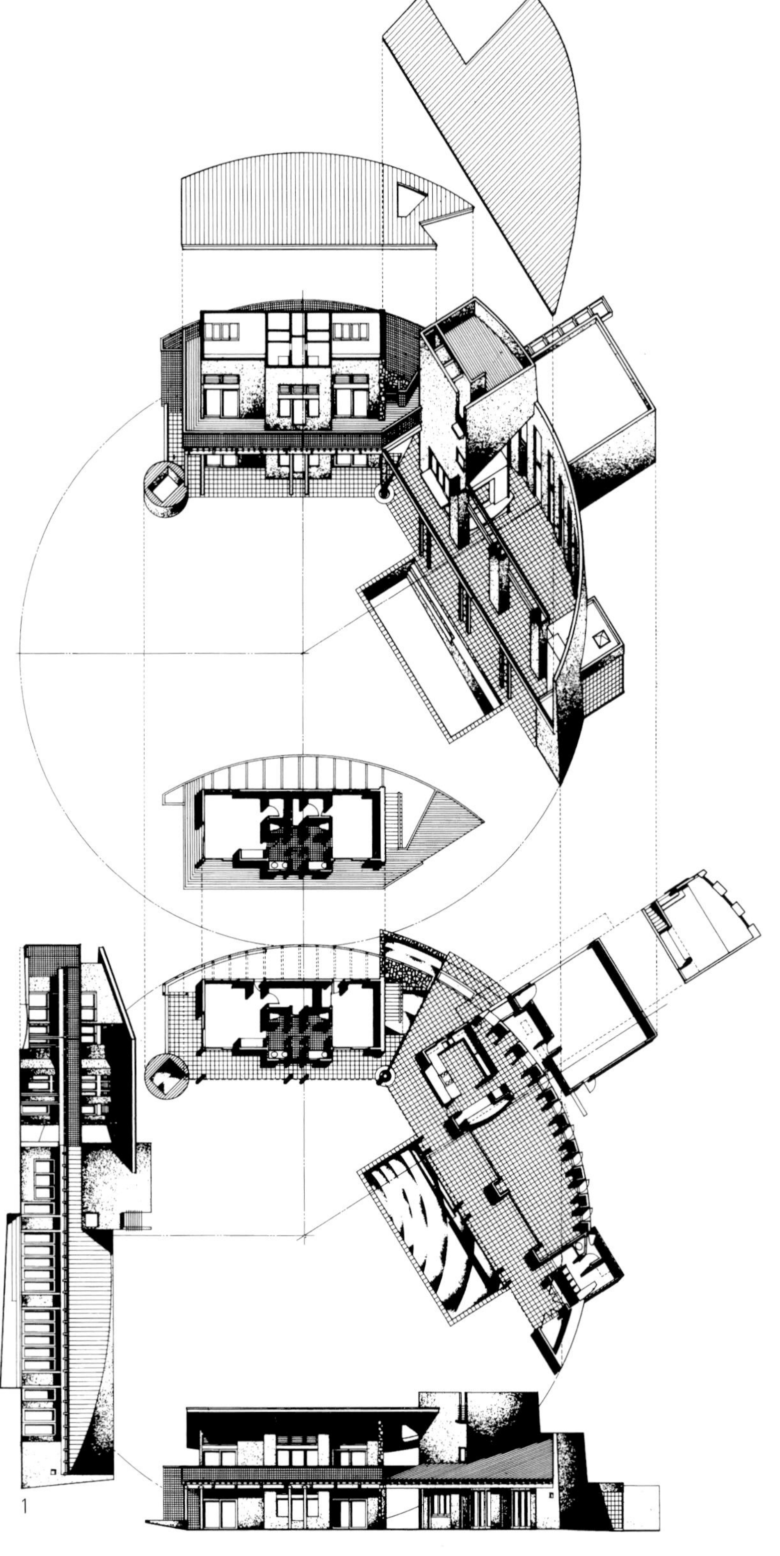

1 Axonometric, floor plans and elevations

2 South facade

3 North facade

2

3

4

6

5

7

4 View of west curving wall from south
5 View of lattice screen at entrance
6 View of curving wall at living room
7 Mosaic tile entry fountain
8 View of west curving wall from north
Photography: Michael French

8

Laivapoika Housing Company

Helin & Siitonen Architects

Completion: May 1995

Location: Ruoholahti, Helsinki, Finland

Client: City of Helsinki/Housing Production Office

Area: 12,994 square metres; 139,870 square feet

Structure: Concrete; steel

Materials: Concrete; steel; glass; glass block; metal sheet; Gabro stone

To the south the scheme opens out to the sea with views over the harbour and on the west side there are views towards the nearby park. The built form is therefore surrounded on all sides by public urban space. The new canal, designed by Juhani Pallasmaa, incorporates man-made banks, terraces and bridges and is a particularly important element for this housing scheme and also for Ruoholahti as a whole.

The urban block is divided into three buildings which have a total of six stairwells. The buildings each have six storeys, except for the tower section, which has eight. The buildings are linked by balcony towers which have been constructed of steel and infilled with glass blocks. These towers, together with the glazed balconies, form a light filigree motif which provides a contrast to the massive quality of the concrete structure. As the sun moves towards the west, the glass block tower at the eastern end collects light like a prism; in the morning the prism effect directs the sun towards the yard. The elevations consist of vertical and horizontal planes that create a balanced tension throughout the facades. The divisions within the planes, together with the surface texture, conceal the tectonically problematic joints between the concrete elements.

The choice of the elevational material was based upon authenticity with the addition of colourful metal details. The precast panels are made of coloured concrete, the surface of which is either blue-grey and grooved, or white and completely smooth. The dominant use of blue associates the building with the sea, while the grooving, together with the shadows it casts, renders the heavy elements almost weightless. In accordance with the alternatives given within the master plan, the surface material of the street elevations at ground floor level is matt-polished Gabro. Other major compositional elements include stairwells with uniform glass surfaces, unbroken white walls and dark blue areas of metal sheeting. The window casings are positioned either flush with the exterior surface or recessed in order to achieve relief. The blue-grey colour of the window casings is the same as that of the grooved panels, while some of the frames and balcony handrails are coloured a deep red. The steel parts of the balconies and the glass canopies are dark blue and grey. The doors to the stairwells are also finished with strong, dark colours.

Continued

1

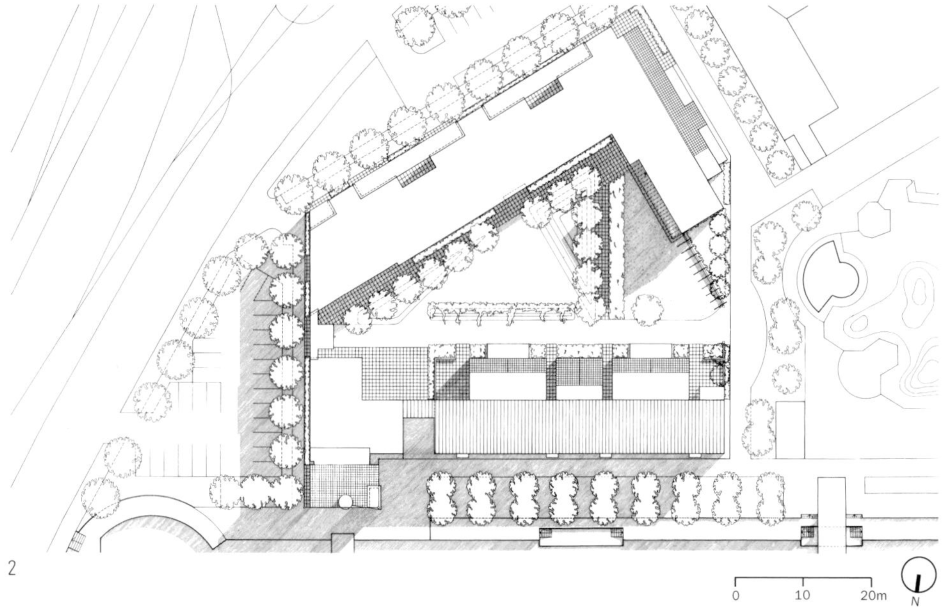

2

3

1 The tower section
2 Site plan
3 View along the Ruoholahti canal
4 Northwestern view across the canal
5 The tower on the northeastern corner of the block

4

5

As is typical in Ruoholahti, the scheme includes free-market owner-occupied flats and government-subsidised owner-occupied and rented flats, ranging from one- to four-bedroom apartments. Each flat has a balcony or a roof terrace that is more spacious than usual. In the internal organisation of the flats, particular attention has been paid to spaciousness, spatiality, light, efficiency of space and flexibility of use. The large flats can usually be divided into two smaller units in order to better accommodate the alterations required by changing families. Some flats have their own saunas, and for others there is a communal sauna attached to a large roof terrace on the top floor.

The scheme also contains a number of special apartments: a group dwelling for the disabled, a 'family home', two artisan flats and flats individually designed for the elderly and the ambient disabled. These flats allow for a more heterogeneous occupancy and are expected to assist the social interaction within the community. There are two common rooms on the ground floor which are reserved for various uses by all occupants.

6

7

8

6 An apartment on the top floor
7 Detail of the ground floor
8 An upper floor in the staircase
9 Staircase seen from the bottom floor

9

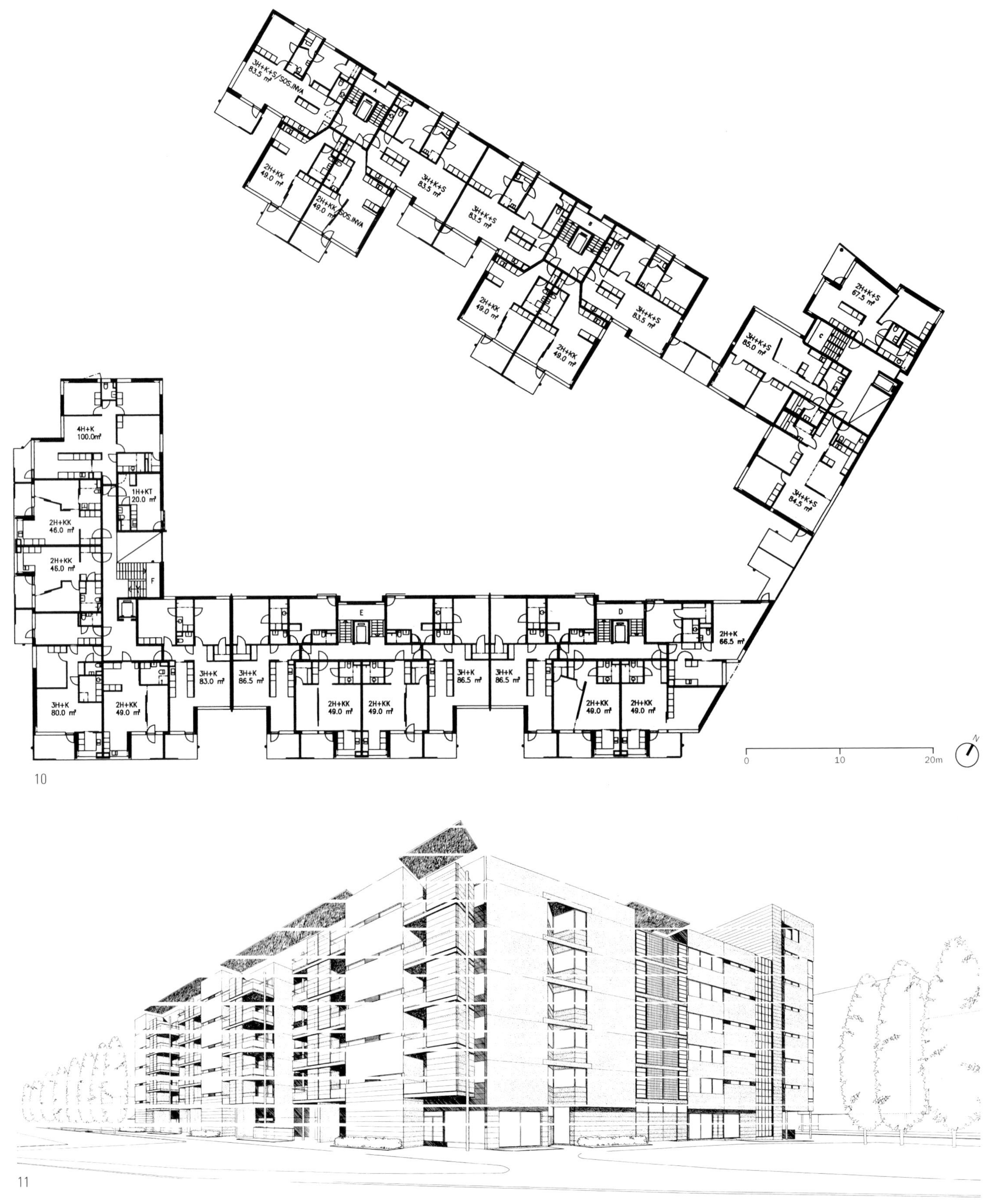

10

11

10 Usual floor

11 Perspective to southeast

12 East elevation

13 Southeast elevation

Photography: Rauno Träskelin

12

13

Mead/Penhall Residence

Bart Prince, Architect

Completion: June 1994

Location: Albuquerque, New Mexico, USA

Client: Mr C. Mead & Ms M. Penhall

Area: 316 square metres; 3,400 square feet

Structure: Concrete slab; wood framing

Materials: Exposed sandblasted concrete; stucco; cedar plywood

Cost: US$204,000

This residence is designed for an infill lot which is 20 metres (65 feet) by 41 metres (135 feet) in size. Houses are built on all of the lots surrounding this one and are 1- and 2-storey contractor designed frame/stucco structures. The lot rises abruptly about 1.5 metres (5 feet) in elevation within the first six metres (20 feet) from the street and is relatively flat from there to the back. This design takes advantage of that by placing the carport under the front portion of the structure. As it was necessary to design for a very low construction budget the structure is kept relatively simple in construction and materials. The walls around the carport are exposed sandblasted concrete block, as are the walls of the fireproof library at the rear of the site. The rest of the structure is of 2x6 framing finished either with stucco and sheetrock or galvanised metal on the exterior and rough-sawn cedar plywood panels on the interior.

The owners are both art historians and have a large collection of photographs, paintings, and 19th century furniture they wanted to display so the design was created with the idea of providing as much wall space as possible for these. The guest bedrooms, master bedroom, and the library/study are on the ground floor and are situated both for privacy and so that they subdivide the site into a series of gardens and courtyards. Above this level is the large curving form of the living spaces anchored at one end by the library/study, and extending over the carport at the streetside. It is this portion of the design which is covered with galvanised metal on the exterior and plywood on the interior with a continuous curving ceiling made of exposed TJI joists and metal. The roof of this part of the house is covered with a membrane roofing which laps over the sides above an undulating line of vertical corrugated metal at the top of the house. There are a series of covered and uncovered decks on this level with emphasis on the distant mountain views to the north and east.

1

2

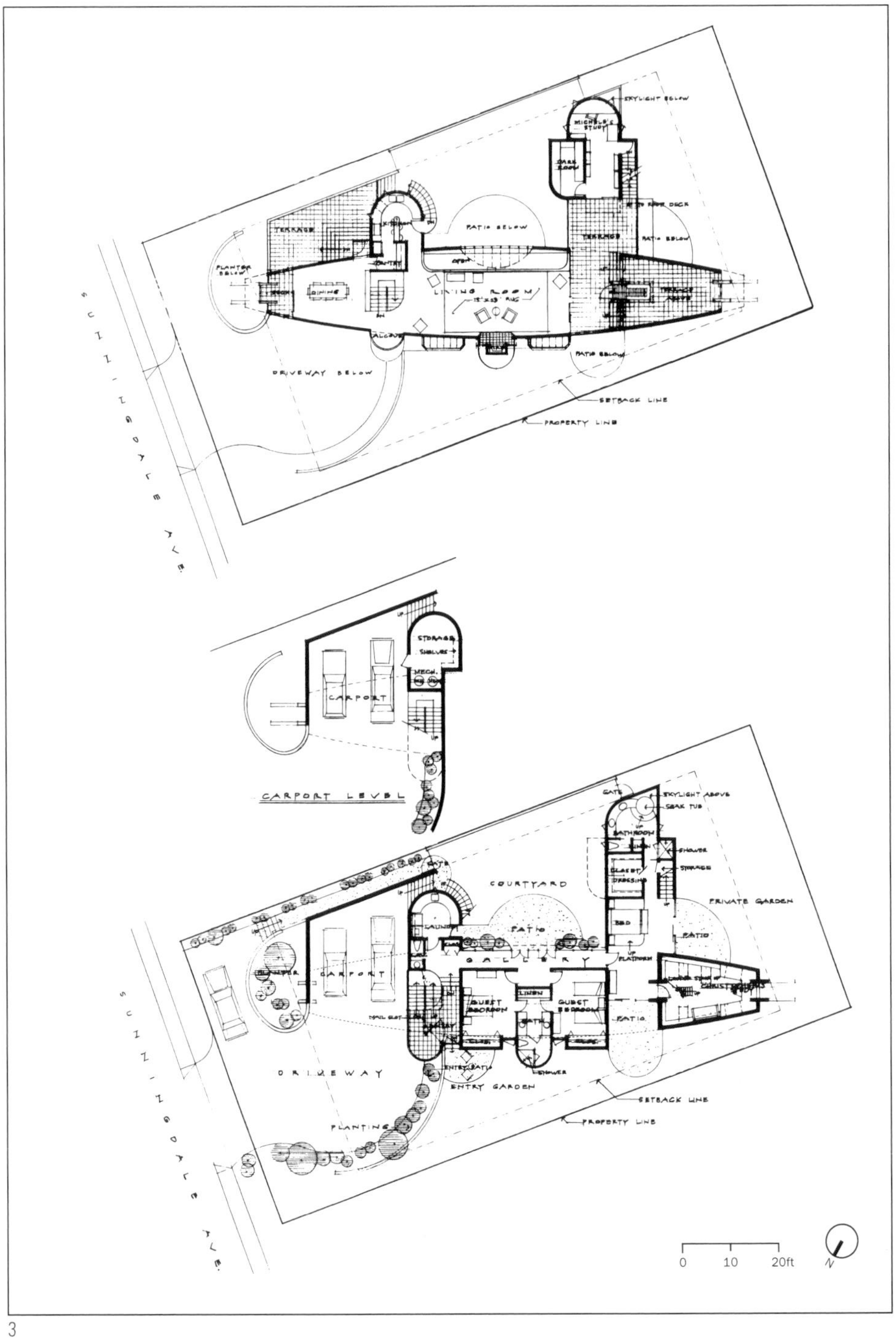

3

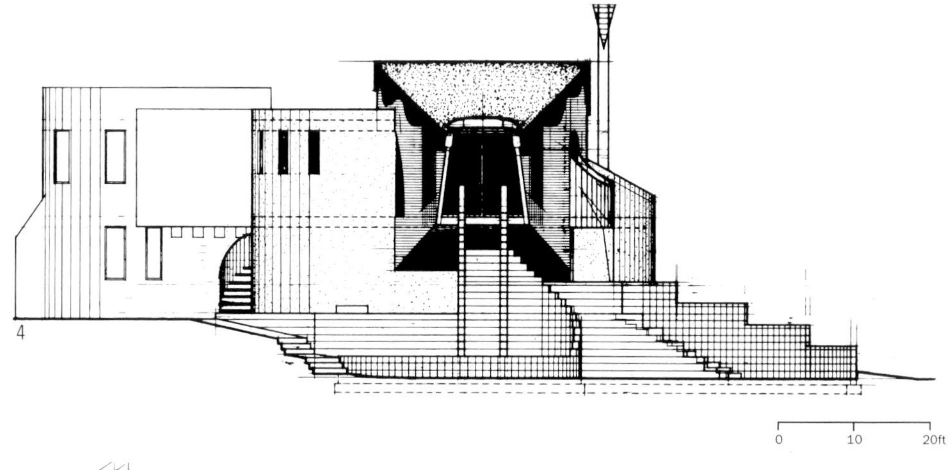

4

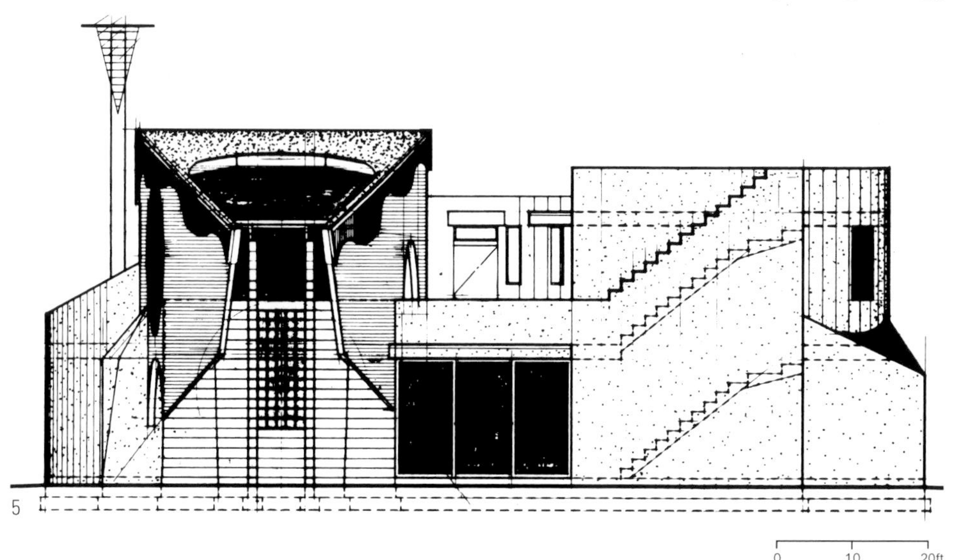

5

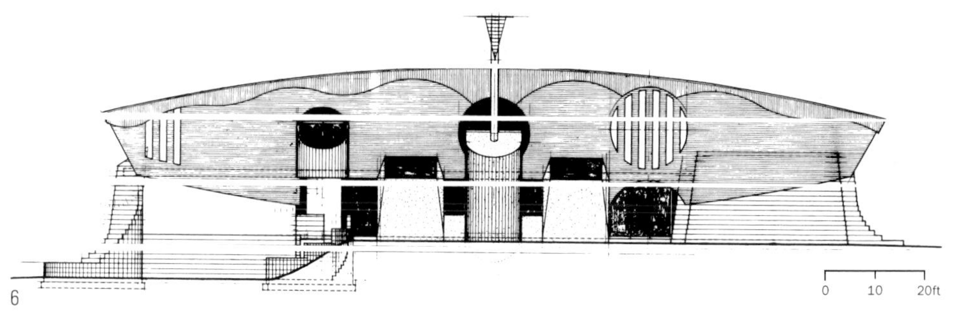

6

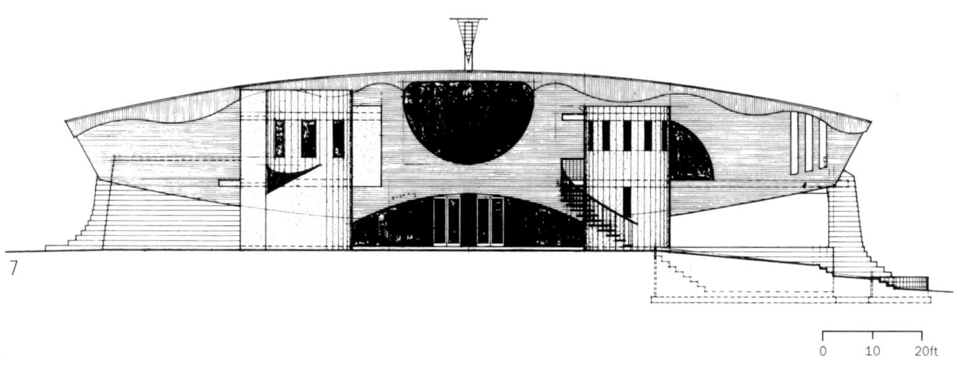

7

8

9

10

11

1 View from the street looking southwest
2 View of the courtyard, stair to kitchen
3 Ground level plan (bottom), carport level plan (middle), upper level plan (top)
4 Northeast elevation (view from the street)
5 Southwest elevation (rear garden)
6 Northwest elevation (side garden)
7 Southeast elevation (courtyard)
8 End view from street
9 Side view from street
10 Interior view of dining area looking towards living room
11 Courtyard view with fountain in foreground

Photography: Christopher Mead

Mexx Farm

Gujrals

Completion: December 1994
Location: New Delhi, India
Client: M/s Mexx International
Area: 5,000 square metres; 53,820 square feet
Structure: Brick
Materials: Exposed brick; local stone; plaster

This project covering 22.5 acres of countryside was planned to provide six independent units with servant quarters. While three of the houses belonged to a single family having 15 acres, the other three were to house individual families.

With all four families sharing a common boundary wall and other services, the placing of each house was to be taken into consideration. Each family owned two and a half acres of an angularly defined land piece which had to be respected to avoid any unforeseen property dispute. Therefore, house numbers one, two and three are located above, while house numbers four, five and six are woven to make a single complex. This was achieved by building an elevated road that encircles the three and provides entry at a middle level to each house. The common area in the centre is designed like a centre court with a swimming pool.

The project was started in 1990 and completed in 1994. The time taken in building was longer than expected due to the location, which was about 24 kilometres (fifteen miles) from the centre of New Dehli.

The material used was exposed brick and a local stone quarried in the vicinity. The client brief only asked for a design as a local identity and a large amount of open area and vegetation.

1 Front side view
2 Rear side view with pool seen at the rear
3 Side elevation as seen from swimming pool
4 Front view
5 Rear view
6 Side elevation
7 Front elevation

1

2

3

4

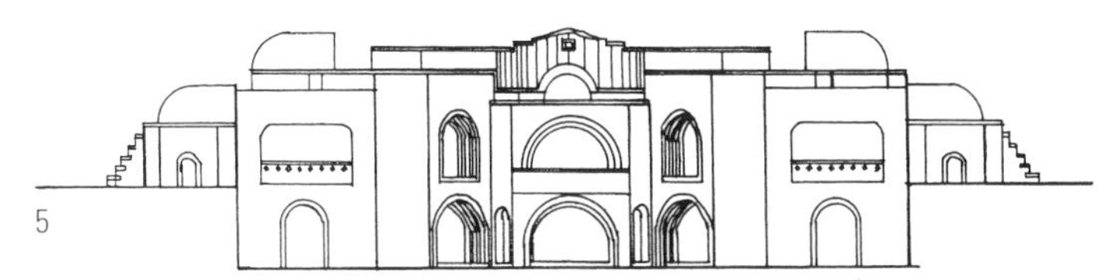
5

6

7

Millot-Gomez House

A.H. Ravazzani

Completion: March 1995

Location: Punta del Este, Uruguay

Client: Ms N. Gomez, Mr R. Millot

Area: 240 square metres; 2,500 square feet plus 120 square metres; 1,292 square feet from the deck

Structure: Natural brick; reinforced concrete

Materials: Natural brick; ceramic tiles; stones; wood.

Cost: US$180,000

Awards: 1995-1996 Represented Uruguay in the Architectural Biennial in Chile

Construction of this house respects the surrounding mountainous and hilly landscape of the sierra, also reflecting a detailed care for nature.

The house offers different perspectives throughout the access road, with new angles and details. It opens up to a dramatic landscape, with the intensity of sunset, light and colour changes during the day, and through the different seasons and weather changes. A 120 square metre (1,292 square foot) great wooden deck integrates the house to the landscape.

It consists of two spaces united by a glass hall and an open terrace on ground level. The focal point of the premises is on the lake, which implies that all rooms face this direction.

The property backs onto a steep mountain side. Access is possible from a semicircular patio.

Natural bricks are used in the interior walls, with reinforced concrete and ceramic tiles forming the roof. Local stones are set into the exterior walls, with doors, window frames and floors finished in wood.

This selection of natural materials, with very little or no incorporated technology, all contributes to the continuous dialogue of the site with its surroundings. The plastered finish on the walls was an attempt to highlight the stepped access to the solariums.

1

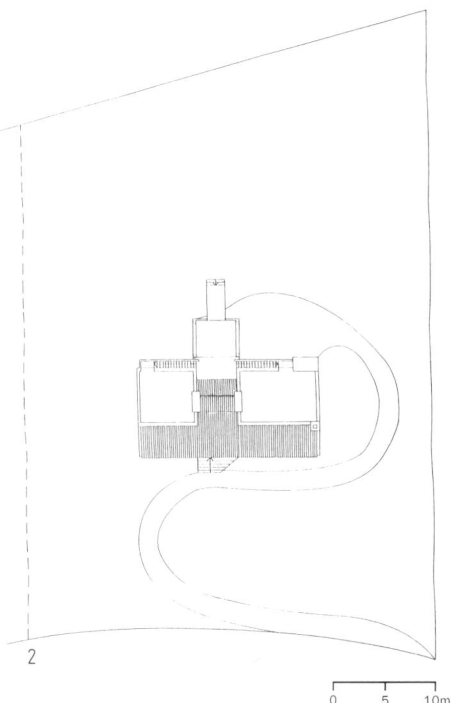

2

3

4

1 Access/semi-circular patio in mountain
2 Site plan
3 East facade detail
4 Main facade
5 Section
6 West facade
7 East facade
8 West facade
9 Detail deck
10 Open terrace/second level
11-12 Detail deck

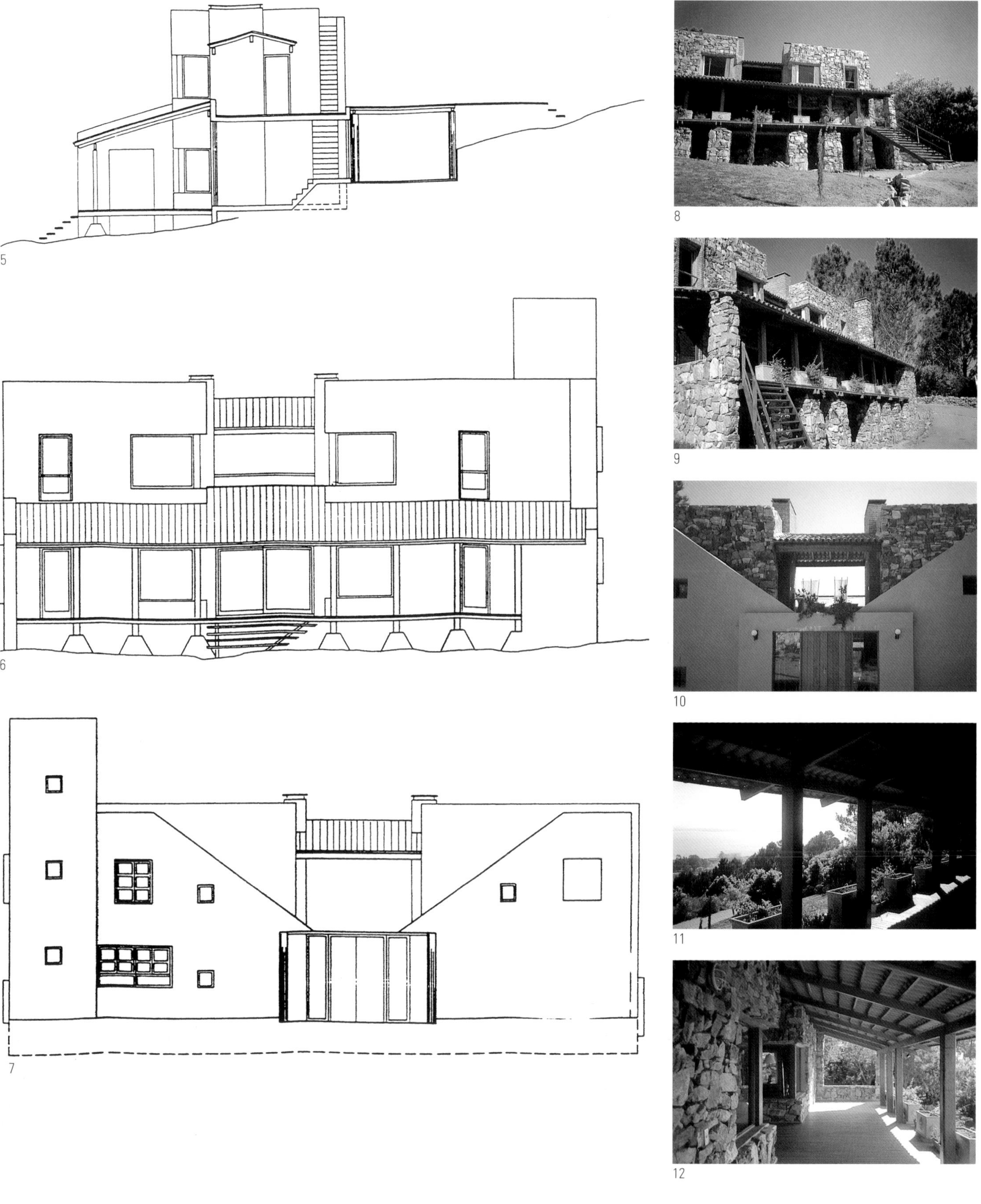
5

6

7

8

9

10

11

12

Mount Royal in Morningside

Adrian Maserow Architects

Completion: May 1995

Location: Morningside, Sandton, South Africa

Client: Hilsam Properties

Area: 10,000 square metres; 107,643 square feet

Structure: Cement; brick

Materials: Plaster; beam and lintel concrete slab; tile

Cost: R14 million

Mount Royal is a low rise, high density residential scheme located in Morningside, an upmarket suburb in Sandton.

This urban development provides a large range of apartments varying from spacious three bedroom ground floor apartments to compact one bedroom loft apartments (in the roofspace). Large balconies are featured and individualised entries to each apartment assist in personalising the scheme, varying it from the traditional corridored apartment block.

The height is 3-storeys (plus the loft)—but a smart sectional use of the contour placed the road entry level at mid level, thereby requiring only a one up level or one down level change to the entrance.

The architectural language used here is a 'free-style' classicism embracing a series of interpreted elements. The distinctive rustication of the base, double and triple volume paired columns, a flared pediment and coping and other icons of the language combine to form a traditional and rich architectural assemblage of this distinctive 'terraced' apartment project.

1

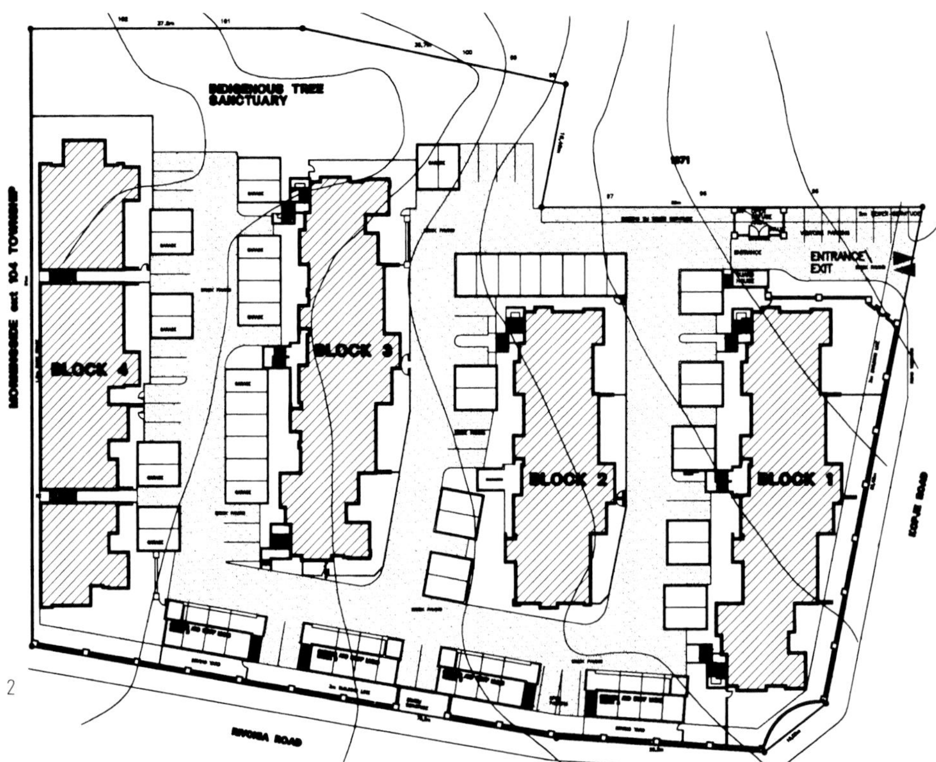

2

3

4

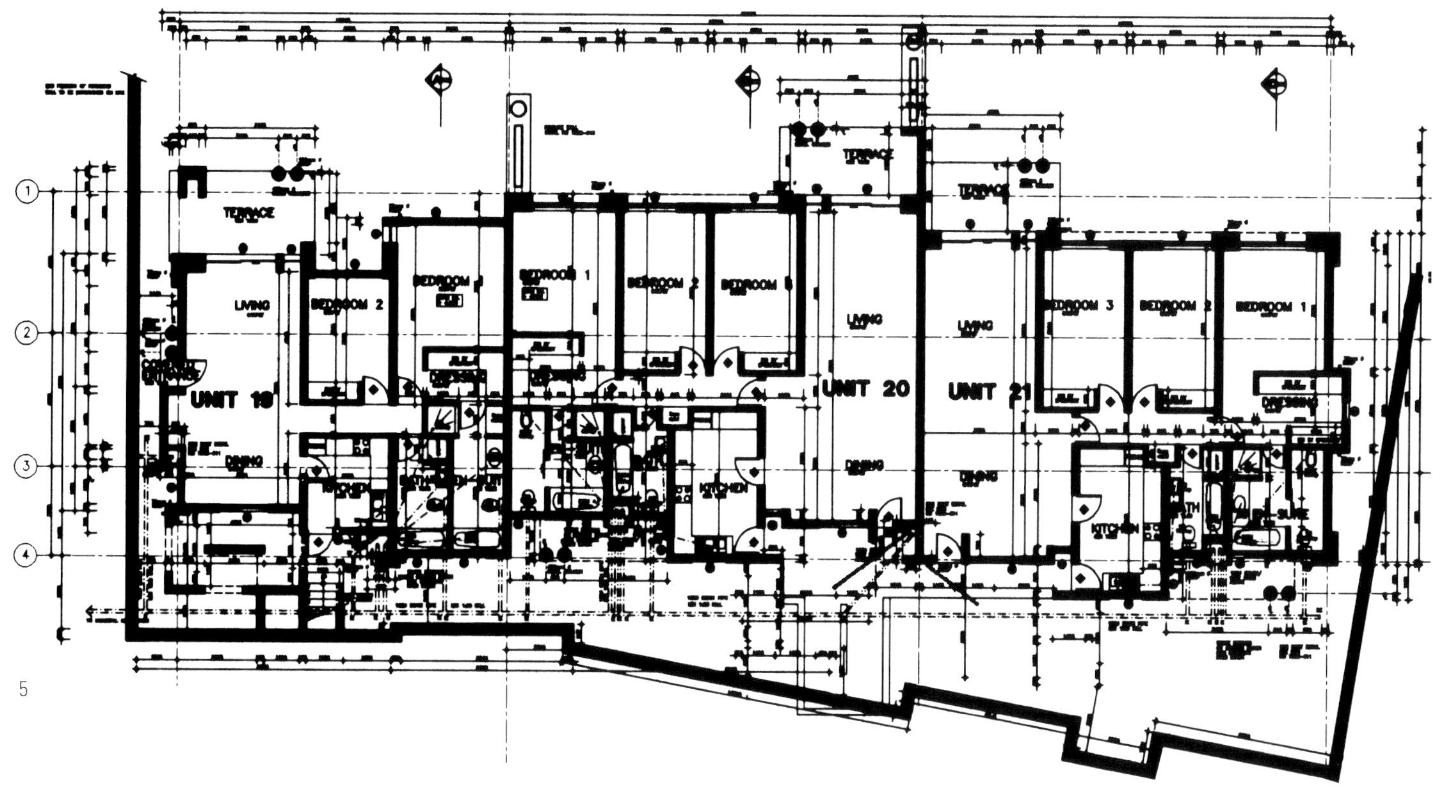

5

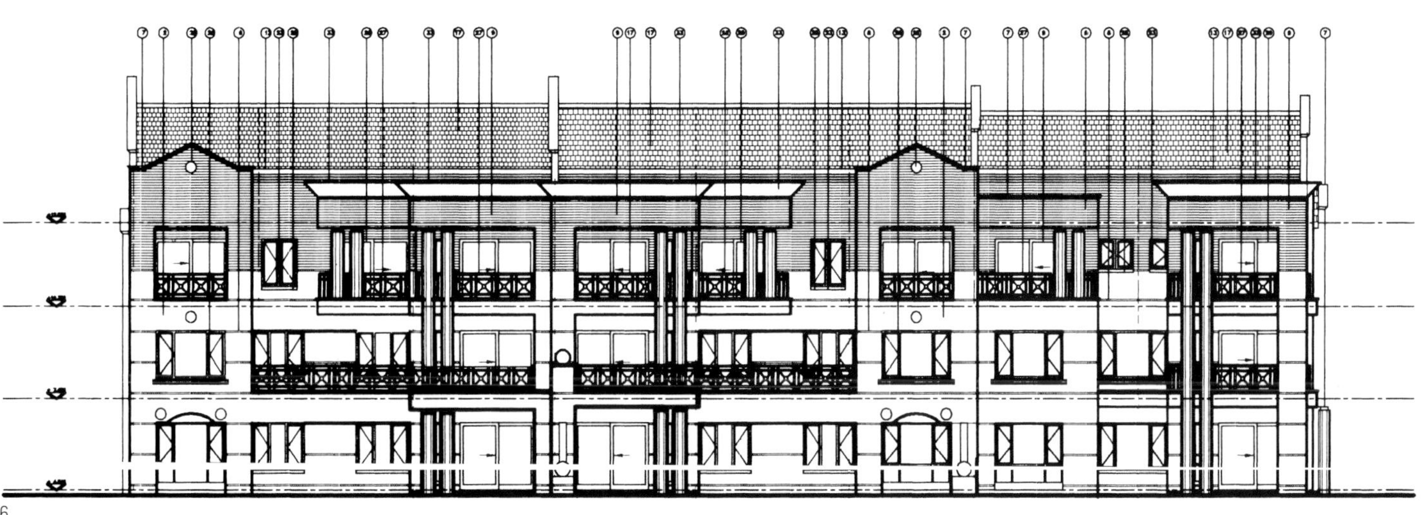

6

7

8

9

1 Perimeter detail and landscape
2 General site layout
3 Internal street corner
4 Architectural perspective
5 Typical floor plan

6 Elevation detail
7 Volumetric assemblages
8 Terraced massing
9 Entrance corner

Photography: Adrian Maserow

Mr Eaton's Residence

Architects 49 Limited

Completion: April 1995

Location: Nichada Thani, Bangkok, Thailand

Client: Mr R. Eaton

Area: 1,200 square metres; 12,917 square feet

Structure: Concrete

Materials: Exposed concrete; glass; aluminium cladding

Cost: 15 million Baht

A private house representing a modern vitality via modern materials and forms creates a new environment to the neighbourhood, mostly of typical Thai style with overhanging roofs. Transparency and composition of simple geometric forms are key words to capture the image of the owner's open-mindedness and his lively personality.

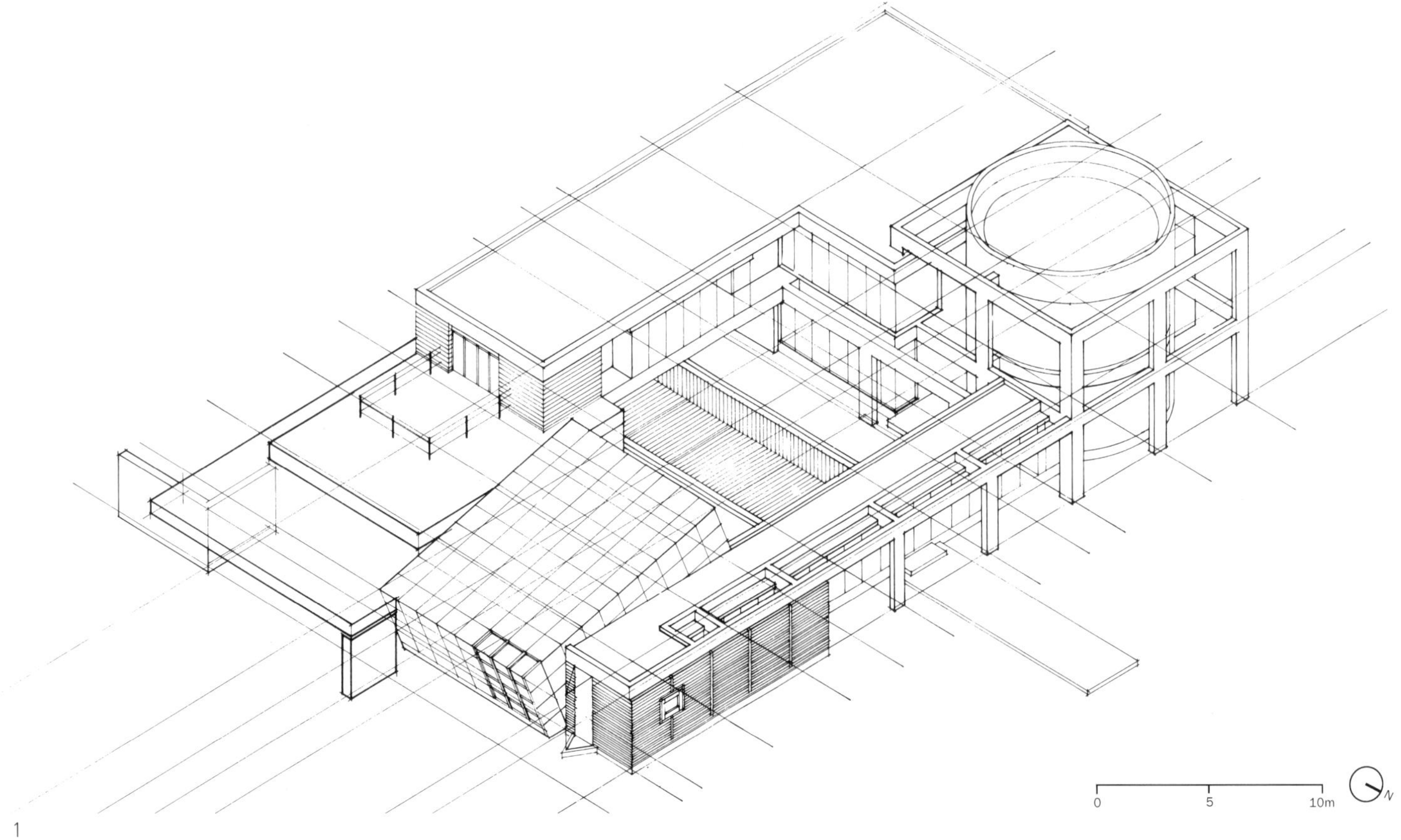

1

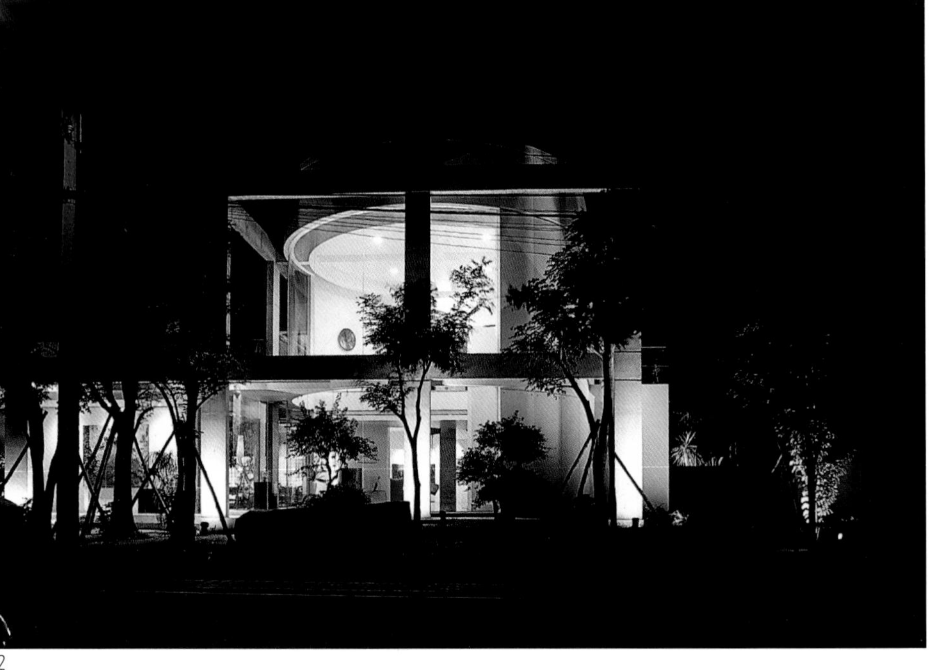

2

1 Isometric
2 Living rotunda at night
3 Cross section
4 North elevation
5 Master bedroom over the pool

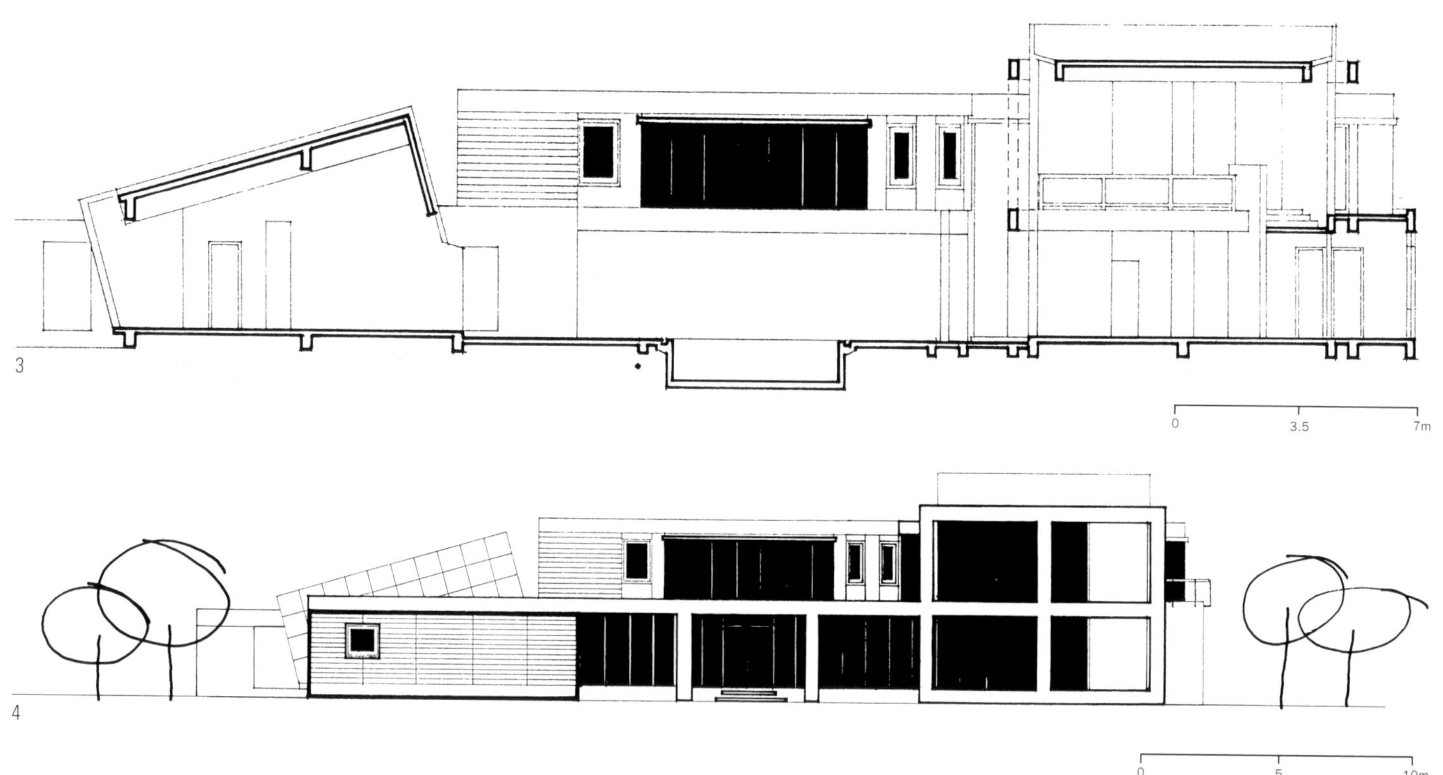

3

4

5

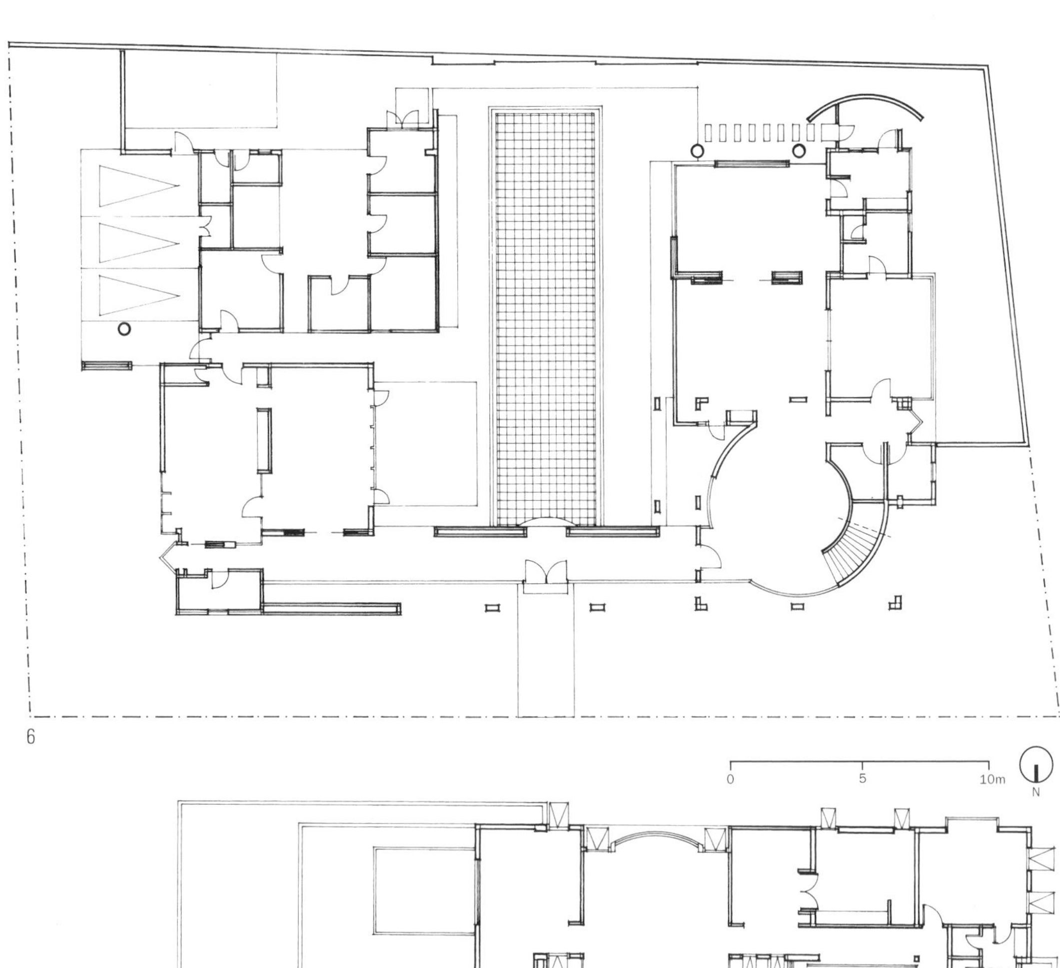
6

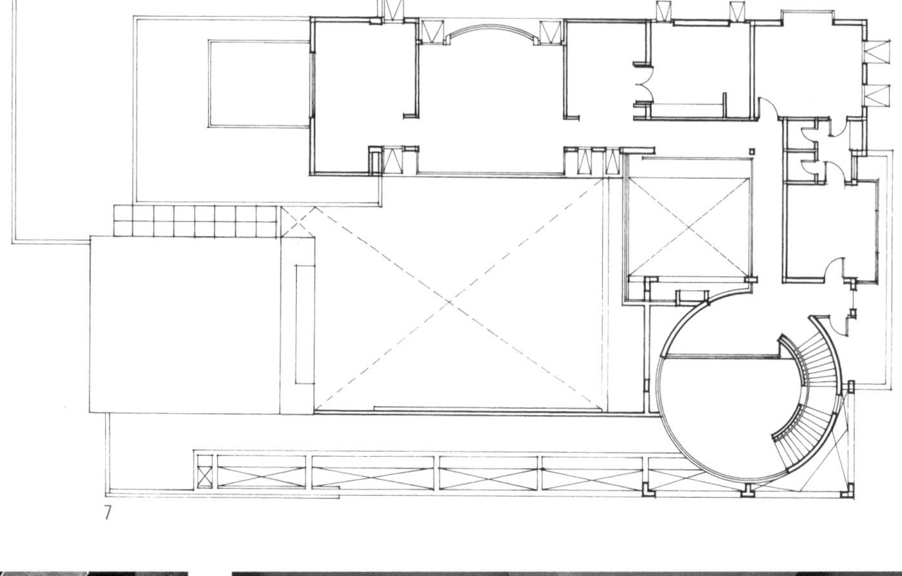

7

8

9

10

11

6 Ground floor plan
7 Upper floor plan
8 Granite floor in living room
9 Living hall
10 Dining room
11 The rotunda
12 Front gallery
Photography: Skyline by Somkid Piampiyachart

12

Ocean View House

Swatt Architects

Completion: May 1995

Location: Oakland, California, USA

Client: Swatt Architects

Area: 279 square metres; 3,000 square feet

Structure: Wood frame

Materials: Multi-coloured stucco; gypsum board; maple hardwood; limestone tile; concrete

Cost: US$350,000

This design is a response to a site which has one view opportunity, and many limitations and constraints.

The building is organised on five levels. The upper levels contain the 'private' bedroom spaces, and the lower levels, which terrace down the sloping site, contain the 'public' living, dining and kitchen spaces. The multi-level design, with two south facing storeys (barely meeting the city's new, reduced, height limit) promotes maximum solar access.

The plan, due to the narrow site, is organised around a double height single loaded circulation spine. This space, modulated by 5.5 metre (18 foot) high by 15 cm (6 inch) wide 'column' windows at 1.2 metre (4 foot) centres, allows morning sunlight to penetrate the interior, and at the same time shields the living spaces from an adjacent over-scaled new residence.

Views of local landmarks to the northwest (U.C. Berkeley's Campanile and the historic Claremont Hotel) are emphasised and framed with large scale mitred glass corner windows.

Formally, the architectural language reflects the functional response: closed, linear and rhythmic on the circulation side; diagonally open, with thin 'reaching' overhangs on the view side; and sculptural and animated on the street side. In the newly-built Oakland Hills, this purely modern response is a refreshing departure from the predominantly traditional approach of the neighbouring residential development.

1

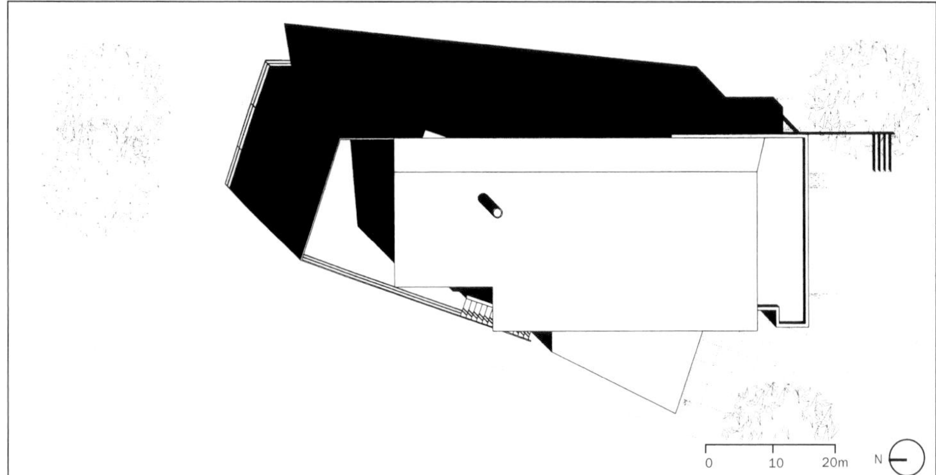

3

2

4

5

6

7

1 Detail
2 North elevation
3 Site plan
4 South elevation
5 Detail
6 View from entry
7 Dining/living area
8 First level plan
9 Second level plan
10 Dining/living area
11 Kitchen

Photography: Mark Darley/ESTO

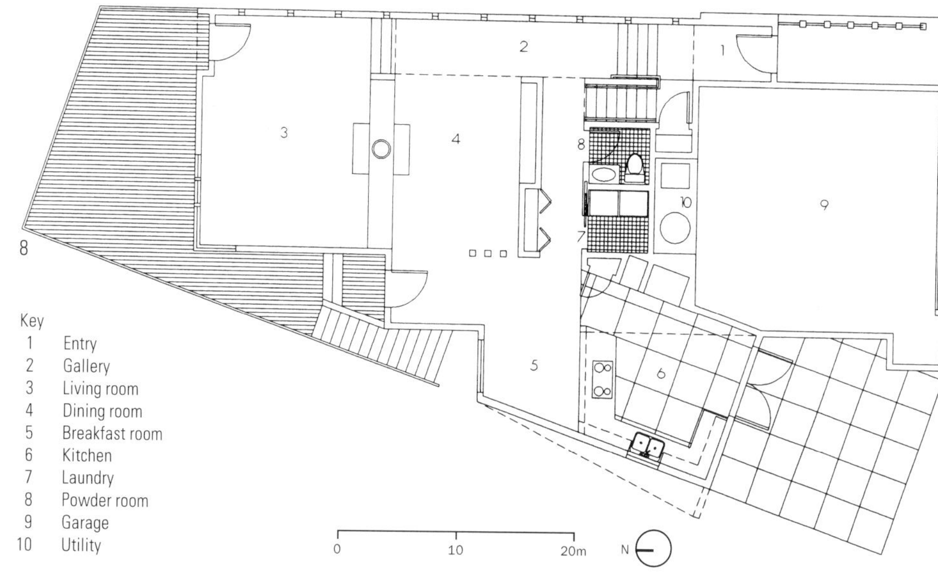

8

Key
1 Entry
2 Gallery
3 Living room
4 Dining room
5 Breakfast room
6 Kitchen
7 Laundry
8 Powder room
9 Garage
10 Utility

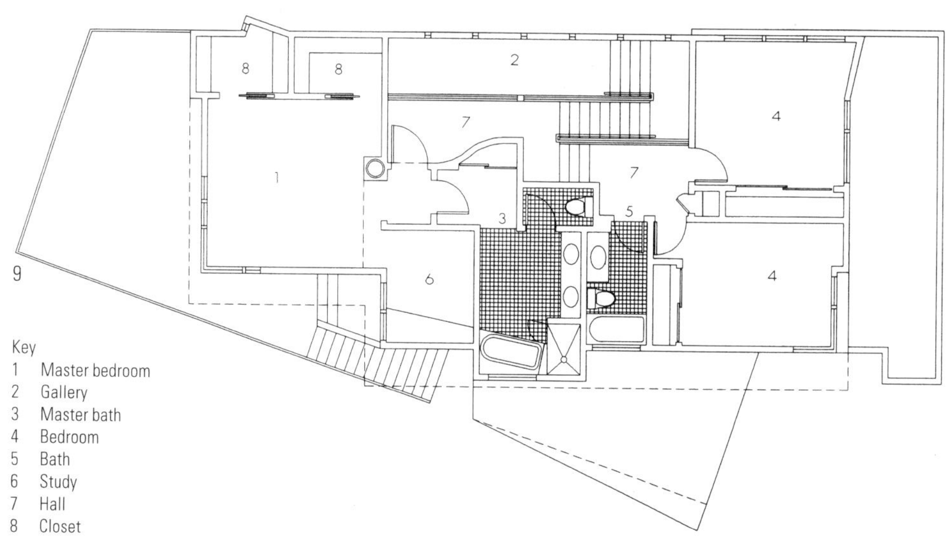
9

Key
1 Master bedroom
2 Gallery
3 Master bath
4 Bedroom
5 Bath
6 Study
7 Hall
8 Closet

10

11

Permata Hijau Apartment

Pacific Adhika Internusa, PT

Completion: February 1994
Location: Permata Hijau, Jakarta, Indonesia
Client: PT Masato Prima
Area: 24,000 square metres; 258,342 square feet
Structure: Reinforced concrete
Materials: Concrete; GRC; brick
Cost: US$20 million

The apartment is located within one of the housing estates in South Jakarta, by the side of a 47 metre (155 feet) wide Arterial road. A variety of plan types and design options offer future residents a choice best suited to their needs.

120 residential units vary in size from 90 square metres (970 square feet) to 190 square metres (2,045 square feet), scattered in three towers surrounding a courtyard. Each tower has two large sized elevators which open to fully air-conditioned lobbies, allowing fast and comfortable access to all units for residents and guests. Services, a coffee shop, and valet parking are provided.

The architectural style sets a new standard in Jakarta for design excellence, with 'Classic Style' as the theme, using mostly local materials.

1

1-2 View from the Artery road
3 Arrival court with the frog fountain
Photography: Yori Antar

2

3

Powell House

Kanner Architects

Completion: March 1995

Location: Malibu, California, USA

Client: R. and A. Powell

Area: 297 square metres; 3,200 square feet

Structure: Wood frame

Materials: Cement plaster; wooden doors and windows

Cost: US$288,000

The Powell House was one of the first houses to be rebuilt after being destroyed in the devastating 1993 Malibu fire. It sits at the end of Big Rock on a terraced site looking onto a stunning view of Malibu and the Pacific. The original 3,200 square foot (297 square metre) residence spread over one-storey, which made it feel deceptively large. The architects largely maintained this plan, and the existing slab; but otherwise transformed what had been a nondescript house—hipped roofed and shingles with projecting eaves—into a low-cost residence, whose beauty lies in its simplicity and the judicious definition of existing, but understated, volumes, entrance ways, details and sequences.

Fire prevention concerns informed the new design, which had to do away first with overhangs—the first house had been immolated due to fire whipping up under the eaves. The result is flush walls and minimal parapets. This unadorned look carries through the rest of the house: shapes that were already implied were accentuated into building platonic solids, canopies extended over doors to highlight them and to create a sense of interlocking platonic solids and to create a sense of interlocking planes; and openings onto the Malibu view were amplified. The asymmetry of the plan becomes a leit-motif that is reflected in the window design; each is a unique composition of irregular planes. The cubist quality of the house is offset, in a modernist way, by soft landscaping that lines undulating paths.

An asphalt driveway became decomposed granite; smooth cement plaster took the place of reconstituted stone by the swimming pool. Inside, the concrete slab was polished to serve as flooring for bathrooms and circulation, while living and family room floors were finished in maple. These were just some of the light touches in a remodel whose overall palette is simple, honest materials and light, warm tones; giving the occupants a bright welcome home.

1

3

2

1 Detail at entry
2 Northwest view of living area
3 Living area with dining/kitchen area in the background
4 Overall view at entry
Photography: Mark Lohman

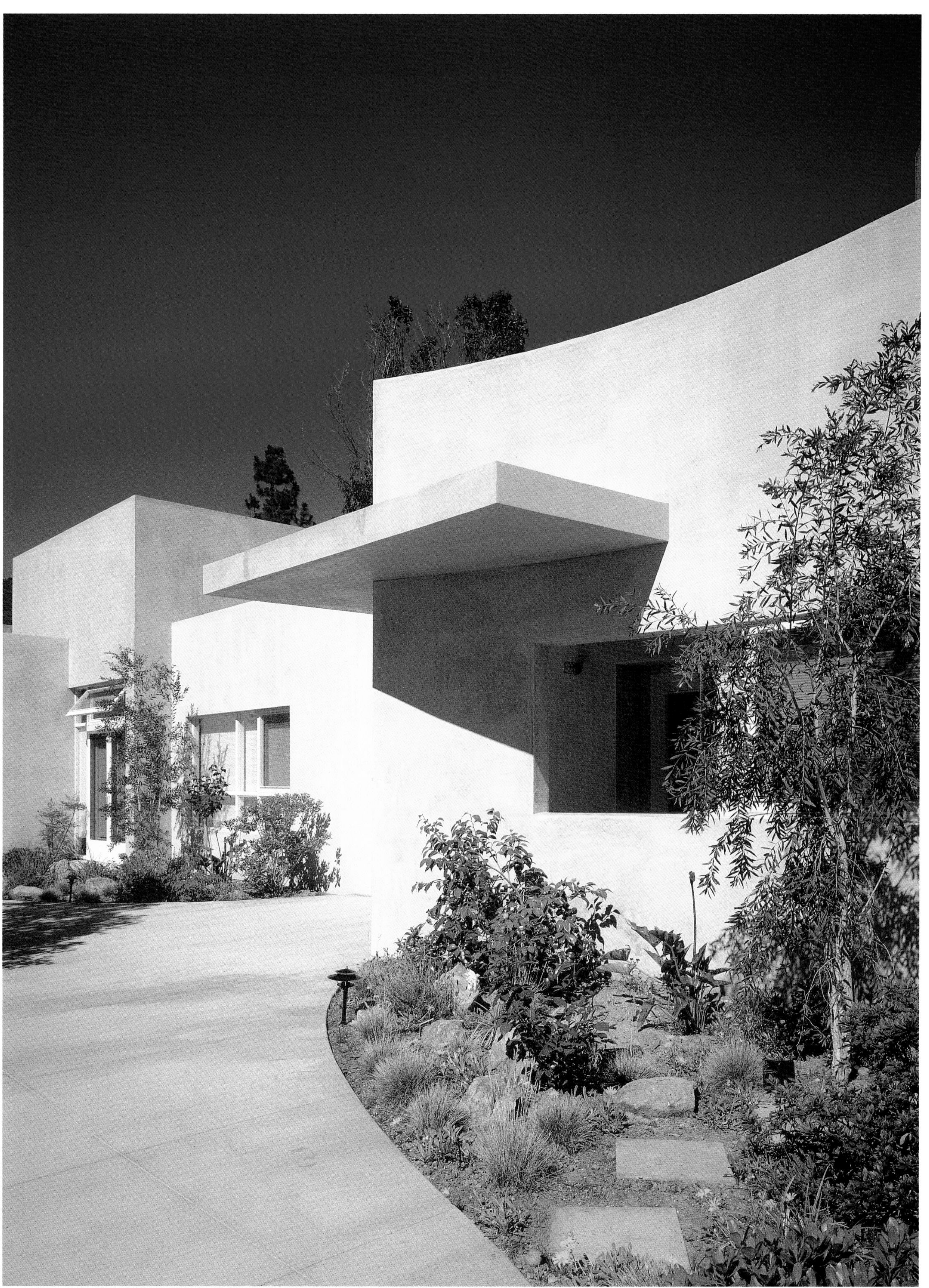

4

Residence in Harvey Cedars

Susan Maxman Architects

Completion: July 1994

Location: Harvey Cedars, New Jersey, USA

Area: 232 square metres; 2,500 square feet

Structure: Wood frame on pilings

Materials: Cedar

Awards: 1995 Honor Award; Philadelphia Chapter of American Institute of Architects

1995 Merit Award; Builder's Choice, Builder Magazine

Due to its spectacular oceanfront location, this summer residence had to comply with strict building height, setback and flood plain requirements. Despite these restrictions, the first floor features generous three metre (ten foot) ceiling heights and a floor elevation that allows for optimal ocean views. Living areas and outdoor deck are oriented to these views.

Trellis and lattice work enhance the wraparound deck space, providing protection from the sun and casting patterns of shadows and light upon the solid geometries of the house.

The interior of the house features naturally finished maple wood built-ins, screen walls and flooring, contrasting with the painted white walls and trim.

1

2

1 View from the beach
2 View from the north
3 Second floor plan
4 First floor plan

Cl
Master bedroom
Cl
W
D
Bedroom
Up
Down
Office
Bedroom
3
Hot tub
Living room
Kitchen
R
Cl
Cl
Guest bedroom
Down
Up
Down
Dining area
Entry below
Screened-in porch
Deck above
Down
4
0
4
8m
N

5

5 View to the northeast
6 Kitchen
7 View from the living room
8 Dining area
Photography: Catherine Bogert

6

7

8

Riverside Apartments

Hayball Leonard Stent

Completion: February 1995

Location: South Melbourne, Victoria, Australia

Client: Bellmist Pty Ltd.

Area: 18,000 square metres; 193,757 square feet

Structure: In situ reinforced concrete slabs; precast concrete

Materials: Unpainted galvanised steel; slate and zinc alume roofing

Cost: A$13.25 million

Awards: 1995 Melbourne City Council Building Awards Merit Award

1995 Royal Australian Institute of Architects Commendation Award

The principal focus was to provide a range of affordable housing which would complement the scale of the historic Jones Bond Store by incorporating a diversity of building form and architectural detail

A residential apartment project located on the southwest edge of the Southbank precinct, Riverside comprises new medium rise apartments adjacent the Bond Store. The architectural treatment does not draw in a literal sense from the historic building but rather provides a low key contrast. This design approach maintains that the architecture of the new construction should not compromise the integrity of the historic building by an attempt to echo its form or detail.

The 5-storey former bond store is included in the Victorian Register of Historic Buildings. Originally a warehouse for the shipping industry, the Store is refurbished to accommodate apartments, a gymnasium and swimming pool, and resident function facilities.

1

2

3

1 Main entry
2 View of southwest
3 Plan
4 Corner residential units
5 View of lower height residential units

4

5

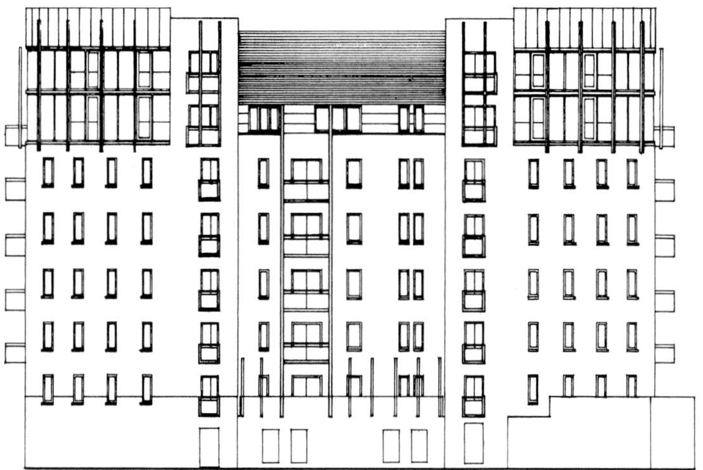

6

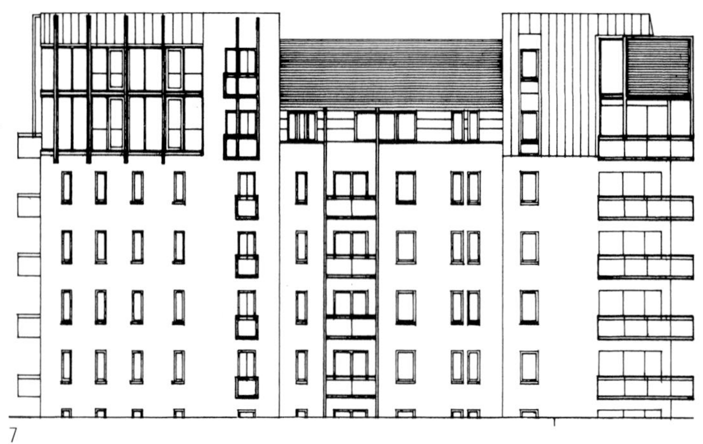

7

8

9

6 South elevation
7 North elevation
8 East elevation
9 West elevation
10 North building from Southbank Boulevard
Photography: Tim Griffith; Hayball Leonard Stent

10

Segal House

Hugh Newell Jacobsen

Completion: July 1994

Location: Hobe Sound, Florida, USA

Area: 446 square metres; 4,800 square feet

Structure: Concrete slab; concrete block

Materials: Wood; glass; stucco

The concept for this Florida house began with the recall of the earlier houses in this region. They were perched on pilings, like a boat pulled up amidst the scattering of sea grass near the water's edge close by. These simple houses were typically enclosed by adjustable shutters alone and roofed in tin, from which a metal chimney servicing the cook stove within, announced the domestic intent.

A traditional and rapidly disappearing form is evoked in this design. The alignment of gable ends recalls the 19th century cracker houses that faced the wind and met the downside of the climate by nearly overcoming it through survival. Shutters are used to encourage the movement of air, while painted block walls are called upon to resist, in many cases, too much of the same.

The Florida house must be designed to face some of the best and some of the worst nature can present.

This house, built from the palette above, overlooks a fairway with the full advantages of glass and the necessary built-in protection of shutters that speak quietly of the threatening winds.

The living room pavilion is truly a hollowed out shell of the early cracker house expressing a volume of moving light and air within. The shingled form of the roof is expressed and not withheld within each of the spaces inside this white gathering of Floridian forms and materials. The white coral fossil floors extend the eye and the interior spaces beyond the physical limits of glass, and bounce a wonderfully reflected light through the glass walls, protected from the direct light by sunscreens.

1

1 View of east elevation over the pond

2 Plan

Photography: Robert Lautman

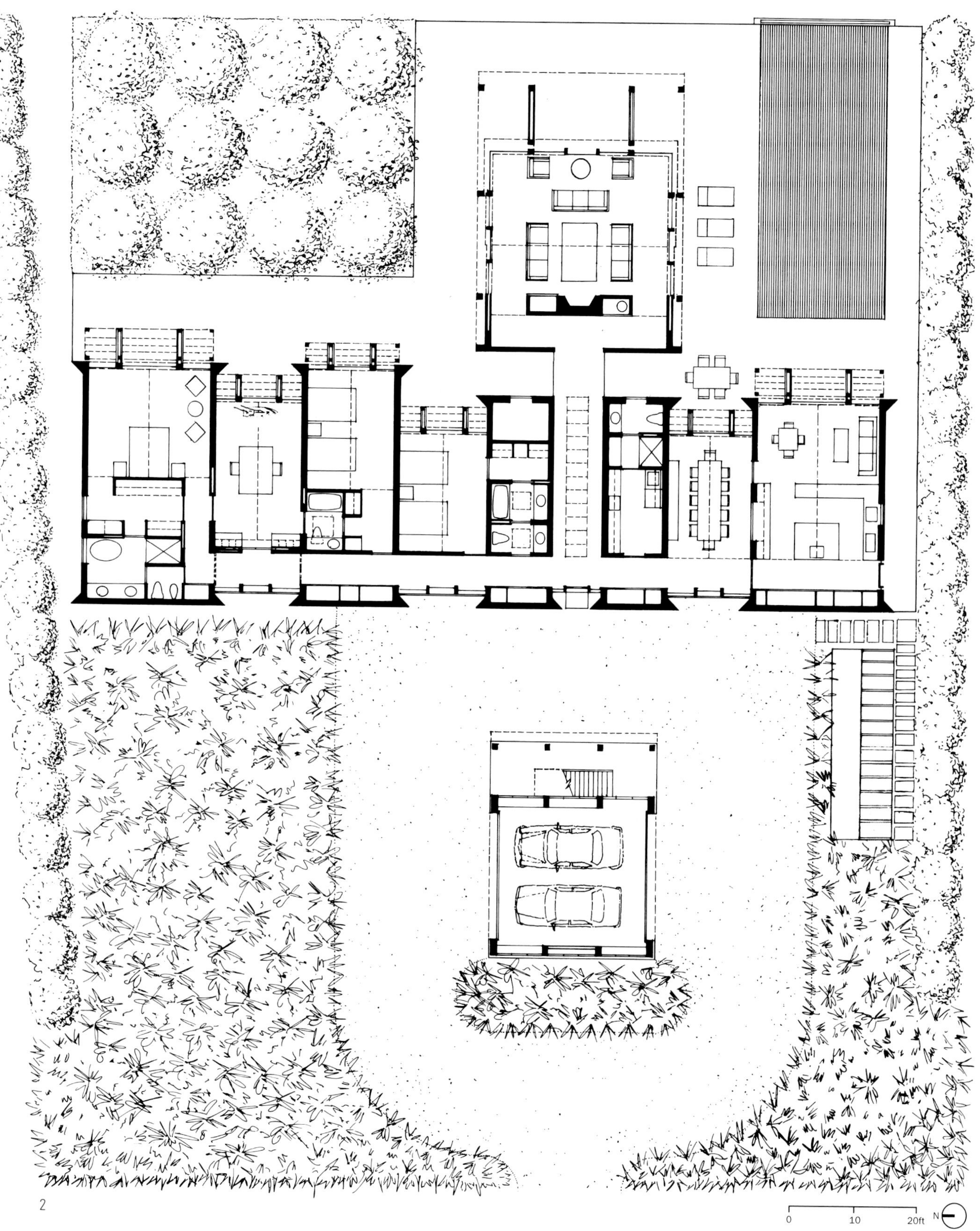

2

Singer Residence

Kanner Architects

Completion: January 1995

Location: Malibu, California, USA

Client: P. and J. Singer

Area: 184 square metres; 1,982 square feet

Structure: Wood and steel frame

Materials: Cement plaster; galvanised metal standing seam roof; wood doors and windows; steel canopies

Cost: US$178,000

The Singer Garage/Guest House is a mini-residence intended as an interim home/construction staging area for the yet to be constructed main house.

The architectural character of this Garage/Guest House is inspired by the owner's desire to have the project read as a contemporary expression of a European hill town.

The architects decided to break apart (function by function) the project's massing into gabled, vaulted, flat and curvilinear volumes and planes. The site walls have a compositional role as a part of this group of forms.

The building and site walls are wrapped in three different shades of integrally coloured putty coat plaster. The natural patina resulting from the hand trowelled application process was intentional. Douglas Fir ash, bleached, then varathaned with a marine varnish is deeply recessed into the home's thick exterior walls.

The arced, cantilevered steel deck is infilled with grey stained Douglas Fir decking. The railing is composed of both steel and wood members. Large steel compression braces support the cantilevered deck. Canted steel awnings with perforated metal infill panels shade the living and bedroom window walls at the warmest time of day.

Exterior volumes express the ceiling geometrics of the interior. Gabled forms are supported by white painted triangular trusses. Barrel vaulted forms are supported by arced glue-laminated trusses.

The guest house, as well as its future big brother, are designed to capture light and view. Both exterior and interior geometrics are pure and the forms are simple, so as to provide the background for the artistic expression and living requirements of the client.

1

2

3

1 Front view from the west
2 Rear detail
3 Living area
4 Side composition

Photography: Mark Lohman

4

Waldhauer Residence

House + House, Architects

Completion: October 1994

Location: Woodside, California, USA

Client: Fred & Ruth Waldhauer

Area: 260 square metres; 2,800 square feet

Structure: Wood frame

Materials: Cedar siding; integral colour stucco; maple cabinetry; galvanised metal

Energy conservation, a thoughtful use of natural resources and poetic harmony with the site were the guiding project requirements for this house for an inventor/musician and an environmental scientist with varied and fascinating interests.

The house is located within California's 'scenic corridor' on the crest of the coastal range overlooking the Pacific Ocean. A beautiful grove of oak trees, a protected meadow, the windswept grassy hillside, and large sandstone boulders with ancient Indian mortars have all been preserved. The building forms derive from a geometric framework inspired by site characteristics. The sloping roof follows the topography and tree lines and deflects occasional gale force winds while the curving living wing provides a wind break for a protected outdoor garden at the entrance. Alignments organise the building to acknowledge sunset at the winter solstice when the family gathers. The solar orientation of major living spaces takes advantage of heat gain in the winter, while a deep trellis on the west provides protection from the summer sun. Convection pulls cool air from the canyon below to flow naturally up into the low-set awning windows and out the high clerestory windows and the tower, providing natural cooling and ventilation.

Building materials are specifically selected for their low toxicity, local availability, low maintenance and compatibility with the environment. All paints and stains are non-toxic. The wood floor, manufactured from recycled lumbermill scraps, draws the golden hues of the native grasses into the house. Weathered grey cedar siding reflects the shades of earth and the integrally coloured grey-green stucco matches the lichen covered boulders.

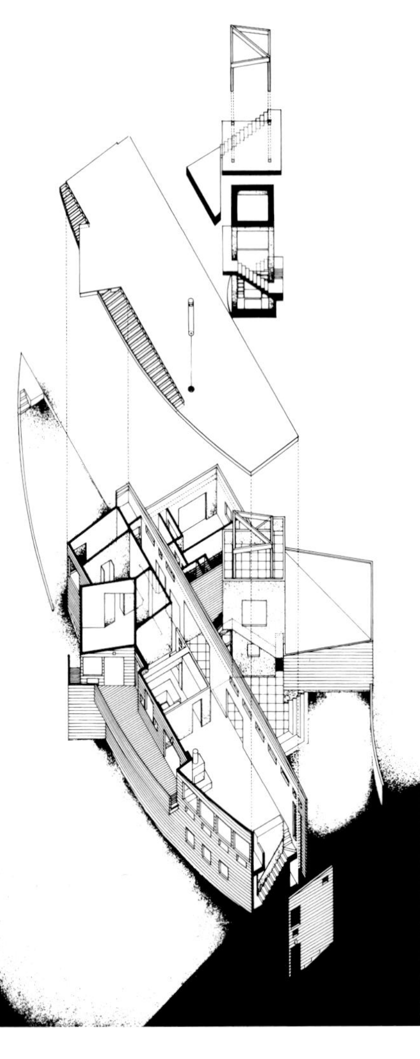

1

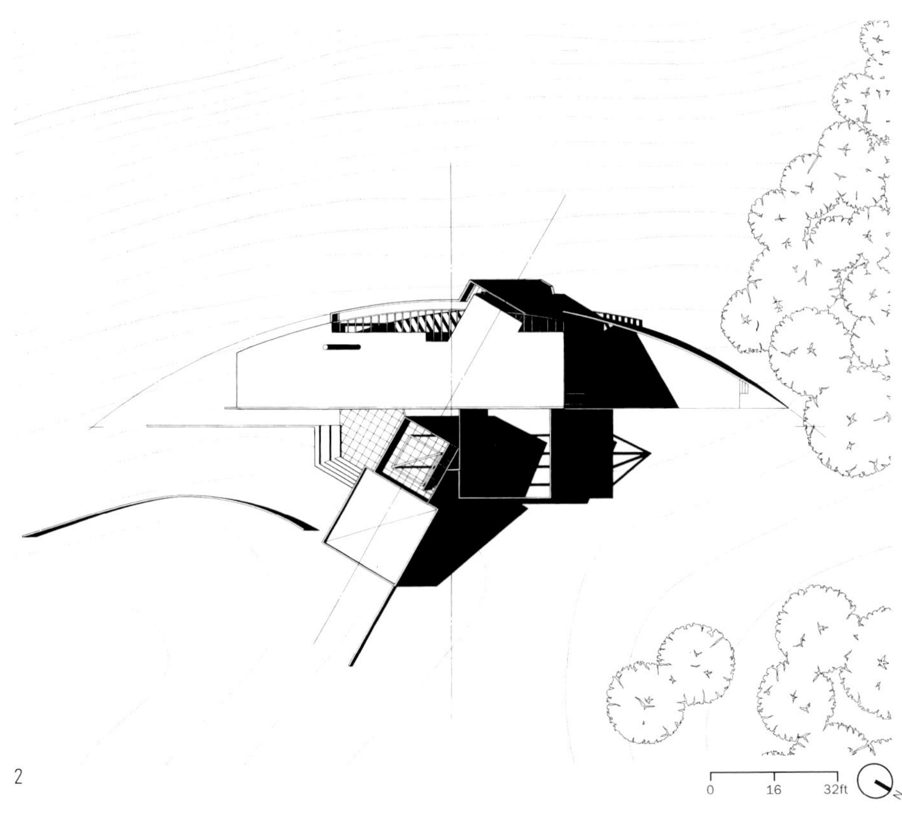

2

3

1 Exploded axonometric view
2 Site plan
3 South facade
4 West facade

4

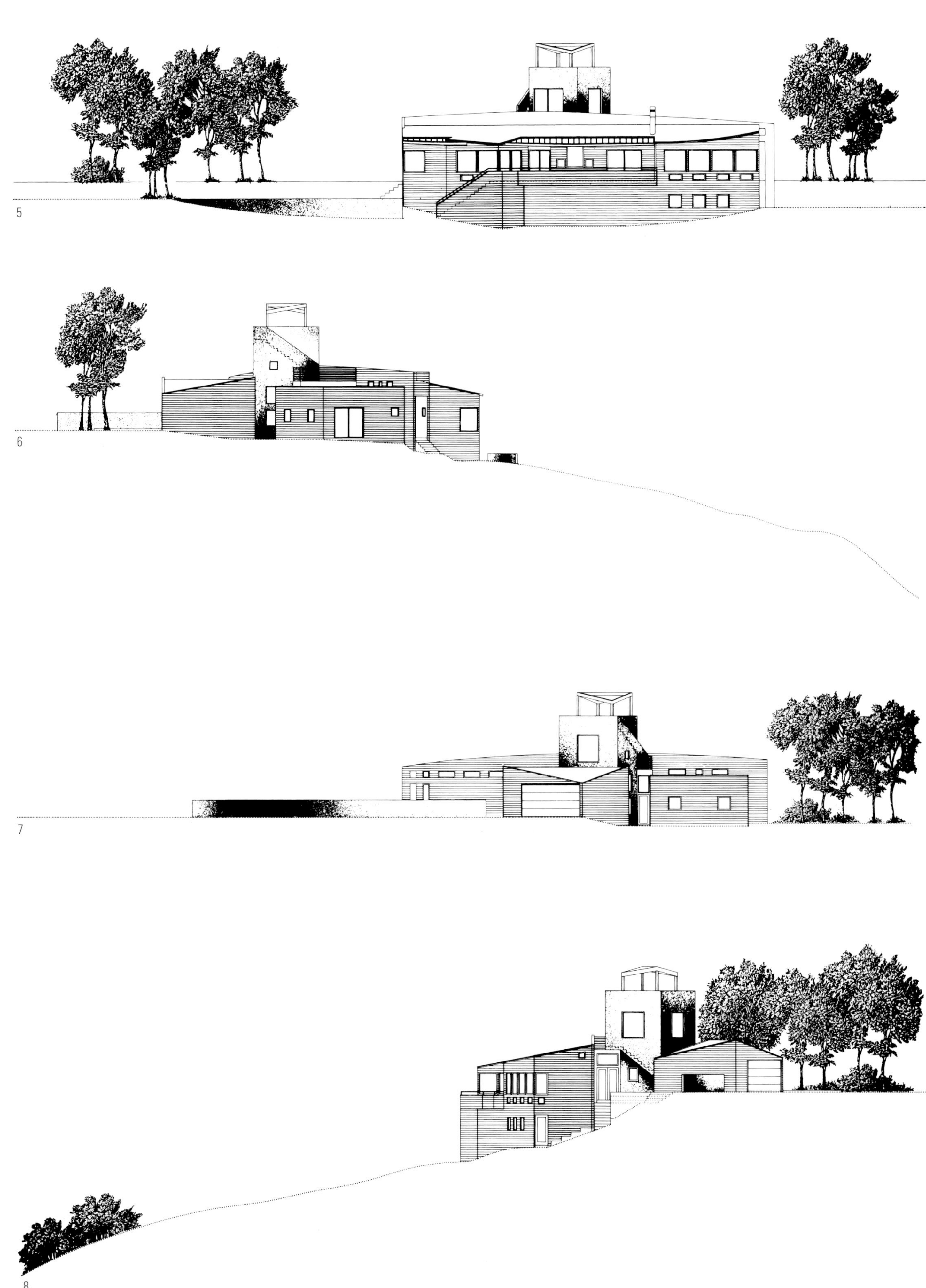
5
6
7
8

9

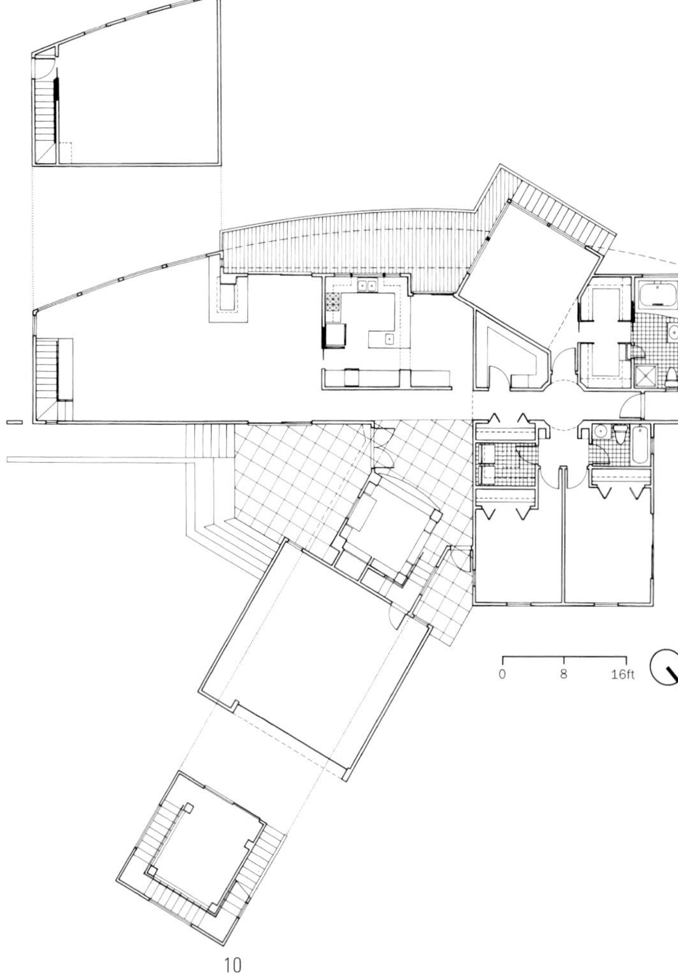

10

11

12

5 West elevation
6 North elevation
7 East elevation
8 South elevation
9 View of trellis from deck
10 Floor plans
11 View of living room
12 View of entry from library
Photography: Alan Weintraub

Villa Nuottaniemi

Arkkitehtitoimisto Paatela-Paatela & Co

Completion: July 1994
Location: Helsinki, Finland
Client: M. Paatela
Area: 260 square metres; 853 square feet
Structure: Concrete; steel frame
Materials: Brick; wood; tiles

The building is a single family house located on a sloping site by the seashore, approximately 15 minutes drive from downtown Helsinki.

The building emphasises the scenery to the Gulf of Finland in the south while it is relatively closed with only one opening to the north.

The living spaces follow the profile of the sloping site in two levels with the living room, dining and kitchen on the lower floor level and the bedrooms with the main entrance on the upper floor level.

The master bedroom has a view to the sea through the upper part of the living room. The sauna, hobby rooms and storage areas are on the basement floor level. The children's bedroom section with the basement can be separated to an independent apartment as the family concept changes in the future.

The building is constructed of concrete with steel frame structure, double brick external walls and roof structure of wood with roof tiles.

The living area of the house is approximately 260 square metres (853 square feet).

1

2

3

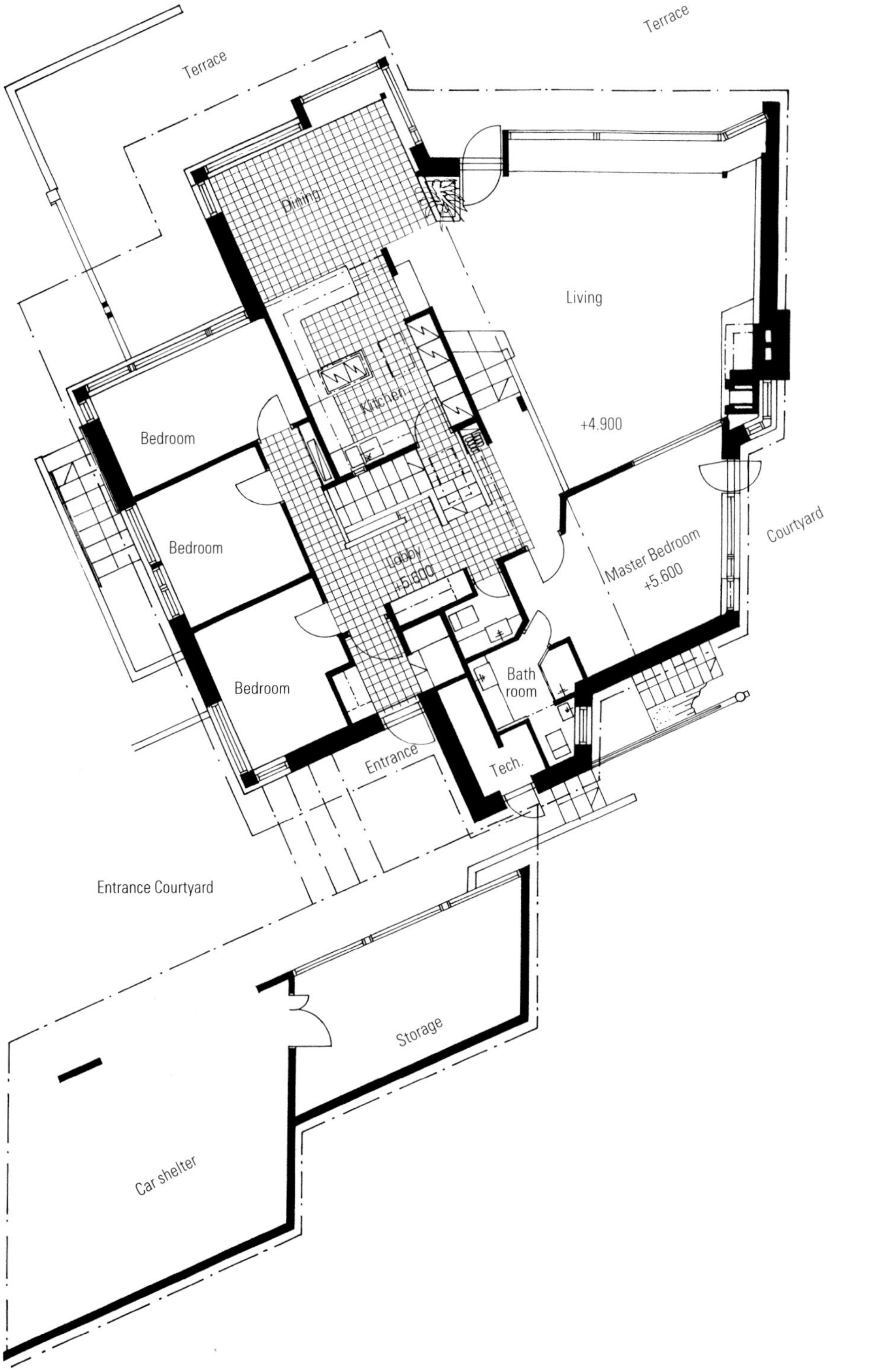

Terrace
Terrace
Dining
Living
Kitchen
+4.900
Bedroom
Bedroom
Lobby
+5.600
Master Bedroom
+5.600
Courtyard
Bedroom
Bath room
Entrance
Tech.
Entrance Courtyard
Storage
Car shelter

4

5

6

7

1 Facade to the sea (south)
2 Entrance, facade to east
3 Stairs to the kitchen and lobby
4 Site plan
5 View from kitchen through dining room
6 Living room, dining in the back
7 Living room

Ever Commonwealth Commercial Complex

G&W Architects, Engineers, Project Development Consultants

Completion: December 1994
Location: Quezon City, Philippines
Client: Gotesco Properties, INC.
Area: 71,500 square metres; 769,645 square feet
Structure: Reinforced concrete

A shopping complex, Ever Commonwealth has four levels of commercial space, together with a bowling centre, 10 cinemas, a department store, commercial spaces, restaurants and an amusement centre.

1

1 Shopping complex facade
2-3 Shopping mall main atrium

2

3

Future Park Plaza

Architects 49 Limited

Completion: March 1995

Location: Rangsit, Prathumthani Province, Thailand

Client: Rangsit Plaza Co., Ltd.

Area: 550,000 square metres; 5,920,344 square feet

Structure: Concrete; precast wall; space frame roofing

Materials: Mosaic on precast concrete wall; steel frame metal sheet roof; reflective glass

Cost: 1,230 million Baht

Future Park Plaza the largest commercial and entertainment complex in the country.

The Plaza consists of two prominent department stores; Central and Robinson, and a hypermarket, entertainment theme park, convention hall and retail stores.

These facilities were distributively placed to create magnets along its 500 metre (1,640 foot) long facade.

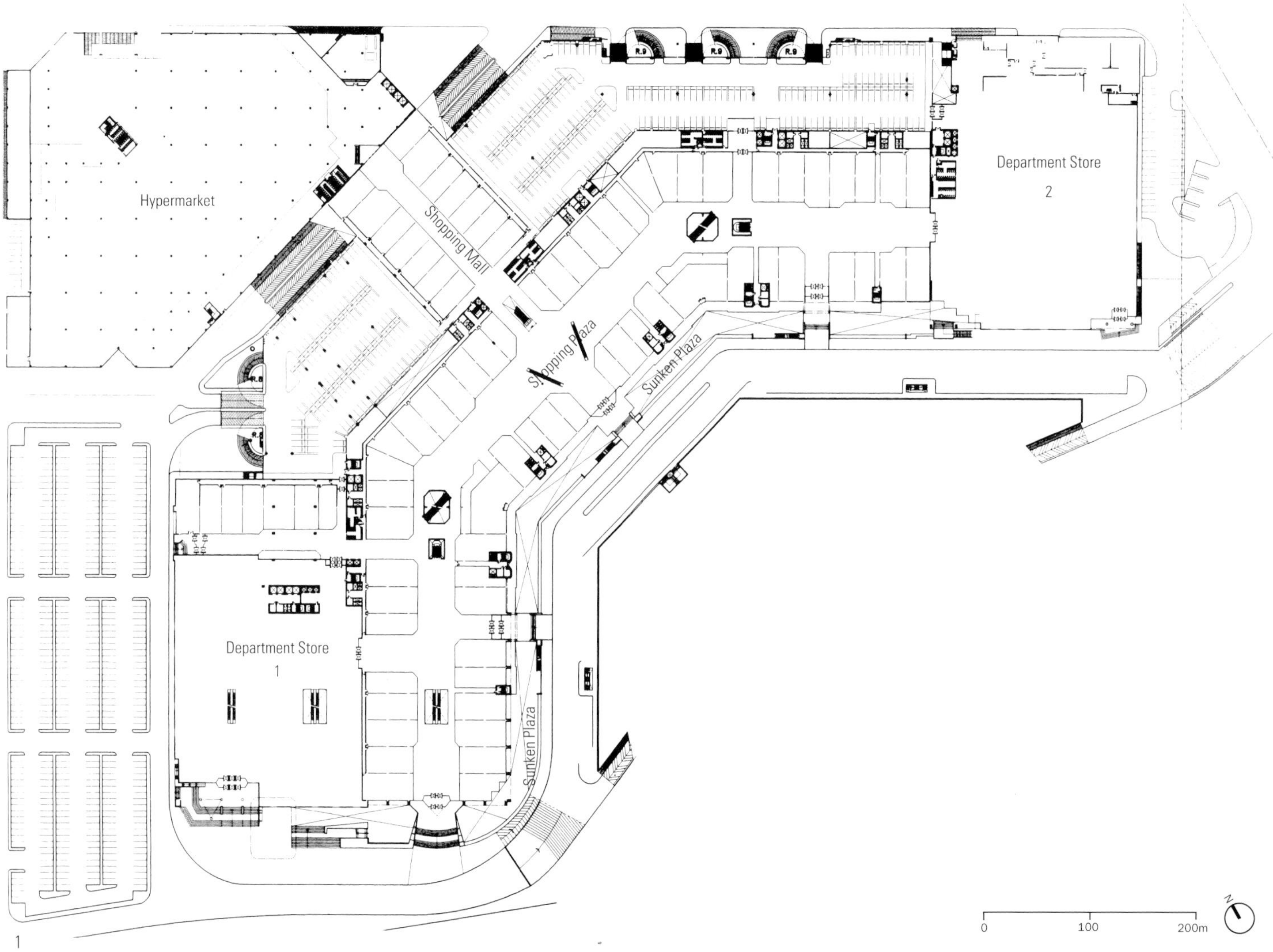

Hypermarket

Shopping Mall

Shopping Plaza

Sunken Plaza

Department Store 2

Department Store 1

Sunken Plaza

0 100 200m

1

2

1 Layout plan
2 View from front plaza
3 Southwest elevation
4 South elevation
5 Skylight in main atrium

Photography: Skyline by Somkid Piampiyachart

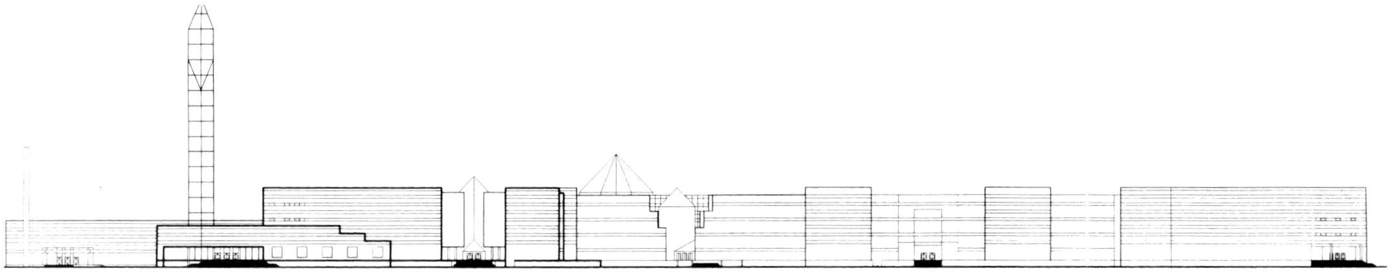

3

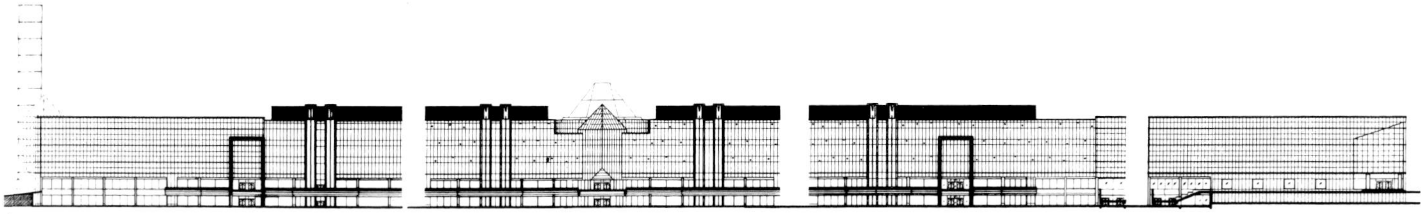

4

5

Phototime Processing Laboratory & Studio

House + House, Architects

Completion: October 1994

Location: Palo Alto, California, USA

Client: Stephen Shepard

Area: 185 square metres; 2,000 square feet

Structure: Steel frame

Materials: Stainless steel; maple; neon signage; cable railings; steel truss frame lighting supports; coloured plaster

Awards: ASID Design Excellence Award
Renaissance Design Award
Best in American Remodelling Award

Sensual materials, sculptural forms and layers of colour enrich a dynamic new environment for this 185 square metre (2,000 square foot) photographic laboratory facility which provides state-of-the-art technology for film processing, computer graphics and a portrait studio. A two and a half metre (eight foot) rotated square, designated by a charcoal grey accent carpet, sets up critical alignments for lighting, furniture and walls, defining specific work zones within an open plan. At the focal point is a curving, paneled and riveted brushed stainless steel wall sliced open at one end to emit a magenta neon glow. A steel column, hand ground to a sensual texture reflects in the mirrored finish behind. The reception desk for the portrait studio greets customers with its sleek curving steel surface, wildly ground into a magical hologram effect, topped with natural maple. An adjacent maple work table with a sliced, canted front provides ample layout space and conceals detailed storage. At the waiting area a maple top table is etched with the floor plan in diagram.

A bold one and a half metre (five foot) diameter cylinder in the processing area, concealing existing ductwork, is hand-finished in layers of purple and green plaster and crowned with three neon rings. The stair railing is burnished steel with cables and hardware typically used in ship rigging. Stringent functional requirements demanded the careful selection and placement of light fixtures to simulate balanced daylight. Truss frames carry a battery of fluorescent and halogen, task and ambient light fixtures. To further accentuate the high-tech nature of the facility, neon signs and accents were incorporated to designate work zones.

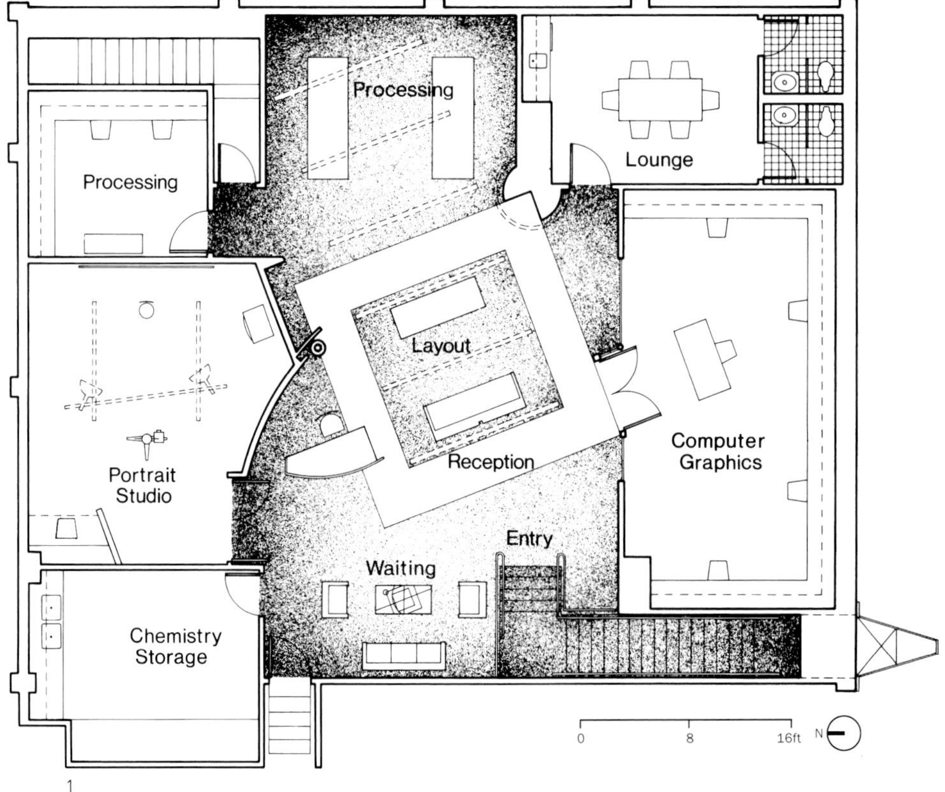

1

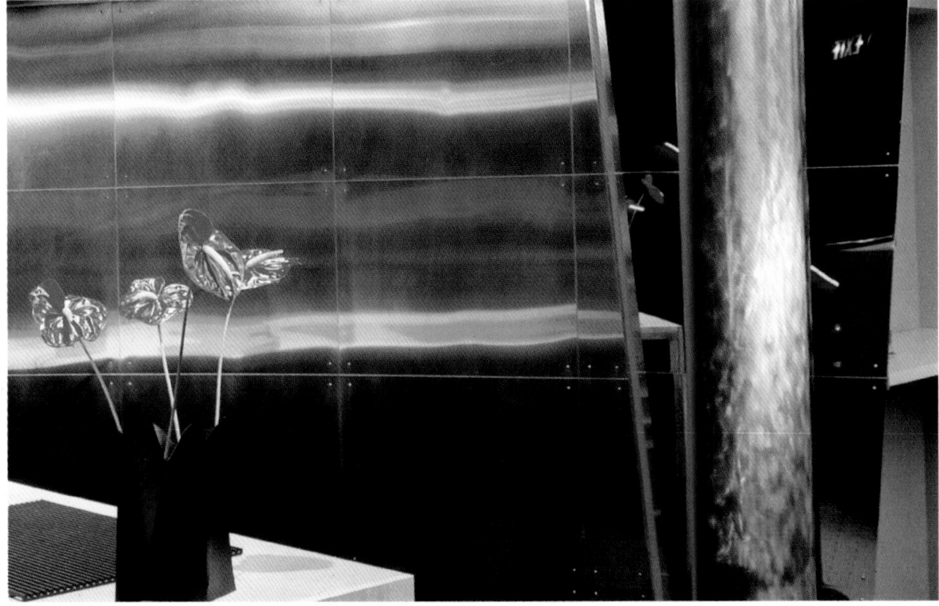

2

1 Floor plan
2 Detail of stainless steel wall
3 Axonometric view
4 View to reception and processing areas
5 View from stairway to computer graphics area
6 Reception desk and stainless steel wall

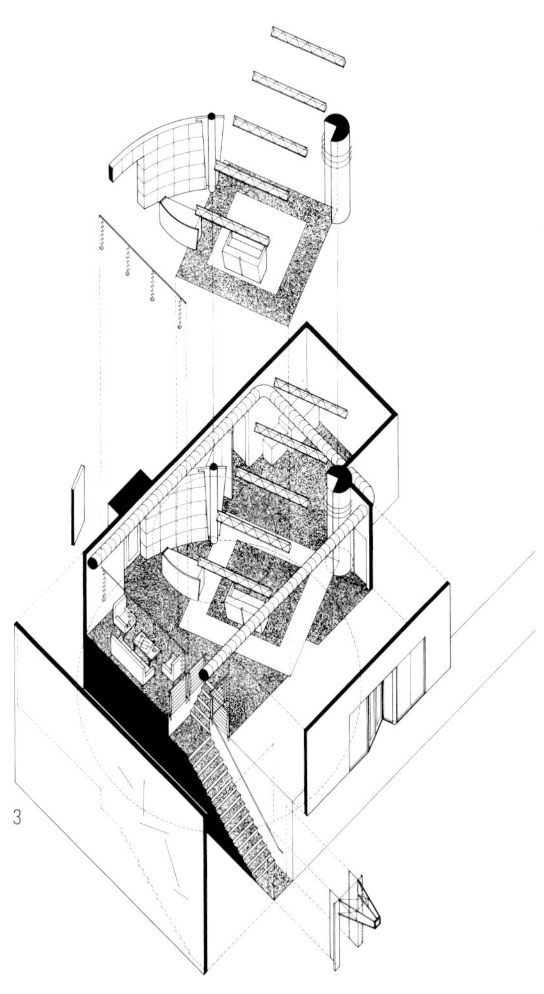

3

4

5

6

7 Steel cable railing detail
8 View to computer graphics area
9 Detail of cable railing support
10 Overall view of processing laboratory
11 View to portrait studio and reception
Photography: Stephen Shepard, Jr.

7

8

9

10

11

Sainsbury's Supermarket

Terry Farrell and Partners

Completion: July 1994

Location: Harlow, Essex, United Kingdom

Client: J. Sainsbury PLC

Area: 6,503 square metres; 70,000 square feet

Structure: Steel frame; concrete slabs on metal decking

Materials: Architectural masonry; flat and profiled metal cladding; structural glazing; render; membrane roof

Cost: GB£10 million

The proposals for a new supermarket on a nine acre site adjoining Harlow Town Centre are based on urban design principles. The scheme comprises a store, car parking, and a new petrol filling station. Access is from a new roundabout and section of dual carriageway, with separate service access off the existing northern boundary road. The proposed site layout relates strongly to the context. The store is located in the northwest corner, adjacent to an existing mature woodland. Parking is divided into two main areas crossed by axial routes relating the store entrance to the site perimeter. The entrance is treated as a collection of individual components linked to the main building, clearly visible at the heart of the site. Along the northern boundary, the building steps down to meet the adjoining road, and staff accommodation below the main sales level animates the existing faceless retaining wall.

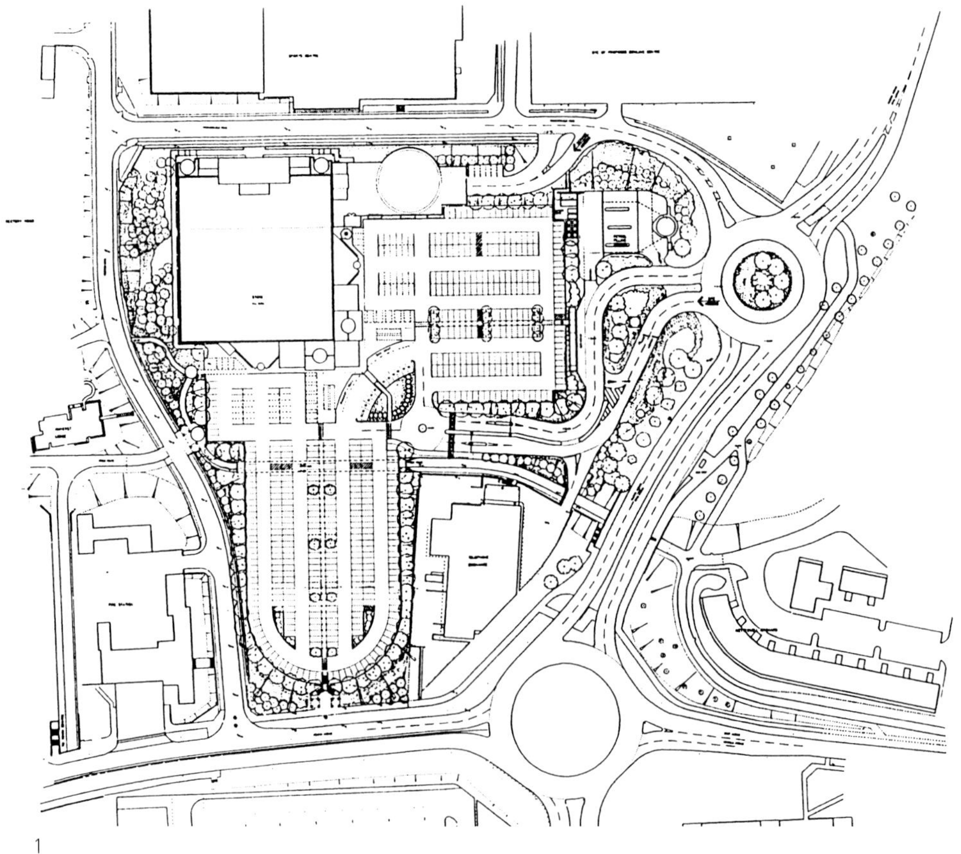

1

2

1 Site plan
2 View from cycleway footbridge
3 Shopfront entrance: isometric projection viewed from below
4 Shopfront entrance: isometric projection viewed from above
5 Shopfront entrance glazed canopy and revolving door: isometric view from below

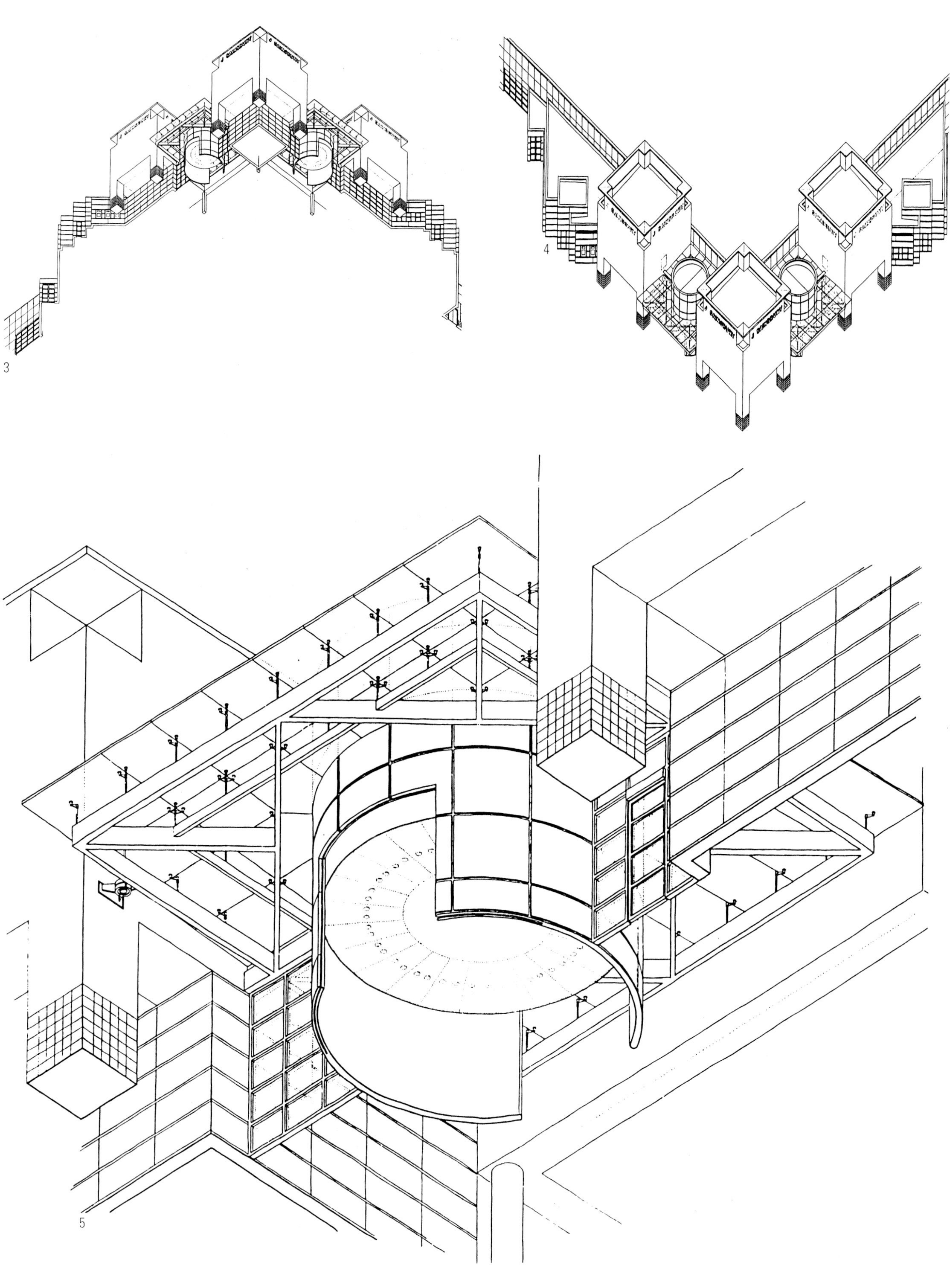
3
4
5

6 Colour model studios from the northeast
7 Site entrance pavilions
8 Detail of glazed entrance canopy

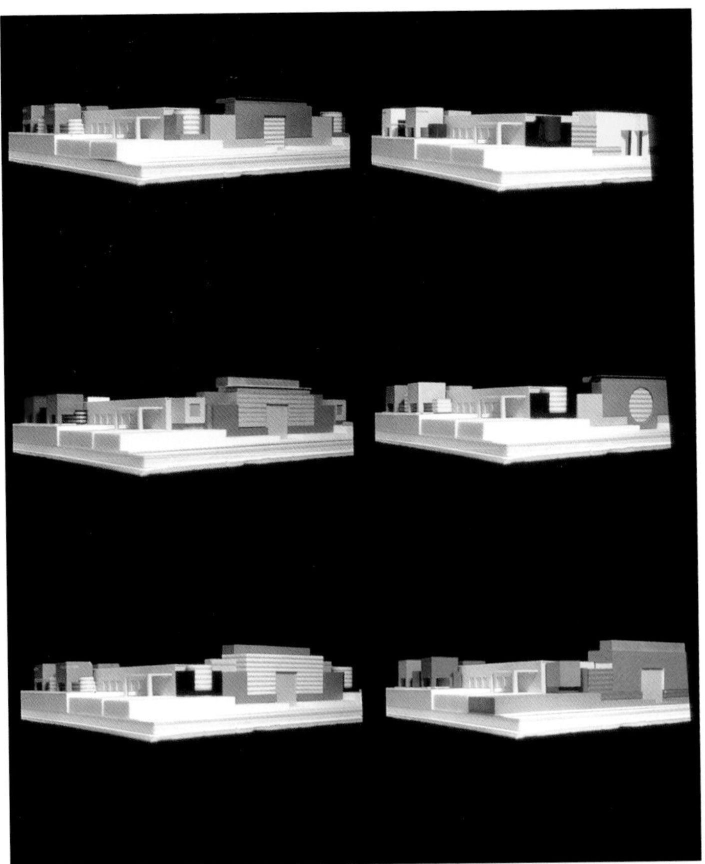

6

7

8

9 Glazed entrance canopy and revolving doors
10 External illumination
11 Entrance cubes
12 Store entrance
Photography: Peter Cook; Nigel Young

9

10

11

12

Tanglin Place

TSP Architects + Planners

Completion: January 1995

Location: Singapore

Client: Tanglin Place Development Pte Ltd (A Subsidiary of Kuok (S) Pte Ltd)

Area: 4,930 square metres; 53,068 square feet

Structure: Reinforced concrete columns; beams

Materials: Painted cement plaster; aluminium framed windows

Cost: S$10 million

The plan of this 4-storey shopping development is rather simple, consisting of open plan shops accessed by escalators and two stair cores (one with an adjoining lift). In terms of making a gesture to the outside world, however, the problem is one of how to avoid the urban 'blindness' of this type of building. TSP here takes a set designer's approach and provides an eclectic facade. The client believes that this modified tudor facade, with corner towers and a segmented half-timbered facade with a hint of steeply pitched roof, is the correct language for his shopping centre.

TSP does maintain that in contemporary architecture, there is a place for mannerist solutions like this when a client clearly shows a preference for it. Furthermore, the design establishes a sense of continuity with the adjacent Tudor Court.

1

2

3

4

5

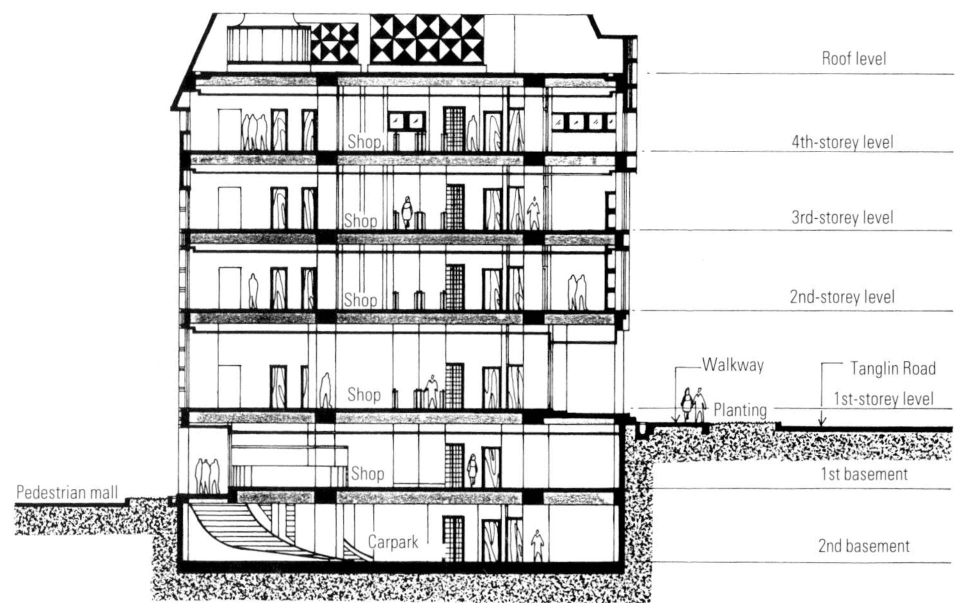

6

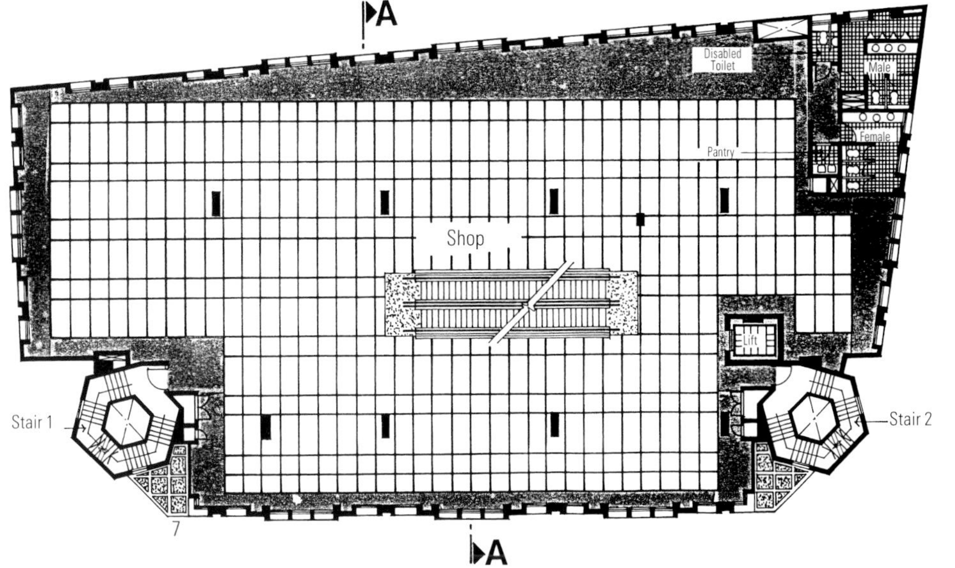

7

8

9

10

1 Tanglin Place
2 Continuity with adjacent Tudor Court
3 Tudor walkway
4 Modified Tudor facade
5 Entrance
6 Section A-A
7 Typical floor plan
8 Shopfront
9 Open plan interior
10 Shopping interior

Apartment Building and Jeanine Manuel Bilingual Active School

Architecture Studio

Completion: June 1994

Location: Paris, France

Client: Semea XV, Sagi

Area: 9,000 square metres; 96,878 square feet

Structure: Concrete; aluminium roof; steel; glass; metal girder

Cost: 57.7 million French francs

The facade of the building can be described in terms of theatrical space such as a decor, a backdrop. The curtain falls in front of the facade, opening slightly to reveal a darker mass that evokes the focal point of the visual axis. By parting at the lower edge like a raised veil, this volume clears the vast portico of the entrance to the Bilingual Active School. The remainder of the facade, slightly in retreat from the street, blends in with the neighbouring buildings.

The school and apartments are spatially and clearly situated and dissociated: the school, which has its own separate entrance, is located on the ground floor and organised around an atrium with a glass roof.

The apartments occupy the upper stories, offering a vertical stacking of several types of dwelling; apartments in length on the first levels, and duplexes on the higher levels facing south towards the Edgar Faure street, freeing up space in the attic for technical control rooms without any structure jutting out from the roof.

The metal roof comes down the northern facade of the building like a very smooth skin.

1

2

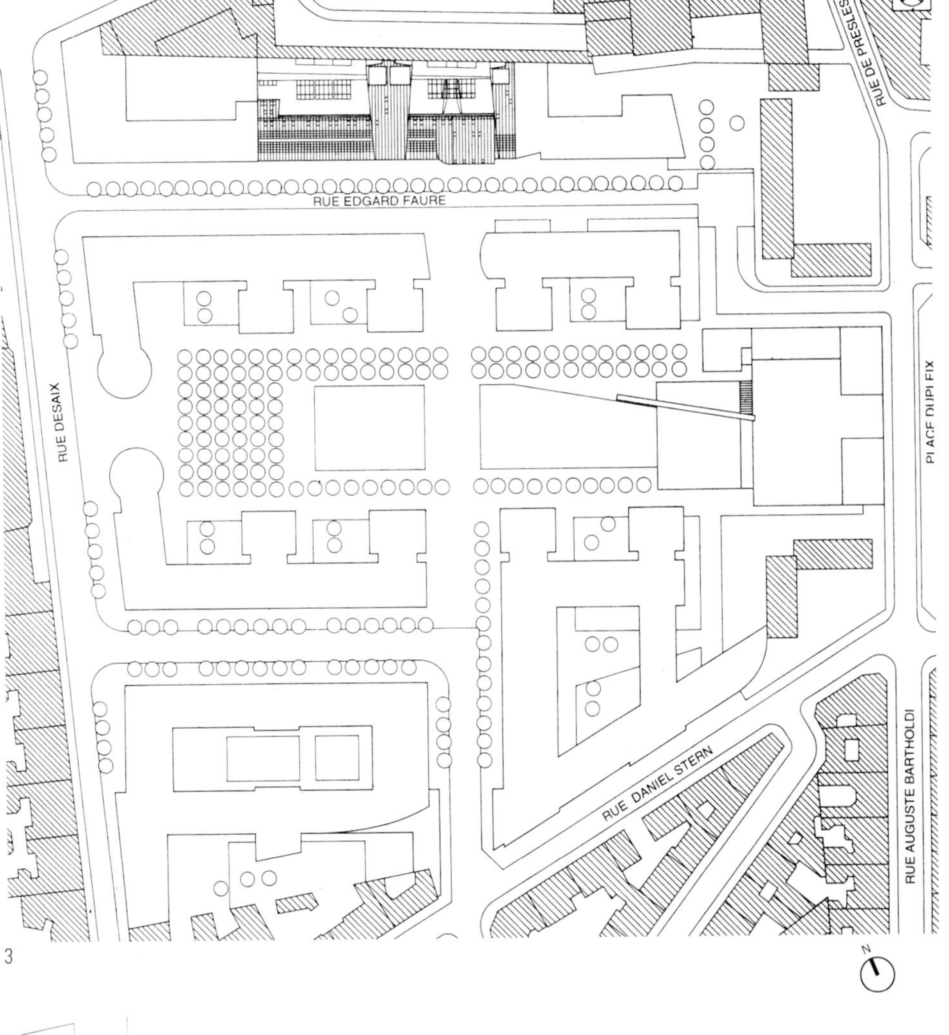

3

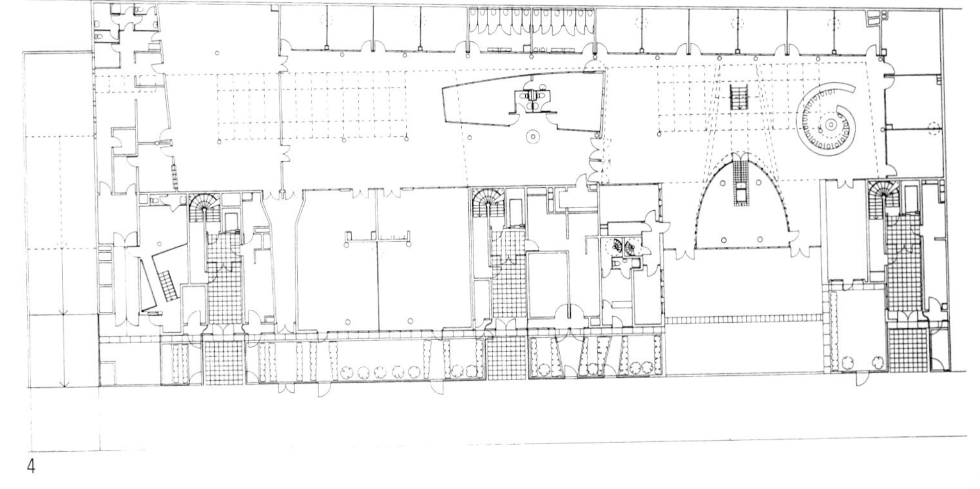

4

1 View from the Eiffel Tower
2 Detail of loggias on southern frontage
3 Block plan
4 Ground floor plan
5 View from the south

5

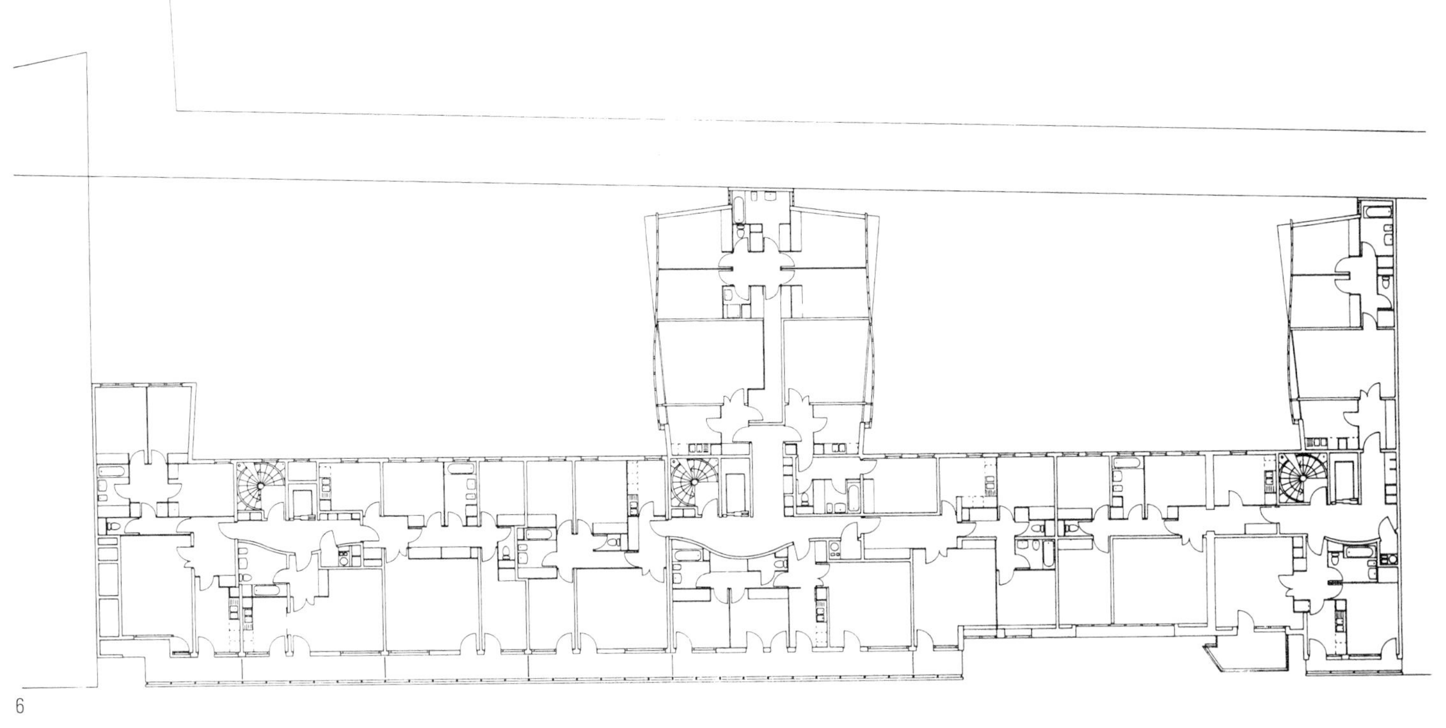
6

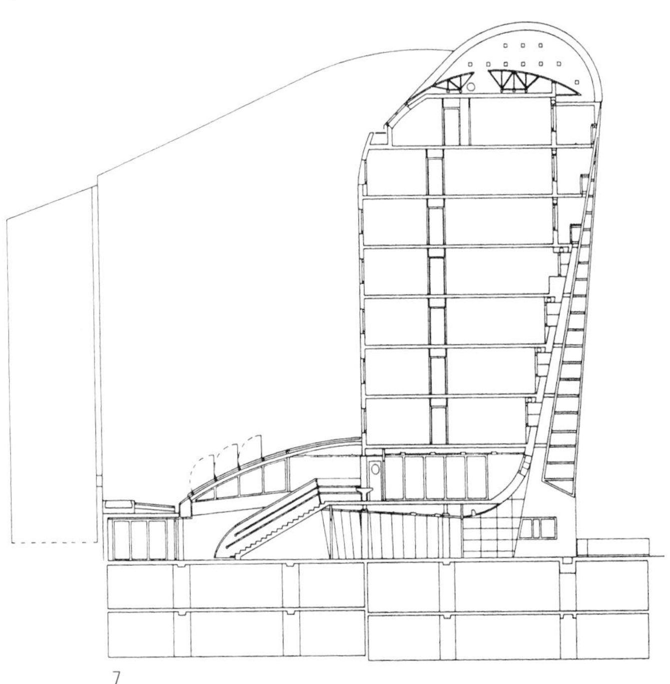
7

8

6 Stock floor plan
7 Cross section
8 Southern frontage
9 School entrance
10 School central space

9

10

Bamboo House (Restaurant) and Bamboo Gallery

Young-sub Kim

Completion: June 1995

Location: Kang Nam-ku, Seoul, Korea

Client: Bamboo House

Area: 516 square metres; 5,556 square feet

Structure: Reinforced concrete

Located in the residential district of Seoul, the height of Bamboo House could not exceed more than 2-storeys, or 11 metres (36 feet). However, it is not the unelevated height which prompts the feelings of intimacy, rather, the architect has carefully designed the house to the surrounding neighbourhood, so that it creates an atmosphere of familiarity.

The building has two distinctive programs; one is a restaurant, and the other, an exhibition gallery. In order to neutralise the building's identity one over the other, a 'mid-zone' (connecting hall) has been placed between the programs which plays an important role within the building.

Occupiers gain various experiences moving through the Bamboo House and Gallery. Unexpected places or space emerges throughout the building, yet its overall organisation is well composed shifting from the small scale to the large scale space. Rather than the additive thinking of assembling one space next to the other, the Bamboo House is organised in a continuous manner which provides for new experience.

The intimacy and familiarity of the Bamboo House projects lie in the disjunction of these intimate and known elements. These concepts were taken from Korean classical architecture, and reinterpreted in modern reality.

1

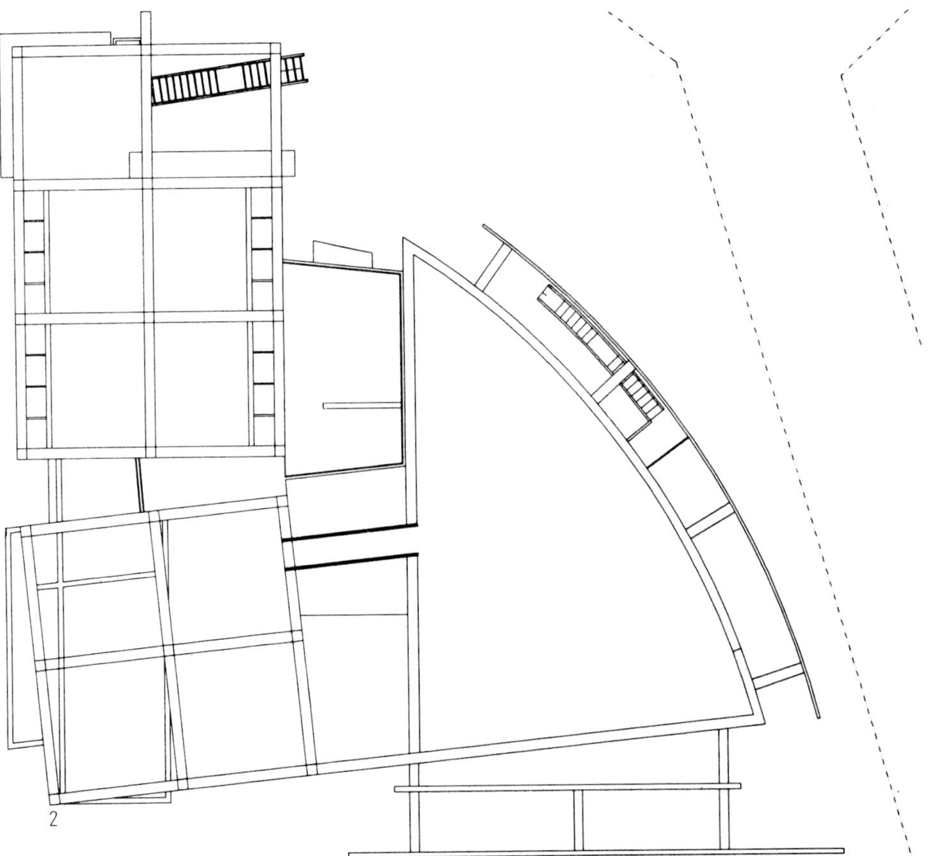
2

3

1 Aerial view
2 Site plan
3 Front view
4-5 Detail of entrance
6 Front view at night

4

5

6

7 West elevation
8 South elevation
9 North elevation
10 Rear walls
11 Bamboo Garden, glass block wall

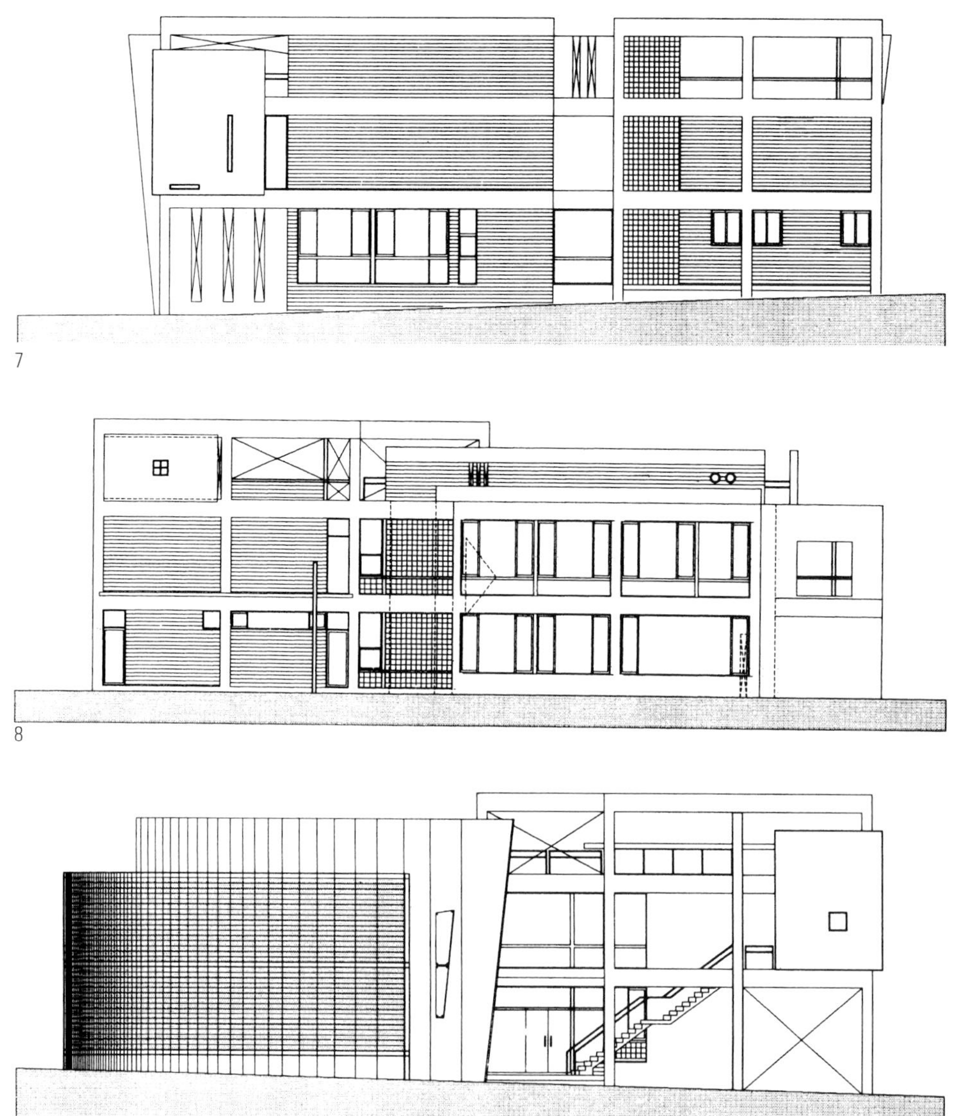

7

8

9

10

11

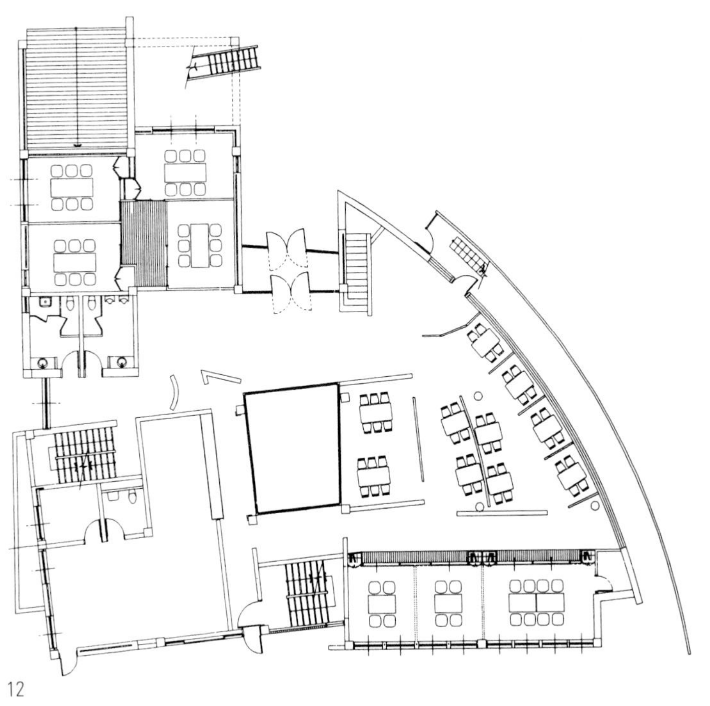

12

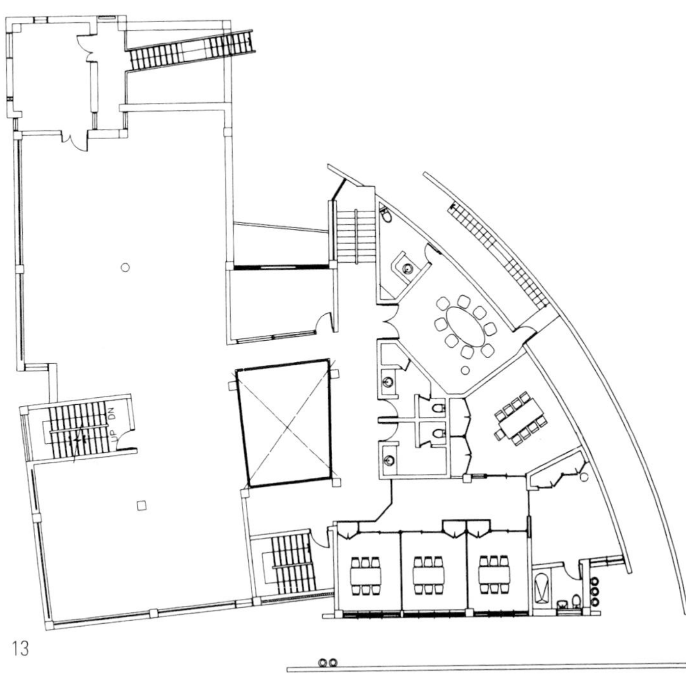

13

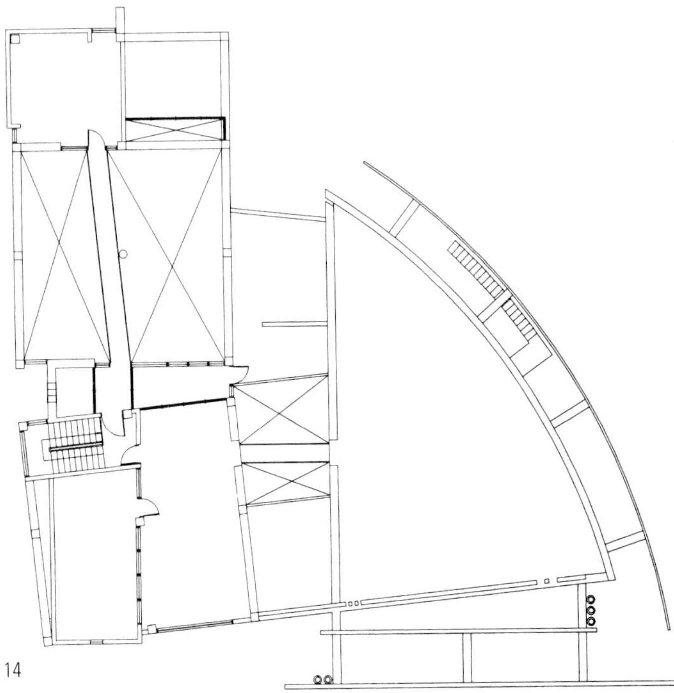

14

15

12 First floor plan
13 Second floor plan
14 Roof floor plan
15 Bamboo Gallery roof bridge
16 Restaurant, entrance hall
17-18 Restaurant, detail of interior

16

17

18

19

20

21

19 Entrance hall and patio, view from counter
20 Patio and sky bridge on second floor
21 Corridor on second floor
Photography: Chal Soo-ook; Kim, Jae-Kyeong; Kim, Young-sub

Bugis Junction

DP Architects Pte Ltd

Completion: February 1995

Location: Singapore

Client: Bugis City Holdings Pte Ltd

Area: 112,000 square metres; 1,205,597 square feet

Structure: Post and beam reinforced concrete structural frame; pre-stressed concrete

Materials: Granite cladding; glazed membrane roof; timber; retractable perforated PVC sun screen; terracotta tiles

Cost: S$300 million

Located in one of Singapore's historical areas this project was developed from a careful analysis of colourful characteristics and qualities of old Bugis Street; the result is an exciting illustration of how well the commercial and community needs of today can go hand in hand with the older patterns of the past.

Accommodation includes a 400-room hotel, offices, shops and leisure activities. The functional mix is simply but strongly stated. Two high rise blocks located at the extreme ends of the rectangular site create a low rise zone of shophouses in between which provide an intimate pedestrian scale and ambience. Existing pedestrian routes were enclosed beneath a very light structure which does not obscure the rich detail of the shop facades and allows the space to be air-conditioned. At Bugis Square, the computer controlled fountain is a great attraction. Constructed flush with the surrounding floor level, it entices spectators to venture and participate.

1

2

3

4

5

6

7

1 Overview of development from the northeast
2 View of the restaurant component and the InterContinental Hotel from the road to the south
3 View from Bugis Square to the covered street with the InterContinental Hotel behind
4 View along an internal street in the retail component
5 The fountain at Bugis Square
6 View of the entrance to the covered street
7 Interior view along the covered street

Photography: Chan Sui Him

Evercrest Golf Club & Resort

G&W Architects, Engineers, Project Development Consultants

Completion: August 1995
Location: Batangas, Philippines
Client: Evercrest Resort, Inc.
Area: 7,500 square metres; 80,732 square feet
Structure: Reinforced concrete

This Triple-A resort boasts of a par 72, 18-hole golf course designed by the renowned Arnold Palmer. The hotel and clubhouse overlook the scenic golf course.

The resort's amenities include a helipad; a hotel complete with 10 suites and 75 regular rooms, in addition to a function room and banquet hall; and a club house including coffee shop, golf shop, a sauna with massage room, and a hot and cold Japanese bath.

1 Resort club house
2 Hotel facade
3 Hotel main lobby

1

2

3

Pepperdine University Student Dormitory

David Jay Flood Architect

Completion: September 1994

Location: Malibu, California, USA

Client: Pepperdine University

Area: 6,875 square metres; 74,000 square feet

Structure: Wood frame

Materials: Cement plaster over wood; concrete tile; aluminium frame windows

Cost: US$5.8 million

The campus of Pepperdine University is located on the southern and western faces of the Santa Monica Mountains in Malibu as it slopes down to the Pacific Ocean. With a mandate to expand its on-campus student housing, the university selected a long, narrow, irregularly shaped shelf jutting out of a steep hillside for the site of its new 278-bed co-ed student dormitory.

The serpentine building, sited to the outermost edge of the shelf, follows the natural contours of the hillside and has spectacular views of the Pacific Ocean and the campus below. Automobile and pedestrian access, parking and recreational areas are located on the north side of the building protected from the strong prevailing winds. The dormitory's main entry is centrally located and is defined by a semi-circular colonnade.

The undulating plan for this 2-, 3- and 4-storey building is created by alternating wedge-shaped nodes housing common areas and vertical circulation cores between standard modules of student suites. This design helps reduce the visual impact of the 6,875 square metre (74,000 square foot) building and allows for greater privacy between rooms.

Each suite sleeps four people in two bedrooms with a shared bath. The suite plans are designed so that each bedroom has two semi-private yet contiguous areas, which allow for great flexibility in layout and usage of the room.

The building's exterior materials and colours, which conform to the university design standards, are a soft pastel stucco with terra cotta coloured roof tiles. The response to site conditions, the unique design solutions and the material and colour palette create a building that twists and turns and steps down the hillside, evoking the atmosphere of a coastal hilltown.

1

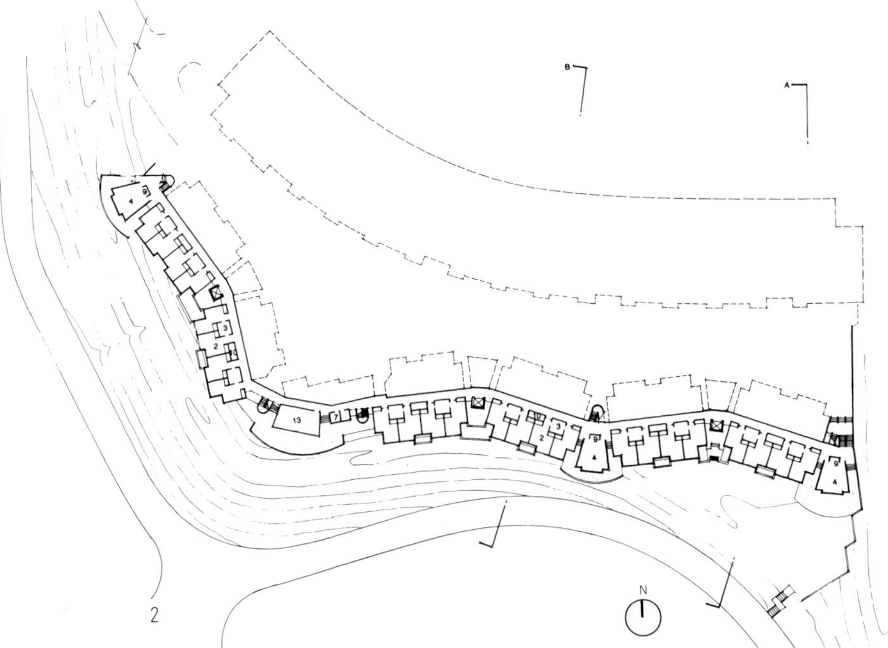

2

3

1 View of Student Dormitory from the southeast

2 Site plan

3 View of Student Dormitory from the west

4 Floor plan of a typical study lounge and room module

5 Interior view of student lounge

Photography: Michael Arden Photography

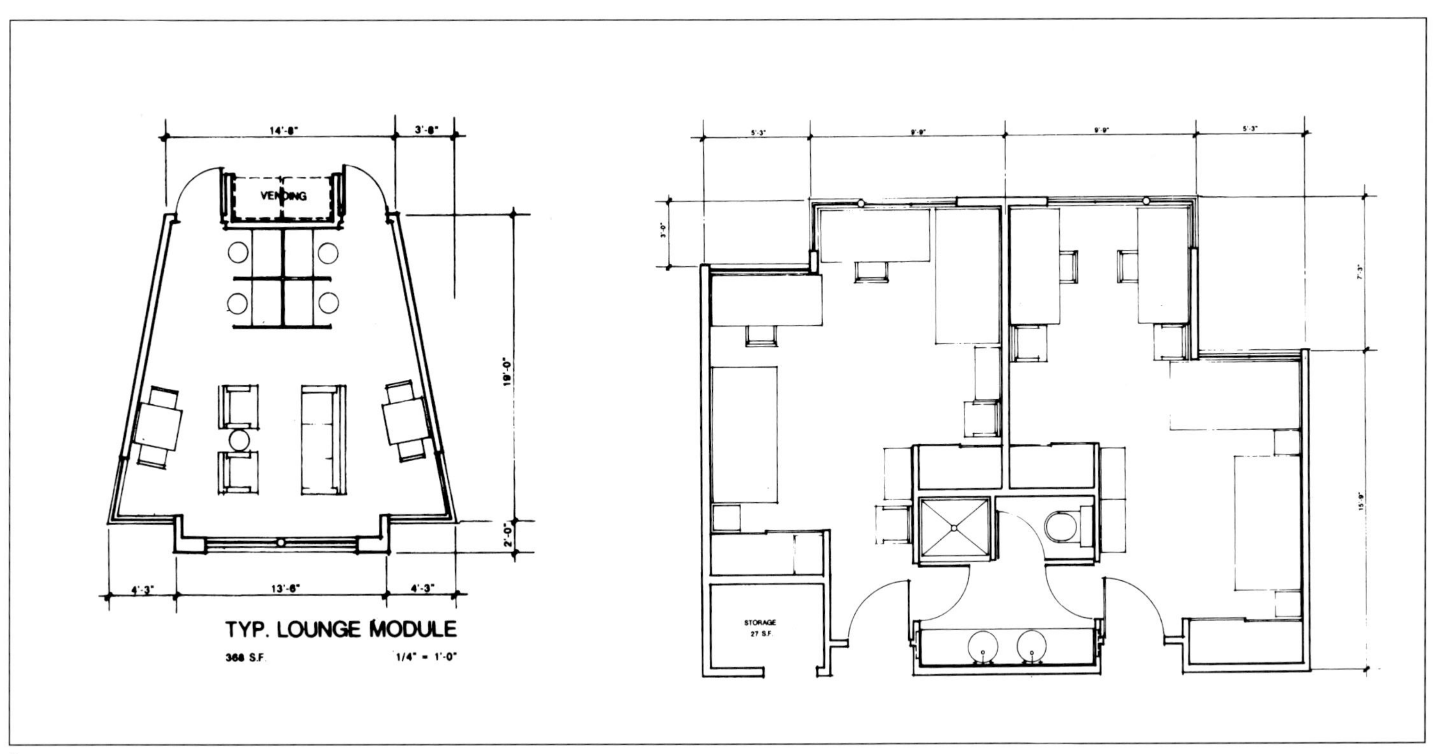

14'-8"
3'-8"
VENDING
19'-0"
2'-0"
4'-3"
13'-6"
4'-3"
TYP. LOUNGE MODULE
368 S.F.
1/4" = 1'-0"
STORAGE
27 S.F.

4

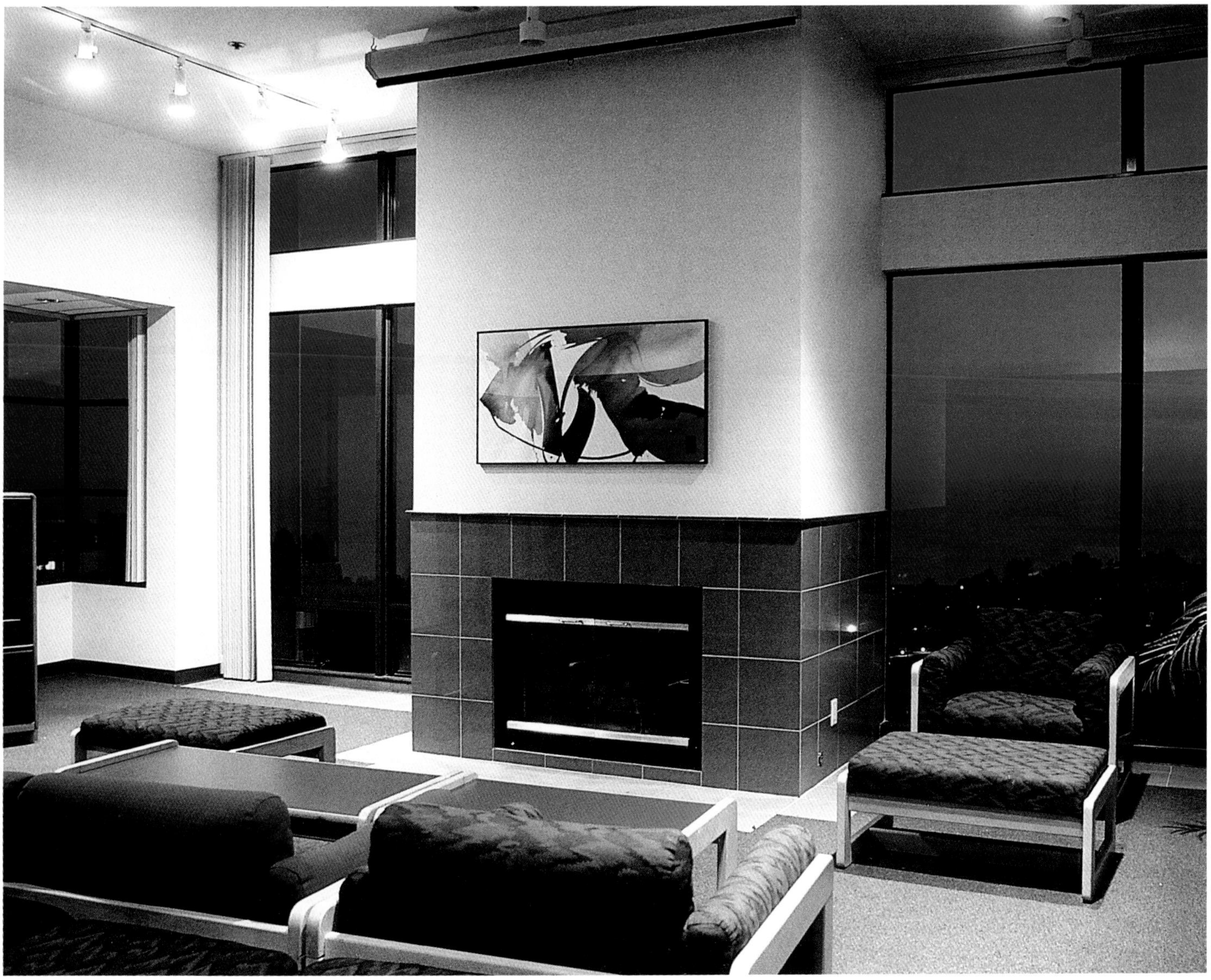

5

Youth Hostels Association of Queensland Brisbane City Hostel

Bligh Voller Architects

Completion: July 1995
Location: Brisbane, Queensland, Australia
Client: Youth Hostels Association of Queensland
Area: 980 square metres; 10,550 square feet
Structure: Reinforced concrete; steel
Materials: Plasterboard; steel; concrete block
Cost: A$1,112,000

The purpose of the project was to develop a quality, budget accommodation/backpacker facility which brought travellers together in the spirit of hostelling, but also provided greater privacy and more amenity through the use of twin and double rooms, some with ensuites.

As the flagship of YHA Queensland, the building had to reflect the culture and lifestyle of the region and be innovative in the style of accommodation and facilities it provided to the backpacker industry. The architecture therefore had to be progressive and memorable to complement the spirit of the project.

The Hostel contains accommodation for the manager and a duty manager, reception, laundry, public cafe and lounge, disabled facilities, and will accommodate up to 50 persons. Facilities are generally shared except for the provision of four private bathrooms incorporated into the double rooms.

The building is sited over an existing railway tunnel which has had several implications over the structure, namely vibration isolation of the building, maximum loading limits on the tunnel, and foundation support.

Concrete piers pass through loose fill and are supported by the rail tunnel and adjacent rock. The ground floor waffle pod slab is isolated at points of contact to these piers by rubber blocks. Ground floor walls are load-bearing exposed blockwork supporting a suspended slab. The first floor and roof structure are steel framed to reduce the building mass and external walls are a combination of face blockwork, bagged blockwork, and corrugated zincalume steel sheeting. All internal wall sheeting to the first floor is fire rated plasterboard with internal wall finishes to the ground floor either left as face blockwork or bagged and painted. Colour features extensively throughout the building in key locations. Structural steel elements are generally hot dipped galvanised. Intentionally the building utilises a limited range of generally raw and robust materials, and this aids in minimising building costs.

1

2

3

4

5

6

7

8

9

10

11

12

1 View to entry and managers' residence
2 View on arrival
3 Curved metal-clad wall, sunscreens
4 Sunshade detail, northwest rooms
5 Northwest elevation, street frontage
6 Carpark ramps
7 Cafe, view to lounge and tea room
8 View to lounge and entry
9 Entry, reception and stair to first floor
10 Lounge area, reception beyond
11 Cafe
12 View to lounge

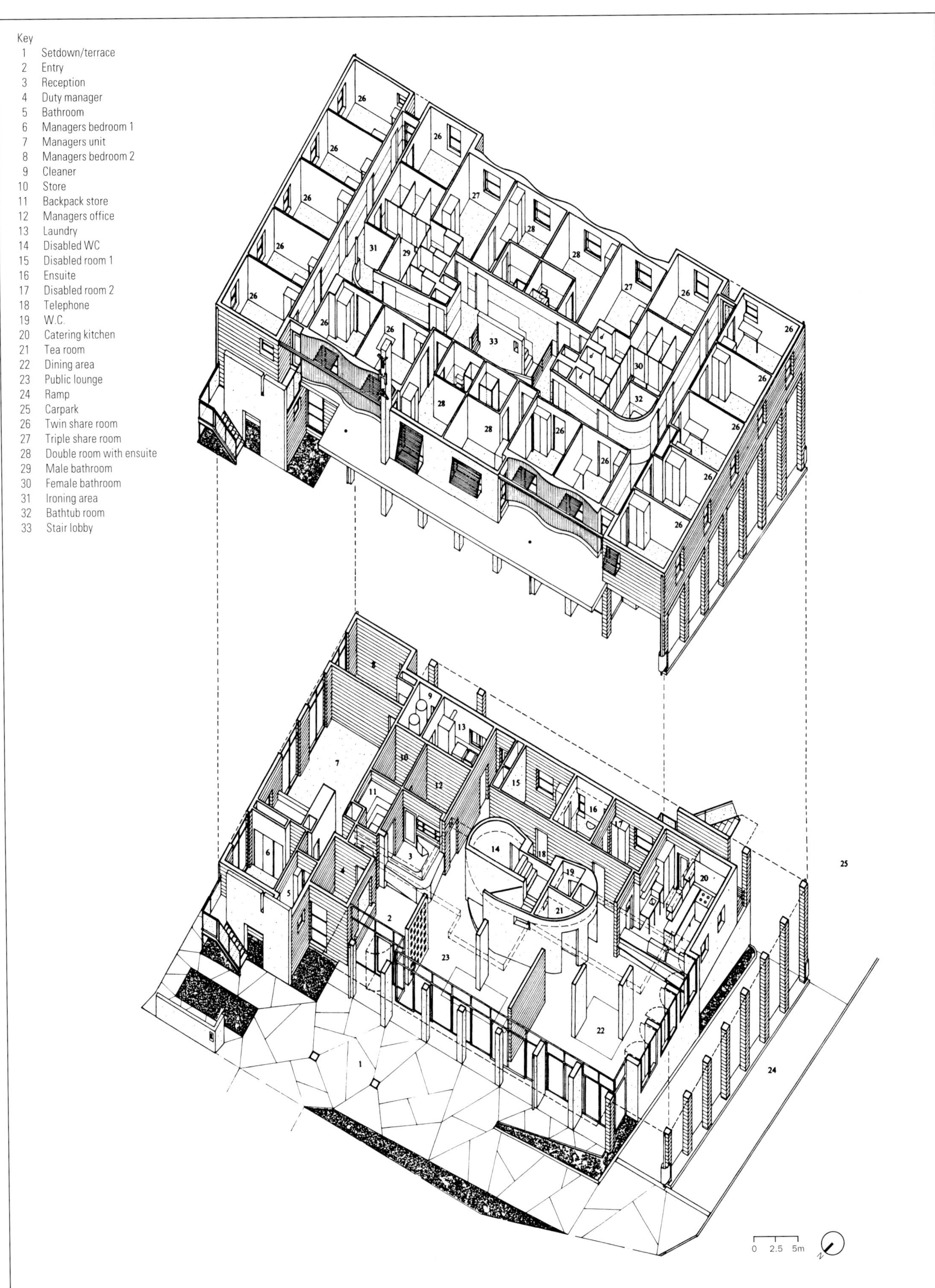
Key
1 Setdown/terrace
2 Entry
3 Reception
4 Duty manager
5 Bathroom
6 Managers bedroom 1
7 Managers unit
8 Managers bedroom 2
9 Cleaner
10 Store
11 Backpack store
12 Managers office
13 Laundry
14 Disabled WC
15 Disabled room 1
16 Ensuite
17 Disabled room 2
18 Telephone
19 W.C.
20 Catering kitchen
21 Tea room
22 Dining area
23 Public lounge
24 Ramp
25 Carpark
26 Twin share room
27 Triple share room
28 Double room with ensuite
29 Male bathroom
30 Female bathroom
31 Ironing area
32 Bathtub room
33 Stair lobby
0 2.5 5m
N

13

14

16

17

15

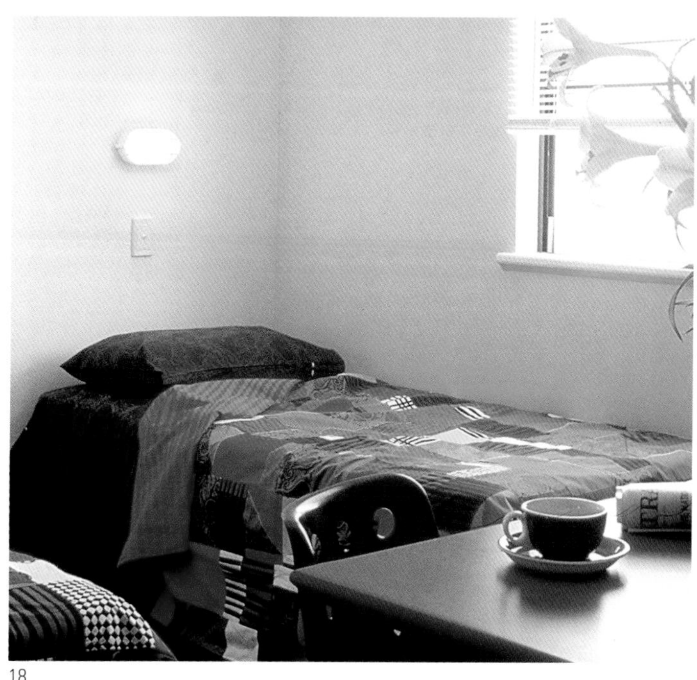
18

13 Exploded axonometric view from the street
14 Ground floor view of connecting stair to first floor rooms
15 First floor stairwell
16 Double room interior
17 Typical bathroom facilities
18 Typical twin share room
Photography: Andrew Bock; David Sandison

Biographies

A.J. Diamond, Donald Schmitt and Company

A.J. Diamond, Donald Schmitt and Company provide full services in programming, planning, architecture and interior design. Located in Toronto, Canada, the firm was established in 1975 and is comprised of two partners, Jack Diamond and Donald Schmitt, 24 architects, and a support staff of six.

The firm has made significant contributions in the fields of architecture, urban planning, landscape architecture, building conservation, and interior design. Projects such as the Metro Central YMCA (1984), the York University Student Centre (1990) and the Richmond Hill Central Library (1993), all located in the Greater Toronto area, have set high standards for user satisfaction and architectural excellence which are internationally recognised. The firm has recently completed the new Jerusalem City Hall in Israel and is currently engaged in the design of the new Jewish Community Centre in Manhattan, the Fine Arts building at the University of British Columbia and the 470-bed Baycrest Hospital in Toronto.

A.J. Diamond, Donald Schmitt and Company have received over 50 regional, national and international awards in design for projects in North America and the Middle East. These awards include four Governor General's Awards, the Credit Foncier Prize and an Olympic Arts Gold Medal.

Ahrends Burton and Koralek

Since forming their partnership in 1961, Ahrends Burton and Koralek have undertaken a great variety of projects in Britain and abroad which include planning studies and development plans, housing (both government-financed and private), university and other higher educational buildings, hospitals, schools, libraries, transport, commercial and industrial buildings, specialising in energy conservation. Current work includes the new British Embassy in Moscow.

Ancher/Mortlock/Woolley

The practice began in 1946 and Ken Woolley, who joined in 1964, is now the senior director. Steve Thomas, Dale Swan and Phil Baigent are the other directors and there are now three associates.

The core group are all active project directors enabling the high level of design quality to be maintained. The firm has been responsible for a large number of projects of greatly varying size, cost and function. Its outstanding special skill is the development of briefs for special buildings which, with the reputation for excellence and quality, ensures that client needs are met. With this experience, Ancher Mortlock & Woolley is familiar with all the innovations in project delivery and control. It has a substantial CADD installation, ample premises and a Quality Assurance system certified in compliance with AS 9001. The firm has been a recipient of all the major architectural industry awards for excellence, including on three occasions the Gold Medal of the Royal Australian Institute of Architects, in recognition of its dedication to the highest standards of design and professional practice.

Andrews Scott Cotton Architects

Andrews Scott Cotton Architects formed their practice at its current location in 1953, and have a continuous history of involvement in residential and community buildings in addition to commercial work.

The firm operates from an historic building in central Auckland and a branch office in Wellington. Andrews Scott Cotton Architects provides architectural and interior design services for projects throughout New Zealand. Staff currently number approximately 33, and include Computer Aided Design resources.

Almost all commissions take advantage of the full range of planning, architecture, interior design and contract management services offered. Creative answering of client needs and aspirations is supported by a team experienced in documentation, cost control and programming. Budgets and programming targets are held firmly in view.

The practice enjoys a high proportion of repeat clients. Over the years Andrews Scott Cotton Architects' projects have reflected the successful integration of aesthetics, practicality and functionality, producing buildings that have exceeded their clients' expectations, and received national recognition and awards.

Architects 49

Architects 49 was established in 1983. Its overriding objective has always been to provide truly professional and comprehensive services in all fields of architecture. These services cover a wide range, and are related to such matters as preparation of master plans, urban planning, design of buildings and complexes, and construction management. They also include counselling on the feasibility and viability of a project, and on other aspects for its development and management. In other words, Architects 49 offers to work for its clients faithfully, from the beginning of a project until its successful completion.

Since the founding of Architects 49, team work has been the watchword for them when they perform their tasks. A 'team approach' system was adopted, under which each project would be handled by a team of suitably experienced professionals, and their work closely supervised by a senior executive of the firm. This was to ensure that every project under their responsibility would be completed on time, within the planned budget, and in accordance with the clients' requirements.

Architects 49 has, from 1989-1995, added nine affiliated firms as follows: P 49 Interior and Associates Co., Ltd.; P 49 Deesign and Associates Co., Ltd.; 49 Engineering Consultants Ltd.; 49 Construction Management Ltd.; Landscape Architects 49 Ltd.; 49 Graphic and Publications Ltd.; 49 Model Presentation Studio Ltd.; Interior Decoration Construction Management Co., Ltd.; and Skyline Studio Ordinary Partnership.

Most of these companies are housed under the same roof; the remainder are located nearby. They are all affiliated to work side by side, so that the client may be assured of best quality and fast, efficient and comprehensive service.

Architectural Resources Cambridge, Inc.

Architectural Resources Cambridge, Inc. (ARC), founded in 1969, provides professional services in the fields of architecture, planning and interior design. These include feasibility and land-use planning, site design, master planning, programming, conceptual design, construction documentation, construction administration, space planning, furnishings selection and design, and equipment selection and design.

A major focus of ARC's work has been the planning and design of laboratory, office, research and development, manufacturing, training and conference facilities for corporate clients. In addition to corporate projects, ARC specialises in the planning and design of academic facilities for schools, colleges and universities.

Located in Cambridge, Massachusetts, ARC's professional staff of 40 architects, planners and interior designers bring a strong and broad foundation of experience to their work. ARC uses CAD extensively in the design, documentation and analysis of client requirements. Nationally recognised for excellence in architecture, ARC has received numerous design awards from the American Institute of Architects.

Architecture Studio

Founded in 1973, Architecture Studio today comprises six associates and many young architects of different nationalities. The six associates are Martin Robain, Rodo Tisnado, Jean-François Bonne, Alain Bretagnolle, René-Henri Arnaud and Laurent-Marc Fischer.

Recently completed projects include the High School of the Future at Jaunay-Clan (1987); the French Embassy in Muscat, Oman (1989); the Institute of the Arab World in Paris (1991); the Citadel University in Dunkerque (1990); the Arènes High School in Toulouse (1991); the Jules Verne High School in Cergy-le-Haut (1993); the Apartment Building and Jeanine Manuel Bilingual Active School in Paris (1994); and the Fire Station at Gennevilliers (1995).

Projects under construction include the École des Mines in Albi-Carmaux (late 1995); Universitate Residency in Paris (1996); the Church Notre-Dame de l'Arche d'Alliance in Paris (1997); the Law Courts in Cael (1996); the National Judo Institute in Paris (1997); the Business Centre 'La City' in Besançon (2000); the General Hospital in Cannes (2000); and construction has commenced on the European Parliament in Strasbourg, which is expected to be completed in 1997.

Bates Smart Pty Ltd

Bates Smart (formerly Bates Smart McCutcheon) is a practice of over 100 Architects and Interior Designers operating in Melbourne and Sydney. Established in 1851, Bates Smart has developed a broad client base in Melbourne, which has expanded to Sydney where an office opened in 1995.

Bates Smart's fundamental goal is to achieve quality design solutions through a totally client-focused approach. Each project evolves from the specific client requirements and innovation emerges through the design process.

This approach is combined with strong technical and management skills to provide cost effective and personal service.

The practice embraces architecture, interior design and facility planning and includes project experience in fitout, health, educational, residential and special purpose buildings.

Herbert Beckhard Frank Richlan & Associates

Herbert Beckhard and Frank Richlan formed the firm after long associations with the late Marcel Breuer, a major figure in 20th century architecture. Avoiding specialisation, the firm designs many project types, including houses, university buildings and industrial facilities, as well as office buildings. This diversity allows Beckhard and Richlan to remain fresh and alert to new ideas and techniques, strengthening their ability to develop innovative solutions, unaffected by whims of fashion.

The partners maintain a highly personal level of service, from design concepts to the development of projects and their technical resolution. HB+FR works over large distances, dealing with locales of varying cultures, climates and construction techniques. Recent or current projects are located in Russia, Guam (South Pacific), Europe and all over the United States.

HB+FR has received numerous awards for design excellence, including two prestigious American Institute of Architects' Awards, and has been published internationally. Beckhard has been elected to the highly prestigious National Academy of Design.

Bernhard Blauel Architects

This practice aims to maximise the potential of any brief and encourages an efficient dialogue from the outset between client, user and the building team.

Established in London in 1985 Bernhard Blauel Architects have worked on complex and intricate projects ranging from the design of contemporary furniture to the conversion of listed buildings and large fitouts for clients in the UK and abroad. Completed buildings show not so much a concern for the dictates of fashion, but for the most economical use of space and materials combined with the application of modern building techniques.

This approach has resulted in a light and airy architecture, whatever the size of circumstances and led to the practice being selected for the prestigious *40 under forty* exhibition at the Royal Institute of British Architects. Members of the practice engage in teaching as well as in the continuing study of contractual and production methods.

Current projects include a number of corporate office refurbishments, leisure and new residential developments in the City of London, Manchester, Birmingham as well as in Turkey, France and Germany.

Bligh Voller Architects

Bligh Voller's mature approach to architecture, interior design and urban planning has developed over its life of 68 years. The original practice was founded by Arthur Bligh in 1926 and today the design leadership is derived from the two second-generation partners, Graham Bligh and Jon Voller.

The organisation is managed by nine partners and 12 associates. All work remains under the control of the partners who are active, experienced design architects. Offices are located in Canberra, Sydney and Brisbane directly employing 76 staff, with joint ventures in Cairns as Bligh Voller James, Hong Kong as Chan Bligh Voller, and Papua New Guinea as Bligh Voller Richardson Proctor.

Each project brings with it a new client, a new brief and special cost constraints. To achieve the desired solution, the design process must be a collaborative effort between the designer and the client. Bligh Voller ensures that clients take an active role in defining their needs and goals and in this way act as a catalyst in bringing client and solution together. Their approach relies on clients dealing with a professional who has individual skills and a support team with an established capability of responding rapidly to project demands.

Michael Adams is the Managing Partner of Bligh Voller. His concern is with sustaining a high level of technical and project management skills for all Bligh Voller staff, and in the achievement of a high quality of service in design excellence and budget objectives. Michael has been with Bligh Voller for seven years and prior to this he spent six years with Mitchell/Giurgola and Thorp working on the Parliament House project in Canberra.

Jon Voller has been a partner in the firm for 20 years and has as his primary responsibility the management and design of major projects. During his time with the practice, he developed a strong interior design capability as a fully integrated discipline within the firm. He brings to the practice a strong belief that experience and design skills must be used to act as a catalyst in adding value to clients' business endeavours through responsible design.

BOORA Architects, P.C.

Established in 1958, BOORA Architects, P.C. is an 80 person architectural, planning and interior design firm based in Portland, Oregon. Nationally recognised as a leading designer of cultural arts and educational facilities, BOORA has worked on 25 college and university campuses throughout the country and completed $100 million in design of public arts facilities. The firm's buildings are known for their clarity of design and for fitting their unique context while having an individual character and feel.

Current clients include Nike, Aegean Corporation, Regional Center of the Arts, Sacramento, California Redevelopment Agency, Cheney Cowles Museum, General Services Administration, Kaiser Permanente, Seattle University, University of Washington, University of California, Riverside, and the University of California, Santa Cruz, among others. A measure of BOORA's success is the excellent record of award-winning designs, on or under budget, on schedule, with quality construction documents and, most importantly, satisfied clients.

Consultants Incorporated Architects + Planners

Consultants Incorporated Architects + Planners was established in 1982 by its founding partners Edwin Clay and John Chou, having reorganised from an earlier company that was in practice since 1958. The firm provides professional services in architecture, design, planning, development consultancy and project implementation, both in Singapore and the region.

The firm has serviced the Singapore Zoological Gardens for some 20 years—from the planning and design of Singapore's first zoo in the early 1970s, to the yearly additions of new exhibits and most recently, the planning and design of the Night Safari. The firm is currently working on a number of further projects including the Amazing World of Insects for the zoo.

The firm designs and implements an extremely wide range of projects. Some major completed works include the premier Mt Elizabeth Hospital & Medical Centre; Liang Court Complex comprising Hotel New Otani, Daimaru Departmental Store and a 26-storey Service Apartment Tower; Mazda, Renault and Volvo car showrooms; Factory and Warehouse Complex for Rothmans of Pall Mall; some major exhibits at the Jurong Bird Park and the 54-hole Palm Resort Golf & Country Club, its Recreational Centre and the resort's 360-suite Hotel Sofitel in Johor, West Malaysia. Other completed works include high-rise office buildings, residences and condominiums, colleges and schools, churches and mosques.

Cooper•Lecky Architects, PC

Cooper•Lecky Architects, PC is a design firm providing architecture, planning and interior design services to institutional, federal, state and local governments; corporate and private clients. W. Kent Cooper, AIA established the firm in Washington, D.C. after completing his work for the office of Eero Saarinen in the design and construction of the Dulles International Airport. Mr Cooper was joined by William P. Lecky, AIA in 1963. The firm has since worked on such notable projects as the Vietnam Veterans Memorial, the National Zoo's Amazonia Exhibit building, the National Children's Center, and the recently dedicated Korean War Veterans Memorial. The firm specialises in architecture that nurtures culture and community. Such work extends beyond the nation's capital to include a national and international audience.

Cox Architects

Cox Architects began in 1964 as Philip Cox & Associates, part of the well-known Sydney School of Architects which focused architecture on issues of regional and cultural identity. The company's reputation grew primarily from education, housing and conservation work until the 1980s when it began to draw such large commissions as Yulara Tourist Resort at Ayers Rock and the Canberra National Stadium and Sports Centre. This work was the feature of the Australian Architecture Exhibition at the Venice Biennale in the pavilion designed by the firm.

The Australian Bicentenary in 1988 was a major catalyst for public projects, and in 1985 the practice began work on the Sydney Exhibition Centre, the Australian National Maritime Museum, the Sydney Football Stadium and the National Tennis Centre. In recognition of the quality of these projects and changing demands, Cox Architects expanded into South-East Asia where it has undertaken major master planning and commercial work. The organisation is one of the main pioneers of Computer Aided Design facilities and possesses one of the Southern Hemisphere's most sophisticated production technology systems to ensure that clients are provided with efficient, accurate and cost-effective solutions.

The organisation has offices in Sydney, Canberra, Brisbane, Perth, Melbourne and Jakarta.

Leo A. Daly

Leo A Daly is an internationally recognised planning, architecture, engineering and interior design firm with 11 US offices and international offices located in Hong Kong, Tokyo, Dubai, Madrid and Berlin. Recipients of national and international design and engineering awards, the 80-year old privately held firm, headed by Leo A. Daly III, FAIA, RIBA, RAIA, has nearly 700 design and engineering professionals—graduates of more than 100 colleges and universities. Daly has completed projects in more than 50 countries establishing offices worldwide in response to client requirements. Areas of most significant focus include; North America, Southern Asia, East Asia, the Pacific and Western Europe.

Organised on a full-service integrated team basis, Daly's teams are permanent organisational units consisting of Architects and Interior Designers; Civil, Structural, Mechanical and Electrical Engineers; and Cost Estimating and Specifications Experts. Teams are led by Project Managers, who report to Project Officers. They are supported by administrative, clerical and computer technology.

The Daly firm shares its clients' concern for the practical aspects of the business world. Recognising the importance of remaining within budget, controlling costs, and adhering to deadlines, Daly's professionals use diligence and ingenuity in fulfilling client expectations.

Daryl Jackson Pty Ltd

Daryl Jackson Pty Ltd is an interdisciplinary design practice of professional architects, urban planners and interior designers. Established in Melbourne in 1964, the firm has offices in Brisbane, Canberra, Sydney, and an office in London to undertake work in the United Kingdom and Eastern Europe. The practice has gained both a national and international reputation for high quality consultation recognised in the consistent receipt of awards and citations.

The most recent awards include the 1992 Sir Zelman Cowan Award for the Melbourne Cricket Ground; the 1993 Canberra Medallion for the Boiler House lecture theatre, University of Canberra; and the 1993 National Building Owners and Managers Award for 120 Collins Street, Melbourne.

Other Sir Zelman Cowan Awards are for the Australian Institute of Sport Swimming Halls, Canberra, 1984; and Canberra School of Art, 1981.

In 1990, Daryl Jackson became an Officer of the Order of Australia and in 1987, the Royal Australian Institute of Architects honoured him with its highest award, the Gold Medal.

The offices operate as a series of teams of highly-skilled architects under the leadership of the directors and Daryl Jackson.

Douglas Roberts Peter Loebenberg

Douglas Roberts Peter Loebenberg, established in 1964, now has over 60 members in Johannesburg and Cape Town offices. The partners, while all South African, have worked and studied in various countries including the USA and UK.

Projects historically and currently are in all the major South African cities, southern African centres and recently China and Thailand.

Current and recently completed work includes specialty shops, retail malls, office blocks, wholesale distribution depots, warehouses and private hospitals.

While the staff complement includes specialists in construction management, interior design and town planning, the main thrust is architecture, and the specialist skills available are used to support the architectural teams.

The practice has established good working relationships with British, American and Canadian architectural and multi-disciplinary design studios who are working jointly on a number of current projects.

DP Architects Pte Ltd

Design Partnership was established in Singapore in 1967. The subsequent expansion of the firm led to its being incorporated as DP Architects in 1975. Regional offices currently operate in Kuala Lumpur, Jakarta and Manila.

The firm's range of professional services comprises all aspects of architecture, urban planning, interiors and graphic design.

The range of design experience includes colleges, conservation projects, hotels, recreation and resort facilities, residential developments, industrial complexes, major shopping centres, office buildings, transport facilities, convention and exhibition centres and technology parks.

The office has an extensive and a very advanced CADD system. It is applied throughout different work stages from schematic design and design development, which includes rendering and 3D modelling studies, to contract documentation and project administration.

Ellenzweig Associates

Ellenzweig Associates is an architectural firm with a staff of 60 professionals located in Cambridge, Massachusetts. The firm provides comprehensive professional design services, including programming, feasibility studies, master planning, and full architectural services—schematic design, design development, contract documents and construction administration.

Established in 1965, Ellenzweig Associates specialises in complex, technically challenging projects—research facilities for academic, medical and corporate clients; teaching facilities for academic clients; and transportation-related facilities such as parking structures and subway stations for municipal clients. Initial commissions at Harvard University and the Massachusetts Institute of Technology launched the firm's continuing focus on designing research laboratories. Ellenzweig Associates' commitment to design excellence and client satisfaction is reflected in long-term relationships with many repeated clients.

The firm has won over 50 design awards in the last eight years, including American Institute of Architect Honor Awards for Post Office Square and Joslin Diabetes Center, and has had projects published in *Architecture, Architectural Record, Progressive Architecture* and *The Wall Street Journal.*

Ellerbe Becket, Inc.

Ellerbe Becket's tradition for excellence began in 1909. Today, their international presence is growing with offices in Minneapolis, San Francisco, Los Angeles, Kansas City, Chicago, New York, Washington, D.C., Tokyo, England and Indonesia. Ellerbe Becket is an integrated, full-service firm providing sound technical, artistic and practical solutions. They are recognised throughout the world for their expertise and experience. One of the largest planning, design and construction services firms in the United States, their personalised approach is closer to the kind of dedication customers expect from smaller firms.

Ellerbe Becket encourages diversity and exploration in design. As a result, their work environment is energised and interactive. The challenge of blending creative ideas with the practical needs of customers keeps them on the creative edge.

Ellerbe Becket values function as well as aesthetics, and creates environments that work. Ellerbe Becket's unique ability to offer construction services provides customers with single-source accountability, continuity and consistency throughout the project process. Their comprehensive design/build, construction management and program management services virtually guarantee a quality facility solution.

Elliott + Associates Architects

Established in 1976, Elliott + Associates Architects is a full-service architectural firm staffed by licensed architects, interior designers, graphic designers, marketing and public relations people, and support personnel. The firm draws expertise from its staff primarily in the area of commercial projects and renovations.

Elliott + Associates Architects specialises in three separate areas of design: (1) architectural design and planning; (2) interior design; and (3) graphic design. These three areas of expertise enable the firm to provide either a package of design services, or individual design services—whatever the client needs. Elliott + Associates' computer system allows for efficient production of construction documents and gives the client an opportunity to view of the project in three dimensional terms, before the project is constructed.

Elliott + Associates will encompass the client's total needs for design and planning services in order to centralise the decision-making process.

Successfully fulfilling the clients' total needs for design and planning services requires the staff to be 'creative listeners'. Through creative listening, Elliott + Associates Architects provides the highest quality architectural services available, while keeping the clients' needs and budget foremost. This philosophy allows each and every project, large or small, to have its own individual personality reflecting that client's image.

Enviro•Tec

Established in Singapore in early 1972, Enviro•Tec has matured into a regional practice with commissions in Singapore, Malaysia, Indonesia, Saudi Arabia, Sri Lanka and the People's Republic of China.

The partners of Enviro•Tec are registered Architects with more than 24 years of experience in design, planning and project administration/management.

Projects undertaken include town planning, resort planning, urban centre planning, shopping malls, office parks, condominium development industrial complexes, hospitals, real estate and hotel development.

To enhance the quality of design services, Enviro•Tec has embarked on a restructuring exercise to concentrate on pre-contract planning and architectural design services.

In 1991, a wholly owned representative office was established in Jakarta, Indonesia to bring its expertise closer to the local investors. By the third quarter of 1995 the representative office was again restructured into a local PMA company assuming the title of PT Enviro•Tec Indonesia with the admission of three local directors. By the end of 1996, the company, which is now fully independent and CAD based, is expected to move into its new headquarters building to better serve its growing number of clients in Indonesia.

Enviro•Tec has a strong belief in achieving a more conducive built-environment through continuing education of the architectural students and has been committed to providing training opportunity to the local architectural students since 1991.

ETV Arkitektkontor AB

ETV Arkitektkontor was founded in 1968 after having won first prize in the Scandinavian architectural competition for a new central hospital for the Jönköping County Council. Gösta Eliasson; architect SAR; the managing director has been responsible for the firm's operations since its formation. Over the years ETV has designed a wide variety of projects, but hospitals and health care related buildings have been the firm's most important sector. ETV has won most of the hospital architectural competitions in which it participated. The Visby General Hospital was also the result of the first prize in a national architectural competition.

Today the office has a staff of 14, whose services include architectural and interior design. Almost all projects, renovations as well as new buildings, are CAD-designed. ETV's policy is to combine careful analysis and logistical study with aesthetic creativity to design high quality buildings that are economical to operate as well as to build.

Terry Farrell & Partners

The practice was established by Terry Farrell in 1965. The company has offices in London, Edinburgh and Hong Kong.

The practice provides to its clients a comprehensive consultancy which includes architectural, urban design, planning and management services. The highest standards are applied to every aspect of their appointment from the initiation of a project right through to its finalisation and occupation.
Their commissions have been for new buildings, refurbishment, restoration and interiors as well as for master planning, urban design and town planning schemes. The company has been responsible for a diverse range of projects which span from the major office redevelopment schemes of up to 500,000 square feet which was recently undertaken in London at Charing Cross, Alban Gate and Vauxhall Cross through to such small specialist buildings as the Henley Royal Regatta Headquarters Building, TVam Television Studios in Camden and the Thames Water Authority Building in Reading. Their experience includes a broad range of building types including shopping; conference centres, including Edinburgh International Conference and Exhibition Centre; exhibition halls; offices; museums; cultural and tourist buildings; housing; television studios; theatres and industrial buildings.

Over the last ten years it has developed a leading reputation in urban design and in recent years has been involved in a wide range of urban design studios and master plans for complex or sensitive sites.

Feilden & Mawson

The practice carries out the services of architecture, planning, project management and has opened a health and safety department to deal with the new CDM regulations. Established in 1957 by Sir Bernard Feilden, the practice has seven partners and 50 staff with offices in London and Norwich. The firm has designed for most sectors including commerce, retail, education, health, housing, industrial, leisure and public facilities, winning over 40 major architectural awards and commendations. In 1995 the University of Sussex selected Feilden & Mawson as architects for the design of the extension to Sir Basil Spence's Library and the student community centre with auditorium and commercial outlets.

C.W. Fentress J.H. Bradburn and Associates, P.C.

C.W. Fentress J.H. Bradburn and Associates, P.C. (Fentress Bradburn), maintains a full-service office in Denver with a staff of 60, including 25 registered architects and six interior designers, 25 of which are CADD literate.

The firm's reputation is backed by 103 regional, national and international awards for design excellence. Recently, the firm was selected as the 1994 Firm of the Year Award, a distinguished award presented by the AIA Colorado. Fentress Bradburn produces buildings that are as cost efficient and functional as they are ambitious in their design.

Curt Fentress graduated with honours in 1972 from North Carolina State University School of Design, where he received a Bachelor of Architecture degree. Following graduation, Mr Fentress joined the firm of I.M. Pei and Partners of New York. As a senior designer he participated in the design of various architectural projects, as well as in master planning for major site development plans.

Jim Bradburn graduated in 1966 from Rensselaer Polytechnic Institute in Troy, New York, where he received a Bachelor of Science degree in building construction and a Bachelor of Architecture degree. In 1968 he joined the Hamden, Connecticut firm of Kevin Roche John Dinkeloo and Associates. During his 12 year association, he served as Project Architect on projects such as the Helen Bonfils Theater Complex at the Denver Center for the Performing Arts, the Metropolitan Museum of Art in New York City, the University of Michigan's Power Center for the Performing Arts and the World Headquarters Building of Richardson-Merrell Corporation in Wilton, Connecticut.

The principals are licensed in 31 states and the firm is currently working on projects in California, South Dakota, Wyoming, Oklahoma, Nevada, Colorado and Seoul, Korea. The work ranges from US$3 million to US$500 million on a single project with the majority of projects from US$3 million to US$25 million.

Flad & Associates

Established in 1927, Flad & Associates is an architectural, planning, engineering, and interior design firm based in Madison, Wisconsin, with offices in San Francisco, California; Stamford, Connecticut; and Gainesville, Florida.

Serving a long list of Fortune 500 and 100 clients, the firm's project teams are composed of architects, interior designers and planners with experience in corporate office, research, university and healthcare environments.

Flad & Associates believes that each project is the result of collaboration between client and the design team and produces a building uniquely suited to its site and the people who occupy it.

David Jay Flood Architects

David Jay Flood, FAIA, president of David Jay Flood Architects, recipient of the Elliott Noyes and E.S. Heller architectural scholarships, received his Bachelor of Architecture from the University of California Berkeley in 1959.

Prior to initiating private practice in 1967, Mr Flood was a Designer/Project Architect with Welton Becket & Associates and Senior Planner and Architect for the Janss Corporation.

Since establishment in 1967, Mr Flood's firm has developed a widespread reputation in multi-residential housing design, winter/summer resort planning and design, educational residential institutions and specialised corporate design in both industrial and office fields.

In 1980, he was the first appointed Sports Commissioner for the 1984 Olympics held in Los Angeles. He is a director of the Los Angeles Sports Council and USOC Olympic Training Centres.

The company has received over 20 national and regional design awards.

Richard Fleischman Architects, Inc.

Richard Fleischman Architects, Inc., founded in 1961, is a multi-faceted design and management firm of innovative professionals committed to excellence. The firm is organised to provide broad architectural and planning services, including research and programming, program management, feasibility/threshold studies, land use analysis, facilities evaluation, master planning, space planning, graphic and interior design. Richard Fleischman Architects' services also include cost estimating, value engineering, scheduling, competitive bidding and contract negotiation, co-ordination and observation of construction activities, and financial management.

The spaces Richard Fleischman Architects creates reflect the firm's ideology and their clients' expectations. The timelessness of Richard Fleischman Architects' designs have been achieved through a creative blend of technology and imagination. Facilities designed early on still have maintained their design integrity for the past three decades. Economic, political and technological factors will continue to impact upon the future of the art of building and the perception of our environment. Although futurists remind us that planning is essential to ensure positive growth, it is the firm's imagination and understanding of technology that allows them to anticipate change, to channel their intellectual resources in positive directions.

Richard Fleischman Architects believes the initial phase of planning permits the firm greater freedom to participate completely and logically in the synthesis of final recommendations.

Sir Norman Foster and Partners

Sir Norman Foster and Partners employs about 320 staff worldwide with about 200 located in their London office. The practice is led by a Board of Directors. Each design Director is actively involved in the design of particular projects and in the overall design control of all projects. Sir Norman Foster and Partners has, since its inception in 1963, received over 120 awards and citations for excellence and won 21 international competitions.

Their projects range in scale from master plans for regenerating and expanding cities to individual buildings, interior design, furniture and product design, corporate graphics and exhibitions and have major projects in the United Kingdom, Japan, Hong Kong, France, Germany, the Netherlands, Spain, the United States and Saudi Arabia.

In 1990, the practice moved into its own custom-designed double height studio on the south bank of the River Thames and currently has offices in Glasgow, Berlin, Frankfurt, Hong Kong and Tokyo.

Sir Norman Foster and Partners believe that design excellence can only be achieved through active collaboration with the client. In addition to their prime skills of architecture and urban planning, they are supported by a sub-structure of other disciplines.

The firm attaches importance to models, both as design tools and as a means of communicating ideas to the client. In addition to scale models of buildings they regularly produce full size mock ups of components as part of the firm's policy of testing everything.

Sir Norman Foster and Partners has an extensive network of the latest Intergraph CAD workstations, which are used for 2D and 3D design and co-ordination, 3D modelling, visualisation and rendering. Output is in the form of monochrome or colour A0 size plots, or 35mm slides. They have used their 3D models for animated video production and photo-montage work.

Sir Norman Foster and Partners maintains that architecture and interior design are indivisible and they retain control of all details of the interior of their buildings down to fire exit signs. There is hardly a building completed by the practice in which the interior has not also been designed by its teams. The studio is capable of handling the full range of interior design requirements.

Goody, Clancy & Associates

Established in 1955, Goody, Clancy & Associates is one of Boston's largest architecture and planning firms. GC&A has gained national and international recognition for the design of distinguished urban buildings, including signature commercial office towers, state-of-the-art research facilities, contextual additions to university campuses, award winning housing communities and revitalised neighbourhoods, and the preservation and restoration of national historic landmarks.

Every project undertaken at Goody, Clancy & Associates is under the direct supervision of one or more of the three principals: Joan Goody, John Clancy and Robert Pelletier. The principals, working with the firm's ten associates, oversee both project design and management, from inception to completion. With a professional and technical staff numbering 50, the firm has the resources to handle large and complex projects, and yet is small enough to give each project full attention, including an unusually high level of principal involvement and expert management by an experienced project managers.

Michael Graves Architect

Michael Graves, a native of Indianapolis, received his architectural training at the University of Cincinnati and Harvard University. In 1960, Graves won the Rome Prize and studied at the American Academy in Rome, of which he is now a Trustee. Graves is the Schirmer Professor of Architecture at Princeton University, where he has taught since 1962. He is a fellow of the American Institute of Architects.

Since the beginning of his practice in Princeton, New Jersey, Graves has been in the forefront of architectural design. His work has directly influenced the transformation of urban architecture from the abstract modern architecture towards more contextual and traditional themes. In his projects, Graves has consistently demonstrated his ability to create designs sympathetic to both the general program of use and the context of the site. He is also well known for his design of furniture, furnishings and artefacts.

Gujrals

Gujral's firm 'Design Plus' was founded by Satish Gujral, a painter and sculptor by training, who had won international acclaim long before he branched into architecture in the mid 1970s. It was in 1975 that Gujral, after winning the commission to design the Embassy of Belgium in New Delhi, took to architecture seriously. His design of the Belgium Embassy was universally hailed and won him the 'Order of the Crown' from the Belgian Government in addition to an honorary fellowship from the Indian Institute of Architecture.

In the mid 1980s Gujral was joined by his son Mohit Gujral who had architectural training at Ahmedabad. Since then both father and son have created building after building in an amazing unison. In fact, both admit that it is impossible to draw a line as to which part could be accredited to one or the other.

Their contribution to architecture has been hailed internationally as the most serious attempt to develop a contemporary idiom for Indian architecture, with its roots in the past.

Hartman Cox

Hartman-Cox Architects was founded by George E. Hartman Jr and Warren J. Cox in 1965. Over the past two and a half decades the firm has grown slowly to a size averaging 25 architects, and major institutions and developers have become clients. In addition to their corporate, academic, library, law school and museum buildings, the firm completed a series of major commercial office buildings during the 1980s and at the same time the restoration of or addition to a number of prominent historic structures.

Current work includes a significant number of academic, library, law school and museum commissions in progress throughout the country.

George Hartman received his BA from Princeton University in 1957, followed by his Master of Fine Arts in architecture in 1960. Warren Cox received his BA, *magna cum laude*, from Yale University in 1957, following with his Master in Architecture in 1961, again at Yale.

In 1988 Hartman-Cox Architects received the American Institute of Architects' Architectural Firm Award, the highest award for architectural design a firm can receive from the Institute. Over the years, the firm has received over 90 other regional and national design awards including six American Institute of Architects' National Honour Awards and some 16 historic preservation awards.

Hayball Leonard Stent

Hayball Leonard Stent are committed to a rational design approach. Their methodology is specific to site and context, and also informed by an understanding of human space, modern culture and contemporary values. In this way the functional objectives of the brief can be satisfied in a manner which also invokes a subjective response.

The establishment of Hayball Leonard Stent Pty Ltd in 1983 was the culmination of a long association between Len Hayball, Richard Leonard and Robert Stent. From 1974 to 1983, Len Hayball was the managing partner at Gunn Hayball Pty Ltd, a firm of architects and planners in which Richard and Robert were also involved. Since the firm's inception, the complementary attributes of experience, pragmatism and creativity have combined to provide innovative and efficient solutions to a broad spectrum of built environments.

Helin & Siitonen Architects

Since the firm's founding in 1979 its work has included cultural institutions, offices, commercial and recreational development and housing. The scale of projects range in size from summer cottages to corporate headquarters of 50,000 square metres (538,215 square feet) and master plans for multi-functional centres.

The work is committed to creative design, backed up by particular research in every project, and thorough knowledge of processes and technology in the field of building. The emphasis is in the quality of the design, careful supervision of the execution and the close collaboration with the client. Each project is given the same individual attention and is treated as an unique opportunity to improve conditions of space or a certain function.

The office is fully equipped with modern CAD facilities.

The Hillier Group

The Hillier Group is a multi-faceted architectural firm offering clients a wide range of services in the areas of architecture, interior design, master planning, facility management, landscape architecture, project management, construction management, engineering and land-use planning.

Founded in 1966 by CEO J. Robert Hillier, The Hillier Group is ranked the fourth largest architecture firm in the United States, with projected revenues for 1995 in excess of US$40 million. The staff of approximately 325 is headquartered in Princeton, with offices in Philadelphia;, New York City; Clarks Summit, Pennsylvania; Washington, D.C.; Dallas; Kansas City, Missouri; and Sydney, Australia. Hillier has worked on projects of all sizes in 31 states and 15 foreign countries.

To date, the firm has won more than 170 state, national and international design awards. Over 80 percent of its annual revenue come from repeat clients.

HKS Inc.

HKS Inc. is a Dallas based firm with offices in Tampa, Richmond and Los Angeles. HKS provides professional services in architecture, planning, interior architecture, and structural engineering. Founded in 1939, the firm has executed commissions for structures valued in excess of US$9 billion. During its 56 year period, HKS has grown to be the fifth largest architectural and engineering firm in the nation with projects in over 170 cities located in 39 states, the District of Columbia and seven foreign countries.

Experience of the firm includes office buildings, health care facilities, hotels, corporate headquarters, banks, correctional facilities, public buildings, multi-family housing, and a variety of projects for education and industry. Over 90 percent of HKS' current work is for repeat clients.

HKS' business philosophy emphasises performance in achievement of client goals. The deliberate and effective application of this philosophy of service has resulted in the ability to consistently deliver economically successful projects that are well designed, technically well executed, and completed within budget and on schedule.

HMC Group

HMC Group, a Californian architectural firm founded in 1940, has earned numerous design awards for hospital and school projects. Other projects include government and commercial designs. With offices in Ontario, Sacramento, San Diego and San Jose, HMC provides a comprehensive range of design services including architecture, interiors and planning throughout the western United States.

Ranked as the fourth largest architectural firm in California by *Engineering News Record* magazine in 1994, HMC employs nearly 150 professionals, including 97 registered architects. Current projects include the US$60 million, 18,580 square metre (200,000 square foot) Ontario Convention Center and a US$25 million high school in Oakley, California.

Birgitta Holm Architects Inc./STADION Architects Inc.

Birgitta Holm Architects Inc. is a middle sized company, formed in 1987 (known as Loggia Architects Inc. from 1989 to 1994). Examples of their projects in recent years include an Upper Secondary School in Härryda (with Bergström architects), and refurbishments of schools in Västerås, Stockholm, Tyresö and Botkyrka. They have also completed a new school, child day-care centre and community centre in Tyresö Strand outside Stockholm, and a program for restoration of Medieval buildings around the Cathedral of Strängnäs.

STADION Architects Inc. is a company with eight architects, formed in 1988. Examples of recent projects completed in Stockholm include buildings for the University of Technology Division Electronics, Butchers Museum, low energy housing for the elderly, renewal of the Vårbergs Hospital, and a day-care centre for the mentally retarded.

House + House Architects

Steven and Cathi House and their associates endeavour to create beauty, serenity and amazement in their work and in the process of architecture. They find their greatest inspiration in the subtleties of each site and in the deepest recesses of their client's souls—and with intimate analysis discover how to mould each project into that unique environment that embodies magic and harmony. In each project they find new opportunities to lift themselves and their clients to a higher level of perception of the world...not through the latest technology, but through their skilful manipulation of form, light and texture.

Recognised for their innovative work, House + House has designed projects ranging from custom homes throughout the San Francisco Bay area, the Sierra Nevada mountains, Los Angeles and Hawaii, to state of the art retail facilities, to a Caribbean Island resort. They have received numerous design awards and have been published extensively. Steven and Cathi House have co-authored *Mediterranean Indigenous Architecture - Timeless Solutions for the Human Habitat*, a major exhibition which has travelled throughout the United States. The poetic quality of their work derives from the simpler side of life...the magic sparkle of sunlight raking across a textured wall...

Hugh Newell Jacobsen

Hugh Newell Jacobsen has practised architecture under his own name since 1958. His projects have been built and published worldwide, winning over one hundred awards for excellence in design. Among these are six National Honor Awards from the American Institute or Architects and 20 awards for excellence in house design from Architectural Record.

Mr Jacobsen received his Masters Degree in Architecture at Yale in 1955 and the Certificate of the Architectural Association School of Architecture in London in 1954. He is a Fellow of the American Institute of Architects and an Academician of the National Academy of Design. He has been a member of the Joint Committee on Landmarks of the National Capital, a consultant on historic preservation to the cities of Charleston and Savannah, and serves on the board of the International Hassan Fathay Institute. He lectures extensively throughout the United States and abroad and has served on numerous design award juries. He was the editor of *A Guide to the Architecture of Washington, D.C.*.

Mr Jacobsen is personally responsible for all phases of each project, from analysis and design through detailing and construction, with his staff providing day-to-day management. His office also provides interior design and landscape architecture.

The buildings he produces are noted for their precision, clarity, elegant formality, style and wit, and all have an inherent respect for their environs. Throughout his career, Mr Jacobsen has practised a distinctive and intensely personal brand of contextual and allusionist architecture. Recent buildings also partake of a frank revivalism that includes broad references to classical styles as well as the rich idiom of the vernacular.

Kanner Architects

Kanner Architects is an award-winning, widely-published architectural practice based in Westwood, Los Angeles. Kanner Architects has built a variety of projects—residential, institutional, governmental and commercial buildings—in a wide range of styles.

Much of Kanner Architects' work is inspired by the optimistic modern architecture of 1950s and 1960s Los Angeles. They have synthesised the restrained commercial modernism of the 1950s and Googie-style popular modernism into strong, soundly-planned but unabashedly spirited designs that Steven Kanner describes as "...a combination of pure modernism and our own brand of Pop modernism that is intended to be playful, optimistic and positive. It's a pure expression of the way we feel about the city".

Kanner Architects was established in 1946 by I. Herman Kanner AIA, and will celebrate its fiftieth anniversary in 1996. Charles G. Kanner FAIA became president of the firm in 1974, and his son and partner, Steven Kanner AIA, joined the firm in 1984.

Kaplan/McLaughlin/Diaz

Founded in 1963, Kaplan/McLaughlin/Diaz (KMD) has developed an award winning international practice in architecture, planning and urban design. The firm has offices in San Francisco, Los Angeles, Portland, Seattle, Tokyo, Seoul, Mexico City and Kuala Lumpur, and has designed and completed construction in 25 states in the United States and in France, Japan, China, Malaysia, Singapore, Indonesia, Korea and Mexico. The practice encompasses a wide range of building types including office, retail, mixed-use, hotels/resorts, academic, housing, healthcare, government, entertainment, historic restoration and adaptive re-use and urban design. Within the past ten years, the firm has won more than 100 design awards, including 37 awards from the American Institute of Architects.

KMD's talent for 'working-at-a-distance' has assisted the firm in moving towards a worldwide project base. Kaplan/McLaughlin/Diaz's international activities reflect the breadth of the firm's experience and its unique design philosophy. International projects range from winning a design competition for a 139,350 square metre (1,500,000 square foot) mixed-use project in Shanghai to preparing the plan for Mexico's Marina Vallarta waterfront resort.

Juhani Katainen Architects

Juhani Katainen Architects was founded in 1968.

From the very first, the office concentrated on major public building design projects, and has regularly participated in design competitions with great success.

Design work is based on an exact analysis of the user's needs, and the plans, construction costs, schedules and technical implementation are tailored to fit those needs.

The office aims to produce high-quality professional design and architecture. It strives to recognise its responsibility towards the client and to optimise design concepts with regard to the life span of the building.

Working practices are based on an atmosphere of openness and co-operation, respecting the views of the client and of colleagues.

Most of the office's projects have been presented in detail in architectural journals, both Finnish and foreign.

Juhani Katainen has been professor in the Department of Architecture at Tampere University of Technology since 1988.

In 1995, the Ministry of Education appointed Professor Katainen Finland's representative on the European Community Advisory Committee on Education and Training in the Field of Architecture; also, the Finnish Association of Architects appointed him their representative in the Architects' Council of Europe, Standing Committee no. 2 'Profession of Architecture'.

Kisho Kurokawa

Kisho Kurokawa was born in Nagoya, Japan in 1934, and graduated in Architecture from Kyoto University in 1957 and from graduate school, Tokyo University, in 1964. He began his career in the late 1950s and first came to public notice in 1960 as a founder of the influential Metabolism movement. His philosophy has been in practice, the paradigm shift to the 'Age of Life Principle' from the 'Age of Machine Principle'. The key concepts, Metabolism, Metamorphosis, and Symbiosis express the characteristic of the 'Age of Life Principle'.

Kurokawa's architecture has won numerous prizes around the world. He has been awarded a Prize of Architectural Institute of Japan, Prize of Japan Art Academy in Japan, a gold medal from the Academy of Architecture in France and the Richard Neutra Award from the United States. He was nominated as an Honorary Fellow of both the American Institute of Architects and the Royal Institute of British Architects.

MacLachlan, Cornelius & Filoni, Inc.

MacLachlan, Cornelius & Filoni, Inc. is a full-service architectural firm providing architectural design, master planning, programming, interior design and construction administration services since 1889.

The vitality of the firm is maintained by practising architecture with a diverse clientele which includes educational and religious institutions, performing arts and health care organisations, parks and recreational facilities, commercial and housing clients, and developers and community groups. Notable Pittsburgh area projects designed by the firm include Point State Park, Heinz Hall, the Benedum Center for the Performing Arts, and the Mercy Hospital of Pittsburgh. Through vast experience and expertise, MCF has gained a regional reputation and works with repeat clients from North Carolina to Michigan and Illinois to Delaware.

Through respecting the client's aspirations, needs, budget, and schedule, MacLachlan, Cornelius & Filoni, Inc. is able to embody firmness (structure and shelter), commodity (function and utility) and delight in every enduring architectural work.

Martinez Cutri & McArdle International (MCM International)

MCM Corporation—MCM Planners & Architects, MCM Interiors, MCM International—is an interdisciplinary firm engaged in the practice of architecture, planning, urban design, and interior architecture. With a core staff of 20 architects, urban and regional planners, designers, landscape architects, interior designers and technical personnel, MCM is in the position to offer its clients services on a person-to-person basis. The firm was established in 1980 and maintains its corporate headquarters in San Diego, California, USA.

MCM has designed over 200 projects with a construction value in excess of US$1.5 billion; the firm provides design services worldwide. Areas of specialisation include: mixed-use developments, educational and institutional facilities, master planning and urban design, hotel and resort facilities, governmental and corporate offices, multi-family residential projects, and industrial/research developments.

The practice is guided by strong beliefs and principles. These beliefs are based on the simple concept that the design of forms in space should be generated by the context of their surroundings, while the principles of design should advance our culture.

Their intent as a firm is to create good design; that is to create spaces and structures which exhibit a timeless quality. MCM design environments that are inviting regardless of typology and locale. It is their contention that the vitality and beauty of the built environment plays a crucial role in a productive and healthy community, and as design professionals, they must assume this responsibility.

The Principals of MCM are the recipients of numerous design awards, citations, and prizes from the American Institute of Architects, American Planning Association, Progressive Architecture, as well as local commendations.

Adrian Maserow Architects (Pty) Ltd

Adrian Maserow Architects has been in private practice in Johannesburg since 1983, and has pursued a distinctive design career through combining theoretical and practical architectural knowledge.

Formed in 1983, and together with associates Jonathan Liebowitz and Leigh Reid, Adrian Maserow Architects (Pty) Ltd has been recognised as a leading architectural firm in Sandton, Gauteng, the economic powerhouse of Southern Africa.

In 1985 Adrian obtained a Master's Degree at the University of the Witwatersrand under the renowned Professor Guedes.

This 15 person firm embodies the entrepreneurial spirit of the day with the timeless concerns for composition, character, form, scale and meaning.

Each member of the firm is selected for their commitment to excellence in design and with a passion to continually renew and not just repeat works of architecture.

Adrian Maserow Architects is currently involved a diverse range of projects, from stylish residential projects to corporate office parks, health clubs and retail developments and works throughout Southern Africa from the Sandton based headquarters.

Adrian Maserow Architects is committed to the creation of an exuberant contemporary architecture characteristic of its time and place. The enigmatic quality of this highveld is critical to the time and spirit of this firm's work. The pioneering spirit of the New South Africa, and a rare fusion of cultures and economies make each commission process intensive. Adrian Maserow Architects works with a strong focused vision in its pursuit of the celebration of architecture.

Susan Maxman Architects

Susan Maxman Architects is a medium-sized firm located in Philadelphia, Pennsylvania. The firm offers a full range of design services for both new construction and renovation projects including master and site planning; feasibility studies; programming; historic preservation, restoration and rehabilitation; interior design; and ADA assessment and evaluation. Comprehensive architectural services range from conceptual design through construction administration.

The firm has always practised environmentally responsive architecture. Each design problem is uniquely approached in a way that responds to the context in which it is placed, is compatible to the needs of the users, and is in harmony with the elements that reinforce and support a thriving community. Through continuing education and active research, firm members have become specialists, practising a design philosophy that emphasises quality of life, cost effectiveness and a concern for the future. By evaluating building materials and systems, with an effort to conserve natural resources, decrease environmental degradation and create healthy buildings, the firm is planning now for future generations.

Susan Maxman Architects has been presented with numerous awards, including an American Institute of Architects Honor Award for its design work at Camp Tweedale, a cabin complex and activity building for the Freedom Valley Girl Scout Council. Building on that experience, the firm has developed a sensitivity and expertise for projects in natural settings. The National Park Service, several Girl Scout Councils and the USDA Forest Service have become repeat clients. Among the firm's awards for restoration and preservation are the McArthur Award for the adaptive reuse of the Robert Lewis House; and the National Trust for Historic Preservation's Grand Prize for the restoration of the Pennock Farmstead. For the design of a residence in Harvey Cedars, New Jersey, the firm has recently been awarded an Honor Award from the Philadelphia Chapter of the American Institute of Architects, in addition to a Merit Award from *Builder* magazine.

Mitchell/Giurgola Architects

Mitchell/Giurgola Architects was formed in 1958 and established an office for general practice in New York City in 1968. The practice offers a comprehensive range of architectural services including master planning and urban design, research and programming, new buildings, renovations and additions, interior design and graphic design.

Mitchell/Giurgola has practised in a wide geographical area including 21 states in the United States and seven foreign countries. Recent commissions include The Lighthouse Headquarters in New York City, the Ciba-Geigy Pharmaceuticals Life Sciences Building in Summit, New Jersey and the Belvedere, a new waterfront park at Battery Park City in Lower Manhattan.

The practice has been characterised by a constant commitment to an architecture based on humanistic principles. Values inherent to particular program and to a particular locale and culture are explored and celebrated, resulting in a unique architectural solution for each project.

Mitchell/Giurgola received the Architectural Firm Award of the American Institute in 1976, the highest honour bestowed upon an American practice, and the Medal of Honour Award from the New York Chapter of the AIA. The firm has received over 75 professional honour awards for its architecture and planning work. The Life Sciences building on the Ciba-Geigy Pharmaceuticals campus in Summit, New Jersey received *R&D Magazine's* 1995 Lab of the Year Award. The Lighthouse Headquarters is the recipient of a 1996 National AIA Honour Award for Interior Design. The Belvedere is also the recipient of a 1996 National AIA Honour Award winner for Urban Design, as well as the recipient of the Waterfront Center's 1995 International Award for Excellence on the Waterfront.

Morris Architects

The firm was established in Houston, Texas in 1938 as Wilson and Morris Architects. After years of experience and growth the firm became Morris Architects. In addition to their Houston home office, Morris Architects had a full-service regional office in Orlando, Florida. They provide architectural design, interior architectural design, programming, master planning and graphic design services.

Their professional practice is national, with projects and registration in 20 states. Their specialties include a wide variety of project types with a current focus on entertainment/recreation, corrections, healthcare and interiors.

Over the past 57 years, the firm has served as architect for many of Houston's landmark buildings such as the Astrodome, Pennzoil Place, Transco Tower, the Wortham Theater Center, and Galleria II. The high percentage of major projects they have done for repeat clients attests to the quality of their work and the responsiveness of their staff.

Murphy/Jahn

Helmut Jahn has earned a reputation on the cutting edge of progressive architecture in the 1970s and 1980s. Murphy/Jahn's buildings have received numerous design awards and have been represented in architectural exhibitions around the world.

Born in Germany, Jahn graduated from the Technische Hochschule in Munich. He came to the United States for graduate studies in architecture. In 1976, his first major high-rise building in Chicago, the Xerox Centre, won great critical acclaim.

Today, as President and Chief Executive Officer of Murphy/Jahn, he has been called Chicago's premiere architect who has dramatically changed the face of Chicago. His growing national and international reputation has led to commissions across the United States, Europe, Africa and Asia. He is committed to design excellence and the improvement of the urban environment. His projects have been recognised globally for design innovation, vitality and integrity. From the numerous publications on his work, one understands the excitement his work has generated in the public eye as well as professional journals and press.

Jahn's professional activities are highlighted by numerous lectures and juries for various universities, professional societies and civic and commercial groups. He is a Fellow in the American Institute of Architects in which his work has received four AIA National Honour Awards, and a total of 55 Distinguished Building Awards from the local chapters of the AIA.

Jahn's work has been included in exhibits worldwide since 1980. He has taught at the University of Illinois Chicago Campus, was the Elliot Noyes Professor of Architectural Design at Harvard University, the Davenport Visiting Professor of Architectural Design at Yale University and Thesis Professor at the Illinois Institute of Technology.

His design is both rational and intuitive; it attempts to give each building its own philosophical and intellectual base and establishes an opportunity to exploit its particular elements to achieve a visual and communicative statement. The rational part deals with the realities of a problem. The intuitive aspect deals with the theoretical, intellectual aspects—a sub-conscious ability to sense the intrinsic structure of a problem and establish priorities for the elements of design that deal with space, form, light, colour and materials and the way architecture communicates through symbol and meaning of architectural language.

Hans Murman Arkitektkontor AB

In the office of Hans Murman the projects range from design and interior design to houses and shopping malls.

During the last few years the main issues have been offices and interior design, the head office of EF Education, in Stockholm, having been the largest project.

In Ramundberget, a ski resort in northern Sweden, 25 small modern wooden vacation houses have been built of natural and local materials, grouped together in a way that makes them feel as though they belong to the landscape.

A warm atmosphere, human scale and proportions that feel right are the prime objectives in all projects from the office. A lot of work is done with interior and exterior detailing, design and finding the natural place for the building.

Barton Myers Associates, Inc.

The firm of Barton Myers Associates, Inc. was established in Toronto, Canada, in 1975. A Los Angeles practice was opened in 1981, and in 1987 the practice moved full-time to Los Angeles. The diversified practice ranges from large-scale planning to unique architectural projects. The firm is particularly known for its architectural design within complex urban contexts involving combinations of old and new developments. Major clients include universities, cultural and institutional organisations and private corporations.

Recent major projects include the Art Gallery of Ontario Expansion in Toronto, completed in 1993, which was the result of a limited design competition; the Cerritos Center for the Performing Arts in Cerritos, California, a flexible theatre completed in early 1993; and, the New Jersey Performing Arts Center in Newark, New Jersey, a multi-theatre facility featuring a 2,750-seat concert hall, currently under construction. Barton Myers received the 1994 Gold Medal from the Royal Architectural Institute of Canada.

Nikken Sekkei Ltd.

Nikken Sekkei is the oldest and largest architectural firm in Japan. Descended from a predecessor firm established in 1900, Nikken Sekkei was incorporated in its present firm in 1950 and today employs a multi-disciplinary staff of some 1,800 planners, architects and engineers responsible for the design and construction administration of projects valued at over ¥165 billion (US$1,650 million at an exchange rate of ¥100 to US$1) per year. To date, Nikken Sekkei has undertaken commissions for more than 13,000 projects in Japan as well as some 40 countries all over the world, ranging from private museums to public housing, and from high technology factories to Nikken's specialty, corporate headquarters buildings. The quality of work is confirmed by the numerous national awards and international competitions won by Nikken Sekkei.

Paatela-Paatela & Co Architects Ltd

Founded originally in 1912, Paatela-Paatela & Co Architects Ltd is one of the oldest architect's offices in Finland.

Throughout decades, Paatela-Paatela & Co Architects Ltd has been Finland's leading specialist in hospital and health care design. In addition to that, the company has designed a variety of projects for research, education, corporate and industry sectors. Besides complexes implemented in Finland, Paatela-Paatela & Co Architects Ltd has designed several projects in the Middle East, Africa and Russia.

In addition to larger projects, it has also been quite usual for them to design private houses and recreational buildings for their customers. Designing a recreation villa in Lapland, made of 60 centimetre (2 foot) thick dried up Siberian pine logs, can be as testing as that of a major public housing.

Today, the use of computers and company's new Quality Control system has significantly improved the methods and quality of design work. Paatela-Paatela & Co Architects Ltd utilises the latest computer-aided design methods to provide constantly up-to-date drawings and bills of quantities for each project.

Pacific Associates International PT.

Pacific Associates International PT. (PAI) is an architectural, planning and interior design firm with a broad range of experience in master planning, housing of all types, resorts, offices, retail and interiors. Located in Jakarta, Indonesia and established in 1985, the firm is directed by four partners who are involved on a daily basis with every project.

PAI's reputation for innovative design work and reliability is a result of its commitment of responsibility towards the client and the understanding of how to apply creative design solutions that are practical and developed to real budgets. The firm approaches each project without preconceived notions of architectural style, preferring to evolve the design tailored to the client's needs together with the climatic and physical requirements of the site.

Services provided by PAI include master planning, feasibility studies, programming, design, construction documents and construction administration. Clients include developers, corporations, government agencies, banking institutions as well as private individuals.

Perry Dean Rogers & Partners

Perry Dean Rogers & Partners is a 40 person architectural and interior design firm established in 1923 as Perry Shaw and Hepburn. Since that time, college and university projects have formed the core of Perry Dean's practice. Over the past 70 years, the firm has completed or is currently involved in designs for more than 100 academic institutions. Projects have ranged from feasibility studies for small, independent colleges to master plans for universities, to major renovations or additions to existing buildings and the associated management of complex phasing programs, to designs for new buildings. In the past five years alone, PDR&P has designed over US$200 million worth of academic projects, and work for schools and colleges has comprised 80 percent of their workload.

The concentration of academic commissions at Perry Dean Rogers & Partners ensures a staff thoroughly versed in the particulars of college and university design. They are experienced in working with large user constituencies and are accustomed to the budgetary and schedule constraints common to the academic world.

PDR&P has received numerous design awards for its college buildings, including the prestigious Harleston Parker Award for the Wellesley College Science Center and a 1989 AIA/ALA Honor Award for the Olin Memorial Library—an addition to an existing library at Wesleyan University.

Bart Prince

Bart Prince was born in Albuquerque, New Mexico where he began at an early age to make architectural designs. Several early residential projects were designed and built before he completed high school at the age of 17. He apprenticed with architect Bruce Goff in Kansas City, Missouri during the summers while attending the School of Architecture at Arizona State University from which he graduated in 1970. He continued his work with Mr Goff in Tyler, Texas after graduation until his return to Albuquerque in 1972. He opened his own office in 1973 and was licensed to practise architecture in 1974.

His work has consisted of a variety of projects built primarily throughout the western United States including Hawaii. The designs are expressive of the requirements of individual clients, sites, and climates and result in unusual buildings which have been designed from the 'inside, out'.

Quantrell Mullins & Associates Inc

Quantrell Mullins & Associates Inc, a female owned interior architectural planning and design firm, was established in 1974 by Bianca Quantrell. Its staff includes registered architects, interior designers and support personnel.

Quantrell Mullins was founded in response to the need for an independent interior architectural specialist. The firm has no allegiance to any architect, manufacturer or dealer; the principals believe it is this independence which provides the complete freedom of design so important in creating optimum space usage, efficient layout, and aesthetically pleasing environments. A state-of-the-art, full colour Sun 3/60 computer-aided design (CAD) system enables Quantrell Mullins to offer its clients leading edge technology rapidly and accurately.

Quantrell Mullins & Associates serves the planning and design needs of a wide variety of clients worldwide, including publicly and privately-held corporations, professional firms, financial institutions, medical facilities, hotels, clubs and retail shops. It has successfully completed more than 20 projects in the United States and Europe for 15 international clients. Much of the firm's work is regularly featured in both local and national publications.

RTKL International Ltd.

RTKL International Ltd. is one of the largest and most comprehensive design firms in the world. To serve a global clientele, the firm offers the expertise of more than 500 design professionals strategically located in its Baltimore, Maryland headquarters and in Washington, Dallas, Los Angeles, London, Tokyo and Hong Kong and at affiliate locations in Brisbane, Köln and Guadalajara.

An award-winning portfolio coupled with a comprehensive service including architecture, planning and urban design, engineering, interior architecture, landscape architecture, and environmental graphic design, has led to projects in over 40 countries. Among the firm's specialties are projects for mixed-use, retail, government, hospitality, entertainment, health and sciences, residential and transportation.

From designing a retail-driven mixed-use complex in Asia to a business centre in the United States, RTKL crosses cultural and physical frontiers. While the firm's portfolio is diverse, a commitment to meeting client needs and making a lasting statement of quality permeates each project.

SAC International, Ltd.

Award winning SAC International, Ltd., Architects-Consulting Engineers in Seoul is a 150 person practice established in 1977. The firm has won many awards for its work including the Hilton International Seoul, Korea Military Academy Library, Weightlifting Gymnasium for the 1988 Seoul Olympics, Sonje Museum of Contemporary Art in Kyongju, Korea, Seoul National University Museum, Ajou University Hospital in Suwon, Korea and the Hilton International d'Alger in Algeria.

Jong-Soung (John) Kimm who heads SAC International, Ltd. was educated at Seoul National University and the Illinois Institute of Technology (IIT) under Mies van der Rohe, and served on the Faculty of Architecture at IIT before assuming the direction of SAC International.

The firm has under construction a 20,000 square metre (215,285 square foot) museum for the City of Seoul; an 80,000 square metre (861,140 square foot) office tower in downtown Seoul; and a 1,000-bed teaching hospital is in its planning stage.

The Stubbins Associates

Established in 1949, The Stubbins Associates (TSA) has successfully completed an unusually broad range of project both nationally and internationally. Professional services include feasibility studies; programming and master planning; architectural, interior and landscape design; and technical services including construction documentation and construction administration. The firm utilises the most advanced CAD technology, including 3D modelling, on all projects.

Directed by six principals, the TSA's highly qualified and experienced professional staff take pride in their teamwork with clients, consultants, and contractors. The firm believes in working with each client to explore the full potential for a project, whatever its site, program, budget or schedule. TSA does not impose preconceived design solutions or styles. The design process is tempered with a deep respect for the client's needs, aspirations, functional requirements and constraints. For all of their clients, TSA seeks to provide something special—the immeasurable quality that lifts the human spirit.

TSA is one of the few firms in the United States to have been awarded the prestigious 'Architectural Firm Award' by the American Institute of Architects, placing it at the highest echelon of the profession. In addition, TSA's projects have won more than 150 awards for design excellence, both nationally and internationally.

Studio J.J. International

John W. Sugden Professor Emeritus from the Graduate School of Architecture at the University of Utah and member of the College of Fellows of the American Institute of Architecture is at the present time practising as Principal Architect in the firm of Studio J.J. International—Architecture, Planning and Visual Communication.

He earned a BS and a MS degree in Architecture at the Illinois Institute of Technology in Chicago under the tutelage of Mies van der Rohe and L. Hiberseimer. During this time he also worked as a draftsman and assistant to Mies in his Chicago office.

Since leaving Chicago he has produced over 50 architectural projects, receiving many awards—most recently the award of Merit from the American Institute of Architecture and the Honor Award from the Utah society of the AIA. His work has appeared in many national and international publications, including magazines such as *Bauen und Wohnen*, *l'Architecture d'Aujourd'hui* and *La Nuvoa Citta*.

STUDIOS Architecture

Established in 1985, STUDIOS Architecture is a recognised industry leader with a worldwide reputation for excellence in architectural design. Providing services in strategic design, architecture and interior architectural design, STUDIOS combines creative problem solving with a clear focus on the client's strategic objectives.

With offices in San Francisco, Washington, D.C., New York, Paris and London, STUDIOS has established a strong international presence with many projects completed and underway in Europe and Asia. STUDIOS' clients include Apple Computer, Silicon Graphics Computer Systems, 3Com Corporation, American Express, Morgan Stanley, Credit Suisse First Boston, Andersen Consulting, The Clorox Company, AirTouch Communications and MCI.

The firm has garnered more than 70 design awards and has been featured in more than 100 publications for its work around the world. STUDIOS was recently chosen by its peers as one of the five 'most respected' interior architecture firms in the United States.

Swatt Architects

Swatt Architects was founded in 1975 by Robert M. Swatt, FAIA, to provide comprehensive services in architecture, planning and interior design. The firm has completed a wide range of projects for residential, industrial, commercial and institutional clients. Major projects have been completed throughout California and in Georgia, Nevada, Texas and Utah.

Swatt Architects' objective is to create environments that are distinctive, appropriate to their purpose, and reflect a genuine concern for the people who live and work within them. They believe that the most successful architectural projects respond first to client and user needs, and then combine the most appropriate technology and materials, along with sensitive design, to achieve architecture of lasting value. Their dedication to service and design excellence has been the basis of 20 years of successful professional practice where the vast majority of Swatt Architects' commissions are for repeat clients.

Swatt Architects has been recognised with over 25 local, regional and national design awards for projects throughout the USA.

Thompson, Ventulett, Stainbeck & Associates

Thompson, Ventulett, Stainbeck & Associates, Inc. was established in 1968 to offer professional services in the areas of planning, architecture, and interior design. The primary goal of TVS&Associates is to provide design that fulfils the client's aspirations in a way that is aesthetically distinctive and contextually responsive. The firm strives to combine philosophical objectives with economic and functional consideration to create environments of lasting value.

TVS&Associates is an internationally recognised, 152 person design organisation with projects in 25 states and a number of foreign countries. The firm's organisation is structured around the studio concept. Each project is served by a team tailored to the specific requirements of the client, the project type, and its program. The team remains with the project from conceptual design through construction documents to completion of the project.

Studio principals at TVS&Associates present a level of experience and expertise which is expressed by their work in various special project types. The studio principal represents the highest professional stature within the firm. Studios, acting as small offices, provide the client with clear communication, continuity and a single source of contact throughout the life of the project. The studio design approach also offers an owner the availability and responsiveness of a small practice while allowing the benefits of larger corporate resources.

TVS&Associates' design practice has been built on repeat work from satisfied clients and encompasses a myriad of project types, sizes and complexities. The firm's experience fills the spectrum of an architectural/interior design practice—from convention/conference centres, commercial offices, hotels and retail centres to highly specialised educational, civic, corporate and laboratory/computer facilities.

TVS&Associates' reputation for design quality has been recognised by their receipt of over 120 national and local design awards for planning, architecture and interior design excellence.

Early principal projects for TVS&Associates included the Omni Arena, Omni International (now CNN Center), and the Georgia World Congress Center. From its beginning, a major focus of the firm has been in urban design and complex mixed-use developments. Often these projects included the planning and design of civic and convention facilities, sports arenas, retail centres, hotels and office buildings.

TRO/The Ritchie Organization

For more than 40 years, TRO/The Ritchie Organization has been one of the country's leading consultants to the healthcare community, devoting 100 percent of their talents, resources and capabilities to providing both public and private institutions with a full range of planning and design services.

TRO's corporate headquarters is located in Boston, Massachusetts with regional offices in Birmingham, Alabama and Sarasota, Florida.

Since the founding of TRO three-quarters of a century ago, the firm has successfully completed more than US$1 billion worth of healthcare construction, spanning well over 400 major projects.

The key to their success over the years has been their ability to bring diverse talents and resources of a national practice to meet specific client needs. Unique problems demand the kind of custom solutions and personal attention that they consistently deliver—which is why the majority of clients choose to utilise their expertise on a continuing basis.

TSP Architects & Planners Pte Ltd

TSP Architects & Planners Pte Ltd is a long established regional practice with successful building, urban design and planning projects in Singapore, Malaysia, Indonesia, Brunei, Thailand and Hong Kong.
The practice was formed in 1946 under the name of E.J. Seow steadily growing in size and stature and eventually in 1970, renaming itself as SLH Partners. Upon retirement of E.J. Seow, the firm was reorganised to Timothy Seow & Partners in 1974. In 1988 the practice was further reorganised, abbreviating the name to TSP Architects & Planners to reflect a more corporate image. In 1995 the practice was became incorporated to enable a multi-disciplinary practice and an enhanced competitive edge.

TSP treats each project as a unique combination of opportunities. The client's values, aspirations and policies are the springboards for architectural ideas. Discussions with clients involve frank exchange of views, often leading to the raising of the 'sights' of both clients and the architect. Finding the best answer to the client's needs, providing the best quality of life for all users and ensuring the greatest usefulness of the building are the key issues of architecture. A great deal of effort is put into the understanding of clients' daily operations and long-term plans.

For each client, TSP aims to arrive at the optimum building form and appropriate architectural language achieved by the careful selection and adaptation of constructional vocabulary. The aim in each case is to bring together in a creative way, visual quality and economy of means.

Teamwork is the essence of TSP's approach which leads to projects being more than the sum of the inputs of individual members.

Staff from TSP are constantly involved in architectural education through part-time teaching and as examiners which enable them to be in touch with emergent theoretical ideas in the field of architecture. In addition, involvement with the Singapore Institute of Architects and arbitration works enables TSP to be professionally in contact with all aspects of the practice.

The Wischmeyer Architects, Inc.

The Wischmeyer Architects, Inc. is committed to creating well planned, cost-effective architectural solutions. An extensive scope of experience is the result of projects for schools, colleges, laboratories, hospitals, office buildings, manufacturing facilities and computer facilities; the firm's specialty, however, lies in the design of healthcare environments.
The long-standing philosophy of The Wischmeyer Architects is to provide sound design based on logic, study and a comprehensive understanding of the client's needs.

Since its founding in 1951, the firm has maintained a size which is small enough to allow principals to be intimately involved with each client, yet large enough to facilitate the accumulation of knowledge in a time of rapidly developing technology. The current staff of 40 includes architects, planners, designers and technical support personnel in three regional offices.

Wong & Ouyang

Wong & Ouyang is a well established group of architectural and engineering practices with a staff of 320 professional and support personnel located in Hong Kong and Singapore. The Group handles many different types of building projects from feasibility studies through to final construction, and offers consultancy services in architecture, geotechnical engineering, structural engineering, building services engineering, interior design and graphic design.
Wong & Ouyang & Associates, formed in 1972, is a successor to the firms Wong Ng & Associates, founded in 1957, and Wong Ng Ouyang & Associates, founded in 1964. Wong & Ouyang & Associates has expanded into the present group of practices: Wong & Ouyang (HK) Ltd., Wong and Ouyang (Civil-Structural Engineering) Ltd., Wong & Ouyang (Building Services) Ltd, Wong & Ouyang (Design) Ltd, Wong & Ouyang & Associates (S) Pte Ltd, and Wong & Ouyang (Malaysia) Sdn Berhad.

Projects undertaken by the Group include large scale residential developments, prestigious office and commercial buildings, international hotels, government buildings, educational buildings, industrial buildings, apartment buildings and individual residences.
While the majority of the projects are located in Hong Kong and China, the Group is also active in overseas projects, particularly in the areas of hotel, commercial and condominium developments. The Group has successfully completed projects in Singapore, Seoul, Vancouver, Penang, Johore Bahru, Karachi, Islamabad and the Gold Coast, Australia.

The Group utilises the most recent advances in technology via an advanced CAD system and office computer network, and also maintains a large comprehensive library containing current technical data, catalogues, reference materials and selected samples.

Wong Tung & Partners Ltd.

Wong Tung & Partners Ltd. was established in Hong Kong in 1963. The firm is structured to provide multi-disciplinary services including planning, architectural, engineering and related professional services and has fulfilled this role for a wide variety of projects throughout South-East Asia, the United States, Saudi Arabia and the People's Republic of China. The total construction cost of projects already completed, under construction or in the design stage is in excess of US$4 billion.

The firm has extensive experience in master planning and architectural design of city size community developments. Projects completed have provided residential accommodation for over quarter of a million occupants since 1968. One example is the Taikoo Shing development comprising residential, office, commercial and institutional components.

With a Hong Kong based staff of over 200 professional personnel, the firm is in a position to offer services for all aspects of architectural design of residential, hotel, office, commercial, recreational, institutional and industrial projects.

Young-sub Kim

Kim Young-sub who is well known in Korea as a specialist in church architecture, was born in Mokpo in 1950. He studies at Sung Kyun Kwan University and graduated there in 1974.

After establishing Kunchook-Moonhwa Architects and Engineers in 1982, he has been awarded several prizes with various projects. His work was shown at 'SIAC' in Rome in 1986. He taught history of western arts and interior design at Myungi College (1982-1985) and Kuk-Min University (1986-1994) as a guest lecturer.

His interests have been reflected in various fields including art and music. He as a president of the Committee for Holy Music in Myung Dong and a consultant in music at MBC radio FM program.

He is not only an architect who is theoretical as well as practical, but also a professor at Innovative Design Lab of Samsung and a music columnist.

He wrote *The Architectural History of Myung Dong Cathedral* in 1984.

ARCHITECT/PROJECT	CATEGORY	PAGE
A.J. Diamond, Donald Schmitt & Company		
Jerusalem City Hall Square	Public	276
Richmond Hill Central Library	Public	286
Ahrends Burton and Koralek		
Techniquest	Public	288
Ancher Mortlock & Woolley Pty Ltd		
Control Tower, Sydney Airport	Public	248
Andrews, Scott, Cotton Architects Ltd		
Ronald McDonald House	Institutional	234
Architects 49 Limited		
Future Park Plaza	Retail	376
Mr Eaton's Residence	Residential	346
Architectural Resources Cambridge, Inc.		
Genzyme Corporation Biopharmaceutical Plant	Industrial	180
Architecture Studio		
Apartment Building and Jeanine Manuel Bilingual Active School	Other	390
Fire Station, Gennevilliers	Public	272
Bates Smart		
Cabrini Hospital	Institutional	192
Herbert Beckhard Frank Richlan & Associates		
Memorial Drive Flex-Use Industrial Facility in association with Brandt-Kuybida Architects	Industrial	184
Manufacturing Facility, Toppan Printing Company America, Inc. in association with Brandt-Kuybida Architects	Industrial	186
Bernhard Blauel Architects		
Hypo Bank London	Corporate	46
Bligh Voller Architects		
Brisbane Airport International Terminal	Public	244
Youth Hostels Association of Queensland Brisbane City Hostel	Other	408
BOORA Architects, P.C.		
Pacific Northwest Museum of Natural History	Public	284
Consultants Incorporated		
Night Safari	Recreational	300
Cooper•Lecky Architects, PC		
Korean War Veterans Memorial	Public	282
The National Children's Center	Institutional	230
Philip Cox Richardson Rayner and Partners Pty Ltd		
Brisbane Convention and Exhibition Centre	Corporate	16

ARCHITECT/PROJECT	CATEGORY	PAGE
Leo A. Daly		
Westside Middle School	Educational	174
Daryl Jackson Architects		
Arts/Law Building, Northern Territory University in association with Woodhead (Aust) NT Pty Ltd	Educational	112
Douglas Roberts Peter Loebenberg Architects		
Truworths Head Office	Corporate	100
DP Architects Pte Ltd		
Bugis Junction	Other	402
Construction Industry Training Institute	Institutional	196
Institute of Micro-Electronics/Information Technology Institute	Institutional	214
North View Primary School	Educational	152
Permanent Stage for the Botanic Gardens Symphony Lake	Public	242
St. Andrew's Junior College	Educational	164
Ellenzweig Associates, Inc.		
Joslin Diabetes Center Research and Clinical Facility Expansion	Institutional	216
National Center for Polymer Research, University of Massachusetts, Amherst Whitney Atwood Norcross, Inc., Architect of Record	Educational	168
Ellerbe Becket, Inc.		
Augusta Medical Center	Institutional	188
Children's National Medical Center, Children's Research Institute	Institutional	194
Gund Arena	Recreational	296
Kiel Center Arena	Recreational	298
Moscow Bank of the Russian Federation Savings Bank	Corporate	74
Northern States Power Company World Class Control Center	Corporate	76
Porto Europa Wakayama Marina City	Recreational	302
State Farm Mutual Automobile Insurance Company South Texas Regional Office	Corporate	96
WestHealth	Institutional	238
Elliott + Associates Architects		
ESEO Federal Credit Union	Corporate	38
The Heierding Building	Corporate	42
Enviro•Tec		
Emerald Apartments	Residential	310
ETV Arkitektkontor AB		
The Visby General Hospital	Institutional	236
Terry Farrell and Partners		
Edinburgh International Conference and Exhibition Centre	Corporate	30
Sainsbury's Supermarket	Retail	382
Feilden & Mawson		
Eastern Counties Newspapers New Press Centre	Industrial	178

ARCHITECT/PROJECT	CATEGORY	PAGE
C.W. Fentress, J.H. Bradburn and Associates		
Denver International Airport	Public	260
Flad & Associates		
Genentech Process Science Center	Institutional	204
Modern Woodmen of America	Corporate	70
David Jay Flood		
Jay and Marilee Flood Residence	Residential	320
Pepperdine University Student Dormitory	Other	406
Richard Fleischman Architects, Inc.		
Ohio Aerospace Institute	Institutional	232
Sir Norman Foster and Partners		
New Wing and Renovation of the Joslyn Art Museum in association with Henningson Durham and Richardson	Public	278
G&W Architects, Engineers, Project Development Consultants		
Evercrest Golf Club & Resort	Other	404
Ever Commonwealth Commercial Complex	Retail	374
Imperial Palace	Residential	316
Goody, Clancy & Associates, Inc.		
Biology Building No. 68, Massachusetts Institute of Technology	Educational	120
Michael Graves Architect		
Denver Central Library - Phase 1 Addition	Public	256
Engineering Research Center, University of Cincinnati	Educational	140
Gujrals		
Jindal House	Residential	322
Mexx Farm	Residential	340
Hartman-Cox Architects		
Tulane University Law School in association with The Mathes Group	Educational	166
Hayball Leonard Stent		
Riverside Apartments	Residential	360
Helin & Siitonen Architects		
Laivapoika Housing Company	Residential	332
The Hillier Group		
Princeton Theological Seminary Henry Luce III Library	Educational	156
HKS Inc.		
Health Central	Institutional	210
Mary Washington Hospital	Institutional	224
Yuma Regional Medical Center	Institutional	240

ARCHITECT/PROJECT	CATEGORY	PAGE
HMC Group		
Congressman Jerry Lewis Elementary School	Educational	132
Birgitta Holm Architects Inc.		
Kungsängsskolan Upper Secondary School in association with STADION Architects Inc.	Educational	144
House + House, Architects		
Alta Residence	Residential	308
Ka Hale Kukuna Residence	Residential	328
Phototime Processing Laboratory & Studio	Retail	378
Waldhauer Residence	Residential	368
Hugh Newell Jacobsen		
Segal House	Residential	364
Kanner Architects		
Powell House	Residential	354
Singer Residence	Residential	366
Kaplan/McLaughlin/Diaz		
Grady Memorial Hospital in association with URS Consultants, Carl Trimble Architects, Stanley Love-Stanley and The Burlington Group	Institutional	206
Juhani Katainen Architects		
The Biocentre	Educational	114
Kisho Kurokawa Architect and Associates		
Ehime Museum of Science	Public	268
MacLachlan, Cornelius & Filoni, Inc.		
Thomas Phillips Johnson Health & Recreation Center	Recreational	304
Martinez Cutri & McArdle		
Bonita Professional Center	Institutional	190
Perkins Elementary School	Educational	154
San Diego State University, Imperial Valley Campus	Educational	160
Adrian Maserow Architects		
Mount Royal in Morningside	Residential	344
Susan Maxman Architects		
Joseph Pennock Farmstead Restoration	Residential	326
Residence in Harvey Cedars	Residential	356
Mitchell/Giurgola Architects		
The Belvedere	Recreational	294
The Lighthouse Headquarters	Institutional	220
Morris Architects		
Hirsch, Robinson, Sheiness, Glover, PC., One Houston Center	Corporate	44

ARCHITECT/PROJECT	CATEGORY	PAGE
Murphy/Jahn, Inc. Architects		
Kurfürstendamm 70	Corporate	58
Kurfürstendamm 119	Corporate	60
Hans Murman Arkitektkontor AB		
Årsta Haninge Strand Golf Clubhouse	Recreational	290
Office in Helsinki	Corporate	78
Barton Myers Associates, Inc.		
The Ice House Renovation	Corporate	54
Nikken Sekkei Ltd.		
Crane Park Izumi	Public	250
Dunhuang Cave Cultural Asset Reservation and Exhibition Center	Public	264
Osaka World Trade Center Building	Corporate	80
Arkkitehtitoimisto Paatela-Paatela & Co		
Villa Nuottaniemi	Residential	372
Pacific Adhika Internusa, PT		
Permata Hijau Apartment	Residential	352
Perry, Dean, Rogers & Partners: Architects, Inc.		
City University of New York, New Library	Educational	126
Bart Prince, Architect		
Hight Residence	Residential	312
Mead/Penhall Residence	Residential	338
Quantrell Mullins & Associates Inc		
Lancaster Group Worldwide	Corporate	62
A.H. Ravazzani		
J. Tezzanos Pinto House	Residential	318
Millot-Gomez House	Residential	342
RTKL Associates Inc.		
Embassy of Sweden in association with Stintzing Arkitekter, AB	Corporate	36
Surdiman Tower in association with PT. Airmas Asri	Corporate	98
SAC International, Ltd.		
Energy Systems Research Centre, Ajou University	Educational	138
Seoul National University Museum	Educational	162
The Stubbins Associates, Inc.		
Medical Research Building II in association with Earl Swensson and Associates	Educational	146
Studio J.J. International		
Building on the Prairie	Industrial	176

ARCHITECT/PROJECT	CATEGORY	PAGE
STUDIOS Architecture		
Silicon Graphics Entry Site	Corporate	90
Swatt Architects		
The Icehouse	Corporate	48
Ocean View House	Residential	350
Thompson, Ventulett, Stainback and Associates Inc		
Charlotte Convention Center	Corporate	20
Long Beach Convention Center	Corporate	66
Pennsylvania Convention Center	Corporate	84
United Parcel Service Corporate Office	Corporate	104
TRO/The Ritchie Organization		
Cullman Regional Medical Center	Institutional	202
TSP Architects + Planners		
Tanglin Place	Retail	388
The Wischmeyer Architects, Inc.		
Cox Medical Center South Outpatient Center	Institutional	198
Wong & Ouyang (HK) Ltd		
Gateway I, Harbour City	Corporate	40
Wong Tung & Partners Limited		
Dragon Centre	Corporate	26
Li Po Chun Chambers Redevelopment	Corporate	64
Young-sub Kim		
Bamboo House (Restaurant) and Bamboo Gallery	Other	394
Catholic University, Library and Lecture Hall	Educational	122

IMAGES wish to thank all participating firms for their valuable contribution to this publication and especially Michael Graves, Architect for the use of the cover photograph by Steven Brooke Studios.